Research Anthology on Game Design, Development, Usage, and Social Impact

Information Resources Management Association
USA

Volume II

Published in the United States of America by
    IGI Global
    Information Science Reference (an imprint of IGI Global)
    701 E. Chocolate Avenue
    Hershey PA, USA 17033
    Tel: 717-533-8845
    Fax: 717-533-8661
    E-mail: cust@igi-global.com
    Web site: http://www.igi-global.com

Library of Congress Cataloging-in-Publication Data

Names: Information Resources Management Association, editor.
Title: Research anthology on game design, development, usage, and social
    impact / Information Resources Management Association, editor.
Description: Hershey, PA : Information Science Reference, [2023] | Includes
    bibliographical references and index. | Summary: "Videogames have risen
    in popularity in recent decades and continue to entertain many all over
    the world. As game design and development becomes more accessible to
    those outside of the industry, their uses and impacts are further
    expanded. Games have been developed for medical, educational, business,
    and many more applications. While games have many beneficial
    applications, many challenges exist in current development processes as
    well as some of their impacts on society. It is essential to investigate
    the current trends in the design and development of games as well as the
    opportunities and challenges presented in their usage and social impact.
    The Research Anthology on Game Design, Development, Usage, and Social
    Impact discusses the emerging developments, opportunities, and
    challenges that are found within the design, development, usage, and
    impact of gaming. It presents a comprehensive collection of the recent
    research, theories, case studies, and more within the area. Covering
    topics such as academic game creation, gaming experience, and violence
    in gaming, this major reference work is a dynamic resource for game
    developers, instructional designers, educators and administrators of
    both K-12 and higher education, students of higher education,
    librarians, government officials, business leaders and executives,
    researchers, and academicians"-- Provided by publisher.
Identifiers: LCCN 2022040888 (print) | LCCN 2022040889 (ebook) | ISBN
    9781668475898 (h/c) | ISBN 9781668475904 (eISBN)
Subjects: LCSH: Video games--Design--Research. | Video games--Social
    aspects--Research.
Classification: LCC GV1469.3 .R47 2023 (print) | LCC GV1469.3 (ebook) |
    DDC 794.8/3--dc23/eng/20220930
LC record available at https://lccn.loc.gov/2022040888
LC ebook record available at https://lccn.loc.gov/2022040889

British Cataloguing in Publication Data
A Cataloguing in Publication record for this book is available from the British Library.

The views expressed in this book are those of the authors, but not necessarily of the publisher.

For electronic access to this publication, please contact: eresources@igi-global.com.

List of Contributors

Table of Contents

Section 2
Development and Design Methodologies

Section 3
Tools and Technologies

Section 5
Organizational and Social Implications

Section 6
Critical Issues and Challenges

Preface

Gaming has gained popularity in recent years as more areas of society discover the benefits and opportunities it offers in various sectors. More research is emerging in this area in designing and developing games in order to increase the utility across sectors, and technology is being developed to increase both utility and enjoyment from these games. Recently, the practice of gamification has been applied to education, the medical field, business, and more. However, games, specifically online and video games, often face criticism for a perceived negative impact on society.

It is critical to understand the best practices, challenges, and strategies of gaming design and development to ensure games are utilized appropriately. Research on the social impact of games is also of importance so that a complete view is gained of both the positive and negative attributes of gaming in society.

Staying informed of the most up-to-date research trends and findings is of the utmost importance. That is why IGI Global is pleased to offer this four-volume reference collection of reprinted IGI Global book chapters and journal articles that have been handpicked by senior editorial staff. This collection will shed light on critical issues related to the trends, techniques, and uses of various applications by providing both broad and detailed perspectives on cutting-edge theories and developments. This collection is designed to act as a single reference source on conceptual, methodological, technical, and managerial issues, as well as to provide insight into emerging trends and future opportunities within the field.

The *Research Anthology on Game Design, Development, Usage, and Social Impact* is organized into six distinct sections that provide comprehensive coverage of important topics. The sections are:

1. Fundamental Concepts and Theories;
2. Development and Design Methodologies;
3. Tools and Technologies;
4. Utilization and Applications;
5. Organizational and Social Implications; and
6. Critical Issues and Challenges.

The following paragraphs provide a summary of what to expect from this invaluable reference tool.

Section 1, "Fundamental Concepts and Theories," serves as a foundation for this extensive reference tool by addressing crucial theories essential to understanding the concepts and uses of games and game design in multidisciplinary settings. Opening this reference book is the chapter "A Primer on Gamification Standardization" by Prof. Carlos Filipe Portela from the University of Minho, Portugal; Prof. Alberto Simões of Polytechnic Institute of Cávado and Ave, Portugal; and Profs. Ricardo Alexandre Peixoto de Queiros and Mário Pinto from ESMAD, Polytechnic Institute of Porto, Portugal, which presents a systematic study on gamification standardization aiming to characterize the status of the field, namely describing existing frameworks, languages, services, and platforms. This section ends with "Towards Better Understanding of Children's Relationships With Online Games and Advergames" by Dr. Ali Ben Yahia from LIGUE, Tunis, Tunisia; Prof. Sihem Ben Saad of Carthage Business School, Université Tunis Carthage, Tunisia; and Prof. Fatma Choura Abida from Institute of Computer Science of Tunis, Tunisia, which favors an in-depth understanding of the child's relation with online games and advergames through an exploratory qualitative approach.

Section 2, "Development and Design Methodologies," presents in-depth coverage of the design and development of games for their use in different applications. This section starts with "Augmented Reality Games" by Prof. Baris Atiker from Bahcesehir University, Turkey, which evaluates how augmented reality games interpret gaming concepts and principles through field research methods, new applications, and studies that deal with gamification, presence, immersion, and game transfer phenomena. This section ends with "Eye of the Beholder: Analyzing a Gamification Design Through a Servicescape Lens" by Prof. Adam Palmquist from the School of Informatics, University of Skövde, Sweden and Dr. David Gillberg of Insert Coin, Sweden, which uses the theories from environmental psychology and the servicescape methods to construct a lens to suggest improvements in gamification design for a learning management system used in higher education.

Section 3, "Tools and Technologies," explores the various tools and technologies used within game design. This section begins with "Applied Alternative Tools and Methods in the Replacement of the Game Design Document" by Profs. Pedro Henrique Roscoe Lage de Oliveira and Carlos Alberto Silva de Miranda from Minas Gerais State University, Brazil and Prof. Joao Victor Boechat Gomide from the Universidade FUMEC, Brazil, which proposes alternatives to replace or optimize the use of the game design document (GDD). This section ends with "Towards a Role-Playing Game Procedural Dungeon Generation Strategy to Help Developing Working Skills" by Profs. Esteban A. Durán-Yañez and Mario A. Rodríguez-Díaz from Tecnológico Nacional de México IT Aguascalientes, Mexico and Prof. César A. López-Luévano from the Universidad Politécnica de Aguascalientes, Mexico, which describes the insights towards a proposal to integrate a procedural content generation strategy in a computer role-playing usable and accessible learning video game for gaining replayability to encourage engagement and motivation in learners.

Section 4, "Utilization and Applications," describes how gaming is used and applied in diverse industries for various applications. The opening chapter in this section, "Probability and Game," by Prof. Alessio Drivet from Geogebra Institute of Turin, Italy, emphasizes not only the theoretical aspects but above all the certainty that you always play "against the dealer" with an expected loss assessable for the various games. This section ends with "On Computerizing the Ancient Game of Ṭāb" by Profs. Ahmad B. Hassanat, Ghada Altarawneh, Baker Al-Rawashdeh, and Mohammed Alshamaileh from Mutah University, Jordan; Prof. Ahmad S. Tarawneh from Eotvos Lorand University ELTE, Hungary; Prof. Hossam Faris of The University of Jordan, Jordan; Prof. Mahmoud B. Alhasanat from Al-Hussein Bin Talal University, Jordan; Prof. Alex de Voogt of Drew University, USA; and Dr. Surya V. B. Prasath from Cincinnati Children's Hospital Medical Center, USA, which develops three versions of the game tab—human versus human, human versus computer, and computer versus computer—and employs a genetic algorithm (GA) to help the computer to choose the 'best' move to play.

Section 5, "Organizational and Social Implications," includes chapters discussing the impact of gaming on society. The chapter "Institutions as Designers of Better Social Games" by Prof. Albena Antonova from Sofia University, Bulgaria, discusses how institutions can transform into designers of new types of rules and social arrangements that will be more just and efficient for all within social games. The closing chapter, "The Effects of Fully and Partially In-Game Guidance on Players' Declarative and Procedural Knowledge With a Disaster Preparedness Serious Game," by Prof. Ting Zhou from Fort Hays State University, USA and Prof. Christian S. Loh of Southern Illinois University, USA, investigates the effects of players' gaming frequency, prior knowledge, and in-game guidance received on their declarative and procedural knowledge in a disaster preparedness serious game.

Section 6, "Critical Issues and Challenges," presents coverage of academic and research perspectives on the challenges and issues of games and gaming design. Starting this section is "Gamification Research: Preliminary Insights Into Dominant Issues, Theories, Domains, and Methodologies" by Prof. Kingsley Ofosu-Ampong from the University of Ghana, Ghana and Prof. Thomas Anning-Dorson of the University of the Witwatersrand, South Africa, which explains the idea of game design elements in information systems and provides real-world examples of gamified systems outcomes from developing countries. This section ends with "Digital Games and Violence" by Prof. Arzu Kalafat Çat from Abant Izzet Baysal University, Turkey, which discusses violent elements in digital games within the framework of relevant theoretical approaches through three games that children play most.

Although the primary organization of the content in this multi-volume work is based on its six sections, offering a progression of coverage of the important concepts, methodologies, technologies, applications, social issues, and emerging trends, the reader can also identify specific content by utilizing the extensive indexing system listed at the end of each volume. As a comprehensive collection of research on the latest findings related to games and gaming design, the *Research Anthology on Game Design, Development, Usage, and Social Impact* provides game developers, instructional designers, educators and administrators of both K-12 and higher education, students of higher education, librarians, government officials, business leaders and executives, researchers, and academicians with a complete understanding of the applications and impacts of games and gaming design. Given the vast number of issues concerning usage, failure, success, strategies, and applications of gaming design and development, the *Research Anthology on Game Design, Development, Usage, and Social Impact* encompasses the most pertinent research on the applications, impacts, uses, and development of games.

Chapter 24
Mapping Game Mechanics for Learning in a Serious Game for the Energy Transition

Cristina Ampatzidou

University of Groningen, Faculty of Spatial Sciences, Groningen, Netherlands

Katharina Gugerell

University of Groningen, Faculty of Spatial Sciences, Groningen, Netherlands

ABSTRACT

The integration of learning goals with game mechanics in serious games used in urban and spatial planning processes has the potential to enable game designers and planners to create games with narratives tightly aligned to particular processes and lead to increased learning outcomes. This study presents the results from testing Energy Safari, a serious game for the energy transition in the province of Groningen, and empirically associates specific game mechanics with learning events, derived from players' reports. The research is based on the analysis of post-play questionnaires. Play-testing Energy Safari illustrates that different learning events can be triggered by the same game mechanics, an observation which can be applied in serious game design to facilitate players with different learning needs and styles. In addition, play testing to evaluate the learning performance of serious games should be integrated in the game design process. However, to achieve lasting learning and actionable knowledge, serious games should be used complementarily with other civic participation methods.

INTRODUCTION

The application of serious games spans a range of topics including healthcare, military training, resources management, energy literacy, risk governance, raising awareness on the energy transition to name a few. Serious games are increasingly used as educational resources within urban planning and policy making to promote the understanding of complex urban issues and facilitate negotiations among stakeholders, or to motivate citizens to participate (Devisch, Poplin, & Sofronie, 2016; Mayer, 2009; Poplin,

DOI: 10.4018/978-1-6684-7589-8.ch024

2012; Tan, 2014; Thiel & Fröhlich, 2017). Their learning potential is connected to games' capacities to produce skill-based, cognitive, and affective learning outcomes (Kraiger, Ford, & Salas, 1993), and combine learning with entertainment (Abdul Jabbar & Felicia, 2015; Boyle, Connolly, Hainey, & Boyle, 2012). Co-located gaming especially facilitates learning because players are physically present at the same location and interact with each other while playing either analogue (i.e. board games), digital or hybrid games (digital and analogue mixed). In such co-located settings, games have been reported to improve the interpersonal relations among players (Fang, Chen, & Huang, 2016) and contribute to the 'fun aspect' (Gajadhar, de Kort, & Ijsselsteijn, 2008), which is considered a fundamental condition for learning (Abdul Jabbar & Felicia, 2015; Dahlgren, 2009; Whitton, 2011). A number of authors discuss spatial and urban planning, and civic engagement as collective learning processes (e.g. Friedmann, 1984; Horelli, 2002; Kuhk, Dehaene, & Schreurs, 2015) that are expected to foster problem-solving skills, enhance spatial understanding, establish stakeholder networks, and test out difficult scenarios (e.g. Crookall, 2010; Erhel & Jamet, 2013; Gee, 2005; Granic, Lobel, & Engels, 2014; Luederitz et al., 2016; Shaffer, Squire, Halverson, & Gee, 2005). Over the last four decades planners have experimented with games, to investigate their potential in supporting and facilitating such learning processes (e.g. Gugerell, Jauschneg, Platzer, & Berger, 2017; Medema, Furber, Adamowski, Zhou, & Mayer, 2016; Sakonnakron, Huyakorn, & Rizzi, 2014).

Much existing game literature discusses the gaming-learning experience as one entity. Some authors take a differentiating approach advocating for the importance of a strong integration of game mechanics and explicit learning goals within the game structure (e.g. Habgood & Ainsworth, 2011; Denham, 2016; Malone & Lepper, 1987; Dörner et al., 2016). Also, only few empirical case studies (e.g. Habgood & Ainsworth, 2011; Denham, 2013) demonstrate the practical integration of learning goals within the game structure during the design process. These stress that the selection and balancing of game mechanics is one of the most difficult steps in the design process that requires careful attention.

This study evaluates the learning experience of the players of the serious game 'Energy Safari' and identifies associations between specific game mechanics and specific learning outcomes. The research question of this article thus concerns the impact of specific game elements on the learning experience of the players. We approach this question via the analysis of the game mechanics, gameplay and reported triggered learning events (Leclercq & Poumay, 2005) of Energy Safari. The serious board game Energy Safari is a multi-player, co-located game, embedded in the narrative of the energy transition in the province of Groningen (The Netherlands). The mapped connections between specific game mechanics and learning events can be used prescriptively in future research on serious game design, making the design process more effective. By connecting a prescriptive model of learning to game design, our goal is to contribute to the more systematic integration of learning mechanics within serious game design, and thus in games that deliver the intended learning outcomes. The results confirm the activating and learning potential of the game that allows an entry point in civic, participatory processes, but also calls into question the high expectations on games to deliver sustainable learning outcomes and trigger behavioural change.

LEARNING IN GAMES

'Serious games' combine educational goals with entertainment (Abt, 1969). Game-based learning is often discussed from a holistic perspective, where learning outcomes and gameplay are analysed together as an integrated whole. However, gameplay is a complex experience conditioned by different factors, like the nature of the game, the specific game mechanics, or the context in which it takes place. Hence, the game structure, the gameplay and the positioning of the game within a broader learning process can be carriers of a player's learning experience (Clark, Tanner-Smith, & Killingsworth, 2014; Hays, 2005; Vogel, et al., 2006). Previous research examines the potential of games for learning, covering the spectrum from direct information transfer to open-ended learning (Harteveld & Bekebrede, 2011), the development of particular skills such as problem solving, visual thinking, spatial skills, persistence, reflecting on complex issues, media literacy and network-building skills (Cooper, 2014; Crookall, 2010; Gee, 2005; Granic, Lobel, & Engels, 2014; Hamari et al., 2016; Erhel & Jamet, 2013; Shaffer, Squire, Halverson, & Gee, 2005; Shute, Ventura, & Kim, 2013). However, the academic debate remains controversial: some researchers emphasize the value of games for cognitive and social learning (e.g. Erhel & Jamet, 2013; Gee, 2005; Granic, Lobel, & Engels, 2014; Hamari et al., 2016; Prensky, 2006; Shaffer, Squire, Halverson, & Gee, 2005), while others such as Juul (2011) illustrate the conceptual capacity of games to transfer knowledge and skills between game and real world. However, rigorous empirical evidence that proves this capacity of games is still lacking (Buckingham & Sefton-Green, 2003; Egenfeldt-Nielsen, Heide Smith, & Pajares Tosca, 2008), which might result in a general overassessment and overly positive bias towards games' actual learning effects (Raphael et al., 2010). Also, it remains still unclear how and when exactly learning happens during gameplay, and which role game facilitators, specific game features, and game mechanics play in learning processes (e.g. Mayer, 2009; Ke, 2016). Thus, there is demand for research that evaluates the effects of individual game attributes and features on learning outcomes in order to determine the effectiveness of games as learning tools (Bedwell, Pavlas, Heyne, Lazzara, & Salas, 2012; Clark, 2007).

One possible model for the mapping and analysis of learning in serious games is the 8 Learning Events Model (8LEM) (Leclercq & Poumay, 2005). The value of the 8LEM is based on the direct observability of quantitative and qualitative dimensions of learning (Dörner, et al. 2016). The 8LEM proposes a series of eight learning events (Table 1) covering a range from unintentional or incidental knowledge to more complex forms of learning (Leclercq & Poumay, 2005). Learning events that contribute to factual knowledge and routine practice can be considered simple forms of learning, learning events that entail understanding of a process or phenomenon are of intermediate complexity, and learning events that allow for interpretation and invention of new ideas are complex learning events. During a specific activity, more than one event may take place at the same time. Hence, the model can be used descriptively to trace a diverse spectrum of learning experiences; but also, prescriptively, where each learning event can be triggered by specific actions of the instructor or game facilitator. These qualities allow the 8LEM framework to be used in both, the analysis of games and of gameplay, where a diversity of learning experiences takes place, and in the design of games, where several and diverse learning experiences must be prepared and offered.

LEARNING AND GAME MECHANICS

The gameplay emerges from the interaction among players, the players with the game and how different game elements respond to the players' actions. These interactions are driven by combinations of different game mechanics. Game mechanics are the various actions, interactions, roles, relationships and control mechanisms that are afforded to the players of a game (Hunicke, Leblanc, & Zubek, 2004). Hence, game mechanics are the core building blocks for games as artificial, rule-based systems (Cook, 2006) which turns balancing game mechanics into one of the most crucial activities during the design and playtesting phase. In many educational games the learning goals remain external to the gameplay. These games tend to struggle with instigating learning, compared to games where the learning goals are deeply embedded in the game narrative and driven by specific game mechanics (Denham, 2016; Habgood & Ainsworth, 2011; Kafai, 2001; Malone & Lepper, 1987).

Table 1. The 8 Learning Events in the 8LE Model by (Leclercq & Poumay, 2005). To maintain a level of abstraction in the analysis performed in this paper the eight learning events are addressed in three groups of simple, intermediate, and complex learning events, following similar categorizations found in other frameworks (e.g. Argyris, 1977; Posch & Steiner, 2006).

	Learning Event (8LEM)	Description
Simple Learning	Imitation / Modelling	Incidental or intentional learning through observation, impregnation, and imitation
	Reception / Transmission	Language based learning from communication and reception of information
	Exercising / Guidance	Learning by creating and practising procedures or routines
Intermediate Learning	Exploration / Documenting	Search among available material with a certain degree of freedom
	Experimentation / Reactivity	Learning by exhausting and combining available possibilities, and testing scenarios
Complex Learning	Creation / Confrontation	Creating texts, objects, compositions etc. that are new to the learner
	Self-Reflection / Co-reflection	Interpretation, analysis and judgement of a situation or one's own knowledge and skills
	Debate / Animation	Learning through social interaction, discussion and negotiation of conflicting views

As the learning experiences are contingent to the core game mechanics (Cook, 2006; Järvinen, 2008; Mildner & Mueller, 2016; Sicart, 2008), frameworks that establish connections between specific game mechanics and learning goals have been developed. Such frameworks are, among others, the Game Mechanics – Learning Mechanics framework by Lim et al. (2013) or the Games, Motivation and Learning framework by Garris et al. (2002).

The Game Mechanics – Learning Mechanics Framework (Lim, et al., 2013) suggests that specific pedagogical goals can be translated to specific game mechanics. The authors map out pedagogical theories and strategies and establish a descriptive model, which allows free associations between game and learning mechanics. Lim et al.'s (2013) framework consists of four steps: defining (i) which game mechanics are present, (ii) to which learning mechanics they correspond, (iii) how these specific mechanics have been implemented within the game and (iv) what is the expected usage of these features by the prospective players (see also Arnab et al., 2014).

Another framework that analyses the learning impact of game mechanics is the 'Games, Motivation and Learning Framework' (GML), developed by Garris et al. (2002). It proposes a model with six types of game mechanics, called 'Game Dimensions' (Table 2), based on their expected contribution to motivation and learning. Game mechanics in the dimension 'Fantasy' facilitate focalisation of attention, self-absorption and learning through analogies and metaphors (Driskell & Dwyer, 1984; Malone & Lepper, 1987). A game's 'Rules and Goals' must provide a clear game structure and feedback that can enhance the player's motivation and performance but must also allow for enough diversity of strategies and movements to choose from. The graphics, sound effects and other aesthetic qualities of a game, collected under the 'Sensory Stimuli' dimension, contribute to an experience that is different from the real world and help retain the player's engagement. 'Challenge' ensures that games provide meaningful goals and an appropriate level of difficulty and performance feedback, while mechanics of 'Mystery' are meant to activate curiosity-driven learning. Finally, the dimension of 'Control' refers to mechanics that stimulate the ability to regulate, command or direct something.

Table 2. Game dimensions in the games, motivation, and learning framework. Taken from (Garris, Ahlers, & Driskell, 2002).

Game Dimensions	Descriptors
Fantasy	Imaginary or fantasy context, themes, or characters
Rules / Goals	Clear rules, goals, and feedback on progress toward goals
Sensory Stimuli	Dramatic or novel visual and auditory stimuli
Challenge	Optimal level of difficulty and uncertain goal attainment
Mystery	Optimal level of informational complexity
Control	Active learner control

GAME PROTOTYPE AND METHODOLOGY

The serious game prototype 'Energy Safari' targets the aspiration for the energy transition in the Dutch province of Groningen. The energy transition is a large-scale structural policy change towards an increased use of renewable energy sources, the introduction of energy saving measures, and the significant reduction of dependency on fossil energy (Hauff, Bode, Neumann, & Haslauer, 2014). The energy transition is operationalized through centralized policies, corporate responsibility, and a widespread instigation of citizen-driven, local, energy initiatives. The province of Groningen is home to the largest natural gas field in Western-Europe, making the province the natural gas powerhouse of the Netherlands. However, the steady depletion of the resource and the negative impact on local livability (increasingly frequent earthquakes that damage property and increase the risk of flooding) combined with an international reorientation of energy policy, have fuelled a regional debate on how to achieve a transition away from mineral resources and towards renewable energy. The local and regional governments aspire Groningen to become the 'energy valley' of the Netherlands, so they have recently introduced development strategies addressing the topic of renewable energy and transitioning to a low-carbon economy at large (Spijkerboer, Trell, & Zuidema, 2016). Tapping onto this local and regional debate, the learning goals of Energy Safari are (i) to communicate the complexity of the energy transition, by making players aware of the multiple scales in which the transition is operationalised, (ii) to inform the players on the policy vision for the energy transition in the region, (iii) to introduce existing opportunities to engage in local and regional energy projects, and (iv) to stimulate debate and exchange of real-world and personal experiences regarding energy behaviour and social practices.

ENERGY SAFARI GAME PROTOTYPE

Energy Safari is a four to six-player board game played with the support of a facilitator, usually a member of the research team. Each game session starts with an introduction by the facilitator, explaining that the game is part of a research project, the game rules and the game props. The facilitator also explains the goal of the game: collecting energy and community points and coins by joining different project consortia and implementing energy projects in the province of Groningen (Figure 1).

Figure 1. Activity diagram detailing individual players' options during one round of Energy Safari

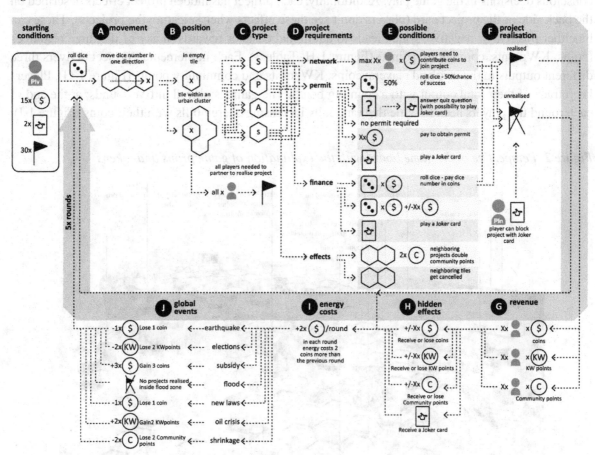

The game board is an abstracted map of the province of Groningen. It is divided in a hexagonal grid where different colours represent different policy areas (red for energy saving, yellow for renewable energy production, green for large scale industrial or agricultural projects and blue for infrastructure and supporting projects). Three special areas are also outlined based on actual zoning: three urban clusters (Groningen, Delftzijl & Eemshaven), a flood risk zone and an earthquake zone (Figure 2). When their turn comes, each player rolls a dice and must move their avatar the rolled number; players can choose in which direction to move on the game board (Figure 1-A). The colour of the tile they land on, determines the type of project they can realise (Figure 1-B, C). Since the projects are presented face up, players can evaluate different project types (see Table 7 in the Appendix) based on their implementation requirements and output and decide which project to implement before they move.

There are three general steps required to implement a project: creating a network of partners who co-finance the project (among the other players), obtaining a permit (either by rolling a dice or answering a multiple-choice quiz question) and paying the implementation costs (determined by rolling the dice) (Figure 1-D). If all requirements are met, the project gets implemented: a token is placed on the tile and all involved players place a flag on it (Figure 2). Every project has different spatial effects. For example, implemented bio-based projects have major spatial impacts: an implemented project cancels out surrounding tiles, so no other projects can be realised; increasing scarcity nudges the player to make more conscious decisions in the game play. Additionally, each project has hidden project effects described on the back side of the project card (players don't see these effects when selecting the projects). These can be either positive or negative, which leads to additional costs or rewards in any of the three resources (coins, KWpoints, community points) (Figure 1-H, Table 3). Each implemented project delivers three different outputs to the involved players: coins, KWpoints and community points (Figure 1-G). Players keep track of their total output with a counting board. The game is played in five rounds; at the end of each round the players need to settle their annually increasing energy bills with their coins (Figure 1-I).

Figure 2. Perspective of the game board with the explanation of game props and tokens

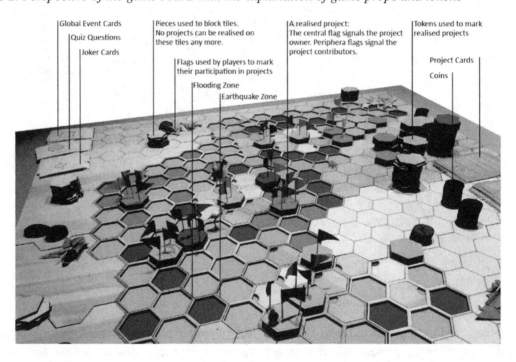

Different types of game cards are used in the game (Figure 2). Joker cards enable players to overcome obstacles in the game: for example, players do not have to pay the implementation costs, or they can receive a permit without rolling the dice. Joker cards can be played by any player at any time. Event cards are played at the end of each round and represent global events such as political changes, natural disasters, or newly implemented taxes or subsidies. Global events affect all the players (Figure 1-J). Multiple choice quiz questions, also in cards, are used to obtain permits. Quiz questions are designed in a way that players can calculate and gauge the correct answer based on common sense (see also Ampatzidou et al., 2015). At the end of the game players count their energy and community points and their coins: the Business Mind is the player with the most coins, the Energy Tycoon is the player with the most KW-points and the Community King or Queen is the player with the most community points. Since there is not a single game target (i.e. collect as many community points as possible), players must choose their own game goal, which allows a reflection on their personal strategy, goals and motives and their links to real-world practises during the debriefing (see also Gugerell, Jauschneg, Platzer, & Berger, 2017).

METHODS AND DATA

The evaluation and testing of the game followed a mixed approach combining (i) a standardized questionnaire (n=87), (ii) participant observation during the gameplay, (iii) audio records of game sessions and (iv) a debriefing in the form of a focus group at the end of each playing session (n=18). Various methods for recruiting players were used (no incentives offered), including social media, personal invitations, and snowball sampling. Game sessions lasted between 1.5-3 hours. The sample (Table 3) covers different individuals ranging from lay people, participants in energy initiatives, public servants, researchers etc. The sample is skewed towards higher levels of education and male participants. Almost 60% were between 19 and 30 years old, which represents the project's focus group of young adults. The sample is balanced regarding gaming experience but with rather modest experience in serious games.

Table 3. Overview of participants

Gender	
- female	30 (35%)
- male	56 (64%)
- no answer	1 (1%)
Age	
- 19 – 30 years	50 (58%)
- 31 – 40 years	21 (24%)
- 41+ years	16 (18%)
Educational Level	
- MBO/HAVO/VWO or similar,	11 (12%)
- HO/WO Bachelor,	18 (21%)
- WO Master	54 (62%)
- Doctor/PhD	4 (5%)
Gaming Experience	
- frequently	32 (37%)
- occasionally	26 (30%)
- rarely or never	29 (33%)

The standardized questionnaire is literature based (Nordin, Denisova, & Cairns, 2014), querying (i) sociodemographic data, (ii) knowledge and environmental attitudes towards energy and participation, (iii) BrainHex player types (Nacke, Bateman, & Mandryk, 2014) and gaming preferences (see also Gugerell, Funovits, & Ampatzidou, in press), (iv) gaming experience and strategy (Brockmyer, et al., 2009; Downs, Vetere, Howard, & Loughnan, 2013; de Kort, IJsselsteijn, & Poels, 2007), and (v) learning impact (Bellotti, Kapralos, Lee, Moreno-Ger, & Berta, 2013; Shute, Ventura, Bauer, & Zapata-Rivera, 2009). Learning impact was sampled by gamers' self-evaluation. The surveys were coded with SPSS. Participant observation took place via note taking by a second researcher not involved in game play; audio records of the game sessions and debriefings were transcribed. The debriefings were guideline based (Crookall, 2010; Lederman, 1992) and addressed three different aspects: (i) What (describing the game play, situations, players' observations), (ii) So what (what was the meaning of the game play related to real-world practices, values, actions, interests), (iii) Now what (anticipating the future, what would "this" mean for the real world, behaviour, transforming interpretation into actionable knowledge). Content analysis (Mayring, 2015; Gläser & Laudel, 2010; Drisko & Maschi, 2016) was performed on the transcribed audio records and the open-ended survey questions, using an analytical framework based on Garris et al (2002) and Leclerque and Poumay (2005).

Analytical Framework

The analytical framework combines two approaches: the Games, Motivation and Learning (GML) framework by Garris et al (2002) and Leclerque and Poumay (2005). The GML framework contains a limited amount of clearly defined game elements, which makes it suitable for this analysis. The 8LEM was selected because it focuses on the learner, because any didactic strategy can be reduced to one or more of the proposed eight learning events, and because it covers both intentional and incidental learning (Dörner, et al., 2016). In this study, the GML framework and the 8LEM model are intersected (Figure 3) in order to link game mechanics (organised according to the GML model) and observed learning events (organised according to the 8LEM).

Each Game Dimension is translated into one or more Game Mechanics (Mx) of the Energy Safari game. Consequently, Player Statements (PxSy), derived through the content analysis, are associated both with the game mechanics they refer to and with the Learning Events players associated them with. Because different players might associate the same mechanic with a different learning event, the grey bands connect different mechanics to different learning events, via the player statement that contained this specific association.

The operationalization of the framework was based on a three-step process (Table 4). First the game mechanics of Energy Safari were categorized along the six game dimensions of the GML framework (Garris, Ahlers, & Driskell, 2002). Subsequently open-ended questionnaire responses and statements the players made during the gameplay or the debriefing were coded in two ways: first, according to the game mechanics of Energy Safari to which they referred to, and then they were regrouped and organised according to the 8LEM (Leclercq & Poumay, 2005) learning experiences that they related with. Reoccurring patterns in the statements associated specific game mechanics to reported learning experiences, identifying the connections between specific game mechanics and learning events. To illustrate: "The effects on the projects, but also the game-wide effects, showed how something went in an unexpected positive or negative way." (1606150102). The "effects on the projects" refers to the mechanic 'hidden project effects' and "game-wide effects" refers to the mechanic 'Global Events', both located in the category 'Mystery' of the GML framework. The fragment "showed how something went in an unexpected positive or negative way." is associated with the learning event 'imitation' because it describes that the player learned something by observing the impact this specific game mechanic had on other projects.

Figure 3. Methodological model combining the game dimensions by Garris, Ahlers and Driskell (2002), and the 8LEM by Leclerq and Poumay (2005) in the framework of this study

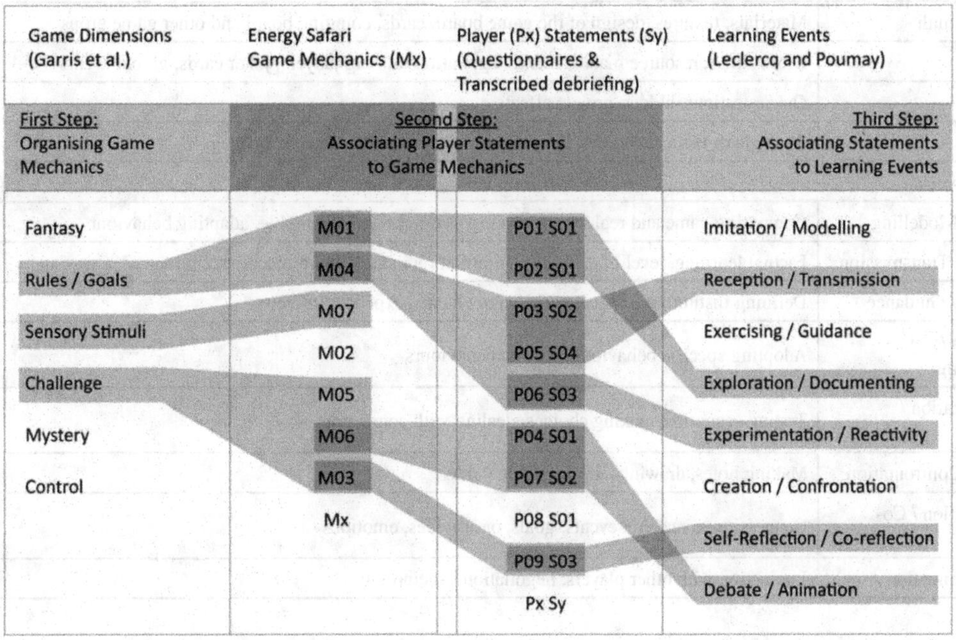

LEARNING IN ENERGY SAFARI

The main aim of Energy Safari is to communicate the complexity of the energy transition as a process that spans multiple scales and includes multiple stakeholders, a goal that was positively assessed. Overall, playing Energy Safari was positively evaluated with 92% of the players reporting that they enjoyed playing the game much or very much, 71% that they would play it again and 70% that they would recommend it to their family or friends. Players remarked that "[Energy Safari] makes the complexity of the energy transition comprehensible" (1606210103) and "really gives more insights into energy and energy transition." (1606220104). Linking serious content and fun in serious games is a pertinent challenge in game design, which the game delivered to the surprise of some players: "I actually liked that it's still really a game and it's fun to play and it doesn't feel that I am only here to learn something. So that I like because that I think is a very difficult balance. If you go too much towards this serious gaming and learning thing, then I would be too bored too soon I guess. I 'm here to play a game still." (160605-02) and "You almost forget it's educative as well, it really feels like a game" (160617-01).

With regards to their learning experience (Table 5), 42% of the players reported that playing the game inspired them to learn more about the energy transition in their region and 29% that the game improved their understanding about the realisation of urban development projects.

Table 4. Operationalization of the methodological model for the content analysis: Codes used to analyse player statements, identifying references to specific game mechanics in Energy Safari during the second coding step, and learning events during the third coding step

	Player Statements Referring to:
Game Elements & Game Mechanics	
Fantasy	Game board, project descriptions, player attitudes
Rules / Goals	Completing projects, selecting game goal, finding partners, territorial effects, yearly energy bill
Sensory Stimuli	Materials, textures, design of the game board, cards, counting board and other game props
Challenge	Dice rolling, resource management, negotiations among players, joker cards, global events
Mystery	Quiz questions, hidden project effects
Control	Strategic or tactical choices, investing on other players' projects, bribing
Learning Events	
Imitation / Modelling	Comparing game and real world, making a complex issue tangible, adapting behaviour
Reception / Transmission	Factual learning, level of difficulty, information included in project descriptions
Exercising / Guidance	Defining institutional space, ad-hoc agreements, expecting effects
Exploration / Documenting	Adopting specific behaviours, testing behaviours
Experimentation / Reactivity	Testing scenarios, making choices, dealing with constraints
Creation / Confrontation	Making notes, drawings, inventing new rules
Self-Reflection / Co-reflection	Connection to real-life events, goals, or attitudes, emotions
Debate / Animation	Interaction with other players, negotiations, reciprocity

The results on reported learning through the interactions among players show that according to 57% of the players the gameplay supported learning from each other through interaction with other players and by watching their strategies during gameplay. Players already active in community projects evaluated the game slightly more positively than uninvolved ones. 56% of the players indicated that the game introduced new possibilities for civic participation in general and 37% indicated that they became more interested in energy initiatives in particular. Still, only 15% would consider becoming more involved in a local or regional energy initiative. Thus, though the game indeed triggers learning, the results remain moderate in instigating a 'call-for-action' in the real-world.

Game Mechanics' Contribution to Learning

When analysed on the level of individual game mechanics, players have been very specific in reporting how individual mechanics have contributed (or not) to their learning experience. However, it is not possible to establish a direct relation of one specific type of game mechanics with one particular learning event as, depending on how players referred to specific mechanics in their statements, the same mechanics have sometimes led to different learning events. Most learning events occurred through experimentation (Table 6), which refers to learning by manipulating different elements and observing the effects of one's actions (Leclercq & Poumay, 2005). This is expected given the nature of the game, which is focused on trying out different strategies. However, the more complex forms of learning, for example debate and self-reflection, occurred by a combination of mechanics, such as negotiating partnerships with other players, while also debating the nature of the project that should be realised.

Table 5. Overview of the reported learning experience of the Energy Safari players

Survey Questions	Relative Frequency				
	Strongly Disagree	Disagree	Neither	Agree	Strongly Agree
Did you obtain and explore new perspectives on the topic of energy?	5	29	34	31	1
Through the game I understand more about realizing urban development projects.	8	28	36	28	1
Through the game I learned something new about the Energy Transition in Groningen.	7	26	37	23	7
Through the game I have a better understanding of energy policy in my region.	15	28	31	24	2
Through the game I am inspired to learn more about the Energy Transition in my region.	3	15	40	38	3
Through the game I have a better understanding of possible projects in my city/neighbourhood that contribute to the Energy Transition.	9	22	45	23	1
Through the game I am more interested in energy projects.	5	15	44	32	5
Would you recommend this game to your family, friends or colleagues?	2	6	22	41	29
Would you play Energy Safari again?	2	8	19	44	27
Because of the game I would like to be more involved in the Energy Transition in my region.	7	23	55	12	3
Did the game show possibilities for participation and involvement?	2	18	23	45	11
Through the game I learned more about the other players.	2	17	24	45	11
Watching the strategies of other players helps me to understand the game better.	6	9	28	36	22
Playing the game demonstrated to me that only through cooperation with others environmental problems could be solved.	6	8	24	41	21
I learned things I didn't know about the Energy Transition from other players.	5	30	22	34	9
Did the game show you a new perspective on the interests and concerns of other players?	3	28	33	29	7

Fantasy and Mystery for Simple Learning Events

Learning events of Imitation and Reception were mainly identified in relation to mechanics of Fantasy and Mystery, such as the abstracted map of the province, the simplified steps in setting up an energy project, and the possibility to adopt attitudes that they do not normally practice (Table 6). Players reported that the abstraction of the territory in the game board "gave a real feel to the world and could result in tactical choices" (1606280306), while they acknowledged that some of their actions could only take place within the game context: "Playing a game makes you do other things than you would do in

Table 6. Positioning of the game mechanics of Energy Safari based on the games, motivation and learning and 8 Learning Models frameworks, based on player statements

			Game Dimensions, Based on Garris, Ahlers & Driksell (2002)					
			Fantasy	Rules/ Goals	Sensory Stimuli	Challenge	Mystery	Control
8LEM, Leclerque & Poumay (2005)	Simple Learning	**Imitation**	Abstraction of provincial map Participation in projects that one does not have the possibility to participate in real life	Yearly energy bill			Hidden project effects Global Events	
		Reception					Quiz Questions Different types of projects	
		Exercising			Counting Board		Different types of projects	
	Intermediate Learning	**Exploration**	Adopt attitudes that one does not practice in real life	Selection of goal (energy, money, community)				
		Experimentation	Participation in projects that one doesn't have the possibility to participate in real life	Finding Partners Territorial effects among neighbouring projects		Managing Resources		Investing in other players projects Using Joker cards
	Complex Learning	**Creation**						
		Self-reflection		Selection of goal (energy, money, community)				
		Debate		Finding Partners		Negotiations for establishing partnerships		

real life." (1607050201). Mystery mechanics can be found in the project cards, and the quiz questions players have to answer to advance with a permit for their projects. The questions were recognized as an immediate trigger for learning during the game, based on reception of information: "The easy part of the learning of course is the questions. If in a short period of time the same question pops-up I would probably get the right answer." (160615-01). In spite of that, quiz questions were also criticized as often not corresponding to a level of knowledge suitable for the players: "It was impossible to answer some questions if you are not from the field" (1606280301); as not coherently related to the project they were connected to: "But I feel it doesn't really… it's just random questions." (160617-01); and mostly, as being too factual and not focusing on values or opinions: "Well some questions are very difficult. It may be possible to give some questions that can be answered in an open question way." (1606140204) and "The questions were sometimes a bit hard to follow (large numbers) and feel a bit quantitatively oriented, to technical measures. There could also be some questions about cultural, social, psychological aspects." (1606150104). The projects' hidden effects (i.e. noise pollution, environmental impact, NIMBY effects) are either positive or negative impacts to a project's neighbours or investors of the project. They have also instigated the Imitation learning event, where players can understand that projects can occasionally go wrong or can have unexpectedly good spin offs: "The effects on the projects, but also the game-wide effects, showed how something went in an unexpected positive or negative way." (1606150102). In general, players appreciated the mechanic 'hidden project effects' and emphasized its value for the game, but also noted that its impact could be even stronger: "The side effects of projects should be more impactful, especially biomass on land use." (1606140203).

Rules and Goals, and Control for Exploration and Experimentation

Learning events of 'Exploration' and 'Experimentation' were mostly associated with mechanics under the 'Rules/Goals', and 'Control' dimensions (Table 6). One important game mechanic that instigated exploration is the 'Selection of goal': players could choose whether to focus on one resource (e.g. energy) and maximise that one; or to pursue resource balance between energy, community points, and coins as their goal. This option is unusual compared to other serious games, which either allocate different player roles or prescribe a single game goal. Even though it does not influence the spatial or strategic exploration in the in-game behaviour, this mechanic conceptually supports the reflection and connection to players' individual real-world practices and values: "[I chose this goal] Because this corresponds with my personal beliefs of doing business, and the game setting encouraged me to do so." (1606280204) and "That's my personal goal for the energy transition" (1606160104). However, the material illustrates that one third of the players didn't follow any specific strategy but adjusted their goal throughout the game. Making strategic choices is a reoccurring activity in the game: it involves selecting the direction a player should move, selecting the type of project to realise, deciding good moments to use joker cards, and whether to join partnerships for other players' projects. Players explicitly referred to those decisions as "the strategic part" (1606280102) of the game, "(…) to invest in the right project, the ones that were adjacent to my already realized projects" (1606210102) and the "choice of investments / how much you pay (or bribe), continuously consider what is the best option" (1606280203). Other mechanics that facilitated exploration and experimentation include territorial effects between neighbouring projects, global events, and the yearly energy bill. A specific mechanic designed to establish balance between player agency and chance was implemented: in order to secure permit for their projects, players could often choose between answering a quiz question or throwing a dice. Game mechanics related to resource management and the scarcity of resources (i.e. coins, knowledge) exhibited capacity to trigger exploratory learning; increasing scarcity would urge players to deliberate their choices: "Maybe make money more scarce to make it so that you really have to make bigger decisions" (1606170101).

Challenge, Rules and Goals for Complex Learning Events

More complex learning events, such as 'Self-reflection' and 'Debate' occurred especially in relation to mechanics of the game dimension 'Rules and Goals' and 'Challenge', such as those that allowed the players to select and pursue a strategy, or to negotiate and cooperate with other players. Learning events of 'Self-reflection' were mostly evident when game mechanics urged players to deal with uncertainties such as dealing with projects' hidden effects or global events and triggered the need to adjust individual strategies: "...throughout the game you get a lot of surprises where you see that your tactic doesn't make much sense at all. And yes, somehow this is reality also when you are in a project or in policy." (160605-02). Reflection and debate on the need of in-game and real-life cooperation and competition was prevalent: "Community Force is needed for the transition" (1606050101), "Collaboration, include different perspectives on an energy project" (1606220205) or "that you need each other and that you need to balance money, knowledge, permits" (1610300108), illustrate characteristic remarks. Particularly, the negotiations for creating partnerships with other players sparked social interaction, debate and collaborative action among the players: "You talk, negotiate and have fun while doing so!!!" (1606280303), "It's a serious game but there was room for socializing." (1606150103) and "The social component, choosing who to involve was in the beginning based on social norms, at the end it was based on game tactics" (1606150101), illustrate that the reflection on behavioural aspects and norms such as social reciprocity also occurred during the gameplay.

Collaboration was a core topic and one of the most obvious complex learning outcomes observed during the gameplay, where players linked in-game and real-world practices: "I would say it's sort of like a real life setting and it's nice to get partners along to accomplish projects that's sort of the... sometimes it's easy if there is a lot to gain." (160615-01); "That's maybe the big learning effect of the game: selected alliances with people and stakeholders that are needed to get through with something. That's what you learn from it." (160605-02) and "I think what I learned most is that it really makes very explicit that it requires cooperation or that you have to interact with other people in a governance landscape or in a governance network, to keep these goals. These are not goals that you can achieve by yourself." (160616-01). Overall 62% of the players reported that the game demonstrated that environmental problems can only be addressed through cooperation with others. It was also a topic that was strongly debated during the debriefing sessions: "I think the game tries to bring across the message that you can only achieve things collectively" (160605-02) and "Cooperation is more beneficial than trying to work for yourself. So that's the message that comes across, right?" (160615-01).

However, the broad perception of the positive value and the need for collaborative behaviour was also scrutinized. The game dimension "Selection of goals" enabled players to choose and play the game either in a collaborative or competitive fashion: "I had another expectation of the game because I am focused on using games for more cooperative (sic) and then this is not working." (160614-02) and "In the beginning (we played) more cooperative because you know you need each other for a longer period of time but when you know that time is running out why bother?" (160615-01). Thus, using mechanics that offer players the choice to select their own goal, act in different fashions and reflect on them, might be a powerful learning element that mirrors real-world complexities in the game.

CONCLUSION

Game-based learning is a complex phenomenon that emerges during the gameplay. Players simultaneously imitate the behaviours of other players, receive and process information, make decisions, explore different strategies, and engage in negotiations, conflicts and discussions with other players. Energy Safari advantages strategic attitude and exchange between players in the form of negotiations and discussions. These learning events resulted from game mechanics such as selecting goals, deciding on project types, and answering quiz questions designed in a way that allow collaboration and competition, common sense and creative approaches. Though the research indicates that Energy Safari evoked simple, intermediate, and complex learning events, some of the 8LEM learning events occurred rather modestly. This limitation did neither harm the run-time behaviour nor the overall learning outcome, which has also been illustrated in another study on a game from the "Safari" family (Gugerell, Jauschneg, Platzer, & Berger, 2017). However, we speculate that there might be an effect on the game enjoyment of different player types, and subsequently on their willingness to engage in serious learning games: while 'Socialisers' and 'Seekers' might be well served with the reflective and discursive game play, 'Daredevils' might be insufficiently challenged by the few mechanics in the 'Challenge' dimension (Gugerell, Funovits, & Ampatzidou, 2019; Nacke, Bateman, & Mandryk, 2014). On the other hand, the same mechanics have sometimes triggered more than one learning event. For example, the quiz questions were associated with reception of information, but they also prompted players to reflect on their own practices, or debate with other players trying to find the correct answer.

The research shows that the same game mechanic can trigger different learning events in a complex web of player and player-game interactions. Hence, play testing the game prototype in different stages of the design phase is crucial to identify the playability of the game and tune the game mechanics, but also to sufficiently evaluate if the selected game mechanics appropriately trigger the anticipated learning events and meet the established learning goals. Linking to other research (Gugerell, Funovits, & Ampatzidou, 2019), we also suggest including player type testing already in the stage of game design and play-testing for an adequate selection and balancing of game mechanics to achieve a balance between entertainment and leaning goals of serious games. Combining and balancing game mechanics is not only a necessary condition for a more coherent and pleasant gaming experience, but it is also necessary to facilitate a diverse learning experience, including challenges, which align to the players' skill level and adapt to the players' skill development (Kiili, 2005; Hwang, Sung, Hung, Huang, & Tsai, 2012). However, this is easier to achieve in single player games than in multiplayer games, which have to facilitate players with diverging skill levels at once. Hence, a serious game that caters into a broader variety of educational levels might face difficulties regarding matching an appropriate player skill level. The research confirms this mismatch: some elements, such as the quiz questions were identified both as too easy and too difficult by players of different backgrounds, whereas other players found that the game would profit from increased complexity and fidelity to realistic situations. Even though the sample of players were predominantly highly educated, the current version of the game prototype failed to adapt to their different skills and literacy. Consequently, it might be necessary to develop and implement tailor-made game mechanics, that match different literacy levels (i.e. different difficulty levels of quiz questions) and skill sets, such as beginner or advanced versions, or different game levels to sustain an enjoyable gaming and learning experience.

As more than 2/3 of the players reported their willingness to replay the game and recommend it to their friends and family, and a bit less than half of the players reported that playing the game inspired them to learn more about the energy transition in their area, it is safe to assume that Energy Safari functioned well as an engaging and motivating medium. Hence, the research on Energy Safari confirms the results of studies reporting short-term learning improvement. However, the fact that only 15% of the players would be interested to become more involved in a local or regional energy initiative, based on their experience of the serious game indicates that the game falls short in terms of triggering behaviour change. This may partly be attributed to the fact that most players in this study played Energy Safari only once. One-time play is a common limitation in the majority of studies looking into the use of games for learning (Ke, 2016). Thus, the question of long-term impact, such as behaviour change, needs to be studied further. The data illustrates that the current assemblage of game mechanics only modestly trigger learning events that may lead to change of social practises in real world settings. We speculate that this shortcoming might be linked to players' inability to assess what exactly they have learned, and that players often did not recognise these activities as learning events, explaining the players' low self-evaluation of learning. Consequently, if learning outcomes remain subliminal, their translation to actionable knowledge is exacerbated or even not possible at all. On the other hand, one might argue that the game performs well, since players don't even notice that they are learning (Aldrich, 2005). We thus conclude that there is a delicate tension in the design of serious games: achieving an adequate balance between subliminal and tacit learning to sufficiently manage run-time behaviour, fun, and also allow a transformation of learning to actionable knowledge and call for action.

As such, the role of the game facilitator in transforming learning events into sustained learning experiences and actionable knowledge appears pivotal. In the 8LEM (2005), Leclercq and Poumay argue for the importance of the tutor in instigating and coordinating the learning events in multiple ways, including being a model to be imitated, providing the message to be transmitted, motivating the learners to act and supporting them in interpreting the consequences of their actions, providing access to information, animating the debates and more (Leclercq & Poumay, 2005). Other studies, focused at classroom use of games, have shown that the role of the teacher is essential in correcting false impressions, covering knowledge gaps and encouraging discussion on key topics (e.g. Egenfeldt-Nielsen, 2007; Squire & Barab, 2004). Future research should then focus on experimental settings, including a control group playing the game without the support of a facilitator, to empirically establish possible differences and depth of the gameplay and learning, and on determining facilitators' roles, tasks, challenges for their area of responsibility, and necessary skills and trainings for successful applications of serious games (see Ampatzidou, et al., 2018).

To summarize, this study points to some meaningful connections between game mechanics and learning events and views the educational possibilities of serious games with optimism. However, it also opens up some directions where further research is necessary to evaluate the long-term learning effectiveness of games and the more coherent integration of game mechanics and learning goals. Particularly when aimed at civic participation processes with intended impact on participants' behaviour, applications of games should take into account a broader diversity of audience, with different learning needs and styles, and should be used complementarily with other methods.

ACKNOWLEDGMENT

The article is a delivery of the research project "Playing with Urban Complexity. Using co-located serious games to reduce the urban carbon footprint among young adults", funded by JPI Urban Europe.

REFERENCES

Abdul Jabbar, A., & Felicia, P. (2015, December). Gameplay engagement and Learning in Game-based Learning: A Systematic Review. *Review of Educational Research*, *85*(4), 740–779. doi:10.3102/0034654315577210

Abt, C. (1969). *Serious Games*. New York: Viking Press.

Aldrich, C. (2005). *Learning by Doing: A Comprehensive Guide to Simulations, Computer Games, and Pedagogy in e-Learning and Other Educational Experiences*. Pfeiffer: John Wiley and Sons.

Ampatzidou, C., Gugerell, K., Constantinescu, T., Devisch, O., Jauschneg, M., & Berger, M. (2018). All Work and No Play? Facilitating Serious Games and Gamified Applications in Participatory Urban Planning and Governance. *Urban Planning*, *3*(1), 34–46. doi:10.17645/up.v3i1.1261

Ampatzidou, C., Gugerell, K., Diephuis, J., Devisch, O., Constantinescu, T., Jauschneg, M., & Berger, M. (2015). *The Mechanics of Playful Participatory Processes. In Design, Social Media and Technology to foster Civic Self-Organisation* (pp. 185–196). Hasselt: University of Hasselt.

Argyris, C. (1977). Double loop learning in organizations. *Harvard Business Review*, (September-October), 115–125.

Arnab, S., Lim, T., Carvalho, M. B., Bellotti, F., de Freitas, S., Louchart, S., ... De Gloria, A. (2014). Mapping learning and game mechanics for serious games analysis. *British Journal of Educational Technology*, *46*(2), 391–411. doi:10.1111/bjet.12113

Bedwell, W. L., Pavlas, D., Heyne, K., Lazzara, E. H., & Salas, E. (2012). Toward a Taxonomy Linking Game Attributes to Learning: An Empirical Study. *Simulation & Gaming*, *43*(6), 729–760. doi:10.1177/1046878112439444

Bellotti, F., Kapralos, B., Lee, K., Moreno-Ger, P., & Berta, R. (2013). Assessment in and of Serious Games: An Overview. *Advances in Human-Computer Interaction*, *2013*, 1–11. doi:10.1155/2013/136864

Boyle, A., Connolly, M. T., Hainey, T., & Boyle, M. J. (2012). Engagement in digital entertainment games: A systematic review. *Computers in Human Behavior*, *28*(3), 771–780. doi:10.1016/j.chb.2011.11.020

Brockmyer, J. H., Fox, C. M., Curtiss, K. A., McBroom, E., Burkhart, K. M., & Pidruzny, J. N. (2009). The development of the Game Engagement Questionnaire: A measure of engagement in video game-playing. *Journal of Experimental Social Psychology*, *45*(4), 624–634. doi:10.1016/j.jesp.2009.02.016

Buckingham, D., & Sefton-Green, J. (2003). Gotta Catch 'em all: Structure, Agency and Pedagogy in Children's Media Culture. *Media Culture & Society*, *25*(3), 379–399. doi:10.1177/0163443703025003005

Clark, D. B., Tanner-Smith, E. E., & Killingsworth, S. (2014). *Digital Games, Design and Learning: A Systematic Review and Meta- Analysis. Executive Summary*. Menlo Park: SRI Education.

Clark, R. E. (2007). Learning in serious games? Arguments, evidence, and research suggestions. *Educational Technology, 47*(3), 56–59.

Cook, D. (2006, October 23). What are Game Mechanics? *Lost Garden*. Retrieved from http://www.lostgarden.com/2006/10/what-are-game-mechanics.html

Cooper, S. (2014). *A Framework for scientific discovery through video games*. New York: Morgan & Claypool Publishers. doi:10.1145/2625848

Crookall, D. (2010). Serious Games, Debriefing, and Simulation / Gaming as a Discipline. *Simulation & Gaming, 41*(6), 898–920. doi:10.1177/1046878110390784

Dahlgren, P. (2009). *Media and Political Engagement: Citizens, Communication, and Democracy*. New York: Cambridge University Press.

de Caluwe, L., Geurts, J., & Kleinlugtenbelt, W. (2012). Gaming Research in Policy and Organization: An assessment from the Netherlands. *Simulation & Gaming, 43*(5), 600–626. doi:10.1177/1046878112439445

de Kort, Y. A., IJsselsteijn, W. A., & Poels, K. (2007). Digital Games as Social Presence Technology: Development of the Social Presence in Gaming Questionnaire (SPGQ). In *Proceedings of PRESENCE 2007: The 10th International Workshop on Presence* (pp. 195-203).

Denham, A. R. (2013). Strategy instruction and maintenance of basic multiplication facts through digital game play. *International Journal of Game-Based Learning, 3*(2), 36–54. doi:10.4018/ijgbl.2013040103

Denham, A. R. (2016). Improving the design of a learning game through intrinsic integration and playtesting. *Technology, Knowledge. Learning, 21*, 175–194.

Devisch, O., Poplin, A., & Sofronie, S. (2016). The Gamification of Civic Participation: Two Experiments in Improving the Skills of Citizens to Reflect Collectively on Spatial Issues. *Journal of Urban Technology, 23*(2), 81–102. doi:10.1080/10630732.2015.1102419

Dörner, R., Martin-Niedecken, A., Kocher, M., Baranowski, T., Kickmeier-Rust, M., Göbel, S., . . . Gebelein, P. (2016). Contributing Disciplines. In R. Dörner, S. Göbel, W. Effelsberg, & J. Wiemeyer (Eds.), Serious Games. Foundations, Concepts and Practise (pp. 35-82). Springer International Publishing Switzerland. doi:10.1007/978-3-319-40612-1_2

Downs, J., Vetere, F., Howard, S., & Loughnan, S. (2013). Measuring audience experience in social videogaming. In *Proceedings of the 25th Australian Computer-Human Interaction Conference: Augmentation, Application, Innovation, Collaboration* (pp. 217-220). Adelaide: ACM.

Driskell, J. E., & Dwyer, D. J. (1984, February). Microcomputer videogame based training. *Educational Technology, 24*(2), 11–17.

Drisko, J. W., & Maschi, T. (2016). *Content analysis*. New York, NY: Oxford University Press.

Egenfeldt-Nielsen, S. (2007). *The educational potential of computer games*. New York: Continuum.

Egenfeldt-Nielsen, S., Heide Smith, J., & Pajares Tosca, S. (2008). *Understanding videogames: The essential introduction*. New York: Routledge.

Erhel, S., & Jamet, É. (2013). Digital game-based learning: Impact of instructions and feedback on motivation and learning effectiveness. *Computers & Education, 67*, 156–167. doi:10.1016/j.compedu.2013.02.019

Fang, Y.-M., Chen, K.-M., & Huang, Y.-J. (2016). Emotional reactions of different interface formats: Comparing digital and traditional board games. *Advances in Mechanical Engineering, 8*(3), 1–8. doi:10.1177/1687814016641902

Friedmann, J. (1984). Planning as Social Learning. In D. C. Korten & R. Klauss (Eds.), *People-centered development, Contributions towards Theory and Planning Frameworks* (pp. 189–194). West Hartford, CT: Kumarian Press.

Gajadhar, B., de Kort, Y., & Ijsselsteijn, W. (2008). Influence of social setting on player experience in digital games. In J. Kientz, S. Patel, B. Jones, E. Price, E. Mynatt, & E. Abowd (Eds.), *CHI '08 extended abstracts on Human factors in computing systems* (pp. 3099–3104). New York: ACM. doi:10.1145/1358628.1358814

Garris, R., Ahlers, R., & Driskell, J. E. (2002). Games, motivation, and learning: A research and practice model. *Simulation & Gaming, 33*(4), 441–467. doi:10.1177/1046878102238607

Gee, J. (2005). Why Are Videogames Good for Learning? *Spectrum (Lexington, Ky.), 32*, 25–32.

Gläser, J., & Laudel, G. (2010). *Experteninterviews und qualitative Inhaltsanalyse*. VS Verlag für Sozialwissenschaften. doi:10.1007/978-3-531-91538-8

Granic, I., Lobel, A., & Engels, R. C. (2014). The Benefits of Playing Video Games. *The American Psychologist, 69*(1), 66–78. doi:10.1037/a0034857 PMID:24295515

Gugerell, K., Funovits, P., & Ampatzidou, C. (2019). Daredevil or socialiser? Exploring the relations between intrinsic motivation, game experience and player types in serious games with environmental narratives. In *O. Devisch, L. Huybrechts, & R. De Ridder (Eds.), Participatory Design Theory*. Routledge.

Gugerell, K., Jauschneg, M., Platzer, M., & Berger, M. (2017). Playful Participation with Urban Complexity - Evaluation of the Co-located Serious Game Mobility Safari in Vienna. *REAL CORP*, 413-420.

Habgood, J. M., & Ainsworth, S. E. (2011). Motivating children to learn effectively: Exploring the value of intrinsic integration in educational games. *Journal of the Learning Sciences, 20*(2), 169–206. doi:10.1080/10508406.2010.508029

Hamari, J., Shernoff, D. J., Rowe, E., Coller, B., Asbell-Clarke, J., & Edwards, T. (2016). Challenging Games Help Students Learn: An Empirical Study on Engagement, Flow and Immersion in Game-Based Learning. *Computers in Human Behavior, 54*, 170–179. doi:10.1016/j.chb.2015.07.045

Harteveld, C., & Bekebrede, G. (2011). Learning in Single- versus Multiplayer games: The more the merrier? *Simulation & Gaming, 42*(1), 43–63. doi:10.1177/1046878110378706

Hauff, J., Bode, A., Neumann, D., & Haslauer, F. (2014). *Global Energy Transitions - a comparative analysis of key countries and implications for the international energy debate.* Berlin: Weltenergierat. Retrieved from www.atkearney.com/documents/10192/5293225/Global+Energy+Transitions.pdf/220e6818-3a0a-4baa-af32-8bfbb64f4a6b

Hays, R. T. (2005). The Effectiveness of Instructional Games: A Literature Review and Discussion. *Defense Technical Information Center.* Retrieved from http://oai.dtic.mil/oai/oai?verb=getRecord&metadataPrefix=html&identifier=ADA441935

Horelli, L. (2002). A Methodology of participatory planning. In R. Bechtel & A. Churchman (Eds.), *Handbook of Environmental Psychology* (pp. 607–628). New York: John Wiley.

Hunicke, R., Leblanc, M., & Zubek, R. (2004). MDA: A formal approach to Game Design and Game Research. In *Proceedings of the AAAI workshop on Challenges in Game.* AAAI Press.

Hwang, G.-J., Sung, H.-Y., Hung, C.-M., Huang, I., & Tsai, C.-C. (2012). Development of a personalized educational computer game based on students' learning styles. *Educational Technology Research and Development, 60*(4), 623–638. doi:10.100711423-012-9241-x

Iten, N., & Petko, D. (2016). Learning with serious games: Is fun playing the game a predictor of learning success? *British Journal of Educational Technology, 47*(1), 151–163. doi:10.1111/bjet.12226

Järvinen, A. (2008). *Games without Frontiers: Theories and Methods for Game Studies and Design.* Tampere: Tampere University Press. Retrieved July 13, 2015, from http://urn.fi/urn:isbn:978-951-44-7252-7

Juul, J. (2011). Half-Real: Video Games between Real Rules and Fictional Worlds (1st paperback ed.). Cambridge, MA: MIT Press.

Kafai, Y. B. (2001). The Educational Potential of Electronic Games: From Games–To–Teach to Games–To–Learn. *Cultural Policy Center, University of Chicago.* Retrieved from https://culturalpolicy.uchicago.edu/sites/culturalpolicy.uchicago.edu/files/kafai.pdf

Ke, F. (2016). Designing and integrating purposeful learning in game play: A systematic review. *Educational Technology Research and Development, 64*(2), 2019–2244. doi:10.100711423-015-9418-1

Kiili, K. (2005). Digital game-based learning: Towards an experiential gaming model. *The Internet and Higher Education, 8*(1), 13–24. doi:10.1016/j.iheduc.2004.12.001

Kraiger, K., Ford, K. J., & Salas, E. (1993). Application of cognitive, skill-based, and affective theories of learning outcomes to new methods of training evaluation. *The Journal of Applied Psychology, 78*(2), 311–328. doi:10.1037/0021-9010.78.2.311

Kuhk, A., Dehaene, M., & Schreurs, J. (2015). Collective learning experiences in planning: the potential of experimental living labs. In AESOP 2015 - Definite Space - Fuzzy Responsibility. Prague.

Leclercq, D., & Poumay, M. (2005). *The 8 learning events model and its principles.* University of Liège. Retrieved from www.labset.net/media/prod/8LEM.pdf

Lederman, L. (1992). Debriefing: Toward a Systematic Assessment of Theory and Practice. *Simulation & Gaming, 23*(2), 145–160. doi:10.1177/1046878192232003

Lim, T., Carvalho, M. B., Bellotti, F., Arnab, S., de Freitas, S., Louchart, S. . . . De Gloria, A. (2013). The LM-GM framework for Serious Games Analysis. *Information Technology Services, Office of Teaching, Learning and Technology, University of Iowa*. Retrieved from https://teach.its.uiowa.edu/file-resource/836

Luederitz, C., Schäpke, N., Wiek, A., Lang, D. J., Bergmann, M., Bos, J. J., ... Westley, F. R. (2016). Learning through evaluation – A tentative evaluative scheme for sustainability transition experiments. *Journal of Cleaner Production*, 1–16.

Malone, T. W., & Lepper, M. R. (1987). Making Learning fun: a taxonomy of intrinsic motivations for learning. In R. E. Snow, & M. J. Farr (Eds.), Aptitude, Learning, and Instruction Volume 3: Conative and Affective Process Analyses (pp. 223-253). Hillsdale, NJ: Lawrence Erlbaum.

Mayer, I. S. (2009). The Gaming of Policy and the Politics of Gaming: A Review. *Simulation & Gaming*, *40*(6), 825–862. doi:10.1177/1046878109346456

Mayring, P. (2015). *Qualitative Inhaltsanalyse: Grundlagen und Techniken*. Beltz.

Medema, W., Furber, A., Adamowski, J., Zhou, Q., & Mayer, I. (2016). Exploring the potential impact of serious games on social learning and stakeholder collaborations for transboundary watershed management of the St. Lawrence River Basin. *Water (Basel)*, *8*(175).

Milam, D., & Howell-Moroney, M. (2010). Ordering Stakeholder Relationships and Citizen Participation: Evidence from the Community Development Block Grant Program. *Public Administration Review*, *70*(4), 601–609. doi:10.1111/j.1540-6210.2010.02181.x

Mildner, P., & Mueller, F. '. (2016). Design of Serious Games. In R. Dörner, S. Göbel, W. Effelsberg, & J. Wiemeyer (Eds.), Serious Games, Foundations, Concepts and Practice (pp. 57-82). Springer. doi:10.1007/978-3-319-40612-1_3

Nacke, L. E., Bateman, C., & Mandryk, R. L. (2014). BrainHex: A neurobiological gamer typology survey. *Entertainment Computing*, *5*(1), 55–62. doi:10.1016/j.entcom.2013.06.002

Nordin, A., Denisova, A., & Cairns, P. (2014). Too Many Questionnaires: Measuring Player Experience Whilst Playing Digital Games. In *The Seventh York Doctoral Symposium on Computer Science and Electronics*.

Poplin, A. (2012). Playful public participation in urban planning: A case study for online serious games. *Computers, Environment and Urban Systems*, *36*(3), 195–206. doi:10.1016/j.compenvurbsys.2011.10.003

Posch, A., & Steiner, G. (2006). Integrating research and teaching on innovation for sustainable development. *International Journal of Sustainability in Higher Education*, *7*(3), 276–292. doi:10.1108/14676370610677847

Prensky, M. (2006). *Don't bother me, Mom, I'm learning!: how computer and video games are preparing your kids for twenty-first century success and how you can help!* St. Paul, MN: Paragon House.

Raphael, C., Bachen, C., Lynn, K.-M., Balwin-Philippi, J., & McKee, K. A. (2010). Games for Civic Learning: A conceptual Framework and Agenda for Research and Design. *Games and Culture*, *5*(2), 199–235. doi:10.1177/1555412009354728

Sakonnakron, S., Huyakorn, P., & Rizzi, P. (2014). Urban Gaming Simulation for Enhancing Disaster Resilience. A Social Learning Tool for Modern Disaster Risk Management. *Tema - Journal of Land Use, Mobility and Environment*, 841-851.

Shaffer, D. W., Squire, K. R., Halverson, R., & Gee, J. P. (2005). Video Games and the Future of Learning. Wisconsin Center for Education Research, School of Education, University of Wisconsin, Madison, WI.

Shute, V. J., Ventura, M., Bauer, M., & Zapata-Rivera, D. (2009). Melding the Power of Serious Games and Embedded Assessment to Monitor and Foster Learning: Flow and Grow. In U. Ritterfeld, M. Cody, & P. Vorderer (Eds.), *Serious Games: Mechanisms and Effects* (pp. 295–321). New York: Routledge, Taylor and Francis.

Shute, V. J., Ventura, M., & Kim, Y. (2013). Assessment and learning of qualitative physics in Newton's playground. *The Journal of Educational Research*, *8*(2), 1–14.

Sicart, M. (2008). Defining Game Mechanics. *The International Journal of Computer Game Research*, *8*(2).

Spijkerboer, R., Trell, E.-M., & Zuidema, C. (2016). Rural resilience and renewable energy in North-East Groningen, the Netherlands: in search of synergies. In *C. Mose, A. Reichert-Schick, U. Grabski-Kieron, & A. Steinführer (Eds.), European rural peripheries revalued: governance, actors, impacts* (pp. 313–341). Berlin: LIT publishing house.

Squire, K., & Barab, S. (2004). Replaying history: engaging urban underserved students in learning world history through computer simulation games. In *ICLS '04 Proceedings of the 6th international conference on Learning sciences* (pp. 505 - 512). Los Angeles, CA: UCLA Press.

Tan, E. (2014). *Negotiation and Design for the Self-Organizing City*. Delft: TU Delft.

Thiel, S.-K., & Fröhlich, P. (2017). Gamification as Motivation to Engage in Location-Based Public Participation? In G. Gartner & H. Huang (Eds.), *Progress in Location-Based Services - Lecture Notes in Geoinformation and Cartography* (pp. 399–421). Cham, Switzerland: Springer. doi:10.1007/978-3-319-47289-8_20

Vogel, J. J., Vogel, D. S., Cannon-Bowers, J., Bowers, C. A., Muse, K., & Wright, M. (2006). Computer Gaming and Interactive Simulations for Learning: A Meta-Analysis. *Journal of Educational Computing Research*, *34*(3), 229–243. doi:10.2190/FLHV-K4WA-WPVQ-H0YM

Whitton, N. (2011). Encouraging engagement in game-based learning. *International Journal of Game-Based Learning*, *1*(1), 75–84. doi:10.4018/ijgbl.2011010106

This research was previously published in the International Journal of E-Planning Research (IJEPR), 8(2); pages 1-23, copyright year 2019 by IGI Publishing (an imprint of IGI Global).

APPENDIX

Table 7. Examples of projects included in the project cards, along with the implementation conditions required to realise each project, their hidden effects and their output. The projects vary in scale and type and are based on a survey of existing local energy initiatives, regional policies and a co-creative process with relevant stakeholders.

Project Description	Implementation Conditions	Hidden Effects	Output
Energy Saving Projects			
Install a solar heater on your roof to get warm water from the sun.	Network: Get 1 of your neighbors to join you in this project. Each player (including you) has to pay 1 coin to join the initiative.	Block the green tiles around your project. Your project has a multiplier effect on neighboring Energy Saving projects. Participants in existing projects win 1 coin.	2 coins / project owner & 1 coin / contributor 1 KW point/ contributor 1 Community point/ contributor
	Permit: Ask the Housing Corporation for permission: Roll the dice: - 1,2,3 you don't get the permit this time - 4,5,6 you get the permit - If you sacrifice your community points and pay 1 extra coin you can go ahead without a permit.		
	Finance: Check out different retailers. Roll the dice: pay the number you roll in coins.		
Insulate your windows with double glass.	Network: You don't really need your neighbors to do that. But you can double your community points if you find 2 more collaborators.	Pick a Joker card.	2 coins / project owner & 1 coin / contributor 3 KW point/ contributor 1 Community point/ contributor
	Permit: Ask the Housing Corporation to coordinate this: Roll the dice: - 1,2,3 they don't agree to go ahead - 4,5,6 they will support your claim or Answer a Quiz Question.		
	Finance: Negotiate the installation price with a contractor: Roll the dice: pay the number you roll in coins.		
Energy Production Projects			
Make a neighborhood initiative to collectively install solar panels on your rooftops.	Network: Get 2 of your neighbors to join you in this project. Each player (including you) has to pay 1 coin to join the initiative	Your neighbors are inspired by your example. Neighboring projects get 2 Community points per contributor and you get to pick a Joker Card.	2 coins / project owner & 1 coin / contributor 2 KW points/ contributor 5 Community points/ contributor
	Permit: Apply for a subsidy to continue with the project. Answer a Question to prove your knowledge to the committee.		
	Finance: Negotiate the installation price with a solar panel manufacturer. Roll the dice: pay the number you roll minus 2 coins.		
Gather your neighbors to collectively install a windmill in the countryside.	Network: Get 3 of your neighbors to join you in this project. Each player (including you) has to pay 1 coin to join the initiative	you need to take compensatory measures to avoid harm to protected bird species in your area. Pay 1 coin extra.	2 coins / project owner & 1 coin / contributor 1 KW point/ contributor 3 Community points/ contributor
	Permit: Ask the Province for permission. Roll the dice: - 1,2,3 you don't get the permit this time - 4,5,6 you get the permit or Answer a Quiz Question		
	Finance: Collecting the capital necessary can be quite tricky. Apply for a loan to the Bank. Roll the dice: pay the number you roll in coins.		
Agricultural and Industrial Projects			

continues on following page

Table 7. Continued

Project Description	Implementation Conditions	Hidden Effects	Output
Start a small biomass production unit.	Network: Find 2 more partners for this project. Each player (including you) has to pay 1 coin to join the initiative.	Neighbors still complain about the smell. Lose your community points or pay an extra coin for further improvements.	2 coins / project owner & 1 coin / contributor 5 KW points/ contributor 1 Community point/ contributor
	Permit: Ask the City Hall for permission. Roll the dice: - 1,2 you don't get the permit - 3,4 you get the permit - 5,6 you get the permit but the neighbors are afraid that biomass production stinks! It costs you 2 coins extra for time to convince them and the upgrades to your infrastructure.		
	Finance: There are several costs involved in this project. Roll the dice: pay the number you roll in coins.		
Set up a company that will collect municipal solid waste and convert it to biofuel.	Network: Find 3 more partners for this project. Each player (including you) has to pay 2 coins to join the initiative.	That smells bad! You have to pay 3 coins extra to run a campaign about the positive impact of this project.	2 coins / project owner & 1 coin / contributor 7 KW points/ contributor 2 Community points/ contributor
	Permit: The Municipality would love to have something like this in the city, but they want to make sure they commission the right company. Answer a Quiz Question to prove your knowledge.		
	Finance: There are several costs involved in this project. Roll the dice: pay the number you roll in coins.		
Infrastructural and Supporting Projects			
Start an energy cooperation to facilitate other people who want to start their own energy projects.	Network: Find 3 more people to get started. It takes a lot of time to organize this, so it costs 2 coins to you and your partners to get started.	Your project actively supports Energy Production and Saving projects. Contributors in neighboring existing projects win 1 coin and 1 KW point for every investment they have done in Energy Production and Saving projects.	2 coins / project owner & 1 coin / contributor 3 KW points/ contributor 4 Community points/ contributor
	Permit: No permit needed for this but you have to prove your knowledge on local energy issues. Answer a Quiz Question to move on.		
	Finance: There are several costs involved in this project. Roll the dice and pay the number you roll in coins.		
Invest in a start-up testing out special cooling systems for servers based on excess heat from households.	Network: Find 2 more partners for this project. Each player (including you) has to pay 1 coin to join the initiative	You can use your neighbors as a pilot project. Neighboring projects get 2 KW points per participant.	2 coins / project owner & 1 coin / contributor 2 KW points/ contributor 1 Community point/ contributor
	Permit: You don't really need a permit to start a business! But you do need to be well informed about recent tech developments. Answer a quiz question to go on!		
	Finance: There are several costs involved in this project. Roll the dice: pay the number you roll in coins.		

Chapter 25
Towards the Development of a Game for Computational Thinking:
Identifying Students' Needs and Interests

Panagiotis Kosmas

*Center for the Advancement of Research and Development in Educational Technology, Cyprus &
School of Education, University of Nicosia, Cyprus*

Andrea Philippou

Center for the Advancement of Research and Development in Educational Technology, Cyprus

Panagiotis Psomos

University of the Aegean, Greece

ABSTRACT

Computational thinking (CT) is now considered an essential approach for developing critical thinking and 21st-century skills. CT as a teaching methodological approach is more connected to STEM education as it provides clearer conceptual and practical considerations to understand science, computer, and mathematical concepts. Based on the recent literature, educational robotics, applications, and serious games are the means of applying CT in teaching practice. This study examines students' needs, interests, and motivations for using a game in the context of CT. Quantitative analysis from an online questionnaire to 394 students from secondary education in different five countries (Greece, Cyprus, Italy, Poland, United Kingdom) demonstrate the students' game interests and needs that guide us to develop a game for CT's implementation in the classroom. Essential insights, considerations, and implications are providing for the design, development, and use of games for the CT in an educational environment.

DOI: 10.4018/978-1-6684-7589-8.ch025

INTRODUCTION

Nowadays, in the digital society of the 21st century, the exponential onset of computers is forcing a transition in which digital literacy is now a necessary ability to cultivate (Shute, Sun, & Asbell-Clarke, 2017; Angeli & Giannakos, 2020). Most of us use computers regularly and we need to learn how to work with them to get the most out of their computing power (Shute et al., 2017).

It seems that CT is the new literacy. Wing (2006) acknowledged CT as a vital skill cultivated by all literate people attending compulsory education to supplement the other three key competencies: reading, writing, and mathematical skills. Since then, several research studies have been published and many scientific discussions among scholars have been started on how CT can be integrated into the school practice. CT is considered as a thinking process (or otherwise a human thinking ability) that uses analytical and algorithmic methods to formulate, evaluate and solve problems (Bocconi et al, 2016). CT, also, has been advocated by most educational policy makers as a capability that is equally important for all as numeracy and literacy (Bocconi et al, 2016). Not only it is the core for the STEM disciplines and courses (Science, Technology, Engineering and Mathematics), but it is also useful in daily life. The human brain itself is wired to think computationally; therefore, our development and future prospects need to learn how to use its full potential (Henderson, Cortina & Wing, 2007).

In an academic setting, the use of various game tools and educational robotics can be a fun and motivating technique and is recommended to support teaching and learning in the context of CT (Ioannou & Makridou, 2018). Specifically, serious games applications can support teachers' practices providing further understanding and meaningful experiences to students (Anastasiadis, Lampropoulos & Siakas, 2018). As educators continue to unlock their skills, serious and other mobile games, tools or applications are becoming increasingly widespread (Kazimoglu, Kiernan, Bacon, & Mackinnon, 2012). In parallel, students are getting used to gaming in their everyday lives, and technology is even more present around us. Minimizing or eradicating the "digital gap" is vital by promoting more significant involvement in the growing digital environment. Along the same lines, educational robotics is closely related to the CT approach, as it offers to students opportunities to think, develop, construct, communicate, collaborate, and critically reflect on their creations and solutions (Alimisis 2013; Bers, Flannery, Kazakoff, & Sullivan, 2014; Eguchi, 2010).

There are several grey areas in the literature and lots of definitions and explanations, including the definition of CT and mainly how CT can be incorporated into the school curriculum. The use of tools such as robotics posit CT as a very promising area to support learning outcomes at schools (Angeli & Giannakos, 2020). Despite that, different kinds of serious games have been proposed as another way to cultivate students' CT. Based on the existing empirical literature, this chapter aims to provide an important set of considerations regarding the development and the use of robotics and serious games to promote the development of CT in educational contexts. The innovation of this study is the provision of significant conclusions based on secondary education students' perspectives regarding the design and development of a game to be used in the classroom in the context of CT. Educators or researchers could use our findings and conclusions to develop an interesting, meaningful and attractive learning experience applying CT's concepts and approaches.

What follows is first the provision of some theoretical underpinnings, principles, and definitions in CT. After that, the chapter offers an overview of recent empirical studies on the application of games to enhance CT and discusses what the literature demonstrates on the implementation of CT in education. The following section describes the methodology used in this research and presents the most important findings based on the quantitative analysis. Finally, based on the students' responses, the chapter concludes with some important implications for the design, development and use of games for the CT in an educational environment.

COMPUTATIONAL THINKING: DEFINITIONS AND THEORETICAL UNDERPINNINGS

Having as the primary goal to 'foster the 21st century skills necessary to fully participate in the digital world' Bocconi et al., (2016) mentioned that CT is a concept that has been gaining attention recently. Closely linked to coding, programming, algorithmic thinking, CT has been promoted by educational stakeholders along with other skills that are regarded as fundamental for all, such as numeracy and literacy, as well as a means for developing new skills for integration into the employment market (Bocconi et al., 2016), for learning STEM (Weintrop et al., 2014) and for coping with the challenges of the twenty first century (Angeli & Giannakos, 2020). Since it can help youngsters develop skills linked to problem-solving (Henderson, Cortina, & Wing, 2007) and decision-making (Kules, 2016; Wing, 2008), CT has been a subject of attention in studies from various fields in recent years. As a result, CT is a necessary ability for everyone (Hsu, Chang, & Hung, 2018).

In the literature, there is not one current unanimous concept of CT that is being used. Wing (2006) defined the 'computational thinking' as it "*...involves solving problems, designing systems, and understanding human behavior, by drawing on the concepts fundamental to computer science. Computational thinking includes a range of mental tools that reflect the breadth of the field of computer science*" (p.33). Wing, (2006) also, asserted that CT "*represents a universally applicable attitude and skill set everyone, not just computer scientists, would be eager to learn and use*" (p. 33). She also claimed that, "*to reading, writing, and arithmetic, we should add computational thinking to every child's analytical ability*" (Wing, 2006, p. 33). Similarly, Wing (2011), introduced another definition of CT and defined CT as "*the thought processes involved in formulating problems and their solutions so that the solutions are represented in a form that can be effectively carried out by an information-processing agent*" (p. 1).

Although there is currently no distinct unanimous definition of CT, based on the research literature CT is a thought process that applies some core features (Angeli et al., 2016; Wing, 2006; Barr et al., 2011; Bers et al., 2014; National Research Council, 2010; Selby and Woolard, 2013). The features mutual among researchers are four, namely abstraction, decomposition, algorithmic thinking, and debugging. Table 1 defines the core features of computational thinking.

COMPUTATIONAL THINKING AND STEM EDUCATION

For many educators, CT is a relatively new concept. The goal of CT in education is to teach students how to think like computer scientists so that they can solve problems in a way that a computer might (Shuchi & Roy, 2013). The core features of CT as proposed by many researchers are critical and have a strong link with STEM education and learning because of their connection to the STEM disciplinary processes of modelling, reasoning, and problem solving (Foster, 2006; Henderson, Cortina, Hazzan & Wing et al, 2007; Sengupta et al., 2013).

Table 1. Core features of computational thinking

Feature	Definition
Abstraction	The ability to determine what data to preserve for an entity/object and what to neglect (Wing, 2011).
Decomposition	The ability to break down a complicated problem into easier parts in order to comprehend and solve it (National Research Council, 2010; Wing, 2011).
Algorithmic thinking **a. Sequencing** **b. Flow of control**	The capability to prepare a step by step series of actions to solve a problem (Selby, 2014). The ability to place actions in the right order (Selby, 2014). The sequence in which to perform instructions/actions (Selby, 2014).
Debugging	The ability to recognize, delete, and correct mistakes (Selby, 2014).

In addition, the STEM subjects provide a natural setting for CT instruction (Grover & Pea, 2018) and CT was acknowledged as a core scientific practice by the Next Generation Science Standards (NGSS Lead States, 2013). Through CT-embedded scientific inquiry, the integration of CT for science, technology, engineering, and mathematics (STEM) curriculum has the potential to improve science learning and boost student engagement in STEM learning (Yang, Swanson, Chittoori, & Baek, 2018). By promoting innovation and problem solving, incorporating CT into the classroom helps students prepare for the future (Fessakis, Gouli, & Mavroudi, 2013; Kosmas & Zaphiris, 2019). Computation is an indispensable component of STEM disciplines as they are practiced in the professional world (Jona et al., 2014). As a result, to sustain continuous discovery, thinking skills set among STEM educators and students must be developed (Swaid, 2015). Thus, research needs to focus on CT in STEM education (Tang, Yin, Lin, Hadad, & Zhai, 2020). The question that research in STEM education needs to answer is not why we must integrate CT, but how. As a result, it's vital to look for effective ways to include CT in our STEM teaching.

COMPUTATIONAL THINKING AND EDUCATIONAL ROBOTICS

The research in this field has led to many dialogues and thoughts on the best way to teach CT as learners face many academic difficulties (Bonar & Soloway, 1983; Coull & Duncan, 2011). There is a lot of interest in educational robotics currently, as seen by the constant introduction of new educational robots and articles in the media (Komis, Romero, Depover, & Karsenti, 2019). Naturally, academics have begun to investigate the contribution of educational robotics in promoting CT development (Bers, 2010; Grover & Pea, 2013; Kazakoff, Sullivan, & Bers, 2013; Lee et al., 2011). According to research, children who program robots acquire and apply key CT principles including abstraction, automation, analysis, decomposition, modularization, and iterative design (Bers, 2010, Kazakoff et al., 2013; Lee et al., 2011).

In addition to that, research involving younger children found that children as young as four years old may develop modest robotics projects while learning about important principles in engineering, technology, and computer programming (Bers et al., 2010; Bers et al., 2014). For example, Bers et al., (2014) used Lego WeDo robots and the CHERP (Creative Hybrid Environment for Robotics Programming) language in a study with 53 kindergarten children and found that the children were engaged in the process and understood basic programming and CT concepts relevant to sequencing and selecting the correct instructions. Also, in young children's education, the programming of toy robots (e.g., Bee-Bot) is widely applied (Atmatzidou & Demetriadis, 2016). For this activity, in particular, the learner needs to organize the actions (that wants the robot is to carry out) in a sequence of movements, paying attention to spot similar actions in different situations that can be repeated without re-programming them. Hence, the learner carries out useful practices of abstraction and decomposition. This resonates with the different affordances of physical and virtual environments supporting multiple pathways to CT. Angeli and Valanides (2019) looked at the effects of learning with Bee-Bot, a floor-programmable robot, on the computational thinking of young boys and girls. Because Bee-Bot does not provide a visual representation of the command's children use to program it, scaffolding was expected to play a crucial role in developing children's computational thinking skills when learning with it. The findings displayed CT gains among children.

Studies on the development of CT skills in older children have also yielded promising findings. Recent research by Angeli and Makridou (2018) demonstrated that educational robotics (using the kit LEGO WeDo) was an efficient technique for teaching elementary school students CT skills, even in a short intervention period. What is more, two studies were conducted by Constantinou and Ioannou (2018) at a primary and a secondary school in the Eastern Mediterranean to discuss CT gains of students related to their involvement in educational robotics activities. It was found that students participating in the ER interventions showed substantial development in their CT abilities.

Moreover, a research by Ioannou and Angeli (2016) described the efforts towards designing technology-enhanced instruction (using educational robotics and a 3D interactive programming environment) for teaching Computational and Algorithmic Thinking in 8th graders coming from different secondary education schools in Cyprus. Based on the results, the Technological Pedagogical Content Knowledge framework and the Technology Mapping approach, which guided the design of the instructional intervention, were effective in promoting the development and understanding of computational and algorithmic thinking skills and concepts by students, respectively. Ioannou and Makridou (2018) reviewed published literature explicitly focusing on the use of educational robotics to advance the CT skills of students in K-12. The articles reviewed illustrate empirical evidence indicating that educational robotics can promote students' cognitive and social skills.

However, while robotics appears to be an efficient tool for teaching and learning and a fascinating topic for students of all ages, robotics pedagogy is still in its infancy. Despite the fact that the use of Educational Robotics different kinds of other serious games activities has been proposed as a different way to cultivate students' CT. For example, Bellegarde, Boyaval, and Alvarez (as mentioned in Komis, Romero, Depover, & Karsenti, 2019) give a comparative analysis of cognitive mediations at work in the context of an educational device aimed at introducing robotics and computer science to kindergarten students (5-6 years old). The experimental device is a robot named «Blue Bot,» which features three modalities in the realm of serious games: the body, the robot, and the digital tablet (Komis, Romero, Depover, & Karsenti, 2019).

COMPUTATIONAL THINKING AND SERIOUS GAMES

Screening through limited literature, there was found that games existed long before CT was popularized and labelled as an essential skill. Moreover, games that were once disconnected from schools are now being adopted by teachers as a key teaching tool, while such serious games are incorporated into traditional lesson plans so that students learn concepts through playing (Kazimoglu et al., 2012). This comes as no surprise because computer games contain interactive, engaging and immersive elements that have educational affordances (Frazer, Recio, Gilbert, & Wills, 2014). Most of these games involve a scenario designed to cover a basic programming task and learn algorithmic thinking and help students communicate and collaborate with their classmates, whereas some games address more advanced learning objectives (Malliarakis, Satratzemi, & Xinogalos, 2014). The main idea is to close the gap between theory and practice, merge abstract concepts with practical experiences, and inspire students to learn (Vahldick, Mendes, & Marcelino, 2014).

The concept of 'serious games' has been first introduced by Abt (1970); in his book Serious Games Abt suggested that simulations and games can improve education in the classroom as well as in an informal environment. The definition of the' serious game' has been updated many times since 1970. Sawyer (2002) linked serious games with the connection between a serious purpose and the knowledge and technology now present in the video game industry. Nowadays, there is not one unanimous definition of "serious games". The term is currently established and is becoming increasingly popular. Zyda's (2005, p.26) definition of serious games, stated that entertainment is undoubtedly a component: *"Serious game: a mental contest, played with a computer in accordance with specific rules, that uses entertainment to further government or corporate training, education, health, public policy, and strategic communication objectives."* Zyda (2005) states that serious games supplement pedagogy including activities that teach, thereby transferring information or skills and as a result makes games serious. Additionally, he emphasizes, however, that pedagogy must be secondary to the story and that the entertainment aspect comes first (Zyda, 2005).

The emphasis on the entertainment element contrasts with the definition of serious games proposed by Michael and Chen (2006). Michael and Chen (2006, p.21) defined Serious Games as *"games that do not have entertainment, enjoyment, or fun as their primary purpose"*. This definition is consistent with that proposed by, e.g., PIXELearning (PIXELearning.com, 2006); *"The use of computer game and simulation approaches and/or technologies for primarily non-entertainment purposes"*. However, Michael and Chen (2006) noted that this is not to suggest that serious games are not amusing, entertaining, or enjoyable, only that there is an added objective over and above the entertainment aspect.

According to more recent literature, Gouin-Vallerand, Ferreira, & Hotte, (2018) created a serious game to provide students with education as a supplement to everyday school learning. A mobile serious game was created and tested with children to introduce ideas in mathematics and English. The findings demonstrated the serious game's usefulness in persuading youngsters to participate in the educational activity and suggested that their understanding had improved. It also highlighted aspects of the game's design. Also, Hart Margheri, Paci, & Sassone, (2020) supported that serious games provide an engaging, enjoyable teaching environment in which participants learn cyber security theory and ideas and put them into practice while playing the game. During the last decade, the importance of using computer video games in secondary and tertiary education has grown significantly, with the dual focus of sharing theoretical and applied knowledge while delivering lessons, as well as offering a means to attract students and maintain their interest in core subjects at the same time (Kazimoglu et al., 2012). Meanwhile, few studies have explored the usefulness of serious games as technological means to enhance computational thinking.

Curricula that used serious games to specialize in learning programming have found positive effects on students as well as on learning outcomes (Ater-Kranov et al., 2010). In their work, *"A serious game for developing computational thinking and learning introductory computer programming"*, Kazimoglu et al. (2012), created a serious game, through the use of video game technologies, which promotes the development of CT skills in order to make teaching and learning basic computer programming easier.

The main pedagogical advantages presented to emphasize the fact that 'games are engaging and motivational, thus students will be encouraged to learn programming constructs in an entertaining and potentially familiar environment. Then, students will be able to transfer their learning outcomes from that environment into learning introductory computer programming with a programming language'.

Additionally, a study by Wu and Richards (2011) examined the use of a digital game-based curriculum on the emergence of CT skills in middle school students in Taiwan. Specifically, researchers mentioned that the students would be able to perform the essential abilities of CT (decomposition, pattern recognition, pattern generalization and abstractions, algorithm design, and data visualization) and would demonstrate their ability to apply computational thinking skills to problems that were not within the scope of the game. Also, Cano and colleagues (2021) created a serious game (Perdi-Dogs) for children aged 7 to 11 with hearing impairment. The findings illustrated that children were highly motivated to play.

The most frequently occurring outcomes and impacts seem to be knowledge acquisition/content understanding and affective and motivational outcomes (Basawapatna, Koh, & Repenning, 2010; Combefis, Beresnevičius, & Dagienė, 2016). Moreover, playing serious games to learn programming is linked to a range of perceptual, cognitive, behavioral, affective and motivational impacts and outcomes (Theodoropoulos, Antoniou, & Lepouras, 2017). However, the CT education domain is still in its infancy and requires research for developing theories of the learning mechanisms occurring in computer games (Kazimoglu et al., 2012).

Although for the field of CT education, it is clear that serious games lead to a variety of positive outcomes and impacts; it is also acknowledged that the literature on such games is fragmented and lacks coherence. Hence, the impact of serious games on CT development has only been evaluated to a small extent. It should also be taken into account that CT education is particularly challenging for students underrepresented in computing and engineering, such as girls and other learners from nondominant groups (Eordanidis, Gee, & Carmichael, 2017). For these students, programming learning methods and digital games have been used together in such a way that one benefits from another. Last, although robotics and serious games seem to be different tools or techniques to achieve CT skills, both intend to encourage users to deal with tasks computationally through playing.

DESIGNING A SERIOUS GAME

When creating a serious game for children, it's crucial to think about the aspects of the game that will fulfil their demands. The idea that well-designed digital games can help students learn is supported by research (Prensky, 2001, 2006; Gee, 2007, 2008). According to previous studies, a fundamental issue in serious game design is to strike a balance between learning and fun (Arnab et al., 2015). Klopfer, Osterweil, and Salen (2009) advise that design teams should focus on both learning and game play simultaneously from the start of the design process. The balance between instruction and enjoyment can be achieved by "*connecting the learning goals and skills with the mechanics in a non-superficial way*", and by "*recognizing the minimum requirements to maintain user engagement with a given outcome/objective*" (Dimitriadou et al., 2021, p. 142). In order for the game to be entertaining and deliver "individualized feedback for learners," the games must also be interactive. Educators have voiced a desire to present learners with a simulation of reality within a serious game where they may apply what they've learned. Considerations about the best approach to display content in the game, adapting the numerous game components for the target audience, handling all age groups, having back-up activity options for different students, retaining engagement, and playtesting were among the other design issues (Dimitriadou et al., 2021).

Previous research has identified features of children's cognitive development that should be considered when building tablet applications for them, such as holding only one item in memory at a time (Chang, Tilahun, & Breazeal, 2014) or manifesting concentration, or focusing their attention on only one trait at a time. Other studies have discovered a number of concerns with children with tablets that can be linked to their ongoing development of motor skills, such as difficulty with multi-touch (McKnight & Fitton, 2010), drag and drop interaction (Humphries & McDonald, 2011), not recognized gestures (Anthony, Brown, Nias, & Tate, 2013), and misinterpreting touch movements (Anthony, Brown, Nias, & Tate, 2013; McKnight & Fitton, 2010).

Immediate feedback, a sandbox, customizability, and customizable complexity encourage players to work within their own zone of competency when dealing with the game's issue area (Gee, 2003). It's important to strike a balance between addressing these needs and the game's mechanics. When this balance is not achieved, one of two things can happen: (1) if the challenges are too complex for the individual's skills, the game becomes too difficult, causing anxiety; or (2) if the game is too simple, the player's skills are too far above the game's challenges, the child becomes bored and loses motivation. Furthermore, interaction with tangible objects piques children's interest and can motivate them; yet, digital apps have not yet to be widely adopted in children's learning. Children's social interactions provide a wealth of information for their learning, not just in terms of language but also in terms of behavioral, cognitive, and social dynamics (Cano et al., 2016). CT as a serious game can be a useful tool in the teaching–learning process for children. Designing a serious game necessitates a technique that entails the collaboration of several experts in the subject in order to identify goals that can be applied to the context of use.

METHODOLOGY

The study follows a quantitative approach (Roni, Merga, & Morris, 2020) with the aim to identify the needs and interests of the students in secondary education in order to start working on the designing of a serious game.

An online survey was distributed to secondary students in five countries (Cyprus, Greece, Poland, Italy, UK). Participants were 394 students (N=394) who attended five countries' lower and upper secondary education in the private and public sectors. Namely, 47 students from Cyprus, 39 students from Greece, 190 students from Poland, 98 students from Italy, and 20 students from the United Kingdom. The survey aimed to explore the gaming interests of the students in lower and higher secondary education to use this knowledge to develop an attractive game concept and learning environment in the context of CT.

The educators, through a link, administered the questionnaire to the participants for approximately 10-15 minutes. The questionnaire was created in English and it was translated to Greek, Italian and Polish. The survey included both close-ended and open-ended questions that allowed participants to express their satisfaction on specific aspects of game interests.

First of all, at the beginning of the questionnaire, participants were informed about the aim of the study, issues regarding GDPR and they were asked about their informed consent. After that, they were asked to answer some background information questions, for example, about age, sex and school grade. Then, participants were asked 11 closed ended questions regarding games: 1) if they have played an education game before, 2) if they think that solving problems related to mathematics in a game is important, 3) how much time they spend playing games, 4) why they are playing games, 5) their preferred device, 6) their preferred type of game and 7) setting as well as questions in terms of 8) interaction and 9) comparison with other players, 10) features of games that find most appealing and 11) if they would like to create their own character. To manipulate the game aspects that keep players immersed through the educational content of the game, participants were instructed to rate ten statements about games. For example, "I learn better if I can relate the experiences of an educational game to experiences in real life", on a scale from 1 ('Strongly Agree') to 5 ('Strongly Disagree'). Finally, one open-ended question was used to allow the participants to express their comments, suggestions, and opinions on any other game elements that they would consider important to be included in the game to make it more engaging and attractive.

The survey questionnaire was developed online using the Google Forms software to be able to be administered online. This option works well in terms of saving time as the online software automatically collects the questionnaires and allows visual representation of the data. Also, it offers convenience and easy access to participants as they can fill the questionnaire from everywhere and when they choose according to their own time schedules.

As for the analysis of the results, descriptive analysis was performed in some significant findings regarding the students' responses in the survey (Petscher, Schatschneider, & Compton, 2013).

RESULTS

In this section, we present the main results that emerged from the analysis of the online questionnaire, focusing on data regarding some demographics data, game characteristics and features and students' preferences and interests.

Starting with demographic data, it seems that the majority of students that answered the survey were female. This applies to all countries except the UK, where the majority of students were male. The gender of students that participated in the survey in all countries is shown in figure 1.

Next, the students were asked to report how much time per week they spend online or playing games or using technology devices. A lot of time is spent by children playing, which is as was actually expected. It seems that the majority of the students play games on average for 4 to 6 hours weekly. Specifically, students in the UK spend more time playing games (average time 6 hours) than the other countries that participated in the research. Students from Greece spend less time playing games (average 4 hours), while in Cyprus, Italy, and Poland the average time is 2-4 hours (see figure 2). Of course, that is a positive indicator that we should use learning through playing. Even better we believe that this could be done through hiding learning in the playing. Mobile or serious games is a way to achieve that goal.

In the question "Would you like the fact that you could compare your performance with that of other players?", the majority of students answered yes. From the responses, it is evident that students want their performance to be compared with other players during the game. As we can see in all countries, competition is an element that students prefer during playing (see figure 3). Thus, adding the competition factor in gaming enhances the motivation of students which is key to learning.

Figure 1. Participants' gender

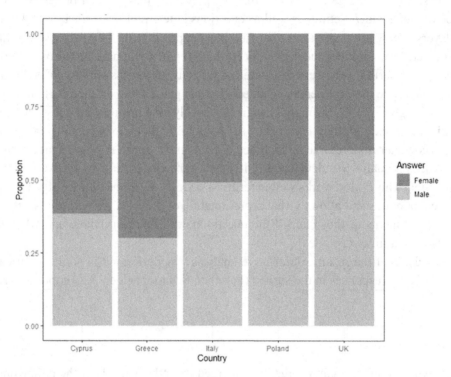

Figure 2. Time spent per week on playing games

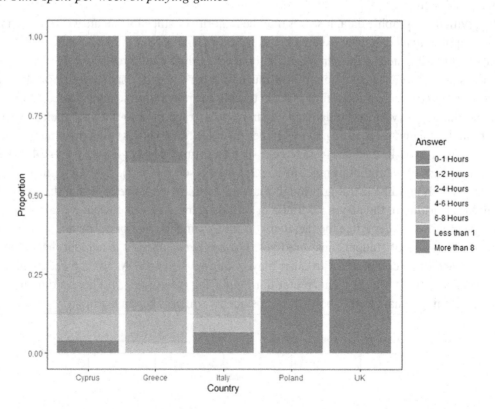

Figure 3. Competition during playing

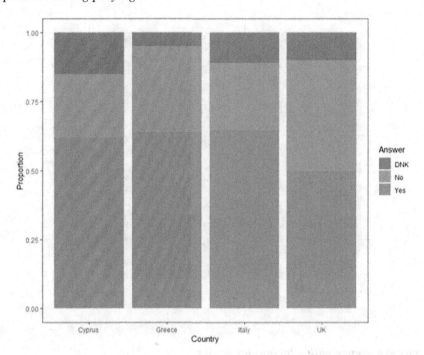

In the following question, students shared their opinion regarding the most appealing features in a game. Namely, students had to select among the following features: challenges, clear goal, feedback, graphics, reality, sound, and storyline. The storyline is the most important feature based on students' responses, followed by challenges and graphics. Notably, in Greece and Italy the most appealing feature is the storyline, while in UK and Cyprus the proffered feature is the possibility of playing the game through challenges. One also important feature, according to the students, is the graphics that games have. A less important feature for students is the sound and the clear goal of the game (see figure 4). That's really important for the design and development of the game since the storyline seems to be an excellent feature for all students. Therefore, one consideration for the development is to add a good story in a game since our minds are hardwired to store information in a storytelling format.

In the question "Have you played an educational game before in the classroom?" the majority of students from all countries gave a positive answer. It seems that almost all participating students have previous experience with educational games. Only in Greece and Italy a high percentage of students said no compared to the students from Cyprus, the UK, and Poland (see figure 5). The real challenge when developing a game for learning purposes is to create a really engaging game and create a flow to students and not just presenting educational information in a media format.

As shown in figure 6, the smartphone is the most common answer regarding the preferred device for playing games, followed by PC. Specifically, students from Cyprus, Greece, and Italy preferred to play games using a smartphone, while students from Poland preferred to use a PC. Students from the UK claimed that the preferred device for them is Xbox (see figure 6).

Figure 4. Appealing features in a game according to students

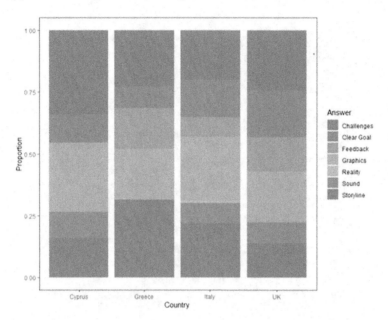

Figure 5. Previous experience with educational games

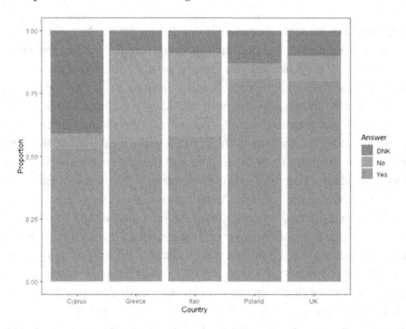

One crucial characteristic/element of such educational games is the possibility to create your own character. As shown in figure 7, it is profound that the vast majority of participating students from all countries, would like to have the option to create their own character while playing a game. Only a small number of students said no. It is undoubtedly a feature that should be added in every online game since the game's personalization is enhanced in that way.

Figure 6. Students preferred devices for playing games

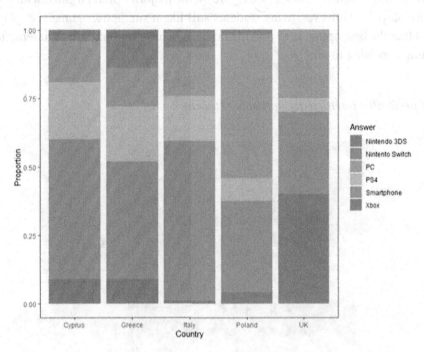

Figure 7. Would you like to create your own character?

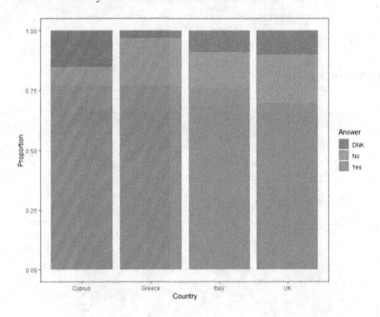

Furthermore, interactivity is one of the most important aspects that we need to consider when designing or developing a game to be used by students in the classroom. Students were asked to answer a question related to whether they prefer a single user or multiplier game. Students' options were three: playing the game alone, two players, more than two players. We report only the responses from students in Cyprus,

Italy and UK. According to the responses (see figure 8), the majority prefer a game with multiple players (i.e. two or more players). However, many students still like a single user game (i.e. playing the game alone). It seems that the best option is to provide both single user and multi-user interaction to students to make the game appealing to all.

Figure 8. Most preferable interactivity option for students

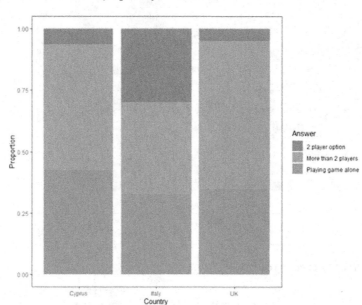
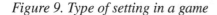

Figure 9. Type of setting in a game

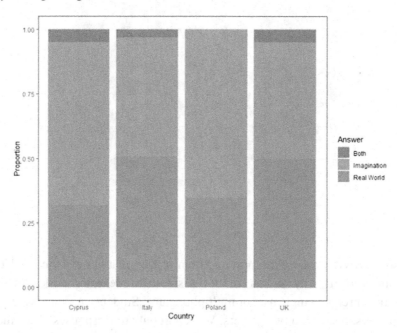

Last, in the question "what type of setting do you prefer?" students hat to choose whether they prefer an imagination setting or a Real World or both settings. As shown in figure 9, imagination is the most popular answer for all students except for Italian students who prefer real world settings. Almost none of the participating students chose the option for both settings (imagination and real world). Therefore, it seems that imagination with some real-world elements could be the best option when developing a game for students.

DISCUSSION

CT in education is emerging worldwide. It seems to be a promise for the education of the new generation of children. Based on the research many countries are introduced CT or they currently planning to introduce it and/or related concepts into compulsory primary and secondary education and proceed to the curricula reforms.

Moreover, teaching CT may require new pedagogical approaches that put students at the centre of the learning process. The employment of educational robotics and serious games in an educational gaming setting are some techniques advocated to help with teaching and learning. The research was conducted investigating the use of Educational Robotics and CT gains. Specifically, the use of educational robotics is demonstrated by recent research (e.g. Angeli & Valanides, 2019; Angeli & Makridou, 2018; Constantinou & Ioannou, 2018; Ioannou & Angeli, 2016; Ioannou & Makridou, 2018) as an efficient technique for teaching students CT skills. The use of serious games is considered a helpful technique as well. The reasoning behind this is that because games are engaging and motivating, children will be motivated to learn in a fun and possibly familiar setting (Frazer et al, 2014). Furthermore, a curriculum that uses serious games has proven good benefits for students and learning results (Ater-Kranov et al., 2010; Kazimoglu et al.,2012). Serious games seem to contribute effectively to this experience (Gouin-Vallerand et al., 2018; Hart et al., 2020), however more research is needed given that the CT education domain is still in its infancy and requires research for developing theories of the learning mechanisms occurring in computer games.

This chapter conducted a literature review on the role of CT, the role of educational robotics and serious games and the relationship between CT and the state-of-the-art of educational robotics and serious games as a didactical approach for students to learn CT ways and principles. Also, this chapter conducted a field research on students' game interests. Specifically, based on students' responses, a game's specific features and characteristics will make the learning more interesting and engaging for students. This will aim to create a serious game concept that will improve students' CT skills.

Considering everything, it is evident that most of the students have played a game in the classroom before. The majority of students spend playing games on average 4 to 6 hours per week, but a significant percentage of students play more than 8 hours. The majority of the students preferred to use a smartphone to play a game and they prefer to play action, strategy games, sports games, and FSP games in a real-world or imagination setting. In terms of interaction, they prefer to play a game with two or more players, and they would like to compare their performance with that of other players. Most of them they would like to create their own character. The students, also, mentioned that, the most appealing features of the games are challenges, graphics, storyline and clear goal. The majority of them play for pleasure, excitement, competition, challenge, relaxation and leisure.

Additionally, students supported that they learn better if they can relate the experiences of an educational game to experiences in real life and when each new piece of knowledge builds on pre-existing knowledge. Furthermore, they enjoy games that seem too hard and they find feedback on their actions in-game help them to progress. They prefer playing games that have clear goals to achieve. They feel that they learn more when they are engaged in a role they play in a game and they can understand a subject being taught to them if they can experiment with the ideas that are taught. Finally, they are more engaged in games when using knowledge about the game's story and the world to solve problems and if the rewards/bonuses are adjusted to the difficulty of the performance.

Limitations

Although the research has reached its aims, there are some limitations to be addressed in future research. First, our findings are mainly focused on the gaming characteristics that students choose for a serious game, which is a major limitation of this study. Given that the serious game is intended for instructional reasons, additional factors such as students' learning styles may have an impact on their gaming preferences. Future research could gather qualitative data on students' gaming experiences, habits, and interests in order to conduct more extensive analyses and get new insights. On the other hand, obtaining this information is vital and will be the next step for us to fit the game to its educational objective successfully. Also, another limitation of the study is that the questionnaire didn't include topics or questions in relation to STEM or CT. We wanted to create a simple questionnaire for students as a preliminary part of our research. The aim was to examine the students' interests and motivation in playing an educational game in the classroom. Our future intention is to involve teachers in our analysis to see their perspective on the implementation of CT through a game.

FUTURE RESEARCH DIRECTIONS AND IMPLICATIONS

This research provides some important quantitative data regarding the game interests of secondary education students. Future directions involve designing or developing a game by applying all of the above preferences raised by the research participants. Some of the essential considerations when designing a game for CT that need to be taken into account include:

- *Interactivity.* It seems that this is one of the most important features that a serious or mobile game provides. The level of interaction is crucial for the game's success. According to the students, the game must offer opportunities for interaction with other players, but not as a mandatory choice. Players could have the possibility to choose if they want to interact with other players or not.
- *Storyline.* According to students, it is one attractive game feature. Narrative and storytelling attract students' attention and curiosity. Interesting storytelling also motivates students to continue and complete the game to investigate what happened and why. Students can write a story about a topic and act it out with various robots.
- *Challenge-based approach.* A game should have some real-world challenges. During the game students must be faced with a real problem that needs to be solved. This would allow students to critically think, identify the possible alternatives, investigate, and finally propose solutions. The

challenges will enable students to gain deep knowledge and develop their skills. The challenge-based approach can be used for designing educational robotics as well.

- *Creativity.* The game should offer possibilities to the students to create or develop something, for example, a character of the game. This is also something that could attract students' interest to play an educational game. Educational Robotics foster students' creativity as it gives the opportunity them to create and develop something.
- *Competition.* Students claimed that it is interesting for them to compete with other players during the game. When a competitive environment is created in a serious game, students' motivation and academic performance improve significantly (Cagiltay, Ozcelik, & Ozcelik, 2015). Robotics Competitions are organized as well in order to increase students' motivation.
- *Educational robotics.* Some numerous games and applications engage students in robotics, teaching them how to code with robotics. Students through the use of robots involved in problem-solving situations and systems thinking. It is now time to consider how a serious game could adopt the logic of robots and provide valuable learning experiences to students. Many characteristics of educational robotics could serve as principles in the development of a game for CT. For example, characteristics such as teamwork, collaboration, problem-solving approaches etc. Could be some basic principles when designing a game in the context of CT.
- *Programming.* The process of producing a set of instructions that inform a computer how to complete a task.

In addition, future endeavors need to be implemented on how educational robotics and serious games could be connected. Although educational robotics and serious games are different techniques to achieve CT gains, both could be considered as methods to achieve 21st century skills through playing. Future studies could explore methods, strategies and approaches on how serious games and robotics can be integrated in the classroom.

Finally, to give a systematic and structured evaluation of the game concept, a set of rigorous experiments needs to be constructed. These will provide analytic data to see if the game successfully supports the development of CT abilities and, as a result, if the game aids students in learning and applying the essential ideas in their lessons. The results need to be analyzed to be able to determine the impact of this game approach and any advantages that can be derived from it.

CONCLUSION

CT has become a buzzword that seems to promise the education of a new generation of children with a much deeper understanding of our digital world. Through the above field research, we looked at the role of CT in education, the relationship between CT and the serious games as a didactical approach for students to learn CT ways and principles. The information collected stresses a clear tendency; the educational landscape is changing fast, and we are now at a tipping point. Various initiatives centered on CT in education are emerging worldwide. Serious games seem to contribute effectively to this experience; however, more research is needed given that the CT education domain is still in its infancy and requires research for developing theories of the learning mechanisms occurring in computer games. We believe that this research offers a clearer understanding of CT in education and provides useful implications for researchers and educators who want to apply CT concepts using games in their practices.

ACKNOWLEDGMENT

This paper was created within Erasmus+ Project CTApp: Teaching Students Computational Thinking Through a Mobile Application [Project Number: 2020-1-PL01-KA201-081924]

REFERENCES

Abt, C. C. (1970). *Serious Games*. Viking Press.

Alimisis, D. (2013). Educational robotics: Open questions and new challenges. *Themes Science and Technology Education*, 6(1), 63–71.

Anastasiadis, T., Lampropoulos, G., & Siakas, K. (2018). Digital game-based learning serious games in education. *International Journal of Advances in Scientific Research and Engineering*, 4(12), 139–144. doi:10.31695/IJASRE.2018.33016

Angeli, C., & Giannakos, M. (2020). Computational thinking education: Issues and challenges. *Computers in Human Behavior*, 105, 106185. doi:10.1016/j.chb.2019.106185

Angeli, C., & Makridou, E. (2018). Developing Third-Grade Students' Computational Thinking Skills with Educational Robotics. In E. Langran & J. Borup (Eds.), *Proceedings of Society for Information Technology & Teacher Education International Conference* (pp. 1-8). Association for the Advancement of Computing in Education (AACE). Retrieved January 20, 2021 from https://www.learntechlib.org/primary/p/182493/

Angeli, C., & Valanides, N. (2020). Developing young children's computational thinking with educational robotics: An interaction effect between gender and scaffolding strategy. *Computers in Human Behavior*, 105, 105954. doi:10.1016/j.chb.2019.03.018

Angeli, C., Voogt, J., Fluck, A., Webb, M., Cox, M., Malyn-Smith, J., & Zagami, J. (2016). A K-6 Computational Thinking Curriculum Framework- Implications for Teacher Knowledge. *Journal of Educational Technology & Society*, 19(3), 47–57.

Anthony, L., Brown, Q., Nias, J., & Tate, B. (2013). Examining the need for visual feedback during gesture interaction on mobile touchscreen devices for kids. *Proceedings of the 12th International Conference on Interaction Design and Children -IDC '13*, 157–164. 10.1145/2485760.2485775

Arnab, S., Lim, T., Carvalho, M. B., Bellotti, F., De Freitas, S., Louchart, S., Suttie, N., Berta, R., & De Gloria, A. (2015). Mapping learning and game mechanics for serious games analysis. *British Journal of Educational Technology*, 46(2), 391–411. doi:10.1111/bjet.12113

Ater-Kranov, A., Bryant, R., Orr, G., Wallace, S., & Zhang, M. (2010). Developing a community definition and teaching modules for computational thinking: accomplishments and challenges. *Proceedings of the 2010 ACM conference on Information technology education*. 10.1145/1867651.1867689

Atmatzidou, S., & Demetriadis, S. (2016). Advancing students' computational thinking skills through educational robotics: A study on age and gender relevant differences. *Robotics and Autonomous Systems*, 75(Part B), 661–670. doi:10.1016/j.robot.2015.10.008

Basawapatna, A. R., Koh, K. H., & Repenning, A. (2010). Using scalable game design to teach computer science from middle school to graduate school. *Proceedings of the Fifteenth Annual Conference on Innovation and Technology in Computer Science Education*, 224–228. 10.1145/1822090.1822154

Bers, M. U. (2010). The TangibleK robotics program: Applied computational thinking for young children. *Early Childhood Research & Practice*, *12*(2), 2.

Bers, M. U., Flannery, L., Kazakoff, E. R., & Sullivan, A. (2014). Computational thinking and tinkering: Exploration of an early childhood robotics curriculum. *Computers & Education*, *72*, 145–157. doi:10.1016/j.compedu.2013.10.020

Bocconi, S., Chioccariello, A., Dettori, G., Ferrari, A., & Engelhardt, K. (2016). *Developing computational thinking in compulsory education-Implications for policy and practice* (No. JRC104188). Joint Research Centre (Seville site).

Bonar, J., & Soloway, E. (1983, January). Uncovering principles of novice programming. In *Proceedings of the 10th ACM SIGACT-SIGPLAN symposium on Principles of programming languages* (pp. 10-13). ACM.

Cagiltay, N. E., Ozcelik, E., & Ozcelik, N. S. (2015). The effect of competition on learning in games. *Computers & Education*, *87*, 35–41. doi:10.1016/j.compedu.2015.04.001

Cano, S., Arteaga, J. M., Collazos, C. A., Gonzalez, C. S., & Zapata, S. (2016). Toward methodology for serious games design for children with auditory impairments. *IEEE Latin America Transactions*, *14*(5), 2511–2521. doi:10.1109/TLA.2016.7530453

Chang, A., Tilahun, L., & Breazeal, C. (2014). Visualisations of Data from the Literacy Tablet Reading Project in Rural Ethiopia. In *Proceedings of the Electronic Visualisation and the Arts (EVA)*, 142–149. 10.14236/ewic/EVA2014.35

Combefis, S., Beresnevičius, G., & Dagienė, V. (2016). Learning programming through games and contests: Overview, characterisation and discussion. *Olympiads in Informatics*, *10*(1), 39–60. doi:10.15388/ioi.2016.03

Constantinou, V., & Ioannou, A. (2018). Development of Computational Thinking Skills through Educational Robotics. In *EC-TEL*. Practitioner Proceedings.

Coull, N. J., & Duncan, I. M. (2011). Emergent requirements for supporting introductory programming. *Innovation in Teaching and Learning in Information and Computer Sciences*, *10*(1), 78–85. doi:10.11120/ital.2011.10010078

Dimitriadou, A., Djafarova, N., Turetken, O., Verkuyl, M., & Ferworn, A. (2021). Challenges in serious game design and development: Educators' experiences. *Simulation & Gaming*, *52*(2), 132–152. doi:10.1177/1046878120944197

Eguchi, A. (2010). What is Educational Robotics? Theories behind it and practical implementation. In Society for information technology & teacher education international conference (pp. 4006-4014). Association for the Advancement of Computing in Education (AACE).

Eordanidis, S., Gee, E., & Carmichael, G. (2017). The effectiveness of pairing analog and digital games to teach computer science principles to female youth. *Journal of Computing Sciences in Colleges, 32*(3), 12–19.

Fessakis, G., Gouli, E., & Mavroudi, E. (2013). Problem solving by 5–6 years old kindergarten children in a computer programming environment: A case study. *Computers & Education, 63*, 87–97. doi:10.1016/j.compedu.2012.11.016

Foster, I. (2006). 2020 Computing: A two-way street to science's future. *Nature, 440*(7083), 419–419. doi:10.1038/440419a PMID:16554785

Frazer, A., Recio, A., Gilbert, L., & Wills, G. (2014). Profiling the educational value of computer games. *Interaction Design & Architecture (s) Journal-IxD&A, 19*, 1–19.

Gee, J. P. (2003). *What Video Games Have to Teach Us about Learning and Literacy*. Palgrave Macmillan. doi:10.1145/950566.950595

Gee, J. P. (2007). *Good video games + good learning: Collected essays on video games, learning and literacy*. Peter Lang. doi:10.3726/978-1-4539-1162-4

Gee, J. P. (2008). *What video games have to teach us about learning and literacy, revised and updated*. Palgrave Macmillan.

Gouin-Vallerand, C., Ferreira, S. M., & Hotte, R. (2018, November). Towards a mobile serious game environment for children self-learning. In *Proceedings of the 4th EAI International Conference on Smart Objects and Technologies for Social Good* (pp. 100-105). 10.1145/3284869.3284901

Grover, S., & Pea, R. (2013). Computational thinking in K–12: A review of the state of the field. *Educational Researcher, 42*(1), 38–43. doi:10.3102/0013189X12463051

Grover, S., & Pea, R. (2018). Computational thinking: A competency whose time has come. In S. Sentance, E. Barendsen, & C. Schulte (Eds.), *Computer science education: Perspectives on teaching and learning* (pp. 19–38). Bloomsbury Academic. doi:10.5040/9781350057142.ch-003

Hart, S., Margheri, A., Paci, F., & Sassone, V. (2020). Riskio: A serious game for cyber security awareness and education. *Computers & Security, 95*, 101–827. doi:10.1016/j.cose.2020.101827

Henderson, P. B., Cortina, T. J., & Wing, J. M. (2007). Computational thinking. In *Proceedings of the 38th SIGCSE Technical Symposium on Computer Science Education-SIGCSE '07*, 195–19. 10.1145/1227310.1227378

Hsu, T. C., Chang, S. C., & Hung, Y. T. (2018). How to learn and how to teach computational thinking: Suggestions based on a review of the literature. *Computers & Education, 126*, 296–310. doi:10.1016/j.compedu.2018.07.004

Humphries, L., & McDonald, S. (2011). Emotion faces: the design and evaluation of a game for preschool children. *Proceedings of the 2011 annual conference extended abstracts on Human factors in computing systems (CHIEA '11)*, 1453. 10.1145/1979742.1979790

Ioannou, A., & Makridou, E. (2018). Exploring the potentials of educational robotics in the development of computational thinking: A summary of current research and practical proposal for future work. *Education and Information Technologies, 23*(6), 2531–2544. doi:10.100710639-018-9729-z

Ioannou, I., & Angeli, C. (2016). A Framework and an Instructional Design Model for the Development of Students' Computational and Algorithmic Thinking. In MCIS (p. 19). Academic Press.

Jona, K., Wilensky, U., Trouille, L., Horn, M. S., Orton, K., Weintrop, D., & Beheshti, E. (2014, January). Embedding computational thinking in science, technology, engineering, and math (CT-STEM). In Future directions in computer science education summit meeting, Orlando, FL.

Kazakoff, E. R., Sullivan, A., & Bers, M. U. (2013). The effect of a classroom-based intensive robotics and programming workshop on sequencing ability in early childhood. *Early Childhood Education Journal, 41*(4), 245–255. doi:10.100710643-012-0554-5

Kazimoglu, C., Kiernan, M., Bacon, L., & Mackinnon, L. (2012). A serious game for developing computational thinking and learning introductory computer *programming. Procedia: Social and Behavioral Sciences, 47*, 1991–1999. doi:10.1016/j.sbspro.2012.06.938

Klopfer, E., Osterweil, S., & Salen, K. (2009). *Moving learning games forward*. The Education Arcade.

Komis, Romero, Depover, & Karsenti, (2019). Robotics in Primary Education–Robotique en Éducation Primaire: Introduction. Review of Science. *Mathematics and ICT Education, 13*(1), 3-6.

Kosmas, P., & Zaphiris, P. (2019, September). Embodied interaction in language learning: Enhancing students' collaboration and emotional engagement. In *IFIP Conference on Human-Computer Interaction* (pp. 179-196). Springer. 10.1007/978-3-030-29384-0_11

Kules, B. (2016). Computational thinking is critical thinking: Connecting to university discourse, goals, and learning outcomes. *Proceedings of the Association for Information Science and Technology, 53*(1), 1–6. doi:10.1002/pra2.2016.14505301092

Lee, I., Martin, F., Denner, J., Coulter, B., Allan, W., Erickson, J., Malyn-Smith, J., & Werner, L. (2011). Computational thinking for youth in practice. *Acfm Inroads, 2*(1), 32–37. doi:10.1145/1929887.1929902

Malliarakis, C., Satratzemi, M., & Xinogalos, S. (2014). Educational games for teaching computer programming. In *Research on e-Learning and ICT in Education* (pp. 87–98). Springer.

McKnight, L., & Fitton, D. (2010). Touch-screen Technology for Children: Giving the Right Instructions and Getting the Right Responses. *Proceedings of the 9th International Conference on Interaction Design and Children -IDC '10*, 238. 10.1145/1810543.1810580

Michael, D., & Chen, S. (2006). *Serious games: Games that educate, train, and inform*. Thomson Course Technology.

National Research Council. (2010). *Committee for the workshops on computational thinking: Report of a workshop on the scope and nature of computational thinking*. National Academy Press. doi:10.17226/12840

NGSS Lead States. (2013). *Next Generation Science Standards: For States, by States*. The National Academies Press.

Petscher, Y. M., Schatschneider, C., & Compton, D. L. (Eds.). (2013). *Applied quantitative analysis in education and the social sciences.* Routledge. doi:10.4324/9780203108550

Prensky, M. (2001). *Digital game-based learning.* McGraw-Hill.

Prensky, M. (2006). *Don't Bother Me, Mom, I'm Learning! How Computer and Video Games Are Preparing Your Kids for 21st Century Success and How You Can Help!* Paragon House.

Roni, S. M., Merga, M. K., & Morris, J. E. (2020). *Conducting quantitative research in education.* Springer. doi:10.1007/978-981-13-9132-3

Sawyer, B., & Rejeski, D. (2002). *Serious Game Initiative.* Academic Press.

Selby, C. C. (2014). *How can the teaching of programming be used to enhance computational thinking skills?* (Unpublished doctoral dissertation). University of Southampton, Southampton, UK.

Sengupta, P., Kinnebrew, J. S., Basu, S., Biswas, G., & Clark, D. (2013). Integrating computational thinking with K-12 science education using agent-based computation: A theoretical framework. *Education and Information Technologies, 18*(2), 351–380. doi:10.100710639-012-9240-x

Shuchi, G., & Roy, P. (2013). Computational Thinking in K–12: A Review of the State of the Field. *Educational Researcher, 42*(1), 38–43. doi:10.3102/0013189X12463051

Shute, V. J., Sun, C., & Asbell-Clarke, J. (2017). Demystifying computational thinking. *Educational Research Review, 22,* 142–158. doi:10.1016/j.edurev.2017.09.003

Swaid, S. I. (2015). Bringing computational thinking to STEM education. *Procedia Manufacturing, 3,* 3657–3662. doi:10.1016/j.promfg.2015.07.761

Tang, X., Yin, Y., Lin, Q., Hadad, R., & Zhai, X. (2020). Assessing computational thinking: A systematic review of empirical studies. *Computers & Education, 148,* 103798. doi:10.1016/j.compedu.2019.103798

Theodoropoulos, A., Antoniou, A., & Lepouras, G. (2017). How do different cognitive styles affect learning programming? Insights from a game-based approach in Greek schools. *ACM Transactions on Computing Education, 17*(1), 3. doi:10.1145/2940330

Vahldick, A., Mendes, A. J., & Marcelino, M. J. (2014). A review of games designed to improve introductory computer programming competencies. *2014 IEEE Frontiers in Education Conference (FIE) Proceedings,* 1–7.

Weintrop, D., Beheshti, E., Horn, M. S., Orton, K., Trouille, L., & Jona, K. (2014). *Interactive assessment tools for computational thinking in High School STEM classrooms.* Paper presented at the international conference on intelligent Technologies for interactive entertainment. 10.1007/978-3-319-08189-2_3

Wing, J. (2008). Computational thinking and thinking about computing. *Proceedings of the IPDPS 2008: 22nd IEEE International Parallel and Distributed Processing Symposium,* 14–18.

Wing, J. M. (2006). Computational thinking. *Communications of the ACM, 49*(3), 33–35. doi:10.1145/1118178.1118215

Wing, J. M. (2011, March). *Computational thinking.* Retrieved from https://csta.acm.org/Curriculum/sub/CurrFiles/WingCTPrez.pdf

Yang, D., Swanson, S., Chittoori, B., & Baek, Y. (2018). Work-in-Progress: Integrating computational thinking in STEM education through a project-based learning approach. *Proceedings of 2018 American Society for Engineering Education (ASEE) Annual Conference and Exposition.* 10.18260/1-2--30091

Zyda, M. (2005). From visual simulation to virtual reality to games. *Computer, 38*(9), 25–32. doi:10.1109/MC.2005.297

KEY TERMS AND DEFINITIONS

Algorithmic Thinking: It is a method of solving by clearly defining the procedures required. Instead of coming up with a single solution to a problem, students create algorithms. When followed precisely (by a person or a computer), they are instructions or rules that lead to solutions to the original and related problems.

Coding: It is the process of using programming languages to create instructions for computers.

Computational Thinking: Computational thinking is a collection of problem-solving techniques that describes problems and solutions in a way that a computer can understand.

Digital Literacy: It refers to a person's capacity to find, assess, and clearly transmit information on a variety of digital platforms using typing and other media. It is based on a person's grammar, composition, typing skills, and ability to use technology to create text, images, audio, and designs.

Educational Robotics: Educational robotics, also known as pedagogical robotics, is a discipline that aims to teach children robotics and programming through hands-on activities starting at a young age.

Mobile Games: A mobile game is a video game that is played on a mobile device.

Serious Games: Serious games are games in which their primary goal is to study or practice a skill rather than to have fun.

This research was previously published in Designing, Constructing, and Programming Robots for Learning; pages 136-158, copyright year 2022 by Information Science Reference (an imprint of IGI Global).

Chapter 26
What Can Gamification Learn From Sensory Marketing?
In the Context of Servicescapes

Miralem Helmefalk
Linnaeus University, Sweden

ABSTRACT

While gamification research is multidisciplinary and has grown in popularity during the last decade, it still requires further evidence and direction on which and how much various game mechanics impact on cognitive, emotional, and behavioral outcomes in digital and physical servicescape contexts. To shed light on this problem, a novel perspective on sensory marketing and gamification was chosen. This chapter has discussed and analyzed the similarities and differences between sensory marketing and gamification, as well as what theoretical perspectives and practices gamification can borrow from sensory marketing. Six issues have surfaced that require more research on this matter: (1) The interaction effects, (2) Weight and impact, (3) Congruency, (4) Complexity, (5) (sub)Conscious/(non)visible elements, and (6) The causal chain. This chapter explains and discusses these issues and offers future research avenues.

INTRODUCTION

During the last decade, gamification has gained considerable attention in research and practice (Nacke & Deterding, 2017). During the same decade there has also been an increasing interest in sensory marketing and how it can aid in better understanding consumers' minds and actions (Krishna & Schwarz, 2014). While both domains may at first seem distant to each other, there are similarities in the underlying logic of modifying and designing elements in a digital/physical place. Despite being about motivating and engaging people to train, or (un)consciously triggering certain purchasing behaviors (e.g. Hamari & Koivisto, 2015; Spence et al., 2014), both domains follow a logic of modifying existing services, environments, atmospheres or servicescapes to impact various behaviors (Helmefalk & Marcusson, 2019).

DOI: 10.4018/978-1-6684-7589-8.ch026

While gamification is studied rigorously and across disciplines, such as in *crowdsourcing, health, computer science, software development, tourism, sustainability, and marketing* (e.g. Kasurinen & Knutas, 2018; Matallaoui et al., 2017; Morschheuser et al., 2017; Sardi et al., 2017), more is required in the context of servicescapes, as underlined by Huotari and Hamari (2012). To contribute research on this matter, there is a need to bridge different domains together, as has been partly done in recent years (Hofacker et al., 2016; Högberg, Shams, et al., 2019; Olsson et al., 2016). However, to advance the interdisciplinary gamification theory, currently overrepresented in digital contexts, new insights are required on bridging physical and digital servicescapes with gamification. To gamify servicescapes appropriately, these environments should be carefully designed, with people's thoughts and emotions in mind (Burke, 2016; Dale, 2014).

To unveil potential new insights, sensory marketing is one potential and fitting candidate that examines how consumers think, feel and act when subjected to sensory stimuli (Krishna & Schwarz, 2014). As sensory marketing is saturated with consumer behavior, gamification has an excellent opportunity to help us understand current gaps and develop a more coherent perspective, especially in regard to how people think, feel and their subsequent outcomes in servicescape contexts.

Mullins and Sabherwal (2018a, p. 1237) state that, "there is a need to understand how more specific emotions, both positive and negative, may help achieve the goals of gamification". The same issue is emphasized in Nacke and Deterding (2017, p. 7) who raise the specific need for research in gamification. The author pinpoints, "Yet we are still dearly lacking studies with rigorous designs that assess both psychological mediators and behavioural outcomes […]". Accordingly, this chapter aims to shed new light on gamification in servicescape contexts and what concepts and methods can be employed to develop gamification theory further. To address these issues, this chapter discusses, deconstructs and analyzes various sensory marketing and gamification issues, which will guide further research on gamification in servicescape contexts. To further explain and elaborate on this argument, these subjects will be briefly presented and contrasted with each other.

BROADLY DEFINING SENSORY MARKETING AND GAMIFICATION

Sensory Marketing

Sensory marketing is a subject comprising studies in neuroscience, marketing, psychology and many other domains. It bears resemblance to consumer behavior theory that investigates how consumers think, feel and behave in different consumption situations. What separates sensory marketing from these popular theories is the sheer focus on the human senses and how sensory stimuli, in terms of visual, auditory, olfactory, gustatory and haptic cues, impact on people's psychology and purchasing behaviors (Krishna, 2012). In a way, sensory marketing tries to delve into the "black box" of consumers, namely the minds and to investigate the causal effects from certain semantic and sensory stimuli. Variables that are frequently measured are for instance, how music impacts people's arousal states, their eating or walking behavior (Herrington, 1996). Other common studies are on perceptual illusions, such as the size of products and retail spaces. To exemplify a sensory marketing study, Raghubir and Krishna (1999) examined biases of volume and container shape, which showed that the shape of glass affects, choice, preference and satisfaction. Ample research has defined potential sensory stimuli, or sensory cues, where these are categorized within a sensory category, such as the sense of hearing or the sense of

531

taste. Besides the five common senses, vision, hearing, smell, touch and taste, other senses are balance, hunger, temperature, pain, orientation, acceleration and others. In some cases, these are also categorized within the five sensory categories, which are generally perceived as acceptable in marketing literature.

While no clear and widely accepted definition of sensory marketing exists, there is one well-known definition referred to in Krishna (2012, p. 333) review, "marketing that engages the consumers' senses and affects their perception, judgment and behavior." However, it must be noted, that technically all marketing engages the human senses and perceptions of marketing communication through the input of sensory channels. Therefore, it is difficult to categorize and position sensory marketing as a single framework or a domain, but rather a way of considering, thinking and reflecting upon existing marketing. In regard to studies in neuroscience, psychology or general marketing (e.g. Gallace & Spence, 2014; Imschloss & Kuehnl, 2017), all have their own specific niches of interest. With the exception of a few studies (e.g. Hultén, 2011), scant research has been conducted on strategies and sensory marketing and how broader strategies can be implemented and executed to guide whole markets, the greater bulk of literature is still inquiring into one or several sensory stimuli and how they alone or combined impact consumers (Mattila & Wirtz, 2001; Spangenberg et al., 2005). In terms of servicescapes, sensory marketing has for a long time considered various digital and physical spaces and places, where these sensory cues impact various consumer experiences and purchasing behaviors (Allmér, 2014; Ballantyne & Nilsson, 2017; Mari & Poggesi, 2013). Servicescapes can constitute anything from retail stores, spas, cinemas, but could also be a homepage or an application.

Gamification

Similar to sensory marketing, gamification is interdisciplinary. Being highly interdisciplinary, the literature on gamification has been rather eclectic, resulting in the concept of gamification being more of a context than a theory (Helmefalk, 2019). The classical definition of gamification are the implementation of game mechanics in non-game contexts (Deterding et al., 2011) or as Burke (2014, p. 6) writes, "the use of games mechanics and experience design to digitally engage and motivate people to achieve their goals" (p. 6). Huotari and Hamari (2012, p. 19) instead define gamification in service contexts as: "a process of enhancing a service with affordances for gameful experiences in order to support user's overall value creation". Needless to say, these definitions portray how various processes or services can be modified to be more engaging and to intrinsically motivate people to conduct certain tasks. In contrast to sensory marketing, gamification is a broader concept, covering domains as diverse as *crowdsourcing, health, computer science, software development, tourism, sustainability, and marketing* (e.g. Kasurinen & Knutas, 2018; Matallaoui et al., 2017; Morschheuser et al., 2017; Sardi et al., 2017). The vast spectrum of different viewpoints on gamification, explains the explosive growth of studies that has surfaced during the last decade. However, as Helmefalk (2019) explains, there seems to be a systematic use of gamified mechanics and their impact on the psychology of users which subsequently mediate different outcomes.

Mechanics refer to the game-congruent elements and processes that can be implemented to enhance experiences and engage users in activities. These game elements, can consist of leaderboards, points, badges, progression, chance, cooperation and many other. (Werbach & Hunter, 2012). As Helmefalk et al. (2019) mention in their study, these mechanics are more or less popular across the different domains. Still the most common ones are leaderboards, badges, pins and points and have become standard elements/mechanics in the gamification discourse (Harwood & Garry, 2015; Seaborn & Fels, 2015). Several authors put forward risks when embedding gamification into organizations or marketing, as many practitioners and researchers think that it is enough to apply gamified elements for imminent success (Burke, 2016). In reality, success is rather built upon complex adjustments. Research shows that gamification does not always work *everywhere* and for not for *everybody* (Hamari, 2013; Koivisto & Hamari, 2014). Consequently, the same logic and questions should be asked for *when* implementing mechanics. Marketeers have been quick to adapt new technologies (see TV, Internet, Social media, AI), likewise the adaptation rate for gamification.

DECONSTRUCTING SENSORY MARKETING AND GAMIFICATION CONCEPTS IN SERVICESCAPES

Sensory Marketing Research in a Servicescape Context

In sensory marketing, especially in servicescape contexts, a well-utilized conceptual model is used to explain the impact of the environment, its stimuli and their effect on emotions and behaviors. Some have even stated it as a paradigm framework (Mari & Poggesi, 2013), which has facilitated considerable research. More specifically it refers to the stimulus (S), organism (O) and response (R) framework (S-O-R) by Mehrabian and Russell (1974). The framework has its foundation in environmental psychology and explains how the surrounding stimuli in an environment impact on the inner beings' emotions, called as the organism which facilitates an response.

Sensory Cues in Servicescapes

The stimuli (*S*) in the environment has been continuously and conceptually interchanged with the concept of atmospherics, which refers to different elements in-store that impacts on how consumers feel and behave (Andreu et al., 2006; McGoldrick & Pieros, 1998; Michon et al., 2008; Pan et al., 2008). In servicescape literature, the term coined by Bitner (1992), discusses various elements inside a store that can impact on consumers, such as music, colors and other potential variables. While the framework is tested and evidenced in retail stores (Donovan, R. J. et al., 1994; Spangenberg et al., 2006), several studies have tried to separate and categorize these elements. Turley, L. W. and Milliman (2000) well-cited study reviewed retailing research and identified 57 (n) elements instore that have an impact on consumers, mostly by categorizing them according to external variables, interior variables, layout and design variables, point-of-purchase decoration variables and lastly human variables.

In contrast to servicescape and atmospherics, sensory marketing is embracing the human senses and the stimuli which is sent through a medium, such air, reaching people with coded information by electromagnetic waves (light), vibrating gases (sound), dispersed molecules in air (scent), physical objects (touch) and with food (taste). It is assumed that elements, cues or/and atmospherics can be deconstructed into even smaller parts. It is this notion that saturates sensory marketing, namely to understand how consumers react on these stimuli (Krishna, 2012). To understand *how* these cues ought to be constructed to be effective is more complicated. This will be more elaborated in the next section.

However, neither marketeers nor researchers can perceive elements in their smallest or purest form, such as light as electromagnetic waves, sound as pitch, tempo and tonality, and this would indeed be immensely impractical (e.g. temperature and sounds Velasco et al., 2013). These cues are instead categorized into larger entities, common and well employed variables, for example music (Spangenberg et al.,

2005), which by itself consists of tempo, genre, tonality, pitch and many other sub elements. Therefore, it is assumed that cues and stimuli are also partly learned, categorized and semantic in their embedded meaning, and not entirely physically restrained. Moreover, cues can be more or less complex across several dimensions. The main point is that marketing communication may be received by different sensory channels and that the senses may provide different types of experience that when combined can enhance that experience (Helmefalk & Berndt, 2018; Krishna et al., 2010; Spence & Gallace, 2011). Moreover, these multisensory properties have been shown to have crossmodal interaction in terms of causing stronger effects on consumers' cognition, emotion or behavior. Moreover, while there is a separation in literature concerning living or nonliving properties in an environment, both service literature and retailing literature consider the importance of people and interactions (Bitner, 1992; Kearney et al., 2013). In particular, sensory marketing discusses social interaction in terms of voice (North et al., 2004; Wiener & Chartrand, 2014), clothing (Rahman, 2012), or touch during service interactions (Guéguen et al., 2007).

Regardless of which one perspective is selected, calling it atmospherics (Kotler, 1973), servicescapes (Lin, 2004; Mari & Poggesi, 2013), cues (Ballantine, P. et al., 2015; Ballantine, P. W. et al., 2010; Herrmann et al., 2013) or stimuli (Soars, 2009), all are essentially the same in terms of the elements in a servicescape that facilitate these effects.

Thinking and Feeling in Servicescapes

The organism (O), in S-O-R, is defined as the emotional states caused by stimuli in an environment, and has received a considerable amount of attention in sensory marketing (Vieira, 2013). While in research there is no consensus with regard to how feelings and emotions should be defined (Cabanac, 2002), especially the issues of the validity of self-reports and emotions (Laros & Steenkamp, 2005). These have generally in servicescape context been examined as arousal, valence and dominance (Donovan, R., 1994). According to research, these emotional states cause and mediate approach or avoidance behaviors (Chebat & Michon, 2003). Although some studies have neglected the concept of dominance as important for explaining the mediating effect of stimuli on behavior, valence and arousal, as measures, have persisted (Mari & Poggesi, 2013). Some have however tried to overcome the limitations of self-reported studies, which usually inquire into these psychological and attitudinal studies (Di Muro & Murray, 2012; Gorn et al., 2001). To decrease the gap between what you feel and what you do, many studies use experimental designs to explain purchasing behaviors with cognition and emotion (Spence et al., 2014).

Behaving in Servicescapes

The response (R) refers to the behavioral responses and activities in a servicescape, regardless of whether it considers mouse clicks, time spent or amount of spent resources (Bucklin & Sismeiro, 2003; Helmefalk & Hultén, 2017; Morrison et al., 2011). While it is arguably difficult to pinpoint whether a response is emotional or not, responses are also occasionally perceived as both emotional or cognitional (see models in Krishna, 2012; Spence et al., 2014). Although approach and avoidance behaviors were central for a long time (Chebat & Michon, 2003; Gulas & Bloch, 1995; Summers & Hebert, 2001), studies have evolved the framework of the S-O-R model into various concepts, including cognitive variables. In retailing literature, which arguably also discuss servicescapes (Mari & Poggesi, 2013), these frameworks are fundamentally built upon the logic of S-O-R. Research, modifies and investigates different angles with different variables, such as impulse purchasing (Chang et al., 2011), online shopping (Peng & Kim, 2014), and many others.

Multisensory, Intensity and Congruency

Two critical aspects that saturate sensory marketing is the (1) *multisensory* integration and how different stimuli and senses interact together for enhancing experiences. The second aspect, that of (2) *congruency*, will be discussed in the next section. Firstly, it is assumed in research that environments that stimulate more senses are generally more pleasant (Helmefalk & Hultén, 2017; Lindstrom, 2005; Raz et al., 2008). It is explained that the brain processes information from the surrounding world making it more comprehensible. For instance, a horror movie is less scary without sounds or food does not taste much without smell. These viewpoints are discussed and examined in neurological, physiological and psychological literature (Driver & Noesselt, 2008). Briefly explained, it must be noted that consumers perceive objects and environments as multisensory which gives a broader spectrum of information that lessens purchasing risks (e.g. with touch, Bhatnagar et al., 2000; Spence & Gallace, 2011). Providing an opportunity to experience the servicescape via additional senses, besides vision, the intensity of these stimuli can be minimized while still being efficient.

Secondly, congruency refers to the correspondence between sensory cues and their relationship to each other and the environment (Helmefalk, 2016). As mentioned earlier, it is possible to examine correspondence between properties, such as between taste and texture (Piqueras-Fiszman et al., 2012) or sounds and temperature (Velasco et al., 2013). These matchings, fit, or congruency can also involve semantic combinations, such as between Christmas scent and Christmas music (Spangenberg et al., 2005). Whether something fits or not is a complex discourse involving concepts such as cognitive fit, crossmodal correspondence, priming, mental models, synesthesia and sound symbolism (Garaus et al., 2014; John et al., 2006; Walker, 2016). A ground stone in marketing has been associations, uniformity and the relatedness between consumers' self-image, brands, as well as in other brand alignment theories (Branaghan & Hildebrand, 2011; Campbell et al., 2010; Errajaa et al., 2018; Jamal & Goode, 2001; Obeng et al., 2015; Turley, Lou W. & Chebat, 2002).

Sensory Marketing Framework in a Servicescape Context

Following the same rationale and logic of the S-O-R framework, many sensory marketing studies and models follow somewhat similar patterns, of a stimulus, being perceived and interpreted, then judged and felt, that levers a behavioral or situational outcome in a servicescape contexts. Although there are several different frameworks in sensory marketing (Hultén, 2015; Krishna & Schwarz, 2014; Spence et al., 2014), one particular example is presented in literature specifically showing these mediating effects of cognition and emotion between stimuli and behavior. Spence et al. (2014) comprehensive literature review of sensory marketing in servicescapes (atmospheres), discusses various aspects of sensory stimuli and how the five senses work together or alone in order to impact cognition and emotion, thus mediating purchase behavior. The model, illustrated in fig 1., shows how sensory stimuli together impact emotion or/ and cognition which subsequently impact shopping behavior. Shopping behavior can constitute approach/ avoidance behaviors, time spent, actual purchasing, touching and many other variations (Helmefalk & Hultén, 2017; Holzwarth et al., 2006; Lin, 2004; Mari & Poggesi, 2013). Spence et al. (2014) review highlights the difficulty of measuring emotions and that it sometimes is more relevant to use general positivity, which by itself consists of different concepts. The term "optimal stimulation" refers to the right amount of stimulation to make the best impact. Regarding cognition, "association" bears a similar notion of the associative elements between stimuli. For instance, what represents what and how close the relationship is between two semantic and sensory cues (e.g. *red* color and *love*). Lastly, shopping behaviors are multifaceted and include a variety of potential behaviors in shopping contexts.

Figure 1. Framework for multisensory shopping behavior (Spence et al., 2014, p. 473)

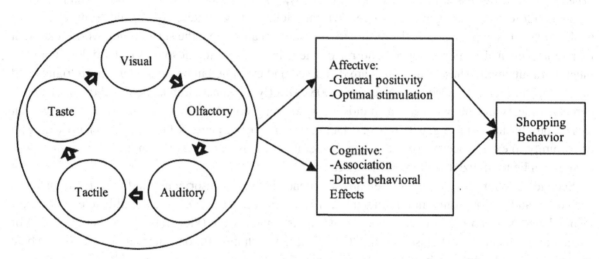

As mentioned, a central point in sensory marketing is to break open the black box to understand how consumers react and behave in different environments. The more evidence that is revealed, the more complex the cause-and-effect map becomes.

Gamification Research in a Servicescape Context

Except for some studies (Helmefalk & Marcusson, 2019; Huotari & Hamari, 2017), little attention has been placed on conceptualizing gamification in servicescape contexts. Despite some digital services being perceived as servicescapes (Allmér, 2014), more research is required in physical environments, stated by Huotari and Hamari (2017) as in line with Bitner (1992) call. As gamification is a multidisciplinary subject, it has many possible perspectives on servicescapes. With regard to marketing, Ballantyne and Nilsson (2017) discuss the need of adjusting current servicescape models to the new era of digital solutions, and that the line between physical and digital servicescapes are blurred out. In their review, they also list gamification as a future trend in servicescape research. Similarly, Huotari and Hamari (2017) call for expanding the servicescape research in gamification. Since their calls for research, only a few studies have tried to conceptualize and synthesize gamification and servicescape research. The study of Helmefalk and Marcusson (2019) reviewed literature on gamification in various business servicescapes and followed the framework of environmental psychology and gamification in service contexts (Huotari & Hamari, 2012; Mehrabian & Russell, 1974), while synthesizing literature to a conceptual model. They illustrate how the S-O-R model, also commonly used in business contexts, is portrayed in gamification literature. Through this, they highlight the process from gamified mechanics and their mediating impact through cognition and emotion, consisting of engagement, motivation and flow. Through these mediators several different outcomes are achieved, such as actual behaviors, shopping experiences and customer loyalty.

Another, more overarching conceptual model, lists similarly the causal effects of mechanics on outcomes. Being an interdisciplinary literature review, Helmefalk (2019) covered studies in "Health and wellness, Crowdsourcing, Sustainability, Computer science, Software development, Marketing and Tourism" and conceptualized similar patterns. Following the same rationale as in Hamari et al. (2014), the review identified the causal chains from the mechanics (M), via psychological mediators (PM) and on the outcomes (O). The relationships in the M-PM-O model are however more complex, as choosing appropriate mechanics should be derived from the desired outcome, something that is highly dependent on the goals, strategy and visions from the designer or actor. By implementing appropriate and congruent mechanics, psychological mediators are aimed for. It is only by understanding these mediators that outcomes can be achieved. As the literature depicts, there is still scarce research on understanding which mechanic impacts on what psychology mediator. Therefore, further research is required to understand and pinpoint exactly how mechanics should be best implemented (Sailer et al., 2017).

Figure 2. Adapted from Helmefalk (2019, p. 18)

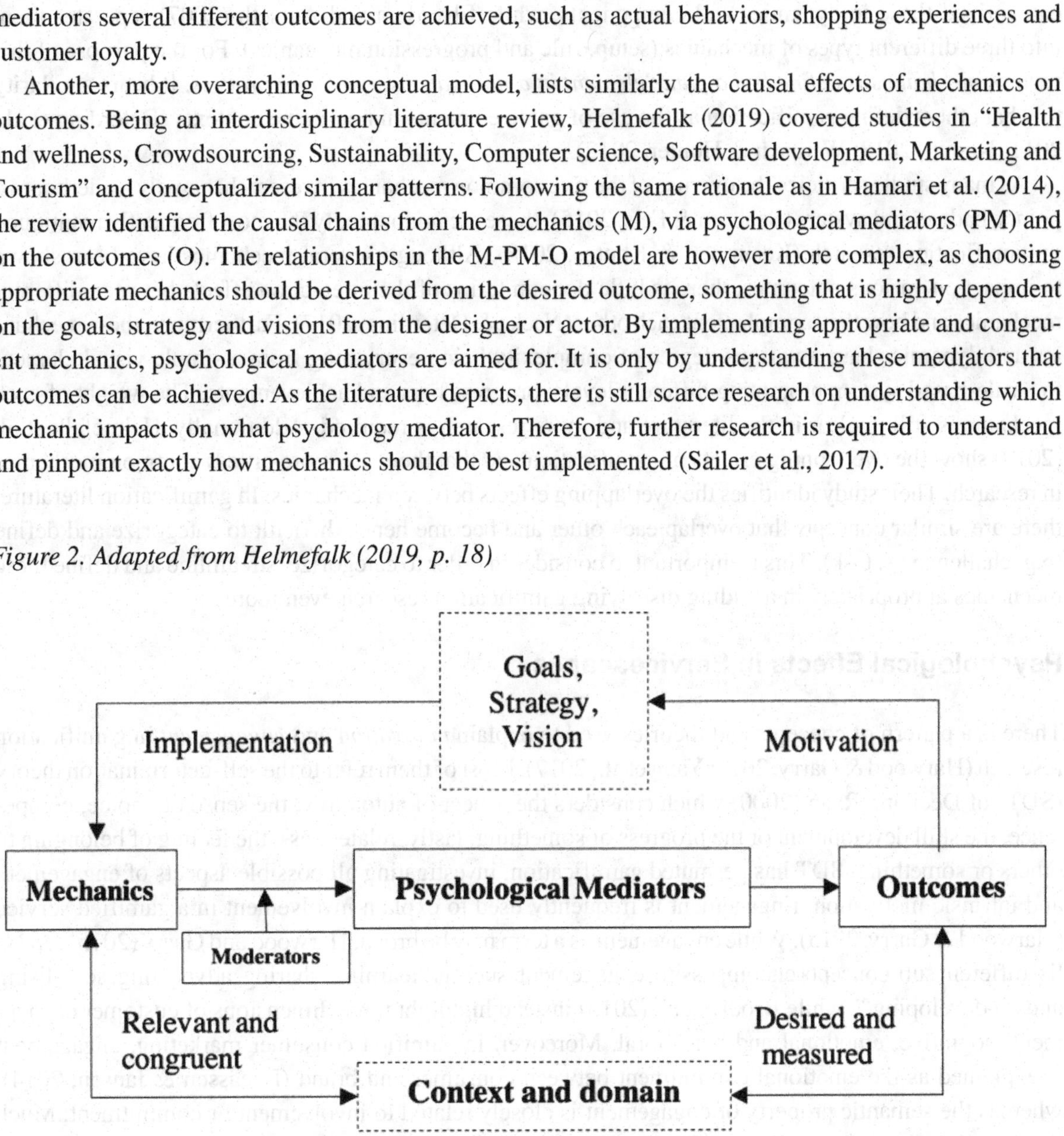

Mechanics/Dynamics/Elements in Servicescapes

As mentioned in the literature, there are several dimensions in a game engine, covering the range from the actual mechanics which constitute the rules and concepts, namely the components of the game. In addition, there are the dynamics reacting to player inputs and provided outputs. Lastly there are the aesthetics that are the emotional responses from the game (Hunicke et al., 2004). However, during the last decade, mechanics has been vaguely incorporated and depicted, sometimes even being eclectic in specifically characterizing a mechanic (Helmefalk et al., 2019). However, Werbach and Hunter (2012) categorized these in dynamics and components, while Elverdam and Aarseth (2007) separates them into three different types of mechanics (setup, rule and progression mechanics). For the purpose of this review, *mechanics is defined as a game element in a non-game service and process*. It bears similarity to what others define gamification as the use of game elements in non-game contexts (Deterding et al., 2011; Kumar, 2013; Werbach & Hunter, 2012)

As many studies criticize the overuse of the five common mechanics in research, namely leaderboards, points, badges and avatars (Seaborn & Fels, 2015), these are undoubtedly the most frequently mentioned in gamification research (Kasurinen & Knutas, 2018). Although several mechanics have been shown to impact on various outcomes, there is little done in terms of the interaction effects between different mechanics and how they complement each other (Nacke & Deterding, 2017). Furthermore, these mechanics and dynamics have a various degree of complexity being everything from a simple visual element to a rule-based system promoting different levels, progress bars and achievements. The weight of each mechanic is still unclear in the literature and more research is required. Additionally, Helmefalk et al. (2019) show the overlapping effects of gamification and that there are more or less common mechanics in research. Their study identifies the overlapping effects between mechanics. In gamification literature, there are similar concepts that overlap each other and become hence difficult to categorize and define (e.g. challenge vs. task). This is important to consider in order to categorize, streamline and define these mechanics appropriately in avoiding dissolving gamification research even more.

Psychological Effects in Servicescapes

There is a pattern of concepts and theories used to explain *motivation* and *engagement* in gamification research (Harwood & Garry, 2015; Yang et al., 2017). Most of them refer to the self-determination theory (SDT) of Deci and Ryan (2000) which considers the aspect of autonomy; the sense of choice; competence, the skill development or the progress of something; lastly, relatedness, the feeling of belonging to others or something. SDT has permuted gamification, investigating all possible aspects of engagement and intrinsic motivation. Engagement is frequently used to explain involvement in a gamified service (Harwood & Garry, 2015). While engagement as a term may be broad, Harwood and Garry (2015, p. 534) list different sub-concepts encompassing engagement, such as "learning, sharing, advocating, socialising and co-developing.", while Brodie et al. (2013) instead highlight three dimensions of customer engagement: cognitive, emotional and behavioral. Moreover, in gamified consumer marketing, engagement is explained as the emotional commitment between consumer and brand (Lucassen & Jansen, 2014), whereas the semantic property of engagement is closely related to involvement or commitment. Much literature ignores defining the specific type of engagement that is investigated. This in turn may increase the risk of confusion. It can be compared to what Seaborn and Fels (2015, p. 28) raise about the issues in gamification research, "the majority of applied research on gamification is not grounded in theory and did not use gamification frameworks in the design of the system under study".

Engagement is partly also interconnected to the concept of flow which is commonly employed to explain the immersion when using a service or process. Flow is described by (Harwood & Garry, 2015, p. 535) as "[...] a key component of gamification, which arises out of comprehension and experiential mastery of the challenges within a particular environment and the accompanying emotional, i.e., positive sensation of competence, through endeavour and labour that this engenders.". Flow involves the cognitive involvement in a specific task, balancing the need for skill and difficulty, where a task being too easy is boring, being too hard increases anxiety. Reaching this balance, induces enjoyment and concentration (Witt et al., 2011).

Although social mechanics trigger various psychological states, arguably belonging to relatedness in STD (Deci & Ryan, 2000; Deci et al., 2001; Ryan & Deci, 2000), there is still an uncertainty as to how these mediators are categorized, being either a mechanic or a psychological mediator. For instance, Hamari (2017), discussed that social comparison may be a force that is facilitated by badges, increasing the user activity on the platform.

Interestingly, attitudinal and emotional dimensions, such as arousal and valance are underemployed in gamification research and which, according to other behavioral theories, have been shown to impact on intent and behavior (Kaltcheva & Weitz, 2006). However, a recent study by Mullins and Sabherwal (2018b) tackles these issues by synthesizing cognitive-emotional theories highlighting the need of exploring and empirically examining different cognitive and emotional frameworks to better understand the effects of gamification. The conceptual paper discusses attention, memory, and how agents, objects and consequence of events interrelate to impact on cognition and emotion. Their framework proposes new insights on how to deeper understand the psychology of users. At present, however, little is empirically evidenced in gamification contexts.

Various Outcomes in Servicescapes

As there are several hundred studies examining the effect of gamification on people, each one of them aims to study a specific mechanic in a specific context, hence the variety of outcomes. In the M-PM-O framework it is difficult to always pinpoint what a mediator is and what an outcome is. In some cases, several psychological states can mediate on each other leaving the outcome as a behavior, but also a concept that bears a relevance to the given domain, such as measuring customer engagement experience (Harwood & Garry, 2015), or the success of online connections (Osipov et al., 2015) and many others. Therefore, it is difficult to accurately isolate an outcome. In learning, learning behavior is measured, in software development, coding or the time it took to finish a task (Burke, 2014; Pettit et al., 2015; Su & Cheng, 2015). What is important is to understand that research has shown that gamification has the ability to alter behavior and by doing so, it is crucial to understand how it does that and what mechanics are causing the reaction.

Moderators and Dimensions in Gamified Servicescapes

Understanding which mechanics are appropriate and effective is consequently dependent on understanding the potential moderators that alter these relationships, making them more or less effective. Several studies depict different moderating effects, such as a study emphasizing the differences in cultures (Matallaoui et al., 2016), or age, favoring younger users as more prone to gamification (Swan, 2012). It may also be that people with a need for cognition may be more subjected to games in advertising if implemented correctly (Vashisht, 2017). Even time alters the influence of gamification, showing that gamification works well as a novelty element and then diminishes with time (Koivisto & Hamari, 2014). These moderating effects indicate the multidimensional nature of gamifying services and servicescapes. It is not far from what Dale (2014) states of the need to understand the customer, to fully and proficiently implement appropriate mechanics into the process.

Nevertheless, as platforms and places are moderators of the efficiency of gamification, these are very related to the nature of servicescapes, being digital or physical. Irrespective of whether the servicescape involves physical tasks, such as map hunting (Wakao et al., 2015), Pokémon GO, or being purely digital, such on online e-learning systems (Osipov et al., 2015), the line between digital and physical is indeed becoming blurred. What is currently non-existent in gamification research is the understanding on the transfer of mechanics between the physical and digital world. In the case of ordinary games, such as chess, this is more evident, but other elements in gamification literature still need to be explored.

DISCUSSION AND ANALYSIS

As the aim is not to conceptualize the two frameworks into a new one, their similarities can however be compared and contrasted where gamification, as a relatively new subject, can incorporate underlying concepts of sensory marketing to adapt and develop its fundamental understanding in order to open new doors for future inquiry. Sensory marketing and gamification may both be perceived as processes or activities in a space, both are also used to modify services or servicescapes. To do so, both sensory marketing and gamification require understanding the user (consumer) to investigate the effects from mechanics or stimuli.

The Interaction Effects of Cues and Mechanics

A common issue raised in sensory marketing is the complexity of including several stimuli. Ballantine, P. W. et al. (2010) discuss the exponential need of treatment groups to investigate 57 (n) atmospheric elements listed in Turley, L. W. and Milliman (2000). Many have thus neglected this notion and instead adapted the gestalt principle (Koffka, 2013), which states that it is difficult to separate cues from each other and the larger context. Modifying offerings and services is not an easy task where the designer or manager can easily predict the outcome of implementing a single sensory cue and expect a certain outcome (Turley, Lou W. & Chebat, 2002). The cue becomes highly dependent on other variables in the servicescape, such as the brand, the physical layout, the products within, the people and a myriad of other factors. Consequently, many have studied whole servicescapes as a unitary experience or a journey (Ballantine, P. W. et al., 2010). Despite this, research is still examining how single or multiple cues together impact on consumers (e.g. Herrmann et al., 2013; Mattila & Wirtz, 2001). In many cases, this is done with factorial experimental designs, often with field experiments where the confounding variables may influence the outcome. Similarly, gamification and its mechanics have posed several calls for research, where not much is known on how these mechanics integrate with each other in servicescapes. Following the logic of sensory marketing, similar designs can be examined, where 1x2, 2x2 or 3x3 factorial designs (as in Högberg, Shams, et al., 2019) can be employed to give more perspective on mechanics and their effects. Nacke and Deterding (2017, p. 7) portray the need for elaborating the complexity that exists within different systems: "To explain these systems, we will also need more complex explanations than the mere understanding of how each element functions individually".

In sensory marketing, multisensory interaction has become a popular topic (Spence et al., 2014), emphasizing the complexities of involving more cues. However, what is peculiarly unique for sensory marketing is how an experience can be enhanced by involving more sensory channels conveying the same type of information. In sensory marketing, cues are often tested in already existing environments, where the meaning and purpose of the given servicescape is already established. In contrast, gamification still has difficulties to implement appropriate mechanics (Robson et al., 2015). As such, designers or actors who implement mechanics are bound by the current type of service, which may not always be easily gamified. Assumedly, increasing the number of mechanics stated in literature, such as implementing avatars, points, badges and rules in a service would eventually end up in a fully-fledged game, contrary to the purpose of gamification. Thus, there seems to be a transformative scale where and when a gamified servicescape becomes a game environment. To understand the tipping point of when there are too many mechanics, more investigation is required.

As mentioned, the building blocks of cues are not simply measured with the fundamental basic elements, such as electromagnetic waves or vibration of gas, but include a variety of combinations, which embrace larger entities. Music is an example, which may be measured by tone, pitch, tonality, and many other components (Crisinel et al., 2013; Spence, 2012), yet is still defined as a cue when measured in experimental conditions. The same logic saturates gamification. The difficulties are twofold: firstly to define whether a "mechanic" is a psychological mediator or a mechanic (Helmefalk, 2019), secondly to depict and to deconstruct existing terminology and semantic meanings of the currently used mechanics. For instance, leaderboards comprise a broad system that includes gathering of input of data, gathering statistics and presenting the data appropriately. The concept and aim of leaderboards can further be deconstructed into sub-concepts and sub-systems. It can be further deconstructed and designed to incorporate comparative or competitive elements, either between users or against the user him/her-self. Each part and sub-part of what constitutes a leaderboard may be altered in order to enhance the efficiency of it. This example presents research opportunity to investigate more specific parts of mechanics, something which until recently has been ignored. It may also be the other way around that there are unexplored systems that only work when combined.

Moreover, while sensory marketing has shown that multiple congruent cues in environments exert most effect on consumer emotion and behaviors (Guéguen & Jacob, 2010; Krishna et al., 2010), the same may be applied to gamification, which may include stimulating more senses with present mechanics. This is mostly relevant in physical environments, where involving spatial and bodily activities may increase experiences, such as kicking balls for coupons, or throwing waste into garbage holes for points. A central part of gamification is instant feedback in the form of a sound or activity which responds immediately. By involving more senses into the feedback process, there is an opportunity to increase engagement and other outcomes.

Weight, Congruency and Complexity

The perception of servicescapes and cues are not uniform and linear, in the sense that all cues have equal effect on cognition, emotion and behavior. Although many studies have shown that when cues correspond to each other, they have greater effect (e.g. Seo & Hummel, 2011). Looking at past studies, there is no doubt that the beta or mean value of cues and their effect on dependent variables are unequal (see Mattila & Wirtz, 2001; Spangenberg et al., 2005; Spangenberg et al., 2006). Equal effect or weight are improbable as to the myriad of complex confounding variables and situations in a servicescape. Thus, it is assumed that the properties of cues are unequal in terms of their effect on people, and different in different environments. For instance, the tempo of music in servicescapes has been shown to alter the movement of people where slower and faster tempo correlates to slower and faster movement (Milliman, 1982). Consequently, some servicescapes are better fitted for quick or slow movement and should be employed with the appropriate and most effective cues, thus similar to how mechanics ought to be employed (Burke, 2016; Helmefalk et al., 2019). Therefore, it seems that to determine the weight or significance of cues and mechanics among others in a given situation is greatly, if not entirely, dependent on the environment and context in which the cue is implemented. Other examples are Mitchell et al. (1995) showing when an odor congruent it increases variety seeking contrary to when incongruent.

A great bulk of literature recognizes the aspect of fit, appropriateness and congruency with regard to cues and how they fit in environments (Demoulin, 2011; Guéguen & Jacob, 2010; Seo & Hummel, 2011). While environments are more difficult to alter than single or several cues, environments become hence a starting point when modifying servicescapes. Moreover, Pedreira et al. (2015) highlight the risks of how poor implementation, poor understanding of users, implementing appropriate design methods and simple schemas will lead to unsatisfactory outcomes.

As mentioned, gamification as a tool has been shown to increase engagement and participation and has also interested practitioners and scholars in how to use it for the best outcome. However, being a tool generates an extent of incomparability. It can be speculated that it is easier to alter and change a mechanic instead of modifying a whole service and this would seem sound, as gamification would be deemed pointless without a base and functioning offering providing value to users. Therefore, gamification is better used as a complementary aid in achieving outcomes in line with the desired outcomes of the service in the servicescape. All these arguments are rooted in either implementing existing congruent mechanics to the service or modifying both the service and the mechanic to be congruent and compatible to each other. In the literature, congruency and combability are undertaken by implementing systems in which the application of mechanics and dynamics with context analysis is looped until satisfaction is reached (Morschheuser et al., 2018). However, there is little evidence on the fundamental rationale of congruency and fit within gamification literature. There are no clear evidence or studies regarding which methods are required in finding appropriate mechanics for different services. In marketing, congruency is sometimes achieved with brand maps, or cognitive semantic mapping techniques identifying options for product or brand extensions (John et al., 2006).

Besides congruency, complexity is another factor which influences the perception of environments. Complexity refers to the richness of elements in a setting or environment (Rosen & Purinton, 2004) and may be (up/down)scaled to different dimensions in a servicescape, including the visual aesthetics (Manganari et al., 2009) or the complexity of an scent (Herrmann et al., 2013). In physical servicescapes complexity is referred to by Spies et al. (1997, p. 2) as "[…] environmental stimuli that determine their complexity are information rate and layout. By information rate we mean the number of information units that are presented within a certain time interval. The information rate usually is higher for new and unusual than for familiar stimuli". Furthermore, in the book of Berlyne (1971) he explains that the attractiveness of environmental stimuli is highly dependent on the level of complexity, where more or less of it influences the attractiveness of environments. This rationale is also related to the optimal level of stimuli discussed by Raju (1980), where the top of an inverted u shape facilitates approach behavior. In contrast to the properties of games and the need of challenge to facilitate flow (Hamari & Koivisto, 2014), the optimal number of mechanics in services is much harder to design and implement in terms of the increasing number of interaction effects. Further research is recommended to find out which and how many mechanics are appropriate and optimal in different servicescapes.

(Sub)Conscious/(Non)Visible Elements and Sensory Adaption

Although often being visually oriented, mechanics do not need to be visually evident in order to have effect. Examples of mechanics that can be incorporated into services and do not interfere with services could be instant feedback, such as playing a sound when throwing waste into a bin (e.g. Berengueres et al., 2013).

While sub-minimal marketing has shown to be pointless and immoral (Broyles, 2006; Hawkins, 1970; Trappey & Marketing, 1996), the influence on the subconscious mind is still present. Several studies have shown that although people are not aware of the manipulated setting, they still influence behaviors, such as the tempo of music, preference of wine, product choice, walking behavior and others (Milliman, 1982; North et al., 1997). It may be an issue of attention, facilitated by contrast in an environment. Contrast is usually achieved by creating incongruent elements in a setting, such as playing an unfitting song, unexpected colors, or an apple smelling like a banana. On another note, there are lot of opportunities to develop guidelines for gamification designers or actors that want to implement gamification in a physical servicescape, as it could be perceived as a manipulative tactic and hence should be treated with caution (Kim & Werbach, 2016; Shahri et al., 2014)

Consequently, the subconscious impact of cues on people are possible (Krishna, 2012), though this is a complex discussion. It could be argued that many elements in a person's environment are constantly impacting on the subconscious mind. Needless to say, cues can be noticed or unnoticed and still may impact on behaviors.

Sensory adaptation is another concept that refers to the ability to get used to a certain stimulus after a while, such as not noticing a scent after a time or the clothes on the skin. By overcoming sensory adaptation, a change is required in order to evoke (in)voluntary attention. While a mechanic is a completely different concept, it is related to time, impact on pleasantness and has also been shown to diminish over time (Farzan et al., 2008). Koivisto and Hamari (2014) investigated how people perceive enjoyment and usefulness from gamification in health contexts. Their study showed that the effects of gamification weakens after a while and that age influences how fast this diminishing effect occurs.

In regard to the discussion, a parallel can be drawn between the intensity of a stimulus and the intensity of gamification. Both may have a stronger or weaker effect on the outcomes, but can be perceived on a non-binary scale, indicating the level of intensity or the level of gamification. For now, there is no clear scale of determining how evident a mechanic is and the optimal level of it.

The Causal Chain

With regard to the S-O-R and M-PO-O framework, there are clear paths from which a stimulus or mechanic impacts on a mediator and this in turn impacts on a response or outcome. Both frameworks highlight a causal chain that is not always so clear to define. Studies are continually inquiring into causal effects that lead to an outcome. For instance, in a retail context Högberg, Ramberg, et al. (2019) show that by gamifying a section instore, consumers are more prone to engagement though hedonic value, which is usually desirable when leisure shopping. This has been shown to increase the link to brand engagement which is crucial for retailers. There are many other examples in research that portray the cause and effects of gamification.Similar to the difficulties of defining whether music is one stimulus or consists of other sub-elements, the same issues persist in gamification research where several concepts are not clearly categorized or positioned. While the literature is constantly renewing the definition on mechanics, more evident testing and conceptualization are needed so that gamification can achieve a consistency, especially in becoming empirically valid and reliable. It is similar to what Nacke and Deterding (2017, p. 7) state, "Yet we are still dearly lacking studies with rigorous designs that assess both psychological mediators and behavioural outcomes –and do so long-term and in the wild, not just short-term and in the lab. Finally, many studies are still to some extent comparing apples with oranges, testing different implementations of design elements with different effect measures".

What Can Be Learned and Needs to Be Examined?

This chapter has discussed various aspects of sensory marketing and gamification in servicescapes. Six main issues were brought up that would benefit gamification research, namely:

Issue 1: The interaction effects

It is difficult to test and investigate all potential interaction effects between mechanics, dynamics and the servicescape. To contribute more empirical evidence on gamification, field experiments are recommended with 1x2, 2x2 2x3 factorial designs. Developing a broader knowledge of the interaction effects between various mechanics would potentially shed more light on how many mechanics are required to work, or before the effect of the gamification diminishes. It illuminates the distinction between a gamified servicescape and a game environment. A more detailed and more refined mapping on each mechanic is essential, foremost to be able to deconstruct a single mechanic in more parts to test and modify it to improve efficiency.

Issue 2: Weight

A mechanic may have different effects on people in different servicescapes, depending on the situation and context. The same applies between different mechanics. To understand the relevance of each mechanic in different contexts, a more detailed comparison between mechanics in different servicescapes is needed.

Issue 3: Congruency

While the risks of poor implementation of gamification in servicescapes has been discussed, congruency has been a concept discussed to aid the appropriate modification of services and servicescapes. However, how mechanics should fit into services and servicescapes is a matter still relatively unexplored. Thus, there is a need of examining how congruency as a concept can aid gamification, either by developing more reliable scales or other methods in achieving compatible solutions.

Issue 4: Complexity

Complexity is another potential factor that may interfere with or aid the effect of gamification. It is similar to the other discussion, but could still impact on how gamified solutions are implemented and perceived by people.

Issue 5: (sub)Conscious/(non)visible elements

Although, it can be argued that there are non-visual mechanics that have an effect on people, there is no clear research on how conscious and unconscious mechanics are perceived and what effect they have. While there is an aspect of engagement and involvement, it is of extra interest to explore whether (sub)conscious elements are at work, or if there is an opportunity for those who want to gamify processes without shifting focus or disturbing the service process. Consequently, this also becomes an issue of ethics.

Issue 6: The causal chain

These issues highlight the present scarcity of research that shows potential mediating and moderating effects on outcomes. Considerable research is needed where cognitive and emotional elements are treated as mediators on the outcomes. Addressing these issues would enrich the scant evidence.

CONCLUSION

This chapter has discussed the similarities and differences between theoretical concepts in the domain of sensory marketing and gamification, as well as what gamification can learn from sensory marketing in servicescape contexts. Through this discussion, six issues have surfaced that requires more research. (1) The interaction effects, (2) Weight and impact, (3) Congruency, (4) Complexity, (5) (sub)Conscious/(non)visible elements and (6) The causal chain. Following the framework of sensory marketing, there are ample opportunities for gamification research to deconstruct and map out different congruent mechanics; examine the amount of impact these have in isolation or when in interplay.

Managerial implications

Following the discussion and analysis in this chapter, there are several potential implications for managers to consider. To find out whether it is worth to implement mechanics into the servicescape, it may be of value to examine whether a wanted mechanic is congruent to the overall servicescape, its individual components and other possible confounding elements, such as the brand fit or type of platform.

As emphasized in the chapter, the number of potential variables that can interfere and work in interaction are endless. To navigate this uncertain landscape, it may be of relevance to first study the desired outcomes, and then to work backwards, in terms of understanding for which behavioral outcomes are desired in the servicescape. The next step is to understand which psychological mediators are inflicting on the outcomes. Lastly, it is crucial to study the vast map of potential mechanics that are congruent in the servicescape context. The chapter has also discussed that gamification does not need to be visually evident, but can be integrated on a level that is in line with the service, such as including the aspect of points, exploration, ranking, leaderboards, or competition without using game related visual cues.

To exemplify the implementation of gamification in a servicescape; a retail store wants to implement an augmented reality (AR) service in their retail app which offers hidden discounts (congruent to stores). This gamified service engages consumers to explore otherwise hidden areas instore, combining both physical and virtual elements. While this idea may generate exploratory behavior and purchasing, it also potentially risks disturbing ordinary purchasing patterns, hence needs to be carefully implemented. A way of considering how consumers value the use of mechanics in servicescapes, a perspective of sensory adaptation and novelty may be applied, where the effects of these mechanics will diminish over time. Consequently, this signifies that the AR experience can be limited and used for special events in order to have a long-term effect.

REFERENCES

Allmér, H. (2014). *E-servicescape is Plausible.* Paper presented at the IRIS Selected Papers of the Information Systems Research Seminar in Scandinavia: Issue nr 5 (2014). IRIS Association.

Andreu, L., Bigné, E., Chumpitaz, R., & Swaen, V. (2006). How does the perceived retail environment influence consumers' emotional experience? Evidence from two retail settings. *International Review of Retail, Distribution, and Consumer Research, 16*(5), 559–578. doi:10.1080/09593960600980097

Ballantine, P., Parsons, A., & Comeskey, K. (2015). A conceptual model of the holistic effects of atmospheric cues in fashion retailing. *International Journal of Retail & Distribution Management, 43*(6), 503–517. doi:10.1108/IJRDM-02-2014-0015

Ballantine, P. W., Jack, R., & Parsons, A. G. (2010). Atmospheric cues and their effect on the hedonic retail experience. *International Journal of Retail & Distribution Management, 38*(8), 641–653. doi:10.1108/09590551011057453

Ballantyne, D., & Nilsson, E. (2017). All that is solid melts into air: The servicescape in digital service space. *Journal of Services Marketing, 31*(3), 226–235. doi:10.1108/JSM-03-2016-0115

Berengueres, J., Alsuwairi, F., Zaki, N., & Ng, T. (2013). Gamification of a recycle bin with emoticons. In *Proceedings of the 8th ACM/IEEE international conference on Human-robot interaction.* 10.1109/HRI.2013.6483512

Berlyne, D. E. (1971). *Aesthetics and psychobiology* (Vol. 336). Appleton-Century-Crofts New York.

Bhatnagar, A., Misra, S., & Rao, H. R. (2000). On risk, convenience, and Internet shopping behavior. *Communications of the ACM, 43*(11), 98–105. doi:10.1145/353360.353371

Bitner, M. J. (1992). Servicescapes: The Impact of Physical Surroundings on Customers and Employees. *Journal of Marketing, 56*(2), 57–71. doi:10.1177/002224299205600205

Branaghan, R. J., & Hildebrand, E. A. (2011). Brand personality, self-congruity, and preference: A knowledge structures approach. *Journal of Consumer Behaviour, 10*(5), 304–312. doi:10.1002/cb.365

Brodie, R. J., Ilic, A., Juric, B., & Hollebeek, L. (2013). Consumer engagement in a virtual brand community: An exploratory analysis. *Journal of Business Research, 66*(1), 105–114. doi:10.1016/j.jbusres.2011.07.029

Broyles, S. (2006). Subliminal advertising and the perpetual popularity of playing to people's paranoia. *The Journal of Consumer Affairs, 40*(2), 392–406. doi:10.1111/j.1745-6606.2006.00063.x

Bucklin, R. E., & Sismeiro, C. (2003). A model of web site browsing behavior estimated on clickstream data. *JMR, Journal of Marketing Research, 40*(3), 249–267. doi:10.1509/jmkr.40.3.249.19241

Burke, B. (2014). Gamify: How Gamification motivates people to do extraordinary things. Bibliomotion. *Inc., Apr.*

Burke, B. (2016). *Gamify: How gamification motivates people to do extraordinary things.* Routledge. doi:10.4324/9781315230344

Cabanac, M. (2002). What is emotion? *Behavioural Processes, 60*(2), 69–83. doi:10.1016/S0376-6357(02)00078-5 PMID:12426062

Campbell, C., Papania, L., Parent, M., & Cyr, D. (2010). An exploratory study into brand alignment in B2B relationships. *Industrial Marketing Management, 39*(5), 712–720. doi:10.1016/j.indmarman.2010.02.009

Chang, H.-J., Eckman, M., & Yan, R.-N. (2011). Application of the Stimulus-Organism-Response model to the retail environment: The role of hedonic motivation in impulse buying behavior. *International Review of Retail, Distribution and Consumer Research, 21*(3), 233–249. doi:10.1080/09593969.2011.578798

Chebat, J.-C., & Michon, R. (2003). Impact of ambient odors on mall shoppers' emotions, cognition, and spending: A test of competitive causal theories. *Journal of Business Research, 56*(7), 529–539. doi:10.1016/S0148-2963(01)00247-8

Crisinel, A.-S., Jacquier, C., Deroy, O., & Spence, C. (2013). Composing with Cross-modal Correspondences: Music and Odors in Concert. *Chemosensory Perception, 6*(1), 45–52. doi:10.100712078-012-9138-4

Dale, S. (2014). Gamification: Making work fun, or making fun of work? *Business Information Review, 31*(2), 82–90. doi:10.1177/0266382114538350

Deci, E. L., & Ryan, R. M. (2000). The" what" and" why" of goal pursuits: Human needs and the self-determination of behavior. *Psychological Inquiry, 11*(4), 227–268. doi:10.1207/S15327965PLI1104_01

Deci, E. L., Ryan, R. M., Gagné, M., Leone, D. R., Usunov, J., & Kornazheva, B. P. (2001). Need satisfaction, motivation, and well-being in the work organizations of a former eastern bloc country: A cross-cultural study of self-determination. *Personality and Social Psychology Bulletin, 27*(8), 930–942. doi:10.1177/0146167201278002

Demoulin, N. (2011). Music congruency in a service setting: The mediating role of emotional and cognitive responses. *Journal of Retailing and Consumer Services, 18*(1), 10–18. doi:10.1016/j.jretconser.2010.08.007

Deterding, S., Sicart, M., Nacke, L., O'Hara, K., & Dixon, D. (2011). Gamification. using game-design elements in non-gaming contexts. In *Proceedings of the CHI'11 Extended Abstracts on Human Factors in Computing Systems.* 10.1145/1979742.1979575

Di Muro, F., & Murray, K. B. (2012). An Arousal Regulation Explanation of Mood Effects on Consumer Choice. *The Journal of Consumer Research, 39*(3), 574–584. doi:10.1086/664040

Donovan, R. (1994). Store atmosphere and purchasing behavior. *Journal of Retailing*, *70*(3), 283–294. doi:10.1016/0022-4359(94)90037-X

Donovan, R. J., Rossiter, J. R., Marcoolyn, G., & Nesdale, A. (1994). Store atmosphere and purchasing behavior. *Journal of Retailing*, *70*(3), 283–294. doi:10.1016/0022-4359(94)90037-X

Driver, J., & Noesselt, T. (2008). Multisensory interplay reveals crossmodal influences on 'sensory-specific' brain regions, neural responses, and judgments. *Neuron*, *57*(1), 11–23. doi:10.1016/j.neuron.2007.12.013 PMID:18184561

Elverdam, C., & Aarseth, E. (2007). Game classification and game design: Construction through critical analysis. *Games and Culture*, *2*(1), 3–22. doi:10.1177/1555412006286892

Errajaa, K., Legohérel, P., & Daucé, B. (2018). Immersion and emotional reactions to the ambiance of a multiservice space: The role of perceived congruence between odor and brand image. *Journal of Retailing and Consumer Services*, *40*, 100–108. doi:10.1016/j.jretconser.2017.08.016

Farzan, R., DiMicco, J. M., Millen, D. R., Dugan, C., Geyer, W., & Brownholtz, E. A. (2008). Results from deploying a participation incentive mechanism within the enterprise. In *Proceedings of the SIGCHI conference on Human factors in computing systems*. 10.1145/1357054.1357145

Gallace, A., & Spence, C. (2014). *In touch with the future: the sense of touch from cognitive neuroscience to virtual reality*. Oxford University Press. doi:10.1093/acprof:oso/9780199644469.001.0001

Garaus, M., Wagner, U., & Kummer, C. (2014). Cognitive fit, retail shopper confusion, and shopping value: Empirical investigation. *Journal of Business Research*, *68*(5), 1003–1011. doi:10.1016/j.jbusres.2014.10.002

Gorn, G., Tuan Pham, M., & Yatming Sin, L. (2001). When arousal influences ad evaluation and valence does not (and vice versa). *Journal of Consumer Psychology*, *11*(1), 43–55. doi:10.1207/S15327663JCP1101_4

Guéguen, N., & Jacob, C. (2010). Music congruency and consumer behavior: an experimental field study. *International Bulletin of Business Administration*, (9), 56-63.

Guéguen, N., Jacob, C., & Boulbry, G. (2007). The effect of touch on compliance with a restaurant's employee suggestion. *International Journal of Hospitality Management*, *26*(4), 1019–1023. doi:10.1016/j.ijhm.2006.12.004

Gulas, C. S., & Bloch, P. H. (1995). Right under our noses: Ambient scent and consumer responses. *Journal of Business and Psychology*, *10*(1), 87–98. doi:10.1007/BF02249272

Hamari, J. (2013). Transforming homo economicus into homo ludens: A field experiment on gamification in a utilitarian peer-to-peer trading service. *Electronic Commerce Research and Applications*, *12*(4), 236–245. doi:10.1016/j.elerap.2013.01.004

Hamari, J. (2017). Do badges increase user activity? A field experiment on the effects of gamification. *Computers in Human Behavior*, *71*, 469–478. doi:10.1016/j.chb.2015.03.036

Hamari, J., & Koivisto, J. (2014). Measuring flow in gamification: Dispositional flow scale-2. *Computers in Human Behavior*, *40*, 133–143. doi:10.1016/j.chb.2014.07.048

Hamari, J., & Koivisto, J. (2015). "Working out for likes": An empirical study on social influence in exercise gamification. *Computers in Human Behavior, 50*, 333–347. doi:10.1016/j.chb.2015.04.018

Hamari, J., Koivisto, J., & Sarsa, H. (2014). *Does gamification work?--a literature review of empirical studies on gamification.* Paper presented at the 2014 47th Hawaii International Conference on System Sciences (HICSS).

Harwood, T., & Garry, T. (2015). An investigation into gamification as a customer engagement experience environment. *Journal of Services Marketing, 29*(6/7), 533–546. doi:10.1108/JSM-01-2015-0045

Hawkins, D. (1970). The effects of subliminal stimulation on drive level and brand preference. *JMR, Journal of Marketing Research, 7*(3), 322–326. doi:10.1177/002224377000700306

Helmefalk, M. (2016). Congruency as a mediator in an IKEA retail setting: Products, services and store image in relation to sensory cues. *International Journal of Retail & Distribution Management, 44*(9), 956–972. doi:10.1108/IJRDM-03-2016-0035

Helmefalk, M. (2019). An interdisciplinary perspective on gamification: Mechanics, psychological mediators and outcomes. *International Journal of Serious Games, 6*(1), 3–26. doi:10.17083/ijsg.v6i1.262

Helmefalk, M., & Berndt, A. (2018). Shedding light on the use of single and multisensory cues and their effect on consumer behaviours. *International Journal of Retail & Distribution Management, 46*(11/12), 1077–1091. doi:10.1108/IJRDM-03-2018-0057

Helmefalk, M., & Hultén, B. (2017). Multi-sensory congruent cues in designing retail store atmosphere: Effects on shoppers' emotions and purchase behavior. *Journal of Retailing and Consumer Services, 38*, 1–11. doi:10.1016/j.jretconser.2017.04.007

Helmefalk, M., Lundqvist, S., & Marcusson, L. (2019). The Role of Mechanics in Gamification: An Interdisciplinary Perspective. *International Journal of Virtual and Augmented Reality, 3*(1), 18–41. doi:10.4018/IJVAR.2019010102

Helmefalk, M., & Marcusson, L. (2019). Gamification in a servicescape context: A conceptual framework. *J International Journal of Internet Marketing, 13*(1), 22–46.

Herrington, D. (1996). Effects of music in service environments: A field study. *Journal of Services Marketing, 10*(2), 26–41. doi:10.1108/08876049610114249

Herrmann, A., Zidansek, M., Sprott, D. E., & Spangenberg, E. R. (2013). The Power of Simplicity: Processing Fluency and the Effects of Olfactory Cues on Retail Sales. *Journal of Retailing, 89*(1), 30–43. doi:10.1016/j.jretai.2012.08.002

Hofacker, C. F., de Ruyter, K., Lurie, N. H., Manchanda, P., & Donaldson, J. (2016). Gamification and Mobile Marketing Effectiveness. *Journal of Interactive Marketing, 34*, 25–36. doi:10.1016/j.intmar.2016.03.001

Högberg, J., Ramberg, M. O., Gustafsson, A., Wästlund, E. J. J. O. R., & Services, C. (2019). Creating brand engagement through in-store gamified customer experiences. *50*, 122-130.

Högberg, J., Shams, P., & Wästlund, E. (2019). Gamified in-store mobile marketing: The mixed effect of gamified point-of-purchase advertising. *Journal of Retailing and Consumer Services*, *50*, 298–304. doi:10.1016/j.jretconser.2018.07.004

Holzwarth, M., Janiszewski, C., & Neumann, M. M. (2006). The Influence of Avatars on Online Consumer Shopping Behavior. *Journal of Marketing*, *70*(4), 19–36. doi:10.1509/jmkg.70.4.019

Hultén, B. (2011). Sensory marketing: The multi-sensory brand-experience concept. *European Business Review*, *23*(3), 256–273. doi:10.1108/09555341111130245

Hultén, B. (2015). *Sensory Marketing: Theoretical and Empirical Grounds* (Vol. 1). New York: Routledge. doi:10.4324/9781315690681

Hunicke, R., LeBlanc, M., & Zubek, R. (2004). *MDA: A formal approach to game design and game research.* Paper presented at the Proceedings of the AAAI Workshop on Challenges in Game AI.

Huotari, K., & Hamari, J. (2012). Defining gamification: a service marketing perspective. In *Proceedings of the 16th International Academic MindTrek Conference.* 10.1145/2393132.2393137

Huotari, K., & Hamari, J. (2017). A definition for gamification: Anchoring gamification in the service marketing literature. *Electronic Markets*, *27*(1), 21–31. doi:10.100712525-015-0212-z

Imschloss, M., & Kuehnl, C. (2017). Don't ignore the floor: Exploring multisensory atmospheric congruence between music and flooring in a retail environment. *Psychology and Marketing*, *34*(10), 931–945. doi:10.1002/mar.21033

Jamal, A., & Goode, M. M. (2001). Consumers and brands: A study of the impact of self-image congruence on brand preference and satisfaction. *Marketing Intelligence & Planning*, *19*(7), 482–492. doi:10.1108/02634500110408286

John, D. R., Loken, B., Kim, K., & Monga, A. B. (2006). Brand concept maps: A methodology for identifying brand association networks. *JMR, Journal of Marketing Research*, *43*(4), 549–563. doi:10.1509/jmkr.43.4.549

Kaltcheva, V. D., & Weitz, B. A. (2006). When should a retailer create an exciting store environment? *Journal of Marketing*, *70*(1), 107–118. doi:10.1509/jmkg.70.1.107.qxd

Kasurinen, J., & Knutas, A. (2018). Publication trends in gamification: A systematic mapping study. *Computer Science Review*, *27*, 33–44. doi:10.1016/j.cosrev.2017.10.003

Kearney, T., Coughlan, J., & Kennedy, A. (2013). An Exploration of the Effects of the Servicescape on Customer and Employee Responses in a Grocery Retail Context. *Irish Journal of Management*, *32*(2), 71–91.

Kim, T. W., & Werbach, K. (2016). More than just a game: Ethical issues in gamification. *Ethics and Information Technology*, *18*(2), 157–173. doi:10.100710676-016-9401-5

Koffka, K. (2013). *Principles of Gestalt psychology*. Routledge. doi:10.4324/9781315009292

Koivisto, J., & Hamari, J. (2014). Demographic differences in perceived benefits from gamification. *Computers in Human Behavior*, *35*, 179–188. doi:10.1016/j.chb.2014.03.007

Kotler, P. (1973). Atmospherics as a marketing tool. *Journal of Retailing*, *49*(4), 48–64.

Krishna, A. (2012). An integrative review of sensory marketing: Engaging the senses to affect perception, judgment and behavior. *Journal of Consumer Psychology*, *22*(3), 332–351. doi:10.1016/j.jcps.2011.08.003

Krishna, A., Elder, R., & Caldara, C. (2010). Feminine to smell but masculine to touch? Multisensory congruence and its effect on the aesthetic experience. *Journal of Consumer Psychology*, *20*(4), 410–418. doi:10.1016/j.jcps.2010.06.010

Krishna, A., & Schwarz, N. (2014). Sensory marketing, embodiment, and grounded cognition: A review and introduction. *Journal of Consumer Psychology*, *24*(2), 159–168. doi:10.1016/j.jcps.2013.12.006

Kumar, J. (2013). Gamification at work: Designing engaging business software. In *Proceedings of the International Conference of Design, User Experience, and Usability*. 10.1007/978-3-642-39241-2_58

Laros, F. J. M., & Steenkamp, J.-B. E. M. (2005). Emotions in consumer behavior: A hierarchical approach. *Journal of Business Research*, *58*(10), 1437–1445. doi:10.1016/j.jbusres.2003.09.013

Lin, I. Y. (2004). Evaluating a servicescape: The effect of cognition and emotion. *International Journal of Hospitality Management*, *23*(2), 163–178. doi:10.1016/j.ijhm.2003.01.001

Lindstrom, M. (2005). Broad sensory branding. *Journal of Product and Brand Management*, *14*(2), 84–87. doi:10.1108/10610420510592554

Lucassen, G., & Jansen, S. (2014). Gamiðcation in Consumer Marketing-Future or Fallacy? *Procedia: Social and Behavioral Sciences*, *148*, 194–202. doi:10.1016/j.sbspro.2014.07.034

Manganari, E. E., Dennis, C., Siomkos, G. J., & Vrechopoulos, A. P. (2009). Store atmosphere in web retailing. *European Journal of Marketing*, *43*(9/10), 1140–1153. doi:10.1108/03090560910976401

Mari, M., & Poggesi, S. (2013). Servicescape cues and customer behavior: A systematic literature review and research agenda. *Service Industries Journal*, *33*(2), 171–199. doi:10.1080/02642069.2011.613934

Matallaoui, A., Hanner, N., & Zarnekow, R. (2016). Gamification: Using Game Elements in Serious Contexts. In S. Stieglitz, C. Lattemann, S. Robra-Bissantz, R. Zarnekow, & T. Brockmann (Eds.), (pp. 3–19). Springer.

Matallaoui, A., Koivisto, J., Hamari, J., & Zarnekow, R. (2017). How Effective Is "Exergamification"? A Systematic Review on the Effectiveness of Gamification Features in Exergames. In *Proceedings of the 50th Hawaii International Conference on System Sciences*. 10.24251/HICSS.2017.402

Mattila, A. S., & Wirtz, J. (2001). Congruency of scent and music as a driver of in-store evaluations and behavior. *Journal of Retailing*, *77*(2), 273–289. doi:10.1016/S0022-4359(01)00042-2

McGoldrick, P. J., & Pieros, C. P. (1998). Atmospherics, pleasure and arousal: The influence of response moderators. *Journal of Marketing Management*, *14*(1-3), 173–197. doi:10.1362/026725798784959372

Mehrabian, A., & Russell, J. A. (1974). *An approach to environmental psychology*. Cambridge: the MIT Press.

Michon, R., Yu, H., Smith, D., & Chebat, J.-C. (2008). The influence of mall environment on female fashion shoppers' value and behaviour. *Journal of Fashion Marketing and Management, 12*(4), 456–468. doi:10.1108/13612020810906128

Milliman, R. E. (1982). Using background music to affect the behavior of supermarket shoppers. *Journal of Marketing, 46*(3), 86–91. doi:10.1177/002224298204600313

Mitchell, D. J., Kahn, B. E., & Knasko, S. C. (1995). There's something in the air: Effects of congruent or incongruent ambient odor on consumer decision making. *The Journal of Consumer Research, 22*(2), 229–238. doi:10.1086/209447

Morrison, M., Gan, S., Dubelaar, C., & Oppewal, H. (2011). In-store music and aroma influences on shopper behavior and satisfaction. *Journal of Business Research, 64*(6), 558–564. doi:10.1016/j.jbusres.2010.06.006

Morschheuser, B., Hamari, J., Koivisto, J., & Maedche, A. (2017). Gamified crowdsourcing: Conceptualization, literature review, and future agenda. *International Journal of Human-Computer Studies, 106*, 26–43. doi:10.1016/j.ijhcs.2017.04.005

Morschheuser, B., Hassan, L., Werder, K., & Hamari, J. (2018). How to design gamification? A method for engineering gamified software. *Information and Software Technology, 95*, 219–237. doi:10.1016/j.infsof.2017.10.015

Mullins, J. K., & Sabherwal, R. (2018a). Beyond enjoyment: A cognitive-emotional perspective of gamification. In *Proceedings of the 51st Hawaii International Conference on System Sciences.* 10.24251/HICSS.2018.152

Mullins, J. K., & Sabherwal, R. (2018). Gamification: A cognitive-emotional view. Journal of Business Research.

Nacke, L. E., & Deterding, C. S. (2017). The maturing of gamification research. *Computers in Human Behaviour*, 450-454.

North, A. C., Hargreaves, D. J., & McKendrick, J. (1997). In-store music affects product choice. *Nature, 390*(6656), 132. doi:10.1038/36484

North, A. C., Mackenzie, L. C., Law, R. M., & Hargreaves, D. J. (2004). The Effects of Musical and Voice "Fit" on Responses to Advertisements. *Journal of Applied Social Psychology, 34*(8), 1675–1708. doi:10.1111/j.1559-1816.2004.tb02793.x

Obeng, E., Prescott, J. E., Hulland, J., Gilbert, R., & Maxham, J. (2015). Retail capability systems. *AMS Review, 5*(3), 103–122. doi:10.100713162-015-0067-7

Olsson, M., Högberg, J., Wästlund, E., & Gustafsson, A. (2016). *In-Store Gamification: Testing a Location-Based Treasure Hunt App in a Real Retailing Environment.* Paper presented at the 2016 49th Hawaii International Conference on System Sciences (HICSS). 10.1109/HICSS.2016.206

Osipov, I. V., Nikulchev, E., Volinsky, A. A., & Prasikova, A. Y. (2015). Study of gamification effectiveness in online e-learning systems. *International Journal of Advanced Computer Science Applications, 6*(2), 71-77.

Pan, F.-C., Su, S.-J., & Chiang, C.-C. (2008). Dual attractiveness of winery: Atmospheric cues on purchasing. *International Journal of Wine Business Research, 20*(2), 95–110. doi:10.1108/17511060810883731

Pedreira, O., García, F., Brisaboa, N., & Piattini, M. (2015). Gamification in software engineering–A systematic mapping. *Information and Software Technology, 57*, 157–168. doi:10.1016/j.infsof.2014.08.007

Peng, C., & Kim, Y. G. J. J. o. I. C. (2014). Application of the stimuli-organism-response (SOR) framework to online shopping behavior. *13*(3-4), 159-176.

Pettit, R. K., McCoy, L., Kinney, M., & Schwartz, F. N. (2015). Student perceptions of gamified audience response system interactions in large group lectures and via lecture capture technology. *BMC Medical Education, 15*(1), 92. doi:10.118612909-015-0373-7 PMID:25997953

Piqueras-Fiszman, B., Laughlin, Z., Miodownik, M., & Spence, C. (2012). Tasting spoons: Assessing how the material of a spoon affects the taste of the food. *Food Quality and Preference, 24*(1), 24–29. doi:10.1016/j.foodqual.2011.08.005

Raghubir, P., & Krishna, A. J. J. o. M. r. (1999). Vital dimensions in volume perception: can the eye fool the stomach?, *36*(3), 313-326.

Rahman, O. (2012). The Influence of Visual and Tactile Inputs on Denim Jeans Evaluation. *International Journal of Design, 6*(1), 11–25.

Raju, P. S. (1980). Optimum stimulation level: Its relationship to personality, demographics, and exploratory behavior. *The Journal of Consumer Research, 7*(3), 272–282. doi:10.1086/208815

Raz, C., Piper, D., Haller, R., Nicod, H., Dusart, N., & Giboreau, A. (2008). From sensory marketing to sensory design: How to drive formulation using consumers' input? *Food Quality and Preference, 19*(8), 719–726. doi:10.1016/j.foodqual.2008.04.003

Robson, K., Plangger, K., Kietzmann, J. H., McCarthy, I., & Pitt, L. (2015). Is it all a game? Understanding the principles of gamification. *Business Horizons, 58*(4), 411–420. doi:10.1016/j.bushor.2015.03.006

Rosen, D. E., & Purinton, E. J. J. o. B. R. (2004). Website design: Viewing the web as a cognitive landscape. *57*(7), 787-794.

Ryan, R. M., & Deci, E. L. (2000). Intrinsic and Extrinsic Motivations: Classic Definitions and New Directions. *Contemporary Educational Psychology, 25*(1), 54–67. doi:10.1006/ceps.1999.1020 PMID:10620381

Sailer, M., Hense, J. U., Mayr, S. K., & Mandl, H. (2017). How gamification motivates: An experimental study of the effects of specific game design elements on psychological need satisfaction. *Computers in Human Behavior, 69*, 371–380. doi:10.1016/j.chb.2016.12.033

Sardi, L., Idri, A., & Fernandez-Aleman, J. L. (2017). A systematic review of gamification in e-Health. *Journal of Biomedical Informatics, 71*, 31–48. doi:10.1016/j.jbi.2017.05.011 PMID:28536062

Seaborn, K., & Fels, D. I. (2015). Gamification in theory and action: A survey. *International Journal of Human-Computer Studies, 74*, 14–31. doi:10.1016/j.ijhcs.2014.09.006

Seo, H. S., & Hummel, T. (2011). Auditory-olfactory integration: Congruent or pleasant sounds amplify odor pleasantness. *Chemical Senses, 36*(3), 301–309. doi:10.1093/chemse/bjq129 PMID:21163913

Shahri, A., Hosseini, M., Phalp, K., Taylor, J., & Ali, R. (2014). Towards a code of ethics for gamification at enterprise. In *Proceedings of the IFIP Working Conference on The Practice of Enterprise Modeling.* 10.1007/978-3-662-45501-2_17

Soars, B. (2009). Driving sales through shoppers' sense of sound, sight, smell and touch. *International Journal of Retail & Distribution Management, 37*(3), 286–298. doi:10.1108/09590550910941535

Spangenberg, E. R., Grohmann, B., & Sprott, D. E. (2005). It's beginning to smell (and sound) a lot like Christmas: The interactive effects of ambient scent and music in a retail setting. *Journal of Business Research, 58*(11), 1583–1589. doi:10.1016/j.jbusres.2004.09.005

Spangenberg, E. R., Sprott, D. E., Grohmann, B., & Tracy, D. L. (2006). Gender-congruent ambient scent influences on approach and avoidance behaviors in a retail store. *Journal of Business Research, 59*(12), 1281–1287. doi:10.1016/j.jbusres.2006.08.006

Spence, C. (2012). Managing sensory expectations concerning products and brands: Capitalizing on the potential of sound and shape symbolism. *Journal of Consumer Psychology, 22*(1), 37–54. doi:10.1016/j.jcps.2011.09.004

Spence, C., & Gallace, A. (2011). Multisensory design: Reaching out to touch the consumer. *Psychology and Marketing, 28*(3), 267–308. doi:10.1002/mar.20392

Spence, C., Puccinelli, N. M., Grewal, D., & Roggeveen, A. L. (2014). Store Atmospherics: A Multisensory Perspective. *Psychology and Marketing, 31*(7), 472–488. doi:10.1002/mar.20709

Spies, K., Hesse, F., & Loesch, K. (1997). Store atmosphere, mood and purchasing behavior. *International Journal of Research in Marketing, 14*(1), 1–17. doi:10.1016/S0167-8116(96)00015-8

Su, C. H., & Cheng, C. H. (2015). A mobile gamification learning system for improving the learning motivation and achievements. *Journal of Computer Assisted Learning, 31*(3), 268–286. doi:10.1111/jcal.12088

Summers, T. A., & Hebert, P. R. (2001). Shedding some light on store atmospherics: Influence of illumination on consumer behavior. *Journal of Business Research, 54*(2), 145–150. doi:10.1016/S0148-2963(99)00082-X

Swan, C. (2012). Gamification: A new way to shape behavior. *Communication World, 29*(3), 13–14.

Trappey, C. J. P., & Marketing. (1996). A meta-analysis of consumer choice and subliminal advertising, *13*(5), 517-530.

Turley, L. W., & Chebat, J.-C. (2002). Linking retail strategy, atmospheric design and shopping behaviour. *Journal of Marketing Management, 18*(1-2), 125–144. doi:10.1362/0267257022775891

Turley, L. W., & Milliman, R. E. (2000). Atmospheric Effects on Shopping Behavior. *Journal of Business Research, 49*(2), 193–211. doi:10.1016/S0148-2963(99)00010-7

Vashisht, D. (2017). Effect of nature of the game on ad-persuasion in online gaming context: Moderating roles of game-product congruence and consumer's need for cognition. *Internet Research, 27*(1), 52–73. doi:10.1108/IntR-10-2014-0271

Velasco, C., Jones, R., King, S., & Spence, C. (2013). The Sound of Temperature: What Information do Pouring Sounds Convey Concerning the Temperature of a Beverage. *Journal of Sensory Studies, 28*(5), 335–345. doi:10.1111/joss.12052

Vieira, V. A. (2013). Stimuli–organism-response framework: A meta-analytic review in the store environment. *Journal of Business Research, 66*(9), 1420–1426. doi:10.1016/j.jbusres.2012.05.009

Wakao, A., Matsumura, K., Suzuki, M., & Noma, H. (2015). Treasure hunt game to persuade visitors to walk around a shopping mall. In *Proceedings of the 2015 IEEE 4th Global Conference on Consumer Electronics (GCCE)*. 10.1109/GCCE.2015.7398555

Walker, P. (2016). Cross-sensory correspondences and symbolism in spoken and written language. *Journal of Experimental Psychology. Learning, Memory, and Cognition, 42*(9), 1339–1361. doi:10.1037/xlm0000253 PMID:26913934

Werbach, K., & Hunter, D. (2012). *For the win: How game thinking can revolutionize your business.* Wharton Digital Press.

Wiener, H. J. D., & Chartrand, T. L. (2014). The Effect of Voice Quality on Ad Efficacy. *Psychology and Marketing, 31*(7), 509–517. doi:10.1002/mar.20712

Witt, M., Scheiner, C., & Robra-Bissantz, S. (2011). Gamification of online idea competitions: Insights from an explorative case. *Informatik schafft Communities, 192.*

Yang, Y., Asaad, Y., & Dwivedi, Y. (2017). Examining the impact of gamification on intention of engagement and brand attitude in the marketing context. *Computers in Human Behavior, 73,* 459–469. doi:10.1016/j.chb.2017.03.066

ADDITIONAL READING

Chou, Y. K. (2019). *Actionable gamification: Beyond points, badges, and leaderboards.* Packt Publishing Ltd.

Hultén, B. (2015). *Sensory marketing: Theoretical and empirical grounds.* Routledge. doi:10.4324/9781315690681

Huotari, K., & Hamari, J. (2012, October). Defining gamification: a service marketing perspective. In *Proceeding of the 16th international academic MindTrek conference* (pp. 17-22). ACM. 10.1145/2393132.2393137

Krishna, A. (2013). *Customer sense: How the 5 senses influence buying behavior.* Springer. doi:10.1057/9781137346056

• Lindstrom, M. (2006). Brand sense: How to build powerful brands through touch, taste, smell, sight and sound. *Strategic Direction, 22*(2).

• Mehrabian, A., & Russell, J. A. (1974). *An approach to environmental psychology.* the MIT Press.

Raju, P. S. (1980). Optimum stimulation level: Its relationship to personality, demographics, and exploratory behavior. *The Journal of Consumer Research, 7*(3), 272–282. doi:10.1086/208815

• Sailer, M., Hense, J., Mandl, J., & Klevers, M. (2014). Psychological perspectives on motivation through gamification. *Interaction Design and Architecture Journal*, (19), 28-37.

Chapter 27
Eye of the Beholder:
Analyzing a Gamification Design Through a Servicescape Lens

Adam Palmquist

iD https://orcid.org/0000-0003-0943-6022

School of Informatics, University of Skövde, Sweden

David Gillberg

iD https://orcid.org/0000-0003-0087-5205

Insert Coin, Sweden

ABSTRACT

Gamification, the idea of using game design elements to make tasks more engaging, is used in many contexts. The enthusiasm for gamification and its potential uses can be seen in different research—as well as business fields. As of this day, there exists no dominant design principle or standard on how to construct a gamified solution. However, there seem to exist generic dogmas on what a gamification solution should include, look, and feel like. The theories used to explain the gamification techniques often originate from the field of game design and psychology. It is possible that more research fields could be used as a lens to magnify the effects of gamified information systems. In this report, we use the theories from environmental psychology and the servicescape methods to construct a lens to suggest improvements in gamification design for a learning management system used in higher education.

INTRODUCTION

According to the researchers O'Donnell, Deterding, Kappen, Fitzpatrick, Nacke and Johnson (2017) the use of gamification is multidisciplinary. Research about gamification has been conducted within a broad range of different areas, such as marketing (Hamari & Lehdonvirta, 2010; Huotari & Hamari, 2012; Hofacker, De Ruyter, Lurie, Manchanda, & Donaldson, 2016), learning (Cruaud, 2017; Dichev & Dicheva, 2017; Denny, 2013) digital health (Johnson et al., 2016; Von Bargen 2016) and human resources (Armstrong, Landers, & Collmus, 2015). The above-cited studies show through various research

DOI: 10.4018/978-1-6684-7589-8.ch027

methods that gamification can be somewhat useful in increasing user engagement through the use of game elements. However, the design process of gamification is yet vague. There are suggestions that the methods of how to design gamification come from game design and various psychological theories (Robson et al. 2015; Morschheuser et al. 2017; Shahri et al. 2019). There are approaches that suggest other theories from the field of informatics and behavioral economy (Liu, Santhanam, & Webster, 2017), as well as learning and communication (Treiblmaier, Putz, & Lowry, 2018), could be used as lenses for viewing, explaining or magnifying gamification design. This chapter adds a servicescape lens to the multidisciplinary research approach of gamification design theories, as well as a perspective for practitioners when designing a gamified implementation.

An early Gartner report claims that 80 percent of current gamified applications will fail to meet business objectives primarily due to poor design (Mora et al, 2015). Despite the existence of good and poor gamification design, only a few studies have been conducted on a variety of gamification design choices (see Sailer et al, 2017). It seems that previous studies have discussed gamification as a generic construct, neglecting the fact that different game designs can result in very diverse applications of game design elements. However, even if the technology and methodology have proven to be useful (Hamari, Koivisto, & Sarsa, 2014), questions about why they work, how they work and how they can be improved have been raised (Landers, Bauer, Callan, & Armstrong, 2015).

Gamification and servicescape are new terms for old ways of affecting people's behaviors. By altering the design of an existing system, both methods aim to affect people's retention and engagement. Even though there are related purposes of the two methods, the design of the servicescape and the design of gamification have been sparsely discussed (Huotari & Hamari, 2017). This chapter examines whether a case of gamification design for a learning management system (hereafter LMS), with the purpose to increase students' completion rates, could benefit from the use of a servicescape lens. The constructed lens in the chapter examines the design of gamification elements in a studio specialized in gamification design. The gamification design in this chapter undergoes a servicescape analysis to see how the lens theoretically can improve the design outcome. The real-world case is a research project conducted in 2018-2019, with the purpose of increasing the student retention and completion rates in higher education, with the aid of gamification.

BACKGROUND

The Student Retention Crisis and the GARFIEID-Project

Student completion rates in higher education are a growing problem. In the last decade, the completion rates in higher education have suffered from a downward trend (European Commission, 2015). According to the OECD, an average of 39% of students complete their bachelor's program within its theoretical duration (three years), increasing only to 67% given three additional years (OECD Indicators, 2019) within tertiary education of OECD-countries in 2017. This is problematic in relation to the development of society as a whole. As more and more workplaces become increasingly digital and automated, there will be a significant need for individuals to attend tertiary education (Manyika et al., 2017).

In the EU 2020 education strategy, one of the goals is to have more individuals completing higher education. Reducing dropout- and increasing completion rates in higher education is one of the key strategies for achieving this goal. This is regarded as crucial, both for the high-level skills that Europe's knowledge-intensive economic sectors need as well as for Europe's capacity to innovate and foster productivity and social justice (European Commission Education and Culture, 2015).

To meet the problem of early dropouts, the Swedish Innovation Agency, Vinnova, granted the project GARFIElD - Gamification of Automation stRategies For InDustry 4.0 in 2018.[1]

One of the aims of the GARFIElD project was to increase the completion rate and to reduce student dropouts in higher education through a gamified digital learning tool, GWEN. GARFIElD used gamification methods throughout the projects' learning processes and courses with the aim to increase student engagement and universities' completion rates without lowering the knowledge requirements that the Swedish manufacturing and automotive industry poses.

The expected result was that the students would have a greater chance of completing the course during the predetermined study period if the course material was gamified.

In the project, the gamification studio Insert Coin assisted Chalmers University, a Swedish university that focuses on research and education in technology, natural science, architecture and maritime studies, with the design, implementation and construction of pilot tests, by holding workshops and courses that explore, examine and analyze the needs of the university. The knowledge that transpired from workshops and courses was transformed into a game-based implementation in Chalmers' current learning platform Canvas, a web-based learning management system (LMS). The GARFIElD project ran for approximately one year. In that year, different courses tested to utilise gamification in their LMS. The courses ran for about 4-8 weeks. In this chapter studied case, the gamification implementation in the Canvas LMS resulted in an 8% increased completion rate and a 294% increase of A-grades compared to four previous instances of the same course without gamification.

Definition of Gamification in the GARFIElD-Project

The term gamification was initially used by Nick Pelling in 2002 but started to gain popularity in the academic world around 2010 (Treiblmaier, Putz, & Lowry, 2018). As of today, there are different definitions of the term. The definition of gamification in the GARFIElD project was "the use of game design elements in non-game contexts". This broad definition was coined by Deterding, Dixon, & Nacke (2010) and draws the lines around a common idea and understanding of gamification. It is worth to note that this definition sets gamification aside from the term "serious games"; games created with a purpose other than just entertainment (Susi & Johannesson, 2007). With this in mind, gamification is not a game. It functions similarly to a game, however, creating a game-like experience by incorporating game elements in applications. The purpose is to enhance the value of an experience and stimulate further user engagement in order to bring out certain behaviors. Some examples of game elements are points, badges and/or leaderboards, meant to encourage various user behaviors within a gamified experience (Werbach & Hunter, 2012).

How to Design Gamification

The design of gamification is not just a matter of adding points, badges and leaderboards to a software product, but to knowledgeably design a system that will facilitate preferred user-behaviors (Werbach & Hunter, 2012). One way to facilitate preferred user-behaviors is indeed through the use of game elements or game mechanics; the rules that oversee the interaction between users and the game system (Teh, Schuff, Johnson, & Geddes, 2013). Nevertheless, the game elements and game mechanics need to be structured as an ecosystem, not just randomly added, to have a chance to affect the desired user behavior (Palmquist, 2018). However, even with a designed gamification eco-system, there is no guarantee that users will react in the way the designer had in mind (Kim & Werbach, 2016). There are a lot of examples of gamification failures in various fields, e.g., in employee performance, onboarding and training (Callan, Bauer, & Landers, 2015). How then shall gamification be designed to avoid disappointments and information systems' commercial failures?

The studies regarding how to design gamification give a mixed impression of the process, likewise there are discrepancies on what separates a good gamification from a bad one. Gamification practitioners, as well as researchers, acknowledge that gamification is challenging to design and to implement (Koivisto & Hamari, 2019; Palmquist, 2019). The challenge of designing gamification includes divergences regarding gamification designers' and stakeholders' backgrounds, goals, and understanding of gamification (Hassan, Morschheuser, Dreidev, & Hamari, 2018). However, Mora, Riera, Gonzalez, & Arnedo-Moreno (2015) claim that many gamification-based solutions fail because they have been created on an impulse or by mixing designs features from different digital games without a proper design process. An issue with gamification is that there is no well-defined design method, despite the abundance of approaches on how to design gamification.

From academia, there have been attempts to delineate and frame how the design process works. Investigations into how to design gamification have been conducted by Morschheuser, Hamari, Werder, & Abe (2017), as well as Shahri, Hosseini, Phalp, Taylor, & Ali (2019). These studies attempt to reveal how gamification professionals work, how gamification is produced, and what knowledge designers have to possess. By analyzing different articles and surveys, and doing interviews with professional gamification designers, Morschheuser et al. (2017) found that designers need to understand their end-users' needs, incentives and behaviors, in addition to the context characteristics. With this said, Morschheuser et al. (2017) found that there are discrepancies in the published literature on gamification design, as well as in the gamification specialist interviews (e.g. the design process). Morschheuser et al. (2017) conclude their study with the following takeaway: gamification design should follow an iterative and user-centered design process with a high degree of user involvement as well as early testing of design ideas. Morschheuser et al. (2017) also identify that in order to design functioning gamification, the designer needs to have a profound knowledge of game-design and human psychology.

Shahri et al. (2018), using a similar method as Morschheuser et al. (2017), although with a larger dataset, discovered that there is a need to assimilate gamification with the contexts in which it is being applied to. Otherwise, it will not be as effective. Shahri et al. (2018) conclude that due to the gamification objective (to affect the end-users' choices through design interactions), the gamification design body of knowledge should include the field of psychology, not just game design. Psychology could give knowledge about which approaches the gamification design should use in order to be successful in affecting the end-users' behavior, as well as increasing the users' motivation and engagement. In their meta-study about gamification in various information systems, Koivisto & Hamari (2019) also stated that given that the goal of gamification is to affect behavior, it is beneficial if the gamification designer has an understanding of psychology. This is also proclaimed by Liu et al. (2017); gamification design in an information system, as well as research on the topic, could be strengthened from an understanding of the underlying psychological theories that relate to gamification.

Other studies show that gamification professionals claim that in order to successfully design gamification, the designer has to have psychology in mind (Palmquist, 2019; Richter et al., 2015). Even though there does not exist a dominant method for designing gamification, the connecting thread in research about gamification design is that the designer should have knowledge in psychology and game design to be a successful gamification designer. However, the field of psychology is large. Which psychological theories and methods should be used in a gamification design? Different psychological theories have been put in relation to gamification and why it is engaging (Heinzen et al., 2015). Explanation models for how gamification should be designed are Operant Conditioning/Behaviorism, SDT and Flow-theory.

With the expanding multidisciplinary approach to gamification, there are suggestions of other theories that could be beneficial, for designers as well researchers, to understand. These theories are from, e.g., the field of informatics, behavioral economy, learning and communication (Liu, Santhanam, & Webster, Treiblmaier, Putz & Lowry, 2018).

In a study, Huotari & Hamari (2017) approach service systems and the service landscape with a gamification lens, concluding that gamification could contribute to a marketing context. If gamification were to be more connected to the overall business strategy, it could add important pieces to the puzzle between game studies and marketing. However, the benefits gained probably work more than one-way. The servicescape lens could possibly enhance a gamification design, as much as a gamified lens could benefit a servicescape design.

Table 1. Three psychological theories referenced in different gamification litterateur

Psychological theory	Descriptions	Reference papers and literature
Behaviorism/Operant Conditioning	A method of response learning through feedback. It works by giving the individual rewards and punishments for different behaviors. An individual creates an association between a particular behavior and a consequence (Holland & Skinner, 1961), e.g., rewards and positive feedback. Gamification practices relate to the method. When the end-user is receiving points in a gamified context, the end-user is expected to repeat that behavior.	(Werbach & Hunter, 2012; Seaborn & Fels, 2015; Landers et al., 2015; Richter et al., 2015; Robson, Plangger, Kietzmann, McCarthy, & Pitt, 2015)
Flow	The Flow theory describes a mental state in which individuals performing an activity are fully immersed. This state is called flow. The state is characterized by the absorption in what one does, resulting in the loss of space and time awareness (Csíkszentmihályi, 1992). Flow is a multidimensional construct, including perceptions of user control, concentration, arousal of curiosity and individual interest. The theory highlights the balance between easy and too hard. The flow state will emerge when users are optimally challenged; if the interaction is too demanding, it may produce anxiety, and if it is not challenging enough, boredom (Csíkszentmihályi, 1992).	(Werbach & Hunter, 2012; Deterding, 2015; Sailer et al, 2017; Seaborn & Fels, 2015; Meske, Brockmann, Wilms, & Stieglitz, 2017; Matallaoui, Hanner, & Zarnekow, 2017; AlMarshedi, Wanick, Wills, & Ranchhod, 2017; Landers et al., 2015; Koivisto & Hamari, 2019)
Self Determination Theory (SDT)	SDT is an established theory of human motivation, with empirical support across different contexts (Deci & Ryan, 2000). The theory focuses on various types, rather than the amount, of motivation that affects engagement, problem-solving, psychological health, and satisfaction (Deci & Ryan, 2000). SDT distinguishes between autonomous and controlled motivation. With the former, people experience a self-endorsement of their actions, while in the latter, they experience pressure to think, feel or behave in particular ways. Three primary intrinsic needs involved in self-determination include the need for competence, autonomy and relatedness.	(Werbach & Hunter, 2012; Deterding, 2015; Seaborn & Fels, 2015; Meske et al., 2017; Matallaoui et al., 2017; Landers et al., 2015; Richter et al., 2015; Mora et al., 2015; Koivisto & Hamari, 2019)

Definition of Servicescape and E-Servicescape

The servicescape is an S-O-R (Stimuli, Organism, Response) framework that has its roots in the research area of environmental psychology, mainly in the theories regarding the three emotional dimensions of pleasure, arousal and dominance, and approach-avoidance behavior (Mehrabian & Russell, 1974).

The three emotional dimensions are viewed as an orthogonal spectrum, where the extremes are mutually exclusive; pleasure-displeasure, dominance-submissiveness and where arousal is defined as "a feeling state varying along a single dimension ranging from sleep to frantic excitement".

Approach, within the approach-avoidance behavior model, is defined broadly to include "physical movement toward, or away from, an environment or stimulus, degree of attention, exploration, favorable attitudes such as verbally or nonverbally expressed preference or liking, approach to the task (the level of performance), and approach to another person (affiliation)" (Mehrabian and Russell, 1974).

The tendency of increased approach behavior in relation to arousal should be understood as an inverted U curve, where extremely low arousal, under-stimulation, and extremely high arousal, overstimulation, diminish the approach behavior (Mehrabian and Russell, 1974).

Figure 1. The approximate relationship between arousal and approach-avoidance behavior, based on an illustration by Russel & Mehrabian (1978)

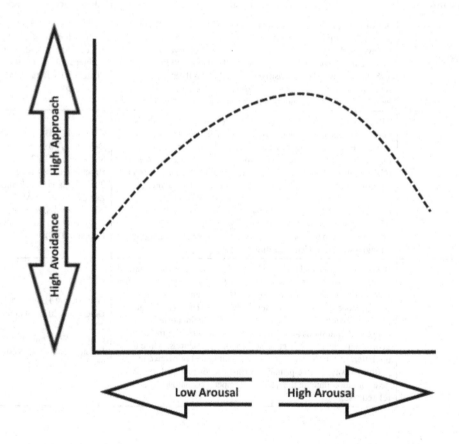

The term servicescape was originally defined as "how the built environment (i.e., the man-made, physical surroundings as opposed to the natural or social environment) ... affects both consumers and employees in service organizations" (Bitner, 1992). Since the coining of the term, there have been several studies that use the servicescape framework as a lens through which to view various service environments, such as hospitals (Loureiro, Sarmento, Lopes, & Jin, 2015), airports (Fodness & Murray, 2007; Park & Ryu, 2019) and hotels (Jessica Hwang, 2007; Avan, Uyar, Zorlu, & Özmen, 2019), to mention a few. They look at how customers are affected by everything from the presence of art to the quality of lighting or how easy signs are to read and understand.

Since the early 2000's, the research into servicescapes have also begun to investigate areas of digital interaction between providers and customers, also known as e-servicescapes or e-scapes, such as websites and mobile apps (Hopkins, Grove, Raymond, & Laforge, 2009; Wang, Tsai, & Tang, 2018; Koernig, 2003, Lee & Jeong, 2012). The same theories that have been used for physical servicescapes, and the approach-avoidance model it is based on, seem to apply here as well. Well communicated information, clear design and pleasing aesthetics all contribute to approach behaviors (Clark et al, 2009).

SERVICESCAPE PERSPECTIVES ON A GAMIFICATION DESIGN

Even though the theories of gamification and servicescape have different origins and applications, they have a lot of commonalities. Both focus on human responses to designed situations or stimuli and are used to elicit specific wanted actions (Butler, 2015; Bitner, 1990). The main difference between the two is that servicescape design is rooted in behaviors that are directly beneficial to the service provider (Bitner, 1990) while gamification is used to motivate people to achieve their own goals (Burke, 2014; Kumar, 2013). The goals of an organization that uses gamification are mainly achieved by identifying goals that are shared by both user and organization and focusing the gamification effort on them (Kumar Roy, Singh Jindal, & Harrigan, 2019; Kumar, 2013, Burke 2014). The approach differences do not mean that there is an inherent opposition between the two. While gamification is often used as a means to reach an organization's goal, it does it mainly by helping the users to reach personal goals that are also beneficial to the organization (Burke, 2016).

Gamification is never meaningful in itself; it always requires a context in which to reside. Since the context of this case study is an e-servicescape, a servicescape analysis of the gamification design could help to increase the efficacy of the gamification effort.

The servicescape analysis in this chapter is based on previous research performed within the fields of physical servicescapes and e-servicescapes. The previous findings can be grouped under three major labels.

Tangibility

There is a positive relationship between the tangibility of the e-scapes and the users' attitude towards the service, their attitude toward the web site, their behavioral intent and unaided recall of attributes of the service. There also exists an inverse relationship between tangibility and the perception of risk (Koernig, 2003).

Useful and informative content

Useful and informative website content fosters positive purchase behaviors (Hopkins, Grove, Raymond, & Laforge, 2009). One specific area of informative communication that has been studied is the usage of signage, as in signs (explicit signs), symbols (for example implicit indications through colors, material, lighting and sound) and artifacts. Signage has been deemed particularly important when it comes to forming first impressions, for communicating new service concepts and repositioning a service, as well as in highly competitive industries where customers are looking for cues to differentiate the organizations (Bitner, 1992).

Approach behaviors due to Pleasure and Arousal

Emotional responses to the servicescape can be captured by two dimensions; pleasure and arousal. While both pleasure and arousal increase approach behaviors, arousal will not do so when combined with unpleasantness.

High pleasure and high arousal consumers (i.e., how pleasant and how energized the consumers feel about an experience) will report significantly more exploration of the servicescape than other consumers. High pleasure and high arousal consumers will report significantly more satisfaction with the servicescape and the service than other consumers (Dawson & Bloch, 1990).

Pleasure and arousal can be increased through many means. In this analysis, the focus has been on two parameters that are highly relevant in relation to gamification:

- Perceptions of greater personal control in the servicescape increase pleasure.
- Complexity in the servicescape increases emotional arousal (Bitner, 1992).

From this theoretical base, the following hypotheses have been formulated:

H1: There is a positive relationship between tangibility in images and texts within the gamification elements, the student's attitude towards education in general and the particular gamified content, as well as between positive student activity and the student's unaided recall of attributes of the service.

H2: There is an inverse relationship between the tangibility of gamified elements and the perception of risk.

H3: Useful and informative content in the gamified elements fosters positive student activity.

H4: Signs (actual signs or indicators of meaning or action), symbols (aesthetic cues with symbolic meaning, such as rarity indicators of items) and artifacts (representations of physical objects, such as avatars or trophies) are particularly important in forming first impressions and for communicating new concepts.

H5: Perceptions of greater personal control in the e-servicescape increase pleasure which in turn increases positive student activity.

H6: Complexity in the e-servicescape increases emotional arousal which in turn increases positive student activity, except when combined with unpleasantness.

H7: High pleasure & high arousal students (i.e., those students experiencing high pleasure or arousal) will report significantly more exploration of the gamified e-servicescape than other students.

H8: High pleasure & high arousal students will report significantly more satisfaction with a gamified e-servicescape, and the educational content in general, than other students.

In the following case study, we will investigate how this constructed servicescape approach could benefit a gamified LMS-environment.

A Gamification Implementation in The LMS Canvas

To investigate the hypotheses that gamification design could be benefited from a servicescape lens, the focus is on a gamification design proposal for the gamified course. The Insert Coin gamification team constructed a gamification platform called GWEN based on different game modules or game elements patterns. As an example, the levels module is a combination of the game elements points, progress bar, and avatar. The modules are stand-alone, in the sense that they can be implemented individually in a software system, but they can also be implemented together for a more game-like experience. It is possible for a client to choose which module/-s they want to use or combine in a GWEN-implementation, together with the design team. In the investigated case, the LMS Canvas communicates with the modules by sending messages that indicate the user's activity. If more than one module is implemented, the modules communicate with each other. The gamification is visualized through a widget that presents the results of the logic applied to the messages about the user's activity. The case study in this chapter is investigated with a theoretical method with no empirical user data analysis. Therefore, the study proposed lens is discussed in accordance with the design of the gamification in the LMS and not with user data or user reactions to the gamified course.

Figure 2. The Canvas LMS without a gamified layer

Figure 3. The Canvas LMS with a gamified layer

ANALYSIS

This section gives an overview of the gamification design in the GARFIElD project. It discusses the gamification modules and presents a critical read of how the gamification module design could benefit from a servicescape lens. The focus for the analysis is on five distinct gamification design choices (modules) in relation to the Canvas LMS.

Design Choice One: The Tutorial Module

In computer games, the player is often presented with an introductory phase. These introductions are applied in games as a series of tasks that must be completed to advance in the game environment. The reason for this is that the player should learn the basis of the game before the real game begins, and so, the introductory phase serves as a type of onboarding to the game.

 According to the gamification studio, the tutorial module is essential for the onboarding of a service (Insert Coin, 2019). The module facilitates the usage of the product by presenting different tasks that the user has to complete in order to start their gamified experience.

 The gamification studio describes the tutorial module as follows:

The tutorial module is designed to support the end-user to get a flying start together with your software product. The module urges your clients to learn about your product as well as to provide a better understanding of its service. The goal of the module is to faster onboard the end-user in your software product. (Insert Coin, 2019)

Figure 4. In the gamification implementation in Canvas, the tutorial module and the tasks presented were designed so that the students could have an onboarding to the course at the university as well as to the LMS

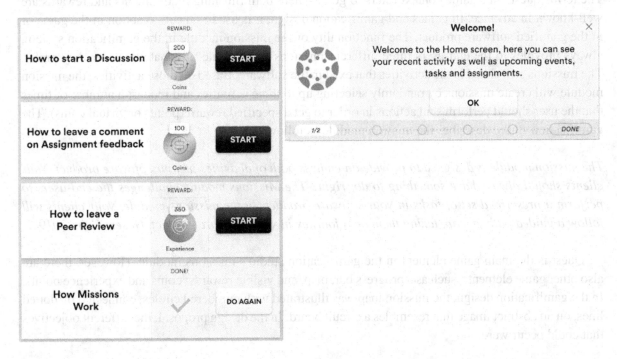

Servicescape Analysis

The usage of tutorials is in line with the hypothesis "useful and informative website content fosters positive student activity" (H3). The proposed tutorials act as a kind of signage, showing the way through the e-servicescape and thereby helping the student to get acquainted with the environment (H4). However, when writing the tutorial texts and choosing images to go with them, it would, from a servicescape perspective, be beneficial to take into account the actual learning content of the course as well as the learning environment in which the course takes place, not just describe the issue at hand. There are two factors to consider for the tutorials' texts and images. First off, to highlight tangible elements in the subject being discussed, e.g. machines on an assembly line for a course on automation or a roman palace for a course in antique architecture. Secondly, to highlight physical attributes of the university such as characteristic buildings on campus or physical elements of a typical lecture hall.

Making these additions should increase the students' behavioral intent and unaided recall of attributes.

It should also decrease the perception of risk, making the student feel more at ease in the learning environment (H2).

A well-designed tutorial could allow a higher level of complexity in a software product. A gamified tutorial could potentially facilitate technology acceptance in an e-servicescape context. According to the 6th, 7th and 8th hypotheses, this in turn, would likely increase both the level of exploration, as the satisfaction with the e-servicescape and the learning experience (H6-8). The use of step-by-step introductions as a form of signage could, according to hypothesis four, also ease the user's onboarding for a product (H4).

The Mission Module

The term "quest" in a game context refers to goals where both finishing requirements and rewards are well-known in advance. In games and gamification design, it is used as a call to action in the game or in the gamified software product. The functionality of the mission module in the gamification system, always provides to the end-users three different missions to complete, in whatever order they prefer. The missions are related to the activities that exist in the software. Based on those activities, the mission module will create missions by randomly selecting up to three activities and request a number of times that the user should perform said actions in order to get a specified reward (points or virtual coins). The gamification studio describes the mission module as follows:

The mission module is designed to provide an endless path of activities in your software product. Your clients should always have something to do, right? The Missions module challenges the end-users to perform a prescribed set of tasks in your software product. In the missions module, your clients will follow a guided path, a map, taking them on a journey in your software product. (Insert Coin, 2019)

Quest is the main game element in the gamification studio's missions module. However, there are also other game elements, such as a progress bar, map, and visible rewards; coins and experience points. In the gamification design, the mission map was illustrated with numbered circles, connected by dotted lines, on an abstract image that resembles a circuit board. In the design proposal, the different objectives that could occur were:

- Complete an assignment
- Leave a peer review on an active assignment
- Comment on assignment feedback

Servicescape Analysis

The mission module has the potential to increase the student's level of arousal through a concept called nudging (Thaler, R. H., & Sunstein, 2009). An example of that, would be that the objectives in the missions, give students indirect advice on how to behave, followed by positive reinforcement when the objectives are completed. To get positive stimuli for performed actions in a gamified context, which derives from the theory of operant conditioning, has proven to give the end-user positive emotions and self-satisfaction (Werbach & Hunter, 2012; Landers et al., 2015).

Just as with the tutorial module, how the texts are formulated, and which images are used is important. If the gamification elements are to reach their full potential from a servicescape perspective, both texts and images should relate to the subject at hand and to tangible elements of the teaching environment. The generic graphics of the map could, for example, be substituted with a background consisting of an assembly line, where the checkpoints are stations along the way to completing a product. This would relate more to the subject being taught, automation of production systems, making the mission map more tangible. The objectives themselves lack images altogether, which may be a missed opportunity to increase the perception of tangibility.

Figure 5. The mission map, showing the progression through a theoretically never-ending list of missions. The student is presently on the second mission. The objectives shown in the image are simply illustrations of the functionality, not intended to be the final product

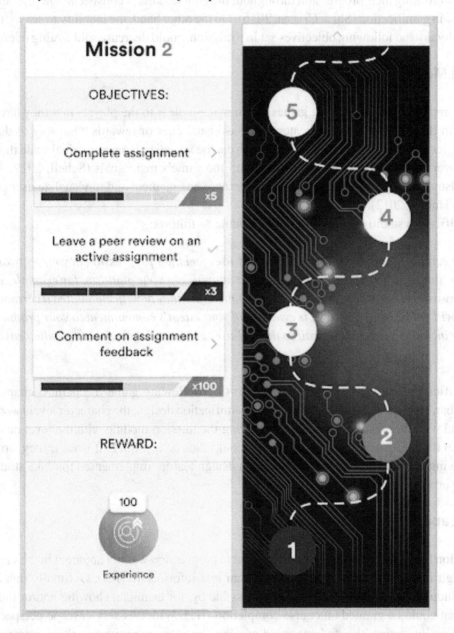

The subjects for the mission objectives clearly state the wanted action, which is in line with the hypothesis that "useful and informative content in the gamified elements fosters positive student activity" (H3). The objectives refer to activities that are common in school settings, such as assignments. Since these activities often have physical components, in the case of assignments that might be a handwritten article, it would be fairly simple to add images to the objectives that increase its tangibility in accordance with H1.

The mission module also has the benefit of increasing the students feeling of control and autonomy, since they can choose to fulfill individual objectives in any given order and at any given time, thereby themselves controlling their progression throughout the course. This is consistent with the self-determination-theory in gamification (Shi & Cristea, 2016). On the other hand, the inability to set your own goals as a student, by instead following objectives set in a mission, could decrease said feeling of control (H5).

The Level Module

Games, and in particular role-playing games, often make it clear to the players that they have achieved a milestone in the game by using indicators such as visual cues or rewards. One way of doing this is through a player-character level progression, which can be visualized as a numerical scale that increases based on player performed actions compatible with the game's main goals (Schell, 2019). This game element is also used in gamification as a way to increase engagement and to visualize user progression (Werbach & Hunter, 2012).

The gamification studio describes the level module as follows:

The levels in gamification are used to make the end-user feel their progression in your software product. The rules are simple; when your clients do various activities in your platform, for example, completing missions, they will get rewarded with experience points. After they have accumulated a certain number of points, they will gain a level. The level is evidence of your client's commitment to your product. Also, the level module includes an avatar-portrait so the end-user can associate with your product easier."(Insert Coin, 2019)

The gamification studio's level module contains the following game mechanics: character levels, progression bar, visible rewards and avatar. In the gamification design, the character levels were designed to correspond with the actual course week, mirroring the mission module with the level module. If the course was in its third week, the student's level should thus be level 3. If it wasn't, they would clearly not be following the intended syllabus. This was a design feature implemented to make students aware of how their progression related to the courses.

Servicescape Analysis

The connection between the user's level and the course progression was not apparent in the visual design, neither though images nor texts, making the design less informative (H3). Optimally this illustration and/or text should also be made as tangible as possible by, for example, showing and/or talking about a diploma that could be granted on course completion (H1). With this servicescape perspective added on the gamification design, the students could possibly get more committed to their course material.

The avatar in the gamification is displayed in the design proposal as a generic face with no significant connection to either the course automation of production systems or the specific university where the course was held (H1, H4). Further studies would be needed to investigate whether or not the students would get more engaged in the system if the avatar could be customizable by the user (H4-H6), representing famous individuals with a connection to the school and/or subject (H1), or some other design paradigm altogether.

Figure 6. The student has received 675 experience points since the last level up, and needs 325 more in order to reach level 3. Experience points will be rewarded by completing tasks such as missions or other significant activities. Having reached level 3, the student will receive a reward consisting of 250 virtual coins that can be used in the shop module

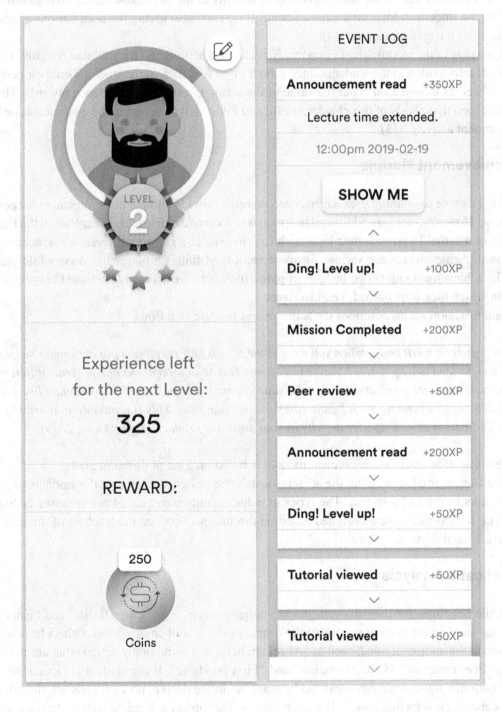

The event log in the module shows previously performed actions and their related rewards. This gives useful information for the students since it gives feedback to the students on their performed actions and indicates the value of the action through experience rewards (H3). Expanding a notification gives more information, as well as the ability to navigate directly to the page most related to the notification, thus giving the student an increased sense of control (H5) and also giving the notifications a secondary functionality as navigational signs (H4).

The event log in the module shows previously performed actions and their related rewards. This provides useful information to the students since it both gives feedback to the students on their performed actions, as well as information about the value of the action through the experience rewards. This supports the second hypothesis of this chapter; useful and informative content in the e-servicescape fosters positive student activity (H3).

The Achievement Module

Completing a game or winning over adversaries can often provide enough encouragement for people to play a game. However, there are additional techniques to motivate individuals to explore all the functions and levels of a game. To provide the player with cues to explore a game in different ways, achievements can be used. Achievements are various forms of records of things a player has done while playing a game. The achievement indicators; badges, trophies, pins, etc., are accessible outside the specific game context in which they were earned, i.e., in a roster.

The gamification studio describes the achievement module as follows:

Have you ever got a merit badge when you were in the Scouts? Or received a pin at summer swim camp? Did you feel noticed and approved? You're not alone! The Achievement module presents different milestones in your software product. It will make your clients try to achieve different goals like log in on different devices or attending social gatherings in your platform. This is a module that wants to build end-user dedication as well as user activity in your software product. (Insert Coin, 2019)

The gamification studio's achievement module is based on a set of different goals.

For the Canvas implementation, the achievements were designed to engage the students to perform different tasks in the LMS-system. The types of achievements were, e.g., Peer reviewer or Statistics master. The achievements were designed based on discussions between the teachers of the course and the gamification designers.

Servicescape Analysis

Some of the headlines for the achievements are rather generic, e.g., "close finish" and "game-based design" and have no explicit connection to the course or the school environment. Others have a clearer connection to the subject at hand, such as "AI researcher", and some imply actions that are possible to perform; "Peer reviewer", "Quiz champion" and "First purchase". If the student clicks on the "View Details" button, a more descriptive text can be read, but in the design, no such texts are shown. Of the examples above, the ones that have a clear connection to the subject at hand, as well as the ones referring to actions possible to perform, are preferable from a servicescape perspective (H1).

Figure 7. A list of achievements in the LMS design. Those marked with a checkmark, such as "Close Finish" and "Researcher", have been completed

When writing the titles and descriptions shown by clicking "view details", it is important to not only describe the actions needed to complete the achievement, but also to make the relationship to the subject and the school environment as tangible as possible (H1, H3).

The fact that all achievements are predefined, increases the chance of the actions to become meaningful in relation to the overall goal of course completion and high grades (H3). Just as with the mission module, the student cannot influence which objectives are included in an achievement. This makes an active or passive relationship to the achievements the only real choice, possibly decreasing the feeling of personal control (H5).

The number of different achievements with different objectives increases the overall complexity of the e-servicescape, which can be seen as beneficial (H6).

Some of the images in the design shown above have a certain connection to the wanted actions, but most are either related to games or are generic icons without connection to either the course or the school. From a servicescape perspective, the images would have benefited from being more closely related to a physical representation of the objectives, such as an image of a calculator for the achievement "Math 1 completed" (H1, H3).

The Shop Module

In games where players control characters inhabiting game worlds, they may have a need for various services, such as trading. This mechanic is called (self-service) kiosks, which are places where players can go to get these services and represent an interaction like that of a vending machine. The kiosks are locations in the game worlds where players can, on their own, do transactions or receive services. In the gamification design, the kiosk-mechanic was represented as a shop, where the users in the gamified software product could spend their earned coins, obtained from gaining levels.

The gamification studio describes the shop module as follows:

Getting feedback is crucial to get motivated for different tasks. Rewards are a kind of feedback that makes us want to pursue more important things. But one thing is for sure; not everybody wants the same thing. If you can choose what type of reward you will get after a hard day's work, you get a feeling of agency. This is how we designed the shop module. End-users are different, so why should they not be able to choose their own rewards? When your end-users use your software product, they get rewarded with a fictive currency called GWEN-Coins. In the shop, they can spend them on what they want – do they want a t-shirt or do they want a free subscription month? It's their choice. (Insert Coin, 2019)

The gamification studio's shop module contains different tangible and intangible rewards. The rewards are bought with the users' earned virtual coins. In the design proposal for Canvas, the titles and descriptions for the items that students could buy were:

- Extended deadline – "A one-time use voucher for extending your next upcoming deadline."
- Limited edition t-shirt – "A cool limited edition Chalmers T-shirt."[2]
- Science Avatars – "New cool science-themed avatar pack".
- Lecturers Assistant (sic!) – "A free one-on-one session with the teacher assistant to get help with the course"

Figure 8. The shop module. At the top, the student can see the current balance of virtual coins in the wallet. The larger area in the middle contains items available in the shop, with the possibility to scroll down in order to find more items

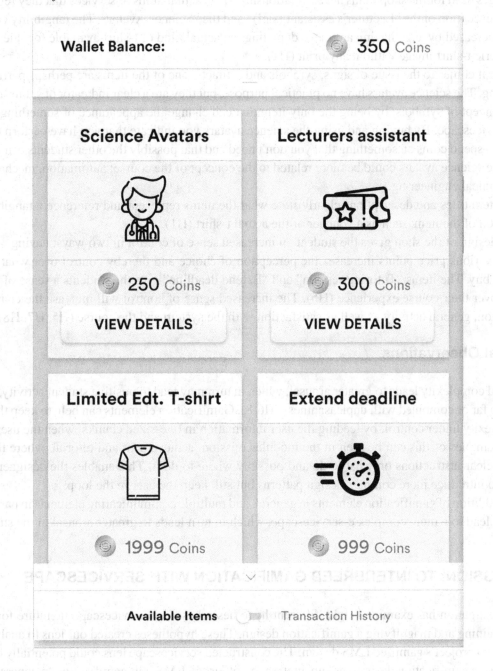

Servicescape Analysis

The images used for the shop items have a relationship to the actual items or services that they represent, with the exception of the "Lecturer's assistant (sic!)" and the "Science Avatar". The tangibility could be further increased by, e.g., having an image depicting the actual kind of t-shirt available for sale instead of a generic t-shirt image without any print (H1).

When it comes to the issue of signs, symbols and artifacts, one of the items are perhaps particularly interesting. The science avatars have no practical purpose, but they are a clear indicator of status, relating to the concept of symbols, by being the only item that can change the appearance of something within the e-servicescape. By buying and using the science avatars you indicate that you have performed well enough to spend coins on something that you don't need and that possibly the other students can't afford (H4). The science avatars could be more related to the concept of the course; automation, mechatronics or mechanical engineering.

The item titles and descriptions clearly state what the items represent and reference a tangible representation of the item, such as a voucher or the actual t-shirt (H1).

The design of the shop gives the student an increased sense of control in two ways; having multiple items at various price points increases the perception of choice and thereby control over what to buy or not to buy. The items "Tutoring session" and "Extend deadline" give the students a sense of greater control over their course experience (H5). The increased sense of control will increase the chances of exploration, general activity as well as satisfaction with the system and the course (H5, H7, H8).

General Observations

Increased complexity leads to greater arousal, which in turn may lead to positive student activity, unless taken too far or combined with unpleasantness (H6-8). Gamification elements can help to keep the level of complexity under control, by feeding the user information in bite-sized chunks, when the user needs them. Examples of this can be seen in the modules mission, achievement and tutorial, where the user is given clear instructions on what to do and possibly where to do it. This enables the designer of the system to introduce more complex design patterns but still keep the user in the loop.

The addition of gamification elements in general, and multiple communicating elements in particular, will also lead to a more complex e-servicescape, which in turn leads to greater arousal in the students.

DISCUSSION: TO INTERBREED GAMIFICATION WITH SERVICESCAPE

This investigation has examined eight different hypotheses based on servicescape literature for viewing, explaining and magnifying a gamification design. These hypotheses created our lens to analyze the GARFIElD project's gamified LMS design. The constructed servicescape lens could potentially be used to improve a gamification design implementation in not just an LMS, but gamification in general. With this chapter we propose several focus areas that gamification researchers and gamification professionals could use in their line of work:

- Increase the user's level of arousal, but avoid extreme levels, since that will lead to stress reactions and avoidance behavior.

- Increasing the user's level of pleasure will not only increase the level of activity, but also the user's level of exploration, unaided recall of information and general liking of the servicescape and the service.
- Use tangibility to yours and the user's benefit. Be specific and concrete where possible.
- Use signs, symbolism and artifacts to enhance first impressions and help guide the user through the experience. This can take many forms, such as actual signs or help texts, links from information to the area discussed, color coding of items to show which ones are more valuable to the user, etc.
- Give the user a feeling of control over both the environment and the experience. Examples include giving the user the ability to influence the missions and achievements that are available, giving the user the ability to modify the environment such as avatars, visualization of trophies and the number of notifications that the system shows the user.
- Increase the level of complexity but do it in a way that does not cause overload. A higher level of complexity helps to stave off boredom and increases the likelihood of achieving a flow state (Csíkszentmihályi, 1992).

Being well-aware that the studied case is limited and that various of the above propositions could already exist in different present gamification implementations, our discoveries should be viewed with some caution. This lens may not turn the psychological paradigm concerning gamification design upside down. Nonetheless, for scholars, this lens could provide a tool for understanding why different gamification designs succeed and why some fail, even though they use similar game elements. For gamification professionals, this lens adds to the body of knowledge of gamification and should be viewed as an additional tool in the toolbox of gamification design. If the main goal of gamification is to support the user to reach their goals, and by doing so, the organization's overarching goals, this lens could prove useful.

FUTURE RESEARCH

A potential theoretical advancement of this chapter is that gamification design and research could relate more to the literature and research on servicescape and environmental psychology. The literature on servicescape touches on the practice of designing settings for achieving desired behavioral responses. In this context, the servicescape is the first aspect of a service that is perceived by the end-user. It is at the first meeting that end-user is likely to form impressions of the level of service they will receive in a context.

By contrast, the literature on psychological motivation theories and gamification design centers more on the use of non-pecuniary motivations, such as the need for challenge (Werbach & Hunter, 2012), stimulation (Deterding, 2015), self-determination (Koivisto & Hamari, 2019), immersion (Seaborn & Fels, 2015) and social image (Liu, Santhanam, & Webster, 2017) in different settings.

If gamification designers want to use our servicescape lens to enhance their gamification design, or if researchers try to explain why some gamification implementations succeed or fail by looking through our servicescape lens, they must be aware of the limitations of this study. Further research on more gamification cases is required, including using the lens in a design process to test if the lens is useful. Furthermore, our selected case is limited, and more research would need to be conducted on real-world cases in other contexts than education, e.g., Marketing, Human Resources or Digital Health.

Also, we recommend that further research on other existing psychological theories and methods could also be explored to extend the body of knowledge for gamification design, e.g., Need for achievement, Goal Setting, PERMA-V and Expectancy theory. It could also be beneficial to explore theories from behavioral economics like nudge and prospect theory.

CONCLUSION

This chapter examines how the use of a servicescape lens in gamification design potentially could improve the user experience within a gamified LMS. Even though the term servicescape, as well as gamification, are relatively new, the idea of affecting human behaviors through design choices have been used for centuries. The analysis of gamification from a servicescape perspective implicates that gamification designs could benefit from being more content specific and tangible than generic, both when it comes to descriptions and visualizations. The hypothesis is that the engagement of the end-user, with regards to the course and its material, could be improved through the use of a servicescape informed gamification design. This relates to the findings of Morschheuser et al. (2017), as well Shahri et al. (2019), that gamification should have a focus on end-users, and their needs. Applying gamification without a deep understanding of users could turn to be harmful to the user's experience. This chapter adds to the findings that if the gamification development team would have a more profound knowledge about the content that is gamified, the gamification could be applied on a more detailed level, which would probably enhance the user experience. The gamification modules that were used in the case study have the potential to integrate many of the elements that have been identified as positive from a servicescape perspective. But to do so requires that individuals within the implementation team, be it from the gamification studio or the target product's organization, put in the time and effort to identify which tangible elements that would be most fitting to integrate into texts and imagery.

ACKNOWLEDGMENT

The study was partly supported by the Swedish innovation agency, Vinnova (grants number 2018-02953).

REFERENCES

AlMarshedi, A., Wanick, V., Wills, G. B., & Ranchhod, A. (2017). Gamification and Behaviour (pp. 19–29). doi:10.1007/978-3-319-45557-0_2

Armstrong, M. B., Landers, R. N., & Collmus, A. B. (2015). *Gamifying Recruitment* (pp. 140–165). Selection, Training, and Performance Management; doi:10.4018/978-1-4666-8651-9.ch007

Avan, A., Uyar, A., Zorlu, Ö., & Özmen, A. (2019). The effects of servicescape on the emotional states and behavioural responses of hotel guests. Anatolia; doi:10.1080/13032917.2019.1575885

Bitner, M. J. (1990). Evaluating Service Encounters: The Effects of Physical Surroundings and Employee Responses. *Journal of Marketing*, *54*(2), 69–82. doi:10.1177/002224299005400206

Bitner, M. J. (1992). Servicescapes: The Impact of Physical Surroundings on Customers and Employees. *Journal of Marketing*, *56*(2), 57–71. doi:10.1177/002224299205600205

Burke, B. (2016). *Gamify: How gamification motivates people to do extraordinary things*. Routledge.

Butler, C. (2015). Applied behavioral economics: a game designer's perspective. In Gamification in Education and Business (pp. 81–104). Springer; doi:10.1007/978-3-319-10208-5_5.

Callan, R. C., Bauer, K. N., & Landers, R. N. (2015). How to Avoid the Dark Side of Gamification: Ten Business Scenarios and Their Unintended Consequences. In T. Reiners & L. C. Wood (Eds.), Gamification in Education and Business (pp. 553–568). Cham, Switzerland: Springer International Publishing; doi:10.1007/978-3-319-10208-5_28.

Clark, W., Ezell, J., Clark, J., & Sheffield, D. N. (2009). Stay or leave: Applying approach-avoidance theory to virtual environments. *Journal of Database Marketing & Customer Strategy Management*, *16*(4), 231–240. doi:10.1057/dbm.2009.25

Cruaud, C. (2017). The Playful Frame Design and use of a gamified application for foreign language learning. Retrieved from https://www.duo.uio.no/bitstream/handle/10852/60251/PhD-Caroline-Cruaud--2018.pdf?sequence=1&isAllowed=y

Csíkszentmihályi, M. (1992). Flow: den optimala upplevelsens psykologi. Natur och kultur.

Dawson, S. A., & Bloch, P. H. (1990). Pleasure and Arousal in the Marketplace, (1989), 139–147.

Deci, E. L., & Ryan, R. M. (2000). Self-Determination Theory and the Facilitation of Intrinsic Motivation, Social Development, and Well-Being. *The American Psychologist*, *55*(1), 68–78. doi:10.1037/0003-066X.55.1.68 PubMed

Denny, P. (2013). The effect of virtual achievements on student engagement. In Proceedings of the SIGCHI conference on human factors in computing systems (pp. 763–772). ACM; doi:10.1145/2470654.2470763.

Deterding, S. (2015). The lens of intrinsic skill atoms: A method for gameful design. *Human-Computer Interaction*, *30*(3–4), 294–335. doi:10.1080/07370024.2014.993471

Deterding, S., & Dixon, D., & IT, R. K. (2010). Gamification: Toward a Definition Sebastian. *Studies in Computational Intelligence*, *300*, 1–361. doi:10.1007/978-3-642-13959-8_1

Dichev, C., & Dicheva, D. (2017). Gamifying education: what is known, what is believed and what remains uncertain: a critical review. International Journal of Educational Technology in Higher Education. doi:10.1186/s41239-017-0042-5

European Commission. (2015). *Drop-out and completion in higher education in Europe - Main Report*. European Commission Education and Culture; doi:10.2766/826962

Fodness, D., & Murray, B. (2007). Passengers' expectations of airport service quality. *Journal of Services Marketing*, *21*(7), 492–506. doi:10.1108/08876040710824852

Hamari, J., Koivisto, J., & Sarsa, H. (2014). Does gamification work? - A literature review of empirical studies on gamification. Proceedings of the Annual Hawaii International Conference on System Sciences. doi:10.1109/HICSS.2014.377

Hamari, J., & Lehdonvirta, V. (2010). Game design as marketing: How game mechanics create demand for virtual goods.

Hassan, L., Morschheuser, B., Dreidev, N. A., & Hamari, J. (n.d.). First-hand experience of why gamification projects fail and what could be done about it. Retrieved from http://ceur-ws.org/Vol-2186/paper17.pdf

Heinzen, T. E., Gordon, M. S., Landrum, R. E., Gurung, R. A. R., Dunn, D. S., & Richman, S. (2015). A parallel universe: Psychological science in the language of game design. In Gamification in Education and Business (pp. 133–149). Springer; doi:10.1007/978-3-319-10208-5_7.

Hofacker, C. F., De Ruyter, K., Lurie, N. H., Manchanda, P., & Donaldson, J. (2016). Gamification and mobile marketing effectiveness. *Journal of Interactive Marketing*, *34*, 25–36. doi:10.1016/j.intmar.2016.03.001

Holland, J. G., & Skinner, B. F. (1961). The analysis of behavior: A program for self-instruction.

Hopkins, C. D., Grove, S. J., Raymond, M. A., & Laforge, M. C. (2009). Designing the e-servicescape: Implications for online retailers. *Journal of Internet Commerce*, *8*(1–2), 23–43. doi:10.1080/15332860903182487

Huotari, K., & Hamari, J. (2012). Defining gamification: a service marketing perspective. In Proceedings of the 16th International Academic MindTrek Conference (pp. 17–22). ACM; doi:10.1145/2393132.2393137.

Huotari, K., & Hamari, J. (2017). A definition for gamification: Anchoring gamification in the service marketing literature. *Electronic Markets*, *27*(1), 21–31. doi:10.1007/s12525-015-0212-z

Hwang, L.-J. (2007). The hotel servicescape for Chinese female travellers. In Advances in Hospitality and Leisure (pp. 231–241). Emerald Group; doi:10.1016/S1745-3542(06)03014-1.

Indicators, O. E. C. D. (2019).. . *Education at a Glance, 2019*. doi:10.1787/f8d7880d-en

INSERT COIN webpage [Online] Sweden Date viewed 2019-10-15. Retrieved from www.insertcoin.se

Johnson, D., Deterding, S., Kuhn, K.-A., Staneva, A., Stoyanov, S., & Hides, L. (2016). Gamification for health and wellbeing: A systematic review of the literature. Internet Interventions, 6, 89–106. doi:10.1016/j.invent.2016.10.002

Kim, T. W., & Werbach, K. (2016). More than just a game: Ethical issues in gamification. *Ethics and Information Technology*, *18*(2), 157–173. doi:10.1007/s10676-016-9401-5

Koernig, S. K. (2003). E-Scapes: The Electronic Physical Environment and Service Tangibility. *Psychology and Marketing*, *20*(2), 151–167. doi:10.1002/mar.10065

Koivisto, J., & Hamari, J. (2019). The rise of motivational information systems: A review of gamification research. *International Journal of Information Management*, *45*, 191–210. doi:10.1016/j.ijinfomgt.2018.10.013

Kumar, J. (2013). Gamification at work: Designing engaging business software. In International conference of design, user experience, and usability (pp. 528–537). Springer; doi:10.1007/978-3-642-39241-2_58.

Kumar Roy, S., Singh Jindal, G. O., & Harrigan, P. (2019). The Rise of Smart Consumers: Role of Smart Servicescape and Smart Consumer Experience Co-creation. Article in Journal of Marketing Management. Retrieved from https://www.researchgate.net/publication/333106220

Landers, R. N., Bauer, K. N., Callan, R. C., & Armstrong, M. B. (2015). Psychological theory and the gamification of learning. In Gamification in education and business (pp. 165–186). Springer; doi:10.1007/978-3-319-10208-5_9.

Lee, S., & Jeong, M. (2012). Effects of e-servicescape on consumers' flow experiences. *Journal of Hospitality and Tourism Technology*, *3*(1), 47–59. doi:10.1108/17579881211206534

Liu, D., Santhanam, R., & Webster, J. (n.d.). TOWARD MEANINGFUL ENGAGEMENT: A FRAMEWORK FOR DESIGN AND RESEARCH OF GAMIFIED INFORMATION SYSTEMS 1. Retrieved from http://enterprise-gamification.com

Loureiro, S. M. C., Sarmento, E. M., Lopes, R., & Jin, K. N. (2015). Feeling Better While Waiting: Hospital Lobby in Portugal and South Korea. *Asian Journal of Business Research*, *5*(2). doi:10.14707/ajbr.150017

Manyika, J., Lund, S., Chui, M., Bughin, J., Woetzel, J., Batra, P., … Sanghvi, S. (2017). Jobs lost, jobs gained: Workforce transitions in a time of automation. McKinsey Global Institute.

Matallaoui, A., Hanner, N., & Zarnekow, R. (2017). Introduction to Gamification: Foundation and Underlying Theories (pp. 3–18). doi:10.1007/978-3-319-45557-0_1

Mehrabian, A., & Russell, J. A. (1974). *An approach to environmental psychology*. The MIT Press.

Meske, C., Brockmann, T., Wilms, K., & Stieglitz, S. (2017). Social Collaboration and Gamification (pp. 93–109). doi:10.1007/978-3-319-45557-0_7

Mora, A., Riera, D., Gonzalez, C., & Arnedo-Moreno, J. (2015). A Literature Review of Gamification Design Frameworks. VS-Games 2015 - 7th International Conference on Games and Virtual Worlds for Serious Applications. 10.1109/VS-GAMES.2015.7295760

Morschheuser, B., Hamari, J., Werder, K., & Abe, J. (2017). How to Gamify? A Method For Designing Gamification. In Proceedings of the 50th Hawaii International Conference on System Sciences (2017). doi:10.24251/HICSS.2017.155

O'Donnell, N., Kappen, D. L., Fitz-Walter, Z., Deterding, S., Nacke, L. E., & Johnson, D. (2017, October). How multidisciplinary is gamification research?: Results from a scoping review. In Extended Abstracts Publication of the Annual Symposium on Computer-Human Interaction in Play (pp. 445-452). ACM.

Palmquist, A. (2018). *Det spelifierade klassrummet*. Studentlitteratur AB.

Palmquist, A. (2019). A product to gamify other products; implementing gamification in existing software. In 2019 11th International Conference on Virtual Worlds and Games for Serious Applications (VS-Games) (pp. 1–8). IEEE. 10.1109/VS-Games.2019.8864535

Park, J.-W., & Ryu, Y. K. (2019). Investigating the Effects of Airport Servicescape on Airport Users' Behavioral Intentions: A Case Study of Incheon International Airport Terminal 2 (T2). *Sustainability*, *11*(15), 4171. doi:10.3390/su11154171

Richter, G., Raban, D. R., & Rafaeli, S. (2015). Studying gamification: The effect of rewards and incentives on motivation. In Gamification in Education and Business (pp. 21–46). doi:10.1007/978-3-319-10208-5_2

Robson, K., Plangger, K., Kietzmann, J. H., McCarthy, I., & Pitt, L. (2015). Is it all a game? Understanding the principles of gamification. *Business Horizons*, *58*(4), 411–420. doi:10.1016/j.bushor.2015.03.006

Russell, J. A., & Mehrabian, A. (1978). Approach-Avoidance and affiliation as functions of the emotion-eliciting quality of an environment. *Environment and Behavior*, *10*(3), 355–387. doi:10.1177/0013916578103005

Sailer, M., Hense, J. U., Mayr, S. K., & Mandl, H. (2017). How gamification motivates: An experimental study of the effects of specific game design elements on psychological need satisfaction. *Computers in Human Behavior*, *69*, 371–380. doi:10.1016/j.chb.2016.12.033

Schell, J. (2019). The Art of Game Design: A book of lenses. AK Peters/CRC Press.

Seaborn, K., & Fels, D. I. (2015). Gamification in theory and action: A survey. *International Journal of Human-Computer Studies*, *74*, 14–31. doi:10.1016/j.ijhcs.2014.09.006

Shahri, A., Hosseini, M., Phalp, K., Taylor, J., & Ali, R. (2019). How to engineer gamification: The consensus, the best practice and the grey areas. Journal of Organizational and End User Computing (Vol. 31). doi:10.4018/JOEUC.2019010103

Shi, L., & Cristea, A. I. (2016). Motivational Gamification Strategies Rooted in Self-Determination Theory for Social Adaptive E-Learning. In Lecture Notes in Computer Science (including subseries Lecture Notes in Artificial Intelligence and Lecture Notes in Bioinformatics) (Vol. 9684, pp. 294–300). doi:10.1007/978-3-319-39583-8_32

Susi, T., & Johannesson, M. (n.d.). *Serious Games-An Overview.*

Teh, N., Schuff, D., Johnson, S., & Geddes, D. (2013). Can work be fun? Improving task motivation and help-seeking through game mechanics.

Thaler, R. H., & Sunstein, C. R. (2009). *(2009). Nudge: Improving decisions about health, wealth and happiness. Nudge: Improving Decisions About Health.* Wealth and Happiness; doi:10.4324/9781912282555

Treiblmaier, H., Putz, L.-M., & Lowry, P. B. (2018). Research Commentary: Setting a Definition, Context, and Theory-Based Research Agenda for the Gamification of Non-Gaming Applications. AIS Transactions on Human-Computer Interaction, 129–163. doi:10.17705/1thci.00107

Wang, T. C., Tsai, C. L., & Tang, T. W. (2018). Exploring advertising effectiveness of tourist hotels' marketing images containing nature and performing arts: An eye-tracking analysis. *Sustainability (Switzerland)*, *10*(9). doi:10.3390u10093038

Werbach, K., & Hunter, D. (2012). *For the win: How game thinking can revolutionize your business.* Wharton Digital Press.

ENDNOTES

[1]   A full description of the project could be found at:
        https://insertcoin.se/why-gwen/science/project/garfieid
        and
        https://www.vinnova.se/p/garfield---gamification-of-automation-strategies-for-industry-4.0/

[2]   This was a physical t-shirt sporting the university's logo.

This research was previously published in Utilizing Gamification in Servicescapes for Improved Consumer Engagement; pages 86-118, copyright year 2020 by Business Science Reference (an imprint of IGI Global).

Section 3
Tools and Technologies

Chapter 28
Applied Alternative Tools and Methods in the Replacement of the Game Design Document

Pedro Henrique Roscoe Lage de Oliveira
Minas Gerais State University, Brazil

Carlos Alberto Silva de Miranda
Minas Gerais State University, Brazil

Joao Victor Boechat Gomide
Universidade FUMEC, Brazil

ABSTRACT

This chapter proposes and experiments alternatives to replace or optimize the use of the game design document (GDD). The creation and development of a game is accomplished by relying on the GDD, which contains all the information, such as the script, mechanics, and relevant details, so the team can use as a guide. There is no exact formula for creating a GDD, and several formats are proposed and used nowadays. Information misinterpreted or misunderstood at different levels of responsibility can create irreparable problems after the start of production. This chapter proposes the use of analog prototyping associated with benchmarking techniques and agile development as efficient alternatives to GDD, which are tested in the development of the game Forsaken Dungeons, created by one of the authors.

INTRODUCTION

This chapter analyses a set of methods used as efficient and economic alternatives to GDD topics and digital prototyping, to increase the team efficiency, organization and communication. The game design goals and topics are commented on (CRAWFORD: 1982, 49-50): 'A game must have clearly defined goal. This goal must be expressed in terms of the effects that it will have on player. It is not enough to declare that a game will be enjoyable, fun, exciting or good; the goal must establish the fantasies that the

DOI: 10.4018/978-1-6684-7589-8.ch028

game will support and the types of emotions it will engender in its audience. (…)Once you have settled on your goal, you must select a topic. The topic is the means of expressing the goal (…)'

To achieve the goal of developing a game based on the efficiency and economically principles it is assumed that a coordinated set of development techniques and documents are valuable among which we mention benchmarking; analog and paper prototyping; user retention and monetization documents. In addition, it is important to apply agile and vertical improvement techniques during the project development.

The game designer can be defined as the professional who determines the gameplay basic guidelines of the product and the development methods that will be used to produce the final product by the development team (ROUSE: 2001, 18) states that 'at its most elementary level, game design consists of inventing and documenting the elements of a game.'

Jesse Schell shows that the game designer must cultivate many skills, ranging from knowledge in technical writing to mathematics (Schell, 2008: 2-4). The designer will use every skill he has to communicate the ideas and to reach the conclusion of the project with minimum expenses and maximum result.

The first phase of a game development starts before programming, art, marketing or any other subject related to game development. The game designer is responsible for planning the product development strategies, goals and topics, before even involving other professionals. (CRAWFORD. 2016, pg. 51) says that 'during this phase it is critical that you commit little to paper and above all, write no code! (…) You will generate during this phase a great variety of specific implementation ideas for your game. They will not all fit together neatly (…). Indulge yourself in creating implementation ideas, but be prepared to winnow the ruthlessly during design.'

To Ernest Adams, 'a game is designed by creating a concept and identifying an audience in the concept stage, fleshing out the details and turning abstract ideas into concrete plans in the elaboration stage, and adjusting the fine points in the tuning stage (…).' (ADAMS: 2009, 62). Rouse points that 'in many ways, developing a game is all about understanding your limitations and then turning those limitations into advantages.' (ROUSE: 2001, 47-54)

The construction of a digital game depends on the teamwork of a diverse crew with a wide range of technical skills. One of the most delicate parts of development is the efficient and cost-effective use of each member effort. The team must seek a scenario where the professionals work with functional independence and their performances are not limited by product scope, harmonizing each personal set of skills in order to create a coherent product. As observes Rouse, the development team must be organized to divide the product in parts and build the game incrementally. 'Instead of working a little bit on all the different components of the game, you should try to complete one system before moving on to the next. Work on the most basic and essential systems first, and then build the systems that depend on that system. This allows you to implement a system, test it out, see if it 'feels' right, and only then move on to the next system.' (ROUSE: 2001, 254)

Tracy Fullerton (2008: 188) points out 'if you try to design the entire game at once, you might become confused and overwhelmed. There are so many elements in a typical game that it is difficult to know where and how to start. What we recommend is that you isolate the core gameplay mechanics and built out from there.'

The development of game design tools boost the team effectiveness, since the game designer will be able to perform typical gameplay design tasks independently (ROUSE: 2001, 378) notes that 'in order to create superior content, the design team will need to be equipped with well-designed, robust game creation tools. Therefore, one can conclude that designing a good game is about designing good game creation tools'.

In this chapter, analog prototyping, benchmarking and agile development processes are presented as processes for the game designer, which can replace some GDD topics in many productions. Those resources are poorly approached in the literature, never analyzed together, and rarely used by development teams.

GAME DESIGN DOCUMENT

Game development is a multidisciplinary creative process aimed to fulfil the human desire to play and have fun. To develop games it is important that the designer seeks to learn constantly about the most varied subjects. The inspiration for building games come from the most varied academic fields and the ability to listen and learn from your own mistakes.

The game development process is complex, and in practice there will always be scope changes, feature additions and rework. Even in large and consolidated teams these are inevitable constants; however, investing in planning techniques reduces the likelihood of such changes being counterproductive. Good planning generates documents that accurately determine how many arts; songs; animations; levels and how many systems will be needed to achieve the least viable product, which keeps the development team highly producible.

During the development, the design process follows phases of the product creation, starting with the overall planning, designation of responsibilities and set of the tools that will be developed and/or used by the team. The final stage is dedicated to polishing, which involve a large number of iterations with individuals inside and outside the development group.

Writing a GDD is considered a relevant part of the process. It is assumed, in general, that the lack of a GDD guiding the project culminates in failure. There is no perfect formula for a GDD production, along with huge controversies on how to build it. As Adams notes, 'As part of their job, game designers produce a series of documents to tell others about their game design. Exactly what documents they produce and what the documents are for vary from designer to designer and project to project (ADAMS: 2009, 54)

The document has the function of recording decisions and agreements that have been made orally or making explicit the ideas that have been ventilated and approved by the developers. Although there is no standard for composing a GDD, there are proposed structures and recommendations.Those who support the use of GDD as the backbone of game development understand that this document should include several sessions. However, as noted by Rouse, 'different companies may have different standards for what documentation pieces they create in order to assist and guide a game´s development.' (ROUSE. 2001, 302)

The documents that usually are part of the GDD are listed in Adams (ADAMS: 2009, 56-58):High Concept Document, which defines the central concept of the game; Game Treatment Document: the most detailed game description document, considered an extended version of the High Concept Document; Character Design, World Design, Narrative Design and Level Design Documents: those are specifically directed to specific parts of the game; Game Script document: according to Adams, this document cover the stories and mechanics that shape the game core.

Tracy Fullerton (2008: 396) understands that 'You should think of your design document as a living document. You will likely have to make a dozen steps before it is complete, and then you will need to constantly update it to reflect changes that are made during the development process. Because of this, it is important to organize your document on a modular way. If you organize your document carefully from the beginning, it will be easier to update and manage as it grows in size and complexity'.

Some practical issues brought by writing all these documents within the game creation process are justifying the time and effort needed to write them, along with the effectiveness of these documents while producing the game. It is well known that many game developing professionals only read these documents superficially. Others prefer a more informal and intuitive approach, as seen in many productions. The game designer has to be a good communicator to make the others understand the GDD and must track the work of the other professionals, as points (Schell: 2008, 3). Richard Rouse (2001: 292) points out that 'the necessity of game development documentation is a side effect of the increasing size of game development teams. In the early days of game development, when a development team consisted of one multi-talented individual, documenting the functionality of the game was less important. If that one person was able to establish and implement a vision for the project's gameplay, it did not especially matter if she wrote it down or not.'

In recent years, the intensifying of competition and the increasing complexity that has been attributed to products and services have required the developers to adapt their processes with a view to improving quality and reducing time. These adaptations involve management techniques and methods of design, analysis, simulation and optimization. The use of prototypes become an essential condition to increase the company's abilities to identify customer needs as a matter of priority and to provide important subsidies to improve communication among those involved in the process, as well as reduce the chances of failure and increase the chances of success of the enterprise. In addition, prototyping provides the possibility of evaluating the perceptual and sensory experience that will occur in the process of use, in relation to shape, external appearance, color and texture.

In this context, it becomes evident the importance of the prototypes in the development process, considering that these can be used to realize tests that allow the verification of possible problems, besides the opportunities of the optimization of the game functions. Prototyping helps not only to speed up but to make a more secure development, as well as making the investments in subsequent stages more assertive as Medeiros Filho says, 'It does not matter how much experience or talent the professional has in game design, an idea may in practice become quite different from what has been planned, in addition, a number of other elements, previously unseen, may surface, altering the form and scope of the project.'

It is assumed that, in the case of games in genres suitable for analog prototyping, game design documentation coupled with prototyping processes are the most economic and effective way for the development of the product and that the more detailed the prototypes are, the less documentation will be required for the game. A game that can be in its predominance represented by analog and paper prototypes is consequently a game that can have much of its documentation represented by the prototypes, and therefore, communication and the understanding of the game by the team can be made commencing by these prototypes.

ANALOG AND PAPER PROTOTYPING

Prototyping is an essential part of the development since it allows the analysis of its form and functionality before the investments in tooling or definitive platforms. Historically, these representations of products (or simply, prototypes) have been used since the evolution of production processes, evolving from manual representations (sketches, drawings, mockups and physical models, for example) to virtual representations, from the years 80, with the evolution of CAD (computer aided design), and, more recently, with rapid prototypes as comments VOLPATO (2007, p).

In recent years, the intensification of competition and the increasing complexity of the products and services have demanded the companies to adapt their product development processes in order to improve quality and reduce time. The use of prototypes becomes an essential condition to increase the company's abilities to identify customer needs as a matter of priority and to provide important subsidies to improve communication among individuals in the process, as well as reduce the chances of failure of the endeavor. In addition, prototyping provides the possibility of evaluating the perceptual and sensory experience that will occur in the process of use, in relation to shape, external appearance, color and texture, as seen in H. Tai. (TAI, 2017. Pg. 71-86).

Paper prototyping allows designers to quickly test the fluidity of their interface screens by simply using paper and pen so that important creative decisions can be made in the planning phase. Fox notes: 'You are choosing the most important places where you need to spend time and effort.' (FOX, 2005, p.

It is assumed that the materialization of interfaces from paper prototyping will allow them to be approved before the creation of the definitive arts. A well-planned paper prototype will allow all project members to sanction the fluidity of the interfaces presented or, if they believe there is a better way to achieve the desired result, to express their ideas.

Prototyping is an important process for creating a product. The quickness, inexpensiveness and clarity are characteristics of the prototyping process that can be divided into two categories, high fidelity and low fidelity, according to the proximity they have from the final material. Jesse Schell (2008: 86-87) understands that 'every prototype must be created to answer a question and sometimes more than one. (…) Your goal is to loop as usefully and as frequently as possible. So if you can manage it, why not just get the software out of the way? If you are clever, you can prototype your fancy game idea as a simple board game, or what we sometimes call a paper prototype. This lets you spot problems sooner.'

Tracy Fullerton (2008: 176) notes that 'physical prototyping also allows for non-technical team members to participate at a very high level in the design process. No one needs specialized knowledge or expertise in a programming language to give their input, which will allow for a wider variety of perspectives in the design process. Physical prototyping will also allow for a broader and deeper experimentation process simply because it can be done without major cost or use of resources.'

On the subject Kay et al (2003, 6) states that the prototype points out and serves to communicate information and show tangible ideas to the development team, internal management and external clients. Testing and refining the interactions of a game in the prototyping phase means that all other individuals involved in the development are less likely to rebuild parts of the product due to problems identified in later phases.

Digital and analog games have differences, notably the interactions with physical pieces on the first ones and the graphical interface interactions in the second. In addition, there are differences in how they deal with the mechanics and complexity. Digital games have the game system as a final referee for rules. In the other hand, if a rule is contradictory in an analog game, players may discuss and decide what is the best way to apply it. The analog game system is adaptable, while the digital game system is rigid. Moreover, the complexity in digital games can be hidden in the feedback system, which allows the game to remove certain tasks from the player operations, for example, operations that can be made instantly by the computer. On the subject Fullerton (2008: 132) understands that 'when we use the word 'feedback' in general conversation, we often are just referring to the information we get back during an interaction, not what we do with it. But in system terms, feedback implies a direct relationship between the output of an interaction and a change to another system element. Feedback can be positive or negative, and it can promote divergence or balance in the system.'

It is possible to state that a set of systems present in a board game can represent a significant fraction of the systems presented by digital games. As an example, T*he Dark Souls* board game captures the fundamentals of the *Dark Souls* digital game, absorbing its mechanics and translating them into a turn-based combat system.

It is important to note, however, that analog prototyping will be more efficient in developing games with typical board mechanics and are in some cases not recommended (when, for example, the mechanics of a game are based only on combat or running). There are certain game genres that best fit analog prototyping like games with strategy, puzzle, card games, and resource management mechanics.

Tracy Fullerton (2008: 178) understands that: 'Physical prototypes are critical for designing both board games and sophisticated electronic games. Many famous electronic games are based on paper games. The system for digital role-playing games such as Diablo II, Baldur's Gate, EverQuest, Asheron's Call and World of Warcraft are derived from the paper-based system of Dungeons & Dragons.'

Analog prototyping can be used as a key resource in development since it is a quick tool to validate the iteration possibilities of a digital product. Also, the developer must consider that the financial and human expenses implicated in the making of an analog prototype are objectively lower than that of a digital prototype. This method gives the designer superior implementation effectiveness; mechanics can be created and tested without the need to translate them with code, placeholders or art implementation. Furthermore, understanding a game using an analog prototype is easier than reading a GDD, making the game experience perception more fluid to the team since they will actually play the game, being able to perform all critical balancing and mechanics modification before the digital development begins.

Tracy Fullerton (2008: 207) concludes that 'Creating a physical prototype is a critical step in the design of your original game concept. It will save your team tremendous amounts of time because everyone will have a clear understanding of the game you are making. In addition, a physical prototype will enable you to focus your creative energy on the game mechanics without becoming distracted by the production and programming process. And most importantly, making a prototype gives you the freedom to experiment and through experimentation comes innovation.'

(SNYDER: 2003, 12) describes the advantages of paper prototyping for interface prototyping, which she says are good to provide feedback early in the development process, encouraging creativity, promoting rapid iterative development, facilitating communication with the team and customers by enabling a multidisciplinary team to work together since it does not require any technical skills.

BENCHMARKING

Benchmarking techniques can be utilized in the game design process aiming to analyze and applying the best principles in the game development. Benchmarking, according to Elmuti and Kathawala(1997: 229) 'is the process of identifying the highest standards of excellence for products, services, or processes, and then making the improvements necessary to reach those standards, commonly called 'best practices'. The justification lies partly in the question: 'Why reinvent the wheel if I can learn from someone who has already done it?'

Through benchmarking, the game designer can set each goal and topic of his game based on examples of solutions he found in other games, facilitating the set-up of the project and guiding the work of team members. Watson (2007: 3) remembers that benchmarking is a process of comparing in order to learn how to improve. Motivation for a benchmarking study is the desire to improve and become more competitive.'

Elmuti and Kathawala (1997: 229) states that 'the process of benchmarking is more than just a means of gathering data on how well a company performs against others (…). It is also a method of identifying new ideas and new ways of improving processes and, therefore, being better able to meet the expectations of customers.' The benchmarking used in the early phases of development intent to support the team organization. Watson (2007: 8) points out that '(…) benchmarking will provide productivity improvement by concentrating on specific activities that will improve the effectiveness, efficiency, or economy of routine business operations.'

Some tools like Game Analytics can be used for benchmarking the game over time, helping the developer to notice and troubleshoot user retention and other design issues. This tool allows the developer to compare the performance of the game with others in the tool network, helping the developer to make informed decisions with the understanding of the markets the game aim and its individual performance.

By looking outside and researching other games, the designer can identify best practices, qualities and flaws within other games in the same genre typically have, along with ways to fix it. With the use of benchmarking, the game designer can light better ways to reach a high-quality ultimate product. As an example of benchmarking use, there is the game Forsaken Dungeons, created by JetDragon Studios.

The game used as a main reference for the creation of the universe was Battlechasers. Dofus and Dark Quest 2 were the benchmark for scenery, while base gameplay was benchmarked by the board game Gloomhaven and other turn-based tactical games. The Level Design Document was replaced by a Level Editor tool, while the Game Script document was replaced by the analog prototype.

AGILE DEVELOPMENT IN GAME DEVELOPMENT

Analog prototyping and benchmarking are put together in their maximum effectiveness when used inside agile development processes, as opposed to traditional cascade development. The fundamental problem of the cascade development is that game creation is a constant process of learning and iteration. Agile development techniques increase the speed of the development by establishing a workflow capable of allowing the materialization of the project instead of exhaustive documentation, as observed by Clinton Keith (2010: 13): 'We are uncovering better ways of developing software by doing it and helping others do it. Through this work we have come to value: 1.Individuals and interactions over processes and tools; 2.Working software over comprehensive documentation; 3.Customer collaboration over contract negotiation; 4. Responding to change over following a plan.'

Agile development represents a modular structure that makes every effort to build a development progression that is more adaptive and focused on the developers instead of detailed documentation about the game, giving priority to team communication and iterations. Using agile in game development increase the team ability to identify and solve game development problems with efficiency and economy.

On agile development Medeiros Filho comments: 'In the process of game development, different agile production methodologies are adopted by each company. Among them is the SCRUM methodology, an agile production methodology that has become very popular in the gaming industry, where the production focus is characterized by small iteration cycles. The goal is not to define all content at the beginning but to explore possibilities during the process, where teams can even modify the project mindset based on iterations and changes over the course of the cycles. In this sense it is always good or desirable to have some playable prototype. '(MEDEIROS, 2013: page 313).

The creation of a game using agile development is divided into pre-defined time intervals called sprints. Each sprint's objective is to fulfil a specific functionality required by the customer, referred as 'user story'. Each sprint is only completed after development and testing of the corresponding user story features. The next sprint will be planned by prioritizing which features are the most important, and so on, until all the development goals are met. This mindset saves time and removes obstacles that will invariably arise during development.

Analog prototyping and benchmarking work as guides, to define the initial sprints and the first short-term goals, in the agile development process. If the entire team had the opportunity to iterate with the analog product and the benchmark games, the definition of the project scope will be clearer to the developers and much rework will be avoided as the iterations have been already made, ensuring the effectiveness of the game mechanics and the fun of the product-player interactions.

The most commonly methodology used to apply agile development methods and practices is called Scrum. It names three main roles: Product Owner, Scrum Master and Development Team. The Product Owner (usually the game designer) has the final say in the game concepts, while the Scrum Master enables the interaction between all involved parts, removing any obstacles arisen during the development, and the Development Team carries on the technical development of the product.

Game development projects can end up generating unrewarded effort. Usually, among the reasons that cause this problem we can identify: overoptimistic schedules; lack of technical team capacity and feature creep. C. Keith (2010: 17) understands that feature creep is the term given to resources being added to a project inflating the original game scope and impairing the development. The author understands that there are two main reasons for the feature creep, and those are the stakeholder demands and the poor result of implemented features. The feature creep impacts negatively in the game development since it represents the exacerbation of changes widening the project scope. However, it's important to emphasize that the game creation is a practice based on incremental progress and new features and improvements are welcome during the product creation process whenever they don't impact in the development time.

Erik Bethke (2003: 288) says 'Feature creep actually starts during the earliest parts of the Project: requirements gathering and game design. Here it is quite easy to lose track of the core game you are making (because it is still so fresh and new) and start sprawling a bit and tossing in ill-considered, distracting features.'

The game development success comes from the effectiveness of the methodologies applied to detect problems and find solutions during the game creation process. To achieve team-efficiency, the communication between the members is of paramount importance to allow features of the product to be effectively delivered. Furthermore, it is important to integrate potential consumers in the iteration process to ensure the optimal user experience. To achieve these objectives, the use of analog prototyping, benchmarking and agile development techniques can result in the improvement of the team communication and workflow, as well as aiding on solving emergent problems that will during the project evolution.

CASE STUDY

The case study procedures used in this research were divided into stages, they were: definition, planning, execution, data gathering, data analysis and conclusion. Inserted in the case study of this work was made the game development procedure, from its basic concept to the final product following the scheme below: Concept; benchmarking and brainstorming; definition of monetization scheme; definition of user retention mechanics; paper and analog prototyping; mechanical balancing; digital prototyping of interfaces; digital prototyping of basic mechanics and developer tools; agile roadmap; sprint backlogs.

Coming up with ideas is important, but it is just the tip of the iceberg. An idea starts to make sense and be engaging in stages, first the game designer must immerse in the topic he wish to explore (maybe a game about medieval monsters raiding dungeons, or a game about solving murder mysteries in a steampunk setting for example). After preparing the idea the designer will go through an incubation process, this means he will let the idea develop inside the inner of his mind. Then the insight happens, the moment the designer can feel his idea is worth pursuing. Ideas can also be derived from existing games and activities, that's why it is important to research and play many games as possible during this process. Using techniques like benchmarking the developer can understand the 'hot spots' from the games he is analyzing and by doing so he can save himself from a lot of hard work that has been done previously by someone else.

The project definition occurred in the first stage of the research. The game genre chosen was a strategy turn-based game that can have its mechanics easily simulated with the use of analog prototyping.

Game development is a collaborative work. After the basic project definition it's important to make a brainstorming session with the whole team. Working with all the members in that phase not only generates innovative ideas but engage all the crew members in the game creation process. When the project has the basic structures already defined its easier for other members to talk about their own experiences and ideas. Here the designer must exercise one of the most important skills he can have, listen to his team ideas with attention, no criticism or intolerance.

During the brainstorming phase is important to write down the generated insights. During the development of Forsaken Dungeons we made an 'idea deck'. All the ideas we had were transformed into cards with phrases containing them. Then we started picking the ideas one by one and the whole team gave two grades to each card ranging from 1 to 10. The first grade is the appeal of the idea, the 'how cool this idea is metric' (the higher the better) and the second grade is about the complexity and expensiveness of the idea implementation (the lower the better). That does not mean we discarded any idea, we kept all of them in a box, but the idea cards with the appeal and complexity grades would serve as guidelines to the designer during the execution phase.

In the planning phase, the benchmarking process was also done; the basic mechanics of the game were defined; the monetization tactics and the retention techniques that would be applied in the development were established and also brainstormed with the team.

With the benchmarking process is important to study the market opportunities of the game. The benchmarking can heavily persuade the designer to choose a specific monetization model or commonly used retention techniques; these constraints may demand amendments in the overall gameplay.

It is also important to consider during that phase the cost of the game idea. Ideas that are too ambitious should be carefully inspected and most likely scaled down.

In the execution phase, the paper and analog prototypes of the product were made following the ideas gathered with the brainstorming and benchmarking; the pool of ideas were refined and evaluated during the prototyping processes. From the prototypes, screen fluidity tests were performed (using the paper prototypes), and tests were done with the analog prototype (to define mechanics). From the analog prototype all balancing can be done ensuring that the product, at the digital development phase would not need any fundamental changes in its composition.

Forsaken Dungeons mechanics system is composed by a set of modular subsystems. Each unit card have 6 main characteristics, those are:

- Card Base Health Points
- Card Active Skill 1
- Card Active Skill 2
- Card Active Skill 3
- Card Passive Skill 1
- Card Passive Skill 2

To balance the units of the game, each passive and active skill were created and represented by a card in the analog prototype. Each base unit with health point was also represented by a card. By mixing the skill cards with the base unit cards each unit could be balanced and thematically adapted. This unit balancing generated insights regarding the aesthetics of each character; the overall 'average power level' of each unit and also the value of each skill in 'gameplay impact'. During this process it was also possible to define the skill level required to play with each assembled character; each character received grades varying from 1 (very easy to use) to 10 (very hard to use). It's important to highlight that analog prototyping the ideas make the process focus on gameplay rather than technology. Analog prototypes are easier to modify and discard and also allows all the team members independent of their expertises to participate in the iteration process.

With the definition of what the final product will be, a number of user experience tests were done with people inside and outside the development team. Digital development started with the prototyping of the game screens in Photoshop. The paper prototypes provided the basis for their implementation. In addition, from the analog prototypes it was also possible to begin the development of the fundamental mechanics of the game.

It's important to emphasize that digital prototypes are not the finished game, those can be made with bought or free assets, minimal art and sound. The reason to make a digital prototype is to investigate, identify and solve issues related to the game aesthetics, control responsiveness, technology and mechanics. The prototypes may serve as a starting point in the creation of the final product, but its primary function isn't to speed up the development with the reuse of what have been made, but to prevent the project from being delayed due to problems identified too late.

During the digital prototyping was established which developer tools would be important. The need for a level editor; a monsters editor; a skills editor and a player character editor were identified.All these developer tools were subdivided into sprints of 14 days each and in 04 months of development a digital product already existed with a reasonable amount of mechanics implemented; animations; feedback and music. The game progression was meticulously analyzed with a group of 33 individuals who used the product and provided feedback lists to aid development.

During the benchmarking, made in the planning phase, games like Dark Quest 2 (for aesthetics) and Super Mario Maker (for the level builder importance in the game system) were used as conceptual starting points. It was also defined, during this phase, the definitive name of the game, that is, 'Forsaken Dungeons'. Forsaken Dungeons is a dungeon exploration and turn-based strategy game with aspects of RPG, level management and building.

A small document was created, titled 'Base Guidelines' and in it was outlined the shallow concept of the game and also the main mechanics. This document is a summary of the first topics that are usually part of a GDD. In this document the following concept was determined: 'The definitive turn-based strategy game with management and RPG aspects comes to mobile devices powered by a powerful level editor and intense customization of characters within reach of the player's fingers. Explore dungeons, kill monsters, build your city and give birth to true heroes! In Forsaken Dungeons you are the manager of the Brotherhood, a team of atypical adventurers struggling to purge the evil of the world.' This document also specified key product parameters, among which the monetization scheme and retention techniques used.

For monetization the freemium strategy was defined, i.e. the game will be distributed free of charge and players will be able to buy aesthetic products and advantages in an in-game store.

In relation to retention techniques, the following parameters were defined: 'The game will present the following retention techniques in order to keep its users active and engaged in the experience: 1. Progression; 2.Scarcity; 3.Daily Login; 4.Social Reciprocity; 5. Customization.

In terms of Progression and Customization one system do both, i.e., players can customize the skills of their characters; every 30 levels (progression) a new ability is released to the character (customization). The player can choose which ability to attach by modifying the gameplay and adjusting his character to his style of play. In relation to Social Reciprocity, a system was built to connect the game to social networks and the player can ask life potion for his social media friends. The system of Daily login is aimed at the 'Skill Runes'. Every time the player comes into play in a 24 hour period, he will receive a rune that can be used through a crafting system to build a skill (a skill is mounted through 5 runes).

After the 'Base-Guidelines' document, the analog prototype and paper prototypes could be materialized. Mechanics and interface changes were decided with the entire team and with the participation of individuals outside the development team from brainstorming done after iteration experiences with the game. There were 30 days of weekly testing done with punctual changes to the product mechanics to improve gameplay. Individuals outside the development team filled in feedback sheets leaving their opinions on what could be improved in the game. There were nine sessions of controlled playtest (with the developers guiding the gameplay) and four sessions of blindtests (where no developer can guide the gameplay and the users must receive a manual/video with the rules).

Tracy Fullerton (2008: 249) understands that: 'a continual iterative process of play-testing, evaluating and revising is the way to keep the game from straying during that long arduous process of development. Of course, you cannot keep changing the basic game design – after all, the goal is to release the product eventually.'

The product screens were prototyped in Photoshop, based on the paper prototypes, and sought to get as close to the intended end result as possible. The creation of the developer tools also started, which were planned in a brainstorming session marked after the last play-test of the analog prototype made in the execution phase. Sprints were made that lasted 2 months and both the tools and the screens are ready in their entirety. In the 4th month of development it was established that MVP levels would be made using the level editor and also the fundamental screens for the game would be implemented.

Starting from the MVP it is possible to send the product to publishers, which will also require a 'Project Presentation Document', where the proposal is illustrated for potential investors. Illustrations are used in this document through high fidelity prototypes, analog prototypes and other tools to clearly illustrate design, such as a game manual. This document is not a GDD since its purpose is not to present technical aspects of the game and subsystems to the developers. There were two 15-day sprints for completing the MVP; by the 5th month it was done and sent to 33 individuals, including publisher evaluators. Of these submissions, 20 responses were received, which gave shape to a feedbacks list. Questions were included in the feedback document as shown below:

- What is your game first impression
- Can you identify and describe any specially satisfying or frustrating gameplay experience?
- The game duration is good or you feel it could be shorter or longer?
- Did you find the rules easy to understand?
- How the game control feel?
- Is the game looks and music appealing to you?
- You have any ideas for improving the game?

The feedbacks collected were implemented to the game following the priorities and thus continuing with the incremental development of the design sprints.

The methodology applied in the development of Forsaken Dungeons and presented in this work proved to be efficient in the development of digital turn-based strategy products. It got clear that card games and other typically analog games can use this methodology with no problems. The game development process presented in this work can be represented by the graph presented in figure 1.

The advantages of using the methodology proposed in this work are as the diagram in figure 2.

Figure 1. The game development process presented in this work

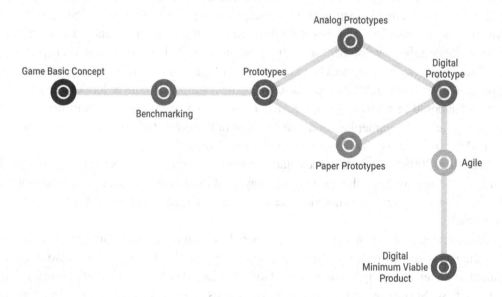

CONCLUSION

This article demonstrates that there are alternative processes to the exclusive use of the game design document, to create and develop a game. Analog prototyping, associated with benchmarking, can replace parts of the GDD depending on the game genre and mechanics, and those methods can be integrated in agile development processes for maximum efficiency. The capability to detect problems and create high-quality communication between the game designer and the rest of the development team and customers makes analog prototyping, benchmarking and agile techniques powerful techniques for creating and iterating with the features of the game.

Figure 2. Advantages of using the proposed methodology

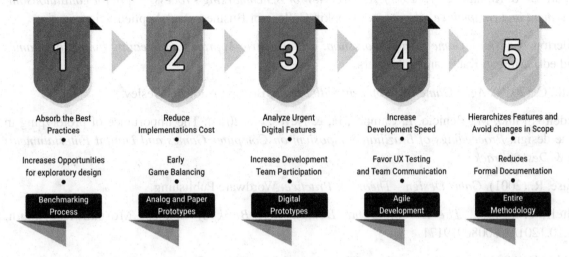

The game design document is in many cases vital for the game development but this use should be analyzed to a greater or lesser extent on a case-by-case basis. Despite being the most used instrument in game development this documentation presents limitations associated with the lack of synergy between the records put on paper and the development stages of a game. There is no single way to work with game design. The alternatives presented in this chapter, although much less used in the mainstream production, have great results when applied especially in genres related to management, strategy and card games. Those methods, when used correctly give as outcome an improvement in the use of human and financial resources, as well as easy and timely identification of flaws during the project, enabling their solution.

ACKNOWLEDGMENT

The authors are grateful to CNPq, FAPEMIG and CoPIC/FUMEC, Brazilian research funding agencies, for the financial support to this work.

REFERENCES

Adams, E. (2009). *Fundamentals of Game Design (2ⁿᵈ ed.). Academic Press.*

Bethke, E. (2003). *Game Development and Production.* Wordware Publishing, Inc.

Buxton, B. (2007). *Sketching User Experiences – Getting the Design right and the Right Design.* Morgan Kaufmann.

Chua, C. K., Leong, K. F., & Lim, C. S. (2003). Rapid Prototyping (2nd ed.). World Scientific. doi:10.1142/5064

Crawford, C. (1982). The Art of Computer Game Design. Vancouver, Canada: Academic Press.

Elmuti, D., & Kathawala, Y. (1997). *An Overview of Benchmarking Process: a tool for continuous improvement and competitive advantage.* Lumpkin College of Business And Applied Sciences.

Fullerton, T. (2008). *Game Design Workshop: a Playcentric Approach to Creating Innovative Games* (2nd ed.). Morgan Kaufmann Publishers.

Keith, C. (2010). *Agile Game Development with Scrum.* Boston: Addison-Wesley.

Medeiros Filho, M., Benicio, I., Campos, F., & Neves, A. (2013). The importance of prototyping in game design. *Proceedings of Brazilian Symposium on Computer Games and Digital Entertainment: Art & Design Track.*

Rouse, R. (2001). *Game Design – Theory & Practice.* Wordware Publishing.

Schell, J. (2008). *The Art of Game Design – A Book of Lenses.* Morgan Kaufmann. doi:10.1201/9780080919171

Snyder, C. (2003). *Paper Prototyping – The Fast and Easy Way to Design and Refine User Interfaces.* San Francisco, CA: Morgan Kaufmann.

Stapenhurst, T. (2009). *The Benchmarking Book – A How-To-Guide to best practice for managers and practitioners.* Oxford, UK: Butterworth-Heinemann.

TAI. (2017). *Hsuan-an. Design: conceitos e métodos.* São Paulo: Blucher.

Watson, G. H. (2007). *Strategic Benchmarking Reloaded with Six Sigma – Improve Your Company's Performance Using Global Best Practice.* John Wiley & Sons.

This research was previously published in the Handbook of Research on Human-Computer Interfaces and New Modes of Interactivity; pages 148-161, copyright year 2019 by Engineering Science Reference (an imprint of IGI Global).

Chapter 29
Serious Games, Meditation, Brain–Computer Interfacing, and Virtual Reality (VR):
Empowering Players to Discover Their Minds

Ryan Murdoch

The Glasgow School of Art, UK

ABSTRACT

Brain-computer interfacing (BCI), the ability to interact with software and technology with our thoughts and feelings, presents an exciting new frontier for serious games and learning. This chapter outlines an approach to incorporating real-time brain-monitoring in educational games. Both outlining and suggesting how technically this can be achieved using affordable and accessible "off the shelf" consumer technology and the popular game engine Unity. By designing such experiences considering pedagogy and serious game theory, we can attempt to classify this new form of user interaction and its value for educational purposes. Specifically, this chapter looks to engage players with ideas of meditation by monitoring their "meditation" using BCI technology and visualizing it in engaging game worlds and experiences. As a valuable tool for addressing mental illness and personal wellbeing, meditation is worth exploring as a learning outcome within serious games.

INTRODUCTION

Today technology marches forward at an ever accelerating pace. Computers that once took up whole floors of buildings now fit snuggly in our pockets, the internet connects people around the globe almost instantaneously to one another and to a nearly endless wealth of information. What impact does this acceleration have on us? Without a doubt it has massive and positive implications for mankind, but so too does it create new issues. This concept of human progress as a double edged sword is not new. Perhaps

DOI: 10.4018/978-1-6684-7589-8.ch029

one of the most powerful speeches ever given on the subject was that of John F. Kennedy at Rice University (1962); his famous speech about putting a man on the moon. With regards to mankind's progress he noted that: 'This is a breathtaking pace, and such a pace cannot help but create new ills as it dispels old, new ignorance, new problems, new dangers'. These words still hold profound truth today. In an ever more connected world what happens to our idea of privacy? In an age of instantaneous gratification, endless media, data and content what happens to the length of our attention? What impact will the endlessness of the digital world have on us and our mental health? In a time with such advanced medicine to fortify our bodies and cure our physical ails, perhaps our mental well-being has been overlooked. The human mind as an unexplored vista is as enticing and mysterious as space to Kennedy, and the world, in the 1960s. This chapter aims to examine the technological tools and innovations that can let us explore and quantify this nebulous space, this space within each of us: the human mind. Since the beginning of time the human mind and understanding it has been one of man's greatest mysteries and challenges. It was often thought that what we now consider the mind; the element of a person that allows the gifts of thought, feelings and consciousness, was one and the same with the soul. In Aristotle's work De Anima he describes the mind as 'the part of the soul by which it knows and understands', in fact Aristotle believed it was human nature to long for knowledge and understanding (Shields, 2016), Thousands of years later our longing to understand the mind has led to many great discoveries; we can now peer into its workings, understanding the brain and mind through the lenses of neurology and psychology. However being able to read the mind is just the beginning, what if we could use that read data to inform computers and technology? That is the premise of Brain-Computer Interfacing (BCI); the science of communicating with machines using brain activity and thought. This chapter hopes to separate the science from the fiction that surrounds this exciting technology. Furthermore it aims to look past the novelty of BCI, to examine its potential in 'serious' or educational games and experiences. Providing an exploration of the unique feedback that can be provided by monitoring the brain, in an attempt to engage users with concepts of meditation and regulation of the mind. Because, even though science has worked hard to separate the mind from the soul, to understand our minds is still to understand ourselves. 'Serious Games do not simply teach their rules, narrative, fictions, metaphors or goals, but they teach the players something about the world, themselves and their own values, beliefs and behaviours' (Mitgutsch, 2011).

Serious Games

'When we think of games, we think of fun. When we think of learning we think of work. Games show us this is wrong' (Gee, 2005). Serious games are games that have scope beyond recreation. They can be for training, teaching and propagating information, in fact games create uniquely customizable environments that excel in all of these areas. So the study of 'serious games', a seeming oxymoron in itself, spans multiple disciplines. From user psychology and pedagogy, the study of learning, to game art, design and narrative (Lim et al., 2014). The virtual world of games offer more than just flexibility with respects to learning, it offers a rich and fun way to present information to new audiences. Games naturally are designed to be fun, but they are also designed to be learned, a good game guides the player, teaching them seamlessly as the game progresses. It is these qualities that serious games draw on to create effective new ways to teach. Mitgutsch (2011) describes serious games using the famous song from 'Mary Poppins' (1964): 'A Spoonful of Sugar'. Which, according to the song, 'helps the medicine go down'. Mitgutsch goes on to describe serious games as: '"esigning a spoonful of sugar and filling it with serious content'.

Meditation

Meditation is the practice of focusing or drawing attention to ones thoughts in order to relax, 'clear the mind' or find peaceful or mindful states. 'Meditation can be defined to include any of a family of practices in which the practitioner trains an individual to consciously calm his/her mind in order to realize some benefit or achieve inner peace or harmony' (Chen, 2011). Serious games require a problem area to be addressed, with intended learning outcomes. So is it possible to teach meditation and mental well-being with serious game approaches? Meditation is a particularly interesting area to attempt to engage learners with, it is very much an experiential phenomena and as tacit knowledge it is hard to verbalize or write about the experience of meditation. This creates a problem when trying to share and 'transfer' knowledge, the key goal of serious game approaches. Additionally as meditation has ancient roots in religious practice it often has a kind of 'mysticism' and associated stigmas. Despite this it has grown increasingly as an academic area of interest, with notable and measurable benefits to those who practice meditation. Despite increased enthusiasm that benefits from developing understandings of psychology and neurology (thanks to brain monitoring approaches), there is still much inconsistency within research across disciplines. Heinz (1981) notes: 'In reviewing the amassed psychological research on meditation, a consistent picture of meditation's purpose and defining features does not readily emerge'. Is it possible to use serious games and brain-computer interfacing technology to engage users with meditation in new, engaging and experiential ways?

Brain-Computer Interfacing (BCI)

Brain-Computer Interfacing is the science of using measurable brain signals to communicate with technology and computers. The term was coined and discussed by Jacque Vidal in his 1973 paper 'Towards Direct Brain-Computer Communication', in his work he asked if 'observable electrical brain signals could be put to work as carriers of information in man-computer communication'. Considering the possibilities of BCI he went on to ponder if such approaches could be used to control 'prosthetic devices or spaceships'. Today prosthetic limbs are indeed being controlled by BCI (Coffey, 2014) and BCI is very much alive in science fiction and popular culture. Aired in 1991 'The Nth Degree', an episode of Star Trek: The Next Generation, featured a popular representation of Brain-Computer Interfacing. Lt. Barclay, a shy and fairly average engineer, is knocked unconscious by a probe. When he awakes he finds his knowledge expanded and influenced by an alien civilization, the Cytherians. Eager to fully utilize the Enterprise's computers he develops a 'neural-scan interface', to interact with the ships computers with greater speed, using his thoughts directly. However the new interface puts the life of not only Lt. Barclay, but the whole crew in danger. Today many approaches for monitoring the brain exist, but these technologies date back as far as the 1920's. The polygraph or lie detector exists as an early example of brain-machine communication and was invented in 1921. There are several possible brain-monitoring techniques that can be considered when creating brain-computer interfaces. Many of these techniques have benefits and draw backs, in particular approaches often trade off on spatial vs. temporal resolution. All brain monitoring approaches that will be discussed are unintrusive; requiring no surgery, as this chapters focus is on exploring accessible educational tools for mental health. In this chapter we will explore the potential of Brain-Computer Interfacing as an educational tool, informed by serious game theory and enhanced using the immersive potential of virtual and augmented reality. Focusing on the history of Brain-Computer Interfacing technology and examining case studies; from teaching meditation and wellbeing to creating useful interventions for attention disorders and even autism. Technology does not always have to serve as a distraction, but instead, as this chapter will show, can act as a means to learn about, reflect upon and combat mental illness in engaging and meaningful ways.

BACKGROUND

Brain-Computer Interfacing (BCI) is the science of using measurable brain signals to communicate with technology and computers. It was coined and discussed by Jacque Vidal in his 1973 paper 'Towards Direct Brain-Computer Communication', in his work he asked if 'observable electrical brain signals could be put to work as carriers of information in man-computer communication'. Considering the possibilities of BCI he went on to ponder if such approaches could be used to control 'prosthetic devices or spaceships'. Today prosthetic limbs are indeed being controlled by BCI (Coffey, 2014) and BCI is very much alive in science fiction and popular culture. Today many approaches for monitoring the brain exist, but these technologies date back as far as the 1920's. The polygraph or lie detector exists as an early example of brain-machine communication and was invented in 1921. There are several possible brain monitoring techniques that can be considered when creating brain-computer interfaces. Many of these techniques have benefits and draw backs, in particular approaches often trade off on spatial vs. temporal resolution. All brain monitoring approaches discussed are unintrusive; requiring no surgery. Intrusive approaches are considered inappropriate within the context of this research.

Functional Magnetic Resonance Imaging (fMRI)

Functional magnetic resonance imaging or fMRI is a neuroimaging approach that uses magnetic resonance imaging to monitor the change in blood as it flows around the brain. This unintrusive approach causes the subject no harm and does not require direct contact with the scalp. First used in the experiments of Roy and Sharrington (1980) it can produce immensely detailed pictures of brain activity with a high spatial resolution. However it can take between 2 and 10 seconds to capture this data, resulting in a sluggish temporal resolution (Kim & Uĝurbil, 1997).

Electroencephalogram (EEG)

EEG or electroencephalogram is a method of using electrodes placed on the scalp to measure electrical brain activity, pioneered by Hans Berger in 1924. When neurons in the brain communicate information to one another the small electrical signals can be detected, together some 10^6 neurons create a measureable reading of a few microvolts that can be monitored this way. Despite being filtered by the meninges, skull and scalp there is a latency of less than a millisecond in this method of monitoring (Woodman, 2010). Giving it a much higher temporal resolution than that off fMRI. EEG is a particularly useful technique in that it is not intrusive, it 'has become one of the most useful tools in the diagnosis of epilepsy and other neurological disorders' (Miranda & Brouse, 2005). Various methods of EEG analysis exist including Hjorth, power spectrum and spectral centroid analysis, these methods take the frequency of the EEG and extrapolate readings from them often using FFT or similar approaches. EEG has some downfalls however; eye movement, eye blink and heartbeat can all cause artefacts in the EEG readings many modern methods of EEG monitoring use algorithms to account for this kind of bodily noise that is introduced. Additionally EEG is not capable of capturing the detailed images of brain function that can be captured with high spatial resolution of fMRI. EEG is the more affordable of the two approaches and EEG is used in almost all consumer BCI solutions.

Event-Related Potential (ERP)

ERP or event-related potential uses EEG to monitor the brains response to specific stimulus. Using this technique specific internal or external events can be measured. It is usually measured using multiple electrodes across the scalp using a few milliseconds temporal resolution (Otten & Rugg, 2005).

This technique is popular for brain-computer interfacing, it allows users to 'think' a specific command that is then monitored and recorded. This command, such as 'up' can then be used to interact with other devices. This approach is used in the consumer Emotiv EPOC EEG headset which has been used experimentally with digital games (Badcock et al., 2013).

Optical Imaging and Mixed Approaches

Several emerging approaches hope to address the failings of existing brain monitoring techniques. Combinations of fMRI and EEG approaches can allow for high spatial and temporal resolutions when gathering data. Additionally there is ongoing research into 'optical imaging', with this approach photons are fired into regions of the brain to gather information. This new approach is being researched in Facebook's 'Building 8' by leading researchers and a former DARPA director. Facebook intends to release a prototype in two years for an unintrusive consumer device that will allow users to type one hundred words a minute using BCI.

BCI in Video Games

With BCI solutions, in particular those that make use of EEG and ERP, becoming increasingly accessible and affordable to developers there has been an increase in the research into BCI in video games over the last twenty years. Examples include 'Brainball' (Hjelm & Browall, 2000) which allowed to players to relax to move a metal ball on a game table, with a visualization of their relaxation as measured by EEG displayed to the players on a projected screen. Krepki et al. (2007) created a series of simple 2D BCI controlled games. Player's wore multi-electrode caps and their EEG feedback was used to allow them interact with various game scenarios. Exploring BCI's 'path towards multimedia applications'. Bos et al. (2010) explored using user focused human-computer interaction approaches in the domain of BCI games. Discussing the increasing availability of BCI solutions and its possible use in games and new mediums. 'Recently, the focal point has shifted to a new group of potential users: the general population. From a commercial perspective, such a large target group could be a very lucrative endeavour. Especially gamers are great potential users, as they are early adopters, willing to learn a new modality if it could prove advantageous' (Bos et al., 2010). Bonnet et al. (2013) experimented with multiuser BCI games, finding that a multiplayer element improved player's engagement in the game and reflecting on the trend of moving from more medical BCI uses towards games and media over the proceeding decade. It can be seen that BCI in video games is an increasing area of academic interest, providing for technical and artistic creativity through the medium of video games.

Consumer BCI and the Age of Neurotechnology

Affordable brain-computer interfaces have seen a significant increase since the start of the millennium. In 2004, Neurosky's two electrode headset can monitor EEG data. InteraXon a company original working with Neurosky's technology released their own 'Muse' EEG headset in 2007. With Emotiv producing a similar product, but with the addition of ERP capabilities in 2011. 2017 has been heralded as the year of 'brain tech' (IEEE Spectrum, 2017). With investment in the technology from the likes of Facebook and Elon Musk causing increasing interest in the field. Significant progress has been made towards creating a platform for games and virtual reality, with Neurable releasing a modified HTC Vive headset with EEG and ERP monitoring capabilities. Promisingly this device supports Unity which is a highly accessible engine, popular amongst game developers.

Neurofeedback: A Tool for Learning

Neurofeedback is the process of providing visual or sonified feedback to a user of their brain activity. This previous use of BCI was limited to experimental use in medical fields, displaying potential in treating ADHD in children (Duric, 2012) and epilepsy (Sterman & Egner, 2006). With a notable increase in interest for BCI, and so neurofeedback, in multimedia applications there has been criticism from the more established fields. "However, the ease in the development of new software programs for feedback functionality and displays, together with the entry into the field of a diverse group of professionals and semi-professionals, has led to an unfortunate lack of consensus on methodology and standards of practice. In turn this has contributed to reluctance by the academic and medical communities to endorse the field." (Sterman, 2006). Despite the criticism of the more creative side of neurofeedback, meaningful work has been carried out within the domain of serious games. Friedrich et al. (2015) created a serious game focused on neurofeedback for children with autism spectrum disorder, monitoring the MU signal via EEG and creating a neurofeedback game. Parents reported improved behaviour in the day to day life of the young participants, support neurofeedback as a powerful learning tool with potential in serious games.

Hinterberger (2010) combined EEG feedback with electrocardiogram (ECG) heart monitoring to create 'The Sensorium: A multimodal Neurofeedback Environment'. Projecting a biofeedback augmented light show onto the walls of the test room of the 'Sensorium' accompanied by a reactive soundscape. This visual and sonified neurofeedback was created to help users interact with their physiological functions, participants reported "An increase in contentment, relaxation, happiness and inner harmony" after using the neurofeedback experience. 'MeditAid' is a wearable neurofeedback devices that provides audio feedback on states of meditation developed by Sas and Chopra (2015). It used dynamic audio to aid users in the practice of deep meditation, using 'binaural beats' a method of brain entrainment that creates a psychoacoustic frequency to encourage similar frequencies neurologically. Brain entrainment methods have been shown to be beneficial for those suffering from cognitive functioning deficits, stress, pain, headache/migraines, PMS, and behavioural problems (Huang-Storms, 2008). MeditAid was shown to benefit the 'deepening of meditative states', helping users engage with meditation and mindfulness (Sas and Chopra, 2015).

METHOD AND DESIGN

The aim of this research is to explore neurofeedback as a tool for serious games. To do this a simple neurofeedback experience was created using a Unity game engine, with design drawing on learning and pedagogical theory. Namely experiential and situated learning. This section will address how brain-computer interfacing can be contextualized within educational game frameworks, game design methodology and importantly how we can attempt evaluate this experience in these given frameworks.

Research Questions

1. Can useable EEG BCI experiences be sufficiently designed using the described approach?
2. Can such an experience support learning, or more specifically the kind of valuable 'transformational' or 'deep' learning described in serious game literature?
3. What insight into this kind of approach can we gather from qualitative analysis of participant experience, does it support potential and future use of BCI and neurofeedback in serious games?

Experience Design and Development

When designing a serious game there are many things to consider. Of course the learning outcomes, in this case engagement with ideas of meditation and its practice, take pride of place in considerations and so do the pedagogical theories that support those outcomes. It could be argued however that something often overlooked in the literature is the quality of the game or experience itself. Today gamers, which is almost everyone and not just young 'digital natives' (Selwyn, 2009), hold games and digital media to a very high standard. Game experiences need to at least attempt to adhere to the high levels of graphical, audio and user-experience quality players are familiar with. An underpinning concept of serious games is that they are fun; this idea of a 'spoonful of sugar'. An obstacle to user engagement and fun, and one that is increasingly becoming a tall order, is creating games of the quality players expect.

Defining Gameplay

When defining gameplay it is important to define player interaction, a player interacts with a game through 'mechanics'. For instance an attack mechanic could consist of a user pushing a button and his/ her on screen avatar performing an attack move. When using BCI as a means of gameplay interaction there are no buttons, only the players mind. So how can we define player interaction within mechanics and therefor gameplay? The gameplay classification work carried out by Djaouti et al. (2007) proposes a simple set of 'game bricks' to represent types of game mechanic, by classifying mechanics we can identify them in other games and implement them knowingly in our own games. For example move, shoot and destroy are represented as individual 'mechanic' bricks, if we put these elements together we can imagine a game similar to 'Space Invaders' where the player moves, shoots and destroys alien spaceships to complete game outcomes. In the designed experience: 'Aurora - Mind over Matter' there is no moving shooting or destroying, so how can we classify the experiences elements? The input from brain-computer interface systems can be erratic, unpredictable and frustrating to manage if high demands are put on the player. For example having to meditate or relax enough to perform an attack in-game would not be a suitable form of gameplay, the spontaneous nature of pressing a button on a game controller is not shared by EEG neurofeedback. ERP methods, as mentioned previously, could more accurately realize this kind of 'cognitive button press'. Two 'game bricks' in particular stand out when trying to suggest mechanics for EEG BCI (Huster et al., 2014). Those are 'manage' and 'match'. The manage mechanic supports the idea of a player managing a resource to perform an action, usually this suggests managing ammo to fire a weapon or resources to build units. Can we consider user meditation a kind of in-game resource? One to be managed in order to achieve the desired outcome? Perhaps more accurate would be the 'match' brick, which requires the player to keep an element in a particular state to achieve outcomes, such as checkmate being achieved by the 'elements' being in the right place to check the enemy king. So perhaps it is better to consider player mediation as an element to be matched to a particular state, rather than resources meant to be managed to allow particular outcomes. To create a neurofeedback 'match' mechanic the experience was designed in such a way that when the players 'meditation' value reached a high enough threshold the game would react positively to the users input. This simple and minimalistic approach meant there were no additional mechanics or game interactions for the player to focus on, the sole purpose of the experience was to encourage the player keep their 'meditation' at the required state.

Challenge, Reward, Growth

Having chosen to use a 'match' mechanic as the means of user interaction, we can then consider how that interaction will affect the gameplay. Games can generally be summarised to have a simple kind of 'gameplay loop' or cycle. Generally this is a challenge, a reward and subsequent growth. For instance the player overcomes a challenge, such as defeating an enemy, they are rewarded perhaps with treasure that enemy had. These rewards allow the player to advance and grow within the context of the game.

So what is the gameplay loop regarding the designed experience using a 'match' mechanic? In the designed experience the player must undergo the challenge of matching their 'meditation' as read in real time using BCI to a certain threshold. Upon completing this challenge or task the player is rewarded by a visual and sonic change in the game environment, acknowledge the players successful interaction and achievement of matching the required state. This success allows the player to achieve knowledge of what strategies, actions or approaches allowed them to achieve this meditative state, with the intention of letting them hone their meditation 'skills' within the context of the game and letting their understanding of the practice grow.

Feedback and Heuristics

To support the player's interaction with the gameplay there must be understandable feedback given to the player, confirming their actions within the game. Here neurofeedback and game feedback cross paths. The feedback provided in neurofeedback allows players to understand and reflect on their cognitive functions, similarly feedback in games supports a player's understanding of their place in the game.

This is done through heuristics. There are two kinds of heuristics to be considered in relation to a game or experience. Positional heuristics that let the player know if they are winning or successfully completing the challenge and directional heuristics that allow the player to understand what strategy or approach to take to progress towards completing the given challenge. In the experience designed players are given directional heuristics through a score displayed on an in-game screen. This score represents their 'meditation' level as input through the BCI system and shows players the level of their meditation and how close they are to triggering the match mechanic. A change in game environment acts as a positional heuristic visually alerting players to their success at overcoming the match mechanic.

Level Design

The game changes between two environments this is, as described above, to assist in showing the player via heuristics their progress and success in the game. This feedback is important to play the game and so learn its outcomes. Additionally with reference to situated learning the environments where created to inforce experiential learning. It also creates a subtle narrative to the game, where by the player clearing their mind, meditating and becoming peaceful causes the virtual environment of the game to mimic that action, and so reinforce it. The starting environment is a plain and mundane room, similar to the situation a player may choose to practice meditation in real life. Compared to the relaxing outdoor environment representing successful meditation.

Importance of Soundscapes

Depending on whether the player chooses to practice deep meditation or mindfulness the players may choose to close their eyes. Therefor it is important that not only should the environment reflect their success when they open their eyes, the audio of the game should provide strong feedback to assist the player. The first bedroom environment has the sound of humming computers and screens and a beeping sound representing the player being 'plugged into the machine', attempting to draw on familiar schemas around BCI, like those in the Matrix. The second environment on the other hand has the sound of the vast outdoors; wind, trees creaking and distant animals. Additionally reaching very high levels of meditation triggers dynamic music, which fades in and out to provide feedback and a relaxing soundtrack for the player.

Creating Flexibility and Encouraging Exploration

To allow players to find a 'meditation threshold' comfortable for them a difficulty setting was created, the difficulty between 1 and 5 is displayed on an in-game screen. Players could adjust this setting to make the 'match' mechanic more or less difficult to suit their own ability. This was intended to reducing the sometimes erratic nature of neurofeedback and make the game more engaging and playable, giving the players the potential to customize the experience. Additionally it was intended to allow the player to try and move between difficulties encouraging experimentation and reflection on their chosen approaches and strategies. Exploration helps facilitate learning within serious games, and engagement in general.

Summary

In summary the experience created could be described as an interactive EEG BCI based neurofeedback experience that uses a customizable match mechanic to allow players to challenge themselves and learn experientially. With underpinning narrative and heuristics supported by visual and audio feedback in 3D situated learning environments.

Testing

Testing was carried out to evaluate the usefulness of the developed approach and to analyse the potential for learning through its application. The testing procedure and practice was informed by the literature in serious games analysis such as Catalano and importantly Mitgutsch's use of Bateson's work to analyse learning 'in, through and beyond serious games'. Testing was focused on the gathering and analysis of qualitative data from the players/participants, with quantitative measures used as a baseline source of data to support general usability.

Participants

This study focuses on the qualitative experience of ten participants aged between 19 and 30, four male participants and six female participants took part. There was various familiarity with meditation across the participants, but being of key importance to the study the participants have been broken down into 'meditation groups' to benefit qualitative analysis. Four categories were determined to help aid analysis. None: participants who had no experience with meditation or meditative practices (3 participants). Tried: one individual had a unique relationship with meditation, having tried it but not had a positive experience, this individual was placed in their own group to reflect this. Fair: participants who had practiced meditation, experienced it through activities like yoga or group meditation and had practiced it on occasion (3 participants). Practiced: participants who regularly practiced meditation or had done so for long periods of time (3 participants).

Procedure

1. Participants were briefed generally on the study, the BCI system and the game experience.
2. Participants were asked to give consent and read through instructions.
3. Participants were asked to fill out a pre-test survey and reflect on their relationship with meditation and their practice of it if applicable and what current tools, if any, the used to engage with meditation. They were asked what might lead them to engage with meditation.
4. The experience was described and outlined to the player, as was the EEG headset they were asked to wear.
5. They were encouraged to play for around five to ten minutes, changing difficulties and reflecting on their experience.
6. Participants then filled out a post-test questionnaire. This includes a system usability scale questionnaire, to consider the general usability and playability of the experience. Additionally they were asked to reflect on the strategies that helped them interact with the game.
7. Participants were interviewed on their experience to gather further qualitative data.

Usability Testing as a Basic Metric

Bateson's framework as reimagined for serious games provides the foundation for this approach to testing, looking to find learning 'in, through and beyond' serious games. To gain 'level zero' the player must be able to respond with ease to the experience and be able to learn its fundamental components. In terms of game design this means the player must feel comfortable to play the game as it was intended, to make sure that this low level of learning was achieved participants were asked fill out a 'system usability scale' (SUS) questionnaire. This was to measure generally for usability to make sure the experience was engaging enough to facilitate the further levels of learning. This SUS scale, created by Brooke (1986) (Usability.gov) is intended to measure the 'appropriateness to a purpose of any given artefact'. Though with only a small number of participants collectively this quantitative data is not particularly useful, within a more qualitative approach to evaluating the developed experience it can provide a baseline for usefulness to each participant and a value of how easy the system was to use. Confirming that 'level zero' could be achieved in the context of the experience with no hindrance.

Qualitative Assessment of Exploration

Participants were observed while playing the game, observations were made on level of apparent relaxation, interest in the game, eagerness to explore the experience and adjust levels of difficulty. The process of engaging with the game and exploring its mechanic through gameplay allowed the players to understand the context of the experience, experimenting and achieve the first level of learning following Bateson's framework. Focusing on observing gameplay and listening to participant accounts provide a means of accessing this learning 'through serious games', allowing us to then consider the next and most important level of learning.

Qualitative Analysis of Learning

The second and final level of learning as considered by Bateson supports the idea of 'deep learning' as described by Gee (2005). It is the level where through relating the learning achieved in previous levels to themselves and their existing knowledge and beliefs they can experience transformative learning. Taking the learning 'beyond' the game and into real world contexts. To monitor and look for traces of this kind of learning player's strategies towards and beliefs around meditation where compared before and after the experience. If the experience could facilitate adequate reflection for the player to reconsider their approach to meditation in a broader sense the game could be suggested to have had a successful, meaningful and individual impact on the player. By separating participants into individual categories based on their own relationship with meditation we can attempt to see this kind of shift in their thoughts and approaches, with reference to their existing knowledge and feelings before using the neurofeedback experience. This explorative approach aims to try to access the usefulness of the experience as a tool for advancing learning and engagement with meditation and potentially realizing how it may be practiced by that individual. Evaluating the overall usefulness of EEG BCI based neurofeedback experiences within the given context of serious games and educational experiences.

Results

Using a SUS questionnaire to get a rough baseline for participant usability was originally intended to support the basic interactions required for 'level zero' learning. However when comparing the perceived usability on average between groups created around experience with meditation practice (no practice: 3, fair practice: 3 and well-practiced: 3) interesting differences appeared.

The questions are separated between agreeing on positive (5) and negative (5) aspects of the experience. With 0 being strongly disagree and 5 to strongly agree when represented below.

Positive Question Agreement

- **I would use this frequently:** On average users agreed that they would like to use the system frequently (4.1/5). Fair (4.3) and well-practiced (4.7) participants were more enthusiastic about using the system when compared to those with no practice (3), who, on average, neither agreed nor disagreed to wanting to use the system again.

- **I thought it was easy to use:** On average participants found the system easy to use (4.6/5). Fair (4.7) and well-practiced (4.7) players found the systems slightly easier than average. While players with no experience still agreed the system was easy to use (4.3) but to a lesser extent when compared to the average and other groups.

- **I found the functions well integrated:** On average players agreed the experience's functions and features were well integrated (4). In this instance no practice and fair practice groups agreed (3.7) to a lesser extent than those well-practiced (4.3).

- **I imagine people would learn to use this quickly:** On average participants agreed that learning to use this system could be done quickly (4.1). Those well-practiced in meditation perceived the system to be easier to learn for others (4.7) when compared to no practice (4) and fair practice (3.3).

- **I felt confident using this:** On average players agreed to feeling confident using the experience (3.6). Well-practiced players (4.3) agreed more strongly than fair practice players (3.3). On average players with no experience leant more towards not being confident using the system (2.7).

Findings

On average players were positive about the experience, however when comparing those that practice meditation frequently with those who have no practice clear differences appear. Regarding agreeing to positive statements regarding the experience found in the SUS questionnaire; those well-practiced were consistently above average. Well-practiced players felt more confident using the system, found it easier to use and learn and they were enthusiastic about using such an experience frequently. Those with no practice where less positive about the experience, with averages consistently falling below the participant average. They were less enthusiastic about using the experience again and found the system less easy to use and more difficult to learn than well-practiced players. These findings could indicate a correlation between experience with meditation and perceived usability of the experience, suggesting that even though participants generally were positive about the experience when answering, players with more experience engaged with the experience more positively overall.

Negative Question Agreement

- **I found this too complex:** On average players disagreed with the experience being too complex (1.3/5). The players with no experience disagreed less than the other two groups (1.7)
- **I feel I would need technical support:** On average players disagreed (2.3/5). However experienced meditators felt they would be less likely to need support (1.6), in comparison those without experience actually agreed that they would need technical support on average (3.3).

- **I thought the experience was inconsistent:** On average players disagreed (2/5). Again comparing well-practiced and no practice players, well-practiced felt there was less inconsistency (1.3), while those without practice felt there was more (2.3).
- **I found it cumbersome:** In general players disagreed (1.9). Well-practiced players actually found slightly more cumbersome than the average (2) and unexperienced players found it significantly more cumbersome when compared (2.3).
- **I need to learn a lot before I get going:** On average players mostly disagreed (2.4). However though well-practiced (2.3) and fair practiced (1.6) felt they did not need to learn a lot, non-practiced players actually agreed to need to learn a lot (3.7).

Findings

Players on average disagreed with the negative questions in the SUS questionnaire. However when examining meditation groups this is not true. Those without practice in meditation actually agreed to feeling a lot of learning was required and that they needed additional support. Again across questions non practiced players felt less positive compared to the average, while those with lots of practice were found to be more positive on average across questions, other than finding the system more cumbersome than participant average.

Qualitative Data

'Meditation groups' are used again when analysing the qualitative reports and interviews provided by participants. This allows a focus on each participant's reflections and potential learning within the context of their current understanding.

EVALUATION

This study has no usefulness if it is not aware of its own scope, this is a small study and though the findings are interesting, an area of research as broad as neurofeedback for educational purposes merits more scrutiny. Though conclusions and relationship can be discussed relating to the results of the study further research must be carried out, with greater numbers of participants, to draw conclusions. What the study may suggest will be the topic of the next chapter. This study can be scrutinized not only for its number of participants but also for elements of game design, development and testing.

Game Design

Originally the contrast between the irritating office environment and the relaxing outdoor environment was intended to add to the narrative and differentiate the environments. It became clear that the soundscape used in the first environment was distracting and not conducive of meditation, though some players seemed to enjoy the challenge, many found it made the experience more difficult. A revised game would have a more peaceful starting environment so not to distract players. Furthermore players, especially those with no experience, felt there needed to be more explanation of the workings of the game. From a game design perspective this can be attributed to the failings of the user interface and the games heuristics. Additionally, as no explanation or description of mediation was given to players before the play session, information in-game could have helped address difficulty understanding the game and its premise. Particularly for players with less experience. Some players also questioned a lack of narrative, especially in the 'relaxing' environment as they felt this would motivate them to play. Overall a revised game would have to address many areas to support a better and more inclusive experience.

Game Development

Problems are also present at a deeper development level. The value sent from the NeuroSky headset is between 0 and 100, that value becomes 0 to 10 by the time it reaches Unity. This results in a 10x reduction of resolution in the system. More important is the nature of that reduced signal, in code it is reduced using simple if statements. A value greater than 0 equals 1, a value greater or equal to 20 equals 2 and so on. This use of general if statements when reducing information to be sent across Arduino microprocessors results in a kind of stepping of the signal drastically from 1 to 2 (and so on) because of the way the signal is processed. This could add to the erratic nature the system sometimes takes, especially with unexperienced players. To address this the headset could send the value (0 to 100) that represents meditation directly to Unity via Bluetooth. This is possible and would remove the degradation of the signal. Resulting in a smoother experience with a greater resolution.

Testing

Testing procedure can also be criticized, the participant group was small, only 10 people. There was an equal number of well, fair and non-practiced players. Though efforts were made to minimize noise players were sometimes distracted by students and other sounds when trying to relax using the experience. Some questions were unclear and had to be further explained to participants during pre and post questionnaires. Reference in questions should have been made to 'the experience' or 'the game' not 'the Aurora Experience' which confused participants, additionally the use of the word 'cumbersome' in the SUS caused difficulty for some participants, some whom did not have English as a first language. A more universal word should have been used for inclusivity.

FUTURE RESEARCH DIRECTIONS

Basic user testing using the SUS questionnaire questions supports that generally players found the system easy to use and interact with. However when looking at result averages with relation to user experience well-practiced players found the system easier to use than those with no practice in meditation. This could suggest that the system was in fact able to measure meditation, with more experienced users having an easier time and perceiving the system to be more useable. It is important to note that no description of meditation practice was given to any of the participants, perhaps if a similar experience was supported by additional learning materials, a workshop or a professional practitioner, engagement could be improved for novice meditators. These findings are in stark contrast to the finding of Sas and Chopra (2015) who found neurofeedback experiences particularly useful for 'novice meditators'. Though the experiential learning tool developed seemed to be usable, and so support Bateson's 'level zero' of learning, it is felt further research into usability with regards to level of experience is needed. Additionally further research to identify the value additional learning materials can add when helping unexperienced players engage with experiential neurofeedback experiences would be valuable. Further studies should aim to record participant EEG levels during gameplay, this could provide quantitative data to define whether or not well-practiced players are better at the game than those with little or no practice. Fair practiced players seemed to have more 'deep' meditation strategies before playing the game, during play they often changed their strategies to a more 'mindful' approach. They were surprised by how little they had to close their eyes and by how much breathing techniques and the kind of calm awareness associated with mindfulness, helped control the experience. Well-practiced players on the other hand seemed to have ideas closer to mindfulness when approaching the experience, instead they used 'deep' meditation strategies such as relaxing the body and closing the eyes while playing the game. These changes in strategy from both fair and well-practiced players could represent a kind of learning or reassessment of their own meditation practices. However, it is felt that a longer study to try and map changes in practice over time would give a greater insight into the potential for 'transformational' learning. Though this study shows what may be traces of learning of this kind and a general usability to support the legitimacy of the system in monitoring meditation, further work must be carried out to create best practice in this emerging field. It is believed that BCI and neurofeedback have great potential for reflective experiential learning and serious games. The responses of practiced players were far more positive than that of those with no practice, this could reflect the accuracy of the system and the closeness of the meditation mechanic in the experience and the practice of meditation in real life. Alternatively those that regularly practice meditation may just have had more enthusiasm and interest in this kind of experience. It is felt the results would suggest the success of this approach, however user testing also highlighted several failings of the experience; from irritating sound design to lack of in-game information. Therefor this study is better seen as a 'toe in the water', an early look at how this kind of experience may benefit the world of serious games. As a heavily experiential method there is much that can benefit neurofeedback games in the experiential learning approaches found within serious game literature. Furthermore by adhering to serious game literature when considering design and development games can be assessed with greater accuracy with regards to their potential for learning. Importantly this study used consumer grade EEG hardware and was still successful in creating working and usable systems. This approach could provide low cost and accessible means for game developers and researchers to explore brain-computer interfacing.

CONCLUSION

Brain-computer interfacing and neurofeedback provide an exciting new area for exploration in serious games. BCI offers a new frontier for learning and importantly learning about ourselves. Experiential neurofeedback games could provide engaging and novel new ways for us to learn about tacit and beneficial practices like meditation, answering age old questions about the human mind, its functions and how we can master them. Consumer facing solutions to brain-monitoring can allow greater access and experimentation in this field and as the fields of neurology and psychology advance serious games can benefit from attempting to frame the growing knowledge and approaches of these disciplines within its own literature and pedagogical theory. Importantly these kinds of solutions and approaches could help engage players with practices that can help them overcome real problems. How to relax when feeling stressed or how to focus when they have to, systems that can help players master these skills as they would master a skill in a game. Serious games often address external problems and knowledge, but through neurofeedback and BCI serious games can empower us to understand the mind.

REFERENCES

Badcock, N. A., Mousikou, P., Mahajan, Y., De Lissa, P., Thie, J., & McArthur, G. (2013). Validation of the Emotiv EPOC® EEG gaming system for measuring research quality auditory ERPs. *PeerJ, 1*, e38. doi:10.7717/peerj.38 PMID:23638374

Bateson, G. (1972). Steps to an ecology of mind: Collected essays. In *Anthropology, Psychiatry, Evolution, and Epistemology*. University of Chicago Press.

Bonnet, L., Lotte, F., & Lecuyer, A. (2013). Two brains, one game: Design and evaluation of a multi-user BCI video game based on motor imagery. *IEEE Transactions on Computational Intelligence and AI in Games, 5*(2), 185–198.

Bos, D. P. O., Reuderink, B., Van De Laar, B., Gurkok, H., Muhl, C., Poel, M., . . . Nijholt, A. (2010). Human-computer interaction for bci games: Usability and user experience. In *Cyberworlds (CW), 2010 International Conference on* (pp. 277-281). IEEE.

Chen, Z., Hood, R. W., Jr., Yang, L., & Watson, P. J. (2011). Mystical experience among Tibetan Buddhists: The common core thesis revisited. *Journal for the Scientific Study of Religion, 50*(2), 328-338.

Coffey, A. L., Leamy, D. J., & Ward, T. E. (2014). A novel BCI-controlled pneumatic glove system for home-based neurorehabilitation. In *Engineering in Medicine and Biology Society (EMBC), 2014 36th Annual International Conference of the IEEE* (pp. 3622-3625). IEEE. 10.1109/EMBC.2014.6944407

Djaouti, D., Alvarez, J., Jessel, J. P., Methel, G., & Molinier, P. (2007). Towards a classification of video games. In *Artificial and Ambient Intelligence convention*. Artificial Societies for Ambient Intelligence.

Duric, N. S., Assmus, J., Gundersen, D., & Elgen, I. B. (2012). Neurofeedback for the treatment of children and adolescents with ADHD: A randomized and controlled clinical trial using parental reports. *BMC Psychiatry, 12*(1), 107. doi:10.1186/1471-244X-12-107 PMID:22877086

Friedrich, E. V., Sivanathan, A., Lim, T., Suttie, N., Louchart, S., Pillen, S., & Pineda, J. A. (2015). An effective neurofeedback intervention to improve social interactions in children with autism spectrum disorder. *Journal of Autism and Developmental Disorders, 45*(12), 4084–4100. doi:10.100710803-015-2523-5 PMID:26210513

Gee, J. P. (2005). Learning by design: Good video games as learning machines. *E-Learning and Digital Media, 2*(1), 5–16. doi:10.2304/elea.2005.2.1.5

Heinz, B. R. (1981). *The origins of meditation: Perspectives beyond the scientific research* (Unpublished doctoral dissertation). Loyola University Chicago. Retrieved July 10, 2018 from https://ecommons.luc.edu/luc_diss/2065

Hinterberger, T. (2011). The sensorium: A multimodal neurofeedback environment. *Advances in Human-Computer Interaction, 3*.

Hjelm, S. I., & Browall, C. (2000). Brainball: Using Brain Activity for Cool Competition. *Proceedings of the First Nordic Conference on Computer-Human Interaction (NordiCHI 2000)*.

Huang-Storms, L. (2008). *Efficacy of neurofeedback for children with histories of abuse and neglect: Pilot study and meta-analytic comparison to other treatments.* University of North Texas.

Huster, R. J., Mokom, Z. N., Enriquez-Geppert, S., & Herrmann, C. S. (2014). Brain-computer interfaces for EEG neurofeedback: Peculiarities and solutions. *International Journal of Psychophysiology: Official Journal of the International Organization of Psychophysiology*, *91*(1), 36–45. doi:10.1016/j.ijpsycho.2013.08.011 PMID:24012908

IEEE Spectrum: Technology, Engineering, and Science News. (2017). *Silicon Valley's Latest Craze: Brain Tech*. Retrieved August, 10, 2017 from http://spectrum.ieee.org/biomedical/devices/silicon-valleys-latest-craze-brain-tech

Kennedy, J. F. (1962). *Moon Speech*. Rice Stadium. Retrieved July 10, 2018 from https://er.jsc.nasa.gov/seh/ricetalk.htm

Kim, S. G., & Uğurbil, K. (1997). Comparison of blood oxygenattion and cerebral blood flow effect in fMRI: Estimation of relative oxygen consumption change. *Magnetic Resonance in Medicine*, *38*(1), 59–65. doi:10.1002/mrm.1910380110 PMID:9211380

Krepki, R., Blankertz, B., Curio, G., & Müller, K.-R. (2007). The Berlin Brain-Computer Interface (BBCI) – Towards a new communication channel for online control in gaming Applications. *Multimedia Tools and Applications*, *33*(1), 73–90. doi:10.100711042-006-0094-3

Lim, T., Louchart, S., Suttie, N., Hauge, J. B., Stanescu, I. A., Ortiz, I. M., ... Ott, M. (2014). Narrative serious game mechanics (NSGM)–insights into the narrative-pedagogical mechanism. In *International Conference on Serious Games* (pp. 23-34). Springer. 10.1007/978-3-319-05972-3_4

Miranda, E., & Brouse, A. (2005). Toward direct brain-computer musical interfaces. In *Proceedings of the 2005 Conference on New Interfaces for Musical Expression* (pp. 216-219). National University of Singapore.

Mitgutsch, K. (2011). Serious learning in serious games. In M. Ma, A. Oikonomou, & L. C. Jain (Eds.), *Serious Games and Edutainment Applications* (pp. 45–58). Springer London. doi:10.1007/978-1-4471-2161-9_4

Otten, L. J. & Rugg, M. D. (2005). Interpreting event-related brain potentials. *Event-Related Potentials: A Methods Handbook*, 3-16.

Sas, C., & Chopra, R. (2015). MeditAid: A wearable adaptive neurofeedback-based system for training mindfulness state. *Personal and Ubiquitous Computing*, *19*(7), 1169–1182. doi:10.100700779-015-0870-z

Selwyn, N. (2009). The digital native–myth and reality. *Aslib Proceedings*, *61*(4), 364–379. doi:10.1108/00012530910973776

Shields. (2016). Aristotle's Psychology. *The Stanford Encyclopedia of Philosophy (Winter 2016 Edition)*. Retrieved July 10, 2018 from https://plato.stanford.edu/archives/win2016/entries/aristotle-psychology/

Sterman, M. B., & Egner, T. (2006). Foundation and practice of neurofeedback for the treatment of epilepsy. *Applied Psychophysiology and Biofeedback*, *31*(1), 21–35. doi:10.100710484-006-9002-x PMID:16614940

Usability (Improving the User Experience). (2018). Retrieved July 10, 2018 from https://www.usability.gov/

Vidal, J. J. (1973). Toward direct brain-computer communication. *Annual Review of Biophysics and Bioengineering*, *2*(1), 157–180. doi:10.1146/annurev.bb.02.060173.001105 PMID:4583653

Woodman, G. F. (2010). A brief introduction to the use of event-related potentials in studies of perception and attention. *Attention, Perception & Psychophysics*, *72*(8), 2031–2046. doi:10.3758/BF03196680 PMID:21097848

KEY TERMS AND DEFINITIONS

Brain-Computer Interfacing (BCI): The ability to interact with software and technology with our thoughts and feelings; it presents an exciting new frontier for serious games and learning.

EEG or Electroencephalogram: Is a method of using electrodes placed on the scalp to measure electrical brain activity, pioneered by Hans Berger in 1924.

ERP or Event-Related Potential: It uses EEG to monitor the brains response to specific stimulus. Using this technique specific internal or external events can be measured.

Functional Magnetic Resonance Imaging or fMRI: It is a neuroimaging approach that uses magnetic resonance imaging to monitor the change in blood as it flows around the brain. This nonintrusive approach causes the subject no harm and does not require direct contact with the scalp.

Meditation: It is the practice of focusing or drawing attention to one's thoughts in order to relax, clear the mind, or find peaceful or mindful states.

Mixed Approaches: Emerging approaches hope to address the failings of existing brain monitoring techniques. They are a combination of fMRI and EEG approaches that can allow for high spatial and temporal resolutions when gathering data.

Serious Games: They are games that have scope beyond recreation. They can be for training, teaching and propagating information, in fact games create uniquely customizable environments that excel in all of these areas.

System Usability Scale (SUS): It provides a reliable tool for measuring the usability. It consists of a ten-item questionnaire with five response options for respondents from "strongly agree" to "strongly disagree." It was originally created by John Brooke in 1986.

This research was previously published in Virtual and Augmented Reality in Mental Health Treatment; pages 32-50, copyright year 2019 by Medical Information Science Reference (an imprint of IGI Global).

Chapter 30
DICE:
A Generic Model for the Design Process of Serious Games

Damien Djaouti

LIRDEF, University of Montpellier, Montpellier, France

ABSTRACT

This article deals with serious game design methods. More specifically, it focuses on the following question: is there any universal series of steps to design a serious game? Or is the availability of several different design methods unavoidable? To try to answer this question, we will study a corpus of ten design methods suited to Serious Games. Most of these theoretical tools are coming from or aimed to industry professionals. This literary review will allow us to perform a comparative analysis over the various steps used by these methods, in order to build a generic model for the design process of Serious Games: the Design / Imagine / Create / Evaluate (D.I.C.E.) model.

1. INTRODUCTION

Serious Games have a formal definition (Michael & Chen, 2005) and are currently seen as a specific type of video game. Thus, per Alvarez (2007), Serious Games are no different from entertainment video games in formal terms; their difference is purely cultural and pragmatic.

Do these particularities imply that specific design methods should be used for Serious Games? Work in the field tends to suggest so: several publications put forward tailor-made process models for Serious Games (Cheruette, 2009; Lhuillier, 2011; Marfisi-Schottman et al., 2010; McMahon, 2009; Sauvé, 2010; St-Pierre, 2006). But are these various methods, which are aimed at creating one and the same object, really different? More precisely, this article intends to explore the following problem: is there a universal series of steps for designing a Serious Game? Or do several design methods need to be used concomitantly?

DOI: 10.4018/978-1-6684-7589-8.ch030

To attempt to address this question, we propose to study a corpus of methods devoted to designing Serious Games, via a literature review. The majority of these theoretical tools are designed by or intended for industry professionals. Initially, we will present a design method that we have experienced personally as part of a project to design a driving simulation Serious Game. We will then review other design methods for Serious Games proposed by scientific and industrial literature on the subject. This literature review will thus allow us to carry out a comparative analysis of the different steps proposed as part of these methodologies, in order to attempt to delineate a generic design process model suitable for Serious Games.

2. LITERATURE REVIEW: DESIGN METHODS FOR SERIOUS GAMES

There are several documented process models for designing Serious Games. In order to carry out a literature review, we assembled a corpus of texts using the keywords "serious game", "design", "methodology" and "method", in English and in French, via the Google Scholar search engine. We choose to use only Google Scholar to perform our literature review as it allowed us to easily search for academic works written in either English or French language, and also because it's currently the largest academic database available (Gusenbauer, 2019). To confine the scope of our study, we selected only texts that were published from 2002 onwards, because the 2002 year marked the start of the current wave of Serious Games (Djaouti, 2014). Among the works identified through this online search, we focused on the ones clearly stating a series of steps to design a Serious Game. This focus was required to later compare the design methods. But it also introduces a scope limitation in our study. Therefore, the current study does not aim to provide an exhaustive view. Instead, our goal is to compare a sample of the available Serious Game design methods to try to devise a generic design process model.

Taking those limitations into account, our literature review enables us to identify nine methods used for designing Serious Games. Those nine methods are mainly taken from academic publications (books, dissertations and articles), although some of them are the fruit of collaborations between companies and universities.

2.1. The GEDRIVER Design Process

We propose to begin this study of design methods for Serious Games with an example coming from a project we personally worked on. While working at OKTAL, a private company designing training simulations, we were involved with a Serious Game project aimed at raising awareness of eco-driving among motorists. This project, baptised GEDRIVER (Green & Efficient Driver), united a consortium of five partners: the car manufacturer Renault, Key Driving Competences (KDC), the LEAD and ARTS laboratories at the University of Burgundy, and OKTAL. By combining realistic interfaces (steering wheel, pedals and gearstick from a real vehicle) and a technical tool for creating automobile simulations, SCANeR (Djaouti, 2011), the aim was to devise a simulator that will allow the general public as well as professionals to learn the principles of eco-driving. These principles are aimed at reducing the CO_2 emissions of a vehicle by changing the habits of its driver (Figure 1).

The design process of this Serious Game was divided in four steps:

Figure 1. The GEDRIVER Serious Game

1. **Defining the serious content:** The serious content of the game was initially formalised during meetings and exchanges with the all the partners. Based on reference documents on the subject, a list of eco-driving principles to be conveyed through the game was drawn up. This list was accompanied by a selection of the vehicles to be made available in the game, in close collaboration with Renault, which supplied the data to enable the behaviour of those vehicles to be simulated: consumption, CO_2 emissions curve depending on the engine speed, etc. During this initial brainstorming phase, it was also decided that another element of serious content would be added to the game: road safety awareness;

2. **Game Design:** Defining the concept of the game. Starting from the serious concept defined by the partners, the second step involved inventing a game concept that would enable this serious content to be transmitted. The concept and the detailed description of its mechanisms were then set down formally on a game design document to enable the developers to create prototypes;

3. **Level Design:** Designing the different levels in the game. All once the game mechanisms have been approved by all partners, the second phase of the design process, Level Design, can begin. This involves inventing scenarios that implement the game mechanisms. In concrete terms, it involves constructing the different levels of the game (hence the name);

4. **Realisation and assessment of prototypes:** Once the design steps are complete, the next step in the process involves realising a prototype to assess the suitability of the Serious Game. This is an iterative process. An initial prototype is realised and then tested. Based on feedback from users, the designer adjusts the design. Another prototype is then realised based on the corrected design, and reassessed. This process continues until user feedback corresponds with the objectives pursued by the designer. For GEDRIVER, this involves assessing whether the serious content defined at the beginning of the brainstorming stage is actually being transmitted by the game.

2.2. An Industrial Model Based on Educational Engineering

The team of researchers working on the Learning Game Factory project developed theoretical tools for the design of Serious Games. In concrete terms, these researchers propose two complementary models. The former model details the entire industrial circuit for creating a Serious Game (Marfisi-Schottman et al., 2009). This model is associated with another similar work that focuses solely on the design steps of a Serious Game, however, particularly for games intended to transmit educational content (Marfisi-Schottman, 2010). This model comprises seven steps (cf. Figure 2).

Figure 2. Serious Game design model by Marfisi-Schottman et al.

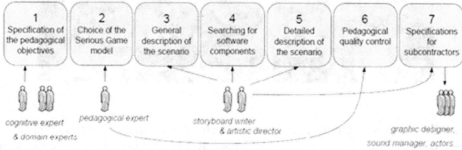

2.3. The Industrial Method of KTM Advance

KTM Advance has extensive experience in this field and also has an industrial design method specifically for Serious Games (Boudier & Dambach, 2010). Under this method, the process of designing Serious Games is broken down into five steps:

1. **Analysis of requirements:** Defining the technical and educational characteristics required of the Serious Game. This stage strives to identify the educational content to be communicated via the game, and to formalise it To do this, the designers at KTM Advance propose to begin with a framework document that sums up the educational requirements expressed by the client. Then, a more in-depth analysis of the content to be communicated is carried out (such as via interviews with specialists in the subject-matter to be handled), and the various elements of this content are compiled in a hierarchical list;
2. **Proposed Game Design:** Based on the elements compiled during the previous stage, the designer invents game mechanisms that will allow this content to be transmitted. This Game Design proposal is formalised in an appropriate document, which sets out the various aspects of the game including: scenario, gameplay, a list of the game boards, interactions in the game, etc.;
3. **Developing a prototype:** Based on the elements imagined during the Game Design phase, the programmers create a prototype of the game. This prototype can be used to test the suitability of the game mechanisms proposed with regard to the educational objectives defined during the initial stage;

4. **Iterative deliveries:** The game is then developed following an iterative process. Both authors hereby state that they have opted for short iteration cycles, where the game is regularly submitted to the client, who then sends back a list of the changes to be made;

5. **Final delivery:** Once the iteration cycles have been completed, the process results in a finished Serious Game, which is guaranteed to be relevant to the objectives pursued by virtue of the continual user tests carried out during stage [D].

2.4. The Two Industrial Models of Paraschool

Another industrial model is proposed by Marc Cheruette, a designer at Paraschool, a company specialising in the design of educational Serious Games (Cheruette, 2009) (Figure 3).

Figure 3. The method for creating a Serious Game used by Paraschool

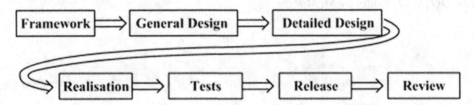

The design work here is divided up into three steps. The first stage, Framework, encompasses the designer's preliminary work: determining the target for the project, identifying the educational objectives, and documentary research on the subject-matter to be covered. The next step is the General design, which aims to sketch out the broad outline of a principle for the game that will allow the educational content to be transmitted: opting for an entertaining video game and choosing the game's universe, objectives, characters, etc. This first draft is then fleshed out during the Detailed design stage by creating all the game's rules, its interface and so on. In their methodological guide, Cheruette proposes to use theoretical tools such as GamePlay bricks (Djaouti & al., 2008) as a basis for this stage. The Serious Game designed in this manner is then realised and tested internally, until it receives the final validation of the client. Even though this model deconstructs theoretical design into a larger number of steps, it puts forwards a series of steps that is not dissimilar to the models described above.

Lhuiller (Lhuillier, 2011) is a former production director at Paraschool and proposes two design process models. Her first model, which is of the waterfall type, basically incorporates the same steps as proposed by Cheruette. Her second model, on the other hand, is inspired by agile development methods and is centred on an iterative process broken down into four steps:

1. **Framework:** Defining the aims of the project using conventional theoretical tools (strategic analysis models, interview forms, etc.);

2. **Design:** See below:
    a. **Educational:** Defining the educational content of the game;
    b. **Technical:** Defining the technical restrictions on the project;
    c. **Game Design:** Writing a game design document;

3. **Prototype(s):** The iterative part of the process, during which prototypes are produced on a regular basis (one per fortnight) and sent to the client for evaluation;
4. **Delivery:** The game is complete and is sent to the client.

2.5. The DODDEL Model

Educational engineering appears to have inspired several approaches to the process of designing a Serious Game. One of its vectors of influence is the generic ADDIE model (cf. 3.). Since some parties in the Serious Game industry have backgrounds in educational engineering, they have drawn inspiration from this generic model in order to put forward a series of steps for designing a Serious Game. One example of this we can identify is the DODDEL model (McMahon, 2009). This acronym for document-oriented design and development of experiential learning is composed of the steps described in Figure 4.

Figure 4. The DODDEL model by McMahon

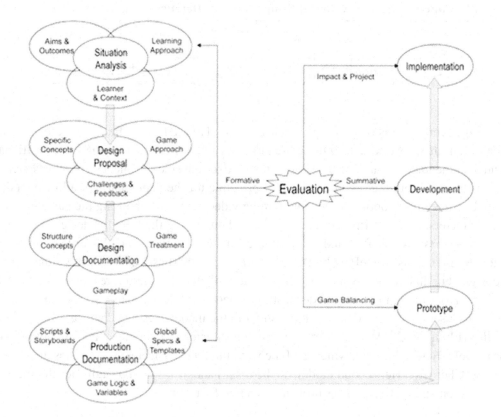

By the author's own admission, the DODDEL model is based on the generic ADDIE model, on which it improves by introducing iterative loops for certain steps of the process. McMahon used this model as a guide for students new to creating Serious Games. This field experiment (McMahon, 2009), which involved a group of twenty students in their first year of a bachelor's degree in Game Design, shows that the DODDEL model appears to be appropriate for helping beginners with two aspects. It begins by defining a common ground in order to facilitate internal communication for each group of students. Most of all, however, this model proposes a full series of steps to be followed when creating a Serious Game. It can thus be used as a roadmap to the creative process for persons who have never produced this type of item before.

2.6. A Model Focusing on Content

A radically different approach to designing Serious Games is put forward by the team of researchers behind the e-Adventure authoring tool. These researchers proceed on the basis that the realisation of Serious Games combines at least two types of skillset: experts in the serious sector; and developers able to handle the technical construction of the game. According to them, if the sector experts are not supervised, the project will encounter technical limitations. If, on the other hand, the programmers define the technical limits in advance, the creativity of the sector experts will be seriously limited. The researchers thus propose a third way, in the form of a *content-centred* model (Moreno-Ger et al, 2008). Rather than following the generic approach, they deliberately focus on a type of video game that, according to them, will allow educational content to be communicated in an appropriate manner: graphic adventure games. The researchers then propose a series of steps for creating such a Serious Game (cf. Figure 5).

2.7. A Model for Designing Educational Video Games

Beyond these focalised approaches to Serious Games, there is the St-Pierre model (St-Pierre, 2006), which forms part of the broader production of multimedia. The researcher begins by describing the various steps in the production process for a multimedia project:

- Analysis and design:
  - **Analysis of requirements:** Identifying and defining the objectives of the product;
  - **Creative development:** Devising a multimedia scenario;
  - **Documentation:** Writing design specifications that describes how the product works so as to allow that product to be manufactured;
- Production and validation:
  - **Production of the media elements:** Creating the video and audio elements of the product;
  - **Integration – programming:** Software implementation of a functional prototype of the product;
  - **Assessment:** Testing the product with users, then amending the product via an iterative process;
- Distribution and maintenance.

With the exception of the final phase, which concerns the distribution of a multimedia product, the various steps comprised in the first two phases more or less recall the design models for Serious Games mentioned above. Indeed, St-Pierre does not put forward a specific production process model for Serious Games, as he deems that the latter constitute multimedia projects. He thus proposes that this general model be used as a basis for designing them.

Figure 5. The design process model of Moreno-Ger et al.

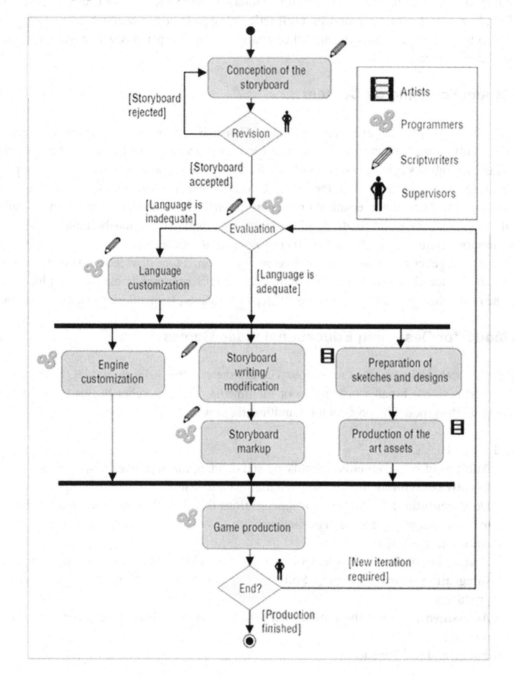

2.8. An Approach Centred on the Use of an Authoring Tool

Authoring tools can also be at the centre of a method for designing a Serious Game, as proposed by the researchers behind the *Adventure Author* and *Flip* tools. As a summary of their study on the creative process, for fields ranging from game design to writing via software engineering, they propose a series of steps for creating video games in an educational context (Robertson & Nicholson, 2007):

- **Exploration:** The designer becomes familiar with the technical tool he will be using, evaluates its potential for creation and begins to consider where this potential is richest in terms of the message he is looking to convey;
- **Idea Generation:** During this stage, the designer puts forward numerous ideas and assesses how appropriate they are. He then selects an ensemble of converging ideas that will enable the basics of the design of a game to be sketched out. During this stage, the designer will return to the previous stage repeatedly in order to evaluate the technical feasibility of his idea;
- **Game Design:** The designer expands on the ideas he adopted to form a detailed game concept: game mechanisms, characters, scenario, contents of levels, etc.;
- **Game Implementation:** The designer uses the technical tool to create the game he has thought up. This stage is iterative: the designer tests the game regularly and corrects it, modifying what was defined during the previous stage if need be. This stage continues until a full game has been created;
- **Game Testing:** The designer then tests his game from beginning to end, in order to identify any general problems such as the balance of the game or any technical issues;
- **Evaluation:** The designer has his game tested by a person taken from the target audience. He then observes that person's reactions, takes note of any positive or negative feedback, and may decide to return to the previous steps in the process in order to improve the game.

The researchers then tested and confirmed the validity of this model by observing children using their technical tools for creating video games (Robertson & Nicholson, 2007). An initial wave of experiments was carried out in the form of optional summer workshops over the course of a week. Adolescents aged between 12 and 16 were given free rein to create video games, without having to include a serious aspect in their projects. A second series of field experiments took place in a school environment, with children aged 10. This time the workshops lasted one hour per week, and took place during normal school hours. Similar to the work of Kafai (1994), these experiments show the educational potential of creating video games in a school situation. Rather than the mere usage of the game being a teaching aid, it is the creation process itself that becomes a teaching vector.

2.9. The Framework Game Methodology for Education

Another approach closely associated with a technical tool has been developed via generic educational game shells (GEGS). The creation of educational Serious Games complies with a specific logic in this regard, in order to simplify the creation process: the framework game methodology (Sauvé, 2010). This approach involves taking an existing game and removing its content (information conveyed by the game) to leave only its structure (way of playing). The framework game thus obtained can then be enriched with new content, such as educational content. According to Sauvé (Sauvé, 2010), the process used for creating framework games that can be used for designing educational Serious Games is broken down into five steps:

- **Preliminary analysis or planning of the GEGS:** Identifying the educational content to be transmitted and selecting a framework game so that its structure can be used;
- **Designing the GEGS:** A detailed description of the components of the framework game to be retained or modified as part of design specifications. These design specifications are composed of

illustrations of the different screens within the game, annotated so as to show the different potential interactions (Sauvé, 2010a);

- **Production of the GEGS:** Programming the various functionalities of the shell to produce an initial functional version;
- **Validation of the GEGS:** The generic shell is assessed by the target designer audience, and the software is revised via an iterative process if required;
- **Formative evaluation of the games created via the GEGS:** An educational game is created using the shell, and that game is then evaluated by the target user group.

The process described here thus does not relate directly to the creation of a Serious Game, but rather to the creation of a theoretical tool used to facilitate the creation of an educational Serious Game. More specifically, it involves designing the entertainment side of an educational game, to allow teachers to concentrate solely on the serious side, and thus making it easy and quick for them to create educational video games.

3. DISCUSSION

3.1. How Can the Process of Designing Serious Games be Formalized?

Now that we have reviewed these different models that formalise the process of designing a Serious Game, can we answer the question asked at the beginning of this article, to whit: is there a universal series of steps for designing a Serious Game?

At first glance, the variety of models that we have just examined would tend to suggest not: the series of steps of these ten models are not identical. A more in-depth analysis nonetheless enables us to give a more nuanced answer. Although the methods of our corpus cannot be used to identify a universal series of steps for designing a Serious Game, certain aspects and steps do seem similar in the models presented. To begin with, these ten models show more or less explicitly the iterative nature of some or all of the process. The notion of prototyping also recurs several times, as does the concept of tests with users during the design process. These observations led us to compare these ten methods in a more structured manner. Although it is impossible to define one single method for designing Serious Games, it might be possible to compare these models and identify similarities. It may even be possible to formalise these similarities in the form of a generic model.

The concept of a generic model comes to us directly from a tool taken from educational engineering: the ADDIE generic model (Molenda, 2003). This is a theoretical framework used for implementing educational curricula. This model comprises five steps: Analysis, Design, Development, Implementation and Evaluation. The Analysis stage incites the educator to identify the educational objective pursued, and to analyse the target audience. During the Design stage, the various steps of the educational curriculum are designed. The Development stage then allows all the educational content of the curriculum to be created. This curriculum will be tested on a sample audience (teachers and students) during the Implementation stage. Finally, the Evaluation stage assesses the suitability of the curriculum using two methods: formative evaluation, which is continuous throughout the creation process; and summative evaluation, which is aimed at testing certain aspects of the curriculum with a specific audience.

The model is deemed to be generic because the five steps it defines are rarely used without further modification. Generally, each educator will define his or her own series of steps based on the framework proposed by this model. As explained by Molenda, this is visibly attributable to the fact that the term ADDIE has no precise or identifiable origins, instead being the fruit of empirical practice in the educational engineering sector. Each educator is therefore free to propose his or her own model of educational engineering and devise a variable number of steps falling within the five generic steps defined by the ADDIE generic model.

This approach to the generic model is particularly suitable for analysing the methods for designing Serious Games that we have studied. We propose to compare the various steps of these ten models, and to attempt to consolidate them thematically. For example, we can see that numerous steps of the ten models studies basically consist of identifying and formalising the serious content that is to be communicated via the game: the Framing stage from the models of Cheruette and Lhuillier, the Analysis of requirements stage from the models of KTM Advance and St-Pierre, or even the Defining the serious content stage used in the design process for GEDRIVER. We thus propose to consolidate the steps of our various models within one generic stage, entitled simply Define. By pursuing a similar approach for all steps in these ten models, we obtain a total of four generic steps:

1. **Define:** Specifying the serious content that is to be transmitted via the game: educational objectives, list of information to be transmitted, list of skills to be acquired, advertising message, etc.;
2. **Imagine:** Starting from the serious content, the creator invents a game design;
3. **Create:** A prototype is realised to test the suitability of this game design;
4. **Evaluate:** The prototype is evaluated with a target audience. The assessment criteria vary from one project to another but, for most Serious Games, the extent to which the content defined during the first stage is transmitted will generally be measured.

Table 1 details how the steps from each model have been consolidated into one of these four generic steps.

3.2. Introducing the DICE Generic Model for Serious Game Design

The combination of the four generic steps *Define, Imagine, Create* and *Evaluate* forms a generic model for designing Serious Games: the DICE generic model.

Figure 6. The DICE generic model for the Serious Game design process

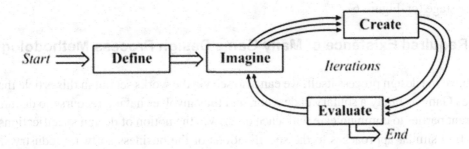

Table 1. Comparison of several design process models for Serious Games

Design Process Model	Define	Imagine	Create	Evaluate
GEDRIVER design process (cf 2.1)	- Defining the Serious content	- Game Design - Level Design	- Realisation of prototypes	- Assessment of prototypes
Model by Marfisi-Schottman *et al* (cf. 2.2)	- Client's need	- Conception - Pedagogical quality control	- Production - Coherence control & debugging	- Test on test group - Use and maintenance
Model by KTM Advance (cf. 2.3)	- Analysis of requirements	- Proposed Game Design	- Developing a prototype	- Iterative deliveries - Final delivery
Model by Cheruette (cf. 2.4)	- Framework	- General design - Detailed Design	- Realisation	- Tests - Release - Review
Model by Lhuillier (cf. 2.4)	- Framework	- Design	- Prototypes	- Delivery
Model by McMahon (cf. 2.5)	- Situation Analysis	- Design Proposal - Design Documentation	- Production doc. - Prototype - Development - Implementation	- Evaluation
Model by Moreno-Ger *et al*. (cf. 2.6)	*Task handled by the domain expert"*	- Conception of the storyboard - Language customization - Storyboard writing/modification - Preparation of sketches and designs	- Engine customization - Storyboard markup - Production of the art assets - Game production	*Continuous Evaluation during the whole process*
Model by St-Pierre (cf. 2.7)	- Analysis of requirements	- Creative development - Documentation	- Assets production - Integration & programming	- Assessment-Distribution and maintenance
Model by Robertson & Nicholson (cf. 2.8)	- Exploration	- Idea Generation - Game Design	- Game Implementation	- Game Testing - Evaluation
Model by Sauvé (cf. 2.9)	- Preliminary analysis or planning of the GEGS	- Designing the GEGS	- Production of the GEGS	– Validation of the GEGS - Games evaluation

Like most of the models studied as part of this article, the DICE generic model is based on an iterative cycle comprising three of its four generic steps. Indeed, we can observe for the models in our corpus that the steps we have consolidated into the first generic step, *Define*, occur once only during the design process. On the other hand, the steps we consolidated under the other three generic steps form part of an iterative cycle beginning with the *Imagine* stage, continuing via the *Create* stage and ending only with the *Evaluate* stage (cf. Figure 6).

3.3. The Required Existence of Many Game Design Process Methodologies

Over and above the design process itself, we can also see via the works set out in this article that designing a Serious Game is rarely a solitary endeavour, and thus involves having recourse to documents that allow different parties to communicate with each other. Via the notion of design specifications, we can, in the end, find similar approaches to the specifications of the business software industry. That said, creating Serious Games also appears to embody an element of artistic creativity, in the same way as creating video games. This aspect partially explains the virtually systematic usage of agile methods in the models presented here: regardless of the design method used, the designer must include user tests in the design loop in order to determine the quality of his or her product. This creativity does however also seem to be one of the reasons for which there are so many design methods in existence. This plurality of methods can also be found in the entertainment video game industry (Djaouti, 2011), so we feel it is interesting to recall the words of game designer Chris Crawford (1982) when describing his own method of designing entertainment video games:

The procedure I will describe is based on my own experiences with game design, and reflects many of the practices that I use in designing a game. However, I have never used this procedure in a step-by-step fashion, nor do I recommend that any person follow this procedure exactly. In the first place, game design is far too complex an activity to be reducible to a formal procedure. Furthermore, the game designer's personality should dictate the working habits she uses. Even more important, the whole concept of formal reliance on procedures is inimical to the creative imperative of game design. [...] I therefore present this procedure not as a normative formula but as a set of suggested habits that the prospective game designer might wish to assimilate into her existing work pattern. (p. 45)

In light of the proximity between video games and Serious Games (Alvarez, 2007), these words seem particularly relevant to our study. Thus, although it is possible to put forward theoretical tools formalising the process of designing Serious Games via a clearly-defined series of steps, none of these attempts at formalisation can claim universality. As Crawford reminds us, the creative nature of the process of designing a game, whether that game is serious or not, implies a certain degree of freedom. This explains why it is possible to identify so many different methods for designing Serious Games: each method reflects a facet of its inventor's personality. The diverse range of tools studied in this article thus means that the requirements of a broad panel of designers can be addressed. Although none of the methods set out here will be satisfactory for any given designer, there is always the option of appropriating an existing model and changing it, or even creating a wholly original model. To this end, we propose to use the DICE generic model as a canvas intended to inspire all designers of Serious Games in search of the series of steps that suits them the best, or that is the most suitable for their current project. By way of example, Table 1 shows the manner in which this generic model can potentially be instantiated and adapted by any Serious Game designer.

4. CONCLUSION

In light of the multitude of methods available for designing Serious Games, this article explores the following problem: is there a universal series of steps for that can be used to design a Serious Game? Or do several design methods need to be used concomitantly?

To provide a response to this question, we set out and analysed ten different design methods: one initial method, which we experienced personally as part of an industrial project, and nine other methods taken from a literature review. At first glance, these methods borrow numerous elements from the business software industry, such as the concept of iterative cycles and user tests inspired by agile methods. The presence of steps such as Game Design, creative development and educational quality control, however, clearly indicate that these design methods have a specific objective in mind: Serious Games.

By observing these ten methods, we thus identified several different process models for designing Serious Games. However, although each of these methods is based on a distinct series of steps, we can nonetheless distinguish certain similarities in the ten models studied. These similarities led us to put forward the DICE generic model, a framework for defining series of steps in the design of Serious Games. This model, based on an iterative cycle, comprises four generic steps: Define, Imagine, Create and Evaluate. It is therefore possible to classify each step of the ten design methods presented in this article within one of these four generic steps. The DICE generic model can thus be seen as a concise framework from which any designer can define their own set of steps for designing a Serious Game. Because, as Crawford (1982) reminds us, the process of designing a game, whether that game is serious or not, implies a certain degree of freedom. Instead of there being a universal design method used by the entire industry, every Serious Game designer ends up defining their own method. This observation highlights the main benefit of identifying the design methods for Serious Games in this manner. Since there is no such thing as a universal theoretical tool, it is essential to identify a broad panel of existing approaches in order to offer guidance to a large number of different designers during their creative process. We suggest that designers who are not satisfied with the existing tools use the DICE generic model as a canvas for creating new methods.

Nonetheless, it may seem a little simplistic to summarise the creative aspect of designing Serious Games as merely being the freedom for each game designer to define their own series of steps. Although this aspect is admittedly important, other dimensions such as having recourse to the users' shared gaming culture, the various methods of incorporating serious content via the rules of the game (Djaouti, 2011), the importance of the fictional dimension of the game (Allain, 2013) or even radical approaches such as games that are deliberately impossible to beat (Lee, 2003) are just as vital. In a similar register, our proposed generic model currently focuses solely on the process of designing, disregarding the very important issue of the products obtained via the methods based on these processes. Would there be a way of carrying out a similar study on the products, so as to devise a generic method for designing Serious Games rather than a generic model?

We will attempt to respond to this question in our upcoming work, where we aim both to explore the creative dimension of designing Serious Games and to carry out a deeper analysis of the products associated with the various methods set out in this article.

ACKNOWLEDGMENT

This research received financial support for English language editing services from the University of Montpellier - Faculté d'éducation.

REFERENCES

Allain, S. (2013). Serious game et perception du réel: lecture documentarisante et potentiel cognitif (PhD Thesis). Genève, Suisse: Université de Genève.

Alvarez, J. (2007). Du jeu vidéo au serious game, approches culturelle, pragmatique et formelle (PhD Thesis). Toulouse, France: Université de Toulouse.

Boudier, V., & Dambach, Y. (2010). *Serious Game: Révolution pédagogique.* Hermès Science Publications.

Cheruette, M. (2009). Vers une méthodologie pour la conception des Serious Games [Master thesis]. Université Paris XIII, Paris, France.

Cook, D. (2007, July 19). The Chemistry of Game Design. Gamasutra. Retrieved from http://www.gamasutra.com/view/feature/1524/ the_chemistry_of _ game_design. php

Crawford, C. (1982). The Art Of Computer Game Design: Reflections Of A Master Game Designer. McGraw-Hill.

Djaouti, D. (2011). Serious Game Design - Considérations théoriques et techniques sur la création de jeux vidéo à vocation utilitaire [PhD Thesis]. Université de Toulouse, Toulouse, France.

Djaouti, D. (2014). De l'utilité de l'appellation "Serious Game". Le jeu est-il l'apanage du divertissement? *Interfaces numériques*, *3*, 409-429.

Djaouti, D., Alvarez, J., Jessel, J., & Methel, G. (2008). Play, Game, World: Anatomy of a Videogame. *International Journal of Intelligent Games & Simulation*, *5*, 35–39.

Gusenbauer, M. (2019). Google Scholar to overshadow them all? Comparing the sizes of 12 academic search engines and bibliographic databases. *Scientometrics*, *118*(1), 177–214. doi:10.100711192-018-2958-5

Kafai, Y. (1994). *Minds in Play: Computer Game Design As A Context for Children's Learning*. Routledge.

Lee, S. (2003). I Lose, Therefore I Think: A Search for Contemplation amid Wars of Push-Button Glare. *Game Studies*, *3*(2). Retrieved from http://www.gamestudies.org/0302/lee/

Lhuillier, B. (2011). *Concevoir un serious game pour un dispositif de formation*. FYP Editions.

Marfisi-Schottman, I., George, S., & Tarpin-Bernard, F. (2010). Tools and Methods for Efficiently Designing Serious Games. *Games Based Learning, ECGBL, 2010*, 226–234.

Marfisi-Schottman, I., Sghaier, A., George, S., Tarpin-Bernard, F., & Prévôt, P. (2009). Towards Industrialized Conception and Production of Serious Games. *Presented at the Internantial Conference on Technology and Education (ICTE)*. Academic Press. Retrieved from http://arxiv.org/abs/0911.4262

McMahon, M. (2009). Using the DODDEL model to teach serious game design to novice designers. *Presented at the ASCILITE 2009*. Academic Press.

Michael, D., & Chen, S. (2005). Serious Games: Games That Educate, Train, and Inform (1st ed.). Course Technology PTR.

Molenda, M. (2003). In Search of the Elusive ADDIE Model. *Performance Improvement*, *42*(5). Retrieved from http://www.eric.ed.gov/ERICWebPortal/detail?accno= EJ676523

Moreno-Ger, P., Martínez-Ortiz, I., Sierra, J. L., & Fernández-Manjón, B. (2008). A Content-Centric Development Process Model. *Computer*, *41*(3), 24–30. doi:10.1109/MC.2008.73

Robertson, J., & Nicholson, K. (2007). Adventure Author: a learning environment to support creative design. *Presented at the 6th International Conference for Interaction Design and Children (IDC 2007)*. Academic Press. 10.1145/1297277.1297285

Rollings, A., & Morris, D. (2003). *Game Architecture and Design: A New Edition*. New Riders Games.

Sauvé, L. (2010a). *La conception d'une coquille générique de jeux éducatifs*. In L. Sauvé & D. Kaufman (Eds.), *Jeux et simulations éducatifs: Études de cas et leçons apprises* (pp. 493–528). Presses de l'Université du Québec.

Sauvé, L. (2010b). *Introduction au guide*. In L. Sauvé & D. Kaufman (Eds.), *Jeux et simulations éducatifs: Études de cas et leçons apprises* (pp. 463–465). Presses de l'Université du Québec.

St-Pierre, R. (2006, January). La conception de jeux vidéo éducatifs: une méthodologie de recherche/création [PhD Thesis]. Université du Québec, Montréal, Canada. Retrieved from http://www.clikmedia.ca/CM/

Tajè, P. (2007, July 27). Gameplay Deconstruction: Elements and Layers. Game Career Guide. Retrieved from http://www.gamecareerguide.com/features/355/gameplay_deconstruction_elements_.php

This research was previously published in the International Journal of Game-Based Learning (IJGBL), 10(2); pages 39-53, copyright year 2020 by IGI Publishing (an imprint of IGI Global).

Chapter 31
How to Track Progress:
Progressive Tracking Games

Charles Westerberg
Beloit College, USA

Tom McBride
Beloit College, USA

ABSTRACT

This chapter introduces a second kind of tracking game: progressive tracking games. In it, the authors show how students can use progressive tracking games to develop tracking skills that will become more sophisticated over time, rather than a simple matter of mastering facts. They introduce four levels of tracking that can be used to enhance learning. The levels take ideas and start with (1) definitions, move to (2) learning methods, build to (3) listing examples, and finish with (4) applying ideas in new ways. They introduce a series of games that teachers can use to help students learn how to track more progressively. They draw their examples from literature (The Great Gatsby), history ("The Gettysburg Address"), philosophy (miracles), and poetry ("I Could Not Tell").

A PROGRESSIVE TRACKING GAME: DOG-WALKING AND FOOD POISONING

So far, all our games have treated conceptual ideas as virtual reality, while non-virtual reality has become their testing ground. This is a feature of the games today's students have grown up with: a journey into a world of challenges—obstacles overcome by perception and, in some games, coordination. There are games where the aim is to find Waldo or build a Sim City, and other games (the ones detailed here) where the aim is to examine pears through the eyes of Trobriand Islanders or ferret out real-life waiters and Sisyphus-types. There are games that occur entirely in virtual reality, and others, like ones detailed here, that split their time between virtual, conceptual reality and examination in non-virtual reality.

DOI: 10.4018/978-1-6684-7589-8.ch031

But there is another feature of games that we have so far not discussed: levels. A common question put to players is, "What level are you?" If our previous games might be categorized as Tracking and Testing, there's now a new game in town, and in this book: Tracking and Progress Games. This is, to a degree, a matter of framing. The underlying idea is a simple one: A progressive tracking game involves the acquisition of a skill at Level One. A second skill is vital at Level Two, but the second skill builds on the first. The third skill builds on the first and second. The fourth skill depends on the first, second, and third. The quicker and more accurate a player is with Skill 1, the better able will she be to achieve a similar proficiency with Skill 2, and so on. That's progress, folks. Digital gamers have a term—Easter eggs, which mean signposts of progress. If you "find an Easter egg," it means you have achieved the requisite progress so far and now have a way onward and upward to the next "egg."

But what are the applications—this feature of digital games—for improving classical learning? For one thing (not the only one), it might simply be the way a course is organized.

For instance, a professor might point out, if she were a sociologist, that the course will entail four stages of growth: learning what social facts are; learning how social facts are established and researched; learning the work of the great practitioners in this field; and learning how to observe and research social facts in one's own environment. In other words: 1. Workable Definition, 2. Research Methods, 3. Historical Examples, and 4. Applied Imagination. Different instructors will want to develop their own growth templates.

But let us go back to our Sociology teacher. She might appear on the first day or class and offer an overview. What is a social fact? The instructor might give an example of one: the maintenance people on this campus wear uniforms, while faculty and students do not. Or: when students take a class they sit while teachers stand. These are social facts, but why are they social facts? So: Level One involves being able to define what is meant by a social fact and pick them out. Is dog-walking a social fact? Is shunning a restaurant where you got food poisoning a social fact? Once you can answer these questions with skill and persuasion, the professor might tell her students, you have passed Level One.

And this is a necessary prep for Level Two: The research and establishment of social facts. If you think dog-walking is a social fact, how would you try to make your case? What research would you do? Whom would you talk to? Is it just walking a dog or is it also a certain way of walking a dog? Is it certain dogs as opposed to others? Is a poodle especially "walkable" in order to communicate something about class, while not walking a Pit Bull is a way of saying something about status? At Level One you gained some facility with the concept and selection of social facts. At Level Two you must contemplate how to get into the tall weeds of survey and research. You will not actually do so yet—not until Level 4—but you have simulated the process in your own mind, with the professor, and with classmates and through readings.

Level Three: Now that you yourself, the instructor goes on during this first day of class, have simulated the roles of a theorist and researcher of social facts, you are ready to read the findings and ideas of other, more skilled and famous, social fact theorists and observers than you may turn out to be. Until students had contemplated this business for themselves, they weren't ready to appreciate and critique social theorists who proposed seminal findings in the estrangements of city life, the links between theology and the profit system, and the myriad ways by which people try to manage the impressions of others. So: a man jumping out of a window to his death after being fired is not a physical fact but a social fact; a person striving to be rich as a sign of God's favor is not an economic fact but a social fact; a person wearing vertical stripes in order to look thinner is not a fashion fact but a social fact. You, the professor says, will be a more thoughtful and critical reader of Durkheim, Weber, and Goffman. So: your Level One skill builds up to your Level Two skill, which builds up to your Level Three skill. Definition leads to Self-Contemplation leads to Illustration, and all three will lead up to Investigation, which is the essence of…

Level Four: In Level Two you spent some time asking what sorts of inquiries you would have to make in order to investigate whether or not this or that (dog-walking, spurning a restaurant that made people sick) were social facts. You enter into this last Level, says Professor X, armed with definitions, contemplations, and examples. You are ready to try investigating social facts on your own. Take, for instance, refusing to go back to the bad restaurant. Surely this could not be a social fact. This is a natural fact: we are physically primed, hard-wired, to avoid repeating the ingestion of sickening foods. Yet right away the investigator might run across a problem. How does the customer know for sure that it was the café that caused all the trouble? How does the customer know that he didn't just pick up a virus from another customer, which could happen anywhere? Yet the customer tends to blame the restaurant—obviously the researcher needs data on these incidents in order to discover a pattern. Where would that data be? But is it possible that the customer blames the restaurant, fairly or unfairly, because he thinks this is part of his role as a consumer? Does he have consumer bias—"I am the buyer, the customer, and in a free market system am always right." Does this color his decision not to go back to the eatery, so that his future avoidance is not just a natural response but a social decision that flows out of a capitalist system?

This is a tough question. But it's precisely the sort of thorny question to be asked and possibly answered at Level Four. One might call this entire game a process of climbing (up levels), but it is really a form of progressive intellectual tracking. It is in the service of a classical learning goal: the ability to define concepts and apply them to situations perhaps not quite dreamt of in the original conceptual formula.

Another Progressive Tracking Game: The Great Gatsby

In the Sociology/Food Poisoning Game we saw how progressive tracking can give students a sense of where they are in the acquisition of skills and where they need and presumably want to be up the level scale. But now we move into a different feature---and virtue—of progressive tracking games: If students turn a text into a progressive tracking game, it will help them grasp the structure of the text and offer insightful ways of following it. Here the progressive tracking game is not so much a measurement of improvement but rather a template for reading. Let us being to see how.

F. Scott Fitzgerald's Great Gatsby is one of the world's great novels, narrated in the 1920s by an American Middle Westerner named Nick Carraway (Fitzgerald, 1995). At the end of Long Island in the 1920s Carraway meets a rich bootlegger named Gatsby, likewise from the Middle West (North Dakota) who has used his ill-gotten gains to take on social pretensions. He gives huge and festive parties in his Long Island mansion. Carraway learns that Gatsby is trying to impress his (Nick's) distant cousin Daisy, whom Gatsby met five years earlier and fell in love with. Daisy is married, but Gatsby still hopes to win her hand. Money, he thinks, will turn the passage of time into renewed eros. This is Gatsby's dream. In the end, however, he not only loses Daisy, once again, but also his life, as he is murdered by a grief-stricken man who thinks Gatsby has run over his unfaithful wife and killed her. The man was misinformed, but Gatsby is found floating, dead of a bullet wound, in his swimming pool.

The plot of Gatsby is quite well-known, but this summary is all one really needs to know in order to consider the novel as a progressive tracking game. In doing so, we will broaden our sense of how instructive progressive tracking games can be in the classroom. In turn, we can build on both the Social Facts Tracking Game and the Gatsby Tracking Game to find still other applications.

The Great Gatsby: A Tracking Game

Player: Nick Carraway

Level One: Nick wonders about Gatsby (sees him in the starlight contemplating the green light at the end of a dock across Long Island Sound: this is where Daisy and her husband live.)

Level Two: Nick befriends Gatsby (goes to one of his parties; hears Gatsby's stories about his past: that he was born rich—only later does Nick learn this isn't true).

Level Three: Nick gets involved with Gatsby (agrees to set up a date between Gatsby and Daisy; is a witness to the conflict between Gatsby and Daisy's husband; learns that Gatsby was really born poor and has made his money through crime in order to re-invent himself as a rich, sporty person)

Level Four: Nick is loyal to Gatsby after Gatsby's death (decides that Gatsby's dream of Daisy, though the foolish one of a crook, was also noble and consistent with the American Dream of being anyone you want to be despite background).

Now, what is the aim of tracking the novel as a progressive game with Nick as the four-levels player. It is clearly not to turn Nick into a sociology student who learns more and more at each level. It is true that Nick does enter a learning process in the four levels: from curiosity to information (some of it false and misleading) to involvement to a moral choice about divided loyalties. Yet at the end of the Sociology Tracking the student ideally has become a good fledgling student of social facts, while at the end of the Gatsby game Nick has not "mastered" anything. He only knows, or thinks he knows, that Gatsby's vision of rekindling timeless romance is both foolhardy and yet gorgeous, and is ennobled by its being a version of an American fantasy built into the mythos of the United States (the pilgrims, the pioneers, the immigrants and other re-invented groups). He has traversed a long way from Level One (idle curiosity) to Level Four (loyalty to a grand hope even in these lurid 1920s circumstances).

Is this progress? Discuss. Debate. Or: if students were to design a digital game based on Gatsby, with Nick as the player (players in the game take on the character of Nick), what options would be given to Nick in the virtual reality game? Would he have the option not to become so involved with Gatsby. Would he have the option of trying to clear Gatsby's name in the press of the time? Would he have the option of confronting Daisy and telling her that she was not worthy of Gatsby's dream? Once we have put Nick into the template of a progressive tracking game, there are opportunities for all sorts of conjectures and insights.

So: While it is true that Nick does not make "progress" as does our sociology student, it is equally true that students can make progress, via the game, in their understanding of a great novel.

But let us not walk away from further insights just yet, for one opportunity these sorts of progressive games offer is to change the identity of the player. Nick is the narrator of the novel, but it's named for Gatsby and is principally about him. So:

Gatsby Game . . . **Player:** Jay Gatsby . . .

Level One: Gatsby meets Daisy, has an out-of-time love affair with her in his uniform, which means that this rich girl does not know that he is poor . . .

Level Two: Gatsby emerges from the Great War, becomes a highly able gangster and re-designs himself as an old money swell (old sport) . . .

Level Three: Gatsby in his new fake persona then pursues Daisy and tries to get her to leave her husband . . .

Level Four: Gatsby loses Daisy and his life.

How does the Gatsby game change when we make Gatsby the player? Well, of course, the events of each level are different. For instance, Nick doesn't die at novel's end, while Gatsby does. We can certainly say that Gatsby "played" a high-stakes game and lost. But there is one thing we cannot say: that in any sense he "won." In a progressive game one can gain information and knowledge, but if at Level Four one dies because the game was poorly played, such increase in facts and wisdom does one no good. So progressive tracking games are for the living, or those who will live on, and not for the dead. To the extent that Nick gains anything in his game—that he decides the American Dream is noble even if Gatsby is a flawed instance of it, and is faithful to Gatsby's ideal but not the man himself—then Gatsby's death is what forces Nick to decide what he thinks. So Gatsby is a feature of Nick's progressive game, but it is really Nick who is the only eligible player.

Thus may we leave this section on progressive tracking games by stating that the identity of the player is as central to learning from these games as is the levels of which they are composed?

The Gettysburg Address Game

First, here's a text, followed by an assignment:

Four score and seven years ago our fathers brought forth on this continent, a new nation, conceived in Liberty, and dedicated to the proposition that all men are created equal.

Now we are engaged in a great civil war, testing whether that nation, or any nation so conceived and so dedicated, can long endure. We are met on a great battle-field of that war. We have come to dedicate a portion of that field, as a final resting place for those who here gave their lives that that nation might live. It is altogether fitting and proper that we should do this.

But, in a larger sense, we can not dedicate -- we can not consecrate -- we can not hallow -- this ground. The brave men, living and dead, who struggled here, have consecrated it, far above our poor power to add or detract. The world will little note, nor long remember what we say here, but it can never forget what they did here. It is for us the living, rather, to be dedicated here to the unfinished work which they who fought here have thus far so nobly advanced. It is rather for us to be here dedicated to the great task remaining before us -- that from these honored dead we take increased devotion to that cause for which they gave the last full measure of devotion -- that we here highly resolve that these dead shall not have died in vain -- that this nation, under God, shall have a new birth of freedom -- and that government of the people, by the people, for the people, shall not perish from the earth (Lincoln, 1995).

Assignment: Dear Students in American Political Theory (Political Science 221), Above you will find the full text of Lincoln's brief but famous speech at the dedication of the cemetery created by the Battle of Gettysburg. The battle occurred in the summer of 1863; the speech in the late fall of 1863. Your task is two-fold. First, count and list the number of words with mathematical implications, such as of course the famed "four score and 7" (87) and "little note nor long remember" ("little" is imprecise, but it refers to a small number, while "long" refers to a much bigger one). Second, turn the speech into a game. Name the player; identity the levels; score the progressive rewards, if any. What happens to the Gettysburg Address when you turn it into a progressive tracking game? Does this transformation change the way you read it? How so, if so?

Now it is easy enough for us to do the first part of the assignment. The only specific number Lincoln mentions is the "four score and seven," but the speech is numerical in the general sense throughout, with, for instance, references to greater or lesser dedication or to a civil war that is "great" (terrifyingly huge). Let us leave aside for the moment why the professor made this the first part of the assignment. The more difficult part of the assigned task involves the re-casting of a speech into a game. Who would be the player?

Of course, we might think of Lincoln as the player, but he would seem better suited as the designer of the game. Is he asking his listeners to play? We have noted in the Great Gatsby game that these games are for the living, not the dead. We eliminated the idea that one could play a game, get to a top level of ambition, and then die. These games are for the living—like Nick, or what we should properly call "the classroom living." This reasoning might lead us to infer that the players of the Gettysburg Tracking Game, if we can find it, would be anyone listening to or reading the speech. All those who did so in Lincoln's time—in the "real time" of the game—are now dead. That leaves only us.

So, if we are the Players, what are our progressive levels? If we try to redesign the speech as a tracking game, with levels and scores, that would that entail? Here is one possibility among others.

Level One: Recalling and then believing that the United States was founded on the proposition of universal equality (Declaration of Independence made the nation "new"). 1 point

Level Two: Showing up at the battlefield dedication/remembrance ceremony; this way you hear the speech, and even if you don't show up physically (which is impossible today for us), you can "show up" by reading the speech. 2 points

Level Three: Acknowledging, and feeling with great emotion, that the Union soldiers (not the Confederate ones) who died in the vicious battle gave more to the cause of equality than you have. 3 points…. so now, if you have completed the first three levels, you have earned 6 points total.

Level Four: Being fully willing to give as much to the cause of equality as the Gettysburg Union soldiers did. 10 (yes, 10) points, though those only somewhat (less than fully) willing might get only between 4-9 points. The winner accumulates 16 total points, and no one can exceed that number. So the winner might join with a lot of co-winners, but to win at all is a great honor and feat.

So sixteen points wins, but no player gets by Level 4 without going through the other levels of remembering, attending, and acknowledging. Lincoln in effect says you cannot "win" the game unless you first qualify at lower levels. Note, also, that the lower levels do not oblige much physical action, or than showing up for the speech or finding it online and reading it. It is only Level 4 that commits players to risk the non-virtual possibility of death. But, as with Gatsby, no one wins the game by dying, but only by being willing to do so. But why "win"? What does it mean to win a game that might result in one's death?

Here it seems impossible, in this recasting of the great speech as a progressive tracking game, to separate winning the game from winning the civil war. This is a rousing speech. Its quiet profundity should not fool its readers. The side that will win is the side that is willing to give "that last full measure of devotion." It is the side that most wants to win. And what does it mean to win? It means keeping the union? And what does that mean? It means keeping united the only nation officially dedicated to the proposition that all are created equal. That's why one gets 10 points on the possible way to 16. He or she is a winner because the United States—the United States—is a winner. This, then, must be why the political science professor insisted that students first find implicitly arithmetical language in the speech: because the speech is ultimately about giving, more or less.

There are other ways of "gaming" the speech. One could read it as a "resurrection game": the soldiers have died but shall rise again if their just cause is won through to victory. This would then turn the game into a sort of "Salvation Game," also with four levels of being familiar with the resurrection story, being willing to hear the story, taking full account of sacrifice, and then rising again with the they who sacrificed. Of course this would be a secular resurrection. In a scared resurrection game one gets more than just 16 points. One gets life eternal.

Let us take stock. What is really involved in turning the Gettysburg Address into a game—in "reading" or "tracking" it as a game. We should begin by thinking about why people like games. They like challenges, especially if nothing much is at stake other than public embarrassment if one isn't very good or fails to go all the way to the top. People like games because they enjoy the satisfactions of taking things one step at a time. It appeals to their sense that it's quite OK to learn slowly. They life the high scores that potentially await them. Lincoln never played a video game, but he seems to have understood this psychology, as he takes his listeners, whom we are now, with some insight, calling players, into the stuff of challenges, step-wise learning, and rewards. This is really an American Citizenship Game: this is how you play and win the game of true civic responsibility.

So, what we have learned for the classroom is: Turning a text into a game in an excellent way to track the contents of the text, as well as the psychological appeal of the text. It is a fine way to read and study, and it is resonant with the game structure with which the current generation has matured.

The Miracles Game

Again, in order to make readers more comfortable with the spirit and methodology of progressive tracking games, we shall offer two more examples: one from the philosopher David Hume and the other from the poet Sharon Olds.

One of the mot off-studied of all Hume's essays is the one called "Of Miracles," published in 1746. In it, Hume outlined his reasoning for a religious age about the believability of miracles, which he doubted. Here is a passage; suppose the professor assigned students to turn it into a progressive tracking game—as a key to understanding the gist of Hume's argument.

Suppose, for instance, that the fact, which the testimony endeavors to establish, partakes of the extraordinary and the marvelous; in that case, the evidence, resulting from the testimony, admits of a diminution, greater or less, in proportion as the fact is more or less unusual. The reason why we place any credit in witnesses and historians, is not derived from any connection, which we perceive a priori, between testimony and reality, but because we are accustomed to find a conformity between them. But when the fact attested is such a one as has seldom fallen under our observation, here is a contest of two opposite experiences; of which the one destroys the other, as far as its force goes, and the superior can only operate on the mind by the force, which remains. The very same principle of experience, which gives us a certain degree of assurance in the testimony of witnesses, gives us also, in this case, another degree of assurance against the fact, which they endeavor to establish; from which contradiction there necessarily arises a counterpoise, and mutual destruction of belief and authority. I should not believe such a story were it told me by Cato, was a proverbial saying in Rome, even during the lifetime of that philosophical patriot. The incredibility of a fact, it was allowed, might invalidate so great an authority (Hume, 1985).

Here is one way, though only one among others, to re-cast this paragraph into a tracking game. The player is the reader, and Hume wants the reader to track his game instructions through progressive levels. If you get to the last level you are a good player in the game designer's eyes. The game designer is David Hume.

Level One: When you hear something not very unusual, assume that there is an alliance between the report and the reporter and credit both. (Note, by the way, the linguistic link between "credit" and "credible": the charge card companies allow us to charge items because they believe it is more credible than not that we will pay for them at some point—the longer, the better, given their interest rates!)

Level Two: Now comes the first test: When you hear something very unusual, something that you yourself have not observed and would not/never expect to observe, assume there is a contest between report and reporter. (For instance, you generally credit "Cato" as a highly reliable and truthful Roman, but now he has said that he saw a butterfly turn into an elephant. So now there is a contest, a game, a conflict, between the unusual quality of the report and the reputation of the reporter.)

Level Three: Realize that the only person who can settle the game, declare a winner, is you, to whom the report has been made. (There are of course things you can do in order to decide. You can read books on whether or not butterflies can turn into pachyderms, or you can ask Cato if anyone else has seen the miraculous transformation or call Cato's shrink to see if you can get any information on how Cato has been feeling of late. But look at the nature of the game. It is not just the normally reliable Cato versus the butterfly/elephant story. It is also Cato and the butterfly/elephant tory versus something else. It is by the standards of this "something else" that you must decide whether or not to credit Cato or discredit him and his report. Only in the final, highest Level (4) do you have a chance to discover what this "something else" is.)

Level Four: Bet, intelligently, against Cato and his story. Or: perhaps, as in the nature of bets, insist on very favorable odds. "I will bet that your story is true, perhaps, but only at a million to one odds—that would be one dollar lost if it isn't true but a million dollars gained if it is." But why is there only a million to one shot that Cato's report is incredible and wrong? Simple: Because butterflies and elephants and human beings with two eyes have been around for eons, but no one has ever reported, before, the sudden transformation of a butterfly into an elephant. No one before Cato has ever seen a butterfly and then a windy mist and a stretch of tissue and behold: where once butterfly flapped, now an elephant trumpets. This long history of not-seeing a butterfly turn into an elephant is sometimes called "the uniformity of nature," but until players have grasped this instrument of assessing credibility they will not reach Level Four. If not, then they are not really good players of the Miracle Game designed by Mr. Hume.

An alternative way of playing this game, which will especially capture its gameiness, is to post a number that both the credibility of the reporter and the credibility of the report must add up to. That number could be 16. If the reporter is unusually trustable, one might give him a 10, but if the story seems preposterous, one might award the story only a 1 for a total of 11. But if the reporter is somewhat reliable, the player might give him a 6 and if his story seems believable, then one might award the whole mélange a 16. That would barely qualify, but a perfect score would be 20 of course. A 16 might mean, "I believe this, but there's a real chance it might be false." A 20 would be a score of absolute confidence. That is the sort of life problem that Hume is up to in this pivotal paragraph from "Of Miracles."

Students of the current generation have a gaming mindset and are accustomed to progressive levels of skill. Educators making assignments to recast texts into progressive games will need to stress the analogies between video games and the task at hand. There is the intro level of skill, which is usually not very demanding.

Here it is fairly easy to grasp that when good old Joe tells us that he saw Bill last week, it is not an usual sighting and Joe (call him Joe Cato) is someone whose word has generally ben trustworthy. Or, at the introductory level of conceptual skill, it is not hard to understand that if all the experts say that wooly mammoths are extinct and no one reports seeing one, it is easy to believe that they are gone.

But higher levels are harder, as in the temporary confusion of being told something quite implausible by someone who is usually reliable. Of course, the example of the butterfly and the elephant is an easy one. Harder would be to deal with a report, from a usually credible person, that your best friend, equally reputable, has embezzled a considerable sum of money from a bank. But Level 2 requires one to acknowledge that now there is a game on: between the reporter and the report. Now the reporter is up against an opponent: the apparent implausibility of what he has to report.

Level 3 is a bit harder still because it requires the player to realize that there are now really three contestants in the game: the reporter, the report, and the person to whom the report has been made, who is also the player. And it is the player, the latter of the three, who must judge and declare a victory: ether it goes to the reporter, who general probity makes his report believable; or it goes against the reporter, whose reputation is exceeded by the sheer preposterousness of what he has reported. Again, in the elephant/butterfly business, that is an easy call to make. In other instances, where the story seems absurd but is surely possible, it is a much harder call for the player—also now a referee—to make.

Level Four is the hardest of all, because it requires an application of the principle of the "uniformity of nature." And here again it is not always an easy thing to apply—that's why it's Level Four material. Nor is it always easy to know for sure. If Joe Cato says that your best friend has called you the world's worst jerk behind your back, then you may have a very difficult time applying the "uniformity of nature" to a situation involving the equally (usually) reliable Joe and your best friend, especially as Joe has said that it was to him, and to him only, that your best friend said you were a jerk.

In "Of Miracles" Hume spoke to a still pious age that still believed in miracles and urged them to believe in the uniformity of nature over miraculous reports (Hume, 1985). But the essay has a long reach and goes beyond, in his implications, the age of miracles. The Belief Game, which is what the Miracle Game has become in contemporary times, is a hard one to play. But students have, as we've noted, a gaming mentality and are presumably ready to learn.

The Bus Stop Game

Assignment from the English professor: Recast the following poem, "I Could Not Tell," by Sharon Olds into a progressive tracking game and show what insights you gained from said transformation.

I could not tell I had jumped off that bus,
that bus in motion, with my child in my arms,
because I did not know it. I believed my own story:
I had fallen, or the bus had started up
when I had one foot in the air.
I would not remember the tightening of my jaw,
the irk that I'd missed my stop, the step out
into the air, the clear child

gazing about her in the air as I plunged
to one knee on the street, scraped it, twisted it,
the bus skidding to a stop, the driver
jumping out, my daughter laughing
Do it again.
I have never done it
again, I have been very careful.
I have kept an eye on that nice young mother
who lightly leapt
off the moving vehicle
onto the stopped street, her life
in her hands, her life's life in her hands (Olds, 1980).

These recasting assignments may be challenging and take work to get proficient at. But there are questions one may ask that will help immediately. One is this: If it's a progressive game, what is the end game—making progress towards what? Leaving aside for the moment the literary side of a literary poem, for but only for a moment, the answer would seem to be obvious: the end game is to get off the bus safely, without accident. And if that's how one would "win" the game, then the poet is presumably the player, and the four levels would be: 1: Recall that when you leave the bus you will be responsible for both your life and that of the child you are holding. 2: Be alert for your stop. 3: Wait until the buss has come to a full stop. 4. Step carefully onto the curb. At poem's end the poet says that she has now mastered this game and learned her lesson from the accident before. If the end game, on the other hand, were "to have an accident without intending to while getting off the bus," then the poem would be that game: 1: Be in a world of your own while on the bus. 2: Be unsure whether you forgot your stop or not. 3: Have not a clue whether or not the bus started moving when you and your child tried to get onto the curb. 4: Fall on the cement and have no idea what had had happened to cause the dangerous incident.

So that's the poem: the difference, the tension between these two games, the one that was played through most of the poem's recounting, and the one the poet says she's playing now. Most of the poem is taken up with Game 2, but there is a vow at poem's end to keep playing Game 1. Also note: Game 1 is played by attending to two major stops: the place to get off and the stationery condition of the bus. Yet for all the stress on safety through stops, the poem runs on and on very rapidly, as though to mock these necessary stops. It's only when the poem "stops" that the poet belatedly honors Game 1, which is based on stops. To play Game 2 well, you have to forget all about stops. You have to flow in a world of your own.

Maybe, in fact, it is the poet who plays Game 2 and the mother who plays Game 1. And once you track the poem this way—by tracking two different bus stop games (a safe Game 1 and a breakneck Game 2), one may see that the poem is a poem about being a poet instead of a mother.

This in turn raises two questions: First, how many texts "track" by playing two games off each other: one with X quality and the other with Y quality. How much argumentative and literary and intellectual energy comes from this dialectic of two tracking games, each with its own steps and levels and end games? Discuss in class. Debate. Second, this poem may be metamorphosed into a Progressive Tracking Game., but it may also be recast as a Thermostatic Tracking Game. Let us see how in the next section, as we move from Testing and Progressive Games to Thermostatic ones.

REFERENCES

Fitzgerald, F. S. (1995). *The great Gatsby*. Scribner Paperback Fiction.

Hume, D. (1985). *Of miracles*. Open Court Classic.

Lincoln, A. (1995). *The Gettysburg address and other speeches*. Penguin Books.

Olds, S. (1980). *Satan says*. University of Pittsburgh Press.

Chapter 32
Playing With Auditory Environments in Audio Games:
Snake 3D

Markus Spöhrer
University of Konstanz, Germany

ABSTRACT

Audio games highlight audio as the major narrative, ludic, and interactive element in the process of gaming. These games enroll the players in the process of gaming and distribute agency by translating auditive cues into interactive "pings" and provide a potential for an auditory virtual space. Designed for either blind persons or as "learning software" for hard-of-hearing people, audio games dismiss graphical elements by using the auditory ludic elements and foreground auditory perception as a main condition for playing the game. Spöhrer demonstrates this by using the example of 3D Snake, which needs to be played with headphones or surround speakers. The game uses verbal instructions and different sound effects to produce an auditory image of a snake that can be moved with the computer keyboard. In this auditory environment, the relation of both human and non-human elements (e.g., controller devices, the arrangement of speakers, cultural practices of gaming, aesthetic devices, and software configurations) produce and translate a specific mode of auditory perception.

INTRODUCTION

Within those branches of Media Studies concerned with digital games, usually labelled *Game Studies*[1], the auditory dimensions of 'digital gaming' have only recently attracted the attention of the academic discourse: Only ten years ago, "articles on video game music [were] few and far between" (Munday, 2007, p. 51) within the upcoming field of *Game Studies* and merely a "niche" (Röber & Masuch, 2005, p. 1). Meanwhile, this situation has changed – at last a bit – with the publication of a range of articles and books on video game sound design, the theory and practice of game sound and music as well as their relation to narrative and gameplay (e.g. Munday, 2007; Collins, 2008; Collins, 2013; Austin, 2016;

DOI: 10.4018/978-1-6684-7589-8.ch032

Summers, 2016, Domsch, 2016). Despite such publications that point out to the crucial role that the auditory aspects play for digital games, it seems that in most of the research dealing with digital games, visual aesthetics is attributed the most important factor in digital gaming. Moreover, if one considers the common and widely accepted definitions of video or computer games, the visual element respectively graphics are a defining attribute or even a condition for 'playing the game'. See for example the following definition of 'video game':

By definition, the video game is a visual medium, and one that combines information processing and interaction, often in such a way that one relies on the speed of the other. A large part of playing a video game involves reading and interpreting the graphics of the game, for navigation and other goal-oriented activities such as collecting or using objects and interacting with the right characters, and so on. (Wolf, 2006, p. 193)

In this respect, the auditory aspects of gaming are frequently considered a 'supporting aesthetic device' or "decorative effects" (Gärdenfors, 2003, pp. 111) only and thus ,seeing' is more important than 'hearing' when it comes to handling the interface or interacting with the game, executing the ludic components as well as following the game's narrative – this might also be related to the recent studies on visual culture or even be considered a symptom of such (e.g. cf. Mirzoeff, 2001). It is true that "[c]urrently game interfaces mostly rely on graphics to convey information to the player" (Garcia & de Almeida Neris, 2013, p. 229). And although some of the most popular and recent 'mainstream' games sporadically implement ludic auditory sequences – such as the blind 'Clicker' creatures in *The Last of Us* (Naughty Dog, 2013), that react to sound only and thus shift the focus on auditory cues –, these games rely heavily on visuals ('graphics') in the interactive process established between the player and the gaming dispositive (cf. Waldrich, 2016): „Many of the game aspects, e.g. player-game interaction, scenery and scenario, guidelines, tutorials and others, are primarily communicated through colors, shapes, text and visual objects" (Drossos, 2014, np) and from a commercial perspective this "is probably due to both user and developer prejudice" (Friberg & Gärdenfors, 2004, p. 149). Thus in most commercially successful games the "audio communication channel appears to be under-utilized, even though it has been shown to be effective as an interface and as a means to entertain" (Drossos et al., 2015).

This argument seems strengthened by the fact that games, such as for example the *The Last of US,* are very hard to not at all to master without the visual information provided by the graphical interface, whereas the absence of sound does not have the same effect. Though weakening the aesthetic experience, most commercially successful games can be played without the presence of sound.

Nevertheless, it would be wrong or at least an incomplete statement to consider the graphical interface of digital games as a defining element of such[2], since there is a whole range of games, so-called 'Audio Games' or sometimes called 'audio only games', that highlight and implement 'audio' as the major narrative, ludic and interactive element and thus foreground auditory perception as a main condition for 'playing the game'.[3] Instead of creating a ludic space by use of a graphical interface, these games' gameplay, immersive quality and interactive situation are conditioned by what can be described as "auditory interfaces" (cf. Garcia & de Almeida Neris, 2013, p. 229). Dependent on the software, the sensory capacities and gaming skills of the players as well as the setup of the socio-technical environment of these games or the peripherals and devices (the 'hardware') that are used, such auditory interfaces can emerge in different forms and shapes or genres – and are not necessarily 'simply' interactive audio books. There are various different ways of generating "auditory objects" (e.g. characters, items or obstacles) and gameplay mechanisms, enabling "navigation and orientation in audio game scenarios or worlds" (e.g. directions or spatial limitations or narration of the game world) or rendering aesthetic elements (Garcia & de Almeida Neris, 2013, p. 230) as well as creating "eye-free" (Rovithis et al., 2014, np) auditory setups and options menus. Audio Games enroll the player in the process of gaming and distribute agency by translating auditive (and tactile) cues into interactive "pings" (Pias, 2005; cf. Manigron & Zhang, 2016) and thus provide a potential for what can be called 'auditory immersion': As Remi Cayatte (2014) puts it, Audio Games enable the players to navigate "in a virtual space that has to be heard opposed to traditional video games in which the virtual space is mostly seen" (p. 204). To put it differently: (true) Audio Games cannot be played without sound. According to Röber and Masuch (2005) the absence of sound in Audio Games or a visual interface respectively even creates an "increased level of immersion. Similar to reading, or listening to audiobooks, this is due to the stimulated listeners phantasy, which envisions the scene in front of the mind's eye" (p. 2). However, I choose to be skeptical as far as the qualitative aspects of immersion are concerned: I agree that audio-only interfaces create a wholly different techno-sensory configuration than those games, in which gameplay is mainly conditioned by visual interactive cues – the same is true for listening to audiobooks and reading written-language books. These media require different kinds of cognitive skills, the acquisition of different kinds of cultural techniques and require a different socio-technical and socio-medial constellation. I thus suggest that Audio Games, by having "unique features" (Friberg & Gärdenfors, 2004, p. 148) – just as any other specific medium (such as literature or audiobooks) - create a very own and specific form of immersion that is beyond comparison – at least a convincing or suitable model that allows such a comparison has not yet been developed.

While the "the field of video game studies is now a healthy and flourishing one" (Perron & Wolf, 2009, p.1), since now all sorts of academic fields are concerned with video games as well as a wide range of approaches is used and tested for digital games, Audio Games are still widely neglected by academic discourse. This is remarkable, since these games not only provide astonishing possibilities for research on accessibility (e.g. blind persons) (Drossos et al., 2015), education (cf. Rovithis et al., 2014; Araujo et al., 2017) and therapeutic uses (cf. Targett & Fernström, 2003), challenges for video game design (cf. Garcia & Almeida Neris, 2013), and insights into socio-technical or techno-sensory translations and interplays,[4] but last not but least, they provide suitable forms of entertainment (cf. Targett & Fernström, 2003).[5] Although the academic interest in Audio Games is steadily growing, "most of the existing literature and research on [Audio Game]-design focuses on accessibility issues and not on mechanics, navigation, plot or narration" (Rovithis et al., 2014, np) or the player's interaction with the socio-technical arrangement of the gaming dispositive (Waldrich, 2016) and the corresponding sensory and medial effects.

On the one hand this paper addresses this issue by focusing on a specific video game example that provides a complex auditory interface – *3D Snake* – and on the other hand, in doing so, this chapter offers an application of Actor-Network Theory for the analysis of (audio)gaming situations.

Audio Games: A Short Overview

Despite the title of this chapter, I will neither give a comprehensive historical overview of Audio Games nor a compilation of different genres of audio-based games. Rather, by discussing a few specific examples, I will point out to the diversity of game mechanics and characteristics of Audio Games and problems and questions they could raise for Game Studies research. Audio Games can generally be intended as 'educational games' (usually for visually impaired persons) such as for example demonstrated by Karshmer and Paap (2010) by the example of the math game *AutOmatic Blocks* or serve as entertainment only such as *Papa Sangre* (Somethin' Else, 2010) to name the game that has gained the most academic attention so far. But of course, educational value does not exclude the entertainment factor.

Now, how do such audio-based games look – or rather: 'sound' like? Audio Games are not a recent invention and come in a great variety of genres, narratives and game mechanics, on a whole range of consoles or output devices and of course, depending on the specific soft- and hardware setups, can be controlled with a whole range of input devices – some of them even audio-based, requiring the players to use their voice in order to interact with the game. The latter also applies for "Music Games" (cf. Austin, 2016) or "rhythm games" (cf. Perron & Wolf, 2009, p. 2) respectively such as *Singstar* (Sony, since 2004), which requires the players to sing into a microphone that can be plugged into the *Playstation* console. Other examples are *Guitar Hero* (Harmonix, since 2005) that uses "other types of peripherals like the guitar-shaped controller used to simulate guitar playing" (Perron & Wolf, 2009, p. 2) or a broad spectrum of recent Audio Game Apps, that make use of the smartphone's or tablet's built-in microphone. However, oftentimes these games, although relying heavily on sound, are supported by visual or tactile interactive elements and thus do not necessarily qualify as true Audio Games or audio-only games.

While a tactile element is basically (almost) always required in a way for playing Audio Games (or digital games in general) – at least one needs to somehow 'turn on', 'feel' or 'touch' the corresponding input device –, visuals are no necessary condition for playing digital games or Audio Games respectively. An early example for such a game is the *Touch Me* – a "memory test" (Hugill & Amelides, p. 356) of which an arcade machine and handheld versions exist - released in 1974 by Atari (cf. Knoblauch, 2016). In this non-narrative mnemonic game, the player is supposed to reproduce either a sequence of blinking lights or sounds by pressing the corresponding buttons. Thus, the game can be played as an audiovisual game, a visual only game or an audio-only game – if one is musically talented enough and capable of memorizing the sequences of the musical notes randomly played by the game without peeking at the lights. One might say the same about Music Games such as *Guitar Hero*, however, it is very hard to memorize the by far more complex sequences of musical notes and their corresponding buttons on the controller-guitar, especially if one cannot *see* the visual representation and the interactive cues of the fast pacing rhythmical patterns and sequences of the songs.[6] Consequently, in contrast to many arcade or home console games with gameplay mechanics that were/are heavily conditioned by visual elements, *Touch Me* was also suited for blind persons. Many of the later Audio Games were actually produced for or by visually impaired programmers and players - in many cases amateurs or small companies:

The majority of [audio-only games] have been developed by and for the blind and visually impaired community and are mostly available as offline computer applications. [Audio-based games] are addressed as offline, online and lately mobile applications to a broader audience, since the limited use of graphics makes them friendlier to players who are not accustomed to eye-free interfaces. (Rovithis et al., 2014, np.)[7]

However, despite or especially because of their eye-free interfaces, audio-only-games, are often attributed with being 'a challenge for people whose perception or gaming experience is mainly conditioned by visuality' and thus somewhat flipping the concepts of disability and accessibility.

An example for a commercially produced game that exclusively relies on auditory elements, gameplay mechanics and narrative is WARP'S 1997 release *Real Sound: Kaze no regret* (cf. Collins, 2013, p. 24), which could be played on both *Sega Dreamcast* and *Sega Saturn*. The game was directed at both visually impaired and visually abled audiences, and was sold with instruction manuals in braille and a bag of the seeds of a typical Japanese pot plant, that could be planted and touched during playing the game (and at some point in the game had narrative relevance). The game can mainly be described as an 'interactive digital novel' or a 'digital gamebook': it featured a narrative that was solely represented by the spoken voices of voice actors and supported by an atmospheric musical score and dismissed graphical elements altogether. During the game, the display of the TV or monitor remained black. Fittingly, according to Röberand Masuch, "[t]hrough the advantages of speech and sound, audio games are especially qualified for the presentation of narrative content, as found in adventure and action adventure games" (2005, p. 2) such as *Kaze no regret*. In *Kaze no regret* the player spends most of the time listening as the adventurous love story unfolds. At critical points in the plot line, a set of bells will ring, alerting the player that he/she is now supposed to choose which way the story is going to take by pressing the corresponding buttons on the controller.

In a sense, *Kaze no regret* could be contextualized in a literary tradition or even a 'cinematic' tradition, if one compares the game to interactive (non-auditory) gamebooks such as those for example written by Steve Jackson and Ian Livingstone or early text-adventure games such as *Zork* (Infocom, 1980) or maybe even interactive movies such as *Under a Killing Moon* (Access Software, 1994). Of course one must keep in mind the translational and transformative processes and the specific characteristics that each mediatization is conditioned by and the differences in the process of perceiving the game and acting with and within the specific gaming situation produced by these conditions (cf. Waldrich, 2016; Giddings, 2008). However, what appears to be striking here, is what I would call the element of time in relation to the gameplay mechanics. In *Kaze no regret* and the other 'interactive' media I briefly mentioned, there is no pressure to react to the 'pings' or 'prompts' directed to the player within a critical time span. The interactive element and the corresponding socio-technical set-up of the Sega consoles certainly adds a ludic component to the game or even allows to consider this game a 'game'. However, in contrast to most of the popular graphics-based games or game genres like Jump 'n Runs, Beat 'em Up Games, Racing Games, Shooters etc. that highlight fast pace and require a series of quick-time-reactions or let's say: a high degree of tactile and perceptive activity and processing, this game rather produces a somewhat 'slow' gameplay-player-relationship. I'm deliberately *not* choosing the word 'passive' here, as I'm aware of the problems that arise with categorizing degrees of activity or even a too hasty differentiation of the attributes 'active' and 'passive'. Moreover I think that the terms ‚active' and ‚passive' in relation to consuming media is highly problematic – no matter whether narrative or non-narrative media are concerned. Even though (video) games are usually characterized by "active involvement" (Liebe, 2013, p. 49), reading books or watching films - activities that are usually considered to be less 'active' or 'interactive' - require active involvement from their users, too. Cognitive, perceptual and emotional involvements that are conditions for reading books or watching films are not less 'active' than handling a game controller or responding to visual, auditory or tactile cues. Especially since these media, just as video games, rely on cultural techniques or "technologies of the body" (Mauss, 1973) – for example turning the pages, holding a book in the right angle or setting up the TV, controlling a Blu-Ray player's menus etc. – that are heavily conditioned by specific bodily functions and their respective use. I suggest that media should not be compared in terms of 'more' or 'less', but instead one should rather describe how they enroll, immerse and configure users and their corresponding socio-technical setups in their very own specific way (Waldrich, 2016). I think in the case of *Kaze no regret* it might be apt to say that it can be contextualized in a literary tradition, but nonetheless interweaves specific interactive moments that are characteristic for digital gaming: In different stages and sequences of the game, *Kaze* configures the player in a specific cognitive and bodily way, that requires them to mostly sit still and listen as the narrative unfolds and prompts them at specific points in the game, allowing the player to take as much time as they want – to 'pause', one might say. As *Kaze* is still a game and as this is merely a sort of 'translation' of the socio-medial configuration of an interactive book, I choose to consider *Kaze*'s gameplay and interactive situation as a mode of 'slow-playing', a deliberate aesthetic- and gameplay-design choice that creates a comparably lower frequency of interactive prompts. This should be kept in mind as it comes to comparing *Kaze*'s gameplay and level of interactivity to those of *3D Snake*, a game that fits the genre label 'action game' and rather requires constant, fast-pacing reaction, because of the shorter intervals of interactive auditory cues.

Actor-Network Theory, Hearing and the Sensory Conditions and Effects of 'Playing With Sound'

As mentioned before and as can be universally accepted, 'sound', 'auditory information', 'auditory interfaces', their respective 'interactive cues' and narrative and ludic situations are unique and incomparable to their visual or even haptic counterparts as they represent distinctive medial situations, conditions and effects. In this respect, it is remarkable how the interplay of human sensory and perceptive capacities and conditions and effects in relation to specific gaming situations/events and dispositives (cf. Waldrich, 2016; Giddings, 2008) – in the case of Audio Games: 'hearing' – have not yet been a concern of academic discourse. Especially Actor-Network Theory (ANT) seems to be a fitting approach to describe both the conditions of playing digital games and their effects (cf. Waldrich, 2016) as well as their "heterogeneous parts, and their relationships with one another, as generative of the Game Event" (Conway & Trevillia, 2015 p. 69). While the application of Actor-Network Theory in Media Studies or for media (cf. Spöhrer, 2016a) respectively proved to be fruitful, research on ANT combined with digital gaming is still limited – notable exceptions are Cypher and Richardson (2006), Giddings (2007, 2008), Taylor (2009), Conway and Trevillian (2015) and Waldrich (2016).

Basically, following the principles of ANT (cf. Callon, 1987), games, players, peripherals or any software, hardware, physical, natural, cultural or virtual elements – be that the types of input or output devices, the spatial constellation of the room the game is played in, specific techniques of the body used to operate the hardware, the software code, the narrative or aesthetic elements of the game etc. – are not to be considered as separate units or entities. Instead playing a digital game needs to be considered an actor-network (Callon, 1987), an "event" (Giddings, 2008) or a "process" (Waldrich, 2016), in which all these elements are reciprocally linked:

The event is constituted by the coming together in play, the collusion of material and imaginary elements: the operations of games (their conventions, rules, and prescriptions), embodied knowledge and technicities (and pleasures, anxieties, frustrations, imagination), play practices (role play, toy play), screen media images and characters, virtual game worlds (and their physics, automata, and affordances), and all sorts of bodies. (Giddings, 2008, p. 13)

As a consequence, a gaming event inextricably entangles non-human as well as human elements (or actors), which are related to each other by constant mutual translations – both human and non-human actors constantly form and shape each other and distribute roles to each other.

Thus, according to ANT, there is no such thing as a permanently fixated entity.[8] Besides that, the innovative assumption of ANT is that all entities – regardless of whether human or non-human entities are concerned – are capable of distributing agency, meaning that all elements enrolled in such networks can and will be acting in some way. Thus, interaction in the event of playing a game can never be ones-sided – neither does the player control the game nor thus the game control the player: "[t]he actions of all agents, be they human, system or machine, have to influence one another in order to establish a process of interaction" (Liebe, 2013, p. 49). In this respect, by applying ANT, "a broader set of relationships must be taken into account when we consider an assemblage of computers, computer games, players, bodies, devices and all manner of other agents" (Cypher & Richardson, 2006, np). In fact, according to ANT, 'single' or 'self-containing' entities that are not interrelated to other elements or enrolled in actor-networks do not exist, but are rather a 'fiction', they are fabricated by means of framing – a necessary, productive and constitutive, yet defamiliarizing, misleading or even "damaging" (Conway & Trivillian, 2015, p. 96) condition for scientific research: the isolation and fixation of 'elements' from the 'whole' of the event for the sake of observation and description. In a lot of cases, especially in the field of Game Studies, this may lead to a range of problematic blind spots, most notably that of the relational and co-constitutional nature of gaming events. Seth Giddings describes this by using the common subject/object distinction:

[S]ubject/object distinctions in gameplay at best allow attention to only some of the gameplay event's components: the screen images but not the human player's behaviors; physical movements but not rule sets, and so on. But at worse, such distinctions deny the coconstitutional nature of gameplay as intense, intimate, and cybernetic—as relations and transformations of speed, slowness, and affect between all part(icipant)s: They break the circuit. (Giddings, 2008, p. 13)

This of course broadens the spectrum of parts or participants a game event can interrelate and be made of. Having said this, one has to note that this by no means renders obsolete the work on 'single' elements or aspects of gaming, but instead provides a valuable basis for pinpointing and interrelating them in the process of mapping the constituents of gaming events. Taylor (2009) provides a non-exhaustive list of possible elements a game event can incorporate:

Games, and their play, are constituted by the interrelations between (to name just a few) technological systems and software (including the imagined player embedded in them), the material world (including our bodies at the keyboard), the online space of the game (if any), game genre, and its histories, the social worlds that infuse the game and situate us outside of it, the emergent practices of communities, our interior lives, personal histories, and aesthetic experience, institutional structures that shape the game and our activity as players, legal structures, and indeed the broader culture around us with its conceptual frames and tropes. (Taylor, 2009, p. 332)

It seems self-evident that a single paper or researcher can never live up to the expectation to encompass all these aspects comprehensively. As Conway and Trivillian (2015) note, "[g]ames are Black Boxes: the accumulation of a vast number of objects that comes together, oftentimes incognito, to produce a Game Event" (p. 95). Thus, as game events theoretically can be made of an infinite number of interrelated elements, it is unavoidable to frame the event and thus 'cut' it and exclude a vast number of elements, in order to be able to describe it *at all*. However, by framing such fragments of events by applying Actor-Network Theory, one is urged to reflect the interrelatedness and theoretical inseparability of these elements as well as the constitutive and selective part the researcher plays in the make-up of actor-networks. As Taylor (2009) puts it:

While in the field assemblages can seem as if they are always somewhat eluding us, giving us glimpses of the whole but often leaving us feeling like we never fully capture it, the conceptual orientation this turn provides is invaluable. Centrally important is the embedded notion of the interrelation of the agents and processes that emerge through them (Taylor, 2009, p. 332).

In the most literal sense: "The presence of the researcher and the research technologies are inseparable from the networks under study" (Giddings, 2008, p. 6).

If all aspects and elements, be they human or non-human, interrelate in actor-networks and condition each other in the process of mutual translations, how then does perception – in our specific case: hearing – correlate to the interactions in gaming situations? I described 'hearing' in relation to specific socio-technical setups before (Spöhrer, 2016b), by using the example of the Cochlear Implant. In this paper, I concluded that hearing is by no means a stable constant or a 'naturally' given or fixed 'faculty'. Instead, by applying the principles of Actor-Network Theory I concluded that perception as well as 'that which is perceived' is inseparably interwoven with cultural techniques, technology and their relation to ever changing bodily 'functions': hearing is highly depending on the 'environment' it is embedded in and vice versa. I propose that the same is true for 'playing with sounds', the gaming situation in general and especially the following example of *3D Snake*, which I will use to strengthen this point.

3D Snake

If we accept this as a heuristic for the analysis of the game/game event in the following, interesting observations can be made by the example of the non-narrative Audio Game *3D Snake* (PB Games, 2004).[9] The freeware game *3D Snake* produced by the Swedish programmer Philip Bennefall is an Audio Game based on the gameplay mechanics of the classic computer and mobile phone game *Snake*. *Snake*, which certainly became most popular with the release of the early Nokia mobile phones, solely relies on visual graphics (and supporting sounds not necessarily relevant to the actual gameplay), following the popular 'casual game' principle 'easy to learn, hard to master'. In *Snake*, the player controls a dot, square, or object on a bordered plane, which visually represents the avatar – a (growing) snake - that can only move within these borders. As it moves forward and by collecting 'fruits', it leaves a trail behind, resembling a moving snake. Usually the end of the trail is in a fixed position, so the snake continually gets longer as it moves. The game is over when the snake runs into the screen border, a trail or another obstacle, or itself. As the trail, representing the tail of the snake, continuously grows longer, it gets harder to avoid the various obstacles – especially the tail itself.

3D Snake in contrast can only be played with a 3D-sound headphone or 3D-sound[10] speakers, as it dismisses the visual component altogether or rather translates the visually based interface and gameplay mechanics into an auditory one, using both verbal instructions and different 'auditory cues' (and corresponding tone pitches, sound locations and volume levels) to produce a „3D aural representations of the space" (Sanchéz & Lumbreras, 1999, p. 101). As in other Audio Games such auditory cues "describe objects, functions and actions" of the game, "[t]hey merge the previous knowledge of the listener with natural auditory associations with sound sources and causes" and "can incorporate a large variety of information simultaneously by combining and processing the audio dimensions of sound amplitude, pitch and timbre and by assigning a meaning to the corresponding objects and situations from the virtual environment" (Balan et al., 2015, p. 4). In the case of *3D Snake* the auditory cues are designed to alert the player to an object or event, though they do not 'sound like' their referents in the real-world. The latter makes senses, as in *3D Snake* such cues are used to produce spatial configurations and usually "positions are abstractions that are not associated with sounds in the real world" (Gärdenfors, 2003, p. 112).

By use of such auditory cues, the specific socio-technical setup of the game and the perceptual and cognitive effects this interplay yields, an auditory 'image'[11] of the snake is produced, which can be moved by the player by using the computer keyboard or a game controller. According to Collins (2013) this is a phenomenon that can be observed for Audio Games and their players in general:

Research into these types of spatially rendered audio-based games has demonstrated that both sighted and visually impaired players are able to conceptualize a physical game space in the absence of visuals. Even without visuals, audio-based games create a mental space in the player's mind that the player can navigate through their mental mapping of the game's environment. (Collins, 2013, p. 24)

Regardless of whether the players are sighted or not, the game thus demands a high degree of skill and capacity of reaction and also requires the cognitive ability to 'imagine' where the snake might hit the obstacle next, in order to move it away from the corresponding obstacle.[12] In this respect, gameplay-wise, *3D Snake* is a fast-paced game, prompting the player to react in a high frequency. A player that sits still for too long or cannot react fast enough is faced with a 'game over' notification and will have restart the game from the beginning.

Similar to *Kaze no regret* the screen of the output device (usually a computer display) remains white during playing the game. The three different options in the game's menu are announced verbally as soon as the application is executed. By giving instructions like 'start new game', the game already creates an auditory yet rudimentary space, which is spatially structured solely by use of auditory cues spoken by a female voice: 'up' and 'down'. However, as soon as the game starts, the gameplay mechanics as well as the binaural interactive cues or pings produced by the game exclusively emerge in the form of non-verbal auditory signals. The game thus relies on the perception and comprehension of binaural sounds by the player, which are created by the specific socio-technical setup of the game (most notably 3D-Headphones and the binaural soundscape the software creates) as well as the 'sound production technique' used to program and produce the game: binaural sound production "replicates the natural hearing cues created by our ears and captures sound with two microphones used to record 3D stereo sound" (Mangiron & Zhang, 2016, p. 86). The game thus relies on an ideal 'normal' hearing player and consequently, in order to enable playing the game, "effectively mimics the way ['normal' hearing] humans actually hear" (Hugill & Amelides, 2016, p. 359) – at least from a perspective that determines the 'ideal player' of such games as a person, whose perception has been conditioned by certain historical and cultural discourses and practices of 'normal hearing'.[13]

In some Audio Games, especially those that are non-narrative or in non-narrative sequences of such games, and most certainly *3D Snake*, "[s]ome objects and events do not relate to sounds in any straightforward way. It can then be necessary to assign the intended meaning to a completely abstract, musical sound" (Gärdenfors, 2003, p. 112). This is especially true for *3D Snake*, as the sounds used to create its auditory spatial configuration are abstract synthetic sounds, but still are in some way associated with certain everyday 'auditory conventions'. Comparable to acoustic park distance control systems, that symbolize 'attention' or 'danger' or a least undesirable, approaching objects, *3D Snake* works with intervals of two distinct sound signals, which change their frequency according to the events during gameplay: the first is a 'wind' sound, representing the distance of the snake to the walls, and the second is a 'bing bing bing' sound, representing the location of the fruits. As soon as the snake starts to move, the distance to a wall or the fruit changes and thus the frequency of the corresponding sound signals change as well: "The effect of the rushing wind sound is that the board sounds like it's suspended in the air; this provides quite an immersive gaming experience and gives credence to the claim that the game is '3D'" (Davies, 2013, p. 39). By use of these sounds, the game produces a "spatial cognitive representation map" (Balan et al., 2015, p. 5-6) that allows to locate both the borders of the field in which the snake can move and the objects within this field. In this respect, it is paramount that a 3D-headset is used to enable binaural 3D-hearing/playing and not for example ordinary stereo-speakers or stereo-headphones:

Stereo positioning is used to spatially distinguish the sounds of objects. It allows the sound to traverse from left to right, and vice versa. These sounds are critical for the player and his/her understanding of the game. Yet stereo positioning only gives the player one dimension, which is a constraint compared to the two dimensions of a screen. On the other hand, binaural localization with four or five channels produces a feeling of being surrounded by a unique sound field. This occurs because every channel conveys different information, a different form of sound, so the user has a sensation of sound coming from one direction. (Delíc & Sedlar, 2016, p. 358)

Thus, with the 3D-headset mounted to the head of the player and in relation to the player's auditory perception and cognitive processes, the game creates an immersive 3-dimensional soundscape, through which the audio-snake can be steered on its mission to collect the randomly emerging fruit-sounds by pressing the up-down-left-right buttons on the keyboard – a mission that highly depends on the reaction skills of the player, the cognitive capacity of the player to imagine this soundscape as an interactive ludic space, as well as its reciprocal relation to the management and handling of the control devices. In contrast to narrative Audio Games like *Kaze no regret* that heavily rely on story elements, *3D Snake* is a non-narrative game. This point relates to discussions on narratology vs ludology, which oftentimes come to the conclusion that as soon as narrative aspects are highlighted in a game, the interactive or ludic elements are consequently repressed and vice versa (cf. Furtwängler, 2001). With *3D Snake* being a purely non-narrative game, it dismisses reliance on literary or oral traditions or 'verbal aids' as a gameplay mechanic or as interactive cues and thus avoids 'slow-pacing' narrative breaks that reduce the interactive and ludic moments. Consequently, by using non-verbal sounds only it produces a gaming situation that resembles other fast pacing and skill intensive digital games.

Interestingly the 'snake avatar' itself is not associated with an auditory cue, but instead is rendered or framed by the two auditory cues that represent the distance to the wall and the location of the fruits. In contrast to other Audio Games, in which the gameplay can be "enhanced by the utilization of audio spatial positioning" (Drossos et al., 2015), in *3D Snake* this is an indispensable condition for playing the game *at all*. As an effect of this auditory environment design and the specific sensory and technological setup (binaural hearing, 3D-Headphones), the game produces – or "translates" (Callon, 1987) - an interesting kind of "allocentric frame of reference": "The allocentric frame of reference emphasizes the characteristics of the surrounding objects and does not depend on the point of view of the player" (Balan et al., 2015, p. 5). Within this "auditory ecology" (cf. Noble, 2013, p. 103), the snake itself thus is paradoxically 'unhearable' (usually one would say 'invisible') or absent and nevertheless present in the presence of the two auditory cues at first glance, but also both absent and present as a result of this actor-network. The snake is an effect of the player's cognitive processing of these cues, a mental representation that is produced by the technological configuration of the game event, the software code, a certain sound production technique (production of synthetic binaural sound and corresponding programming and the 3D-headphones) as well the sensory-motoric (re)action of the player and their influence on the peripherals. With respect to the arguments made in the ANT-section of this paper, the 'snake' is a "quasi-object" (Latour, 1993, pp. 51-55) that comes into being by the very constellation and processes of this arrangement. Fittingly Giddings (2008) describes the avatar-player-relationship as follows:

"I" referring at times to my physical body and sense of self, but at times to my actions in the game. There is a linguistic and experiential blurring of boundaries between human and machines: In the game ''I'' is at once ''myself'', ''my avatar'', and ''myself and avatar''; a hybrid human and technological entity. (p. 3).

Certainly, a specific form of 'hearing' or 'perceiving' respectively that is related to auditory orientation and localization of sound sources is not only required to play this game successfully, but also *produced* within the act of the player and the other non-human actors enrolling and translating in this very gaming situation. It is true that playing this game is conditioned by specific bodily functions – usually considered 'human' bodily functions related to the anatomy of the ear and 'hearing apparatus'. However, with respect to 'the human body', ANT does not consider the physical or biological facets of human actors as elements that can be separated from 'technology': The body, in any case, is a continuously translating, negotiated, transforming and interrelating element in actor-networks, because according to Latour (1994), "the very shape of humans, our very body, is already made in large part of sociotechnical negotiations and artifacts" (p. 59). Thus, in the case of playing *3D Snake* 'hearing', or more specifically '3D hearing', is effected by several specific listening cues, which in turn are perceived and processed in a specific way as 'information' and consequently distribute 'agency', for example hitting a specific button that moves the mental representation of the 'snake' in the supposed aural direction. 'Playing by hearing' – or 'hearing by playing' - is an interactive process that is enabled by "realtime feedback" (Röber & Masuch, 2005, p. 3), the realization of a "cybernetic circuit": "To play a digital game is to plug oneself into a cybernetic circuit. Any particular game-event is realized through feedback between computer components, human perception, imagination and motor skills, and software elements from virtual environments to intelligent agents" (Giddings, 2007, np). The auditory cues, the technological output device, the player's perceptual processes, the mental representation of the soundscape and the moving snake within this *spatial configuration* as well as the motor-sensory actions of the player are inextricably linked and translating and influencing each other in this process of actor-networking the game event: "Game worlds and temporalities, modes of presentation, puzzles and combat, engagement with computer-controlled characters, are all constantly configuring the player's experience and responding to the player's responses (Giddings, 2008, p. 9). As Landay (2014) puts it and as can be stated for this very example: "Activity that is not reciprocal, simultaneous, mutual, interruptible, is not interactivity" (p. 175). It is a gaming situation or event, in which the cognitive and perceptual processes of the player are conditioned and effects of the socio-technical setup, while in turn these processes condition, act on and effect the socio-technical setup and their respective outputs in a distinctive manner – they are mutually constituting and "com[ing] together to generate an event of gameplay" (Giddings, 2008, p .5) – each element is a (part)icipant and composed of each other:

[A] flow of information between organic and inorganic nodes, the initiation of which cannot be identified in either the player or the machine: By definition, a circuit consists in a constancy of action and reaction. In gaming, for example, not only is there the photon-neurone-electron circuit [...] there are

also macroscopically physical components of that circuit, such as the motions of finger, mouse or stick. […] Through the tactile and visual interface with the machine, the entire body is determined to move by being part of the circuit of the game, being, as it were in the loop. (Giddings, 2007, np)

CONCLUSION

A frequent argument made for Audio Games is, that since "players need to focus on aural stimuli, in order to understand and accomplish the game-play tasks", and that these games exclude or reduce visual input, they effectively "enhance the acquisition of skills, such as memory and concentration" (Rovithis et al., 2014, np). Furthermore, sighted players seem to be challenged by games that are audio-only. For example, one player of *3D Snake* states that it is a "slightly addictive, although rather frustrating game" and a "challenge" (Danger, 2017, np), as "[f]or a sighted person, it can be difficult to imagine an unknown space without the help of his/her eyes" (Jäger & Hadjakos, 2017, np). Simply put, most players are not used to playing games without the aid of visual stimuli and thus are not yet as skilled in this genre as they are when playing visually-based games – they have not yet embodied the cultural, perceptual or 'body techniques' to play these games. The abstract rules of *3D Snake* are more or less clear, when one is familiar with the rules and gameplay mechanics of games like *Snake* or similar games: 'use the keyboard and cursors on the keyboard to operate a representation of a snake and move to the direction of representations of fruits'. The knowledge and the internalization of these rule is obligatory for playing the game - regardless of whether one is sighted or not.[14] As a result of their experience with gaming, most players at least understand the goals of the game and the handling of the peripherals, simply because they learned *how these types of games work*. But in the case of *3D Snake* they cannot rely (fully) on this experience, because their knowledge about gaming is conditioned by the cultural technique of 'visual gaming'. They are simply not yet accustomed to the cultural technique of 'auditory gameplay'. I made the experience that (sighted) people who attempt to play original visual *Snake* and have never played video games in their lives before, basically do not know how to play it: they don't know which buttons to hit, they neither intuitively know that the dot represents their avatar, nor do they know what the goal of the game is. They simply cannot make sense of the pixels emerging on the screen. Finally yet importantly, at first they showed to not have the motor skills to collect the fruits in time. Playing digital games then is highly conventionalized and culturally and historically forged and dominated by visual cues and stimuli and at the same time relies on the way perception and motor skills are conditioned by these conventions and one's experience with these conventions.

The same is true for designers, since 'hearing' in relation to interaction and gameplay in the game event relies on different stimuli and cognitive processes than those used in games that mainly feature graphics. For example, Röber and Masuch (2005) note that if "the entire game, including the user interface, is represented through sound, special care has to be taken to not clutter the auditory display with too much information" (p. 4):

There is a risk that a set of continuous object sounds blend into a cacophony that makes very little sense to the listener. Sounds can be separated spatially in a standard stereo sound system. However, as stereo only represents one dimension, the images that can be conveyed are limited. If one wants communicate spatial structures closer to the complexity of graphics on a two-dimensional computer screen, some kind of surround sound system is needed. Still, there are other difficulties with positioning sounds even in a multi-channel sound system, since they tend to mix together if they are not easily distinguished from other simultaneous sounds. (Gärdenfors, 2003, p. 112)

As with actually 'playing digital games', designing games relies on specific cultural conventions or designing conventions that are mutually related to the demands of players, culturally and socio-technically forged ways of playing and the way most player's perception and sensory faculties are configured in relation to these conventions: "The lack of conventions to draw material from is obviously a major obstacle when communication relies on non-speech sound. While Western culture has a rich tradition of visual iconography, there is no well-established auditory counterpart" (Gärdenfors, 2003, p. 114).

Based on the observations made in the analysis of *3D Snake* in this paper, I would argue that when it comes to Audio Games, not only arguments on 'accessibility' (in relation to disability) are of concern, but also the socio-technical, historical, cultural and perceptual relations and conditions that generate the game event and 'playing digital games' – the very conditions of digital gaming. It is probably true that Audio Games are a possibility for visually impaired players and that most sighted players are not accustomed to play such games – although I would argue that blind players nonetheless need to acquire and comprehend the cultural techniques and conventions that condition playing such games in order to play them. However, I'm reluctant to consider any type of game 'more' or 'less' suited, fun, complex or anything else. Rather, each single game and the corresponding constellation "provide[s] a different, challenging and immersive gameplay experience" (Mangiron & Zhang, 2016, p. 91), whereas the emphasis is on *different*: different in relation to specific conventions of playing digital games and the configuration of the gaming event, because the degree of immersion or challenge is probably a matter of perspective and subjective judgements (every game is necessarily 'immersive', else it couldn't be played *at all*). Having said that and taking the premises of ANT seriously, I would say that each game and each gaming event is different, because of their specific perceptual, cultural, personal, psychological and socio-technical conditions. Thus, instead of comparing these games or constellations to each other in the sense of a quantitative evaluation, a description of how a specific gaming event comes into being seems to be the more promising and fruitful approach.

In this respect I would conclude that *3D Snake* is not simply an 'adaption' or a 'lesser" version of the 'original' *Snake*. However, as Cayatte states for other Audio Games and as described in the introduction to this paper, I would argue that such an Audio Game "can potentially neutralize conceptions of even the most inclusive definition of video games" (p. 204), as visuality is not an excluding criterion for defining digital gaming. Also, in contrast to visually-based digital games, the socio-technical and perceptual arrangement of the gaming situation of *3D Snake* can be described as an 'auditory ecology'. A set-up composed of heterogeneous relations between human and non-human elements (e.g. controller devices, the arrangement of headphones or speakers, cultural practices of gaming or specific 'rules', aesthetic devices and software configurations, cognitive processes, software codes, the player's motor skills and reactions etc.) that produce and translate a specific mode of auditory perception (or: hearing), which in turn is reciprocally linked to the environment and the way 'playing' this game is realized. Considering the gaming event of *3D Snake* an auditory environment that enables 'playing a game with and through sounds', allows to describe the avatar-player-environment-constellation as a complex, actor-networking process that comes into being in the course of this very situation. The acknowledgment of such relationships can be a point of departure for future work that allows the researcher to investigate the ongoing processes in gaming situations – be that those of visually-based games, games focused on tactile or haptic stimuli or simply further audio-only-games.

REFERENCES

Araújo, M., Façanha, A. R., Darin, T. C. G., Sánchez, J., Andrade, R. M. C., & Viana, W. (2017). Mobile audio games accessibility evaluation. In Antona, M., & Stephanidis, C. (Eds.), *Universal access in human-computer interaction. Designing novel interactions. 11th International Conference, UAHCI 2017 Held as Part of HCI International 2017 Vancouver, BC, Canada, July 9–14, 2017, Proceedings, Part II* (pp. 242-259). Cham: Springer International.

Austin, M. (Ed.). (2016). *Music video games. Performance, politics and play.* New York, NY: Bloomsbury.

Balan, O., Moldoveanu, A., & Moldoveanu, A. (2015). Navigational audio games: An effective approach toward improving spatial contextual learning for blind people. *International Journal on Disability and Human Development: IJDHD, 14*(2), 109–118. doi:10.1515/ijdhd-2014-0018

Callon, M. (1987). Some elements of an sociology of translation: Domestication of the scallops and the fishermen St. Brieuc Bay. In J. Law (Ed.), *Power, action and belief: A new sociology of knowledge?* (pp. 196–233). London, UK: Routledge & Kegan Paul.

Cayatte, R. (2014). Where game, play and at collide. In N. Garrelts (Ed.), *Understanding minecraft. Essays on play, community and possibilities* (pp. 203–214). Jefferson, NC: McFarland.

Collins, K. (2008). *Game sound. An introduction to the history, theory and practice of video game music and sound design.* London: MIT Press.

Collins, K. (2013). *Playing with sound. A theory of interacting with sound and music in video games.* Cambridge, MA: MIT.

Conway, S., & Trevillian, A. (2015). 'Blackout': Unpacking the black box of the game event. *ToDIGRA: Transactions of the Digital Games Research Association, 2*(1), 67–100. doi:10.26503/todigra.v2i1.42

Cypher, M., & Richardson, I. (2006). *An actor-network approach to games and virtual environments.* Paper presented at Joint Computer Games and Interactive Entertainment Conference, Perth, Australia.

Danger, C. (2017). *3D Snake. Better living through technology.* Retrieved March 24, from https://www.bltt.org/software/games/3dsnake.htm

Davies, K. (2013). 3D Snake. *Cassiopeia, 5,* 38–39.

Delic, V., & Sedlar, N. V. (2010). Stereo presentation and binaural localization in a memory game for the visually impaired. In *Development of multimodal interfaces: Active listening and synchrony* (pp. 354–363). Berlin: Springer. doi:10.1007/978-3-642-12397-9_31

Domsch, S. (2016). Hearing storyworlds. How video games use sound to convey narrative. In Audionarratology. Interfaces of sound and narrative (pp. 185-195). Berlin: deGruyter.

Drossos, K., Zormpas, N., Giannakopoulos, G., & Floros, A. (2015). Accessible Games for Blind Children, Empowered by Binaural Sound. In *Proceedings of the 8th ACM International Conference on PErvasive Technologies Related to Assistive Environments* (pp. 5:1-5:8). (PETRA '15). New York, NY: Association for Computing Machinery (ACM). 10.1145/2769493.2769546

Friberg, J., & Gärdenfors, D. (2004). Audio Games: New perspectives on game audio. *Proceedings of ACM SIGCHI International Conference on Advances in Computer Entertainment Technology*, 148-154. Retrieved March 22, from extrafancy.net/idia612/research/audioGames.pdf 10.1145/1067343.1067361

Furtwängler, F. (2001). "A crossword at war with a narrative". Narrativität versus Interaktivität in Computerspielen. In P. Gendolla (Ed.), *Formen interaktiver Medienkunst. Geschichte, Tendenzen, Utopien* (pp. 369–400). Frankfurt, Germany: Suhrkamp.

Garcia, F. E., & de Almeida Neris, V. P. (2013). Design guidelines for audio games. In Human-computer interaction. Application and services (pp. 229-238). Springer. doi:10.1007/978-3-642-39262-7_26

Gärdenfors, D. (2003). Designing Sound-Based Computer Games. *Digital Creativity*, *14*(2), 111–114. doi:10.1076/digc.14.2.111.27863

Giddings, S. (2007). Playing with nonhumans: digital games as technocultural form. In *Worlds in play: International perspectives on digital games research*. New York: Peter Lang. Retrieved 31 March, from http://eprints.uwe.ac.uk/8361

Giddings, S. (2008). Events and collusions. A glossary for the microethnographic of video game play. *Games and Culture*, *0*(0), 1–14.

Hugill, A., & Amelides, P. (2016). Audio-only computer games: Papa Sangre. In Expanding the horizon of electroacoustic music analysis (pp. 355-375). Cambridge, UK: UP.

Jäger, A., & Hadjakos, A. (2017). *Navigation in an audio-only first person adventure game*. Paper presented at The 23rd International Conference on Auditory Display (ICAD), Pennsylvania State University. 10.21785/icad2017.033

Karshmer, A., & Paap, K. (2010). AutOMathic Blocks: Supporting learning games for blind students. *Business Analytics and Information Systems*. Retrieved March 24, from http://repository.usfca.edu/at/19

Knoblauch, W. (2016). *Simon*: The prelude to modern music video games. In M. Austin (Ed.), *Music video games. Performance, politics and play* (pp. 25–42). New York, NY: Bloomsbury.

Landay, L. (2014). Interactivity. In M. P. Wolf & B. Perron (Eds.), *The Routledge companion to video game studies* (pp. 175–183). New York, NY: Routledge.

Latour, B. (1993). We have never been modern. Cambridge, MA: UP.

Latour, B. (2010). A collective of humans and nonhumans. In C. Hanks (Ed.), *Technology and values. Essential readings* (pp. 49–59). Malden, MA: Wiley-Blackwell.

Liebe, M. (2013). Interactivity and music in games. In P. Moormann (Ed.), *Music and game. Perspectives on a popular alliance* (pp. 41–62). Wiesbaden, Germany: Springer VS.

Mangiron, C., & Zhang, X. (2016). Game accesability for the blind. Current overview and the potential of audio application as the new forward. In Researching audio description. New approaches (pp. 75-96). London: Palgrave MacMillan.

Mauss, M. (1973). Techniques of the body. *Economy and Society*, *2*(1), 70–88. doi:10.1080/03085147300000003

Mäyrä, F. (2008). *An introduction to game studies. Games in culture.* Thousand Oaks, CA: Sage.

Miller, K. (2012). *Playing along: Digitals, YouTube and virtual performance.* New York: Oxford UP. doi:10.1093/acprof:oso/9780199753451.001.0001

Mirzoeff, N. (2001). *The visual culture reader.* London, UK: Routledge.

Munday, R. (2007). Music in video games. In Music, sound and multimedia: From the live to the virtual (pp. 51-67). Edinburgh, UK: UP. doi:10.3366/edinburgh/9780748625338.003.0004

Noble, W. (2013). *Self-assessment of hearing.* San Diego, CA: Plural.

Perron, B., & Wolf, M. P. (2009). Introduction. In B. Perron & M. P. Wolf (Eds.), *The video game theory reader 2* (pp. 1–22). New York, NY: Routledge.

Perron, B., & Wolf, M. P. (Eds.). (2014). The Routledge companion to video game studies. New York, NY: Routledge.

Pias, C. (2005). Die Pflichten des Spielers. Der User als Gestalt der Anschlüsse. In Hyperkult II: Zur Ortsbestimmung analoger und digitaler Medien (pp. 313-342). Bielefeld, Germany: Transcript. doi:10.14361/9783839402740-014

Röber, N., & Masuch, M. (2005). *Playing Audio-only Games. A compendium of interacting with virtual, auditory worlds.* Paper presented at Digital Games Research Conference 2005, Changing Views: Worlds in Play, Vancouver, British Columbia, Canada.

Rovithis, E., Mniestris, A., & Floros, A. (2014). *Educational audio game design: Sonification of the curriculum through a role-playing scenario in the audio game 'Kronos'.* Paper presented at the 9th Audio Mostly Conference, Aalborg, Denmark. 10.1145/2636879.2636902

Sanchéz, J., & Lumbreras, M. (1999). Virtual environment interaction through 3D audio by blind children. *Cyberpsychology & Behavior, 2*(2), 101–111. doi:10.1089/cpb.1999.2.101 PMID:19178246

Spöhrer, M. (2016a). Applications of Actor-Network Theory in Media Studies. A research overview. In M. Spöhrer & B. Ochsner (Eds.), *Applying the Actor-Network Theory in Media Studies* (pp. 1–19). Hershey, PA: IGI Global.

Spöhrer, M. (2016b). A cyborg perspective: The cochlear implant and actor-networking perception. In Applying the Actor-Network Theory in Media Studies (pp. 80-95). Hershey, PA: IGI Global.

Summers, T. (2016). Understanding video game music. Cambridge, MA: UP. doi:10.1017/CBO9781316337851

Targett, S., & Fernström, M. (2003). Audio games. Fun for all? All for fun? *Proceedings of the 2003 International Conference on Auditory Display.* Retrieved March 21, from dev.icad.org/Proceedings/2003/TargettFernstroem2003.pdf

Taylor, T. L. (2009). The assemblage of play. *Games and Culture, 4*(4), 331–339. doi:10.1177/1555412009343576

Waldrich, H. (2016). The home console dispositive. Digital games and gaming as socio-technical arrangements. In M. Spöhrer & B. Ochsner (Eds.), *Applying the Actor-Network theory in media studies* (pp. 174–196). Hershey, PA: IGI Global.

Wolf, M. P. (2006). On the future of video games. In In Digital media: Transformations in human communication (pp. 187-195). Brussels: Peter Lang.

ENDNOTES

[1] See for example Mäyrä (2008) for an earlier introduction to the field or Wolf & Perron (2009) for a more recent, comprehensive overview of the general terminology, concepts and research objects of Game Studies.

[2] Despite the fact that the first video games and gaming systems did not feature sound (cf. Liebe, 2013, p. 41).

[3] I should note that there is a crucial difference between ‚interacting‘ with sound (in the most ludic sense) and listening to sound (cf. Collins, 2013, pp. 2-3), just as there is a crucial difference between listening to music or producing music by playing an instrument, which in fact, even on the etymological level, implies a ludic component (Cf. Austin, 2016). With regard to 'playing the music' (in contrast to listening to music), Kiri Miller (2012) provides the example of the Music game *Guitar Hero*, in which the basic gameplay "involves translating the on-screen notation back into music by pressing buttons on a plastic guitar or striking the pads on a simulated drum kit" (p. 85). Such an interactive process or a translational process established between the player and the socio-technical setup is a constitutive condition of all sorts of digital gameplay (no matter whether visual or Audio Games are concerned) and thus the ludic interaction with sound needs to be considered an entirely different type of action than the non-ludic 'listening'.

[4] I covered this topic, that in itself can be considered a research desideratum in Game Studies discourse, in a talk at the NECS 2017 conference in Paris (July 1, 2017) with the title 'Audio Games: Playing with sound in *Snake 3D*'. For the abstract of the talk see the following link: https://mediaandparticipation.com/2017/06/28/necs2017-panel-sense-app-ility/

[5] Rovithis et al. (2014) state that it is especially the exclusive "concentration on sonic information" that is required from the player that make Audio Games "a suitable medium [...] for entertainment" (np) Also see for example Collins' (2013) and other players' description of the Audio Game *Papa Sangre*: "The lack of images is one element that makes it more frightening than most games, as players and critics comment: 'And even though you can't see anything, or maybe because of it, Papa Sangre is terrifying' (Webster 2010); 'In fact, every time you hear anything in Papa Sangre your heart races, even when it shouldn't. Babies crying, telephones ringing — it's all scary to me now' (Hall 2011); 'The pressure & anxiety really teases out the imagination. Real panic sets in when one steps on a bone. Who needs graphics?' (re7ox in Papa Sangre 2011); 'Enjoying playing Papa Sangre very much. The most I've ever concentrated while playing a game' (rooreynolds in Papa Sangre 2011); 'Papa Sangre is great. I played it at the weekend. It reminds me why the radio has the best pictures' (DominicSmith in Papa Sangre 2011)" (2013, pp. 24-25).

6   In fact there are a range of videos of blind players on *YouTube*, who are very skilled at playing some of the more complex songs of *Guitar Hero*. One problem is, that the keys on the controller-guitar do not correspond with the strings on a 'real' guitar and thus are related to the notes and tunes in the game in an arbitrary manner. The four buttons of the *Touch Me* instead each are firmly related to one of the four notes and thus, as soon as the position of the buttons is memorized, there is no need to memorize the whole pattern of the song, but instead allows for an 'organic' interactive reaction to the sounds being played.

7   Two extensive online libraries for both online and offline audio based games and audio only games can be found on www.audiogames.net and www.blind-games.com.

8   Nevertheless, actors can be 'metastable', meaning that the relationships they forged with other actors in such actor-networks are stable over a longer period of time and somewhat resistant to translations (cf. Latour, 1987, p. 137).

9   The game can be downloaded for free from https://www.bltt.org/software/games/3dsnake.htm

10   According to Balan et al. (2015) for most Audio Games, "playback on headphones is superior to loudspeakers and undoubtedly preferred by blind players, as they perceive the sound more accurately without losing salient directional information" (p. 5).

11   As Collins (2013) states and what is certainly true for sighted players that are experienced with playing the original, visual versions of *Snake*: "The separation of sound from source allows mental imagery to dominate the listener's mind. This mental imagery is a result of our synesthetic experience of sound as a component of a multisensory integration: we typically experience sound in association with image, and thus when the image is not apparent, we might still mentally 'see' that image. The sound without image is not disembodied, in other words, because of its corporeal, haptic, and visual associations (pp. 24-26).

12   In contrast to the original *Snake*, in *3D Snake*, as soon as a fruit is collected, the tail of the avatar does not grow, but instead the snake moves faster within the auditory space. As one player describes: "As each piece of fruit is collected the movement of the snake gets faster and so quickly starts getting much more difficult" (Danger, 2017).

13   This statement was made for the game *Papa Sangre*, which can be considered analogous to *Snake 3D* as far as the technical setup and the sound design as well as a specific 'ideal player' is concerned. Although this statement is tempting, one has to be aware of the fact that 'actual' hearing is a highly normalizing statement. One might weaken this statement by adding that this kind of '3D-hearing' is a cultural technique that is conditioned and stabilized by a practiced way of hearing that, historically and culturally speaking, was stabilized as 'normal', 'actual' or 'natural'. I'm adding this concern since these games and the corresponding research usually raises questions about accessibility and from the perspective of a deaf or hard-of-hearing person or even from a critical academic perspective, binaural Audio Games might be considered as thoroughly excluding.

14   I'm aware that the way sighted and blind players practice such games usually differ significantly, but this does not change the fact that the knowledge of specific rules and gameplay mechanics and the experience with certain (motor) skills condition whether a player perceives a game as 'difficult', 'easy' or 'incomprehensible'.

Chapter 33
The Development of the Online Player Type Scale:
Construct Validity and Reliability Testing

Nazire Burçin Hamutoğlu
https://orcid.org/0000-0003-0941-9070
Kırşehir Ahi Evran University, Kırşehir, Turkey

Yavuz Samur
https://orcid.org/0000-0003-4269-7099
Bahçeşehir University, Istanbul, Turkey

Murat Topal
Sakarya University, Sakarya, Turkey

Deniz Mertkan Gezgin
Trakya University, Edirne, Turkey

Mark D. Griffiths
https://orcid.org/0000-0001-8880-6524
International Gaming Research Unit, Psychology Division, Nottingham Trent University, Nottingham, UK

ABSTRACT

The present study outlines the development of the Online Player Type Scale (OPTS) utilizing a motivational taxonomy developed. This taxonomy was comprehensively reviewed to create scale items, and the conceptual framework of the scale was defined. The study group was comprised of 1,479 students attending grades 5 to 8 of a private school. A purposive sampling method was used to recruit the study group, and playing any videogame frequently was the criterion to be included in the sample. The construct validity and reliability testing showed the OPTS comprised four factors: achievement-oriented (ACH), socialization-oriented (SOC), exploration-oriented (EXP), and competition-oriented (COMP). The Cronbach alpha internal consistency coefficients and composite reliability coefficients were 0.89 and 0.99 for KIL, 0.83 and 0.98 for EXP, 0.83 and 0.98 for SOC, and 0.94 and 0.99 for ACH. It is concluded that the Online Player Type Scale is a valid and reliable instrument for assessing gaming motivation.

DOI: 10.4018/978-1-6684-7589-8.ch033

INTRODUCTION

Videogames are played by millions of individuals all over the world and are types of entertainment digital media which have rules that are independent from the real world (Garris, Ahlers, & Driskell, 2002). With advancements in digital technology, videogames are now more realistic in sound, graphics, and storytelling, and have become increasingly better in simulating reality. Videogames can now be distributed and played online via personal computers, mobile devices (such as tablets and smartphones), and dedicated game consoles. One of the most well-known examples of this is the evolution of multi-user dungeon (MUD) games to massively multiplayer online (MMO) games. Although they are similar in gameplay, the main difference between these types of games are that MMOs can support more online players with better graphical interfaces and virtual worlds (Encyclopedia of Science Fiction, 2018).

MMOs are games in which millions of players can assume one of several roles offered by the game simultaneously in virtual worlds. They are games played within a digital environment comprising 2D or 3D virtual worlds where gamers play with others via their avatar (Steinkuehler and Williams, 2006; Yee, 2006b). There are also predefined boundaries and rules within MMOs (Williams, Ducheneaut et al., 2006). MMO games can be complex games that can require thousands of different decisions and making smart choices about character development (Nardi, Ly, & Harris, 2007). A typical MMO player can walk around a virtual world, go hunting, collect plants and mines, go fishing, carry out tasks, fight, beat their competitors, have a job, and/or increase their level to become stronger in the game either alone or with other players (Steinkuehler & Duncan, 2008). Furthermore, players can join several social groups with short-term objectives to more longstanding groups which can extend to real world and where continuous relationships be established (Cole & Griffiths, 2007; Williams, Ducheneaut et al., 2006). MMOs possess multiple types of motivations and actions that can be present in real life but may be realized more easily via gaming in virtual environments.

One of the most important components in gaming behavior is players' motivations and their corresponding actions (Ghuman & Griffiths, 2012). Studies have shown that various types of action and motivations within games are important variables in predicting individuals' levels of having fun while playing games (Bartle, 1996; Lazarro, 2004). Lazarro (2004) claimed there were four motivation types that unlock emotions. These are (i) hard fun (i.e., players having to overcome difficult obstacles to progress in the game in pursuit of winning), easy fun (i.e., players just enjoying the game even if they do not win), altered states (i.e., players engaging in the game because it makes them feel good psychologically and changes their mood for the better), and the people factor (i.e., players wanting to socially interact with others in the game).

Kim and Ross (2006) identified five different gaming motivation types, namely, fantasy, competition, entertainment, social interaction, and diversion in sport video game playing. Yee (2002) conducted research investigating gamers' motivations for playing massively multiplayer online role-playing games (MMORPGs). His research suggested five motivation types; relationship, immersion, grief, achievement, and leadership. Another study by Yee (2006a) on gaming motivations MMORPGs reduced the number of main gaming motivation types for MMORPG players to three; social motivation, achievement motivation, and immersion. Achievement motivation included mechanics, advancement and competition. Social motivation included teamwork, relationships, and socializing. Immersion included escapism, customization, discovery and role-playing.

More recently, Yee, Ducheneaut, and Nelson, (2012) developed the Online Gaming Motivation Scale (OGMS). The scale has a three-factor structure based on Yee's (2006a) research. These factors are (i) social (i.e., players focus on socializing, teamwork while playing), achievement (i.e., players focus on progress completion and competition while playing), immersion (i.e., players focus on spending time exploration and discovery while playing). The OGMS developed based on the self-reports of *World of Warcraft* game players.

Based on SDT, Lafrenière, Verner-Filion and Vallerand (2012) developed the Gaming Motivation Scale (GAMS) to create a standardized tool for assessing gaming motivation. The scale comprised six dimensions including intrinsic motivation (i.e., desire to perform play activity), integrated regulation (i.e., behavior regulated through external means such as rewards), identified regulation (behavior is emitted out of choice), introjected regulation (i.e., the regulation of behavior through internal pressures such as anxiety and guilt), external regulation (i.e., behavior regulated through external means such as rewards) and amotivation (i.e., relative absence of motivation either intrinsic or extrinsic). The GAMS developed based on the self-reports of 276 video game players who engaged in over 25 different games like *Call of Duty, World of Warcraft, NHL11* (Lafrenière, Verner-Filion, & Vallerand, 2012).

Tondello et al. (2016) developed and validated the Gamification User Type Hexad Scale (GUTHS) based on the Marczewski's (2015) user type hexad framework. Marczewski's (2015) user type hexad framework is a gamification user types model. This framework created based on research on human motivation, player types, and practical design experience for personalize gamified systems, gamification and gameful designs (Marczewski, 2015). The GUTHS focused on six user types: philanthropists (i.e., they are people who altruistic and willing to give without expecting a reward), socializers (i.e., they are people who want to interact with others and create social connections), free spirits (i.e., who motivated by freedom and express themselves and act without external control.), achievers (i.e., they are who seek to progress within a system by completing tasks, or prove themselves by tackling difficult challenges), players (i.e., they are motivated by extrinsic rewards and they will do whatever to earn a reward within a system), and disruptors (i.e., they motivated by the triggering of change. They tend to disrupt the system either directly or through others to force negative or positive changes) (Tondello et all., 2016).

Considering these aforementioned studies, Bartle (1996) presents a more suitable theoretical framework for player types in MMO games. There are different types of MMO games like; MMO Battle Arena (MMOBA; *Heroes of Storm, League of Legends,* etc.), MMO Real Time Strategy Games (MMORTS; *Clash of Clans, Starcraft,* etc.), MMO First Person Shooter Games (MMOFPS; *CS-GO, Destiny,* etc.), MMO Racing Games (MMOR; *Rocket League, Asphalt,* etc.), MMO Role Playing Games (MMORPG; *World of Warcraft, Elder Scrolls Online,* etc.) etc. (Dragon Blogger Technology and Entertainment, 2008). Player types such as socializer, achiever, killer and explorer types could exist in MMO genres. Some of the typologies existing in literature was developed for specific games or games types (Kim, & Ross, 2006; Yee (2006a)). Also, Ryan, Rigby and Przybylski's (2006) typology mainly focus on engagement types and level of motivational emotions not gameplay acting. For example, it focuses on explaining whether the motivation is intrinsic or extrinsic rather than discovering whether it is for socializing. Therefore Bartle's (1996) framework focusing players actions and is more inclusive for MMO game genres. Bartle's (1996) seminal study of MUD players (arguably the forerunners of MMO players) examined players' in-game behaviors defined by the main types of in-game action. Results showed that MUD players interacted in-game in accordance with four types of action-oriented motivation, namely, achievement-oriented, socialization-oriented, competition-oriented and exploration-oriented motivations (Bartle, 1996).

According to Bartle's study, about 10% of MUD players were exploration-oriented, 10% achievement-oriented, 80% socialization-oriented, and 1% competition-oriented (Bartle, 1996). Individuals with an achievement-oriented motivation were described as 'men of duty'. Losing in-game may reduce their interest in the game. Therefore, such individuals are outcome-oriented and do not want to stop playing before achieving the tasks in hand. Individuals with a socialization-oriented motivation were described as interacting with other players socially, and benefited from the advantages of such interaction. For socializers, it is not that important to win the game or beat other players. They would rather cooperate with other players and play as a team. For these players, games are medium for them to achieve long-term social interaction. Individuals with a competition-oriented motivation were described as exhibiting similar behaviors to achievers, but it is not enough for them to achieve. Other players must lose while they are winning. They mostly focus on other players and try to beat them. They may not feel they must follow the rules to beat or eliminate other players. Finally, individuals with an exploration-oriented motivation were described as having a focus on exploring the game rather than other players and tasks. They want to explore everything in-game and discover hidden places. In short, it is fun for them to explore. Bartle's (1996) motivational player types are in Figure 1 and were called achievers, socializers, killers, and explorers.

Figure 1. Player motivation of MUD players (Bartle, 1996)

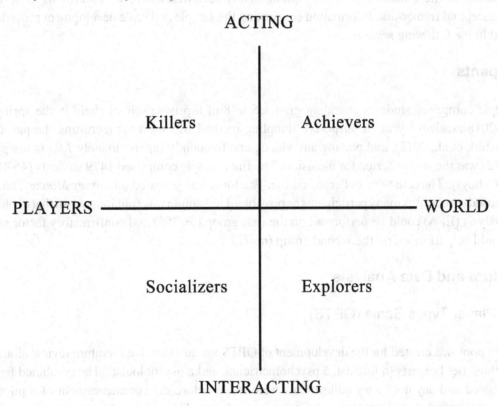

Knowing which motivations individuals are more oriented towards within MMO games and which aspects of MMO games are most attractive help researchers determine the reasons for excessive gaming and potential addiction (Ng & Wiemer-Hastings, 2005; Kuss, Louws, & Wiers, 2012). Studies have shown that different motivations and in-game actions directing the user types can be important variables in determining which motivations are important in the design of games (Orji et al., 2013, 2014), of gamification (Orji et al., 2017), internet gaming disorder (Beard, & Wickham, 2016), and MMO gaming addiction (Hsu, Wen, & Wu, 2009; Caplan, Williams, & Yee, 2009). Game design can be effective in helping players in acquiring information, supporting behavioral changes, and increasing interest in specific topics (Busch et al., 2015).

To date, there is little in the way of player type scales for MMO games in the Turkish literature (Doğan & Şahin, 2017). The Gamification User Types Hexad Scale developed by Tondello et al. (2016) was adapted into Turkish by Akgün and Topal (2018). However, this scale was developed for gamification purposes rather than for MMO-type videogames. Consequently, the present study utilized Bartle's (1996) MUD taxonomy to develop a valid and reliable Turkish instrument for identifying user types in MMO videogames.

METHODS

The present study developed a new scale, based on Bartle's theoretical framework for player types in MMO games. Bartle's taxonomy was comprehensively reviewed to create scale items to define the scale's conceptual framework. Information concerning the sample and scale development procedure are explained in the following section.

Participants

The sample comprised students attending grades 5 to 8 of a private school chain in the spring term of 2017-2018 academic year. A purposive sampling method was used for recruiting the participants (Büyüköztürk et al., 2013), and playing any videogame frequently (approximately *1.93* hours per day, $SD = 0.82$) was the sole criterion for inclusion. The final sample comprised 1479 students (46.4% girls and 53.6% boys). The data were collected online. The form was prepared on *Survey Monkey*, an online platform used to recruit as many participants as possible. The sample was split into two so that exploratory factor analysis (EFA) could be performed on the first group (n=756) and confirmatory factor analysis (CFA) could be performed on the second group (n=723).

Procedure and Data Analysis

Online Player Types Scale (OPTS)

A 45-item pool was created for the development of OPTS via an extensive literature review alongside a team of three field experts (a linguist, a psychometrician, and a psychologist). The combined feedback was evaluated and any necessary adjustments were made before the commencement of a pilot study where a small group of students tested the items for understanding. Any problems that occurred in the pilot phase were dealt with before the finalized scale.

The new scale was then subjected to validity and reliability analyses. Expert opinions were consulted for both content and face validity. EFA and CFA were carried out to test the scale's factorial validity. Kaiser-Meyer-Olkin (KMO) and Bartlett's Sphericity test values were calculated for the suitability of carrying out EFA on the data. The shared factor variance and the factor load values were calculated. The factor construct achieved with the EFA was confirmed using CFA, and the fit indexes were calculated. The results obtained on scale's construct validity were also examined with the convergent and divergent validity testing. Finally, Cronbach's Alpha internal consistency and composite reliability coefficients were used to determine the reliability of the scale. Normality, outlier, multicollinearity, and linearity assumptions that are the prerequisites of analyses were tested. It was found that there are no outliers in any of the items in the scale (Hair, Black, Babin and Anderson, & Tahtam, 2006). Reliability analysis and EFA of the scale were performed in SPSS 20.0 and CFA in AMOS 21. The findings obtained concerning the construct validity were processed using the Excel software package.

Development of the OPTS

The OPTS is a 38-item scale comprising four factors with each item assessed using a 5-point Likert scale where 1 = strongly disagree, 2 = disagree, 3 = neutral, 4 = agree, and 5 = strongly agree. The four factors were achievement-oriented (ACH; 14 items; scoring range 14-70; e.g., "I find it important to solve a puzzle which cannot be solved by anyone in online games"), competition-oriented (KIL; 10 items; scoring range 10-50; e.g., "I find it entertaining to beat the enemy in online games"), socialization-oriented (SOC; 7 items; scoring range 7-35; e.g., "It is important to be someone known in online games") and exploration-oriented (EXP; 7 items; scoring range 7-35; e.g., "The number of areas/places to explore in online games is important"). The factor with the highest mean indicates the individual's dominant player motivation. See Table 1 for the Turkish version and Table 2 for the English translation.

Table 1. Turkish version of the Online Player Type Scale (OPTS)

Çevrimiçi Oyunlar için Oyuncu Tipleri Ölçeği (Online Player Type Scale Items)
1. Çevrimiçi oyunlarda düşmanı yenmeyi eğlenceli bulurum.
2. Çevrimiçi oyunlarda düşmanı yenmeyi önemli bulurum.
3. Çevrimiçi oyunlarda başka bir oyuncunun bana zarar vermeyi planladığını öğrendiğimde, o bana zarar vermeden önce ben ona zarar veririm.
4. Bire bir oyun oynarken en iyi arkadaşımı yenmek benim için eğlencelidir.
5. Çevrimiçi oyunlarda diğer oyuncuları yenmemi sağlayacak bir özelliğe sahip olmak önemlidir.
6. Çok oyunculu bir oyunda mücadelelerde kaç tane oyuncuyu yendiğimle övünürüm.
7. Çok oyunculu bir oyunda savaşçılar grubuna katılmak benim için önemlidir.
8. Savaş oyununda mücadele etmeyi heyecan verici bulurum.
9. Çevrimiçi oyunlarda korkulan kişi olmak önemlidir.
10. Çevrimiçi oyunlarda sahip olduğum güç ile tanınmak isterim.
11. Çevrimiçi oyunlarda yeni bir yer keşfetmek önemlidir.
12. Çok oyunculu bir oyunda bir alanda yalnız başına kalmanın keşfetmek için önemli olduğunu düşünürüm.
13. Çevrimiçi oyunlarda yeni bir mekan/alan/yer açıldığında yeni alanları keşfetmek, bu alanın tarihini öğrenmek isterim.
14. Başka bir oyuncunun beni yenmek için plan yaptığını öğrendiğimde, rakibimin bilmediği yerleri keşfedip hazırlık yaparım.
15. Çok oyunculu bir oyunda "etrafı dolaşıp keşif yapanlar" grubuna katılmayı önemli bulurum.
16. Çevrimiçi oyunlarda keşfedilecek alan/mekan sayısı önemlidir.
17. Çevrimiçi oyun oynarken kimsenin bilmediği şeyleri bilme konusunda yetenekliyim.

continues on following page

Table 1. Continued

Çevrimiçi Oyunlar için Oyuncu Tipleri Ölçeği (Online Player Type Scale Items)
18. Çevrimiçi oyunlarda bir takım, klan veya birliğe kabul edilmeyi önemli bulurum.
19. Çok oyunculu bir oyunda oyun arkadaşlarımla çevrimiçi konuşmak hoşuma gider.
29. Çok oyunculu bir oyunda oyun arkadaşlarımla konuşabileceğim gizli bir alana sahip olmayı önemli bulurum.
21. Çevrimiçi oyunlarda arkadaşsız kalmak kötü bir durumdur.
22. Çevrimiçi oyunlarda zor bir engel ile karşılaştığımda, engeli aşmama yardımcı olacak oyuncuları oyuna dahil ederim.
23. Çok oyunculu bir oyunda zor bir engel ile karşılaştığımda oyun arkadaşımdan bu engeli nasıl geçeceğim konusunda yardım isterim.
24. Çevrimiçi oyunlarda başka birisinin benim hakkımda ne dediğini bilmek önemlidir.
25. Çevrimiçi oyun oynarken deneyim puanı almayı önemli bulurum.
26. Çevrimiçi oyunlarda arkadaşlarımdan daha hızlı bir şekilde oyunu bitirmeyi önemli bulurum.
27. Çevrimiçi oyunlarda herkesten hızlı yüksek deneyim seviyesine ulaşmak önemlidir.
28. Çevrimiçi oyunlarda yeni bir rozet kazanmak hoşuma gider.
29. Çok oyunculu bir oyunda deneyim puanı kazanmak için engelleri kendi başıma aşmak hoşuma gider.
30. Çok oyunculu bir oyunda milyonlarca puan değerindeki bir eve sahip olmayı önemli bulurum.
31. Çevrimiçi oyunlarda yeni bir mekan/alan/yer açıldığında alandaki yeni malzemeye/ekipmana sahip olan ilk kişi olmayı isterim.
32. Çevrimiçi oyunların sonundaki ödülleri almak hoşuma gider.
33. Çevrimiçi oyun oynarken listedeki en yüksek skora sahip olmak önemlidir.
34. Çevrimiçi oyunlarda güçlü olmak isterim.
35. Çevrimiçi oyunlarda kimsenin sahip olmadığı şeylere sahip olmak isterim.
36. Çevrimiçi oyunlarda diğer bütün nesnelerden iki kat daha güçlü bir nesneye sahip olmak önemlidir.
37. Çevrimiçi oyunlarda sahip olduğum oyun seviyesi/deneyim/score/xp puanı ile tanınmak isterim.
38. Çevrimiçi oyunlarda kimsenin çözemediği bir bulmacayı çözmeyi önemli bulurum.

Table 2. English version of the Online Player Type Scale (OPTS)

Online Player Type Scale Items
1. I find it amusing to defeat an enemy in online games.
2. I find it important to defeat an enemy in online games.
3. When I recognize that another player plans to hurt me in an online game, I beat him to the punch before he hurts me.
4. It's funny for me to defeat my best friend while playing one-vs-one.
5. In an online game, it is important to have a feature to defeat other players.
6. I boast about how many players I've defeated in a multiplayer game.
7. It is important for me to join a group of warriors in a multiplayer game.
8. I find it exciting to challenge in a war game.
9. In online game it is important to be a fearful player.
10. I want to be known for the power I have in an online game.
11. It is important to discover new places while wandering in online games.
12. I think being alone in a virtual world in a multiplayer game is important for exploring.
13. I would like to know the history of this area, discovering new areas when a new terrain / space / place is created in online games.

continues on following page

Table 2. Continued

Online Player Type Scale Items
14. When I recognize that another player plans to defeat me, I make preparations to discover and prepare places that my opponent doesn't know.
15. In a multiplayer game, I find it important to join the group of "wanderer & explorers."
16. The number of terrains/places to explore is important in online games.
17. I'm capable of knowing what no-one knows when I'm playing online.
18. I find it important to be join to a team, clan or guild in online games.
19. In a multiplayer game, I like chatting to my friends online.
20. In a multiplayer game, I find it important to have a hidden place where I can chat to my friends.
21. It is a bad situation to stay without friends in online games.
22. When I encounter a difficult task in online games, I rally with players who can help me to overcome it.
23. When I encounter a difficult task in a multiplayer game, I ask my teammates for help on how to overcome it.
24. In online games it is important to know that someone else can talk about me.
25. I find it important to gain experience points when playing online games.
26. I find it important to finish the game faster than my friends in online games.
27. In online games it is important to achieve a high level of experience faster than anyone else.
28. I like to gain a new badge in online games.
29. I like to overcome obstacles on my own to gain experience points in a multiplayer game.
30. I find it important to have a home worth millions of points in a multiplayer game.
31. I like to be the first person to have new material/equipment in the online game when a new terrain/space/place is opened.
32. I like gaining the rewards at the end of online games.
33. It is important to have the highest score on the leaderboard when playing online games.
34. I want to be strong in online games.
35. I'd like to have something in online games that nobody else has.
36. In online games it is important to have an item that is twice as powerful as all other items.
37. I would like to be known by the game level/experience/score/XP score I have in online games.
38. I find it important to solve a puzzle that no-one can solve in online games.

RESULTS

Exploratory Factor Analysis

The data obtained from 756 participants for EFA appeared to be normally distributed (Skewness=-0.780, Kurtosis= 0.607; Tabachnick & Fidell, 2007). The KMO value testing the sample size in the EFA was performed to test the scale's factorial validity which was found to be 0.97. It was then determined that the data differed significantly and were fit for factor analysis by checking Bartlett's Sphericity test (χ^2 = 15608.5, $p = 0.001$) (Büyüköztürk, 2011; Hutcheson & Sofroniou, 1999). Following the EFA, the number of items in the scale was reduced from 45 to 38. The final four-factor construct comprised 38 items with an eigenvalue higher than 1 and explaining 54.34% of total variance with a rotation of 25%.

The explained variance was above 30% and considered sufficient in test development studies in the behavioral sciences (Büyüköztürk, 2011). Values obtained in the EFA are reported in Table 3.

The factor loadings of the 38 scale items varied between 0.311 and 0.719. Factor loading of items in the KIL factor varied between 0.518 and 0.710 and explained 16.84% of total variance. Factor loadings of items in the EXP factor varied between 0.311 and 0.693 and explained 9.59% of total variance. Factor loadings of items in the SOC factor varied between 0.331 and 0.705 and explained 9.80% of total variance. Finally, factor loadings of items in the ACH factor varied between 0.331 and 0.705 and explained 18.11% of total variance. Figure 2 shows the four-factor construct of the scale. As noted above, the results indicated that the OPTS had four factors (KIL items 1-10; EXP items 11-17; SOC items 18-24; and ACH items 25-38).

Table 3. Results of the exploratory factor analysis

Items	Killers		Explorers		Socializers		Achievers	
	Common Factor Variance	Factor Load Value	Common Factor Variance	Factor Load Value	Common Factor Variance	Factor Load Value	Common Factor Variance	Factor Load Value
1	.632	.705						
2	.639	.710						
3	.523	.648						
4	.417	.563						
5	.539	.518						
6	.521	.630						
7	.515	.608						
8	.537	.620						
9	.500	.647						
10	.560	.610						
11			.535	.601				
12			.482	.646				
13			.591	.693				
14			.558	.445				
15			.594	.719				
16			.597	.651				
17			.419	.311				
18					.505	.411		
19					.515	.555		
20					.482	.468		
21					.602	.705		
22					.515	.600		
23					.550	.671		
24					.377	.331		

continues on following page

Table 3. Continued

Items	Killers		Explorers		Socializers		Achievers	
	Common Factor Variance	Factor Load Value	Common Factor Variance	Factor Load Value	Common Factor Variance	Factor Load Value	Common Factor Variance	Factor Load Value
25							.564	.567
26							.467	.577
27							.628	.653
28							.539	.583
29							.468	.577
30							.487	.596
31							.557	.605
32							.598	.569
33							.619	.614
34							.654	.583
35							.679	.712
36							.642	.668
37							.584	.617
38							.461	.570
Variance explained by the factors %	16.84		9.59		9.80		18.11	
Explained Total Variance %	54.34							

Confirmatory Factor Analysis (CFA)

The data obtained from 723 participants for CFA appeared to be normally distributed (Skewness = -0.569; Kurtosis = -0.214 for the KIL factor; Skewness = -0.834; Kurtosis = 0.694 for the SOC factor; Skewness = -0.835; Kurtosis = 0.716 for the EXP factor; and Skewness = -0.763; Kurtosis = 0.229 for the ACH factor). The factor construct achieved in the EFA was confirmed via CFA in the Turkish sample. Normality distribution of the data was taken into account and the "maximum likelihood" method was chosen for the CFA. The factor loadings of the model of scale's four-factor construct achieved in the CFA are shown in Figure 3.

As shown in Figure 3, standard regression weights of items in their factors varied between 0.50 and 0.82. This indicates that the standard values were important in terms of their factors ($p < 0.001$) (Büyüköztürk, 2012). Fit index values of the scale found in the CFA are presented in Table 4. The model appeared to have almost perfect and acceptable fit indexes ($^{1*}\chi^2/SD = 2.48$; CFI = 0.93; GFI = 0.88; AGFI = 0.87; RMSEA = 0.04; SRMR = 0.04) (Bentler, 1980; Bentler & Bonett, 1980; Bollen, 1990; Browne & Cudeck, 1993; Byrne, 2006; Byrne & Campbell, 1999; Hu & Bentler, 1999; Kline, 2011; Steiger, 2007; Tanaka & Huba, 1985; Schermelleh-Engel & Moosbrugger, 2003).

Figure 2. Eigenvalue-factor number graphic of OPTS

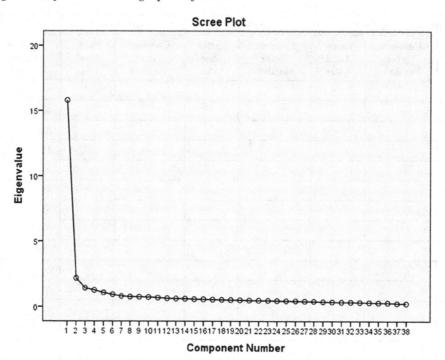

Table 4. Fit index values of the model

Fit Index Values	Perfect Fit	Acceptable Fit	Fit Index Values Achieved in the CFA
X²/DS	$0 \leq \chi^2/SD \leq 2$	$2 \leq \chi^2/SD \leq 3$	2.48
GFI	$0.95 \leq GFI$	$0.85 \leq GFI$	0.88
AGFI	$90 \leq AGFI \leq 1.00$	$85 \leq AGFI$	0.87
CFI	$0.95 \leq CFI \leq 1.00$	$0.90 \leq CFI \leq 0.95$	0.93
RMSEA	$0.00 \leq RMSEA \leq 0.05$	$0.06 \leq RMSEA \leq 0.08$	0.04
SRMR	$0.00 \leq SRMR \leq 0.05$	$0.06 \leq SRMR \leq 0.10$	0.04

Convergent and Divergent Validities

Convergent and divergent validity were investigated for the construct validity regarding whether the OPTS actually assessed its four-factor construct, and average order values (AOVs) were examined for each factor. AOVs were 0.88 for the KIL factor, 0.89 for the EXP factor, 0.87 for the SOC factor, and 0.91 for the ACH factor. Because all these values were higher than .50, its scale factors demonstrated convergent validity (Bagozzi and Yi, 1988). For divergent validity, the AOV square roots of the scale were tested to see whether they were above the correlation between constructs and 0.70 (Fornell and Larcker, 1981). Subsequently, the scale was found to have divergent validity (Table 5).

Figure 3. Values concerning the CFA

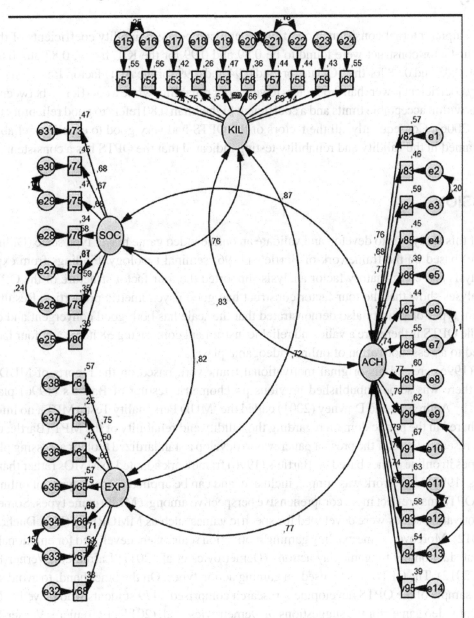

Table 5. Divergent validity values on the Online Player Type Scale (OPTS)

	KIL	EXP	SOC	ACH
Killers	**0.938**			
Explorers	0.604	**0.944**		
Socializers	0.632	0.670	**0.931**	
Achievers	0.754	0.692	0.755	**0.957**

Reliability

Cronbach's alpha internal consistency coefficients and composite reliability coefficients of the scale's 38-item four-factor construct were found to be 0.89 and 0.99 for the KIL factor, 0.83 and 0.98 for the EXP factor, 0.83 and 0.98 for the SOC factor, and 0.94 and 0.99 for the ACH factor. Research shows that a reliability coefficient lower than 0.60 refers to very poor reliability while a coefficient between 0.60 and 0.70 means within acceptable limits and a coefficient higher than 0.80 refers to good reliability (Fraenkel & Wallen, 2006). Consequently, all the factors of the OPTS had very good to excellent reliability. The results obtained in the validity and reliability testing indicated that the OPTS has a consistent structure.

DISCUSSION

The aim of this study was to develop and validate an online video game player type scale (Online Player Type Scale) based on the framework of Bartle's (1996) seminal typology. Findings from exploratory factor analysis and confirmatory factor analysis supported the four-factor structure of the OPTS. Reliability analyses show that the four-factor construct had good psychometric properties. Results regarding different types of validity also demonstrated that the scale has both good convergent and divergent validity. The OPTS is therefore a valid and reliable instrument comprising 38 items and four factors that can be used to assess motivation of online videogame players.

Bartle (1996) created his original motivational framework based on the reports of MUD players. Although there was some unpublished previous psychometric testing of Bartle's (1996) player type framework by Andreasen and Downey (2001) called the 'MUD Personality Test' (MPT), no information has been shared in the public domain regarding the validity and reliability of the MPT (Bartle, undated). Therefore, research focus of the present paper was to develop a standardized tool for assessing player motivation types in online games based on Bartle's (1996) framework adapted to MMOs rather than MUDs.

Bartle's (1996) framework was simple, inclusive, and can be applied to many types of online games. However, OPTS may reflect more comprehensive perspective amongst MMO game types. Some existing gaming motivation scales were developed for specific games such as MMORPGs (Yee, Ducheneaut, & Nelson, 2012). Moreover, some existing gaming motivation scales were developed for emotional engagement for satisfaction not by gameplay actions (Demetrovics et al., 2011; Lafrenière, Verner-Filion, & Vallerand, 2012). The OPTS was focused on gaming action types. On the other hand, to avoid statistical errors, the sample of the OPTS development research comprised 1479 students who played at least several different video games for the suggestions of Demetrovics et al. (2011), Lafrenière, Verner-Filion, & Vallerand (2012), Yee, Ducheneaut, & Nelson (2012). Therefore, the OPTS may contribute to the gaming research field based on its psychometric reliability. At present, there is no valid and reliable instrument developed to identify online player types by motivation type in Turkish literature. Although there is the Gamification User Types Hexad Scale adapted into Turkish by Akgün and Topal (2018) comprising player types such as philanthropists, socializers, free spirits, achievers, players, and disruptors, the scale was developed in relation to gamification rather than motivation. Although there is some crossover in player types, the player types in the two scales arguably have different scopes and fields of application.

A considerable amount of research demonstrates that gaming motivation may have an effect on problematic and addictive game play (e.g., Kuss, Louws, & Wiers, 2012; Ng & Wiemer-Hastings, 2005, (2006a); Caplan, Williams, & Yee, 2009), in-game behaviors (Ryan, Rigby, & Przybylski, 2006), and design of games (Orji et al., 2013, 2014). Knowing which motivations drive individuals to play online games is important for researchers, game designers, and educators studying in the field.

There are of course some limitations to the present study. First of all, the OPTS has limited use in terms of player types. There may be more player types than those examined in the present study because the OPTS only assesses four player types based on their motivational preferences in gameplay based on self-reports. Because players act differently in different games, players may respond to the OPTS differently after playing different types of games. Therefore, the videogame in players' mind at the time of completing the OPTS may provide different responses if tested at a different point in time and with different games. Therefore, test-retest reliability studies need to be carried out. More basic limitations include the fact that the data were self-report (and subject to well-known biases) and only collected from Turkish adolescents. Therefore, the OPTS needs testing on other samples (e.g., emerging adults) from other countries and cultures.

Future studies should focus on cross-cultural studies to validate the OPTS in other countries. This is because existing studies in the literature concerning gaming motivation and player types have focused on specific games or specific people who play videogames from specific regions in the world (as has happened in the present study). In addition to self-report methods, player types could perhaps be verified by diversifying data with different data collection methods such as observations in gameplay, players' in-game and out-of-game conversations, and data from various behavioral monitoring devices (EEG, eye-tracking etc.).

In summary, the OPTS developed in the present study demonstrates good validity and reliability analyses and will be of use in studies on online videogames that need to examine motivational reasons for playing online videogames. Other scales could also be tested alongside the OPTS to see if there is any direct or indirect associations between or among such scales.

REFERENCES

Akgün, Ö. E., & Topal, M. (2018). Adaptation of the Gamification User Types Hexad Scale into Turkish. *International Journal of Assessment Tools in Education*, 5(3), 389–402. doi:10.21449/ijate.379139

Andreasen, E., & Downey, B. (2001). The Mud Personality Test. Retrieved from https://web.archive.org/web/20000818064001/ http://www.andreasen.org/bartle/stats.cgi

Bagozzi, R. P., & Yi, Y. (1988). On the evaluation of structural equation models. *Journal of the Academy of Marketing Science*, 16(1), 74–94. doi:10.1007/BF02723327

Bartle, R. (1996). Hearts, clubs, diamonds, spades: Players who suit MUDs. *Journal of MUD Research*, 1(1), 19–45.

Bartle, R. (n.d.). Bartle Test of Gamer Psychology. Retrieved from http://matthewbarr.co.uk/bartle/

Beard, C. L., & Wickham, R. E. (2016). Gaming-contingent self-worth, gaming motivation, and Internet Gaming Disorder. *Computers in Human Behavior*, 61, 507–515. doi:10.1016/j.chb.2016.03.046

Bentler, P. M. (1980). Multivariate analysis with latent variables: Causal modeling. *Annual Review of Psychology*, 31(1), 419–456. doi:10.1146/annurev.ps.31.020180.002223

Bentler, P. M., & Bonett, D. G. (1980). Significance tests and goodness of fit in the analysis of covariance structures. *Psychological Bulletin, 88*(3), 588–606. doi:10.1037/0033-2909.88.3.588

Bollen, K. A. (1990). Overall fit in covariance structure models: Two types of sample size effects. *Psychological Bulletin, 107*(2), 256–259. doi:10.1037/0033-2909.107.2.256

Browne, M. W., & Cudeck, R. (1993). Alternative ways of assessing model fit. In K. A. Bollen & J. S. Long (Eds.), *Testing structural equation models* (pp. 136–162). Beverly Hills, CA: Sage.

Busch, M., Mattheiss, E., Orji, R., Marczewski, A., Hochleitner, W., Lankes, M., ... Tscheligi, M. (2015, October). Personalization in serious and persuasive games and gamified interactions. In *Proceedings of the 2015 Annual Symposium on Computer-Human Interaction in Play* (pp. 811-816). ACM. 10.1145/2793107.2810260

Büyüköztürk, Ş. (2011). *Sosyal bilimler için veri analizi el kitabı* (14th ed.). Ankara: Pegem Yayınevi.

Büyüköztürk, Ş., Çakmak, E. K., Akgün, Ö. E., Karadeniz, Ş., & Demirel, F. (2013). *Bilimsel araştırma yöntemleri* (15th ed.). Ankara: Pegem Yayınevi.

Byrne, B. M. (2006). *Structural equation modeling with EQS: Basic concepts, application, and programming* (2nd ed.). Mahwah, NJ: Lawrence Erlbaum.

Byrne, B. M., & Campbell, T. L. (1999). Cross-cultural comparisons and the presumption of equivalent measurement and theoretical structure: A look beneath the surface. *Journal of Cross-Cultural Psychology, 30*(5), 555–574. doi:10.1177/0022022199030005001

Caplan, S., Williams, D., & Yee, N. (2009). Problematic Internet use and psychosocial well-being among MMO players. *Computers in Human Behavior, 25*(6), 1312–1319. doi:10.1016/j.chb.2009.06.006

Cole, H., & Griffiths, M. D. (2007). Social interactions in massively multiplayer online role-playing gamers. *Cyberpsychology & Behavior, 10*(4), 575–583. doi:10.1089/cpb.2007.9988 PMID:17711367

Demetrovics, Z., Urbán, R., Nagygyörgy, K., Farkas, J., Zilahy, D., Mervó, B., & Harmath, E. (2011). Why do you play? The development of the motives for online gaming questionnaire (MOCQ). *Behavior Research Methods, 43*(3), 814–825. doi:10.375813428-011-0091-y PMID:21487899

Doğan, E., & Şahin, Y. L. (2017, October). Çevrimiçi Oyuncu Tipi Belirleme Ölçeği: Açımlayıcı Faktör Analizi Çalışması. In *Proceedings of the 5th International Instructional Technologies & Teacher Education Symposium*, İzmir, Turkey. Academic Press.

Dragon Blogger Technology and Entertainment. (2008). 16 Different Types of Massively Multiplayer (MMO) Online Games. Retrieved from https://www.dragonblogger.com/16-types-massively-multiplayer-mmo-online-games/

Encyclopedia of Science Fiction. (2018). Multi user dungeon. Retrieved from http://www.sf-encyclopedia.com/entry/multi_user_dungeon

Fornell, C., & Larcker, D. F. (1981). Structural equation models with unobservable variables and measurement error: Algebra and statistics. *JMR, Journal of Marketing Research, 18*(3), 382–388. doi:10.1177/002224378101800313

Fraenkel, R. J., & Wallen, E. N. (2006). *How to design and evaluate research in education*. New York: McGraw-Hill.

Garris, R., Ahlers, R., & Driskell, J. (2002). Games, motivation and learning: A research and practice model. *Simulation & Gaming, 33*(4), 441–467. doi:10.1177/1046878102238607

Ghuman, D., & Griffiths, M. D. (2012). A cross-genre study of online gaming: Player demographics, motivation for play, and social interactions among players. *International Journal of Cyber Behavior, Psychology and Learning, 2*(1), 13–29. doi:10.4018/ijcbpl.2012010102

Hair, J. F., Black, B., Babin, B., Anderson, R. E., & Tahtam, R. L. (2006). *Multivariate data analysis*. Upper Saddle River, NJ: Prentice Hall.

Hsu, S. H., Wen, M. H., & Wu, M. C. (2009). Exploring user experiences as predictors of MMORPG addiction. *Computers & Education, 53*(3), 990–999. doi:10.1016/j.compedu.2009.05.016

Hu, L. T., & Bentler, P. M. (1999). Cutoff criteria for fit indexes in covariance structure analysis: Conventional criteria versus new alternatives. *Structural Equation Modeling, 6*(1), 1–55. doi:10.1080/10705519909540118

Hutcheson, G. D., & Sofroniou, N. (1999). *The multivariate social scientist: Introductory statistics using generalized linear models*. London: Sage. doi:10.4135/9780857028075

Kim, Y., & Ross, S. D. (2006). An exploration of motives in sport video gaming. *International Journal of Sports Marketing & Sponsorship, 8*(1), 28–40. doi:10.1108/IJSMS-08-01-2006-B006

Kline, R. B. (2011). *Principles and practice of structural equation modeling*. New York: The Guilford Press.

Kuss, D. J., Louws, J., & Wiers, R. W. (2012). Online gaming addiction? Motives predict addictive play behavior in massively multiplayer online role-playing games. *Cyberpsychology, Behavior, and Social Networking, 15*(9), 480–485. doi:10.1089/cyber.2012.0034 PMID:22974351

Lafrenière, M. A. K., Verner-Filion, J., & Vallerand, R. J. (2012). Development and validation of the Gaming Motivation Scale (GAMS). *Personality and Individual Differences, 53*(7), 827–831. doi:10.1016/j.paid.2012.06.013

Lazzaro, N. (2004). Why we play games: Four keys to more emotion without story. Xeodesign. Retrieved from http://www.xeodesign.com/whyweplaygames/xeodesign_whyweplaygames.pdf

Marczewski, A. C. (2015). User Types. In *Even Ninja Monkeys Like to Play: Gamification, Game Thinking and Motivational Design* (1st ed., pp. 65–80). London: Blurb Inc.

Nardi, B., Ly, S., & Harris, J. (2007). Learning conversations in World of Warcraft. In *Proceedings of the Proceedings of the Hawaii International Conference on Systems Science* (pp. 1-10). New York: IEEE Press. 10.1109/HICSS.2007.321

Ng, B. D., & Wiemer-Hastings, P. (2005). Addiction to the internet and online gaming. *Cyberpsychology & Behavior, 8*(2), 110–113. doi:10.1089/cpb.2005.8.110 PMID:15938649

Orji, R., Mandryk, R. L., Vassileva, J., & Gerling, K. M. (2013, April). Tailoring persuasive health games to gamer type. In *Proceedings of the SIGCHI Conference on Human Factors in Computing Systems* (pp. 2467-2476). ACM. 10.1145/2470654.2481341

Orji, R., Nacke, L. E., & Di Marco, C. (2017, May). Towards personality-driven persuasive health games and gamified systems. In *Proceedings of the 2017 CHI Conference on Human Factors in Computing Systems* (pp. 1015-1027). ACM. 10.1145/3025453.3025577

Orji, R., Vassileva, J., & Mandryk, R. L. (2014). Modeling the efficacy of persuasive strategies for different gamer types in serious games for health. *User Modeling and User-Adapted Interaction*, 24(5), 453–498. doi:10.100711257-014-9149-8

Ryan, R. M., & Deci, E. L. (2000). Self-determination theory and the facilitation of intrinsic motivation, social development, and well-being. *The American Psychologist*, 55(1), 68–78. doi:10.1037/0003-066X.55.1.68 PMID:11392867

Ryan, R. M., Rigby, C. S., & Przybylski, A. (2006). The motivational pull of video games: A self-determination theory approach. *Motivation and Emotion*, 30(4), 344–360. doi:10.100711031-006-9051-8

Schermelleh-Engel, K., & Moosbrugger, H. (2003). Evaluating the fit of structural equation models: Tests of significance and descriptive goodness-of-fit measures. *Methods of Psychological Research Online*, 8(2), 23–74.

Steiger, J. H. (2007). Understanding the limitations of global fit assessment in structural equation modeling. *Personality and Individual Differences*, 42(5), 893–898. doi:10.1016/j.paid.2006.09.017

Steinkuehler, C., & Duncan, S. (2008). Scientific habits of mind in virtual worlds. *Journal of Science Education and Technology*, 17(6), 530–543. doi:10.100710956-008-9120-8

Steinkuehler, C., & Williams, D. (2006). Where everybody knows your (screen) name: Online games as "third places". *Journal of Computer-Mediated Communication*, 11(4), 885–909. doi:10.1111/j.1083-6101.2006.00300.x

Tabachnick, B. G., & Fidell, L. S. (2007). *Using multivariate statistics* (5th ed.). Boston: Allyn and Bacon.

Tanaka, J. S., & Huba, G. J. (1985). A fit index for covariance structure models under arbitrary GLS estimation. *British Journal of Mathematical & Statistical Psychology*, 38(2), 197–201. doi:10.1111/j.2044-8317.1985.tb00834.x

Tondello, G. F., Wehbe, R. R., Diamond, L., Busch, M., Marczewski, A., & Nacke, L. E. (2016, October). The gamification user types hexad scale. In *Proceedings of the 2016 annual symposium on computer-human interaction in play* (pp. 229-243). ACM. 10.1145/2967934.2968082

Williams, D., Ducheneaut, N., Xiong, L., Zhang, Y., Yee, N., & Nickell, E. (2006). From tree house to barracks: The social life of guilds in World of Warcraft. *Games and Culture*, 1(4), 338–361. doi:10.1177/1555412006292616

Yee, N. (2002). Five motivation factors for why people play MMORPGs. The Daedalus Project. Retrieved from http://www.nickyee.com/facets/home.html

Yee, N. (2006a). Motivations for play in online games. *Cyberpsychology & Behavior*, *9*(6), 772–775. doi:10.1089/cpb.2006.9.772 PMID:17201605

Yee, N. (2006b). The demographics, motivations, and derived experiences of users of massively multiuser online graphical environments. *Presence (Cambridge, Mass.)*, *15*(3), 309–329. doi:10.1162/pres.15.3.309

Yee, N., Ducheneaut, N., & Nelson, L. (2012, May). Online gaming motivations scale: development and validation. In *Proceedings of the SIGCHI conference on human factors in computing systems* (pp. 2803-2806). ACM. 10.1145/2207676.2208681

ENDNOTE

[1*]χ^2/SD: Chi-square/standard deviation; CFI: Comparative fit index; GFI: Goodness of fit index; AGFI: Adjusted goodness of fit index; RMSEA: Root Mean Square Error of Approximation; SRMR: Standardized Root Mean Square Residual

This research was previously published in the International Journal of Cyber Behavior, Psychology and Learning (IJCBPL), 10(1); pages 15-31, copyright year 2020 by IGI Publishing (an imprint of IGI Global).

Chapter 34
The Application of Intelligent Algorithms in the Animation Design of 3D Graphics Engines

Wenrui Bao

Baoji University of Arts and Sciences, China

ABSTRACT

With the rapid improvement of computer hardware capabilities and the reduction of cost, the quality of game pictures has made a qualitative breakthrough, which has reached or exceeded the picture effect of many dedicated virtual reality engines. On the basis of the design and implementation of the virtual reality 3D engine, the rendering queue management method is proposed to improve the frame rate. Based on the object-oriented design method, emitter regulator particle rendering mode, and traditional bone skin animation technology, the key structure technology in skeletal animation is analyzed, and the animation controller used to control animation playback and key structure interpolation operation is designed, which achieves the ideal animation effect. Finally, a prototype system based on engine is implemented.

1. INTRODUCTION

Virtual reality is an integrated technology, which integrates the latest development of computer graphics, computer simulation, sensor technology and AI technology. It can also be said to be an analog system generated by computer technology (Sun F et al.2015). The 3D engine is the foundation of the virtual reality technology. Virtual reality contains a lot of technology of image processing, including light and shadow computing, animation processing, physical system, collision detection system and rendering system (Baken L et al.2015). At present, the three dimensional game technology maintains a good momentum of development in these aspects (Lau K W.2015). With the growing graphics function of the game engine and the ability of computer hardware, especially the rapid improvement of display capacity, the scene of the 3D game is rapidly developing toward a high sense of reality. So the game engine has been able to fully meet the requirements of the virtual reality in the picture quality (Qin Z et al.2016). Due to the rapid development of the game industry and the maturity of the game engine, the development speed of

DOI: 10.4018/978-1-6684-7589-8.ch034

virtual reality can be greatly shortened and the development cost can be reduced better with the help of game engine (Liu K et al.2017). However, our country's current research on the game engine is relatively backward. If our country don't have a self-developed high-performance game engine, we can't catch up with the international level and resist the impact of a large number of foreign games fundamentally, nor can we drive the development of other industries (Park K B et al.2016). Therefore, independent research and development of solid and high-performance 3D game engine will be of great practical value for the development of our game and virtual reality application platform (Dorta T et al.2016).

2. RELATED WORK

In the 90s of last century, NASA and the United States Department of defense organized a series of research on virtual reality technology and achieved remarkable results. NASA's lab engineered data gloves to made it a high availability product and simulated the operation of Johnson space station in real time, and simulated the test plan of virtual space exploration by Harbert space telescope (Mejía R I et al.2017). At present, NASA has established the aeronautical and satellite maintenance training system, the space station training system and the VR education system for the national use (Konrad R et al.2017). Fujitsu Laboratory Limited is studying the interaction of virtual organisms and the VR environment. They are still studying gesture recognition in virtual reality and have developed a set of neural network posture recognition systems that can identify postures (Diao J et al.2017). Virtual reality technology is a science and technology field with large investment and high difficulty. The research of virtual reality technology in China started relatively late, so there is a certain gap compared with some developed countries. With the rapid development of computer graphics and computer system engineering, virtual reality technology has aroused extensive interest and attention from our government departments and scientists. The 11th Five-Year plan, the National 863 plan, the 973 Plan, the National Natural Science Foundation and the national high technology research and development plan and so on have included the research of virtual reality technology in the scope of funding. China is keeping pace with the new international technology. At the same time, some domestic research institutions and key institutions have carried out virtual reality technology in military, engineering, sports, culture and education.

3. METHODOLOGY

3.1 Grid Model of xVR Engine Renderer

The rendering system designed in this paper consists of three parts and five modules. The first part is the rendering of the primitives management module. The rendering primitives management module is mainly used to manage the rendering primitives, which allows the programmer to use the rendering system efficiently. This part includes two modules: the management of the vertex and the shader, and index management module. These two modules are independent and complementary to each other, but they need to work together. The second part is the part of realizing the rendering function. This section consists of two modules: the material and texture modules and the rendering queue. The material and texture modules are used to manage material and texture, and prevent the renderer from reading the same material and texture repeatedly. The rendering queue mainly plays two roles: one is to ensure the correct drawing order. For example, the sky box is drawn first, then the general object is drawn, and the final drawing interface is made. Two is to improve the efficiency of the rendering. The objects that conform to certain conditions are drawn together to reduce the switching of the rendering state as much as possible. The third part is the grid model, which uses the first two modules to render the model. The system structure diagram is shown in Figure 1. Among them, the original language management module and rendering function module are not specific modules, they are a conceptual module which is abstracted from specific modules according to functions.

Figure 1. Renderer overall structure diagram

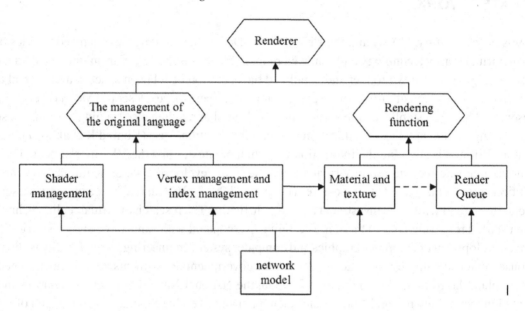

The grid model is one of the most important parts of a game. A game is sure to have a lot of models, such as characters, buildings, plants, etc. Moreover, the mesh model is made up of points set with rendering information through mutual connection. Therefore, programmers are not very realistic in designing a model by constructing their own vertex. Basically all the models in the game are obtained from the model script, so the model must be scripted. In general, the design and modeling of the model are done by modeling software, such as 3dsMax and Maya. The grid files of these modeling software have already scripted the model, so we only need to use the export plug-in to export it into the model format we need. In addition, the fbx file can be used too. The fbx is a relatively new format, which is a free cross platform content exchange format for Autodesk. Both 3dsMax and Maya support export in FBX format, and there are many other 3D content making programs that also support import and export of the format. This format is especially suitable for animated models, bones and skin in XNA. XNA provides two class processing models and grids: Model and ModelMesh. We can manipulate the models created in 3dsMax and Maya with these two classes. The basic flow of the grid model in XNA is shown in Figure 2.

Figure 2. Network model drawing flow chart

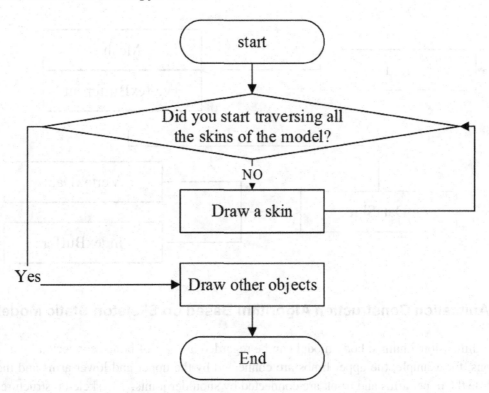

A grid model is a set of vertices with a certain order. For the game engine, efficiency and extendibility are very important. So, it needs to be managed in a different grid in the xVR engine. That is according to different grid material into a plurality of grid data fragments, each fragment of grid data using the same material, all grid data shared vertex buffer fragments of a grid, and a unified starting index buffer counter, each grid data segment has a vertex buffer between them, as shown in Figure 3 shown.

As you can see in Figure 3, the Mesh class has a common vertex buffer that can be shared with a grid data fragment. Each grid data fragment is composed of the instance segment Part and the data fragment DataSlot. Among them, the Part class is responsible for managing the specific instances of the grid and creating and managing the geometric map data. The DataSlot class is mainly responsible for the management of common vertex buffers, vertex data and index buffers, as well as the geometric metafile data for each grid. Each grid data fragment has its own material or texture. For example, you can wear clothes and pants for a human body model and he can change his clothes and pants in the game. In this example, the human model can be placed in the vertex buffer of the grid, and the upper and lower bodies are stored in different Part, respectively. These Part can create different materials or textures, and each Part has a DataSlot that corresponds to the management of vertex data and index buffers. In this way, when you need to change the character's clothes or pants, you only need to change the material or texture of the corresponding half.

Figure 3. Grid model and its data fragment class diagram

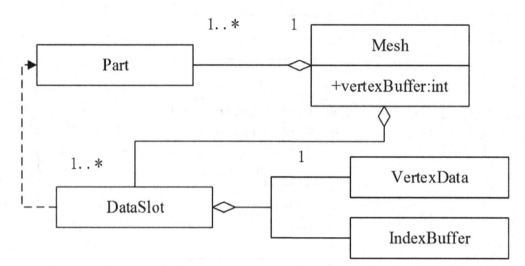

3.2 3D Animation Construction Algorithm Based on Skeleton Static Model

The three-dimensional human body model can be regarded as a set of bones connected by a series of connections, for example, the upper limbs are connected by the upper and lower arms and the elbow joints, while the upper arms and trunk are connected by shoulder joints. The skeleton structure is a series of connected bones that form a hierarchical relationship. In these bone sets, there is the only bone called the root bone, which is the center of the entire skeleton structure. Other bones are attached to the root skeleton as a descendant. When the skeleton is retrieved, it is usually carried out according to the hierarchical relationship. It is first to find the skeleton (pelvis) that forms the skeleton, and then the root bones begin to be retrieved until the needed bones are found. The skeleton is organized into a tree structure according to the hierarchical structure of the father and son. Like a tree structure, all bones in the skeleton structure are connected to the upper bones and eventually connected to the root bones. For the calculation of key structure similarity, the key structure information includes two kinds, one is the coordinate information of touch point and the other is the coordinate information of the touch-controlled component. The video recording of this platform is based on the coordinate information of touch points and driven by events. Therefore, in order to improve the accuracy of adaptive matching, touch point coordinate information needs to be calculated by key structural similarity to determine the key structure of the splicing point. The calculation of similarity is introduced into the distance formula of two points in Euclidean space. It is assumed that x, y is the two point of n-dimensional space, and the Euler distance between them is:

$$dist(X,Y) = \sqrt{\sum_{i=0}^{n}(x_i - y_i)^2} \tag{1}$$

When n=2, the Euclidean distance is the distance between the two points on the plane. When Euclidean distance is used to express similarity, the following formula is generally used: the smaller the distance, the greater the similarity.

$$sim(x, y) = \frac{1}{1 + d(x, y)} \tag{2}$$

So the similarity between the key structure Gi and the Gj (distance difference) Sim C Gi, Gj) is calculated as follows:

$$Sim(G_i, G_j) = \frac{1}{1 + D(G_i, G_j)}$$
$$= \frac{1}{1 + \sqrt{(x_i - x_j)^2 + (y_i - y_j)^2}} \tag{3}$$

In the setting of the threshold, the setting of the threshold can be derived according to the similarity calculation formula. In the described scene, the stitching condition that the locus of the touch point can accept is related to the pixel information of the coordinate points. After a lot of data experiments, the acceptable maximum pixel is 2, and the threshold value is calculated and deduced. The values are as follows:

$$\varepsilon = \frac{1}{1 + \sqrt{2^2 + 2^2}}$$
$$= \frac{1}{1 = 2\sqrt{2}} \tag{4}$$
$$\approx 0.261$$

Therefore, when the similarity is greater than the threshold 0.261, the stitching point which is found at present is the closest matching point. The usual criteria for judging the degree of precocious maturity of chromosomes are the size of the difference between the maximum adaption value and the average fitness of the chromosome, that is:

$$\Delta = f_{max} - f_{ave} \tag{5}$$

When Δ is relatively large, the chromosomes are quite different and the population maintains a good diversity. Otherwise, when people are relatively small, it shows that the chromosome individuals in the population are closer, and the local or global convergence appears. One of the drawbacks of such a criterion is to consider the poor fitness of chromosomes, which do not really reflect the convergence of a good individual. So the criterion is improved to the D-value between the maximum adaptive value and the mean of all the adaptive values of the chromosomes exceeding the average fitness value:

$$\Delta = f_{max} - f_{ave(max)} \tag{6}$$

By calculating the algorithm, the skeleton becomes the final shape that should be presented at this time. The fifth step is to calculate all bones with the transformation matrix as a key step in the skeleton animation, which is responsible for the ability to move the vertex together with the skeleton. In this step, for each vertex in the skin grid, the new position and orientation in the world coordinates need to be calculated one by one.

4. RESULT ANALYSIS AND DISCUSSION

Based on the above analysis, Autodesk's professional modeling software 3dsMax is used to build the geometric model of the virtual scene. V-Ray, Photoshop and other software are applied to render and beautify the model. Then it is exported as a FBX model file, and then in the way of programming in the XVR engine, the model FBX file is loaded into the scene. Finally, after rendering the model by renderer, the final model is displayed in the window, and users can interact with each other through keyboard and mouse, such as field control, switching scenes, etc. Figure 4 is a flow chart of the experiment.

Figure 4. Design flow chart of virtual reality system

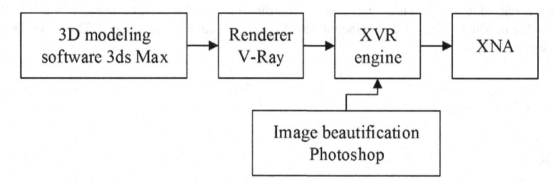

Making a good model in 3dsMax is only the first step in the implementation of the system. The next produced files need to be exported to FBX format, then the exported FBX file is added to the Content folder on the solution resource manager window of VisualStudio2008 development. Finally, the work of adding the model file to the developer is completed. Because the display can support the limitation of resolution, the test was done at 800 X 600, 1024 X 768 and 1280X1024 four resolutions, and at each resolution, the adjustment of the quality of the four level of the model was carried out. In the actual test, the test is performed automatically, and the running picture is moved from the beginning to the end. The FPS engine uses the record function in the whole process to record the time (60 seconds) the average frame range, in order to test the performance of the algorithm under different settings.

Table 1. The advantages of the algorithm

	Node data amount (one)	XML file size (KB)	Traditional brute force algorithm time consuming (S)	This paper studies the time consuming of algorithms (S)	Improvement (%)
Low quality	99	16	0.761	0.171	76.99
Medium quality	210	32			
High quality	288	16		0.522	82.85

X 600 resolution is the lowest resolution of the test. As shown in Figure 5, even under the super high picture quality, the FPS of the system can still remain at about 37, indicating that the XVR engine can run smoothly. The resolution is increased to 1024 X 768, and the FPS of the system can be maintained at 35 when the image quality is super high. Moreover, it can be seen from the graph that the overall operation speed of the system is not much different from that of the 800 X 600 resolution under the same picture quality. Finally, the resolution is increased to 1280 X1024. The test result is shown in Figure 6.10. Even under the super high picture quality, the FPS of the system can remain at 35, and the overall running speed of the system is not much different from that of the 800X 600 with the same picture quality.

Figure 5. The advantages of the algorithm in this paper

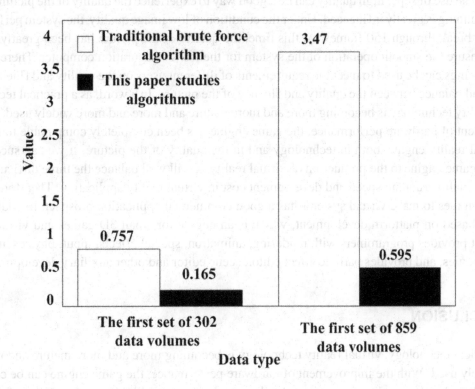

Figure 6. Comparison between the algorithm of this paper and the M-TIGA algorithm

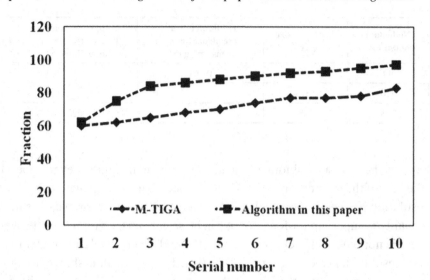

From the above tests, we can see that the virtual reality system built using the XVR engine is not very resource - consuming. But there is a great difference in the performance of the system for different qualities. The use of super high quality can be a good way to experience the quality of the picture, but the speed of running is greatly influenced. Under the condition of low image quality, the system performance can easily break through 150 frames. At this time, the quality of the picture has been greatly lost, but this can ensure the smooth operation of the system for the low configuration computer. Therefore, different drawings can be used to meet the requirements of different users on the quality and fluency of the picture, and balance between the quality and fluency of the picture. In a word, as a practical technology, virtual reality technology is becoming more and more mature and more and more widely used. With the improvement of hardware performance, the game engine has been completely comparable to the high-end virtual reality engine, both in technology and in the quality of the picture. If we can successfully apply the game engine to the production of virtual reality, it will well balance the three difficult factors of picture quality, running speed and development cost in virtual reality application. Therefore, the use of game engines to make virtual systems has a good commercial application prospect. In addition, the engine is based on platform development, which is an engine for small 3D games and virtual reality systems. It provides programmers with rendering, animation, special effects, input, physics and sound effects modules, and provides particle effect editor, scene editor and other auxiliary development tools.

5. CONCLUSION

As a practical technology, virtual reality technology is becoming more and more mature and more and more widely used. With the improvement of hardware performance, the game engine can be compared to the high end virtual reality engine in technology and picture quality. If you can successfully apply the game engine to the production of virtual reality, it will be a good balance of the various factors in the virtual reality application. The application of intelligent algorithm in the animation design of 3D graphics engine is studied in this article. First, the development status of virtual reality at home and abroad is briefly introduced. Meanwhile, the advantage of XNA platform is utilized, and a XVR engine is developed independently, and its overall architecture and core module design are analyzed in detail. The XVR engine is developed on the XNA platform, which is an engine for small 3D games and virtual reality systems. Finally, two different virtual reality design algorithms are implemented using the XVR engine. Then the basic uses of the main functions such as rendering, animation, special effects, GUI, input, physics, AI, and sound effects are described. Finally, the algorithm is tested. The test results show that the engine and corresponding algorithm designed in this article can be effectively applied to 3D animation design, and it is feasible to further promote.

ACKNOWLEDGMENT

This research was supported by the project of Shaanxi Provincial Department of education (No. 19JK0027) and Scientific Research Project of Education Department of Shaanxi Province (No. 19JK0104).

REFERENCES

Baken, L., van Gruting, I. M., Steegers, E. A., van der Spek, P. J., Exalto, N., & Koning, A. H. J. (2015). Design and validation of a 3D virtual reality desktop system for sonographic length and volume measurements in early pregnancy evaluation. *Journal of Clinical Ultrasound Jcu, 43*(3), 164–170. doi:10.1002/jcu.22207 PMID:25041997

Diao, J., Xu, C., & Jia, A. (2017). Virtual reality and simulation technology application in 3D urban landscape environment design. *Boletin Tecnico/Technical Bulletin, 55*(4), 72–79.

Dorta, T., Kinayoglu, G., & Hoffmann, M. (2016). Hyve-3D and the 3D Cursor: Architectural co-design with freedom in Virtual Reality. *International Journal of Architectural Computing, 14*(2), 87–102. doi:10.1177/1478077116638921

Konrad, R., Dansereau, D. G., Masood, A., & Wetzstein, G. (2017). SpinVR: Towards live-streaming 3D virtual reality video. *ACM Transactions on Graphics, 36*(6), 209. doi:10.1145/3130800.3130836

Lau, K. W. (2015). Organizational Learning Goes Virtual? A Study of Employees' Learning Achievement in Stereoscopic 3D Virtual Reality. *The Learning Organization, 22*(5), 289–303. doi:10.1108/TLO-11-2014-0063

Liu, K., Wang, J., & Hong, Y. (2017). Wearing comfort analysis from aspect of numerical garment pressure using 3D virtual-reality and data mining technology. *International Journal of Clothing Science and Technology, 29*(2), 166–179. doi:10.1108/IJCST-03-2016-0017

Mejía, R. I., Olguín-Carbajal, M., & Rivera-Zarate, I. (2017). Virtual reality engine developed in panda 3D for a cave based system. *Journal of Theoretical and Applied Information Technology, 95*(19), 5203–5214.

Park, K. B., & Lee, J. Y. (2016). Comparative Study on the Interface and Interaction for Manipulating 3D Virtual Objects in a Virtual Reality Environment. *Korean Journal of Computational Design & Engineering*, *21*(1), 20–30. doi:10.7315/CADCAM.2016.020

Qin, Z., & Tao, Z. (2016). A Low Memory 3D Animation Technology for "Animation Design" Course. *International Journal of Emerging Technologies in Learning*, *11*(5), 68. doi:10.3991/ijet.v11i05.5697

Sun, F., Zhang, Z., Liao, D., Chen, T., & Zhou, J. (2015). A lightweight and cross-platform Web3D system for casting process based on virtual reality technology using WebGL. *International Journal of Advanced Manufacturing Technology*, *80*(5-8), 801–816. doi:10.100700170-015-7050-1

This research was previously published in the International Journal of Gaming and Computer-Mediated Simulations (IJGCMS), 13(2); pages 26-37, copyright year 2021 by IGI Publishing (an imprint of IGI Global).

Chapter 35

Gamification and Its Application in the Social Environment:
A Tool for Shaping Behaviour

Staling Cordero-Brito

(iD) https://orcid.org/0000-0002-6489-298X

Universidad de Salamanca, Salamanca, Spain

Juanjo Mena

Facultad de Educación, Universidad de Salamanca, Salamanca, Spain & Institute of Psychology and Education, Kazan Federal University, Kazan, Russia

ABSTRACT

This study sets out to conduct a systematic review of the emergence and evolution of gamification in the social environment, its main components, and its application as a learning tool through the motivation and engagement it generates in people. The results were obtained by consulting two major scientific databases, namely, Scopus and the Web of Science, which provided 136 articles published on the social environment from 2011 through to mid-2016 using the term gamification. The results of this study reveal how over time gamification has been gaining importance in the social environment through the use of its components. The highest number of scientific publications come from the United States and Spain. In addition, the use of gaming components increases motivation and engagement. It shows how gamification uses (individual or group) rewards according to the context to achieve the proposed objectives, being successfully implemented in education, health, services, and social learning.

INTRODUCTION

The spread of ICTs in the social environment has involved a series of situations in which new tools are required for addressing social issues, as many people spend a lot of their time playing games on their consoles, laptops and mobile phones. Many of these gamers are digital natives with an interest in the field of learning-based games (Simões, Redondo, & Vilas, 2013) and social applications, with the aim

DOI: 10.4018/978-1-6684-7589-8.ch035

being to find a learning-focused flow state that provides them with a source of motivation and engagement (Hamari & Koivisto, 2015b). According to de-Marcos et al. (2016) and Morford et al. (2014) games provide spaces for conflict resolution, using motivation and commitment. Nevertheless, there is a major difference between the design of learning-based games and the more traditional ones. Learning-based games are designed to generate learning in non-ludic environments, whereas their traditional counterparts are designed to entertain (Day-Black, Merrill, Konzelman, Williams, & Hart, 2015). The inclusion of gaming components in the social environment has therefore expanded in recent times to encourage people to become involved (Bista, Nepal, Paris, & Colineau, 2014), fostering clear objectives, and being divided into goals that are achievable in the short term, involving those participating with a sense of progress, as well as instant feedback and a link to other players (de-Marcos, Domínguez, Saenz-de-Navarrete, & Pagés, 2014).

Gamification means using gaming components in non-ludic environments (Bíró, 2014; Deterding, Dixon, Sicart, Nacke, & O'Hara, 2011; Gatautis, Vitkauskaite, Gadeikiene, & Piligrimiene, 2016; Marache-francisco & Brangier, 2012; Simões et al., 2013; Urh, Vukovic, Jereb, & Pintar, 2015). Hamari and Koivisto, (2015b) and Kapp, (2012) define it as the use of gaming mechanics and dynamics, adding a convincing narrative for the purpose of resolving social issues. Gamification thus exploits the features inherent to games for their use in situations involving a lack of motivation and learning (Dichev, Dicheva, Angelova, & Agre, 2014). Nonetheless, ensuring that these aspects have an impact at social level through a positive knock-on effect requires the community's active involvement, promoting social influence, reciprocity and recognition (Koivisto & Hamari, 2014; Marache-Francisco & Brangier, 2012).

The research proposal here involves conducting a systematic review of the evolution of gamification and its influence on the social environment, with the aim being to boost the achievement of the proposed guidelines and the acquisition of habits in activities that are boring or difficult to do. This article will shed light on those topics with a greater weight in the state-of-the-art. Significant results are provided when finding that gamification increases player learning and participation. Within the social environment, gamification has a major impact through the use of its components, playing an important role in prompting behaviour through motivation (both intrinsic and extrinsic) and engagement. In addition, gamification has a huge potential for its components' implementation in non-ludic contexts.

MATERIAL AND METHODS

The retrieval and review of the literature took place at the end of July 2016. The sample of scientific papers (see Figure 1) was obtained by following the methodological steps applied by Caponetto et al. (2014) and Rickinson and May (2009): scope, search, selection, analysis and presentation of results:

- **Scope:** a) Use of the sample strategy: Title "Gamification"; b) Latitude: Research ambit: Social (Social Sciences), the documents involved in the sampling are articles and reviews (in any language); and c) the timeframe of interest involved all articles and reviews published from 2011 through to the middle of 2016;
- **Search:** A broader spectrum and greater efficiency was achieved by consulting two databases with the highest impact on the publication of scientific articles (Web of Science and Scopus). The search was conducted in both these databases, and 264 studies were retrieved;

- **Selection:** Following an analysis of all the scientific articles and reviews, any duplicates were removed (n = 100), along with any that did not have an abstract (n = 28), thereby providing a final sample of n = 136 articles. Figure 1 shows the databases Web of Science and Scopus.

Figure 1. Sample selection process (adapted from the schema by Miller & Campbell, 2006)

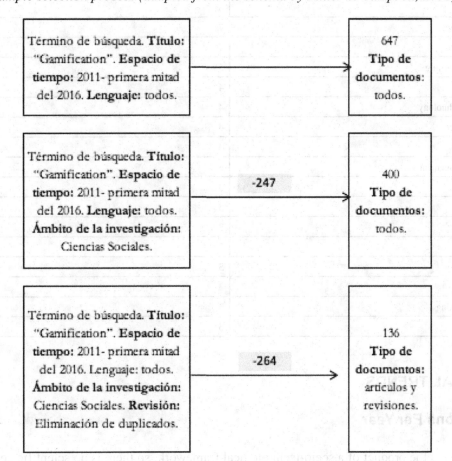

Analysis and Presentation of Results

In order to improve the presentation and analysis of results, the articles were grouped into sections of content, being organised and processed using the following software programs: Mendeley 1.12, Excel 2007, Tableau Public 10.4.2, and Nvivo 10. The sections were created by selecting all the keywords from the articles in the sample (see Table 1), which were then processed in Nvivo 10, with this method providing the topics to be addressed in this article.

Table 1. Keywords of the articles with [3] three matches published in the Web of Science and Scopus databases: Social environment (n = 136) in the period (2011-2016*)

Keywords	Frequency
Learning	10
Education	8
Engagement	8
Game Mechanics	7
Motivation	7
Game-based learning	5
Games	4
Persuasive Technology	4
User Experience	4
Badges	3
Customer Engagement	3
Ehealth	3
Game Design	3
Gaming	3
Mechanics	3
Physical activity	3
Serious Games	3
Social Networking	3
Video Games	3

TEMPORAL TRENDS

Publications Per Year

Gamification is the product of a socio-technological framework, so there is no scientific consensus on the date when it first appeared. According to de-Marcos et al., (2016) and Silva et al., (2013) the concept is a relatively recent one, although the fundamentals of its action are not. The design arose through the development of videogames in the early 1980s (Marache-Francisco & Brangier, 2012).

This review of the main databases for scientific publications (Scopus and Web of Science) has revealed that the term Gamification grew up to prominence in the social environment as from 2011. Figure 2 shows the annual distribution of the publications in the sum of scientific articles produced according to the criteria described in Section 2, compared to a broader category of documents: retrieving all the scientific articles with the word Gamification in the title in the aforementioned databases. The annual breakdown of the scientific articles reveals that there was only one paper in 2011 (0.73% of the sample), six in 2012 (4.41%), 21 in 2013 (15.44%), 26 in 2014 (19.12%), 51 in 2015 (37.5%) with an increase of 96, 13% up on the previous year, and 31 in the first half of 2016 (22.79%). Of the 136 articles, 58 (42,65%) articles were theoretical and 78 (57,35%) were empirical. On Table 2, we can observe that Education was the most studied field of knowledge (n=63; 46,32%), followed by Services (n=41; 30.15%), Health (n=13,24%), and Social learning (n=14; 10,29%).

The reasons for the rapid growth in gamification in the social environment is because at least 50% of the services perceived have one or more gamification components (Hanus & Fox, 2015) and 70% of the world's leading companies use the gaming system (Harwood & Garry, 2015), thereby increasing marginal productivity and consumer loyalty (and sales).

Table 2. Number of articles (sample) be fields of knowledges

Fields of Knowledge	Freq.	References
Education	63	(Attali & Arieli-Attali, 2015; Azmi & Singh, 2015; Barcena & Sanfilippo, 2015; Betts, Bal, & Betts, 2013; Bíró, 2014; Caribe de Oliveira, 2015; Caton & Greenhill, 2014; Challco, Moreira, Bittencourt, Mizoguchi, & Isotani, 2015; Chang & Wei, 2016; Chen, Burton, Mihaela, & Whittinghill, 2015; Coccoli, Iacono, & Vercelli, 2015; Codish & Ravid, 2014; Cozar-Gutierrez & Manuel Saez-Lopez, 2016; da Rocha Seixas, Gomes, & de Melo Filho, 2016; de-Marcos, Domínguez, Saenz-de-Navarrete, & Pagés, 2014; de-Marcos, Garcia-Lopez, & Garcia-Cabot, 2016; Dichev, Dicheva, Angelova, & Agre, 2014; Dicheva, Dichev, Agre, & Angelova, 2015; Domínguez et al., 2013; Erenli, 2013; Fan, Xiao, & Su, 2015; Figueroa Flores, 2015; Gene, Nuñez, & Blanco, 2016; Giannetto, Chao, & Fontana, 2013; Giessen, 2015; González, Toledo, & Muñoz, 2016; Hamzah, Ali, Saman, Yusoff, & Yacob, 2015; Hanson-Smith, 2016; Hanus & Fox, 2015; Ibanez, Di-Serio, & Delgado-Kloos, 2014; Kapp, 2012; Kickmeier-Rust, Hillemann, & Albert, 2014; Kuo & Chuang, 2016; Landers & Armstrong, 2015; Landers, Bauer, & Callan, 2015; Levitt & Piro, 2014; Lieberoth, 2015; Lin & Shih, 2015; Maican, Lixandroiu, & Constantin, 2016; Mavletova, 2015a, 2015b; Morris, Croker, Zimmerman, Gill, & Romig, 2013; Müller, Reise, & Seliger, 2015; Nevin et al., 2014; J. T. Kim & Lee, 2015; Muntasir et al., 2015; Nahl & James, 2013; Nolan & McBride, 2014; Olsson, Mozelius, & Collin, 2015; Sagan, 2014; Schoech et al., 2013; Seaborn & Fels, 2015; Simões, Redondo, & Vilas, 2013; Simon J.D, 2013; Smith-Robbins, 2011; Snyder & Hartig, 2013; C.-H. Su & Cheng, 2015; C. H. Su & Su, 2015; Urh, Vukovic, Jereb, & Pintar, 2015; Veronica Marin Guadalupe Maldonado, 2015; Villagrasa, Fonseca, Redondo, & Duran, 2014)
Services	41	(Baughman, Chuang, Benz, Basilico, & Dixon, 2014; Bittner & Schipper, 2014; Conaway & Cortes Garay, 2014; Di Bartolomeo, Stahl, & Elias, 2015; Faiella & Ricciardi, 2015; Freudmann & Bakamitsos, 2014; Gatautis, Banyte, Piligrimiene, Vitkauskaite, & Tarute, 2016; Gatautis, Vitkauskaite, Gadeikiene, & Piligrimiene, 2016; Hamari, 2013, 2015; Harwood & Garry, 2015; Hofacker, De Ruyter, Lurie, Manchanda, & Donaldson, 2016; Hsu, Chang, & Lee, 2013; Hutton, 2013; Hyypiä & Parjanen, 2015; Insley & Nunan, 2014; Jang, 2015; S. Kim, 2013; T. W. Kim & Werbach, 2016; Korn & Schmidt, 2015; Kumar & Raghavendran, 2015; Levy, 2012; Lucassen & Jansen, 2014; Marache-francisco & Brangier, 2012; Oprescu, Jones, & Katsikitis, 2014; Rapp, 2015; Robson, Plangger, Kietzmann, McCarthy, & Pitt, 2015; Rodrigues, Costa, & Oliveira, 2016; Rodrigues, Oliveira, & Costa, 2016b, 2016a; Roth, Schneckenberg, & Tsai, 2015; Roth & Schneckenberger, 2012; Ruhi, 2015; Sarangi & Shah, 2015; Sigala, 2015a, 2015b; Tcyplakova, 2016; Terlutter & Capella, 2013; Tzimerman, Herer, & Shtub, 2016; Wells, 2016; Werbach & Hunter, 2012)
Health	18	(Allam, Kostova, Nakamoto, & Schulz, 2015; Cruz Junior, 2014; Day-Black, Merrill, Konzelman, Williams, & Hart, 2015; Dembicki, 2016; Gabarron, Schopf, Serrano, Fernandez-Luque, & Dorronzoro, 2013; González et al., 2015; Hamari & Koivisto, 2014, 2015b, 2015a; Jones, Madden, & Wengreen, 2014; Jones, Madden, Wengreen, Aguilar, & Desjardins, 2014; Koivisto & Hamari, 2014; Maturo & Setiffi, 2016; Mokadam et al., 2015; Morford, Witts, Killingsworth, & Alavosius, 2014; Pesare, ROoselli, Corriero, & Rossano, 2016; Uğurel, Morali, Koyunkaya, & Karahan, 2016; Zuckerman & Gal-Oz, 2014)
Social learning	14	(Bista, Nepal, Paris, & Colineau, 2014; Brigham, 2015; Coombes & Jones, 2016; Corcoba Magana & Munoz-Organero, 2015; Ferrara, 2013; Jagoda, 2013; Kerfoot & Kissane, 2014; Love et al., 2016; Mekler, Brühlmann, Tuch, & Opwis, 2015; Procopie, Bumbac, Giusca, & Vasilcovschi, 2015; Santhanam, Liu, & Shen, 2016; Silva, Analide, Rosa, Felgueiras, & Pimenta, 2013; Tolmie, Chamberlain, & Benford, 2014; Yoon, 2013)
Total	136	

Figure 2. Annual distribution of articles with the word Gamification in the title published in the Web of Science and Scopus databases: Social environment (n = 136) in the period (2011-2016*)

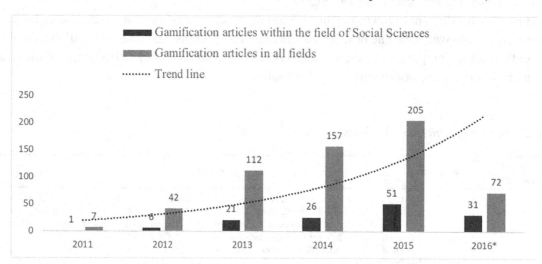

These findings are consistent with those reported by Sigala (2015b), who predicted the rapid growth of gamification, as it had made inroads in the research community.

Publications by Countries and Languages

Millions of users throughout the world are using the gamification system, based on the conviction that everyone can contribute to the discussion, decisions and assessment of results within a social context (Steffen, Dirk, & Chia-Wen, 2015). As regards the 136 scientific articles in the sample in the social environment, the countries with the highest number of publications were as follows: the US (27.94%), followed by Spain (13.24%) and England. It should be noted that the articles in the sample came from 19 countries in all, although none of them, apart from the US, Spain and England, accounted for more than 7%. Figure 3 shows their geographical distribution, with the size of each circle indicated the number of publications produced.

According to Niño-Puello (2013), "80% of the specialised journals indexed in Scopus (scientific research database) are published in English" (p. 247), and specifically, 94.85% of the articles were written in English, with the remaining 5.15% being shared by Portuguese, German, Korean, Spanish, and Russian.

Impact Journals and Authors

A given scientific journal's repercussion often reflects the relative impact it has on the research community within a specific field. In this study, the leading scientific journals were as follows: *Computers in Human Behavior* with 15 publications, followed by *Computers & Education* and *Procedia - Social and Behavioral Sciences* with five documents each. Table 3 shows the impact factor, country of publication, and the database providing the scientific journals; within these, the following authors recorded the highest number of contributions: Hamari, with four, and Koivisto and Su Ch, with three each.

Figure 3. Number of articles published by countries in the Web of Science and Scopus databases: Social environment (n = 136) in the period (2011-2016*)

Table 3. Scientific journals with ≥ three publications in the Web of Science and Scopus databases: Social environment (n = 136) in the period (2011-2016*)

Journal	No. Articles of the Sample (2011-2016)	No. Articles in Social Science (2011-2016)	JCR/ Quartile (2016)	Sjr/ Quartile (2016)	H Index (2016)	Country of Publication	Database
Computers in Human Behavior	15	3,060	Q1	Q1	96	United States	Web of Science/ Scopus
Computers & Education	5	1,376	Q1	Q1	109	United Kingdom	Web of Science/ Scopus
Procedia - Social and Behavioral Sciences	5	23,198	N/a	Q4	22	United Kingdom	Scopus
IEEE Intelligent Transportation Systems Magazine	4	43	Q2	Q2	14	United States	Web of Science/ Scopus
International Journal of Engineering Education	4	1027	Q4	Q1	33	Ireland	Web of Science/ Scopus
International Journal of Game-Based Learning	3	37	N/a	Q4	8	United States	Scopus
Journal of e-Learning and Knowledge Society	3	83	N/a	Q4	8	Italy	Scopus

Design Framework (MDA)

A game's design facilitates the use of gamification in non-ludic ambits (Gatautis, Vitkauskaite et al., 2016). The gaming system may shape players' behaviour (see Figure 4), with a predefined narrative and an effective feedback system, generating a sense of progress through the gaming experience (de-Marcos, Garcia-Lopez et al., 2016). Thus far, there is no scientific consensus on the acceptance of a single gamification design (Rodrigues, Costa, & Oliveira, 2016); hence the reason the design framework to be chosen needs to be consistent with the goals proposed and with users' expectations (Bista et al., 2014).

Figure 4. Progression in the design of gamification: MDA framework (adapted from Hunicke, Leblanc, & Zubek, 2004; Kim & Lee, 2015)

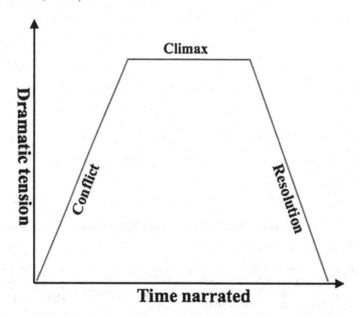

The components are commonly applied in the design of interactive systems (Rapp, 2015), with the aim being to influence users' motivation and engagement (see Figure 5), prompting changes in behaviour (Gatautis, Banyte, Piligrimiene, Vitkauskaite, & Tarute, 2016; Lieberoth, 2015; Rodrigues, Oliveira, & Costa, 2016a) through the incorporation of psychological techniques and gaming components (Procopie & Bumbac, 2015). According to Gatautis et al., (2016) each component has three characteristics: recognition, progression and entertainment. Although there are sundry design frameworks for classifying the gaming components participants use (see the article by González et al., 2016, on types of participants), many researchers and experts have resorted to a formalised design framework for games, referred to as MDA, which stands for mechanics, dynamics and aesthetics, as proposed by the scholars Hunicke, Leblanc, and Zubek. Mechanics involves the rules and components (Ibanez, Di-Serio, & Delgado-Kloos, 2014) that encourage participants to discover and investigate their opportunities through feedback, channelling their behaviour in a predetermined manner. Dynamics is understood to be a key part of the successful creation of videogames, regardless of the platform; it describes the behaviour responding to the mechanics, acting on players, their results (Mora, Riera, González, & Arnedo-Moreno, 2015) and on the social relationships derived from the game (Ruhi, 2015). *Aesthetics* details the emotional responses the player recalls when interacting with the gaming system (Cózar-Gutiérrez & Manuel Sáez-López, 2016; Hunicke et al., 2004; Kapp, 2012; Maican, Lixandroiu, & Constantin, 2016).

Figure 5. Interaction of the components of the game design (adapted from Simões et al., 2013)

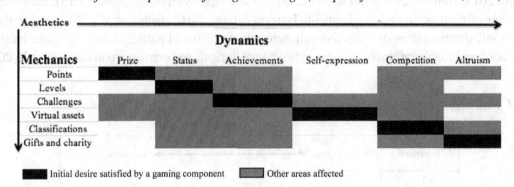

Motivation and Engagement

Social contexts underpin the differences in motivation and engagement both within and between individuals in step with their personal growth, whereby depending on the context there are participants who are more self-determined, energised and integrated than others in response to key drivers such as pleasure, hope, fear, rejection and social acceptance. This means motivation can be heightened by increasing or decreasing these variables (Dichev et al., 2014). Authors such as Giannetto et al., (2013); Kapp, (2012); Robson et al., (2015) and Villagrasa et al., (2014) contend that motivation and engagement are gamification's main objectives. In other words, motivation and engagement are very closely related (Pesare, Roselli, Corriero, & Rossano, 2016) due to the impact in cognitive development, emotional and social areas of the participants studied by self-determination theory (SDT) and the flow. According to cognitive evaluation theory (CET) and organismic integration theory (OIT) (sub-theories of SDT), motivation is divided into intrinsic and extrinsic (Hamari & Koivisto, 2015a; Kapp, 2012; Mekler, Brühlmann, Tuch, & Opwis, 2015; Ruhi, 2015).

Motivation is defined as the level of engagement in relation to the scope of a predetermined objective (Morris, Croker, Zimmerman, Gill, & Romig, 2013). Extrinsic motivation is informed by external regulators, as long as there are significant threats or rewards (Caton & Greenhill, 2014); in other words, motivation comes from outside the individual and refers to the pursuit of an activity (mechanics) with a view to achieving a result (dynamics), regardless of whether the activity is intrinsically motivating it (Yang Chen, Burton, Vorvoreanu, & Whittinghill, 2015). In turn, intrinsic motivation comes from within, as an individual performs an action because it is gratifying in itself, such as altruism, competition, cooperation and collaboration (Sigala, 2015a), reaching the climax of motivation in the form of "behavioral autonomy". In turn, engagement is the inherent desire to achieve a goal, which induces participants to persist within the objectives that they are pursuing, rendering it more difficult to ignore them (Hamari, 2015). It has three components: behavioral, emotional and cognitive (da Rocha Seixas, Gomes, & de Melo Filho, 2016; Pesare et al., 2016).

Authors such as Dichev et al., (2014); Ibanez et al., (2014); Kickmeier-Rust et al., (2014); Sigala, (2015b); Tae Kim, and Lee, (2013) have shown that an increase in external factors makes participants focus on achievements; in other words, when the extrinsic rewards are removed, engagement drops off sharply, as a dependence is created on the external stimulus, whereby participants need to be constantly rewarded in order to continue obtaining results. By contrast, some gaming components (results tables and challenges) may galvanise extrinsic and intrinsic motivation in specific contexts (see Table 4) (Azmi & Singh, 2015; Hamari, 2015; Mekler et al., 2015; Olsson, Mozelius, & Collin, 2015), increasing the acquisition of motivation and engagement (Hanson-Smith, 2016; Ibanez et al., 2014) either through personal self-determination or collective self-determination (social participation). In short, increasing participation and collaboration requires a combination of intrinsic and extrinsic motivation (Sigala, 2015b).

Table 4. Evolution of motivation through regulatory processes

Behaviour	Non-determined ←		→ Self-determined
Type of motivation	Lack of motivation	Extrinsic motivation	Intrinsic motivation
Regulatory factor	Impersonal	External	Internal
Regulatory processes	Dismissive of the activity, loss of control	Rewards, punishments, ego, personal importance	Conscious evaluation, altruism, collective importance

Fields With a Greater Implementation of Gamification

The gamification system has made inroads in several fields in recent years. Thus, depending on the focus, there are dozens of components (see Table 5) in gaming design frameworks that can be used to exert some kind of influence on participants. These components are turned into tools (see Table 6) in order to help and / or support participants as they seek to carry out preset tasks. In this section, it has been considered some of the main components in regard to context, area and the motivation they exercise; Although this may not seem to be the case, all the components and tools are studied equally in the aforementioned disciplines. At the same time, seems that the components of extrinsic motivation appear more in the fields of Services and Education, while those of intrinsic motivation are more common in Health and Social Learning.

Education

Within an educational context, most modern applications use some of the mechanics of gamification to drive participation and the acquisition of knowledge, enabling pupils to decide upon their own goals and shortcomings, adjusting their feedback (positive or negative) depending on the circumstance (Dichev et al., 2014) as a way of learning by playing. Although gamification is not considered a game in education, it is perceived as an innate part of learning. A review of the prevailing components shows that the most common ones are marks (exams), levels (degrees), achievements (scores) and comparative tables. Points and badges are used as external signs of symbolic reward (C.-H. Su & Cheng, 2015), impacting upon students' autonomy. Challenges and competition are used to create a competitive atmosphere, in which ego and reputation conflate, leading to more self-determined behaviour. The group comparison table (Codish & Ravid, 2014) promotes the relationship among students, paving the way for creativity and innovation. With a view to increasing learning (see Table 5, column 2), These components have been used in children's education (Boticki, Baksa, Seow, & Looi, 2015; Nolan & McBride, 2013; Simões et al., 2013), higher education (Domínguez et al., 2013; Müller, Reise, & Seliger, 2015; Nahl & James, 2013; Urh et al., 2015), and foreign-language learning (Coccoli, Iacono, & Vercelli, 2015; Flores, 2015; Perry, 2015). Most of the cases studied have had a positive impact on students' motivation and engagement (Azmi & Singh, 2015; C.-H. Su & Cheng, 2015). Table 5, column 2 contains the gamification tools used within the educational context in the articles in the sample.

Table 5. Number of components used in the fields of knowledge

Components	Education	Services	Health	Social Learning	Total
1) Points	18	6	7	5	36
2) Levels	7	5	3	4	19
3) Badges and medals	17	8	7	5	37
4) Avatars	2	2	2	1	7
5) Leaderboard	16	7	1	4	28
6) Content unlocking	1	2	1	0	4
7) Gifts	3	1	1	1	6
8) Progress bar	6	2	1	1	10
9) Challenges	9	4	3	2	18
10) Missions	3	0	2	1	6
11) Roles	1	0	1	0	2
12) Feedback	5	3	5	6	19
13) Colaboration	12	2		7	21
14) Social networks	1	5	3	2	11
15) Autonomy	2	1	0	1	4
16) Curiosity	1	0	0	0	1
17) Status	4	0	2	2	8
18) Social recognition	3	0	4	2	9
19) Competition	8	1	4	1	14
20) Control	1	0	4	0	5
21) Enjoyment	1	0	0	1	2
Total	121	49	51	46	267

Services

Gamification in service processes adopts a management-by-objectives approach based on a series of strategies to make the design framework more implicit. Its aim is to maximise the loyalty and motivation of customers and employees. Customers are motivated by a series of external rewards, acting as the product's commercial agents through the reception of a good service, albeit creating only short-term loyalty, given that consumers focus more on the reward than on the actual product. This means that when the incentives are withdrawn or changed, there is a sharp drop in motivation (Freudmann & Bakamitsos, 2014; Korn & Schmidt, 2015). Employees are engaged through the target-reward cycle, using comparative tables and action groups, managing and rewarding employees in specific tasks through positive and ongoing feedback (see Table 5, column 3). With a view to achieving the "participant-reward" interrelationship (see Table 5, column 3). These components have been applied with great success in finances (Rodrigues, Costa et al., 2016; Rodrigues, Oliveira, & Costa, 2016b), manufacturing (Korn & Schmidt, 2015; Robson et al., 2015), tourism (Jang, 2015; Sigala, 2015b, 2015a), and marketing (Freudmann & Bakamitsos, 2014; Lucassen & Jansen, 2014; Oliveira, Santos, Aguiar, & Sousa, 2014; Werbach, 2012). It should be stressed that some applications are used to prompt a stimulating experience, creating a mechanics in which aspects of intrinsic motivation prevail, while other games simply focus on creating an experience that will draw customers back over and over again (Freudmann & Bakamitsos, 2014). Table 6, column 3 presents the gamification tools used in the field of services in the articles in the sample.

Health

As in education, the health context (exergames) has successfully converged in the field of videogames through the introduction of gaming components in a range of applications and initiatives related to healthy living (Hamari & Koivisto, 2014). The health system has acknowledged the potential that games have in prevention and in helping patients suffering from an illness or simply adjusting their lifestyles. Most of the external drivers help to reinforce intrinsic motivation (see Table 6, column 4). It uses points and badges as primary rewards to then become stages separated by obstacles, with the reward being to improve or keep their health, helping the state and insurance firms to reduce their costs (Levy, 2012). With the aim being to meet the goals proposed. This design framework has been applied to patients with cancer and diabetes through the conscious use of prescribed medications (Pesare et al., 2016), a reduction in workplace accidents (Levy, 2012), a healthy diet (Bittner & Kulesz, 2015) and exercise (Jones, Madden, & Wengreen, 2014; Zuckerman & Gal-Oz, 2014). Table 6, column 4 shows the gamification tools used in the field of health in the articles in the sample.

Social Learning

Gaming components are applied to social learning with a view to fostering interaction and collaboration (Simões et al., 2013). Their persuasive capacity is determined by social recognition and rewards (Morris et al., 2013). The mechanics and dynamics of gaming are therefore used, being influenced by the objectives of the community involved. In turn, social influence provides the context for developing social interaction, considering how the participant reacts to the group, and how the group can help to establish an influential relationship (Marache-Francisco & Brangier, 2012). In other words, orchestrating the necessary atmosphere to enable participants to learn from observation and from the other members' behaviour: moving from understanding to action. In keeping with network externalities theory, the benefits of social repercussion depend on the number of influential participants the community has (Hamari & Koivisto, 2015b). As regards their social influence (see Table 5, column 5). These components have been used in network learning processes (de-Marcos et al., 2014), sustainability (Corcoba Magaña & Muñoz-Organero, 2015), fuel consumption (Corcoba Magaña & Muñoz-Organero, 2015) and collaboration (Boticki et al., 2015). Table 6, column 5 shows the gamification tools used in social learning in the articles in the sample.

Table 6. Number of tools used in the fields of knowledge

Tools	Fields of Knowledge*					References
	Ed.	Ser.	He.	Sl.	Total	
Duolingo	1	0	0	0	1	(Figueroa Flores, 2015)
GAFU	0	0	0	1	1	(Corcoba Magaña & Muñoz-Organero, 2015)
ONESELF	0	0	1	0	1	(Allam, Kostova, Nakamoto, & Schulz, 2015)
Personalized Tool	8	2	2	1	13	(Bittner & Schipper, 2014; Caton & Greenhill, 2014; Chang & Wei, 2016; Codish & Ravid, 2014; de-Marcos et al., 2014; de-Marcos, Garcia-Lopez, et al., 2016; Dembicki, 2016; Hamzah, Ali, Saman, Yusoff, & Yacob, 2015; Hanus & Fox, 2015; Insley & Nunan, 2014; Jones, Madden, Wengreen, Aguilar, & Desjardins, 2014; Kerfoot & Kissane, 2014; Landers, Bauer, & Callan, 2015)
Schoolcube	1	0	0	0	1	(Azmi & Singh, 2015)
VOKI	1	0	0	0	1	(Barcena & Sanfilippo, 2015)
DeepQA	0	1	0	0	1	(Baughman, Chuang, Benz, Basilico, & Dixon, 2014)
Curatr	1	0	0	0	1	(Betts, Bal, & Betts, 2013)
SEEQ	1	0	0	0	1	(E. Coombes & Jones, 2016)
Next Step	0	0	0	1	1	(Bista et al., 2014)
Miriada X	1	0	0	0	1	(Gene, Nuñez, & Blanco, 2016)
OntoGaCLeS	1	0	0	0	1	(Challco, Moreira, Bittencourt, Mizoguchi, & Isotani, 2015)
CBAL	1	0	0	0	1	(Attali & Arieli-Attali, 2015)
Cogent	1	0	0	0	1	(Y Chen, Burton, Mihaela, & Whittinghill, 2015)
Moodle LMS	1	0	0	0	1	(Coccoli et al., 2015)
MTurk	0	1	0	0	1	(Conaway & Garay, 2014)
Beat the Street	0	0	0	1	1	(Emma Coombes & Jones, 2016)
MinecraftEdu	1	0	0	0	1	(Cózar-Gutiérrez & Manuel Sáez-López, 2016)
ClassDojo	1	0	0	0	1	(da Rocha Seixas et al., 2016)
ClassBadges	1	0	0	0	1	(da Rocha Seixas et al., 2016)
Blackboard	2	0	0	0	2	(de-Marcos, Garcia-Lopez, et al., 2016; De Byl, 2013)
MMBCLS	1	0	0	0	1	(Fan, Xiao, & Su, 2015)
Sjekkdeg.no	0	0	1	0	1	(Gabarron, Schopf, Serrano, Fernandez-Luque, & Dorronzoro, 2013)
QizBox	1	0	0	0	1	(Giannetto et al., 2013)
TANGO:H	0	0	1	0	1	(González, Gómez, et al., 2016)

continues on following page

Table 6. Continued

Tools	Fields of Knowledge*					References
	Ed.	Ser.	He.	Sl.	Total	
Pirate's Island	0	0	1	0	1	(González, Gómez, et al., 2016)
Sharetribe	0	2	0	0	2	(Hamari, 2013, 2015)
Fitocracy	0	0	4	0	4	(Hamari & Koivisto, 2014, 2015b, 2015a; Koivisto & Hamari, 2014)
Samsung Nation Web	0	1	0	0	1	(Harwood & Garry, 2015)
Protagonize.com	0	1	0	0	1	(Hsu, Chang, & Lee, 2013)
Storybird.com	0	1	0	0	1	(Hsu et al., 2013)
Flickspin.com	0	1	0	0	1	(Hsu et al., 2013)
Q-Learning-G	1	0	0	0	1	(Ibanez et al., 2014)
FIT Game	0	0	1	0	1	(Jones, Madden, & Wengreen, 2014)
Gamified survey	3	1	0	2	6	(Love et al., 2016; Mavletova, 2015a, 2015b; Snyder & Hartig, 2013; Veronica Marin Guadalupe Maldonado, 2015; Wells, 2016)
Sonic driver	1	0	0	0	1	(Kickmeier-Rust et al., 2014)
Lopupa	1	0	0	0	1	(Kuo & Chuang, 2016)
TETEM	1	0	0	0	1	(Landers & Armstrong, 2015)
INput	1	0	0	0	1	(Lieberoth, 2015)
Unity3D	1	0	1	0	1	(Lin & Shih, 2015; Uğurel, Morali, Koyunkaya, & Karahan, 2016)
Interactivia.ro	1	0	0	0	1	(Maican et al., 2016)
Tagging platform	0	0	0	1	1	(Mekler et al., 2015)
Top gun	0	0	1	0	1	(Mokadam et al., 2015)
Jeopardy	0	0	1	0	1	(Mokadam et al., 2015)
Lego Mindstorms	1	0	0	0	1	(Müller et al., 2015)
Kaizen-IM	1	0	0	0	1	(Nevin et al., 2014)
Virtual Moodle	1	0	0	0	1	(Olsson et al., 2015)
Foursquare	0	1	0	0	1	(Rapp, 2015)
Nike +	0	1	0	0	1	(Rapp, 2015)
Getblue	0	1	0	0	1	(Rapp, 2015)
Futebank	0	1	0	0	1	(Rodrigues, Costa, et al., 2016)
E-Banking	0	2	0	0	2	(Rodrigues, Oliveira, et al., 2016b, 2016a)
Who Wants to Be a Millionaire? (adapted)	1	0	0	0	1	(Santhanam, Liu, & Shen, 2016)
Tripadvisor	0	2	0	0	2	(Sigala, 2015b, 2015a)
PHESS	0	0	0	1	1	(F Silva, Analide, Rosa, Felgueiras, & Pimenta, 2013)
Google analytics	1	0	0	0	1	(Stavljanin, Milenkovic, & Sosevic, 2016)
Mobile gamification learning system (MGLS)	1	0	0	0	1	(C. H. Su & Su, 2015)
Meaningful Blood Circulation Learning System, called MMBCLS	1	0	0	0	1	(C. H. Su & Su, 2015)

continues on following page

Table 6. Continued

Tools	Fields of Knowledge*					References
	Ed.	Ser.	He.	Sl.	Total	
Step by Step	0	0	1	0	1	(Zuckerman & Gal-Oz, 2014)
Supply ChainSimulator (SCS)	0	1	0	0	1	(Tzimerman, Herer, & Shtub, 2016)
Gamified LABoratorieS GLABS	1	0	0	0	1	Teaching Case of Gamification and Visual Technologies for Education (Villagrasa et al., 2014)
Total	42	20	15	8	85	

*Ed.= Education; Ser.= Services; He.= Health; Sl.= Social learning

It comes to our attention that although Services was the second most frequented field of knowledge studied (in number of components and tools), the health field made use of more components (n=51) number) than Services (n=49) in their gamification strategies. In addition, without reaching the *Points-fication* (Sigala, 2015b, 2015a), most of the tools used in the business field were extrinsic motivation.

CONCLUSION

The review of the literature on gamification in the fields of research in education, health and social learning enables us to briefly confirm the following.

Firstly, it should be noted that the gamified systems in the studies reviewed record better results than more traditional systems (Di Bartolomeo, Stahl, & Elias, 2015), considerably increasing users' involvement. However, it is not enough to simply add a gaming component to an existing application, as this requires choosing a good design framework, accompanied by a convincing narrative and a suitable context. In short, the entire gamification process needs to be seen as a framework subject to modifications (González et al., 2016).

Secondly, one of gamification's conceptual challenges in the social environment is to shape behaviour through the use of rewards, guaranteeing a preordained conduct until the participants acquire the necessary skills, creating a state of flow and learning. Hence the reason a good gamification system should lay the foundations for the development of self-determined behaviour; in other words, transitioning from the gaming components that increase extrinsic motivation to those that effectively provide intrinsic motivation.

Thirdly, it is important to note that the components of gamification with a greater presence in the fields under study are rewards (points, badges), levels, and results tables, as they may use extrinsic motivation to have a quicker, albeit less effective, impact; by contrast, comparison, social recognition and social networks do not have the same repercussion, as these aspects are rarely used in the sample's gamification designs.

A further consideration that deserves to be mentioned is that gamification has proven to be an effective tool for increasing motivation and engagement, with its main focus being the "participant", using design instruments in conjunction with social influence, and having a persuasive effect on the group. Furthermore, it keeps participants engrossed in the gaming experience because they return, share content with the community and influence it, contributing to the collaboration and socialisation of its members.

Limitations

One of the main limitations of this Systematic literature review (SLR) could be the impossibility of having a better selection of the sample, because we used a single word to search "Gamification" in the title, and we only searched in two databases (WOS and SCOPUS). Another limitation of this study could be not having the association of the components and applications used in the fields of knowledge. The last limitation could be not having a category to classify the articles that coincide in several fields of knowledge. In those cases, we classify the articles by the strongest results.

Future Directions

Our future research, for example, would include the association (χ^2) between components of gamification and player type; the association (χ^2) between motivation (extrinsic and intrinsic) and fields of knowledge (Education, Services, Health and Social learning); and the interaction between innovation phases and gamification.

The work is performed according to the Russian Government Program of Competitive Growth of Kazan Federal University.

REFERENCES

Allam, A., Kostova, Z., Nakamoto, K., & Schulz, P. J. (2015). The Effect of Social Support Features and Gamification on a Web-Based Intervention for Rheumatoid Arthritis Patients: Randomized Controlled Trial. *Journal of Medical Internet Research, 17*(1), 14–19. doi:10.2196/jmir.3510 PMID:25574939

Attali, Y., & Arieli-Attali, M. (2015). Gamification in assessment: Do points affect test performance? *Computers & Education, 83*, 57–63. doi:10.1016/j.compedu.2014.12.012

Azmi, M. A., & Singh, D. (2015). Schoolcube: Gamification for learning management system through Microsoft SharePoint. *International Journal of Computer Games Technology*, 1–5. doi:10.1155/2015/589180

Barcena, E., & Sanfilippo, M. (2015). La pildora informativa audiovisual como estrategia de gamificacion en los cursos en linea de segundas lenguas. *Círculo de Lingüística Aplicada a la Comunicación, 63*(0), 122–151. doi:10.5209/rev_CLAC.2015.v63.50172

Baughman, A., Chuang, W., Benz, Z., Basilico, J., & Dixon, K. (2014). DeepQA jeopardy! gamification: A machine learning perspective. *IEEE Transactions on Computational Intelligence and AI in Games, 6*(1), 55–66. doi:10.1109/TCIAIG.2013.2285651

Betts, B. W., Bal, J., & Betts, A. W. (2013). Gamification as a tool for increasing the depth of student understanding using a collaborative e-learning environment. *International Journal of Continuing Engineering Education and Lifelong Learning, 23*(3), 213–228. doi:10.1504/IJCEELL.2013.055405

Bíró, G. I. (2014). Didactics 2.0: A Pedagogical Analysis of Gamification Theory from a Comparative Perspective with a Special View to the Components of Learning. *Procedia: Social and Behavioral Sciences, 141*, 148–151. doi:10.1016/j.sbspro.2014.05.027

Bista, S. K., Nepal, S., Paris, C., & Colineau, N. (2014). Gamification for Online Communities: A Case Study for Delivering Government Services. *International Journal of Cooperative Information Systems*, *23*(02), 1–25. doi:10.1142/S0218843014410020

Bittner, J. V., & Kulesz, M. M. (2015). Health promotion messages: The role of social presence for food choices. *Appetite*, *87*, 336–343. doi:10.1016/j.appet.2015.01.001 PMID:25579221

Bittner, J. V., & Schipper, J. (2014). Motivational effects and age differences of gamification in product advertising. *Journal of Consumer Marketing*, *31*(5), 391–400. doi:10.1108/JCM-04-2014-0945

Boticki, I., Baksa, J., Seow, P., & Looi, C.-K. (2015). Usage of a mobile social learning platform with virtual badges in a primary school. *Computers & Education*, *86*, 120–136. doi:10.1016/j.compedu.2015.02.015

Caponetto, I., Earp, J., Ott, M., & Cnr, I. T. D. (2014). Gamification and Education: A Literature Review. In *Proceedings of the 8th European Conference on Games Based Learning ECGBL2014* (pp. 50–57). Academic Press.

Caton, H., & Greenhill, D. (2014). Rewards and Penalties: A Gamification Approach for Increasing Attendance and Engagement in an Undergraduate Computing Module. *International Journal of Game-Based Learning*, *4*(3), 1–12. doi:10.4018/ijgbl.2014070101

Challco, G. C., Moreira, D. A., Bittencourt, I. I., Mizoguchi, R., & Isotani, S. (2015). Personalization of gamification in collaborative learning contexts using ontologies. *IEEE Latin America Transactions*, *13*(6), 1995–2002. doi:10.1109/TLA.2015.7164227

Chang, J.-W., & Wei, H.-Y. (2016). Exploring Engaging Gamification Mechanics in Massive Online Open Courses. *Journal of Educational Technology & Society*, *19*(2), 177–203.

Chen, Y., Burton, T., Mihaela, V., & Whittinghill, D. M. (2015). Cogent: A Case Study of Meaningful Gamification in Education with Virtual Currency. *International Journal of Emerging Technologies in Learning*, *10*(1), 39–45. doi:10.3991/ijet.v10i1.4247

Chen, Y., Burton, T., Vorvoreanu, M., & Whittinghill, D. M. (2015). Cogent: A Case Study of Meaningful Gamification in Education with Virtual Currency. *International Journal of Emerging Technologies in Learning*, *10*(1), 39–45. doi:10.3991/ijet.v10i1.4247

Coccoli, M., Iacono, S., & Vercelli, G. (2015). Applying gamification techniques to enhance the effectiveness of video-lessons. *Journal of E-Learning and Knowledge Society*, *11*(3), 73–84.

Codish, D., & Ravid, G. (2014). Academic Course Gamification: The Art of Perceived Playfulness. *Interdisciplinary Journal of E-Learning and Learning Objects*, *10*, 131–151. doi:10.28945/2066

Conaway, R., & Garay, M. C. (2014). Gamification and service marketing. *SpringerPlus*, *3*(1), 653. doi:10.1186/2193-1801-3-653 PMID:25392812

Coombes, E., & Jones, A. (2016). Gamification of active travel to school: A pilot evaluation of the Beat the Street physical activity intervention. *Health & Place*, *39*, 62–69. doi:10.1016/j.healthplace.2016.03.001 PMID:26974232

Coombes, E., & Jones, A. (2016). Gamification of active travel to school: A pilot evaluation of the Beat the Street physical activity intervention. *Health & Place, 39*, 62–69. doi:10.1016/j.healthplace.2016.03.001 PMID:26974232

Corcoba Magaña, V., & Muñoz-Organero, M. (2015). GAFU: Using a gamification tool to save fuel. *IEEE Intelligent Transportation Systems Magazine, 7*(2), 58–70. doi:10.1109/MITS.2015.2408152

Cózar-Gutiérrez, R., & Manuel Sáez-López, J. (2016). Game-based learning and gamification in initial teacher training in the social sciences: An experiment with MinecraftEdu. *International Journal of Educational Technology in Higher Education, 13*, 1–11. doi:10.118641239-016-0003-4

da Rocha Seixas, L., Gomes, A. S., & de Melo Filho, I. J. (2016). Effectiveness of gamification in the engagement of students. *Computers in Human Behavior, 58*, 48–63. doi:10.1016/j.chb.2015.11.021

Day-Black, C., Merrill, E. B., Konzelman, L., Williams, T. T., & Hart, N. (2015). Gamification: An Innovative Teaching-Learning Strategy for the Digital Nursing Students in a Community Health Nursing Course. *The ABNF Journal: Official Journal of the Association of Black Nursing Faculty in Higher Education, Inc, 26*(4), 90–94. Retrieved from http://www.ncbi.nlm.nih.gov/pubmed/26665503

De Byl, P. (2013). Factors at play in tertiary curriculum gamification. *International Journal of Game-Based Learning, 3*(June), 1–21. doi:10.4018/ijgbl.2013040101

de-Marcos, L., Domínguez, A., Saenz-de-Navarrete, J., & Pagés, C. (2014). An empirical study comparing gamification and social networking on e-learning. *Computers & Education, 75*, 82–91. doi:10.1016/j.compedu.2014.01.012

de-Marcos, L., Garcia-Lopez, E., & Garcia-Cabot, A. (2016). On the effectiveness of game-like and social approaches in learning: Comparing educational gaming, gamification & social networking. *Computers & Education, 95*, 99–113. doi:10.1016/j.compedu.2015.12.008

de-Marcos, L., García-López, E., García-Cabot, A., Medina-Merodio, J.-A., Domínguez, A., Martínez-Herráiz, J.-J., & Diez-Folledo, T. (2016). Social network analysis of a gamified e-learning course: Small-world phenomenon and network metrics as predictors of academic performance. *Computers in Human Behavior, 60*, 312–321. doi:10.1016/j.chb.2016.02.052

Dembicki, D. (2016). Next Practice in Online Nutrition Education—Gamification—An Inquiry Into the Process of Improving Student Engagement. *Journal of Nutrition Education and Behavior, 48*(7), S53. doi:10.1016/j.jneb.2016.04.143

Deterding, S., Dixon, D., Sicart, M., Nacke, L., & O'Hara, K. (2011). Gamification- Using Game Design Elements in Non-Gaming Contexts. *Chi, 2425–2428*. doi:10.1145/1979742.1979575

Dichev, C., Dicheva, D., Angelova, G., & Agre, G. (2014). From gamification to gameful design and gameful experience in learning. *Cybernetics and Information Technologies, 14*(4), 80–100. doi:10.1515/cait-2014-0007

Domínguez, A., Saenz-de-Navarrete, J., de-Marcos, L., Fernández-Sanz, L., Pagés, C., & Martínez-Herráiz, J.-J. (2013). Gamifying learning experiences: Practical implications and outcomes. *Computers & Education, 63*, 380–392. doi:10.1016/j.compedu.2012.12.020

Figueroa Flores, J. F. (2015). Using Gamification to Enhance Second Language Learning. *Digital Education Review*, (27), 40–61.

Flores, J. (2015). Using Gamification to Enhance Second Language Learning. *Digital Education Review*, (27), 32–54. Retrieved from http://revistes.ub.edu/index.php/der/article/view/11912

Freudmann, E. A., & Bakamitsos, Y. (2014). The Role of Gamification in Non-profit Marketing: An Information Processing Account. *Procedia: Social and Behavioral Sciences*, *148*, 567–572. doi:10.1016/j.sbspro.2014.07.081

Gabarron, E., Schopf, T., Serrano, J. A., Fernandez-Luque, L., & Dorronzoro, E. (2013). Gamification Strategy on Prevention of STDs for Youth. *Studies in Health Technology and Informatics*, *192*, 1066–1066. PMID:23920840

Gatautis, R., Banyte, J., Piligrimiene, Z., Vitkauskaite, E., & Tarute, A. (2016). The Impact of Gamification on Consumer Brand Engagement. *Transformations in Business & Economics*, *15*(1), 173–191.

Gatautis, R., Vitkauskaite, E., Gadeikiene, A., & Piligrimiene, Z. (2016). Gamification as a mean of driving online consumer behaviour: Sor model perspective. *The Engineering Economist*, *27*(1), 90–97. doi:10.5755/j01.ee.27.1.13198

Gene, O. B., Nuñez, M., & Blanco, A. F. (2016). New Challenges for the Motivation and Learning in Engineering Education Using Gamification in MOOC*. *International Journal of Engineering Education*, *32*(1b), 501–512.

Giannetto, D., Chao, J., & Fontana, A. (2013). Gamification in a Social Learning Environment. *Issues in Informing Science and Information Technology*, *10*, 195–207. doi:10.28945/1806

González, C. S., Gómez, N., Navarro, V., Cairós, M., Quirce, C., Toledo, P., & Marrero-Gordillo, N. (2016). Learning healthy lifestyles through active videogames, motor games and the gamification of educational activities. *Computers in Human Behavior*, *55*, 529–551. doi:10.1016/j.chb.2015.08.052

González, C. S., Toledo, P., & Muñoz, V. (2016). Enhancing the engagement of intelligent tutorial systems through personalization of gamification. *International Journal of Engineering Education*, *32*(1), 532–541. Retrieved from http://www.scopus.com/inward/record.url?eid=2-s2.0-84959421037&partnerID=tZOtx3y1

Hamari, J. (2013). Transforming Homo Economicus into Homo Ludens: A field experiment on gamification in a utilitarian peer-to-peer trading service. *Electronic Commerce Research and Applications*, *12*(4), 236–245. doi:10.1016/j.elerap.2013.01.004

Hamari, J. (2015). Do badges increase user activity? A field experiment on the effects of gamification. *Computers in Human Behavior*, *71*, 469–478. doi:10.1016/j.chb.2015.03.036

Hamari, J., & Koivisto, J. (2014). Measuring flow in gamification: Dispositional Flow Scale-2. *Computers in Human Behavior*, *40*, 133–143. doi:10.1016/j.chb.2014.07.048

Hamari, J., & Koivisto, J. (2015a). Why do people use gamification services? *International Journal of Information Management*, *35*(4), 419–431. doi:10.1016/j.ijinfomgt.2015.04.006

Hamari, J., & Koivisto, J. (2015b). "Working out for likes": An empirical study on social influence in exercise gamification. *Computers in Human Behavior*, *50*, 333–347. doi:10.1016/j.chb.2015.04.018

Hamzah, W., Ali, N., Saman, M., Yusoff, M., & Yacob, A. (2015). Influence of Gamification on Students' Motivation in using E-Learning Applications Based on the Motivational Design Model. *International Journal of Emerging Technologies in Learning*, *10*(2), 30–34. doi:10.3991/ijet.v10i2.4355

Hanson-Smith, E. (2016). Games, Gaming, and Gamification: Some Aspects of Motivation. *TESOL Journal*, *7*(1), 227–232. doi:10.1002/tesj.233

Hanus, M. D., & Fox, J. (2015). Assessing the effects of gamification in the classroom: A longitudinal study on intrinsic motivation, social comparison, satisfaction, effort, and academic performance. *Computers & Education*, *80*, 152–161. doi:10.1016/j.compedu.2014.08.019

Harwood, T., & Garry, T. (2015). An investigation into gamification as a customer engagement experience environment. *Journal of Services Marketing*, *29*(6/7), 533–546. doi:10.1108/JSM-01-2015-0045

Hsu, S. H., Chang, J.-W., & Lee, C.-C. (2013). Designing attractive gamification features for collaborative storytelling websites. *Cyberpsychology, Behavior, and Social Networking*, *16*(6), 428–435. doi:10.1089/cyber.2012.0492 PMID:23438264

Hunicke, R., Leblanc, M., & Zubek, R. (2004). *MDA: A Formal Approach to Game Design and Game Research* (pp. 2001–2004). San Jose: Tuning Workshop at the Game Developers Conference.

Ibanez, M.-B., Di-Serio, A., & Delgado-Kloos, C. (2014). Gamification for Engaging Computer Science Students in Learning Activities: A Case Study. *IEEE Transactions on Learning Technologies*, *7*(3), 291–301. doi:10.1109/TLT.2014.2329293

Insley, V., & Nunan, D. (2014). Gamification and the online retail experience. *International Journal of Retail & Distribution Management*, *42*(5), 340–351. doi:10.1108/IJRDM-01-2013-0030

Jang, Y. (2015). A Study on Contents for Leisure Travel Survey Applying Gamification. *International Journal of Tourism and Hospitality Research*, *29*(4), 55–62. Retrieved from http://www.ktra.or.kr

Jones, B. A., Madden, G. J., & Wengreen, H. J. (2014). The FIT Game: Preliminary evaluation of a gamification approach to increasing fruit and vegetable consumption in school. *Preventive Medicine*, *68*(April), 76–79. doi:10.1016/j.ypmed.2014.04.015 PMID:24768916

Jones, B. A., Madden, G. J., Wengreen, H. J., Aguilar, S. S., & Desjardins, E. A. (2014). Gamification of Dietary Decision-Making in an Elementary-School Cafeteria. *PLoS One*, *9*(4), e93872. doi:10.1371/journal.pone.0093872 PMID:24718587

Kapp, K. M. (2012). Games, gamification, and the quest for learner engagement. *American Society for Training and Development Inc.*, *66*(6), 64–68.

Kerfoot, B., & Kissane, N. (2014). The use of gamification to boost residents' engagement in simulation training. *JAMA Surgery*, *149*(11), 1208–1209. doi:10.1001/jamasurg.2014.1779 PMID:25229631

Kickmeier-Rust, M. D., Hillemann, E.-C., & Albert, D. (2014). Gamification and Smart Feedback: Experiences with a Primary School Level Math App. *International Journal of Game-Based Learning*, *4*(3), 35–46. doi:10.4018/ijgbl.2014070104

Kim, J. T., & Lee, W.-H. (2015). Dynamical model for gamification of learning (DMGL). *Multimedia Tools and Applications*, *74*(19), 8483–8493. doi:10.100711042-013-1612-8

Koivisto, J., & Hamari, J. (2014). Demographic differences in perceived benefits from gamification. *Computers in Human Behavior*, *35*, 179–188. doi:10.1016/j.chb.2014.03.007

Korn, O., & Schmidt, A. (2015). Gamification of business processes: Re-designing work in production and service industry. *Procedia Manufacturing*, *3*, 3424–3431. doi:10.1016/j.promfg.2015.07.616

Kuo, M.-S., & Chuang, T.-Y. (2016). How gamification motivates visits and engagement for online academic dissemination – An empirical study. *Computers in Human Behavior*, *55*, 16–27. doi:10.1016/j.chb.2015.08.025

Landers, R. N., & Armstrong, M. B. (2015). Enhancing instructional outcomes with gamification: An empirical test of the Technology-Enhanced Training Effectiveness Model. *Computers in Human Behavior*, *71*, 1–9. doi:10.1016/j.chb.2015.07.031

Landers, R. N., Bauer, K. N., & Callan, R. C. (2015). Gamification of task performance with leaderboards: A goal setting experiment. *Computers in Human Behavior*, *71*, 508–515. doi:10.1016/j.chb.2015.08.008

Levy, M. (2012). Get in the game: Applying gamification to on-the-job safety. *Occupational Health & Safety (Waco, Tex.)*, *81*(10), 46, 48, 50. Retrieved from www.ohsonline.com PMID:23094482

Lieberoth, A. (2015). Shallow gamification testing psychological effects of framing an activity as a game. *Games and Culture*, *10*(3), 229–248. doi:10.1177/1555412014559978

Lin, C., & Shih, J. (2015). Evaluations to the Gamification effectiveness of digital game-based adventure education course- GILT. *Journal of E-Learning and Knowledge Society*, *11*, 41–58.

Love, S., Sanders, M., Turner, K., Maurange, M., Knott, T., Prinz, R., ... Ainsworth, A. (2016). Social media and gamification: Engaging vulnerable parents in an online evidence-based parenting program. *Child Abuse & Neglect*, *53*, 95–107. doi:10.1016/j.chiabu.2015.10.031 PMID:26880281

Lucassen, G., & Jansen, S. (2014). Gamification in Consumer Marketing - Future or Fallacy? *Procedia: Social and Behavioral Sciences*, *148*, 194–202. doi:10.1016/j.sbspro.2014.07.034

Maican, C., Lixandroiu, R., & Constantin, C. (2016). Interactivia.ro – A study of a gamification framework using zero-cost tools. *Computers in Human Behavior*, *61*, 186–197. doi:10.1016/j.chb.2016.03.023

Marache-Francisco, C., & Brangier, E. (2012). Gamification and human-machine interaction: A synthesis. *Le Travail Humain*, *75*(3), 166–189. doi:10.3917/th.753.0225

Mavletova, A. (2015a). A gamification effect in longitudinal web surveys among children and adolescents. *International Journal of Market Research*, *57*(3), 413–438. doi:10.2501/IJMR-2015-035

Mavletova, A. (2015b). Web Surveys Among Children and Adolescents: Is There a Gamification Effect? *Social Science Computer Review*, *33*(3), 372–398. doi:10.1177/0894439314545316

Mekler, E. D., Brühlmann, F., Tuch, A. N., & Opwis, K. (2015). Towards understanding the effects of individual gamification elements on intrinsic motivation and performance. *Computers in Human Behavior*, *71*, 525–534. doi:10.1016/j.chb.2015.08.048

Miller, R. L., & Campbell, R. (2006). of Evaluation Taking Stock of Empowerment Evaluation. *The American Journal of Evaluation*, *27*(3), 296–319. doi:10.1177/1098214006027003003

Mokadam, N. A., Lee, R., Vaporciyan, A. A., Walker, J. D., Cerfolio, R. J., Hermsen, J. L., ... Fann, J. I. (2015). Gamification in thoracic surgical education: Using competition to fuel performance. *The Journal of Thoracic and Cardiovascular Surgery*, *150*(5), 1052–1058. doi:10.1016/j.jtcvs.2015.07.064 PMID:26318012

Mora, A., Riera, D., González, C., & Arnedo-Moreno, J. (2015). A literature review of gamification design frameworks. In Proceedings of the 7th International Conference on Games and Virtual Worlds for Serious Applications (pp. 1–8). Academic Press. Retrieved from https://www.researchgate.net/publication/279059823_A_Literat ure_Review_of_Gamification_Design_Frameworks

Morford, Z. H., Witts, B. N., Killingsworth, K. J., & Alavosius, M. P. (2014). Gamification: The intersection between behavior analysis and game design technologies. *The Behavior Analyst*, *37*(1), 25–40. doi:10.100740614-014-0006-1 PMID:27274957

Morris, B. J., Croker, S., Zimmerman, C., Gill, D., & Romig, C. (2013). Gaming science: The "Gamification" of scientific thinking. *Frontiers in Psychology*, *4*, 1–16. doi:10.3389/fpsyg.2013.00607 PMID:24058354

Müller, B. C., Reise, C., & Seliger, G. (2015). Gamification in Factory Management Education – A Case Study with Lego Mindstorms. *Procedia CIRP*, *26*, 121–126. doi:10.1016/j.procir.2014.07.056

Nahl, D., & James, L. (2013). Gamification in Instruction and the Management of Intersubjectivity in Online University Courses. *International Journal of Web Portals*, *5*(2), 48–62. doi:10.4018/jwp.2013040104

Nevin, C. R., Westfall, A. O., Rodriguez, J. M., Dempsey, D. M., Cherrington, A., Roy, B., ... Willig, J. H. (2014). Gamification as a tool for enhancing graduate medical education. *Postgraduate Medical Journal*, *90*(1070), 685–693. doi:10.1136/postgradmedj-2013-132486 PMID:25352673

Niño-Puello, M. (2013). El inglés y su importancia en la investigación científica: Algunas reflexiones. *Revista Colombiana de Ciencia Animal*, *5*(1), 243–254. doi:10.24188/recia.v5.n1.2013.487

Nolan, J., & McBride, M. (2013, June). Beyond gamification: Reconceptualizing game-based learning in early childhood environments. *Information Communication and Society*, *4462*, 1–15. doi:10.1080/1 369118X.2013.808365

Oliveira, F., Santos, A., Aguiar, B., & Sousa, J. (2014). GameFoundry: Social Gaming Platform for Digital Marketing, User Profiling and Collective Behavior. *Procedia: Social and Behavioral Sciences*, *148*, 58–66. doi:10.1016/j.sbspro.2014.07.017

Olsson, M., Mozelius, P., & Collin, J. (2015). Visualisation and gamification of e-Learning and programming education. *Electronic Journal of E-Learning*, *13*(6), 441–454.

Perry, B. (2015). Gamifying French Language Learning: A Case Study Examining a Quest-based, Augmented Reality Mobile Learning-tool. *Procedia: Social and Behavioral Sciences, 174*, 2308–2315. doi:10.1016/j.sbspro.2015.01.892

Pesare, E., Roselli, T., Corriero, N., & Rossano, V. (2016). Game-based learning and Gamification to promote engagement and motivation in medical learning contexts. *Smart Learning Environments, 3*(1), 1–21. doi:10.118640561-016-0028-0

Procopie, R., & Bumbac, R. (2015, November). The Game of Innovation. Is Gamification a New Trendsetter? *Amfiteatru Economic, 17*, 1142–1155.

Rapp, A. (2015). A Qualitative Investigation of Gamification. *International Journal of Technology and Human Interaction, 11*(1), 67–82. doi:10.4018/ijthi.2015010105

Rickinson, M., & May, H. (2009). *A comparative study of methodological approaches to reviewing literature. The higher education academy.* The Higher Education Academy. Retrieved from https://www.heacademy.ac.uk/sites/default/files/resources/comparativestudy_0.pdf

Robson, K., Plangger, K., Kietzmann, J. H., McCarthy, I., & Pitt, L. (2015). Game on: Engaging customers and employees through gamification. *Business Horizons, 59*(1), 1–8. doi:10.1016/j.bushor.2015.08.002

Rodrigues, L. F., Costa, C. J., & Oliveira, A. (2016). Gamification: A framework for designing software in e-banking. *Computers in Human Behavior, 62*, 620–634. doi:10.1016/j.chb.2016.04.035

Rodrigues, L. F., Oliveira, A., & Costa, C. J. (2016a). Does ease-of-use contributes to the perception of enjoyment? A case of gamification in e-banking. *Computers in Human Behavior, 61*, 114–126. doi:10.1016/j.chb.2016.03.015

Rodrigues, L. F., Oliveira, A., & Costa, C. J. (2016b). Playing seriously – How gamification and social cues influence bank customers to use gamified e-business applications. *Computers in Human Behavior, 63*, 392–407. doi:10.1016/j.chb.2016.05.063

Ruhi, U. (2015). Level Up Your Strategy: Towards a Descriptive Framework for Meaningful Enterprise Gamification. *Technology Innovation Management Review, 5*(8), 5–16. doi:10.22215/timreview/918

Santhanam, R., Liu, D., & Shen, W.-C. M. (2016). Research Note—Gamification of Technology-Mediated Training: Not All Competitions Are the Same. *Information Systems Research, 27*(2), 453–465. doi:10.1287/isre.2016.0630

Sigala, M. (2015a). Applying Gamification and Assessing its Effectiveness in a Tourism Context: Behavioural and Psychological Outcomes of the TripAdvisor's Gamification Users. *Asia Pacific Journal of Information Systems, 25*(1), 179–210. Retrieved from http://www.earticle.net.lib.jejunu.ac.kr:8010/article.aspx?sn=240813

Sigala, M. (2015b). The application and impact of gamification funware on trip planning and experiences: The case of TripAdvisor's funware. *Electronic Markets, 25*(3), 189–209. doi:10.100712525-014-0179-1

Silva, F., Analide, C., Rosa, L., Felgueiras, G., & Pimenta, C. (2013). Gamification, Social Networks and Sustainable Environments. *International Journal of Interactive Multimedia and Artificial Intelligence*, *2*(4), 52–59. doi:10.9781/ijimai.2013.246

Simões, J., Redondo, R. D., & Vilas, A. F. (2013). A social gamification framework for a K-6 learning platform. *Computers in Human Behavior*, *29*(2), 345–353. doi:10.1016/j.chb.2012.06.007

Snyder, E., & Hartig, J. R. (2013). Gamification of board review: A residency curricular innovation. *Medical Education*, *47*(5), 524–525. doi:10.1111/medu.12190 PMID:23574079

Stavljanin, V., Milenkovic, I., & Sosevic, U. (2016). Educational Website Conversion Improvement Using Gamification. *International Journal of Engineering Education*, *32*(1), 563–573.

Steffen, R., Dirk, S., & Chia-Wen, T. (2015). The Ludic Drive as Innovation Driver: Introduction to the Gamification of Innovation. *Creativity and Innovation Management*, *24*(2), 300–3006. doi:10.1111/caim.12124

Su, C.-H., & Cheng, C.-H. (2015). A mobile gamification learning system for improving the learning motivation and achievements. *Journal of Computer Assisted Learning*, *31*(3), 268–286. doi:10.1111/jcal.12088

Su, C. H., & Su, P. Y. (2015). Study on 3D Meaningful Mobile Gamification Learning Outcome Assessment – An Example of Blood Circulation Lesson. *Applied Mechanics and Materials*, *764–765*, 1395–1399. doi:10.4028/www.scientific.net/AMM.764-765.1395

Tae Kim, J., & Lee, W.-H. (2013). Dynamical model for gamification of learning (DMGL). *Multimedia Tools and Applications*, *74*(19), 8483–8493. doi:10.100711042-013-1612-8

Fan, K. K., Xiao, P. W., & Su, C. H. (2015). The Effects of Learning Styles and Meaningful Learning on the Learning Achievement of Gamification Health Education Curriculum. *EURASIA Journal of Mathematics, Science & Technology Education*, *11*(5), 1211–1229. doi:10.12973/eurasia.2015.1413a

Tzimerman, A., Herer, Y. T., & Shtub, A. (2016). Supply Chain Education-the Contribution of Gamification. *International Journal of Engineering Education*, *32*(1), 479–490.

Uğurel, I., Morali, S., Koyunkaya, M. Y., & Karahan, Ö. (2016). Developing and Evaluating Creativity Gamification Rehabilitation System: The Application of PCA-ANFIS Based Emotions Model. *Eurasia Journal of Mathematics. Science and Technology Education*, *12*(2), 203–231. doi:10.12973/eurasia.2016.1523a

Urh, M., Vukovic, G., Jereb, E., & Pintar, R. (2015). The Model for Introduction of Gamification into E-learning in Higher Education. *Procedia: Social and Behavioral Sciences*, *197*, 388–397. doi:10.1016/j.sbspro.2015.07.154

Veronica Marin Guadalupe Maldonado, M. L. (2015). Can Gamification be introduced within primary classes? *Digital Education*, (June), 55–68.

Villagrasa, S., Fonseca, D., Redondo, E., & Duran, J. (2014). Teaching Case of Gamification and Visual Technologies for Education. *Journal of Cases on Information Technology*, *16*(December), 38–57. doi:10.4018/jcit.2014100104

Wells, C. (2016). MRS 'Methodology in context, London, 26 November 2015 'To game or not to game: An investigation of the impact of survey visualisation and gamification. *International Journal of Market Research*, *58*(2), 325–331. doi:10.2501/IJMR-2016-017

Werbach, K. (2012). *How game thinking can revolutionize your business*. Wharton.

Zuckerman, O., & Gal-Oz, A. (2014). Deconstructing gamification: Evaluating the effectiveness of continuous measurement, virtual rewards, and social comparison for promoting physical activity. *Personal and Ubiquitous Computing*, *18*(7), 1705–1719. doi:10.100700779-014-0783-2

This research was previously published in the Journal of Information Technology Research (JITR), 13(3); pages 58-79, copyright year 2020 by IGI Publishing (an imprint of IGI Global).

Chapter 36
Evaluating Social Change Games:
Employing the RETAIN Model

Laurie O Campbell
https://orcid.org/0000-0001-7313-5457
University of Central Florida, Orlando, USA

Glenda A Gunter
The University of Central Florida, Orlando, USA

Robert F Kenny
Florida Gulf Coast University, Fort Myers, USA

ABSTRACT

The RETAIN Model is a game design and evaluation model for serious games. In this study, educators evaluated social change web-based and mobile app games using the RETAIN model rubric. In general, web-based games scored higher on the RETAIN rubric than their mobile app counterparts. In addition, the educators analyzed the social change games for their "hidden curriculum." In some cases, the rubric and "hidden curriculum" contributed to educators altering the way they used the games they had appraised by supplementing context, incorporating discussion, or not using the games at all. The RETAIN model rubric offered educators a tool to evaluate digital games.

INTRODUCTION

As educators pursue active learning options to engage and incentivize students to learn course content, incorporating games in learning has been found to be an active learning option that moves students from being passive recipients to active learners (Koster, 2013). The interactive nature of games, students' motivation to play, increased engagement, and advancing technologies have teachers vested in planning instruction that includes gamification (Dominguez, et al. 2013) and serious games (Gouveia, Lopes, &

DOI: 10.4018/978-1-6684-7589-8.ch036

de Carvalho, 2011; Iten, & Petko, 2016). Research regarding the pedagogy of serious games in teaching and learning is scant. Further, educators are often unaware as to which games are the most effective for transfer of learning (Kenny & McDaniel, 2011) and how to incorporate serious games (Azadegan, 2012). Teacher's dispositions and beliefs towards the academic benefits of games and personal efficacy for implementing games in instruction lags in comparison to the research (Kenny and Gunter, 2011).

As access to mobile devices burgeons in education, through the availability of tablets, smartphones, and laptop programs, the use of mobile and Web-based digital game apps has grown (Seilhamer, Chen, Bauer, Salter, & Bennett, 2015). Increased accessibility, devices ease of use, and students' natural adeptness towards mobile apps and digital learning afford new and multiple active learning opportunities. Additionally, since many apps and Web-based games are free or low cost, instruction of academic content may be supplemented through web and mobile apps with their affordances of personalized and active learning. By fostering, "learning by doing" deeper learning can be promoted (Altamirano and Jaurez, 2013) and learner-centered pedagogies supported (Crompton, 2013).

Mobile and web-based game apps are not only incorporated into learning to compliment core academic content areas, but digital game apps have been assigned to inform and persuade players regarding social and community concerns. Social changes games are characterized by their purpose to develop: (a) a social issue awareness (Schreiner, 2008), (b) personal empathy (Mariani, & Gandolfi, 2016), and (c) positive actions towards community change (Gerber, & Gaitan, 2017). Apps for social change leverage technology to inspire community action (Fogg, 2003). Examining this genre of mobile and Web-based apps has not been examined beyond a pilot case study (Campbell & Gunter, 2017).

Screening the validity of educational mobile apps intended to support classroom instruction offers teachers a rationale for including mobile apps in instruction. For these reasons, the current study was developed to assess the effectiveness of Web-based games and mobile game apps for social change learning. A rubric built on the RETAIN model provided a means for educators to quickly assess social change games for transfer of knowledge. The RETAIN model, which was developed by an instructional designer, an educator, and a game designer (Gunter et al. 2007; Kenny & Gunter, 2011), was chosen because it had previously been utilized to assess console-based and computer-based games (Gunter, 2011; Zhang, Fan, & Xing, 2010). Further, the RETAIN model has been used as a framework for the design of a multi-player tablet application developed to teach students about the water cycle WaterOn! (Dos Santos., Strada, Martina, & Bottino, 2016). Because of these reasons, the following study, utilized the RETAIN model rubric to assess apps for social change for knowledge transfer.

DIGITAL GAMES

Digital games are pervasive in our culture. In the United States, approximately 97% of children and adolescents play games daily for at least one hour (Granic, Lobel, and Engels, 2014). Lee and Hammer (2011), attributed students' motivation to play games to the social, emotional, and cognitive connections that take place when players are engaged in game playing. While motivation can contribute to game play and engagement, motivation does not ensure learning. However, some studies attribute game play to improved cognitive skills such as increased working memory (Barlett et al., 2009) and problem-solving, although multiple studies yielded differing results (Connolly, 2012).

Digital game mechanics such as music, narrative, video, and images contribute to learners' interest and user experience. The storyline, music, and visuals are immersive elements that promote interactivity and are found in most video, console, and game apps, although these elements may have technological limitations (console versus mobile apps). However, when there are technological limitations as realized in mobile application, digital resources like games can be incorporated to gamify the learning experience. Mobile game apps and Web-based games share elements of gamification including but not limited to both are: (a) interactive; (b) problem-based; (c) manual-free; (d) includes visuals; (e) fosters a fail-safe environment; (f) personalized environment; (g) feedback-driven (Kenny, Gunter, & Campbell, 2017).

WEB-BASED SOCIAL CHANGE GAMES

Technology contributes to social change in a myriad of ways (Fogg, 2003). One such way is Web-based games for social change. These scenario-based games immersed the learner in a story that informed the player about social issues from varying perspectives to increase awareness and promote advocacy (Campbell & Gunter, 2017). Further, while playing these games, players are engaged in making choices and experience the consequences of their decisions in a fail-safe environment.

Within the genre of social change games, content varies and may include games to promote sustainability, proper health care, human rights, civics, conservation, and other social problems. Games for social change have been incorporated into teaching and learning in lieu of lectures, as an adjunct to a lecture, or as an introduction to a local social issue prior to community advocacy. These types of games have been identified as influencing explicit and implicit actions and attitudes (Alhabash & Wise, 2012; Edwards, 2015; Shreiner, 2008). Social change games are often designed with a hidden curriculum, teaching in a way that the learner may be unaware of (Portelli, 1993). A hidden curriculum by definition includes implicit values, norms, behaviors, and attitudes (Skelton, 1997). While it is known that students who play social change games tend to be more empathetic and active in social change (Peng, Lee, & Heeter, 2010), it is unknown if games for social change have the capacity for knowledge transfer as measured by the RETAIN model. Therefore, games for social change on mobile app and Web-based platforms were investigated in this study. Because of the moral and ethical aspects of these types of games, additional questions were added to the RETAIN rubric for reviewers to consider the constructs of bias, morals, ethics, and values. The evaluation of these constructs was to inform reviewers of the point of view with the application being reviewed.

THE RETAIN MODEL

Previous research suggested that serious, often called educational, games have the potential to effect learning by increasing interactivity and providing active learning opportunities that engaged students (Kebritchi & Hirumi, 2008). The importance of games and learning were the impetus behind the relevance embedding transfer adaptation immersion and naturalization (RETAIN) Model. RETAIN originated from the systematic evaluation of game design theory in comparison to traditional learning models and strategies. (Gunter, Kenny, & Vick, 2007). Their scrutiny and attention considered representations of the theories, methods, terminologies, and contexts, identified in game design, play, and instructional design.

The RETAIN model theory includes theories, systems, and research of Gagné, Keller, Piaget's, and Blooms'. Gagné's 'Nine Events of Instruction' have been foundational guiding principles for game software development and design (1985). RETAIN valued Keller's (1982) conceptual framework of motivation and Bloom's (1956) hierarchical model of cognitive domains for knowledge acquisition. RETAIN considered the importance of scaffolded instruction, in that academic content acquisition opportunities were built into the design of games; learners/players could advance to the next level (i.e., 'level up' or 'leveling up").

Game developers' primary focus when creating games includes gameplay mechanics through the techniques employed with in a game, challenges and disruptions. Conversely, classroom educators are concerned with academic content found within the game. Story/narrative has been shown to be an effective mechanism for contextualizing content in the learning process (Kenny & Gunter, 2011; Havens, 2007). Gunter, Kenny, and Vick (2007) found that in general, game design ideologies appeared to be missing schema and dis-equilibration as supported by Piaget (1969), as a result, these concepts became a major emphasis in the RETAIN Model. The RETAIN model incorporated game mechanics and content in its scoring schema (See Figure 1.). The E in the RETAIN model (embedding) urged game designers and game reviewers to analyze the story of serious games for convincing fantasy or storyline to contextualize game content (Kenny & Gunter, 2011).

COMPARATIVE GAME ASSESSMENT MODELS

There have been various attempts to create assessments of serious/educational games. Most, however, tend to focus on the technical aspects and processes, rather than instructional/educational theories and best practices. One such attempt to create a value rubric was provided in El Borji and Khaldi' (2015). They presented cases and citations of game designer scholars whose perspectives emanated from the process side of game design as a means to validate their matrix. For example, the design aspects considered included accuracy of content, degree of difficulty, and consistency. All of these are valid perspectives in the process of design; however, while these researchers did approach pedagogy as a process, they never attempted to evaluate the learnability of the content or the implications behind motivation (Keller, 1989). The researchers did consider other important technical aspects such as granularity of the graphics, browsing design, installation, and system requirement. All of these elements are necessary and effect play and the ability of the game to deliver instruction, but these game mechanics are insufficient criteria to assess whether learning takes place.

Other researchers have developed similar frameworks that do touch on some of the components in RETAIN and seem to fail to address or eliminate the elements that would integrate game design theory and instructional design theory with standard learning theories. Yusoff, Crowder, Gilbert, and Wills (2009) proposed a conceptual framework for scenario-based game design for serious games. The theoretical framework focused on the games' design system architecture and related tools in the game development. Various elements are similar in nature to the RETAIN model. There were no clear connections to learning theories or instruction learning theories provided, although the authors do reference the ideas of Gee (2007).

Figure 1. RETAIN model rubric for mobile game apps

Retain Model Rubric
(Gunter, Kenny, Vick, 2008)

Directions: After playing the game being evaluated, complete the Discussion, Level, and calculate the Score similarly to the way it was on the website and/or in the article.

Name of Game: _____

Game Developer: _____   Platform – Android/IOS: _____

Student Evaluator Name: _____

Element	Description	Discussion/ Level	Weight	Score
Relevance	i) Presenting materials in a way relevant to learners, their needs, and their learning styles, and ii) Ensuring the instructional units are relevant to one another so that the elements link together and build upon previous work.	Level =	1	
Embedding	Assessing how closely the academic content is coupled with the fantasy/story content where fantasy refers to the narrative structure, storylines, player experience, dramatic structure, fictive elements, etc.	Level =	3	
Transfer	How the player can use previous knowledge and apply it in other areas.	Level =	5	
Adaption	A change in behavior as a consequence of transfer.	Level =	4	
Immersion	The player intellectually investing in the context of the game.	Level =	2	
Naturalizat ion	The development of habitual and spontaneous use of information derived within the game.	Level =	6	
		Total		**??/63**

Other Notes:

In contrast, the RETAIN Model is simultaneously based on serious game and instructional design best practices. In the original research that led to RETAIN, the researchers determined anomalies and gaps in the design that could potentially prevent satisfaction of the goals and expected outcomes of the game play. In a follow-up gap analysis study, Kenny and Gunter (2011) verified there was a considerable potential for embedding and authenticating the instructional content in game architectures. All, Castellar, and Van Looy (2015) have contributed to the literature on assessment of digital-games by developing a conceptual framework for evaluating learning effectiveness (defined as attainment of effective goals in a real-world context). The elements considered in this framework, although not inclusive game mechanics, did consider learning, motivational, and efficiency outcomes. Through the design and development of the RETAIN Model and rubric the authors addressed the terms and elements used between the educational environments and game industry. The RETAIN Model has been used to evaluate serious computer-based games, console games, and mobile learning apps (Campbell, Gunter, & Braga, 2015; Campbell, Gunter, Kenny, 2015), since it addressed the elements a game must include to teach and support knowledge acquisition (Gunter, Kenny; Vick, 2008; Kenny & Gunter, 2011).

The following investigation utilized the RETAIN model and additional questions to investigate social change Web-based and mobile game apps. The research questions included:

Research Question 1 (RQ1): What were the differences between mobile apps versus Web-based games ratings on the RETAIN model rubric?

Research Question 2 (RQ2): How does using the results of the RETAIN model effect the use of social change games and mobile game apps in the classroom over time?

Research Question 3 (RQ3): When evaluating the "hidden curriculum" of social change games, how did the results effect teachers decisions to incorporate the games for instructional purposes?

METHODS

The overarching purpose of the study was for K-12 teachers to investigate mobile apps and Web-based games for social change for potential knowledge transfer. The study took place over the course of two semesters. The hypothesis for this study: K-12 teachers who analyzed games using the RETAIN Model Rubric would: (a) indicate they would use the rubric again; (b) adopt apps and games that indicate the highest level of knowledge transfer on the RETAIN model rubric; and (c) identify the hidden curriculum.

The study included mobile apps and Web-based scenario games. The study did not include arcade game. Arcade games and apps are most noted for their repetitive actions and relative simplicity. Specific mobile apps and Web-based games were selected based on their stated instructional learning objectives and an analysis of their educational content. Some of the games considered in the study were currently being used in K-12 classrooms. Web-based games were from the genre of games for social change.

Research Design

The study utilized a concurrent triangulation design (see Figure 2). Each semester, all data types (quantitative and qualitative) were collected concurrently (Creswell, 2015). To confirm findings, data were analyzed separately by type (qualitative and quantitative) and by semester. Then the qualitative and quantitative data were combined for triangulation purposes. The study was designed to explain how the RETAIN rubric was used by K-12 teachers to evaluate mobile apps and Web-based games. Teachers' perspectives regarding the immediate and long-term use of the RETAIN model rubric were examined through interviews and focus groups to provide a phenomenological perspective of implementing the RETAIN rubric for curriculum choices.

Figure 2. Study design and data collection points

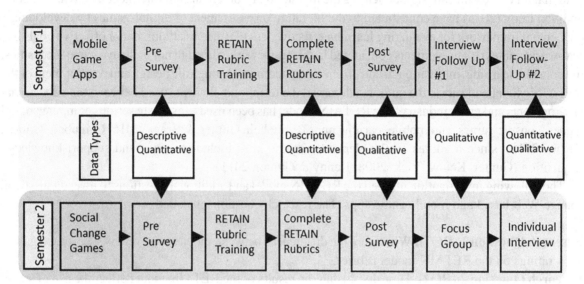

Participants and Settings

Study participants included an intact group of K-12 teachers $N=25$ in a graduate education program at a large university in the southeastern United States. The participants $n=12$ (semester 1) and $n=13$ (semester 2) were either earning their master's degree or completing a certificate program in educational technology, instructional design, or e-learning. Demographics were collected each semester (See Table 1). Eighty percent of the participants were female. Fifty-six percent were under the age of 40. Eighty-four percent had less than 10 years teaching experience. The mode of instruction for these participants was a hybrid environment. Every third week of the semester, the participants were in the face-to-face classroom while the other two weeks they received instruction through an online learning management system.

Table 1. Study demographics

N=25	Female	Male	Age 23-39	Age 40-55	Teaching Experience < 5 years	Teaching Experience < 10 years	Teaching Experience < 15 years
Semester 1	9	3	8	4	6	4	2
Semester 2	11	2	6	7	3	8	2
Total	20	5	14	11	9	12	4

Instrumentation and Timeline

Pre-study Survey

The pre-survey instrument was designed by the researchers to collect baseline data related to: (a) types of devices used in instruction, (b) participants' practices incorporating games in instruction, and (c) prior experiences evaluating games including the RETAIN model. After completing the pre-study survey, students read about the RETAIN model, serious games, and mobile apps and instruction. All quantitative data was collected through Qualtrics and analyzed through SPSS. Online discussions were analyzed through NVivo 11.

RETAIN Model Rubric

The RETAIN model rubric was introduced to the participants after they read the related literature on RETAIN. As a class, participants reviewed a game and completed the RETAIN rubric. The intent of this activity was for the K-12 teaches to practice completing the rubric and to scaffold the K-12 teachers' skills of evaluating games with the RETAIN rubric. In semester two, the RETAIN rubric was slightly modified to collect information specific to social change games (see Figure 3). Participants evaluated either five mobile game apps (semester 1) or three games for social change (semester 2) during a four-week period. Participants shared their evaluations with each other through discussion at the end of the four-week period.

The RETAIN scoring rubric has an assigned point value of 0-3 for the various six elements of game design. Further, each element was weighted according to its perceived importance. As with previous administrations, the weighted order is Relevance, Immersion, Embedding, Adaption, Transfer, and Naturalization with Naturalization assigned the greatest weight. The highest rating an app could receive was 63 points. The higher the score, the stronger the capacity of the mobile game application to support or supplement knowledge transfer. Participants recorded and calculated the appropriate points for each category. Participants followed up with a written rationale that included specific evidence or the lack of evidence to support their score (see Figure 1 and 3).

Post-study Survey

Immediately after the final class discussion related to RETAIN, participants completed the post survey. Questions in the post survey were asked to determine how the K-12 teachers completed the rubrics, the lessons they learned, and to ascertain their position and dispositions regarding mobile game apps and Web-based games. Follow up questions for the post survey were considered from the post-survey analysis.

Post Interviews and Focus Groups

Finally, post interviews were conducted by phone. The focus group in semester 2 was conducted in a face-to-face environment. The interview questions were designed to provide feedback about the long-term effects on both the K-12 teachers (participants) and their students. One person followed up by email.

Figure 3. RETAIN model modified for web-based social change games

Retain Model Rubric
(Gunter, Kenny, & Vick, 2008)

Directions: After playing the game being evaluated, complete the Discussion, Level, and calculate the Score similarly to the way it was on the website and/or in the article.

Name of Game: _____

Game Developer: _____   Platform: _____

Student Evaluator Name: _____

Element	Description	Discussion/ Level	Weight	Score
Relevance	i) Presenting materials in a way relevant to learners, their needs, and their learning styles, and ii) Ensuring the instructional units are relevant to one another so that the elements link together and build upon previous work.	**Level =**	1	
Embedding	Assessing how closely the academic content is coupled with the fantasy/story content where fantasy refers to the narrative structure, storylines, player experience, dramatic structure, fictive elements, etc.	**Level =**	3	
Transfer	How the player can use previous knowledge and apply it in other areas.	**Level =**	5	
Adaption	A change in behavior as a consequence of transfer.	**Level =**	4	
Immersion	The player intellectually investing in the context of the game.	**Level =**	2	
Naturalizat ion	The development of habitual and spontaneous use of information derived within the game.	**Level =**	6	
		Total		**??/63**
Bias Morals Ethics Values	**Comments (Bias and Morals):**	**Comments (Ethics and Values)**		
Would you recommend this game to use in a classroom?	**YES or NO**	**If so or not why or why not?**		

Other Notes:

RESULTS AND DISCUSSION

Research Question 1: What were the differences between mobile apps versus Web-based games ratings on the RETAIN model rubric?

Games are developed for multiple platforms; knowing if platform makes a difference is beneficial when knowledge transfer is a priority. To determine the answer to this question, the overall scores on the RETAIN rubrics were compared. As anticipated, mobile apps scored lower overall as compared to Web-based games. Mobile game apps score ranges for the apps reviewed were from 8 to 52. Web-based games for social change scores ranged from 39 to 63 (which is the maximum amount of points a game can earn on the RETAIN rubric). The technological constraints of the mobile device (smartphone and tablet) may have contributed to the lower overall scores of mobile devices to laptops and Web-based games. Consistently, participants indicated that the mobile game apps lacked Immersion qualities. One participant noted, "The player/learner is not involved cognitively, physically, psychologically, or emotionally in the game play or content." Conversely, participants indicated that some Web-based games had more immersive qualities. "The graphics and game play immerse the learners in the experience, but do not distract from the learning process. The different cases made the learner feel like a true detective." The range of scores support that RETAIN measured Web-based games higher than mobile game apps (See Table 2). While the scores were generally lower in the immersion category, they were also lower in the transfer area.

Table 2. Average score difference for mobile game apps and web-based games by category

		Mobile Game Apps	Web-based Games
R	Relevance	1-3	1-3
E	Embedding	3-6	3-9
T	Transfer	5-15	5-15
A	Adaptation	4-8	8-12
I	Immersion	2-4	4-6
N	Naturalization	6	6-18
	Average Score Range	21-42	27-63

Since the RETAIN model was designed to evaluate and create console and serious games (Gunter, Kenny, Vick, 2007) it is reasonable to consider that Web-based games would score higher than their mobile game app counterparts.

Research Question 2: How does using the results of the RETAIN model effect the use of social change games and mobile game apps in the classroom over time?

All participants had no prior experience with or knowledge of the RETAIN model. Forty-eight percent of the participants had incorporated digital games as part of their curriculum. The other 52% indicated that they did not use games. Their reasons for game usage included the time it took to incorporate games, which would limit their instructional time and focus, and the lack of games for their content area. Games were a part of instruction at all K-12 grades represented. Digital games were most prominent in K-8 grades. Those who did not incorporate digital games mentioned using games for review like *Jeopardy,* or *$100,000 Pyramid.*

The data to answer this research question were analyzed from the post surveys, interviews, and focus group. Open-ended comments were coded as positive, negative, or neutral. These comments were then coded and grouped. The categories that emerged from the post survey after dual-coding included: (a) future usability; (b) content accuracy; (c) student engagement; (d) curriculum support; and (e) prerequisite skills. The comments were counted and reported (See Table 3). Fifty-two unique Web-based games were analyzed along with 43 Mobile game apps.

Table 3. Initial response of all games after completing the study

	Positive	Negative	Neutral	Sample Comments
Future Usability	14	9	4	"The developers suggested using the game with kids who are having trouble adjusting socially. I think it could be used to help teach all kids some social skills." "I would not use this game with my students. It does not have educational value because it lacked content."
Content Accuracy	3	2		"The academic content of the game is closely related to true experiences and reality." "This application was not at all educational and if students were to play this game, they would not learn much other than how to maneuver the phone appropriately to go over or under various obstacles."
Student Engagement	18	5		"It's very simplistic and doesn't hook the user. NO IMMERSIVE QUALITIES." "I can see my students wanting to play this game for hours. It is intriguing."
Curriculum Support	15	3	3	"good source to reinforce preexisting knowledge or post-instructional acquired knowledge"
Prerequisite Skills	5	7		"I would not recommend the game as a primary source of instruction because of the lengthy text learners must read to get to the point of mastery in gameplay."

The middle school teacher/reviewer/participant quoted above recognized that even though the game had instructional qualities and scored in a reasonably high range, the text length may be counterintuitive to gameplay thereby suppressing potential knowledge transfer.

GAMES OVER TIME

During the follow up interviews and focus group for both semesters, a smaller group of participants *n*=7 agreed to be interviewed. The participants were asked how the RETAIN model had impacted their current game choice and usage. Seventy-one percent of the K-12 teacher/participants interviewed incorporated games evaluated with the RETAIN model rubric. These participants had either evaluated previously used curriculum-related digital games or adopted new curriculum-related games that were evaluated based on the RETAIN model. Two participants (teaching Language Arts, and Math) added social change games to support a unit in their curriculum. Of those participants interviewed, all but one participant chose Web-based games instead of apps. Three participants discontinued use of curriculum-related games based on low scores on the RETAIN rubric. One participant indicated that they kept a low scoring Web-based app because the intent of the app was awareness and not knowledge transfer. Finally, of the 23 Web-based games and 14 Mobile game apps reviewed among the participants that participated in follow up interviews and the focus group, only 8 of the Web-based games, and 4 of the Mobile game apps were being utilized within the participants classroom.

Research Question 3: When evaluating the "hidden curriculum" of social change games, how did the results effect teachers decisions to incorporate the games for instructional purposes?

When evaluating social change games, participants were asked to identify explicit and implicit bias, morals, ethics, and values. The data was coded for positive and negative comments. More comments were made about bias than morals, ethics, and values. Areas of perceived bias included gender, ethnicity and race, culture, and social structures. Most comments related to the visuals that the teachers observed.

For instance, the area of ethnicity and race statements that addressed bias included, "Within the game, the clients and lawyers are of various genders and race." Yet another participant noted, "Learners are able to choose the games' guiding avatar's gender and skin color, which is a feature students like and eliminates bias." However, not all comments were positive in this area. When referencing a game about healthy food consumption, the reviewer commented, "While the images for the case files were diverse in nature, there was no Asian or Indian representation. The foods were more Americanized and yet our students are not all American." During the follow-up interview, one teacher explained how they handle this type of bias. She stated, "I tell my students prior to playing the game that not all types of cultures were represented but the principles of the games are important." However, another teacher stated that for some students, playing these games "presents a challenge because of religious or cultural food restriction such as those that do not include dairy or meat." He further stated, "It could indicate to some that those who follow this type of eating are privileged over others who don't."

Social structure bias was observed in several of the games. "For kids living in non-traditional home environments or homes with limited resources, they may not relate to some of the scenarios because the scenarios were not diverse enough." Another participant observed, "Only traditional families were represented." Implicit bias in social structure was observed, but less frequently. Other biases took the form of stereotypes and were related to the avatars' attitudes and values, "Some avatars were written to be self-serving and may come off as insulting and divisive, these avatars were over-simplified to make an exaggerated point."

Comments regarding ethics, morals, and values observed were minimal. In the follow-up interviews the lack of recognition of ethics, morals, and values were addressed. Participants agreed that it was easier to address overt bias than to look at implicit bias, values, ethics, and morals. One teacher/participant had her students critically evaluate an assigned social change game, which led to multiple discussions. The participants in the focus group did concur in every reviewed game that valuing human life was at the forefront. Even if there were destruction of human life, the games would implicitly counterbalance destruction with preserving or uplifting humans. The participants did not eliminate a game because of the hidden curriculum; rather, they altered the implementation of the games.

CONCLUSION

The study confirms previous studies (Campbell & Gunter, 2015a; 2015b; Kenny, Gunter, Campbell, 2017) that teachers' utilizing a tool to review digital games affects the use and implementation in teaching and learning. Benefits of the study for the participants included: (a) thorough evaluation of digital games for evidence of knowledge transfer; (b) gaining new perspectives about the game mechanics; and (c) identifying the hidden curriculum within social change games. Using the RETAIN model rubric during the study translated to authentic learning environments. Participants (K-12 teachers) utilized the RETAIN model rubric after the study to benefit their own K-12 students by choosing a game that met their objective.

The RETAIN model rubric successfully aided in the evaluation of a specific genre of Web-based games supporting the initial intent of the RETAIN model (Gunter, Kenny, & Vick, 2007). It was determined in this study that Web-based games scored higher on the RETAIN model rubric than their mobile game app counterparts. However, this does not suggest that mobile game apps should not be used. There are multiple educational purposes for incorporating games. If knowledge transfer is the aim of incorporating digital games in learning, a higher scoring game or app offers greater potential. The authors recommend in future studies exploration of other genres of games. Further recommendations include formalizing methods for identifying the hidden curriculum of social change games.

The limitations of the present study included all of the participants were in a graduate degree program and were trained to use the rubric. Therefore, the results may not be the same when someone is not trained to use the rubric. In follow-up interviews, the participants expressed increased efficacy in their rubric ratings suggestive that training to use the rubric yielded a more accurate score. The relationship between higher scoring apps and web-based games and improved achievement was not the purpose of the study. Therefore, future studies could include the validation of the RETAIN model related to achievement.

Reviewing games using RETAIN and observing the "hidden curriculum," did influence the way teachers implemented the games they reviewed both in the immediate use and over time. The names of the games reviewed by the teachers in this study were not the focus of this study. Rather, the purpose of the study was to analyze the RETAIN model as a tool to evaluate mobile and Web-based games for classroom use that would best support curriculum. In conclusion, the RETAIN model rubric offers educators a tool to evaluate digital games for transfer of knowledge. While designed for console and stand-alone games, the RETAIN model rubric has been successfully used to evaluate Web-based social change games and mobile apps.

REFERENCES

Alhabash, S., & Wise, K. (2012). PeaceMaker: Changing students' attitudes toward Palestinians and Israelis through video game play. *International Journal of Communication*, 6, 25.

All, A., Castellar, E. N., & Van Looy, J. (2015). Towards a conceptual framework for assessing the effectiveness of digital game-based learning. *Computers & Education*, 88, 29–37.

Altamirano, N. N., & Jaurez, J. J. (2013). Student built games in economic courses: Applying the game design methodology as another approach to deeper learning. *Journal Of Research In Innovative Teaching*, 6(1), 119–135.

Azadegan, A., Riedel, J. C., & Hauge, J. B. (2012). Serious Games Adoption in Corporate Training. In M. Ma, M. F. Oliveira, J. B. Hauge, H. Duin, & K.-D. Thoben (Eds.), *Serious Games Development and Applications*. Springer Berlin Heidelberg. doi:10.1007/978-3-642-33687-4_6

Barlett, C. P., Vowels, C. L., Shanteau, J., Crow, J., & Miller, T. (2009). The effect of violent and non-violent computer games on cognitive performance. *Computers in Human Behavior*, 25, 96–102. doi:10.1016/j.chb.2008.07.008

Bloom, B. S. (1956). *Taxonomy of educational objectives, Handbook I: The cognitive domain*. New York: David McKay Co, Inc.

El Borji, Y., & Khaldi, M. (2014). Comparative study to develop a tool for the quality assessment of serious games intended to be used in education. [iJET]. *International Journal of Emerging Technologies in Learning*, 9(9), 50–55.

Campbell, L. O., Gunter, G., & Braga, J. (2015). Utilizing the RETAIN model to evaluate mobile learning applications. *Paper presented at Society for Information Technology & Teacher Education International Conference* (pp. 670–674). Academic Press.

Campbell, L. O., Gunter, G., & Kenny, R. (2015). The gamification of mobile learning evaluated by the RETAIN model. *Proceedings of Association for Educational Communication and Technology: Accelerate Learning: Racing into the Future Conference*, Indianapolis, IN, November 3–7. Academic Press.

Campbell, L. O., & Gunter, G. (2017). An Evaluation of Social Change Games as viewed through the RETAIN model. In P. Resta & S. Smith (Eds.), *Proceedings of Society for Information Technology & Teacher Education International Conference* (pp. 2552-2556). Austin, TX, United States: Association for the Advancement of Computing in Education (AACE).

Connolly, T. M., Boyle, E. A., MacArthur, E., Hainey, T., & Boyle, J. (2012). A systematic literature review of empirical evidence on computer games and serious games. *Computers & Education*, 59(2), 661–686. doi:10.1016/j.compedu.2012.03.004

Creswell, J. W. (2015). *A concise introduction to mixed methods research*. Los Angeles: Sage.

Crompton, H. (2013). A historical overview of mobile learning: Towards learner-center education. In Berge & Muilenburg (Eds.), Handbook of mobile learning. New York: Routledge.

Dominguez, A., Saenz-De-Navarrete, J., De-Marcos, L., Fernández-Sanz, L., Pagés, C., & Martínez-Herráiz, J.-J. (2013). Gamifying learning experiences: Practical implications and outcomes. *Computers & Education*, 63, 380–392. doi:10.1016/j.compedu.2012.12.020

Dos Santos, A. D., Strada, F., Martina, A., & Bottino, A. (2016). Designing collaborative games for children education on sustainable development. *Proceedings of the International Conference on Intelligent Technologies for Interactive Entertainment* (pp. 3-12). Cham: Springer.

Edwards, R. (2015). Software and the hidden curriculum in digital education. *Pedagogy, Culture & Society*, 23(2), 265–279. doi:10.1080/14681366.2014.977809

Fogg, B. J. (2003). *Persuasive technology: Using computers to change what we think and do*. San Francisco: Morgan Kaufmann. doi:10.1016/B978-155860643-2/50011-1

Gagné, R. (1985). *The conditions of learning* (4th ed.). New York: Holt, Rinehart & Winston.

Gee, J. P. (2007). *What video games have to teach us about learning and literacy* (2nd ed.). New York: Palgrave.

Gerber, H. R., & Gaitan, L. (2017). "Let's Change Already": Community Activism and Pro-Social Play in Egypt. *Educational Technology, 57*(2), 55–61.

Gouveia, D., Lopes, D., & de Carvalho, C. V. (2011). Serious gaming for experiential learning. *Proceedings of the 2011 Frontiers in Education Conference (FIE)*. Academic Press. doi:10.1109/FIE.2011.6142778

Granic, I., Lobel, A., & Engels, R. (2014). The benefits of playing video games. *The American Psychologist, 69*(1), 66–78. doi:10.1037/a0034857 PMID:24295515

Gunter, G., Kenny, R., & Vick, E. (2007). Taking educational games seriously: Using the RETAIN model to design endogenous fantasy into standalone educational games. *Educational Technology Research and Development, 56*(5/6), 511–537.

Gunter, G., Campbell, L., Braga, J., Racilan, M., & Souza, V. (2016). Using the RETAIN Model to evaluate mobile educational games for language learning. *Revista Brasileira de Lingüística Aplicada, 16*(2), 209–235. doi:10.1590/1984-639820168543

Havens, K. (2007). *Story proof: The science behind the startling power of story*. Greenwich, CT: Libraries Unlimited.

Iten, N., & Petko, D. (2016). Learning with serious games: Is fun playing the game a predictor of learning success? *British Journal of Educational Technology, 47*(1), 151–163. doi:10.1111/bjet.12226

Kebritchi, M., & Hirumi, A. (2008). Examining the pedagogical foundations of modern educational computer games. *Computers & Education, 51*(4), 1729–1743. doi:10.1016/j.compedu.2008.05.004

Keller, J. M. (1983). Motivational design of instruction. In C. M. Reigeluth (Ed.), *Instructional design theories and models: An overview of their current status* (pp. 383–434). New York: Lawrence Erlbaum.

Kenny, R., & Gunter, G. (2011). Factors affecting adoption of video games in the classroom. *Journal of Interactive Learning Research, 22*(2), 259276.

Kenny, R., Gunter, G., & Campbell, L. O. (2017). Teachers' assessment of the instructional efficacy of mobile apps: A formative case study. *Journal of Formative Design in Learning, 1*(1), 56–63. doi:10.100741686-017-0003-3

Kenny, R., & McDaniel, R. (2011). The role teachers' expectations and value assessments play in their adopting and integrating video games into the curriculum. *British Journal of Educational Technology, 42*(2), 197–213. doi:10.1111/j.1467-8535.2009.01007.x

Koster, R. (2013). *A theory of fun for game design*. Scottsdale, AZ: Paraglyph Press.

Lee, J. J., & Hammer, J. (2011). Gamification in education: What, how, why bother? Definitions and uses. *Exchange Organizational Behavior Teaching Journal, 15*(2), 1–5.

Mariani, I., & Gandolfi, E. (2016). Negative Experiences as Learning Trigger: A Play Experience Empirical Research on a Game for Social Change Case Study. *International Journal of Game-Based Learning*, *6*(3), 50–73. doi:10.4018/IJGBL.2016070104

Peng, W., Lee, M., & Heeter, C. (2010). The effects of a serious game on role-taking and willingness to help. *Journal of Communication*, *60*(4), 723–742. doi:10.1111/j.1460-2466.2010.01511.x

Piaget, J. (1969). *The mechanisms of perception*. London: Rutledge & Kegan Paul.

Portelli, J. (1993). Exposing the hidden curriculum. *Journal of Curriculum Studies*, *25*(4), 343–358. doi:10.1080/0022027930250404

Schreiner, K. (2008). Digital games target social change. *IEEE Computer Graphics and Applications*, *28*(1), 12–17. doi:10.1109/MCG.2008.4 PMID:18240782

Seilhamer, R., Chen, B., Bauer, S., Salter, A., & Bennett, L. (2015). Changing Mobile Learning Practices: A Multiyear Study 2012–2016. *Educause Review*. Retrieved from https://er.educause.edu/

Yusoff, A., Crowder, R., Gilbert, L., & Wills, G. (2009). A Conceptual Framework for Serious Games. *Proceedings of the 2009 Ninth IEEE International Conference On Advanced Learning Technologies*. IEEE. 10.1109/ICALT.2009.19

Zhang, H. F., Fan, X. Y., & Xing, H. F. (2010). Research on the design and evaluation of educational games based on the RETAIN Model. *Proceedings of the 2010 Third International Symposium on Knowledge Acquisition and Modeling, Knowledge Acquisition and Modeling (KAM)* (pp. 375-378). Academic Press. 10.1109/KAM.2010.5646186

This research was previously published in the International Journal of Game-Based Learning (IJGBL), 9(4); pages 31-44, copyright year 2019 by IGI Publishing (an imprint of IGI Global).

Chapter 37
Therapeutic Gaming for Adolescent Anxiety:
Development and Evaluation of a Mobile Intervention

Steven Barnes
https://orcid.org/0000-0002-5114-2178
University of Bolton, UK

Julie Prescott
https://orcid.org/0000-0001-8612-2495
University of Bolton, UK

ABSTRACT

Anxiety disorders (AD) are the most prevalent of the mental health conditions and are associated with significant and long-lasting burden of disease both for affected individuals and healthcare systems designed to support them. Despite this, barriers to traditional interventions mean less than half of adolescents experiencing ADs seek-treatment, with less than 20% of treatment-seekers ultimately receiving a scientifically validated intervention. Therapeutic games show significant potential to help reduce AD in adolescents, with some concerns remaining over their abilities to engage users, particularly over time. The chapter presents two studies relating to the development of a new mobile gamified intervention for adolescents with AD. This includes a user-feedback study on currently available games for anxiety and depression, followed by a user-feedback, acceptability, and intention-to-use study of a development version of the new intervention.

DOI: 10.4018/978-1-6684-7589-8.ch037

INTRODUCTION

Background

Anxiety Disorders (AD) are the most prevalent of the mental health conditions and are the sixth-leading cause of disability worldwide (Baxter, Scott, Vos & Whiteford, 2014). ADs are associated with significant and long-lasting burden of disease both for affected individuals and the healthcare systems designed to support them (Bandelow & Michaelis, 2015). Among children and adolescents, AD prevalence ranges from 4-20% (Bhatia & Goyal, 2018).

The extant evidence indicates that the proportion of adolescents suffering from AD has increased by up to 70% since the mid-1980s, and that there are now approximately 300,000 young people in the UK with an AD meeting the criteria for diagnosis (Hagell, 2012), making AD the most common disorder of this life-stage (Rapee, Schniering & Hudson, 2009). Prevalence studies show that at any given time, between 3- and 12% of children and adolescents meet the diagnostic criteria for an AD (Rice & Thapar, 2009). As is the case with other psychological disorders including depression, the development of AD increases significantly during adolescent years (Costello & Angold, 1995; Grant, 2013).

A noteworthy heterogeneity in evidence demonstrates that while the initial development of an AD may occur in adulthood, the majority of ADs begin during adolescence, such as social phobia (Kessler, 2005; Beesdo, Knappe & Pine, 2009; Wittchen & Fehm 2003) (where few cases are documented as first instances after adolescent years), and Generalised Anxiety Disorders (Kessler, 2005; de Graaf et al., 2003). At least 50% of adults aged 32-years and meeting the diagnostic criteria for AD show evidence that they would also have met the diagnostic criteria between the ages of 11- and 15-years (Gregory et al., 2007). Therefore, it has been argued that adolescence may be a 'critical period' for AD and future mental health and wellbeing, as the existential identities formed during adolescent years become consolidated as this stage of life closes and adulthood begins (Berman, Weems & Stickle, 2006).

Despite the prevalence of ADs, the short- and long-term implications of AD experience, and the evidence-base demonstrating the efficacy of a range of psychiatric and psychotherapeutic interventions, less than half of adolescents experiencing ADs seek-treatment, with fewer than 20% of treatment-seekers ultimately receiving a scientifically validated intervention (Kessler et al., 2008; Collins, Westra, Dozois & Burns, 2004). Considerable under-recognition, and subsequent under-treatment of anxiety disorders is well-documented, an issue documented by existing literature to be further complicated by a range of social, clinical, and pathological factors including non-disclosure (Corrigan, Druss & Perlick, 2014), the availability of therapeutic provision (Andlin-Sobocki & Wittchen, 2005), and drop-out from existing clinical interventions.

The Role of Digital Interventions and Serious Games in the Therapeutic Process

Electronic Health (eHealth) is defined as "an emerging field in the intersection of medical informatics, public health and business, referring to health services and information delivered or enhanced through the Internet and related technologies" (Eysenbach, 2001). First noted by Abt (1970), serious and therapeutic video games (STVGs) are video games which are designed with a primary purpose other than entertainment, usually to educate or inform the player (Djaouti et al., 2011). Games are increasingly popular and pervasive among adolescents in modern society, with up to 97% of teenagers engaging in some degree of gaming activity (Lenhart et al., 2008). In recent years, a growing focus has been placed on how serious games can be utilised to make positive changes across a range of physical and psychological health-related conditions (Huang & Johnson, 2008).

By harnessing the immersive and entertaining principles of video games, serious games aim to deliver educational material in a gamified context (Thom, Millen & di Micco, 2012). Research has suggested that the fantasy and virtual elements of serious games may enhance learning experiences (Huang & Johnson, 2008) by allowing for multi-sensory hypothesis testing, immediate feedback opportunities, and absence of real-life repercussions of the player's actions (Oblinger, 2004), within a personalisable and adaptable environment (Cannon-Bowers, Bowers & Procci, 2011; Buszewicz, 2006). By affording players ownership over the learning environment, STVGs also provide a critical bridge between access to educational materials and motivating contexts for their delivery (de Smet et al., 2014).

Extant data demonstrates the efficacy of serious games in producing significant and clinically measurable improvements across a diverse range of psychological conditions (Baranowski et al., 2013), for example as tools for reducing psychopathological symptoms associated with gambling disorders (Tárrega et al., 2015), and as a preliminary treatment to cognitive behavioural therapy (CBT) for bulimia nervosa (Giner-Bartolomé et al., 2015). A 2012 review of 38 publications regarding STVG use across a variety of therapeutic frameworks and psychological conditions concluded that game-engagement improved user understanding of their condition, self-management strategy awareness and use, and overall wellbeing, and were in addition a positive distraction-technique from immediate symptom experience (Primack et al., 2012), demonstrating improvement in 69% of cases.

A recent systematic review regarding the use of serious and therapeutic games for adolescent anxiety disorders found that while research into this field appears at present to be extremely limited, as demonstrated by the small number of papers eligible for inclusion in the review, early findings from these studies suggest that therapeutic games have significant potential to help reduce anxiety levels in adolescents (Barnes & Prescott, 2018). However, some concerns remain regarding the capacities of existing protocols to engage users in continued use. Furthermore, digital mental health interventions more widely have been associated with high attrition rates, including rejection after only a single use (Consumer Health Information Corporation, 2011). Participants have also been found to describe learning modules as 'tiring' (Gerrits, van der Zanden, Visscher, & Conjin, 2007) or 'tedious' (Burckhardt, Manicavasgar, Batterham, Miller, Talbot & Lum, 2015).

It has been argued that engaging end users in the development and early testing of eHealth products provides valuable data for their improvement (Ware et al., 2017), with iterative prototyping acting as a form of risk analysis and a requirement for the development of compelling game experiences (Schell, 2008). Despite this, a recent review identified 20 serious games developed for the treatment of anxiety and/or depression, finding half (50%) were developed with some degree of input from intended end-users, with 45% involving users only in the testing phase (Dekker & Williams, 2017). This may explain that, while existing games have shown promise in reducing anxiety symptoms in adolescents (Barnes & Prescott, 2018), their anxiolytic capabilities and capacity to motivate continued play are not always maintained beyond short intervention periods (Schuurmans et al., 2015; Scholten et al., 2016). Consequently, further investigation into how digital interventions, such as therapeutic games, are received by anxious adolescents may help to enhance the continued viability of gamified interventions. The following studies therefore aimed to improve not only the reach of STVGs in terms of better engaging potential users, but also their longitudinal viability, in maintaining user-interest and facilitating the continued practice and maintenance behaviours associated with, and essential for, prolonged remission (HEFCE, 2015; Wiles et al., 2014; Cartwright-Hatton, 2004; James, Soler & Weatherall, 2005).

MAIN FOCUS AND AIMS OF THE CHAPTER

According to Salen and Zimmerman (2004), game design is "the process by which a game designer creates a game to be encountered by a player, from which meaningful play emerges." In this sense, a game cannot be dissociated from its player, as it is the player who constructs narrative and meaning from their experience of play. In this sense, the involvement of potential end-users in the development and review of gamified interventions is essential in understanding the factors which contribute to the emergence of meaningful play.

The present investigations aimed to address the aforementioned shortcomings of existing therapeutic games for adolescent anxiety disorders, by employing potential end-users from the early stages of the development process. User perceptions of existing protocols in terms of platform and game-mechanics, along with their relationships with intention to use, would be utilised in the development of a new intervention. Subsequently, the resulting intervention would also be evaluated on the same basis, in order to maximise its acceptability, and promote prolonged engagement.

Consequently, the first empirical investigation presented in this chapter represents a pre-development exploration of adolescent expectations and requirements of therapeutic games. To this end, user perceptions of game-quality regarding a number of existing and freely available games for anxiety and depression (utilising a number of game-mechanics and therapeutic frameworks) were assessed, along with each game's capability in reducing self-reported anxiety symptoms. Furthermore, given the importance of continued commitment to the development and maintenance of therapeutic gains (HEFCE, 2015; Wiles et al., 2014; Cartwright-Hatton, 2004; James, Soler & Weatherall, 2005), and the value of games in motivating sustained engagement (Sitzmann, 2011), an exploration of user-perceptions of game-quality will be presented in terms of their relationships with intention to use over a subsequent 12-month period.

Further to these findings and drawing on the principles of self-determination theory (Ryan & Deci, 2000), a mobile gamified anxiolytic intervention for adolescents utilising a combination of tasks derived from CBT and attention-bias modification (ABM) will be described. The second empirical study to be discussed in this chapter consisted of a user-evaluation of a developmental pre-release version of the game. Utilising a similar methodology as the first study, the new development game is therefore compared like-for-like with games previously investigated. User-perceptions of quality and intention to use will be discussed, along with an evaluation of the game's anxiolytic capabilities. Finally, the findings of these investigations will be discussed in terms of the next stages for evaluation of the new intervention.

STUDY ONE

Aims

The first study had three primary aims: (1) to establish existing preferences towards specific game-mechanics (e.g. psychoeducation, attention-bias modification, distraction) in adolescents; (2) to assess the relationship between perception of game impact and anxiolytic impact; (3) to establish if measures of objective quality and player expectations (i.e. the perceived impact of a game on the health condition) may be predictive to intention to use over the following 12-month period.

Method

Design

The present study assumed a pragmatist approach employing a convergent mixed design, in order to maximise the usefulness of the findings later in enhancing the implementations of a subsequently developed intervention (Laver, George, Thomas, Deutsch, & Crotty, 2015). Quantitative feedback was collected regarding quality and satisfaction ratings of the games selected for review. Data were supplemented with qualitative data to provide additional support and detail for the numerical ratings, and to offer further insight into the motivations and reasonings underlying them.

A total of eight games purporting the be 'educational', 'informative', 'relaxing' or 'anxiety-reducing' and covering a range of game-mechanics were selected for review. In order to maximise the accessibility of the study to participants, and due to licensing costs and lack of public availability of some existing games for anxiety (e.g. 'Dojo', 'MindLight') or specific hardwares required (e.g. 'PlayMotion'), a convenience sample of games readily available on the public market were selected. As both the development of applications for anxiety and depression (Mohr et al., 2017), and the study of their acceptability/efficacy (Dekker & Williams, 2017; Garrido et al., 2019) is commonplace in this field, and to widen the number of accessible applications for evaluation, games intended for both conditions were used. A summary of the games reviewed can be seen in *Table 1*.

Table 1. Summary of included games, principle game mechanic and mode of delivery.

Game Title	Principle Mechanic	Mode of Delivery
'Mood Mint'	Attention-bias modification	Mobile*
'Guppy'	Distraction	Mobile*
'PsychMeUp'	Attention-bias modification	Mobile*
'Depression Quest'	Psychoeducation	Browser
'Elude'	Psychoeducation	Browser
'Fireboy & Watergirl'	Exposure	Browser
'Echogenesis'	Distraction	Browser
'Drifting Afternoon'	Distraction	Browser

* All mobile games were available on either the Apple iOS or Google Android operating systems at the time of the study being conducted.

Participants

Participants were recruited on a voluntary basis primarily from two academic institutions: a sixth-form college and a university technical college in the North-West of England. Additionally, a small number of participants were recruited via word-of-mouth. Once provided with a full briefing on of the aims of the study, participants gave consent and were allocated a unique anonymous identification code (e.g. S1-001). For participants aged under 16, or not responsible for paying for app-downloads on their mobile device, parental/guardian and/or bill-payer consent was also obtained.

A total of 60 participants were recruited initially. Of these, seven withdrew voluntarily, and twelve were removed by the experimenter as they did not submit any feedback relating to their games, leaving a final sample of $N=41$, including 17 males (41.5%) and 24 females (58.5%). Ages ranged between 13 and 19 years, with the majority of participants aged between 14 and 18 (85.1%).

Materials and Procedure

Following recruitment and consent, participants were randomly allocated two of the candidate games, and were instructed to use these games for a minimum of one-hour over the following seven days, which could be completed in separate play sessions as required. Following the seven-day testing period, data were collected using the User-Version of the Mobile Application Rating Scale (uMARS) (Stoyanov, Hides, Kavanagh & Wilson, 2016). The uMARS is a 20-item, six-point inventory consisting of four objective quality subscales (engagement, functionality, aesthetics and quality of information provided), one subjective quality subscale, and one subscale designed to measure the respondent's perceptions of an application's impact on the health condition. Mean scores can be calculated by averaging the subscale responses, and an overall total quality score can be generated by calculating a mean of the average scores for the four objective quality subscales. In order to supplement and provide further context to the data obtained by the uMARS, a qualitative version was developed.

The uMARS has strong overall internal consistency ($\alpha=.90$) with high internal consistencies across the subscales, as well as good test-retest reliability at .66 at 1- and 2-month intervals and .70 at 3-months (Stoyanov *et al.,* 2016). Additionally, the uMARS does not need respondents to have any relevant formal training in either the health condition, or the virtual health intervention designed to alleviate its symptoms and is therefore accessible to and suitable for a wide number of audiences. For the purposes of this research, references to 'app' were changed to 'game'. For the purposes of the present research, the uMARS would allow not only for an assessment of user enjoyment of the games played, but also their perceptions of the game's ability to make a positive impact on the health condition. Thus, the uMARS would enable the present study to determine the extent to which preferred game-features of adolescents corresponded with features reported to have an impact on health awareness and behaviour.

Participants were also requested to complete the short-form of the Spielberger State-Trait Anxiety Inventory both before and after their trial period (STAI-Y6) (Marteau & Bekker, 1992); a six-item version of the Spielberger State-Trait Anxiety Inventory (Spielberger, Gorsuch & Lushene, 1970; Spielberger, 1983). The STAI-Y6 produces state-anxiety scores comparable to those of the full 20-item variant, and authors of the scale stipulate that 'normal' anxiety scores range between 34 and 36 (Bekker *et al.,* 2003).

Data were obtained via paper printed document or via Google Forms. Social Presence Theory (Short, Williams & Christie, 1976) posits that computer-mediated communications reduce the salience of individuals in online communications without impeding the salience of the ideas under discussion. Moreover, Internet-facilitated de-individuation increases the extent to which an individual will engage in self-disclosure (McKenna & Bargh, 2000) with increased task-focus and reduced self-awareness and self-regulation (Prentice-Dunn & Rogers, 1982).

Following the one-week trial period, participants were given a further week to finalise and submit feedback and were fully debriefed upon completion. Once this period had elapsed, quantitative data were entered and analysed using IBM SPSS (v25.0), while qualitative data were analysed using NVivo (v12).

Results

Quantitative Findings

Of the 41 participants remaining in the study after withdrawals, 21 (51.2%) provided feedback for two games, and 20 (48.8%) provided feedback for one game, leaving 62 total instances of feedback for analysis. The number of instances of feedback per game and per primary game-mechanic can be found in *Table 2* and *Table 3*.

Table 2. Instances of quantitative feedback per game.

Game	Primary Mechanic	Frequency (%)
MoodMint	Attention-bias modification	5 (8.1%)
Guppy	Distraction	13 (21.0%)
PsychMeUp	Attention-bias modification	7 (11.3%)
Depression Quest	Psychoeducation	13 (21.0%)
Elude	Psychoeducation	13 (21.0%)
Fireboy & Watergirl	Exposure	5 (8.1%)
Echogenesis	Distraction	4 (6.5%)
Drifting Afternoon	Distraction	2 (3.2%)

Table 3. Instances of quantitative feedback per mechanic.

Game Mechanic	Games Included	Frequency (%)
Attention-bias modification	MoodMint, PsychMeUp	18 (29.0%)
Psychoeducation	Depression Quest, Elude	26 (42.0%)
Distraction	Guppy, Echogenesis, Drifting Afternoon	13 (21.0%)
Exposure	Fireboy & Watergirl	5 (8.1%)

Average subscale ratings for each game-mechanic were calculated along with a total quality score to assess user-preferences. An overview of the raw data in this regard can be observed in *Table 4*.

The above scores indicated that all games under review scored a moderate overall total quality rating of between 2 and 3. While comparable in terms of total quality score, a number of differences in preferences emerged at subscale level. While exposure games were reported as the most engaging of games (followed by ABM, distraction, and psychoeducation), quality of health information was rated most favourably for games utilising ABM.

Table 4. Average total and subscale quality ratings by game mechanic.

Game Mechanic (N Ratings)	Total Quality Mean (SD)	ENG Mean (SD)	FUNC Mean (SD)	AES Mean (SD)	INF Mean (SD)	SUBJ-QU Mean (SD)	PI Mean (SD)
ABM (N=18)	2.98 (.81)	2.52 (.90)	3.43 (.87)	3.00 (1.09)	2.96 (.93)	2.39 (.83)	2.67 (1.06)
Distraction (N=13)	2.96 (.75)	2.65 (.80)	3.65 (1.16)	2.97 (1.19)	2.33 (1.58)	1.92 (.87)	1.68 (.79)
Psycho-education (N=26)	3.03 (.84)	2.48 (.85)	3.55 (1.03)	3.16 (.78)	2.94 (1.24)	2.14 (.94)	2.81 (1.15)
Exposure (N=5)	3.15 (.91)	3.00 (.40)	3.60 (1.01)	3.20 (1.26)	2.80 (1.73)	3.20 (1.41)	1.97 (1.25)

* EN (Engagement); FUNC (Functionality); AES (Aesthetics); INF (Quality of Information); SUBJ-QU (Subjective Quality); PI (Perceived Impact)

Psychoeducational games were most favoured in terms of subjective quality and most likely to be perceived to be impactful on the health behaviour (although it is worth noting that no mechanic scored higher than '3' in this regard). While some differences emerged when considering functionality and aesthetics, these were more minor.

In terms of their relative abilities to reduce anxiety among players, STAI-Y6 scores were analysed. This analysis was however complicated by high levels of non-compliance in reporting, or incomplete reports. Of the participants who submitted game reviews using the uMARS, 32 (51.60%) also submitted pre- and post-play anxiety ratings. An overview of this data can be found in *Table 5*.

Table 5. Comparison of pre- vs post-play STAI-Y6 state-anxiety scores by game mechanic.

Mechanic	Mean Pre-Play STAI-Y6 Score	Mean Post-Play STAI-Y6 Score	Mean Pre- vs Post-Play Difference (Sig.)
ABM (N=8)	40.00 (8.36)	43.74 (8.25)	+3.74 (p=.426)
Distraction (N=6)	36.67 (10.54)	38.33 (7.53)	+1.67 (p=.415)
Psychoeducation (N=13)	35.64 (13.01)	34.35 (12.43)	-1.28 (p=.594)
Exposure (N=5)	38.67 (11.93)	38.67 (11.93)	0.00 (N/A)

Data were screened for normality across the six domains of the uMARS and the STAI-Y6 using Shapiro-Wilk tests. With regards to the uMARS, while the engagement domain (p=.181), the aesthetics domain (p=.081) and the total quality mean score (p=.096) of the uMARS were normally distributed, the remaining domains were not: functionality (p=.008), information quality (p=.009), subjective quality (p=.003) and perceived impact (p=.001). Of note, the latter two variables demonstrated a notable partial positive skew, with a large number of ratings of '1'. While particular games rated on average notably lower in these domains than others, a notable number of '1' ratings was present across all games and mechanics, suggesting low perceived quality. Both pre- and post-play STAI-Y6 scores emerged as normally distributed. While a number of fractional-power and logarithmic transformations, as recommended by Clark-Carter (1997), were computed, including $\sqrt{x}$, $\sqrt[3]{x}$, x 1/3 and log10(x), the data for these variables remained non-normal.

Initially, a significant moderate positive correlation was found between the total objective quality (OQ) score and intention to use over the following 12 months (r_s=.56, p=<.001). When controlling for perceived impact, the correlation between OQ score and intention to use remained and remained moderate (r_s=.43, p=<.001), albeit with reduced effect (-.122). A moderate significant correlation was also found between the perceived impact of a game and the participant's intention to use it over the following 12-month period (r_s=.44, p=<.001).

Additionally, no significant correlation was found between the perceived-impact of a game, and its actual effect on STAI-Y6 score (r_s=.14, p=.441). Additionally, the correlation between reduction in STAI-Y6 score and intention to use was on the cusp of significance (r_s=.33, p=.054), as was the correlation between total OQ score and anxiety reduction (r_s=.33, p=.056).

Paired-samples *t*-tests revealed no significant differences overall between pre- and post-play anxiety scores. Furthermore, no specific game-mechanic produced a significant change to anxiety rating. This analysis was not extended to exposure-based games owing to the low sample size. Of note, ABM and distraction-based games appeared in fact to increase anxiety scores. While exposure games had been anticipated to increase psychological arousal at least over a short period, no change to anxiety rating was noted.

Qualitative Findings

Thematic analysis was conducted in order to assess the qualitative data collected from the uMARS questionnaire. A total of 36 instances of qualitative feedback was collected from 24 participants, with 12 participants providing qualitative feedback for both of their games, and 12 participants providing feedback for one of their games. The number of instances of qualitative feedback per game and per mechanic can be found in *Table 6*.

Table 6. Instances of qualitative feedback per mechanic.

Game Mechanic	Games Included	Frequency (%)
Attention-bias modification	MoodMint, PsychMeUp	13 (36.11%)
Psychoeducation	Depression Quest, Elude	14 (38.89%)
Distraction	Guppy, Echogenesis, Drifting Afternoon	5 (13.89%)
Exposure	Fireboy & Watergirl	4 (11.11%)

* Figures may not sum to 100% due to rounding.

The analysis of the qualitative data was conducted using the thematic analysis technique as outlined by Braun & Clarke (2006) in order to assess any occurrence or co-occurrence of themes. An overview of the super- and sub-ordinate themes can be found in *Table 7*.

Table 7. Super- and sub-ordinate themes.

	Superordinate Theme	Subordinate Themes	Example Quote
1	Clarity of Use	a) Intuitive nature of game (e.g. instructions on how to use). b) Ease of use (vs anxiety-inducing).	*"...the game appeared to work in the way it was intended to and therefore I liked the game more." (S1-022 – game 'Elude')* *"i do think it did work well however at some points where it told me to select the smiling faces no smiling faces were a option to press which made you lose out on points, this was fustrating [SIC]." (S1-003 – game 'MoodMint')*
2	Variety	a) Important to maintain challenge. b) Customisable and interactive.	*"after a while the game becomes very dull because nothing changes so the player may stop using the game." (S1-002 – game 'Guppy')* *"The game was not very customisable, and this limited how much I liked the game." (S1-022 – game 'PsychMeUp')*
3	Perceived value	a) Anxiolytic value of game (scientific support) and quality health information. b) Need to clearly mark achievement.	*"A how to play page accessible from the start screen to explain what parts of the game are for. How the game helps with anxiety." (S1-007 – game 'Guppy')* *"You don't get much out of the game, when the character reaches the point there are no rewards you just have to keep going. That made me unengaged because I had the attitude of what's the point if there is no reward to the game." (S1-015 – Elude)*
4	Colour & Environment	a) Impact on perception of game usefulness. b) Need for colour to be fitting to the medium.	*"i do think it looked professional but i think if the game wants to be intriguing more colours should be used to make it look less professional and more like a game" (S1-003 – game 'MoodMint')* *[Aspects of the game you found engaging] "the plain colour white mixed with the mint green make it appealing and it also quite a calm combination" (S1-006 – game 'MoodMint')*

Clarity of Use

One of the major themes to emerge from the analysis was a general preference for clarity when using a therapeutic game. Participants frequently reported favourably about games when clear in-game instructions were provided, when control systems were instinctive and produced the anticipated response, and when the nature of the gameplay was, in this sense, predictable.

Participants also frequently commented that games which were perceived to be easier to use were more likely to be anxiety reducing. Contrastingly, and regardless of game-mechanic, games which were perceived to be difficult to use, or were unclear in instructing the player how to navigate the in-game tasks were perceived to be less effective, or in some cases, anxiety provoking. One such example related to the control trials in the game 'MoodMint' where participants on occasions did not realise that, in the absence of a positive stimulus, the correct response was to not select any of the faces. Additionally, participants expressed a preference for in-game instructions to be simple, clear and effective. Explanations deemed too extensive by the player may result in disengagement.

That the participants in this study demonstrated a preference for games which were intuitive and clear in both their instruction and operation is reflective of wider theory regarding acceptance of technology. The Technology Acceptance Model (Davis, Bagozzi & Warshaw, 1989) highlights the importance user perceptions of ease of use, and its subsequent predictive power when considering player-engagement.

Furthermore, such attributes may take on further relevance when considering the context in which therapeutic games operate. When considering the development of games and applications for AD, the simplicity and intuitive nature of the game is likely to take on additional significance, as anxiety conditions are associated with impairments to concentration (Boschloo, Borkulo, Borsboom & Schoevers, 2016), as well as large reductions in motivation (Loonen & Ivanova, 2016). Accordingly, one of the major considerations of therapeutic game development is ensuring that the provision of the game's therapeutic content is done so in a sufficiently clear manner as not to be perceived to be too difficult for the user to comprehend, or in a way which might negatively affect their motivation to engage.

Variety

In addition to the clear and easily navigable nature of a game, participants in this study also expressed a preference towards having the opportunity to engage in a variety of in-game tasks. Furthermore, participants reported that the provision of in-game task-diversity was not only more enjoyable than when games employed a more repetitive style, but that it was also more likely to maintain the game's challenge, and therefore be more effective in retaining their interest over time. However, this was not to say that any repetition was perceived as negative. Providing those recurring elements were not perceived to be too repetitive; some task-recurrence was viewed positively.

The diversifiable and malleable nature of games affords an opportunity for personalising the experience of mental health provision, and the availability of environments which afford and promote user autonomy has been considered to be one of the most important facets of increased motivation (Ryan, Scott Rigby & Przybylski, 2006), allowing users a degree of control over their learning experience. Direct control over the game environment can instil players with a sense of control over their experience and may increase their positive affect while playing the game (Hefner, Klimmt & Vorderer, 2007), enjoyment (Schmierbach, Limperos & Woolley, 2012), and the emotional impact and relevance of the learning material (Mantovani & Castelnuovo, 2003).

Another favourably reported means by which games were able to retain changeability beyond varying the tasks assigned to the player was the provision of customisability options. Effective personalisation of healthcare provision has shown to have positive benefits for individual autonomy and the capacity to self-regulate wellbeing (Schmittdiel *et al.*, 2008). The opportunity for avatar-customisation is another means by which the visual traits and in-game abilities of an avatar present an opportunity for identity-expression or extended identity formation (Turkle, 1995), and have been linked with increased positive identification with the game (Turkay & Kinzer, 2016). Recent research has also demonstrated that motivation for gameplay in young people often involves stress-reduction or a drive to increase autonomy. This is a feature more pronounced in young people with mental health symptoms (Ferguson & Olson, 2013). The present data supports previous investigations into therapeutic apps (Garrido *et al.*, 2019), suggesting that young people place value on autonomy and the capacity of an intervention to afford opportunities for personalisation. Further, in line with Self-Determination Theory, variation in delivery, such as that provided by narrative features (e.g. storylines) provide not only context for gameplay and learning (Kapp, 2012), but may also enhance motivation to learn by fostering relatedness (Baranowski *et al.*, 2008).

However, not all customisability may be of value in designing an effective therapeutic game, particularly when opportunities for individualisation may compromise the validity of the therapeutic delivery, as indicated by one participant playing the game *'MoodMint'*, which allows users to customise the faces used in the attention-bias modification task. Despite this, the present findings mirror wider literature for app research, where poor customisability has been raised frequently as a barrier to engagement (Nicholas, Fogarty, Boydell & Christensen, 2017; Tong, Coiera & Laranjo, 2018). Successful management of the game's presentation (e.g. through varying the in-game tasks to maintain the game's challenge) may help to encourage continued engagement by successfully manipulating the flow state (Csikszentmihályi, 1975). Effective therapeutic game design for AD however must also balance the need to effectively motivate the player through varying task-delivery, with the need for sufficient repetition as to promote cognitive and behavioural change (Roemer & Orsillo, 2002), such as the continued functional exposure to feared stimuli (Foa & Kozak, 1986). Consequently, balancing simplicity and consistency, with opportunities for individual variation is an important design consideration.

Perceived Value

While participants showed a good overall acceptance of the use of games for the delivery of therapeutic content, and their potential in reducing symptom experience, they frequently reported a preference for such games to be explicit in terms of the benefits and value of their engagement for their wellbeing. In this sense, it was not sufficient for games to simply be enjoyable to play, rather participants reported a preference for games to be explicit in such a way the purpose of the game in terms of its health-related benefits could be noticeably and easily extrapolated. Where such information was not provided, or perceived to be insufficient, this was also reported by participants as a negative aspect of their game, and something raised when they were asked about which features should be included in future developments.

The Technology Acceptance Model (Davis, Bagozzi & Warshaw, 1989) highlights the importance user perceptions of usefulness when predicting a user's engagement with an eHealth intervention. In this case also, these findings mirror and inform the quantitative analysis, providing further insight into the underlying perceptions behind the significant moderate correlation between perceived impact and intention to use. Consequently, a further consideration when designing a therapeutic game for this audience, is to consider how the delivery of therapeutic content can be managed in an intuitive and easily discernible manner, without any simplifications in design (such as reductions in long sections of health-related text-information) being of detriment to the perceived usefulness of the intervention.

One means of indicating a player's positive progress is the use of reward and feedback mechanisms. Participants often referred in their feedback to the benefits of using clear feedback mechanisms as a means of indicating where they were making positive progress in the game. However, some participants also noted that such grading mechanisms needed to operate in a manner conscious of the context in which the game was operating. Competitive elements and feedback mechanisms were perceived to be beneficial in driving motivation to engage but may also be detrimental to the benefits of games for health purposes if they were perceived to be too competitive, or when the possibility of loss was perceived too high.

Perceptions of competency can be derived from a number of game-elements. Effective target-setting, along with feedback which recognises the successful completion of incremental steps towards goal satisfaction, has been shown to motivate continued engagement, even as task-difficulty increases (Baranowski *et al.,* 2008). However, incremental increases in the demands placed on the user must be carefully balanced with ability, as repetitive failure, or early task-mastery may reduce motivation, resulting ultimately in player disengagement (Mishra & Gazzaley, 2014). Successful maintenance of this delicate balance is often attributed to preservation of the flow state (Csikszentmihályi, 1975). The extant evidence has pointed to a range of factors responsible for influencing the extent to which STVGs can generate flow, including; competition (Staiano, Abraham & Calvert, 2012), opportunity for co-operative play (Peng & Hsieh, 2012), clear goals (Huang, Johnson & Seung-Hyun, 2013), and clear reward structures (King, Delfabbro & Griffiths, 2010).

As noted by participants in this study however, competency in STVGs however must also be considered in the context of the game's function. Morschheuser *et al.* (2017) advise that games designed for the purpose of psychological intervention (such as therapeutic games) must go beyond basic token economies and player leaderboards (Hamari, Koivisto & Sarsa, 2014) in order to engage the audience. The present findings indicate that beyond the expectation of an engaging play experience, audiences for STVGs hold an additional anticipation that their experiences with the game will exert a perceptible therapeutic effect.

Colour and Environment

The final theme emerging from the data related to the aesthetics of the game, where specific reference was made consistently to the value of colour and game-environment. The colour of the in-game world and avatars, as well as supplementary and functional items such as menus was perceived by many participants to be a key motivating or demotivating factor in determining their continued engagement with the game. Less colourful game-worlds conferred either a sense of game-simplicity and ease of use, or if greyscale, were perceived to have a detrimental effect on the game's potential usefulness. Specifically, participants preferred the in-game environment to be colourful, yet calming, with responses split on preferences towards colour brightness. Of note, while participants preferred games which they perceived to have anxiolytic value, colour and professional appearance was referred as potentially less engaging if it reduced the 'gamified' appearance of a game.

Predicted upon research showing that colours are perceived independently of objects (Siple & Springer, 1983), and that colour such as blue and green are associated with lower state-anxiety than colours such as yellow or red (Jacobs & Suess, 1975), colour psychology suggests that a strong correlation exists between colour properties of objects and the viewer's perceived feelings of joy, sadness, fear and serenity (Geslin, Jégou & Beaudoin, 2016). It suggests that specific colours (such as green) may be associated with positive emotional experiences (such as relaxation and comfort) (Kaya & Epps, 2004). Certain colour combinations may also evoke more favourable perceptions, with research on web-design finding cool colour-combinations to be preferable to warm combinations in this regard (Coursaris, Swierenga & Watrall, 2008). Of note, the games generally commented on most favourably in terms of their use of colour utilised cool colour-combinations, with high prevalence of greens and blues. Games utilising high amounts of dark colours were generally reported on less favourably.

A recent study by Roohi and Forouzandeh (2019) investigated principles of colour psychology when designing an adventure game *'TikTak'*. Two versions of the game were developed: one using colour psychology principles *('TikTakImmersive')*, alongside a second version developed intuitively and without influence of colour-psychology by the game designer alone *('TikTakArbit')*. Participants with normal trichromatic colour vision were then assessed, with findings revealing that *'TikTakImmersive'* produced significantly higher perceived immersion, and significantly fewer in-game task-failures. While participants did spend significantly longer on *'TikTakArbit'*, they completed significantly more tasks on *'TikTakImmersive'*, suggesting that effective use of in-game colour may influence player-performance and immersion, and that game-design may benefit from utilising principles from colour research in order to maximise these outcomes.

Discussion

Principal Findings

The aims of the present study were threefold:

1. To establish any existing preferences towards specific game-mechanics (exposure, psychoeducation, attention-bias modification, distraction) in adolescents when developing a therapeutic game for ADs.
2. To establish if a relationship existed between the perceived impact of a game mechanic, and its actual impact on the health condition.
3. To establish if objective quality measures, and non-specific game-factors such as player expectations (e.g. the perceived impacts of specific game-mechanics on the health condition), may be predictive of an individual's subsequent intention to use the game over a prolonged period (e.g. 12-months).

In relation to hypothesis 1, findings from the quantitative data indicated that, in terms of overall quality scores, the four game-mechanics investigated produced similar overall scores, with all games scoring moderately. More notable differences were however observed at a sub-scale level, with exposure games being rated as most engaging and scoring highest in terms of their perceived subjective quality. Games using ABM and psychoeducation performed well in terms of perceived impact and perceived quality of health information, and distraction games worst, although it is worthwhile noting that no ratings in the present study were 3 or above in this domain. No notable differences between the mechanics were found with regards to functionality or aesthetics, indicating that while not all mechanics were viewed as engaging or impactful as each other, participants found them equally useable and visually appealing. The study therefore reflects the value of surveying potential end-users when designing games for therapeutic purposes.

Regarding hypothesis 2, no significant relationship was found between the perceived impact of a game and its actual effect on STAI-Y6 score. A Of note, psychoeducation games scored highest in terms of PI, and also recorded the largest reduction in STAI score. However, while the games included in this study varied in terms of their perceived impact, none of the reductions made to state anxiety reached statistical significance. The present study therefore suggests that a player's perceptions of a STVGs impact may have no relation to its actual anxiolytic effect. Games also did not always perform as expected with regards to state-anxiety; while ABM games increased state-anxiety as expected, exposure games did not. Distraction games, expected to have an anxiolytic effect in the short-term, also recorded an increase in state-anxiety.

Regarding hypothesis 3, and in light of the positive correlations observed between OQ score, and STAI reduction, with intention to use over the following 12 months, the present study indicates that initial player perceptions and experiences of a game's quality are important variables to consider when predicting engagement. While perceived game impact correlated positively with intention to use at a bivariate level, this was only the case when OQ was not considered. Furthermore, while only included on a speculative basis, regression analyses also appear to highlight the predictive power of OQ when predicting intention to use. Therefore, the present study suggests that while the intention to use a therapeutic game may be predicted from a player's perception of the game's objective quality (engagement value, functionality, aesthetics, information quality), the same cannot be said of the extent to which players perceive the game to have an impact on the health condition.

Qualitative feedback concurred that a game's clarity and intuitive nature (functionality), in-game task variety, and environmental design (aesthetics) were all variables which players considered important in determining a game's quality. While participants in this study frequently cited the need to feel that their use of the game would be beneficial, they often referred to clear demarcation of achievement and objective quality components, such as the provision of quality health information, as ways that this value could be determined. The present data therefore would suggest that, while perceptions of impact are not unimportant, objective quality measures may be important variables to consider when predicting engagement, despite these factors appearing to have no direct significant effects on actual anxiety reductions.

Davis, Bagozzi & Warshaw (1989) found in a study of 107 computer users, that intention to use positively correlated with actual use after 14 weeks, and that perceived usefulness explained approximately half of the variance in an individual's intention to use a program after the same time period. While the present study did not monitor the participants' continued usage of the games included in the present study (if indeed, there was continued usage), and therefore cannot validate or contradict these findings in relation to therapeutic games, both previous research and the present data highlight the importance of user-perceptions for end-product engagement.

Limitations

Despite the contributions of the present study as outlined above, it is not without limitation. Firstly, the relatively small sample size leaves would leave advanced statistical analyses underpowered. Thus, the regression analyses presented are included purely on a speculative and exploratory basis, and caution is required in their interpretation in terms of any predictive value. While the data in the present study did not meet the distribution requirements of a regression analysis, Central Limit Theorem (Cochran, 1947) stipulates that in some situations, the properly normalised sum of independent variables tends toward a normal distribution, even if the individual variables themselves are non-normal. Research investigating the implications of sample size for normal distribution has found that as a sample size grows, sample means become estimators of population means, with distribution curves becoming more normal (Islam, 2018). With specific regard to the present study, Underwood (1997) and Elliot & Woodward (2007) assert that due to regression analysis being one of the most flexible and powerful tests, it is robust against some violations of parametric assumption such as unequal variances with some areas of the dataset. It is in this context, that while the regression analyses for the present study are underpowered, the findings may still provide valuable insight when making key considerations regarding therapeutic game design for this cohort.

The small numbers of participants also providing feedback (of both quantitative and qualitative variety) for specific games (e.g. Drifting Afternoon), or game-mechanics (e.g. exposure) also means that the conclusions drawn in relation to these are somewhat limited. Further exploration of the exposure mechanic is warranted in order to fully ascertain its acceptability, as well as perceived and measured anxiolytic properties in this context.

While efforts were made to recruit across a diverse group of adolescents, the sample is also a notable for its lack of participants at the very young end of the adolescent age range. All participants were also recruited from educational establishments, and thus the participants may not be reflective of individuals at the more severe end of the clinical spectrum, whose needs and preferences may differ from those of adolescents experiencing anxiety, yet still functioning in a mainstream environment.

Additionally, participants only tested a subset of the available games, meaning cross-game comparisons may be somewhat affected by individual differences, unlike in some similar prior investigations (Garrido et al., 2019). Therefore, and in addition to the aforementioned small sample size, the potential exists for the comparisons made in the present study to be partially reflective of such individual differences. This does not however mean that the feedback obtained by such a design does not provide value. In contrast, owing to the increased focus on a small subset of review items, participants did have significantly longer than in previous studies to become familiar with their allocated games, and all played their respective games independently for a minimum of one hour over the one-week period. Some participants reported having used their game(s) every day and for longer in total than the one-hour requirement. The feedback obtained in this study is therefore likely to be further enriched by this increased exposure. Nonetheless, while some anxiolytic measures are of immediate value (such as breathing-control exercises to reduce the immediate physiological aspects of anxiety), even this extended play-period is likely still not sufficient for therapeutic frameworks such as psychoeducation and attention-bias modification to begin exerting their effect. As the present study indicated that expectations and experiences of effect had implications for future intention to use, the acceptability levels of particular mechanics are likely to change as a consequence of further exposure. Future research would benefit therefore from assessing the responses of young people to such games over an extended time period. Assessment may also benefit from focusing solely on games for anxiety, in order for their anxiolytic value to be consistently and fairly compared.

Thirdly, the method of data collection for game-quality relied on the uMARS. The uMARS has proven to be an effective tool for the evaluation of electronic health tools, with good internal consistency and test-retest reliability (Stoyanov, 2016), and is an accessible inventory requiring no training for its use. The use of a consistent measure also allows for easy comparison between games and mechanics and is thus well-suited to the aims of the present study. However, the nature of the questions assessed by the uMARS may also encourage responses regarding the 'low-hanging fruit' of game design (such as graphics and appearance), which may be to the detriment of obtaining valuable feedback regarding the therapeutic aspects of the game. In this sense, further flexibility in data-acquisition, such as using semi-structured interviews, or 'think-aloud' sessions (such as those used by Crane et al., 2017) may allow for clearer focus on the responses of young people to the therapeutic elements of games.

Conclusions

The present study firstly aimed to investigate the preferences of adolescents towards a range of game-mechanics in therapeutic games. Findings indicated that the four mechanics under investigation all similarly produced moderate scores, with some differences emerging at sub-scale level (e.g. perceived impact). Despite the varying expectations of different mechanics in producing beneficial effects for the health condition, no significant correlation however was found between perceptions of a game's impact and its actual effect on STAI-Y6 score. Further analysis also indicated that initial player impressions of objective quality appear important in predicting intention to use over the following 12-month period. Qualitative feedback concurred that young people viewed objective quality variables as important when considering a game's quality, in addition to opportunities for autonomy.

Motivation to change and expectations of outcome are among the biggest predictors of engagement with psychological interventions, and of their outcome (Stice, Rohde, Seeley & Gau, 2010; Lewis, Simons

& Kim, 2012). The present study provides insight into the initial factors considered important by young people when deciding whether to use a therapeutic game and is of value when designing therapeutic games for young people in order to maximise initial engagement.

STUDY TWO

Aims

The second study consisted of a user-evaluation of a developmental pre-release version of the game. Utilising a similar methodology as the first study, the game is therefore compared like-for-like with games previously investigated. User-perceptions of quality and intention to use are explored, along with an evaluation of the game's anxiolytic capabilities.

Development of the New Intervention Game

The principal purpose of this project was to apply end-user-input, to develop and implement an innovative intervention which was effective in reducing symptoms of state- and trait-anxiety in adolescents. In addition, and following from the findings of the previous chapter, the development of the intervention aimed to address some of the primary concerns associated with perceptions of therapeutic games amongst the demographic. By addressing these concerns, a secondary aim of the project was to ensure that player expectations and perceptions of quality were met, in order to facilitate continued engagement with the protocol, thereby affording the best opportunity for its anxiolytic properties to take effect.

The application of clinically verified treatment protocols via electronic games has been shown to elicit significant improvements in health-behaviours including for anxiety conditions in adolescents (Schoneveld et al., 2016; Schuurmans et al., 2015; Li, Chung & Ho, 2011). Secondly, the administration of health-interventions via electronic means, specifically mobile devices, can improve accessibility to treatment over the traditional clinical modes of delivery (Ben-Zeev et al., 2012), which is of additional value considering the avoidance behaviours associated with ADs, the practical and social barriers to treatment faced by anxious adolescents (Kazdin & Rabbitt, 2013; Kaltenthaler, Parry, Beverley & Ferriter, 2008) and the resulting high number of adolescents with ADs who do not receive any form of intervention (Merikangas et al., 2011).

Furthermore, one of the primary advantages of using mobile devices for the administration of health interventions is the ease of delivery, requiring little effort on the part of the recipient (Klasnja & Pratt, 2012). The intervention can be 'pushed' to the user's device, enabling the provision of reminders and motivational messages to further drive engagement, and maintain awareness of current progress and future goals (Bargh, Gollwitzer, Lee-Chai, Barndollar & Trötschel, 2001). Mobile interventions, therefore, compared to traditional desktop computers, make the consistent management of health conditions easier for the user. For these reasons, a mobile game was determined to be the most appropriate medium to achieve the aims of the project.

Game Structure and Design

The game organises a series of tasks and learning exercises into a collection of 'mini-games', which are designed to guide the player gradually through the intervention. Players, irrespective of their current anxiety-status or in-game task-ability, are always presented with the fundamentals of the task itself before the difficulty level is incrementally increased, manipulating the game to adjust to the player's increasing skills and abilities but without providing a challenge so great that it may be overwhelming (Csikszentmihályi, 1975).

Due to the nature and aims of the intervention, the potential exists for the game to be anxiety-provoking in places. Thus, considering the sensitivity of anxious participants towards the potential for, or experiences of, failure, overly challenging tasks may lead to avoidance and reluctance to continue play. The structured design and gradual progression of the game therefore provides a safe and manageable environment for the payer, while providing sufficient repetition as to promote cognitive and behavioural change (Roemer & Orsillo, 2002), such as the continued functional exposure to feared stimuli (Foa & Kozak, 1986).

The game utilises a number of different tasks derived from cognitive-behavioural therapy and attention-bias modification, which are organised into clearly defined spaces in the game and increase in difficulty as the game progresses. The game operates over 31 separate levels contained in a space environment, within which a number of CBT/ABM tasks are delivered as 'mini-games', presented as planets in the in-game world. Progress in the game is saved automatically after the completion of each task, allowing players to pick up where they left previously, and while levels progression occurs in a serial manner, players may return to earlier levels if they so wish. New planets are also introduced gradually over the initial levels as not to be too overwhelming to the player, and to allow for the successful practice and completion of earlier tasks before the introduction of additional ones (see Figure 1). This ensures that more demanding activities are only presented once there has been sufficient opportunity for learning in easier levels to have been demonstrated.

An overview of the mini-games is presented in Table 8, with screenshots of the individual exercises provided in Figure 2.

In-Game Data Acquisition

An additional benefit of modern smartphones is their ability to maintain a constant connection to the Internet. This has enabled the deployment of mobile health interventions to not only become passive providers of health information, but active monitors of engagement and change in parameters relevant to the health condition such as physiological state, or psychological self-reports. The tracking of health information has numerous benefits. Research has suggested that the process of self-monitoring a health condition may in itself be beneficial in reducing the prevalence of undesired behaviours, while increasing the prevalence of desirable behaviours (Kopp, 1988; Gasser et al., 2006), and improve understanding of a health condition and the individual's own behavioural patterns (Consolvo et al., 2008). In mobile applications, self-monitoring can be deployed via self-report measures (such as note-taking) (Mattila et al., 2008), via SMS, or via automated recording systems.

Figure 1. Structural map of the game

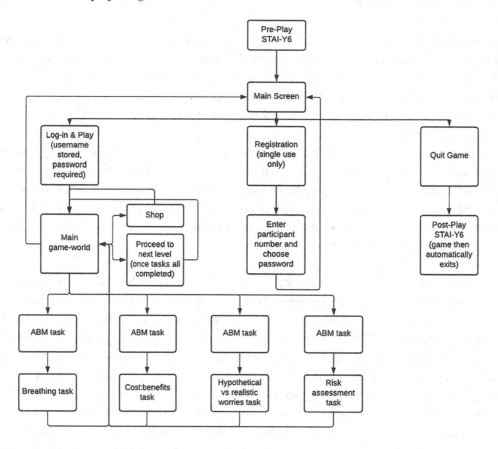

The present game deploys the STAI-Y6 (Marteau & Bekker, 1992) to the user both at the beginning and end of a single play-session, enabling the capture of real-time changes to state anxiety. Performance on the various in-game tasks is also collected by the game and uploaded to a secure server via Amazon Web Services.

Users are identified by a unique anonymised log-in code (e.g. S2-0*xx*) and the game does not offer any opportunity for identifying information to be uploaded. Therefore, the present intervention makes a unique contribution to the field in being the first of its kind to collect real-time 'performance'-data from users. While this feature was developed for use from a research perspective only, enabling the tracking of a number of measures to evaluate the game's efficacy, such acquisitions hold additional value to health-care providers in that they afford a real-time means of tracking users in an outpatient context. In this sense, not only can the efficacy of the game be evaluated by a research team or healthcare provider, but users for whom the game is not operating sufficiently, or who are not using the intervention, can then be directed to additional or alternative support mechanisms as deemed necessary by a qualified professional.

Table 8. Overview of mini-games, aims, and objectives.

Name of Game	Therapeutic Foundation	Objectives	Determinant of Successful Completion
The Happy-Face Task	Attention-bias modification	1. Reduce manifestation of automatic cognitions associated with autonomic arousal and experience of anxiety (Wells & Mathews, 1994) by addressing the subconscious association of neutral stimuli with negative or threatening outcomes (Haddad, Lissek, Pine & Lau, 2011). 2. Provide an easily repeatable method of reducing the manifestation of anxious symptoms through the use of a method shown to exert beneficial effects in a relatively short period of time (Dennis & O'Toole, 2014). 3. Provide a simple and easily accessible method for addressing symptom manifestation, allowing for easy maintenance of treatment gains and relapse reduction (MacLeod et al., 2009).	Successful identification of a positive stimulus within a matrix containing negative stimuli.
Breathing task	CBT	1. Reduce immediate physiological experience of state-anxious symptoms by utilising respiratory patterns, which are closely related to autonomic arousal states (Boiten, Frijda & Wientjes, 1994). 2. Begin engagement with a simple and easily learned technique which requires little cognitive effort yet can provide a sense of accomplishment and progress.	Players are guided through a slow, deep-breathing exercise. Completion of the exercise is determined once the allocated time for the exercise elapses.
Cost vs. benefit analysis	CBT	1. Provide opportunity to engage players in task to exert longer-term changes to trait-anxiety. 2. Encourage engagement with functional/pragmatic disputing with anxiety-provoking ideas and thoughts. 3. Provide a safe and non-threatening environment in which to begin the process of challenging anxiety-provoking cognitions, in the absence of real-world consequences for engagement and failure, and with the benefit of providing an indication of the reality of the therapeutic process, to reduce concern with attending real-world support.	Allocation of stimulus items to either 'cost' or 'benefit' box. Accuracy of answers is reviewed at the end of the exercise.
Hypothetical vs. realistic worrying	CBT	1. Provide opportunity to engage in task designed to exert longer-term changes to trait-anxiety. 2. To expand on the cost:benefits analysis task with more specific functional/pragmatic disputing, considering specific thoughts as opposed to general views on the costs and benefits of the anxiety experience. 3.To provide a safe and non-threatening environment in which to continue the process of challenging anxiety-provoking cognitions without real-world consequence for failure.	Allocation of the stimulus items to either 'hypothetical' or 'realistic' worry. Accuracy of answers is reviewed at the end of the exercise.
Risk-assessment (Iowa Gambling Task)	CBT	1. To practice assessing risk in the absence of real-world consequences. 2. To provide an autonomous decision-making task without clear and specific rules and guidance, to encourage independent decision-making.	Players are provided with a 'loan' of coins. Completion of the exercise is determined once the allocated time for the exercise elapses or if the player runs out of coins. Any remaining coins are awarded as reward.

Figure 2. Screenshots of in-game tasks

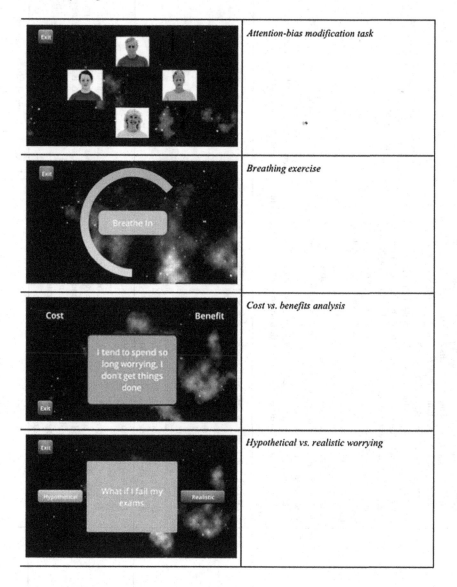

Coins and Reminders

The provision of feedback, reinforcement and reminder structures is a key tenet of serious game design, to foster sufficient intrinsic motivation for further play, particularly as the difficulty of in-game tasks increases (Habgood & Ainsworth, 2011; Kapp, 2012) and the likelihood of avoidance of anxiety-provocation or failure increases. Players were awarded in-game coins for the successful completion of tasks, which initially could be exchanged for badges or medals.

Literature suggests that prompts can be well received by users (Consolvo et al., 2008), providing those reminders are not too obtrusive (e.g. do not contain sound and remain undetectable until the user next picks up their device). While more-obtrusive alerts may also be likeable by some users (Holtz

& Whitten, 2009), users often object to alerts which are considered unnecessarily frequent (Anhøj & Møldrup, 2004). Reminder content should also be motivational (in providing a rationale for continued engagement), direct, and subtle in their content, for instance not referring directly to health conditions in case another person was to see the alert (Curioso, 2009). Well considered and implemented reminders with minimal disruption therefore can drive engagement and motivation, increasing the therapeutic properties of an intervention. For this reason, the game deploys a background reminder to users, though only when considered necessary: (1) when users have missed completing the post-play questionnaire upon leaving the game; (2) if users have not played the game for a near 24-hour period.

In order to determine the game's acceptability to players and their intention to use the game, ability to produce statistically significant reductions to state-anxiety, and to assess any further changes which players may recommend which may improve their engagement, the game underwent an initial evaluation presented below.

Method

Design

The present study assumed a pragmatist approach employing a convergent mixed design, to maximise the usefulness of the findings both in terms of improving the development version of the game (DVG), as well as allowing for comparisons between the new intervention and the games trialled in the first study. Quantitative feedback was again collected via the uMARS and was supplemented with data from a qualitative version to provide additional support and detail to the numerical ratings, and to offer further insight into the motivations and reasonings underlying them.

Participants

Participants were again recruited on a voluntary basis primarily from two academic institutions: a sixth-form college and a university technical college in the North-West of England. Additionally, a small number of participants were recruited via word-of-mouth. Once provided with a full brief of the aims of the study, participants gave consent and allocated a unique anonymous identification code (e.g. S2-001). For participants aged under 16, consent was also obtained from a parent or legal guardian.

A total of 23 participants were recruited initially. Of these, four withdrew voluntarily, leaving a final sample of $N=19$, including 9 males (47.4%) and 10 females (52.6%). Ages ranged between 13 and 19 years, with the majority of participants aged between 14 and 16 ($N=14$, 73.7%).

Materials and Procedure

Following recruitment and consent, participants were given access to the DVG and played this for one hour. In order to determine the ease of use of the DVG and also to control for expectancy effects, participants were only instructed how to use the game in terms of using controls – further instruction or guidance regarding the structure of the game or aims of the tasks was not provided.

As with the previous study, once the one-hour allocated play time had been reached, participants were asked to complete the quantitative and qualitative versions of the uMARS. In addition to the self-report methods, the analysis for the present study also extended to utilising the in-game data capturing systems.

At this point, the game was not connected to Amazon Web-Services, and so data captured were saved as a file directly to the file managing software on the device. This allowed for data to be captured regarding play information, including pre- and post-play anxiety STAI-Y6 scores and additionally reaction time to attention-bias modification tasks, overall score on individual mini-games, and time spent playing.

Upon the completion of the trial period, the data obtained by the game was saved and harvested for analysis, and participants were directed to complete the feedback questionnaires. As previously, data were collected online to preserve anonymity, and to reduce the potential for participants to feel overwhelmed in an interview context. Participants were also instructed to keep a log of any issues (e.g. bugs, crashes, unexpected game-behaviour) which occurred during the trial period.

All participants were reassured that all data supplied in the online questionnaires would be kept strictly confidential, and it was made clear both at the start and end of the study that participants were free to withdraw, up until one week after the trial period, without having to provide a reason.

Results

Quantitative Findings

After withdrawals, the final sample size consisted of 19 participants. Initially, average quality ratings for uMARS subscales were calculated along with total quality score, in order to examine the performance of the game in relation to the existing games trialled in the previous study.

Table 9. Average quality ratings (total and subscale)

Game	Total Quality	ENG	FUNC	AES	INF	SUBJ-QU	PI
Dev. Version (N=19)	3.19 (.64)	2.89 (.85)	3.50 (.72)	3.12 (1.18)	3.22 (1.03)	2.97 (.71)	3.71 (0.57)
ABM (N=18)	2.98 (.81)	2.52 (.90)	3.43 (.87)	3.00 (1.09)	2.96 (.93)	2.39 (.83)	2.67 (1.06)
Distraction (N=13)	2.96 (.75)	2.65 (.80)	3.65 (1.16)	2.97 (1.19)	2.33 (1.58)	1.92 (.87)	1.68 (.79)
Psycho-education (N=26)	3.03 (.84)	2.48 (.85)	3.55 (1.03)	3.16 (.78)	2.94 (1.24)	2.14 (.94)	2.81 (1.15)
Exposure (N=5)	3.15 (.91)	3.00 (.40)	3.60 (1.01)	3.20 (1.26)	2.80 (1.73)	3.20 (1.41)	1.97 (1.25)

 * EN (Engagement); FUNC (Functionality); AES (Aesthetics); INF (Quality of Information); SUBJ-QU (Subjective Quality); PI (Perceived Impact)

 * All figures rounded to 2d.p.

As can be observed in the values in the above table, the DVG performed comparably to existing games, marginally scoring highest in terms of overall quality rating (M=3.19, SD=.64). However, when analysed further, the DVG did not perform significantly better than existing games ($F(4,78)=.086$, $p=.987$). Additionally, Bonferroni comparisons revealed that no individual comparison reached statistical significance. The game also performed comparably against its predecessors in terms of objective quality measures and scored highest for the quality of health information provided (M=3.22, SD=1.03). Similarly, the average perceived impact score for the DVG was considerably higher than in previously assessed games, and distribution of scores lower (M=3.71, SD= .57), than the scores previously attained. When questioned regarding their intention to use the game over the following 12-month period, participants reported a moderate probability of using the game (M=3.37, SD=.68), which compares favourably with previous ABM games (M=2.28, SD=1.02) and Psychoeducation games (M=1.92, SD=1.09).

As the variables of aesthetics and information-quality were not normally distributed (p=.043 and p=.011 respectively) and therefore did not satisfy the demands of parametric testing, no further evaluation in terms of the uMARS sub-domains was pursued.

Data were then analysed to determine the effects of gameplay on STAI-Y6 scores, for which all participants in the present study provided responses. Once more, the data from the present study are presented alongside those from the previous study. Comparisons between the DVG and previous games (grouped by primary mechanic), as well as a full breakdown of the pre- vs post-play anxiety scores can be found in Figure 3 and Table 10 below:

When compared to previous games, the DVG did not significantly outperform existing games in terms of its anxiolytic power (F(1,42)=.365, p=.549). Bonferroni comparisons again revealed that the DVG did not significantly outperform ABM, Distraction, Psychoeducation or Exposure games. However, while previously tested games had produced no significant differences between state-anxiety scores before versus after gameplay, a paired-samples t-test comparison revealed that the DVG did result in a significant reduction in state-anxiety (pre-play M=45.44, SD=17.47 vs. post-play M=36.14, SD=11.82; t(18)=2.251, p=.037). While the large distributions must be noted, both pre- and post-play anxiety scores satisfied the requirements of normal distribution tests for further analysis (Shapiro Wilk pre-play: p=.216, and post-play: p=.140).

Figure 3. Pre-vs post-play STAI-Y6 anxiety ratings for development game vs. existing games (grouped by primary game-mechanic)

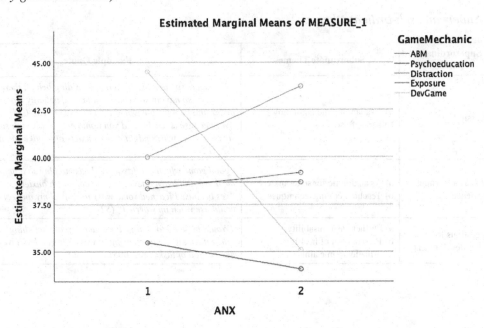

Table 10. Comparison of pre- vs post-play STAI-Y6 state-anxiety scores

Mechanic	Mean Pre-Play STAI-Y6 Score	Mean Post-Play STAI-Y6 Score	Mean Pre- vs Post-Play Difference (Sig.)
Dev. Version *(N=19)*	45.44 *(17.47)*	36.14 *(11.82)*	-9.30 *(p=.037)*
ABM *(N=8)*	40.00 *(8.36)*	43.74 *(8.25)*	+3.74 *(p=.426)*
Distraction *(N=6)*	36.67 *(10.54)*	38.33 *(7.53)*	+1.67 *(p=.415)*
Psychoeducation *(N=13)*	35.64 *(13.01)*	34.35 *(12.43)*	-1.28 *(p=.594)*
Exposure *(N=5)*	38.67 *(11.93)*	38.67 *(11.93)*	0.00 *(N/A)*

* All figures rounded to 2d.p.

Qualitative Findings

Twelve of the participants (63.16%) provided qualitative feedback for the game. As with the previous study, the analysis of the qualitative data was conducted using thematic analysis, adopting the process outlined by Braun and Clarke (2006). The occurrence or co-occurrence of themes was sought, with data initially scanned to generate preliminary codes, which were then re-reviewed and assessed/re-assessed into emerging themes. The outcomes of this procedure are detailed below:

The outcomes of the coding and analysis produced several super- and sub-ordinate themes, which are detailed below with supporting quotes. An overview of the super- and sub-ordinate themes can be found in Table 11.

Table 11. Super- and sub-ordinate themes.

	Superordinate Theme	Subordinate Themes	Example Quote
1	Accessibility	a) Availability and autonomy b) Ease of use	*"Teenagers spend most of there time hiding behind there phones any ways, so having something that could actually make you feel better and be portable would be a life saver" (S2-015).* *"yes because ist easier and you dont need to talk with someone straight away which might cause anxiety and make you not do it" (S2-012).*
2	Game as a learning experience	a) As anxiolytic for state-anxiety b) Teaching coping techniques	*"good game which is relaying and easy to play so it helped calm me down and learn a few things to cope with anxiety" (S2-005).* *"yes because i learned some ways to control my anxiety that i could use when im worried" (S2-007).*
3	Suggestions for further development	a) Further customisability b) Presentation of health information/game aims	*"Would be good to change the spaceship or something" (S2-003).* *"the information was clear but it would be good to have clearer description of tasks" (S2-005).*

Accessibility

Similarly to the previous study, the value of a game's accessibility was raised frequently in the responses. Feedback focused primarily on two ways in which the game's accessibility was beneficial to the user. Firstly, users commented positively on the platform of delivery, remarking that the game would be readily available at the point of symptom experience. Users also remarked on the health information and tasks in the game, and the ease with which these could be chosen and accessed, including during period of symptom experience when other forms of helpful intervention may be deemed too challenging or difficult. Secondly, respondents commented that the game and tasks were easy to use and to understand, making it suitable for use during periods of heightened anxiety. Finally, and consolidating the quantitative feedback, when asked if they would use the game in the future, the accessibility and ease of use of the game was cited as a factor in determining players' future intention to use:

These findings corroborate those of the previous study and, in line with the assumptions of the Technology Acceptance Model (Davis, Bagozzi & Warshaw, 1989), affirm that user-perceptions of the accessibility of a game are a good indication of their intention to continue engaging with it over time. Therapeutic interventions such as ABM and CBT often rely on repetitive training and consolidation activities, with gamified interventions also required to operate in an 'outpatient' context, despite the deficits in concentration and motivation often found in anxiety conditions (Boschloo, Borkulo, Borsboom & Schoevers, 2016; Loonen & Ivanova, 2016). Therefore, the approachability and extent to which games can effectively harness a player's intrinsic motivation to engage is key in determining their ability to exert positive change on anxious symptoms and behaviours.

The Game as a Learning Experience

Confirming the findings of the STAI-Y6 analysis, users commented that they felt that the game had been effective in reducing the level of anxiety that they were experiencing in the moment. Users cited various aspects of the game's design and structure which had created this feeling. The ease of use and accessibility of the game was also raised as a contributing factor to the success of the game as a learning tool. Additionally, users commented that the game had been effective not only as a tool for reducing any anxiety experienced in the moment, but that the tasks had served their educational purpose, i.e. that users' awareness and ability in managing their anxiety had improved.

Finally, and perhaps most significantly, the experience of playing the game was cited not only as being beneficial as a tool for reducing state- and trait-anxiety, but participants suggested that gameplay may also be an educational tool for the therapeutic process itself, a viewpoint which had not been raised with previous games.

The value of the users' positive perceptions of the game's efficacy must be seen in the context of their future engagement with the therapeutic process. CBT is an active treatment which compels clients to challenge enduring and habituated maladaptive beliefs, in a process that can often be perceived by clients as frustrating and discouraging (Becker & Zayfert, 2001). Client satisfaction with the design of their treatment (and failure to account for this) can also result in premature termination and poor treatment outcomes (Swift & Callahan, 2009; Donovan, Kadden, DiClemente & Carroll, 2002). Additionally, a client with positive expectations about the effectiveness and benefits of their treatment has been shown to be more likely to continue their programme (Callahan, Aubuchon-Endsley, Borja & Swift, 2009) and ultimately improve (Borkovec, Echmendia, Ragusea & Ruiz, 2001).

Consequently, and further confirming the findings of the previous study, one of the most important functions of therapeutic game design is to instil in the player a belief that the game makes a valuable contribution to the health behaviour, i.e. that the game reduces feelings of anxiety, while leaving the player feeling better able to cope with future symptom experiences. That the game also resulted in some initial discussion regarding wider engagement with the therapeutic process, suggests that therapeutic games may act as a 'gateway treatment', serving to counteract myths and assumptions about the therapeutic process which may otherwise prevent individuals from seeking further treatment.

Suggestions for Further Development

While the DVG demonstrated its ability to significantly reduce symptoms of state-anxiety and received generally positive feedback, it was not without its initial limitations. Participants also cited a number of areas where they felt the game could be further improved, either in terms of its function, accessibility, or capacity to engage users. These ranged from minor formatting to areas where players requested more meaningful changes, such as access to the app via an official app store or clearer explanation of the in-game tasks.

Following on from the findings of the first study, the initial design of the game had intended to provide players with freedom, choice and autonomy in how they approached the game. While this was commented on positively, users also made frequent request to be able to personalise the game further, referring often to small alterations to the game avatar that could make the game feel more 'their own'. Garrido *et al.* (2019) posited that young people place value on autonomy and the capacity of an intervention to afford opportunities for personalisation. Moreover, the opportunity to personalise healthcare provision is associated with improved individual autonomy and capacity to self-regulate wellbeing (Schmittdiel *et al.*, 2008). The opportunity for avatar-customisation is another means by which the visual traits and in-game abilities of an avatar present an opportunity for identity-expression or extended identity formation (Turkle, 1995), and has been linked with increased positive identification with the game (Turkay & Kinzer, 2016), improving its relatability – a key driver for intrinsic motivation (Ryan & Deci, 2000). Furthermore, the visual traits and in-game abilities of an avatar represents an opening for identity-expression or extended identity formation (Turkle, 1995), and have been linked with increased positive identification with the game (Turkay & Kinzer, 2016).

Finally, participants were asked to provide any experiences of bugs, issues or crashes that they had experienced while testing the DVG. No participants reported encountering any bugs or errors were during the study and all controls, functions and features of the game performed as expected.

Discussion

Principal Findings

The aims of the present study were threefold:

1. To assess the usability of the game in terms of its functionality (e.g. usability of game-mechanics, controls, and to ensure the game operated as expected without the occurrence of bugs or crashes.

2. To assess the acceptability of the game among the target demographic, and to ensure the game addressed feedback obtained in the previous study (e.g. appropriate health-content, feedback structures, difficulty-level, aesthetics, task-variety).

3. To assess whether the game effected significant reductions to state-anxiety when played.

In relation to hypothesis 1, the feedback from the game indicated that users experienced no bugs or errors while using the game and no issues relating to the controls, functions and features of the game were reported. The game operated as expected and all systems including in-game tasks, level progression and coin collection worked as intended. Additionally, the remote data-collection via AWS functioned as anticipated and STAI-Y6 data were successfully collected both pre- and post-play using this mechanism. In this sense, the game performed as expected and satisfied basic pre-rollout checks.

In relation to hypothesis 2, the game received generally very encouraging feedback from users, who commented positively on the game's accessibility, ease of use, quality of health information, task-difficulty, performance as an anxiolytic tool during moments of symptom experience, and ability to provide educational material to assist with the development of coping skills to enable the reduction of anxiety over extended periods. The game scored either comparatively or better when compared to data from the previous study and overall quality ratings were higher. Intention to use scores were also improved, and participants commented positively in qualitative data on the prospect of using the game again. As therapeutic protocols such as ABM and CBT depend on repetitive practice and the continued consolidation of learned material, the improvements made to user-perceptions and the subsequent progress in intention to use data suggest that the DVG is a valuable advancement in providing a gamified intervention for anxiety which users will continue to engage with. These findings are of significant value in the context of the low number of adolescents currently in receipt of a scientifically validated intervention (Kessler et al., 2008; Collins, Westra, Dozois & Burns, 2004), high levels of non-disclosure (Corrigan, Druss & Perlick, 2014), barriers relating to the availability of therapeutic provision (Andlin-Sobocki & Wittchen, 2005), and drop-out from existing clinical interventions.

Finally in relation to hypothesis 3, STAI-Y6 data indicated that the DVG was able to make significant reductions to state-anxiety. This represented an advancement over previously tested games, which had either failed to reduce state-anxiety significantly, made no change, or had increased reported symptoms.

Subsequent Game-Development

To ensure that the final version of the game maximised the value of the user-feedback data collected thus far, a number of minor additional improvements and changes were made to the game to respond to feedback collected in the present study. In order to ensure that any changes made to the game did not impact on the findings above, these changes were kept as minimal as possible, however did intend to address the comments provided by the participants. A summary of the changes made to the game are presented below.

Clearer Description of In-Game Tasks

In the present study, participants indicated that they felt the in-game tasks were not always sufficiently explained and that a lack of clarity may impact on their willingness to engage with the game. Therefore, the descriptions for the in-game tasks were revisited and, where possible, made more concise and direct.

Where players however were encouraged to learn about the tasks as the game progressed (e.g. in the risk-assessment task), the descriptions of the tasks centred more on explaining the controls and basic premise of the game, without revealing too much about the main aim.

Visual Appeal

Some of the participants also indicated that, while the general theme of the game was appropriate and relaxing to play, the plain backgrounds and game-environments could be made more visually appealing. In order to address this, the in-game background was changed for a more colourful variant. In addition, the planets were lined up in a more organised manner to ensure that while players could be free to roam around the map as they wished, the main aim of the game (to approach the planets and complete the tasks) was clear (see Figure 4).

Figure 4. Screenshots of game-environment (main screen) before and after player feedback.

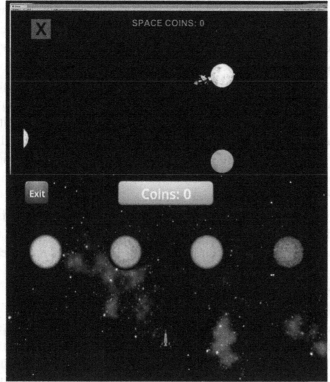

Avatar Customisation

Finally, participants frequently stated while playing the game that they would have liked to have seen more opportunity to customise the game. A number of participants made specific reference to a wish to change the in-game avatar. As the value of the in-game reward coins had also been cited as an area for improved clarity, the in-game store was modified to allow players to change their avatar once they had accrued sufficient coins. The option to accrue badges and medals was removed as this appeared to be less personal to players than avatar customisation and was not cited by any players as an area of interest. A number of alternative spacecrafts were made available to the player for purchase, with the increasing complexity and visual appeal of each craft reflected with increasing cost. Screenshots of the in-game store can be seen in Figure 5 below.

The modifications which players could make to the ship were purely cosmetic, as not to have any impact on the therapeutic aspects of the game. The ability to modify aspects of the game, even if only on a cosmetic level, also addresses the themes of autonomy and customisability emerging from the previous study and is informed by Self-Determination Theory (Ryan & Deci, 2000).

Figure 5. Screenshot of in-game avatar customisation store.

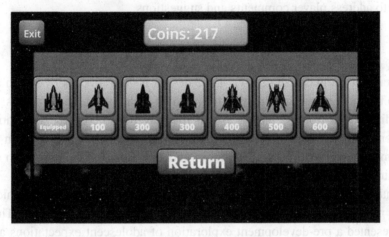

Limitations

While the study was successful in meeting its objectives, there are nonetheless limitations which ought to be considered. Firstly, while the game did achieve significant reductions to state-anxiety, its efficacy with regards to trait-anxiety cannot yet be determined. Players did however provide positive feedback regarding their intention to use the game over a prolonged period, which was supported by intention to use scores from the uMARS. Additionally, while the game was capable of eliciting significant reductions to state-anxiety measures in a controlled environment, it was not possible during the current study to determine the extent to which players would use the game and benefit from it when in a particularly heightened state of arousal. Consequently, further study in relation to these issues is required.

Secondly, the feedback was valuable in determining player intention to use and therefore predicting the future acceptability of the game. However, the present study utilised a sample of both relatively low size. Additionally, the homogeneity of the sample participants (all participants were engaged in full-time mainstream education), means that while the acceptability of the game in this cohort is established, its acceptability in more clinically severe samples is yet to be determined. As individuals with particularly severe cases of anxiety conditions are less likely to be engaging in full-time mainstream education (Patel, Knapp, Henderson, & Baldwin, 2002; Beidel & Turner, 2007), this demographic is likely under-represented in the current study. Future research may determine that while the game was suitable for the present cohort, participants with a more severe symptom presentation may find aspects of the game particularly challenging, such as the risk-assessment tasks which can only be successfully completed by persevering by learning as a product of initial task-failure.

Conclusions

The present study aimed to evaluate a development version of a new gamified intervention for adolescents with anxiety conditions. The findings indicated that the game performed well both in functionality and acceptability; equalling or outperforming previously tested games and producing significant reductions to state anxiety when played. A combination of quantitative and qualitative data were obtained, which in addition to assessing the objectives of the study, also aided in making minor upgrades and modifications to the game to address player comments and suggestions.

Summary

According to Salen and Zimmerman (2004), game design is "the process by which a game designer creates a game to be encountered by a player, from which meaningful play emerges." In this sense, a game cannot be dissociated from its player, as it is the player who constructs narrative and meaning from their experience of play. In this sense, the involvement of potential end-users in the development and review of gamified interventions is essential in understanding the factors which contribute to the emergence of meaningful play.

This chapter has presented the reader with a summary of two investigations which addressed the development of a mobile therapeutic game for adolescents with anxiety disorders. The first empirical investigation represented a pre-development exploration of adolescent expectations and requirements of therapeutic games. To this end, user perceptions of game-quality regarding a number of existing and freely available games for anxiety and depression (utilising a number of game-mechanics and therapeutic frameworks) were assessed, along with each game's capability in reducing self-reported anxiety symptoms. Furthermore, given the importance of continued commitment to the development and maintenance of therapeutic gains (HEFCE, 2015; Wiles et al., 2014; Cartwright-Hatton, 2004; James, Soler & Weatherall, 2005), and the value of games in motivating sustained engagement (Sitzmann, 2011), user-perceptions of game-quality were also assessed in terms of their relationship with intention to use over a subsequent 12-month period.

The second study represented a user-evaluation of a developmental pre-release version of the game. Utilising a similar methodology as the first study, the game was compared like-for-like with those previously reviewed. User-perceptions of quality and intention to use were explored, along with an evaluation of the game's anxiolytic capabilities. Findings revealed the game was both acceptable to the target audience and produced significant reductions to state-anxiety when played. The game also functioned as expected without bugs or crashes. These value of these findings has been discussed in relation to the low number of adolescents currently in receipt of a scientifically validated intervention (Kessler et al., 2008; Collins, Westra, Dozois & Burns, 2004), high levels of non-disclosure (Corrigan, Druss & Perlick, 2014), barriers relating to the availability of therapeutic provision (Andlin-Sobocki & Wittchen, 2005), and drop-out from existing clinical interventions. Additionally, the user-feedback obtained during the study was used to enhance the game's appeal, prior to further longitudinal assessment to determine the extent to which players will continue to engage over time, and the game's capabilities therefore in reducing trait-anxiety in a meaningful and sustained manner in a population often difficult to reach.

FUNDING STATEMENT

This research received no specific grant from any funding agency in the public, commercial, or not-for-profit sectors.

ACKNOWLEDGMENT

The authors would like to thank Joseph Adams for his invaluable contributions to the project in developing the game. We would also like to extend our thanks to Andrew Williams of the Centre for Games Design at the University of Bolton, for his input and guidance during development. Additionally, the authors would like to thank all of the participants from both of the studies discussed in this chapter, for their time in reviewing games, providing feedback and aiding in the development of the new intervention game.

REFERENCES

Abt, C. (1970). *Serious games*. Viking Press.

Andlin-Sobocki, P., & Wittchen, H. U. (2005). Cost of anxiety disorders in Europe. *European Journal of Neurology*, *12*(1), 39–44. doi:10.1111/j.1468-1331.2005.01196.x PMID:15877777

Anhøj, J., & Møldrup, C. (2004). Feasibility of collecting diary data from asthma patients through mobile phones and SMS (short message service): Response rate analysis and focus group evaluation from a pilot study. *Journal of Medical Internet Research*, *6*(4), e42. doi:10.2196/jmir.6.4.e42 PMID:15631966

Bandelow, B., & Michaelis, S. (2015). Epidemiology of anxiety disorders in the 21st century. *Dialogues in Clinical Neuroscience*, *17*(3), 327–335. doi:10.31887/DCNS.2015.17.3/bbandelow PMID:26487813

Baranowski, T., Buday, R., Thompson, D., Lyons, E. J., Shirong-Lu, A., & Baranowski, J. (2013). Developing games for health behaviour change: Getting started. *Games for Health*, *2*(4), 183–190. doi:10.1089/g4h.2013.0048 PMID:24443708

Baranowski, T., Buday, R., Thompson, D. I., & Baranowski, J. (2008). Playing for Real: Video Games and Stories for Health-Related Behavior Change. *American Journal of Preventive Medicine*, *34*(1), 74–82. doi:10.1016/j.amepre.2007.09.027 PMID:18083454

Bargh, J. A., Gollwitzer, P. M., Lee-Chai, A., Barndollar, K., & Trötschel, R. (2001). The automated will: Nonconscious activation and pursuit of behavioral goals. *Journal of Personality and Social Psychology*, *81*(6), 1014–1027. doi:10.1037/0022-3514.81.6.1014 PMID:11761304

Barnes, S., & Prescott, J. (2018). Empirical Evidence for the Outcomes of Therapeutic Video Games for Adolescents with Anxiety Disorders: Systematic Review. *JMIR Serious Games*, 6(1), e3. doi:10.2196/games.9530 PMID:29490893

Baxter, A. J., Baxter, A. J., Vos, T., Scott, K. M., & Ferrari, A. J. (2014). The global burden of anxiety disorders in 2010. *Psychological Medicine*, 44(11), 2363–2374. doi:10.1017/S0033291713003243 PMID:24451993

Becker, C. B., & Zayfert, C. (2001). Integrating DBT-based techniques and concepts to facilitate exposure treatment for PTSD. *Cognitive and Behavioral Practice*, 8(2), 107–122. doi:10.1016/S1077-7229(01)80017-1

Beesdo, K., Knappe, S., & Pine, D. S. (2009). Anxiety and anxiety disorders in children and adolescents: Developmental issues and implications for DSM-V. *The Psychiatric Clinics of North America*, 32(3), 483–524. doi:10.1016/j.psc.2009.06.002 PMID:19716988

Beidel, D. C., & Turner, S. (2007). *Child anxiety disorders: A guide to research and treatment.* Routledge. doi:10.4324/9780203955321

Bekker, H. L., Legare, F., Stacey, D., O'Connor, A., & Lemyre, L. (2003). Is anxiety a suitable measure of decision aid effectiveness: As systematic review? *Patient Education and Counseling*, 50(3), 255–262. doi:10.1016/S0738-3991(03)00045-4 PMID:12900095

Ben-Zeev, D., Drake, R. E., Corrigan, P. W., Rotondi, A. J., Nilsen, W., & Depp, C. (2012). Using contemporary technologies in the assessment and treatment of serious mental illness. *American Journal of Psychiatric Rehabilitation*, 15(4), 357–376. doi:10.1080/15487768.2012.733295

Berman, S. L., Weems, C. F., & Stickle, T. R. (2006). Existential anxiety in adolescents: Prevalence, Structure, Association with Psychological Symptoms and Identity Development. *Journal of Youth and Adolescence*, 35(3), 285–292. doi:10.100710964-006-9032-y

Bhatia, M. S., & Goyal, A. (2018). Anxiety disorders in children and adolescents: Need for early detection. *Journal of Postgraduate Medicine*, 64(2), 75–76. doi:10.4103/jpgm.JPGM_65_18 PMID:29692397

Boiten, F., Frijda, N. H., & Wientjes, C. J. E. (1994). Boiten, F. A., Frijda, N. H., & Wientjes, C. J. (1994). Emotions and respiratory patterns: Review and critical analysis. *International Journal of Psychophysiology*, 17(2), 103–128. doi:10.1016/0167-8760(94)90027-2 PMID:7995774

Borkovec, T. D., Echemendia, R. J., Ragusea, S. A., & Ruiz, M. (2001). The Pennsylvania Practice Research Network and future possibilities for clinically meaningful and scientifically rigorous psychotherapy effectiveness research. *Clinical Psychology: Science and Practice*, 8(2), 155–167. doi:10.1093/clipsy.8.2.155

Boschloo, L., van Borkulo, C. D., Borsboom, D., & Schoevers, R. A. (2016). A prospective study on how symptoms in a network predict the onset of depression. *Psychotherapy and Psychosomatics*, 85(3), 183–184. Advance online publication. doi:10.1159/000442001 PMID:27043457

Braun, V., & Clarke, V. (2008). Using thematic analysis in psychology. *Qualitative Research in Psychology*, 3(2), 77–101. doi:10.1191/1478088706qp063oa

Burckhardt, R., Manicavasgar, V., Batterham, P. J., Miller, L. M., Talbot, E., & Lum, A. (2015). A web-based adolescent positive psychology program in schools: Randomised controlled trial. *Journal of Medical Internet Research*, *17*(7), e187. doi:10.2196/jmir.4329 PMID:26220564

Buszewicz, M., Rait, G., Griffin, M., Nazareth, G., Patel, A., Atkinson, A., Barlow, J., & Haines, A. (2006). Self-management of arthritis in primary care: Randomised controlled trial. *British Medical Journal*, *333*(7574), 879. doi:10.1136/bmj.38965.375718.80 PMID:17040926

Callahan, J. L., Aubuchon-Endsley, N., Borja, S. E., & Swift, J. K. (2009). Pretreatment expectancies and premature termination in a training clinic environment. *Training and Education in Professional Psychology*, *3*(2), 111–119. doi:10.1037/a0012901

Cannon-Bowers, J. A., Bowers, C., & Procci, K. (2011). Using video games as educational tools in healthcare. In S. Tobias & J. D. Fletcher (Eds.), *Computer games and instruction* (pp. 47–72). Information Age Publishing.

Cartwright-Hatton, S., Roberts, C., Chitsabesan, P., Fothergill, C., & Harrington, R. (2004). Systematic review of the efficacy of cognitive behaviour therapies for childhood and adolescent anxiety disorders. *British Journal of Clinical Psychology*, *43*(4), 421–436. doi:10.1348/0144665042388928 PMID:15530212

Clark-Carter, D. (1997). *Doing Quantitative Psychological Research: From Design to Report*. Psychology Press.

Cochran, W. G. (1947). Some consequences when the assumptions for the analysis of variance are not satisfied. *Biometrics*, *3*(1), 22–28. doi:10.2307/3001535 PMID:20240415

Collins, K. A., Westra, H. A., Dozois, J. J. A., & Burns, D. D. (2004). Gaps in accessing treatment for anxiety and depression: Challenges for the delivery of care. *Clinical Psychology Review*, *24*(5), 583–616. doi:10.1016/j.cpr.2004.06.001 PMID:15325746

Consolvo, S., Klasnja, P., McDonald, D. W., Avrahami, D., Froehlich, J., LeGrand, L., Libby, R., Mosher, K., & Landay, J. A. (2008). Flowers or a robot army? Encouraging awareness & activity with personal, mobile displays. In *Proceedings of the 10th international conference on Ubiquitous computing* (pp. 54-63). 10.1145/1409635.1409644

Consumer Health Information Corporation. (2011). *Motivating patients to use smartphone health apps*. Retrieved from: http://www.consumer-health.com/motivating-patients-to-use-smartphone-health-apps/

Corrigan, P. W., Druss, G. G., & Perlick, D. A. (2014). The impact of mental illness stigma on seeking and participating in mental health care. *Psychological Science in the Public Interest*, *15*(2), 37–70. doi:10.1177/1529100614531398 PMID:26171956

Costello, E. J., & Angold, A. (1995). Epidemiology. In J. S. March (Ed.), *Anxiety disorders in children and adolescents* (pp. 109–124). Guilford Press.

Coursaris, C. K., Swierenga, S. J., & Watrall, E. (2008). An empirical investigation of color temperature and gender effects on web aesthetics. *Journal of Usability Studies*, *3*(3), 103–117.

Crane, D., Garnett, C., Brown, J., West, R., & Michie, S. (2017). Factors Influencing Usability of a Smartphone App to Reduce Excessive Alcohol Consumption: Think Aloud and Interview Studies. *Frontiers in Public Health*, 5(39). Advance online publication. doi:10.3389/fpubh.2017.00039 PMID:28421175

Csikszentmihályi, M. (1975). *Beyond Boredom and Anxiety*. Jossey-Bass Publishers.

Curioso, W. H., Quistberg, D. A., Cabello, R., Gozzer, E., Garcia, P. J., Holmes, K. K., & Kurth, A. E. (2009). "It's time for your life": How should we remind patients to take medicines using short text messages? *AMIA ... Annual Symposium Proceedings - AMIA Symposium. AMIA Symposium*, 2009, 129. PMID:21633523

Davis, F. D., Bagozzi, R., & Warshaw, P. R. (1989). User Acceptance of Computer Technology: A Comparison of Two Theoretical Models. *Management Science*, 35(8), 982–1003. doi:10.1287/mnsc.35.8.982

de Graaf, R., Bijl, R. V., Beekman, A. T., & Vollebergh, W. A. (2003). Temporal sequencing f lifetime mood disorders in relation to comorbid anxiety and substance use disorders—Findings from the Netherlands Mental Health Survey and Incidence Study. *Social Psychiatry and Psychiatric Epidemiology*, 38(1), 1–11. doi:10.100700127-003-0597-4 PMID:12563553

de Smet, A., van Ryckeghem, D., Compernolle, S., Baranowski, T., Thompson, D., Crombez, G., Poels, K., van Lippevelde, W., Bastiaensens, S., van Cleemput, K., Vandebosch, H., & de Bourdeauhuji, I. (2014). A meta-analysis of serious digital games for healthy lifestyle promotion. *Preventive Medicine*, 69, 95–107. doi:10.1016/j.ypmed.2014.08.026 PMID:25172024

Dekker, M. R., & Williams, A. D. (2017). The Use of User-Centered Participatory Design in Serious Games for Anxiety and Depression. *Games for Health*, 6(6), 327–333. doi:10.1089/g4h.2017.0058 PMID:28956617

Dennis, T. A., & O'Toole, L. (2014). Mental Health on the Go: Effects of a Gamified Attention Bias Modification Mobile Application in Trait Anxious Adults. *Clinical Psychological Science*, 2(5), 576–590. doi:10.1177/2167702614522228 PMID:26029490

Djaouti, D., Alvarez, J., Jessel, J. P., & Rampnoux, O. (2011). *Origins of Serious Games*. Springer. doi:10.1007/978-1-4471-2161-9_3

Donovan, D. M., Kadden, R. M., DiClemente, C. C., & Carroll, K. M. (2002). Client satisfaction with three therapies in the treatment of alcohol dependence: Results from Project MATCH. *The American Journal on Addictions*, 11(4), 291–307. doi:10.1080/10550490290088090 PMID:12584872

Elliott, A. C., & Woodward, W. A. (2007). *Statistical analysis quick reference guidebook: With SPSS examples*. Sage Publications. doi:10.4135/9781412985949

Eysenbach, G. (2001). What is e-health? *Journal of Medical Internet Research*, 3(2), e:20. doi:10.2196/jmir.3.2.e20

Ferguson, C. J., & Olson, C. K. (2013). Friends, fun, frustration and fantasy: Child motivations for video game play. *Motivation and Emotion*, 37(1), 154–164. doi:10.100711031-012-9284-7

Foa, E. B., & Kozak, M. J. (1986). Emotional processing of fear: Exposure to corrective information. *Psychological Bulletin*, 99(1), 20–35. doi:10.1037/0033-2909.99.1.20 PMID:2871574

Garrido, S., Cheers, D., Boydell, K., Nguyen, Q. V., Schubert, E., Dunne, L., & Meade, T. (2019). Young people's response to six smartphone apps for anxiety and depression: Focus group study. *JMIR Mental Health, 6*(10), e14385. doi:10.2196/14385 PMID:31579023

Gasser, R., Brodbeck, D., Degen, M., Luthiger, J., Wyss, R., & Reichlin, S. (2006). Persuasiveness of a mobile lifestyle coaching application using social facilitation. In *International Conference on Persuasive Technology* (pp. 27-38). Springer. 10.1007/11755494_5

Gerrits, R. S., van der Zanden, R. A., Visscher, R. F., & Conjin, B. P. (2007). Master your mood online: A preventative chat group intervention for adolescents. *Australian e-Journal for the Advancement of Mental Health, 6*(3), 152–162. doi:10.5172/jamh.6.3.152

Geslin, E., Jégou, L., & Beaudoin, D. (2016). How Color Properties Can Be Used to Elicit Emotions in Video Games. *International Journal of Computer Games Technology, 3*, 1–9. doi:10.1155/2016/5182768

Giner-Bartolomé, C., Fagundo, A. B., Sánchez, I., Jiménez-Murcia, S., Santamaría, J. J., Ladouceur, R., Menchón, J. M., & Fernández-Aranda, F. (2015). Can an intervention based on a serious videogame prior to cognitive behavioural therapy be helpful in bulimia nervosa? A clinical case study. *Frontiers in Psychology, 6*, 982. doi:10.3389/fpsyg.2015.00982 PMID:26236261

Grant, D. M. (2013). Anxiety in Adolescence. In W. T. Donohue, L. Benuto, & L. Woodward-Tolle (Eds.), *Handbook of Adolescent Health* (pp. 507–519). Springer. doi:10.1007/978-1-4614-6633-8_32

Gregory, A. M., & Eley, T. C. (2007). Genetic influences on anxiety in children: What we've learned and where we're heading. *Clinical Child and Family Psychology Review, 10*(3), 199–212. doi:10.100710567-007-0022-8 PMID:17503180

Habgood, M. J., & Ainsworth, S. E. (2011). Motivating children to learn effectively: Exploring the value of intrinsic integration in educational games. *Journal of the Learning Sciences, 20*(2), 169–206. doi:10.1080/10508406.2010.508029

Haddad, A. D. M., Lissek, S., Pine, D. S., & Lau, J. Y. F. (2011). How do social fears in adolescence develop? Fear conditioning shapes attention orienting to social threat cues. *Cognition and Emotion, 25*(6), 1139–1147. doi:10.1080/02699931.2010.524193 PMID:21895575

Hagell, A. (2012). *Changing Adolescence: Social trends and mental health*. Policy Press. doi:10.1332/policypress/9781447301042.001.0001

Hamari, J., Koivisto, J., & Sarsa, H. (2014). Does Gamification Work?—A Literature Review of Empirical Studies on Gamification. *47th Hawaii International Conference on System Science*, 3025-3034 10.1109/HICSS.2014.377

Hefner, D., Klimmt, C., & Vorderer, P. (2007). Identification with the Player Character as Determinant of Video Game Enjoyment. In L. Ma, M. Rauterberg, & R. Nakatsu (Eds.), Lecture Notes in Computer Science: Vol. 4740. *Entertainment Computing – ICEC 2007. ICEC 2007*. Springer. doi:10.1007/978-3-540-74873-1_6

Higher Education Funding Council for England (HEFCE). (2015). *Understanding provision for students with mental health problems and intensive support needs.* Retrieved from: http://www.hefce.ac.uk/media/HEFCE,2014/Content/Pubs/Independentresearch/2015/Understanding,provision,for,students,with,mental,health,problems/HEFCE2015_mh.pdf

Holtz, B., & Whitten, P. (2009). Managing asthma with mobile phones: A feasibility study. *Telemedicine Journal and e-Health*, *15*(9), 907–909. doi:10.1089/tmj.2009.0048 PMID:19919198

Huang, W. D., & Johnson, T. (2008). Instructional game design using Cognitive Load Theory. In R. Ferdig (Ed.), *Handbook of research on effective electronic gaming in education*. Information Science Reference. doi:10.4018/978-1-59904-808-6.ch066

Huang, W. D., Johnson, T. E., & Seung-Hyun, C. (2013). Impact of Online Instructional Game Features on College Students' Perceived Motivational Support and Cognitive Investment: A Structural Equation Modeling Study. *Internet and Higher Education*, *17*, 58–68. doi:10.1016/j.iheduc.2012.11.004

Islam, M. R. (2018). Sample size and its role in Central Limit Theorem (CLT). *Computational and Applied Mathematics Journal*, *4*(1), 1–7. doi:10.31295/ijpm.v1n1.42

Jacobs, K. W., & Suess, J. F. (1975). Effects of four psychological primary colors on anxiety state. *Perceptual and Motor Skills*, *41*(1), 207–210. doi:10.2466/pms.1975.41.1.207 PMID:1178407

James, A., Soler, A., & Weatherall, R. (2005). Cognitive behavioural therapy for anxiety disorders in children and adolescents. *Cochrane Database of Systematic Reviews*, *4*, 1–35. doi:10.1002/14651858. CD004690.pub2 PMID:16235374

Kaltenthaler, E., Parry, G., Beverley, C., & Ferriter, M. (2008). Computerised cognitive-behavioural therapy for depression: Systematic review. *The British Journal of Psychiatry*, *193*(3), 181–184. doi:10.1192/bjp. bp.106.025981 PMID:18757972

Kapp, K. M. (2012). The Gamification of Learning and Instruction: Case-Based Methods and Strategies for Training and Education. New York: Pfieffer: An Imprint of John Wiley & Sons.

Kaya, N., & Epps, H. (2004). Relationship between color and emotion: A study of college students. *College Student Journal*, *38*(3), 396.

Kazdin, A. E., & Rabbitt, S. M. (2013). Novel Models for Delivering Mental Health Services and Reducing the Burdens of Mental Illness. *Clinical Psychological Science*, *1*(2), 170–191. doi:10.1177/2167702612463566

Kessler, R. C., Berglund, P., Demler, O., Jin, R., Merikangas, K. R., & Walters, E. E. (2005). Lifetime prevalence and age-of-onset distributions of DSM-IV disorders in the National Comorbidity Survey Replication. *Archives of General Psychiatry*, *62*(6), 593–602. doi:10.1001/archpsyc.62.6.593 PMID:15939837

Kessler, R. C., Heeringa, S., Lakoma, M. D., Petukhova, M., Rupp, A. E., Schoenbaum, M., Wang, P. S., & Zaslavsky, A. M. (2008). Individual and societal effects of mental disorders on earnings in the United States: Results from the National Comorbidity Survey Replication. *The American Journal of Psychiatry*, *165*(6), 703–711. doi:10.1176/appi.ajp.2008.08010126 PMID:18463104

King, D., Delfabbro, P., & Griffiths, M. (2010). Video game structural characteristics: A new psychological taxonomy. *International Journal of Mental Health and Addiction, 8*(1), 90–106. doi:10.100711469-009-9206-4

Klasnja, P., & Pratt, W. (2012). Healthcare in the pocket: Mapping the space of mobile-phone health interventions. *Journal of Biomedical Informatics, 45*(1), 184–198. doi:10.1016/j.jbi.2011.08.017 PMID:21925288

Kopp, J. (1988). Self-monitoring: A literature review of research and practice. *Social Work Research & Abstracts, 24*(4), 8–20. doi:10.1093wra/24.4.8

Laver, K. E., George, S., Thomas, S., Deutsch, J. E., & Crotty, M. (2015). Virtual reality for stroke rehabilitation. *Cochrane Database of Systematic Reviews, 12*(2). Advance online publication. doi:10.1002/14651858. CD008349.pub3 PMID:25927099

Lenhart, A., Kahne, J., Middaugh, E., Rankin-Macgill, A., Evans, C., & Vitak, J. (2008). *Teens, Video Games, and Civics: Teens' gaming experiences are diverse and include significant social interaction and civic engagement*. Pew Internet & American Life Project.

Lewis, C. C., Simons, A. D., & Kim, H. K. (2012). The role of early symptom trajectories and pretreatment variables in predicting treatment response to cognitive behavioral therapy. *Journal of Consulting and Clinical Psychology, 80*(4), 525–534. doi:10.1037/a0029131 PMID:22730951

Li, W. H., Chung, J. O., & Ho, E. K. (2011). The effectiveness of therapeutic play, using virtual reality computer games, in promoting the psychological well-being of children hospitalised with cancer. *Journal of Clinical Nursing, 20*(15-16), 2135–2143. doi:10.1111/j.1365-2702.2011.03733.x PMID:21651633

Loonen, A. J. M., & Ivanova, S. A. (2016). Circuits regulating pleasure and happiness in major depression. *Medical Hypotheses, 87*, 14–21. doi:10.1016/j.mehy.2015.12.013 PMID:26826634

MacLeod, C., Koster, E. H., & Fox, E. (2009). Whither cognitive bias modification research? Commentary on the special section articles. *Journal of Abnormal Psychology, 118*(1), 89–99. doi:10.1037/a0014878 PMID:19222317

Mantovani, F., Castelnuovo, G., Gaggioli, A., & Riva, G. (2003). Virtual reality training for healthcare professionals. *Cyberpsychology & Behavior, 6*(4), 389–395. doi:10.1089/109493103322278772 PMID:14511451

Marteau, T. M., & Bekker, H. (1992). The development of a six-item short-form of the state scale of the Spielberger State–Trait Anxiety Inventory (STAI). *British Journal of Clinical Psychology, 31*(3), 301–306. doi:10.1111/j.2044-8260.1992.tb00997.x PMID:1393159

Matthews, G., & Wells, A. (2016). *Attention and emotion: A clinical perspective*. Psychology Press. doi:10.4324/9781315784991

Mattila, E., Pärkkä, J., Hermersdorf, M., Kaasinen, J., Vainio, J., Samposalo, K., Merilahti, J., Kolari, J., Lappalainen, R., & Korhonen, I. (2008). Mobile diary for wellness management—Results on usage and usability in two user studies. *IEEE Transactions on Information Technology in Biomedicine, 12*(4), 501–512. doi:10.1109/TITB.2007.908237 PMID:18632330

McKenna, K., & Bargh, J. (2000). Plan 9 from cyberspace: The implication of the Internet for personality and social psychology. *Personality and Social Psychology Review, 4*(1), 57–75. doi:10.1207/S15327957PSPR0401_6

Merikangas, K. R., He, J. P., Burstein, M., Swendsen, J., Avenevoli, S., Case, B., Georgiades, K., Heaton, L., Swanson, S., & Olfson, M. (2011). Service utilization for lifetime mental disorders in US adolescents: Results of the National Comorbidity Survey–Adolescent Supplement (NCS-A). *Journal of the American Academy of Child and Adolescent Psychiatry, 50*(1), 32–45. doi:10.1016/j.jaac.2010.10.006 PMID:21156268

Mishra, J., & Gazzaley, A. (2014). Harnessing the neuroplastic potential of the human brain & the future of cognitive rehabilitation. *Frontiers in Human Neuroscience, 8*, 218. Advance online publication. doi:10.3389/fnhum.2014.00218 PMID:24782745

Mohr, D. C., Noth Tomasino, K., Lattie, E. G., Palac, H. L., Kwasny, M. J., Weingardt, K., Karr, C. J., Kaiser, S. M., Rossom, R. C., Bardsley, L. R., Caccamo, L., Stiles-Shields, C., & Schueller, S. M. (2017). IntelliCare: An eclectic, skills-based app suite for the treatment of depression and anxiety. *Journal of Medical Internet Research, 19*(1), e10. doi:10.2196/jmir.6645 PMID:28057609

Morschheuser, B., Riar, M., Hamari, J., & Maedche, A. (2017). How games induce cooperation? A study on the relationship between game features and we-intentions in an augmented reality game. *Computers in Human Behavior, 77*, 169–183. doi:10.1016/j.chb.2017.08.026

Nicholas, J., Fogarty, A. S., Boydell, K., & Christensen, H. (2017). The reviews are in: A qualitative content analysis of consumer perspectives on apps for bipolar disorder. *Journal of Medical Internet Research, 19*(4), e105. doi:10.2196/jmir.7273 PMID:28389420

Oblinger, D. (2004). The next generation of educational engagement. *Journal of Interactive Media in Education, 8*, 1–18.

Patel, A., Knapp, M., Henderson, J., & Baldwin, D. (2002). The economic consequences of social phobia. *Journal of Affective Disorders, 68*(2-3), 221–233. doi:10.1016/S0165-0327(00)00323-2 PMID:12063150

Peng, W., & Hsieh, G. (2012). The influence of competition, cooperation, and player relationship in a motor performance centered computer game. *Computers in Human Behavior, 28*(6), 2100–2106. doi:10.1016/j.chb.2012.06.014

Prentice-Dunn, S., & Rogers, R. W. (1982). Effects of public and private self-awareness on deindividuation and aggression. *Journal of Personality and Social Psychology, 43*(3), 503–513. doi:10.1037/0022-3514.43.3.503

Primack, B. A., Carroll, M. V., McNamara, M., Klem, M. L., King, B., Rich, M., Chan, C. W., & Nayak, S. (2012). Role of video games in improving health-related outcomes: A systematic review. *American Journal of Preventive Medicine, 42*(6), 630–638. doi:10.1016/j.amepre.2012.02.023 PMID:22608382

Rapee, D. M., Schniering, C., & Hudson, J. (2009). Anxiety disorders during childhood and adolescence: Origins and treatment. *Annual Review of Clinical Psychology, 5*(1), 311–341. doi:10.1146/annurev.clinpsy.032408.153628 PMID:19152496

Rice, F., & Thapar, A. (2009). Depression and anxiety in childhood and adolescence: developmental pathways, genes and environment. In K. Yong-Kyu (Ed.), *Handbook of Behavior Genetics* (pp. 379–396). Springer. doi:10.1007/978-0-387-76727-7_26

Roemer, L., & Orsillo, S. M. (2002). Expanding our conceptualization of and treatment for generalized anxiety disorder: Integrating mindfulness/acceptance-based approaches with existing cognitive-behavioral models. *Clinical Psychology: Science and Practice*, 9(1), 54–68. doi:10.1093/clipsy.9.1.54

Roohi, S., & Forouzandeh, A. (2019). Regarding color psychology principles in adventure games to enhance the sense of immersion. *Entertainment Computing*, 30, 100298. Advance online publication. doi:10.1016/j.entcom.2019.100298

Ryan, R. M., & Deci, E. L. (2000). Self-determination theory and the facilitation of intrinsic motivation, social development, and well-being. *The American Psychologist*, 55(1), 68–78. doi:10.1037/0003-066X.55.1.68 PMID:11392867

Ryan, R. M., Scott Rigby, C., & Przybylski, A. (2006). The Motivational Pull of Video Games: A Self-Determination Theory Approach. *Motivation and Emotion*, 30(4), 344–360. doi:10.100711031-006-9051-8

Salen, K., & Zimmerman, E. (2004). *Rules of Play: Game design fundamentals*. The MIT Press.

Schell, J. (2008). *The Art of Game Design: A Book of Lenses*. Taylor & Francis. doi:10.1201/9780080919171

Schmierbach, M., Limperos, A. M., & Woolley, J. K. (2012). Feeling the need for (personalized) speed: How natural controls and customization contribute to enjoyment of a racing game through enhanced immersion. *Cyberpsychology, Behavior, and Social Networking*, 15(7), 364–369. doi:10.1089/cyber.2012.0025 PMID:22687145

Schmittdiel, J. A., Uratsu, C. S., Karter, A. J., Heisler, M., Subramanian, U., Mangione, C. M., & Selby, J. V. (2008). Why don't diabetes patients achieve recommended risk factor targets? Poor adherence versus lack of treatment intensification. *Journal of General Internal Medicine*, 23(5), 588–594. doi:10.100711606-008-0554-8 PMID:18317847

Scholten, H., Malmberg, M., Lobel, A., Engels, R. C. M. E., & Granic, I. (2016). A randomized controlled trial to test the effectiveness of an immersive 3D video game for anxiety prevention among adolescents. *PLoS One*, 11(1), e0147763. doi:10.1371/journal.pone.0147763 PMID:26816292

Schoneveld, E. A., Malmberg, M., Lichtwarck-Aschoff, A., Verheijen, G. P., Engels, R. C. M. E., & Granic, I. (2016). A neurofeedback video game (MindLight) to prevent anxiety in children: A randomized controlled trial. *Computers in Human Behavior*, 63, 321–333. doi:10.1016/j.chb.2016.05.005

Schuurmans, A. A., Nijhof, K. S., Vermaes, I. P., Engels, R. C. M. E., & Granic, I. (2015). A pilot study evaluating "Dojo", a videogame intervention for youths with externalizing and anxiety problems. *Games for Health*, 4(5), 401–408. doi:10.1089/g4h.2014.0138 PMID:26287930

Short, J., Williams, E., & Christie, B. (1976). *The Social Psychology of Telecommunications*. John Wiley.

Siple, P., & Springer, R. M. (1983). Memory and preference for the colors of objects. *Perception & Psychophysics*, 34(4), 363–370. doi:10.3758/BF03203049 PMID:6657438

Sitzmann, T. (2011). A meta-analytic examination of the instructional effectiveness of computer-based simulation games. *Personnel Psychology, 64*(2), 489–528. doi:10.1111/j.1744-6570.2011.01190.x

Spielberger, C. D. (1983). *Manual for the State-Trait Inventory STAI (Form Y)*. Mind Garden.

Spielberger, C. D., Gorsuch, R. L., & Lushene, R. E. (1970). *Manual for the State-Trait Anxiety Inventory*. Consulting Psychologists Press.

Staiano, A. E., Abraham, A. A., & Calvert, S. L. (2012). Motivating Effects of Cooperative Exergame Play for Overweight and Obese Adolescents. *Journal of Diabetes Science and Technology, 6*(4), 812–819. doi:10.1177/193229681200600412 PMID:22920807

Stice, E., Rohde, P., Seeley, J. R., & Gau, J. M. (2008). Brief cognitive-behavioral depression prevention program for high-risk adolescents outperforms two alternative interventions: A randomized efficacy trial. *Journal of Consulting and Clinical Psychology, 76*(4), 595–606. doi:10.1037/a0012645 PMID:18665688

Stoyanov, S. R., Hides, L., Kavanagh, D. J., & Wilson, H. (2016). Development and Validation of the User Version of the Mobile Application Rating Scale (uMARS). *JMIR mHealth and uHealth, 4*(2), e16. doi:10.2196/mhealth.5849 PMID:27287964

Swift, J. K., & Callahan, J. L. (2009). The impact of client treatment preferences on outcome: A meta-analysis. *Journal of Clinical Psychology, 65*(4), 368–381. doi:10.1002/jclp.20553 PMID:19226606

Tárrega, S., Castro-Carreras, L., Fernández-Aranda, F., Granero, R., Giner-Bartolomé, C., Aymamí, N., Gómez-Peña, M., Santamaría, J. J., Forcano, L., Steward, T., Menchón, J. M., & Jiménez-Murcia, S. (1721). Jiménez-Murcia, S. (2015). A Serious Videogame as an Additional Therapy Tool for Training Emotional Regulation and Impulsivity Control in Severe Gambling Disorder. *Frontiers in Psychology, 6*. Advance online publication. doi:10.3389/fpsyg.2015.01721 PMID:26617550

Thom, J., Millen, D., & di Micco, J. (2012). Removing gamification from an enterprise SNS. In *Proceedings of the ACM 2012 Conference on Computer Supported Cooperative Work*. New York: ACM. 10.1145/2145204.2145362

Tong, H. L., Coiera, E., & Laranjo, L. (2018). Using a mobile social networking app to promote physical activity: A qualitative study of users' perspectives. *Journal of Medical Internet Research, 20*(12), e11439. doi:10.2196/11439 PMID:30578201

Turkay, S., & Kinzer, C. K. (2016). The Effects of Avatar-Based Customization on Player Identification. *International Journal of Gaming and Computer-Mediated Simulations, 6*(1), 1–25. doi:10.4018/ijgcms.2014010101

Turkle, S. (1995). Looking toward Cyberspace: Beyond grounded Sociology. *Contemporary Sociology, 28*(6), 643–648. doi:10.2307/2655534

Underwood, A. J. (1997). *Experiments in Ecology: Their Logical Design and Interpretation Using Analysis of Variance*. Cambridge University Press.

Ware, P., Bartlett, S. J., Paré, G., Symeonidis, I., Tannenbaum, C., Bartlett, G., Poissant, L., & Ahmed, S. (2017). Using eHealth technologies: Interests, preferences and concerns of older adults. *Interactive Journal of Medical Research, 6*(1), e3. doi:10.2196/ijmr.4447 PMID:28336506

Wiles, N., Thomas, L., Abel, A., Barnes, M., Carroll, F., Ridgway, N., Sherlock, S., Turner, N., Button, K., Odondi, L., Metcalfe, C., Owen-Smith, A., Campbell, J., Garland, A., Hollinghurst, S., Jerrom, B., Kessler, D., Kuyken, W., Morrison, J., ... Lewis, G. (2014). Clinical effectiveness and cost-effectiveness of cognitive behavioural therapy as an adjunct to pharmacotherapy for treatment-resistant depression in primary care: The CoBalT randomised controlled trial. *Health Technology Assessment*, *18*(31), 1–167. doi:10.3310/hta18310 PMID:24824481

Wittchen, H. U., & Fehm, L. (2003). Epidemiology and natural course of social fears and social phobia. *Acta Psychiatrica Scandinavica*, *417*, 4–18. doi:10.1034/j.1600-0447.108.s417.1.x PMID:12950432

Chapter 38
Can Video Games Be Used as a Stealth Assessment of Aggression?
A Criterion–Related Validity Study

Michael P. McCreery
University of Nevada, Las Vegas, USA

S. Kathleen Krach
iD https://orcid.org/0000-0002-6853-379X
Florida State University, Tallahassee, USA

Catherine A. Bacos
iD https://orcid.org/0000-0002-0653-8982
University of Nevada, Las Vegas, USA

Jeffrey R. Laferriere
iD https://orcid.org/0000-0003-3691-3648
Lebanon Valley College, Annville, USA

Danielle L. Head
iD https://orcid.org/0000-0002-5030-1659
University of Nevada, Las Vegas, USA

ABSTRACT

The current pilot study examined how well a reflective moral-choice video game predicted the rating scale scores of aggression types. To begin, the authors used a coding system to examine in-game proactive and reactive behaviors. This analysis resulted in a tallied score for each construct. These game-based scores were then included in regression models, examining how well within-game behaviors predict scores on a pre-existing rating scale of both proactive and reactive aggression. Findings indicated that game-based proactive scores were not predictive of proactive aggression ratings; however, reactive game-based scores were predictive of reactive aggression ratings. Implications for these findings are discussed.

DOI: 10.4018/978-1-6684-7589-8.ch038

INTRODUCTION

In recent years, researchers have begun to examine whether video games may be employed as stealth assessments (Ke & Shute, 2015; Shute, 2011; Wang, Shute, & Moore, 2015). That is, can a video game be used as a measurement tool for examining psychological constructs *in situ* (Shute, 2011). This growing body of literature has investigated the use of video games to measure a variety of factors including, academic skills (Sabourin, 2015), cognitive abilities (Shute & Wang, 2015), and trait-oriented constructs (Ventura & Shute, 2014). Results across these studies have demonstrated that when video game selection is done with intent (i.e., selected to measure a specific construct), within-game measures significantly correlated with independent psychological instrumentation (DeRosier et al., 2012) or were predictive of measured individual differences (Ventura & Shute, 2014).

The current pilot study aimed to build upon the stealth assessment literature by examining whether the constructs of proactive and/or reactive aggression could be measured through video game-based behaviors. For clarity sake, the purpose of this research was not to examine whether video games cause aggression (see Ferguson 2007, 2013), but whether assessing behavior exhibited within a video game yields similar results to those found with a traditional assessment. The primary reason for such a study is that currently there are limited methods for directly assessing aggression. Instead, aggression has been traditionally examined indirectly through the use of disciplinary counts (e.g., office referrals in children and criminal charges in adults; Pas, Bradshaw, & Mitchell, 2011) or through the use of rating scales (Dodge & Coie, 1987). The first method (i.e., disciplinary counts) requires that the aggression become so intense that it is harmful to society; whereas, the second method relies on the rater to be both truthful (Norfolk & Floyd, 2016) and self-aware (Csikszentmihalyi & Larson, 2014). Given the limitations associated with these traditional assessment techniques, this pilot was designed to examine whether a video game might provide an avenue for the direct assessment of aggressive behavior. By employing a criterion-related validity model, the current study examined the use of in-game behaviors as an *in situ* stealth assessment of proactive and reactive aggression.

BACKGROUND

Proactive-Reactive Aggression

The study of proactive-reactive aggression stems from the social information processing (SIP) model (Crick & Dodge, 1996). This model proposes that when people are presented with a social dilemma, they are required to encode, interpret, evaluate, and respond to a given social situation (Burgess et al., 2006). Over time the misinterpretation of social cues in conjunction with the outcomes associated with enacted responses, result in overlapping but distinct forms of aggression; these forms are referred to as proactive and reactive aggression (Crick & Dodge, 1996; Dodge, 1991).

Proactive aggression (PA) is considered to be an intrinsically motivated form of aggression (Raine et al., 2006). Self-serving in nature, individuals who exhibit proactively aggressive tendencies believe that intentional, goal-oriented, aggressive behavior is a socially effective tool for achieving a desired outcome (Crick & Dodge, 1996). For example, Law et al. (2012) in their study on cyberbullying, describe proactive aggression as the intentional engagement in an aggressive act to obtain resources or achieve a goal. While Hubbard and colleagues (2010) report that people engaging in proactive aggression had both a positive association between the aggressive act and the expected outcome, as well as increased feeling of self-efficacy due to engaging in that proactively aggressive behavior. Taken together, findings such as these suggest that proactive aggression is a 'cold' form of aggression, stressing premeditation or planning on the part of the individual as a way to reinforce feeling of control over their environment (Gardner et al., 2012).

Alternatively, reactive aggression (RA) is considered an impulsive form of aggression (Coie & Dodge, 1998). RA is thought to be the behavioral manifestation of an individual's misinterpretation of ambiguous social cues. For example, an individual exhibiting higher levels of reactive aggression often attribute hostile intent toward others, have difficulty attending to relevant social details, and experience problems with emotional regulation (Hubbard et al, 2010). Calvete and Orue (2012) found that a mistrust schema, as mediated by social information processing, was predictive of reactive aggression. Said another way, as hostile attribution grows (i.e., mistrust), people begin to process information atypically, resulting in a higher likelihood of exhibiting reactive aggression. Rathert, Fite, and Gaertner (2011) found that as the ability to shift and focus attention decreases (i.e. decreases in effortful control), the more likely they were to engage in reactively aggressive behavior. Crapanzano and her colleagues (2010) found that as levels of emotional dysregulation and impulsivity increased so do the corresponding level of reactive aggression. Based on these findings, researchers have begun to characterize reactive aggression as a 'hot' form of aggression that is emotionally laden, impulsive, and often retaliatory in nature; stemming from an individual's propensity to perceive social situations as hostile (Little et al., 2003).

Stealth Assessments

Shute and Ventura (2013) define stealth assessment as using gameplay evidence to assess constructs such as beliefs, feelings, states, and traits. Underlying this definition are several critical factors. First, the assessment component associated with gameplay must be invisible to the player (Shute, 2011). Second, the assessment method must collect real-time evidence as generated by a player's individual differences in responses to a set of tasks, problem, and/or situations (Shute et al., 2017). Third, the tasks, problems, and/or situations must present realistic dilemmas that are aligned with the beliefs, feelings, states, and traits being assessed (Shute & Ventura, 2013).

Using these requirements, researchers have demonstrated the effectiveness of stealth assessments as situated diagnostic tools for a variety of constructs. For example, DeRosier and colleagues (2012) found significant correlations between an in-game social skills assessment and an associated but independent psychological assessment of social skills. Ventura and Shute (2013) found that the video game assessment of persistence, a facet of the personality trait conscientiousness, was predictive of learning. Moreover, Sabourin (2015) found that real-time, in-game assessment, was predictive of cognitive, metacognitive, and motivational factors associated with self-regulated learning. Finally, Shute and Wang (2015) employed an off-the-shelf video game (e.g., Portal 2) to examine problem solving skills. In this study, stealth assessment measures were validated against an external measure of problem solving. Results indicated that in-game measures of problem solving significantly correlated with the external measure (Insight Problems; Chu & MacGregor, 2011).

The Deed as a Stealth Assessment

The Deed (Grab the Games, 2015) is a stylized moral-choice, murder mystery video game with a "Choose-Your-Own-Adventure" design framework. Unlike traditional murder mysteries where the player tries to solve the crime, the objective is to figure out how to commit the perfect murder. Underlying this shift in perspective is a social narrative based on what Heron and Belford (2014) call a reflective moral-choice system. Each game scenario allows the player to engage in a positive, negative, or neutral morally-driven behavior (i.e., choice). This form of game design allows for the capturing of behavioral patterns (i.e., repeated choices).

While its reflective moral-choice system (Heron & Belford, 2014) made *The Deed* a strong candidate for use in a stealth assessment study, there were several additional factors that lead to its final selection. First, the game was designed as a narrative experience, which supports the need for invisibility as reported in previous research (Shute, 2011). Second, as the player works through the narrative, they experience in-game scenarios that are similar to a traditional assessment. That is to say, the in-game scenarios are multiple-choice in design, consisting of a bounded range of positive, negative, and neutral behavioral choices. For example, the in-game maid states, "Your sister is upstairs in her room, I think," and the player may choose between three different responses: (a) "Thank you. (b) "And where can I find you, my pretty?" or (c) "I know my way around my own damn house." Third, all players see the same positive, negative, and neutral behavioral choices for a given scenario (i.e., the response choices are standardized). Finally, because these choices are bounded and standardized to a given situation, data collection does not require the research to make inferences regarding behavior. Rather, data collection consists solely of the documentation of the behavioral choice (i.e., a tally of proactive, reactive, neutral, or prosocial decisions).

Therefore, the current study set out to understand whether in-game behavior was predictive of scores on an external measure of proactive-reactive aggression, resulting in the following questions:

Q1: Does in-game behavior associated with acts of proactive aggression predict scores on the proactive aggression subscale?

Q2: Does in-game behavior associated with acts of reactive aggression predict scores on the reactive aggression subscale?

METHODS

Participants

Prior to the start of the study, a power analysis was conducted to determine the necessary sample size to answer each of the research questions ($f^2 = .15$; level $= .8$; $p = .05$; Cohen, 1992). Results from the analysis indicated that at least 67 subjects were needed to effectively analyze each model.

One hundred and seventy-two participants completed the study. Due to outlier issues or incomplete data sets, 15 participants were removed from the sample. Therefore, the final data set consisted of 157 participants. The gender demographics for the sample consisted of 25% male and 75% female, which is consistent with colleges of education (Snyder et al., 2016). Racial demographics for the sample included: 46% White, 7% Black or African-American, 17% Hispanic or Latino, 17% Asian, 2% Native Hawaiian or Pacific Islander, 10% who reported Two or More races, and 1% who reported Other. The average age of the sample was 24 ($sd = \sim 7$) years old.

Measures

The study consisted of three data collection components: (1) demographics, (2) *Scale of Proactive-Reactive Aggression* (Dodge & Coie, 1987), and (3) coding of gameplay behaviors.

For this study, the *Scale of Proactive-Reactive Aggression* (Dodge & Coie, 1987), which is a 23-Item, 3-point, Likert-type scale, was employed to assess aggression among the participants. Originally designed for a study involving younger male students (ages 7-16), previous research has shown it to be an effective measure of proactive and reactive aggression in adults, regardless of gender (McCreery & Krach, 2018; Miller & Lynam, 2006). Moreover, research has shown acceptable levels of internal consistency, ranging from .86 to .91 for PA, and .84 to .90 for RA (Dodge & Coie, 1987). Normative data for this instrument was not provided.

The bounded and standardized behavioral choices in the "Choose Your Own Adventure" format of *The Deed* allowed for the examination of game-prompt answer choices within the context of their related question stem. In other words, each time a player selected a proactively aggressive, reactively aggressive, neutral, or prosocial response, they received one point for one of these subscales. For example, the player's in-game father asks, "Why can't you ever keep your mouth shut, boy?" and the player may respond in a reactively aggressive manner by stating, "Maybe you're the one who needs to shut his mouth." This response would result in one point (or tally mark) on the within-game RA subscale.

In order to create the within-game proactive/reactive aggression behavior scores, the researchers began by cataloging all the possible choices a player could make during Acts One and Two of the game. These acts are the only sections of the game wherein the reflective moral-choice system exists. Act Three is when *The Deed* is committed, and during Act Four the player finds out the outcome of the game. After the cataloging was completed, each of the behavioral choices were assessed independently by each of the authors for response type (i.e., proactive aggression, reactive aggression, neutral, or prosocial). Interrater agreement was then calculated (.92). Where agreement could not be reached by the authors, the behavioral choice was excluded from the analyses. The culmination of these activities resulted in a codebook that was used to analyze each participant's gameplay. It should be noted that once interrater agreement was reached, all cataloging of behavior was done using a count system (i.e., it either happened [1] or it did not [0]), which is consistent with previous behavioral coding techniques used to examine game play (McCreery et al., 2012; McCreery et al., 2013).

Design

The purpose of the pilot was to examine if in-game behavior could be a valid direct assessment of aggression types. A recent definition of validity is, "the degree to which scores on an appropriately administered instrument support inferences about variation in the characteristic that the instrument was developed to measure" (Cizek, 2012, p. 35). There are several methods of measuring validity. One such method, concurrent / convergent validity, usually refers to assessing if an instrument measures the same constructs as a similar instrument (Messick, 1995). For example, concurrent validity methods have been used for comparing a published assessment instrument to a computer-based, off-the-shelf measurement technique (Clark et al., 2013). Predictive validity usually refers to assessing if findings from an instrument can predict life-related outcomes (Messick, 1995). For example, predictive validity methods have been used to examine how well a computer-based assessment predicts academic improvement (Clemens et al., 2015). Both concurrent validity and predictive validity fall under the umbrella term of criterion-related validity. Given that the current research was a mixture of both concurrent and predictive validity techniques, it would be most appropriate to call it a criterion-related validity study.

Procedures

After receiving IRB approval, participants were recruited from a subject pool at a large university in the southwestern United States. Upon arrival at a computer lab and consenting to the study, participants were asked to sit at one of five identical workstations. Each station was equipped with an identical iMac, two-button mouse, and *The Deed* video game preloaded. Participants began by playing *The Deed*. Upon completion of the game, they were asked to fill out the demographic questionnaire and *Scale of Proactive-Reactive Aggression* (Dodge & Coie, 1987) in Qualtrics (Qualtrics, 2018). This post gameplay administration was done to limit participant priming effects of in-game behavioral choices. All participant gameplay was recorded using Fraps, a video capture software available for Windows (Version 3.5.99; Beepa Pty Ltd., 2013) and coded using the aforementioned codebook. For this study, only the proactive and reactive behavioral responses were included in the analysis.

RESULTS

Standardized Residuals of Proactive-Reactive Aggression

Proactive and reactive aggression have historically demonstrated high correlations (Cima & Raine, 2009; Lobbestael et al., 2013). Therefore, prior to conducting the analysis associated with the current study, a correlation was run between the two subscales ($r = .789$). Due to high correlation between the subscales an exploratory factor analysis (EFA) was necessary to verify construct validity (Raine et al., 2006). This was completed by following the procedures outlined by Lobbestael et al. (2013).

In order to more accurately and realistically represent the Proactive and Reactive Aggression subscales, known to be highly correlated due to previous research (Cima & Raine, 2009), a modification to Lobbestael and colleagues (2013) procedures was made: specifically, the use of an oblique factor rotation (i.e., Promax) was employed to more accurately differentiate the subscales (Costello & Osborne, 2005; Fabrigar et al., 1999; McCreery & Krach, 2018). Adjusted Proactive and Reactive Aggression subscales were then created using EFA results. The Adjusted Proactive Aggression subscale consisted of twelve items (6, 7, 8, 10, 14, 16, 17, 18, 19, 20, 21, and 22), and the Adjusted Reactive Aggression subscale contained eight items (1, 2, 3, 9, 11, 13,15, and 23). Internal consistency was then examined for both the Adjusted Proactive and Adjusted Reactive Aggression subscales ($\alpha = .75$ and $\alpha = .84$, respectively).

Finally, standardized residuals were computed using the Adjusted Proactive and Adjusted Reactive Aggression subscales, by regressing each variable upon the other. These standardized residual scores (i.e., Residual Proactive and Reactive Aggression) are considered "purer" measures of each variable (Gardner et al., 2012). Once completed, an updated corollary analysis was conducted using the Residual Proactive and Reactive Aggression subscales ($r = -.511$, $p < .000$).

Data Normality

Prior to data analysis, data screening was conducted for each of the variables, including skewness and kurtosis. Results of the analyses indicated that data fell within the acceptable limits of an absolute value of two for both skewness and kurtosis (Tabachnick & Fidell, 1996). Please see Table 1 for complete descriptive statistics.

Table 1. Variable means and standard deviations

Variable	N	M	SD	Skewness	Kurtosis
Unadjusted Proactive Aggression	157	6.60	4.42	0.754	.510
Unadjusted Reactive Aggression	157	6.33	4.07	0.747	.800
Adjusted Proactive Aggression	157	2.62	3.13	1.536	2.103
Adjusted Reactive Aggression	157	9.40	5.22	0.392	-.274
Within-Game Proactive Aggression	157	0.80	0.92	1.173	1.132
Within-Game Reactive Aggression	157	0.69	0.95	1.537	2.110

Regression Analyses

To answer Q1, in-game behavior associated with proactive aggression was regressed on the Residual Proactive Aggression subscale. Results were not statistically significant ($p = .453$). Turning to Q2, in-game behavior associated with reactive aggression was regressed on the Residual Reactive Aggression subscale. Results from the analysis indicated that reactively aggressive in-game behavior was predictive of scores on the external measure of reactive aggression ($R^2 = .042$; $F(1,156) = 6.897$, $p = .009$; $b = .217$, $\beta = .206$, $t(156) = 2.618$, $p = .010$).

DISCUSSION

The lack of statistical significance associated with proactive aggression should not be seen as problematic. Rather, when viewed in terms of the theoretical framework associated with the construct of proactive aggression (i.e., self-serving, intentional, and goal-oriented; Arsenio et al., 2009), these results align with expectations. Specifically, it is unlikely the population of a college of education, which serves students training to work within a helping profession field, would attract a student body that consistently demostrates proactively aggressive tendencies. This is borne out in the descriptive statistics (adjusted proactive aggression $\bar{x} = 2.62$; adjusted reactive aggression $\bar{x} = 9.40$). To examine the usefulness of this game to measure proactive aggression, the next steps would be to conduct similar work with a referred or clinical population.

Alternatively, results regarding reactive aggression also appear to align with previous research associated with the construct (Arsenio et al., 2009; Crick & Dodge, 1996; Dodge & Coie, 1987). Specifically, the overall narrative design is grounded in socially interactive experiences. These experiences (i.e., social dilemmas) require players to encode, interpret, evaluate, and respond to a given social situation. This lies at the very core of the SIP model (Burgess et al., 2006). Moreover, in order to complete the game, players are required to engage in reflective moral-choices grounded in social scenarios with no clear correct answer (e.g., when the in-game maid states, "It's just that you have never visited before," the player has to choose between, "I have been busy," "I don't get along with my family," or "[Offended] Just what are you trying to say?"). These ambiguous choices are frequently associated with social experiences, and it is difficulty handling ambiguity that has been consistently found a catalyst for reactive aggression (Dodge & Coie, 1987). Based on these results, it would be prudent to begin examining whether correlates to reactive aggression (e.g., attention, emotional regulation) are also associated with in-game reactively aggressive behavior. This work could not just potentially help to clarify the current stealth assessment work but also provide additional support to the PA-RA theoretical frameworks.

IMPLICATIONS

Given concerns regarding the assessment of aggression, the current pilot was designed to examine whether a video game could work as an *in situ* stealth assessment of proactive-reactive aggression. While the R^2 is indeed small, it is important to recognize that this is an off-the-shelf game that is not designed to purposefully assess aggression. Rather, these findings demonstrate that a reflective moral-choice game may provide a *framework* (emphasis added) to encapsulate or embed a psychometrically sound assessment. Contextualizing the assessment experience in such a manner that it is invisible by design and behavioral in nature (Shute & Ventura, 2013). Thus, potentially limiting the negative impact on validity found with rating scales by potentially removing the confounding effects of truthfulness and self-awareness.

However, despite not being created as an assessment tool, *The Deed's* design does model an assessment through the use of scenarios with bounded multiple-choice answers. It's structure, coupled with the pilot findings would suggest that researchers continue to explore the viability of behavioral stealth assessments. Ultimately, the authors recommend a systematic approach to this process that is grounded in the framework outlined by Shute and Venture (2013), and includes targeted sample selection, examining correlates associated with proactive and reactive aggression, and ultimately the purposeful development of a PA/RA stealth assessment.

REFERENCES

Arsenio, W. F., Adams, E., & Gold, J. (2009). Social information processing, moral reasoning, and emotional attributions: Relations with adolescents reactive and proactive aggression. *Child Development*, *80*(6), 1739–1755. doi:10.1111/j.1467-8624.2009.01365.x PMID:19930349

Burgess, P. W., Alderman, N., Forbes, C., Costello, A., Coates, L. M., Dawson, D. R., ... Channon, S. (2006). The case for the development and use of "ecologically valid" measures of executive function in experimental and clinical neuropsychology. *Journal of the International Neuropsychological Society: JINS*, *12*, 194–209. doi:10.1017/S1355617706060310 PMID:16573854

Chu, Y., & MacGregor, J. N. (2011). Human performance on insight problem solving: A review. *The Journal of Problem Solving*, *3*(2), 119–150. doi:10.7771/1932-6246.1094

Cima, M., & Raine, A. (2009). Distinct characteristics of psychopathy relate to different subtypes of aggression. *Personality and Individual Differences*, *47*(8), 835–840. doi:10.1016/j.paid.2009.06.031

Cizek, G. J. (2012). Defining and distinguishing validity: Interpretations of score meaning and justifications of test use. *Psychological Methods*, *17*(1), 31–43. doi:10.1037/a0026975 PMID:22268761

Clark, R. A., Bower, K. J., Mentiplay, B. F., Paterson, K., & Pua, Y. H. (2013). Concurrent validity of the Microsoft Kinect for assessment of spatiotemporal gait variables. *Journal of Biomechanics*, *46*(15), 2722–2725. doi:10.1016/j.jbiomech.2013.08.011 PMID:24016679

Clemens, N. H., Hagan-Burke, S., Luo, W., Cerda, C., Blakely, A., Frosch, J., ... Jones, M. (2015). The predictive validity of a computer-adaptive assessment of kindergarten and first-grade reading skills. *School Psychology Review*, *44*(1), 76–97. doi:10.17105/SPR44-1.76-97

Cohen, J. (1992). A power primer. *Quantitative Methods in Psychology*, *112*(1), 155–159. doi:10.1037/0033-2909.112.1.155 PMID:19565683

Coie, J. D., & Dodge, K. A. (1998). Aggression and antisocial behavior. In W. Damon & N. Eisenberg (Eds.), 5th ed., Vol. 3, pp. 779–862). Handbook of child psychology New York: Wiley.

Costello, A. B., & Osborne, J. W. (2005). Best practices in exploratory factor analysis: Four recommendations for getting the most from your analysis. *Practical Assessment, Research & Evaluation*, *10*, 1–9.

Crick, N., & Dodge, K. (1996). Social information-processing mechanisms in reactive and proactive aggression. *Child Development*, *67*(3), 993–1002. doi:10.2307/1131875 PMID:8706540

Csikszentmihalyi, M., & Larson, R. (2014). *The collected works of Mihaly Csikszentmihalyi*. Dordrecht: Springer.

DeRosier, M. E., Craig, A. B., & Sanchez, R. P. (2012). Zoo U: A stealth approach to social skills assessment in schools. *Advances in Human-Computer Interaction*, *22*, 1–7. doi:10.1155/2012/654791

Dodge, K. A. (1991). The structure and function of reactive and proactive aggression. In D. J. Pepler & K. H. Rubin (Eds.), *The development and treatment of childhood aggression* (pp. 201–218). Hillsdale, NJ: Lawrence Erlbaum Associates, Inc.

Dodge, K. A., & Coie, J. D. (1987). Social-information-processing factors in reactive and proactive aggression in children's peer groups. *Journal of Personality and Social Psychology*, *53*(6), 1146–1158. doi:10.1037/0022-3514.53.6.1146 PMID:3694454

Fabrigar, L. R., Wegener, D. T., MacCallum, R. C., & Strahan, E. J. (1999). Evaluating the use of exploratory factor analysis in psychological research. *Psychological Methods*, *4*(3), 272–299. doi:10.1037/1082-989X.4.3.272

Ferguson, C. J. (2007). The good, the bad and the ugly: A meta-analytic review of positive and negative effects of violent video games. *The Psychiatric Quarterly*, *78*(4), 309–316. doi:10.100711126-007-9056-9 PMID:17914672

Ferguson, C. J.Entertainment Merchants Association. (2013). Violent video games and the Supreme Court: Lessons for the scientific community in the wake of Brown v. Entertainment Merchants Association. *The American Psychologist, 68*(2), 57–74. doi:10.1037/a0030597 PMID:23421606

Gardner, K. J., Archer, J., & Jackson, S. (2012). Does maladaptive coping mediate the relationship between borderline personality traits and reactive and proactive aggression? *Aggressive Behavior, 38*(5), 403–413. doi:10.1002/ab.21437 PMID:22711314

Grab the Games. (2015). *The Deed* [Computer software]. Retrieved from http://store.steampowered.com/app/420740/The_Deed/

Heron, M., & Belford, P. (2014). 'It's only a game'—ethics, empathy and identification in game morality systems. *The Computer Games Journal, 3*(1), 34–53. doi:10.1007/BF03392356

Hubbard, J. A., McAuliffe, M. D., Morrow, M. T., & Romano, L. J. (2010). Reactive and proactive aggression in childhood and adolescence: Precursors, outcomes, processes, experiences, and measurement. *Journal of Personality, 78*(1), 95–118. doi:10.1111/j.1467-6494.2009.00610.x PMID:20433614

Ke, F. F., & Shute, V. J. (2015). Design of game-based stealth assessment and learning support. In C. Loh, Y. Sheng, & D. Ifenthaler (Eds.), *Serious games analytics* (pp. 301–318). New York, NY: Springer. doi:10.1007/978-3-319-05834-4_13

Law, D. M., Shapka, J. D., Domene, J. F., & Gagne, M. H. (2012). Are cyberbullies really bullies? An investigation of reactive and proactive online aggression. *Computers in Human Behavior, 28*(2), 664–672. doi:10.1016/j.chb.2011.11.013

Little, J. W., Gearhart, M., Curry, M., & Kafka, J. (2003). Looking at student work for teacher learning, teacher community, and school reform. *Phi Delta Kappan, 85*(3), 184–192. doi:10.1177/003172170308500305

Lobbestael, J., Cima, M., & Arntz, A. (2013). The relationship between adult reactive and proactive aggression, hostile interpretation bias, and antisocial personality disorder. *Journal of Personality Disorders, 27*(1), 53–66. doi:10.1521/pedi.2013.27.1.53 PMID:23342957

McCreery, M. P., & Krach, K. S. (2018). How the human is the catalyst: Personality, aggressive fantasy, and proactive-reactive aggression among users of social media. *Personality and Individual Differences, 133*, 91–95. doi:10.1016/j.paid.2017.06.037

McCreery, M. P., Krach, K. S., Schrader, P. G., & Boone, R. (2012). Defining the virtual self: Personality, behavior, and the psychology of embodiment. *Computers in Human Behavior, 28*(3), 976–983. doi:10.1016/j.chb.2011.12.019

McCreery, M. P., Schrader, P. G., Krach, S. K., & Boone, R. (2013). A sense of self: The role of presence in virtual environments. *Computers in Human Behavior, 29*(4), 1635–1640. doi:10.1016/j.chb.2013.02.002

Messick, S. (1995). Validity of psychological assessment: Validation of inferences from persons' responses and performances as scientific inquiry into score meaning. *The American Psychologist, 50*(9), 741–749. doi:10.1037/0003-066X.50.9.741

Miller, J. D., & Lynam, D. R. (2006). Reactive and proactive aggression: Similarities and differences. *Personality and Individual Differences, 41*(8), 1469–1480. doi:10.1016/j.paid.2006.06.004

Norfolk, P. A., & Floyd, R. G. (2016). Detecting parental deception using a behavior rating scale during assessment of Attention-Deficit/Hyperactivity Disorder: An experimental study. *Psychology in the Schools*, *53*(2), 158–172. doi:10.1002/pits.21894

Pas, E. T., Bradshaw, C. P., & Mitchell, M. M. (2011). Examining the validity of office discipline referrals as an indicator of student behavior problems. *Psychology in the Schools*, *48*(6), 541–555. doi:10.1002/pits.20577

Poulin, F., & Boivin, M. (2000). Reactive and proactive aggression: Evidence of a two-factor model. *Psychological Assessment*, *12*(2), 115–122. doi:10.1037/1040-3590.12.2.115 PMID:10887757

Qualtrics. (2018). *Qualtrics Survey Software*. Retrieved from https://www.qualtrics.com

Raine, A., Dodge, K., Loeber, R., Gatzke-Kopp, L., Lynam, D., Reynolds, C., ... Liu, J. (2006). The Reactive–Proactive Aggression Questionnaire: Differential correlates of reactive and proactive aggression in adolescent boys. *Aggressive Behavior*, *32*(2), 159–171. doi:10.1002/ab.20115 PMID:20798781

Sabourin, J. L. (2015). Stealth assessment of self-regulated learning in game-based learning environments. *Dissertation Abstracts International*, *75*.

Shute, V. J. (2011). Stealth assessment in computer-based games to support learning. In S. Tobias & J. D. Fletcher (Eds.), *Computer games and instruction* (pp. 503–523). Charlotte, NC: Information Age Publishing.

Shute, V. J., & Ventura, M. (2013). *Measuring and supporting learning in games: Stealth assessment*. Cambridge, MA: The MIT Press. doi:10.7551/mitpress/9589.001.0001

Shute, V. J., & Wang, L. (2015). Measuring problem solving skills in Portal 2. In P. Isaias, J. M. Spector, D. Ifenthaler, & D. G. Sampson (Eds.), *E-learning systems, environments and approaches: Theory and implementation* (pp. 11–24). New York, NY: Springer. doi:10.1007/978-3-319-05825-2_2

Snyder, T. D., Brey, C. D., & Dillow, S. A. (2016). *Digest of Education Statistics 2014 (NCES 2016-006)*. Washington, DC: National Center for Education Statistics, Institute of Education Sciences, U.S. Department of Education.

Ventura, M., & Shute, V. (2014). The validity of a game-based assessment of persistence. *Computers in Human Behavior*, *29*(6), 2568–2572. doi:10.1016/j.chb.2013.06.033

Wang, L., Shute, V., & Moore, G. R. (2015). Lessons learned and best practices of stealth assessments. *International Journal of Gaming and Computer-Mediated Simulations*, *7*(4), 66–87. doi:10.4018/IJGCMS.2015100104

This research was previously published in the International Journal of Gaming and Computer-Mediated Simulations (IJGCMS), 11(2); pages 40-49, copyright year 2019 by IGI Publishing (an imprint of IGI Global).

Chapter 39

Using an Extended Technology Acceptance Model for Online Strategic Video Games:
A Case of Multiplayer Online Battle Arena (MOBA)

Melanie M. Himang
Cebu Technological University, Philippines

Angie Monterde Ceniza
University of San Carlos, Philippines

Celbert Mirasol Himang
ⓘD https://orcid.org/0000-0002-5663-3304
Cebu Technological University, Philippines

Lanndon Ocampo
ⓘD https://orcid.org/0000-0002-5050-7606
Cebu Technological University, Philippines

ABSTRACT

Due to the rising popularity of online strategic video games, it is crucial to examine the acceptance structure of these games. This study attempts to perform an acceptance evaluation of online strategic video games, particularly multiplayer online battle arena (MOBA), using an extended technology acceptance model (TAM) developed in the current literature and establish a predictive value in determining the behavioral intention in playing online strategic video games. To carry out this objective, a case study consisting of 439 undergraduate students as a sample was conducted. After the data filtering process which involves the removal of insincere responses and non-engaging responses and of those who have not played MOBA games, 278 research participants became the final sample. The questionnaire was created and underwent reliability analysis. Cronbach's alpha coefficient was computed to show the relatedness of each factor as well as to determine its validity and internal reliability. Nine factors were considered in this work that tested for significant relationships and predictive capabilities using structural equation modeling with AMOS software. These factors include altruism, social interaction, use context, perceived ease of enjoyment, perceived ease of use, perceived usefulness, attitude, flow, and behavior intention. Results show that the significant determinants of user behavior intention are the flow, attitude, and per-

DOI: 10.4018/978-1-6684-7589-8.ch039

ceived ease of use while the perceived enjoyment, social interaction significantly influence attitudes in playing online strategic video games, use context, and flow. Furthermore, this work also demonstrates that altruism, social interaction, use context, perceived enjoyment, flow, and attitude are significant factors that can be added to extend TAM. These findings would serve as guidelines in the formulation of principles for game design and development.

1. INTRODUCTION

The rapid availability of the internet leads to the presence of a variety of online video games that attracted players worldwide. Recently, games that are interactive has achieved significant development in the area of game development. Video game players come from various ages, nationality, and occupation. The Entertainment Software Association (2017) found out that video game players are women, comprising 35% to 40% of the population and more than 72% of households play video games. A myriad of motivations exists why they play online video games (Mathews, 2017). These include the following:(1) players are connected to their inner child; (2) players have an outlet to escape from different stress in life; (3) players develop their creativity, strategic skills, and imagination; (4) players can gain friends by playing games; (5) players develop their eye, and hand coordination; and (6) players have something to look forward to. Yee (2006) examined these different motivations. While Granic et al. (2014) comprehensively outlined the benefits of playing video games, playing video games can lead to addiction (Kuss and Griffiths, 2012). This phenomenon is widely documented and reported in the current literature (Anderson and Dill, 2000; Ng and Wiemer-Hastings, 2005; Lemmens et al., 2009; Young, 2009; Kuss and Griffiths, 2012; Wittek et al., 2016; Bean et al., 2017) and will not be discussed here for brevity. Despite its ill-effects, recent works have demonstrated its benefits including cognitive, motivational, emotional, and social ones (Granic et al., 2014), improved working memory (Colzato et al., 2013), disaster learning (Gampell et al., 2017), and probabilistic learning (Schenk et al., 2017), among several others. This list is not intended to be comprehensive. This work aims not to contribute in this debate, but instead, it provides an evaluation of the acceptability of these video games to leverage on their benefits.

One of the most popular strategy video games is the multiplayer online battle arena (MOBA), it is also known as action real-time strategy (ARTS). It is a sub-genre of strategic video games in which player identify his/her character in a team to fight with the other team. The primary objective is to destroy the opposing team with the help of the skills of the chosen character. MOBA has attracted people who desire to put together quick strategies and have a good deal of time for the game. Given the popularity of these MOBA games, it is of full interest to determine an in-depth evaluation of its broad acceptance in the games industry. Lin and Lu (2011), proposed a model that explained the use of social networking sites in incorporating external factors and motivation theory. In the domain of information and communications technology (ICT), scholars are interested in determining the rigorous motivations of acceptance behind the actual usage of information systems. These are some of the models that can be used in explaining such usage: theory of reason action (Ajzen, 1975), motivational model (Davis et al, 1992), model of personal computer utilization (Thompson et al., 1991), unified theory of acceptance and use of technology (Venkatesh et al., 2003), theory of planned behavior (Ajzen, 1991) and technology acceptance model (Davis, 1989).

The technology acceptance model (TAM) (Davis, 1989) is one of the leading techniques used to analyze the behavioral patterns. TAM has been used in the past decade and has proven its validity in predicting the behavioral usage of various information systems. In the past, multiple works have successfully applied TAM and extended TAM models which would explain the user acceptance in many computer application systems (Lin and Lu, 2000; Moon and Kim, 2001; Koufaris, 2002). An extended TAM was suggested by Shin and Shin (2011) that examined the acceptance factors of people in playing social network games. Hsu and Lu (2004) also made use of an extended TAM. Lee and Tsai (2010) investigated people why they continue playing online games using extended TAM. Kwon and Wen (2010) extended the TAM by adding social, identity, altruism, and telepresence. Kim et al. (2011) examined cultural difference as motivation in using different social networking sites. Rosen and Sherman (2006) discussed the acceptance of people's intention to use social networks by extending the TAM. Shin et al. (2011) proposed an extended TAM to investigate factors influencing how user accept the social games. On the other hand, Liang and Yeh (2011) studied the effect of continuous use of mobile services in playing games through mobile phones with an extended TAM. Such extended TAM models are usually context-specific to an application.

Although online strategic video games are becoming more popular as it is played not only teenagers but also elderly (Wang and Sun, 2016) and has influenced the behavioral pattern in spending their free time (Connolly et al., 2012), current literature has not yet addressed a thorough and in-depth understanding of the user acceptability of these games. On this note, Chen et al. (2017) provided insight by arguing that TAM must be a leading and appropriate model in studying the popularity of online games. Chen et al. (2017) performed popularity analysis of mobile social gaming service using extended TAM, and this extension of TAM is the closest representation of user acceptance of online strategic video games. They extended the TAM model by adding factors such as altruism, social interaction, use context, perceived enjoyment, flow, and attitude. They adopted the hypotheses of Fishbein and Ajzen (1975) about the belief- attitude-intention-behavior causal chain in the context of social-based mobile games. The extended model is intended to improve the understanding of the user's intention to play such games. It also provides insights into why most people continue to play mobile social games. They were able to investigate the main determinants and their relationships. The extended TAM of Chen et al. (2017) becomes a more appropriate extension when online strategic video games are taken into context as the additional factors (i.e., altruism, social interaction, use context, perceived enjoyment, flow, and attitude) are straightforward and significant factors in understanding these online games.

Thus, this study aims to evaluate online strategic video games, particularly MOBA, using an extended TAM model proposed by Chen et al. (2017) and to establish a predictive value in determining the behavioral intention in playing these games. The objectives of this work are threefold: (1) to model the user acceptability of MOBA, as an online strategic video game, which has not yet explored in the current literature, (2) to test the replicability of the model of Chen et al. (2017) in MOBA application with an anticipation that crucial insights could be generated for relevant stakeholders, and (3) to provide a better understanding of the acceptance of online strategic video games and to identify a basis that can be used by games industry and game developers on creating strategic video games. Replication, as argued by Goodboy and Kline (2017), is significant for scholars as it precludes confidence of findings for knowledge development in a specific domain field. Likewise, providing insights and better understanding for the acceptability of MOBA is of utmost importance to the game industry as they would be able to develop similar games that could attract the attention of the players to make their video games popular. The contribution of this paper is the acceptance evaluation of online strategic video games as an aid in the formulation of principles for game design and development.

In carrying out the goals, this paper is organized as follows. Section 2 provides a brief review of online strategic video games and the emergence of TAM as a relevant evaluation model of such games. Section 3 discussed the background of the case study and laid the procedure of data collection and analysis. Section 4 presents the top three MOBA games played by the research participants to contextualize the constructs of the extended TAM. Section 5 presents the results and the relevant discussion and implication of these results. This paper ends with a conclusion and a review of possible future works in Section 6.

2. BACKGROUND OF THE STUDY

Over the past half-century, video gameplay has gone from being a somewhat fringe activity to a ubiquitous part of modern culture. In 1972, Magnavox Odyssey released the first dedicated video game console that sold for about 300,000 units. In the mid-2000s, the Xbox 360, the PlayStation 3, and the Wii sold more than 84 million each. Entertain Software Association (2015) examined the presence of strategic video games resulted in a concomitant decrease in time spent watching television and movies. Various works have been dedicated to the advantages and disadvantages of playing online strategic video games. See Yee (2006), Colzato et al. (2013), Granic et al. (2014), Gampell et al. (2017), and Schenk et al. (2017) for some of the benefits and Anderson and Dill (2000), Ng and Wiemer-Hastings (2005), Lemmens et al. (2009), Young (2009), Kuss and Griffiths (2012), Wittek et al. (2016) and Bean et al. (2017) for the discussion of drawbacks related to addiction.

For instance, Green and Sietz (2015) highlighted that playing some video games, mainly "action" video games, results in the general enhancement of cognitive function. It can also provide positive reinforcement such as positive social interactions and feeling of competence (Przybylski et al., 2010) and external reinforcement such as points, badges, among others (King et al., 2013). Video games are highly physiologically arousing and would potentially activate reward systems of the brain that drive brain plasticity (KilgardandMerzenich,1998; Bao et al., 2011). Thus, there is a firm scientific basis that when a video game is appropriately designed. It has the potential to actively alter the brain and behavior. Also, playing video games can promote hand-eye coordination, visual scanning, auditory discrimination, and spatial skills (Johnson et al., 1999; Lisi and Wolford,2002). However, on a negative note, playing video games that are violent can lead to aggression, addiction, and depression (Ferguson, 2007; Anderson et al.,2010). Lemola (2011) found that the constant playing of a computer game at night can be one cause of depressive symptoms. There is evidence showed that violent video games would affect child behavior (Funk, 2011). These games (violent video games) are not appropriate played by children.

One of the most popular strategic online video games is the multiplayer online battle arena (MOBA) games. MOBA games are a subgenre of real-time strategy games in which two teams, typically consisting of five players each, compete against each other with each player controlling a single character. In a typical MOBA game such asDota2 (Frunk,2003), each team consisting of five players are allocated a specific spawning location in their base that is designed to be safe and inaccessible by the opposite team due to a 'fountain' that destroys members of the opposing team almost instantly upon entry. The fountain hook took advantage of this design mechanic through an unlikely combination of abilities from different heroes that purposely pulled an enemy player huge distances across the map and into what was designed to be the forbidden zone of the fountain; thus, killing the opposition outright. Various works have explored why online strategic video games became famous and made a significant leap in the game industry. These are models being adopted in order to explain the acceptance: theory of reason action (Ajzen, 1975), motivational model (Davis et al, 1992), model of personal computer utilization (Thompson et al.,1991), unified theory of acceptance and use of technology (Venkatesh et al., 2003), theory of planned behavior (Ajzen,1991) and technology acceptance model (Davis, 1989).

The technology acceptance model (TAM) (Davis,1989; Davis et al.,1989) adapted from the theory of Reasoned Action (TRA) (Ajzen and Fishbein, 1980; Fishbein and Ajzen, 1975) has received significant attention in IT/IS acceptance literature. TAM focuses on the attitudinal explanations of intention to use a specific technology or service. It posits that two particular beliefs, perceived usefulness (PU) and perceived ease of use (PEOU) are primary determinants of the attitudes (AT)toward using new technology. PU is the degree to which the user believes that using the technology would improve his or her performance on a task, while PEOU is defined as the degree to which a person believes that using a particular system would be free of effort (Davis, 1989; Davis et al.,1989). PEOU and PU are the two key components that have made the TAM one of the most influential research models related to understanding information technology usage (Chau, 2001). They impact attitude toward a technology, which in turn influence the adoption and use of new information technology (Davis, 1989). PEOU and PU were found to be primary factors in adoption in the early days of personal computers in organizational settings(Davis, 1986). Kimetal (2010) discussed the evolutionary process of TAM annually and categorized the characteristics of each proposed models (or extended models) in the aspects of model construction, input variables, application field, and methodology.

Due to the rising popularity of online strategic video games in the form of entertainment, it is essential to examine the acceptance structure of these games. Various works extended the TAM relating to this purpose. For instance, Lin and Lu (2006) found out that the most influential factor that would encourage the users to use social network services is enjoyment, followed by some peers and usefulness. Rose and Sherman (2006) investigated the acceptance of social networking websites to explain the recognition of people's intention to use social networks. Kwon and Wen (2010) revised the TAM Model which revealed three individual differences that would affect the usage of social network services. These are social identity, altruism, and telepresence. Rauniar et al. (2014) conducted an empirical study on Facebook and made use of the technology acceptance model (TAM) and social media usage. They added factors such as users' critical mass, social networking site capability, and trustworthiness. Moreover, Kim et al. (2011) conducted a comparative study of American and Korean college students which shows that using networking sites is useful in seeking friends, social support, entertainment, information, and convenience.

In this work, an extended TAM model proposed by Chen et al. (2017) was adopted which includes traditional factors such as perceived ease of use (PEU), perceived usefulness (PU), attitude (ATT), and behavior intention (BI). This adoption is explained as follows. Since, a game (e.g., MOBA) is different from a regular IT system due to its primary purpose which is for entertainment, enjoyment, and relaxation (Ha et al., 2007), then perceived enjoyment (PE), use context (UC), and flow experience(FL), to provide understanding of pleasure and fun, which are often mentioned in the works of Shin et al. (2011), Lui and Li(2011) and Ha et al.(2007) must be taken into context. Furthermore, since online strategic video gaming is also a kind of social platform for users to share fun and other experience, social interaction (SI) and altruism (ALT) based on the study of Trepte et al. (2012) and Curry et al. (2013) were also added. Lee (2004), on the other hand, found that the flow of the game has a considerable effect in influencing gamers in playing online strategic video games compared to the perceived enjoyment.

There are three individual differences added to the extended TAM of Kwon and Wen (2010), that is, social, identity, altruism, and telepresence. A study by Kim et al. (2011) that cultural difference is a motivation in using different social networking sites. It can influence searching for friends and social support. It can also help influence in entertainment. Rosen and Sherman (2006) examined the acceptance of people's intention to use social networks by extending the TAM. Integrating network externalities and motivation theory found out that enjoyment is one reason in using the social system in the study of Lin and Lu (2011). Shin et al. (2011) proposed an extended model to examine factors influencing how user accept social games.

Recently, Chen et al. (2017) conducted a study about the popularity analysis of mobile social gaming service using an extended technology acceptance model. They extended the TAM model by adding several factors such as altruism, social interaction, use context, perceived enjoyment, flow, and attitude. The proposed model of Chen et al. (2007) is an extension of the current TAM. They adopted the hypotheses of Fishbein and Ajzen (1975) about the belief- attitude-intention-behavior causal chain in the context of social-based mobile games. Altruism is classified as altruism and reciprocal altruism (Ashton et al., 1998). Kin altruism refers to the concept that people sacrifice their benefits to help their genetic relatives. Reciprocal altruism means that people help others because they believe that they would receive similar assistance in return someday in the future. Choi and Kim (2004), on the other hand, to increase customer loyalty to online content it must have an interaction between the computer user and the system and computer user to user interaction.

In predicting the potential use of technology, use context must be considered (van de Wijngaert and Bouwman, 2009). Use context is not just a point in time and space in which a particular action is taken. There is a motivation to use computer software and applications in the workplace either intrinsic or extrinsic as described by Davis et al. (1992). One of the motivations is perceived enjoyment. The intrinsic motivation would refer to the pleasure of using the computer and satisfaction from performing a behavior (Doll and Ajze, 1992). Also, van der Heijden (2003) concluded that perceived enjoyment has a positive influence on users in using a website. In contrast, Ghani (1995) argued that the flow of the game can be measured by enjoyment concentration and found out that perceived control and challenges can predict

Figure 1. Theoretical framework obtained from Chen et al. (2017)

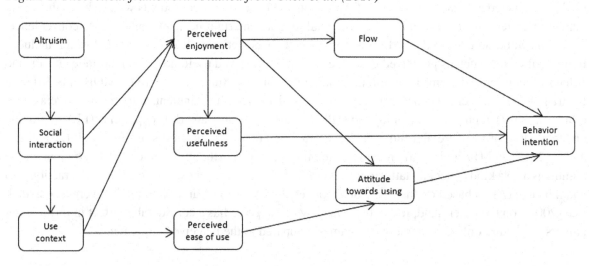

flow. Figure 1 depicts the theoretical framework of the extended technology acceptance model of Chen et al. (2017) being adopted in this work.

Statement of Hypothesis

The following alternative hypotheses were obtained directly from the extended TAM model of Chen et al. (2017). The motivations, as well as the supporting literature in drawing out these hypotheses, were thoroughly discussed by Chen et al. (2017) and are not presented here for brevity.

H1: Altruism (ALT) positively influences social interaction (S) of playing online strategic video games.

H2: Social Interaction(S) positively influences perceived enjoyment (PE) of playing online strategic video games.

H3: Social Interaction(S) positively influences use context (UC) of playing online strategic video games

H4: Perceived enjoyment (PE) positively influences perceived usefulness (PU) of playing online strategic video games.

H5: Perceived enjoyment (PE) positively influences flow (F) of playing online strategic video games.

H6: Perceived enjoyment (PE) positively influences attitude (A) of playing online strategic video games.

H7: Perceived usefulness (PU) positively influences behavior intention (BI) of playing online strategic video games.

H8: Use context (UC) positively influences perceived ease of use (PEU) of playing online strategic video games.

H9: Use context (UC) positively influences perceived enjoyment (PE) of playing online strategic video games.

H10: Perceived ease of use (PEU) positively influences attitude (A) of playing online strategic video games.

H11: Attitude (A) positively influences behavior intention (BI) of playing online strategic video games.

H12: Flow (F) positively influences behavior intention (BI) of playing online strategic video games.

3. METHODOLOGY

This section discusses the case study and the data gathering and treatment procedures.

3.1. Case Study

The case study was conducted at the University of San Carlos, one of the top universities in the Philippines, which is located in the central local region of the country. The University belongs to a class of the country's private universities where annual university fees for college students range from the US $1,200 - $3,000 – a relatively expensive college education. It implies that students have enough resources for playing online games. College students in the Department of Computer and Information Sciences who are players of the MOBA were chosen as the research participants. They are selected as they are the representatives of the population who are inclined to video games with a high degree of computer-related interests. The total population of the department unit is 1,025 and adopting the idea of Smith (2003) of making use of Yamane formula with 95% confidence level and 0.05 margin of error, a random sample 278 college students in the department was obtained. The sample selection process starts by asking individuals from the population of 439 participants if he or she is a MOBA player and 278 of them confirmed as MOBA players. The distribution of the participants according to their degree program shows the following: 130 students taking up Bachelor of Science in Information and Communications Technology (BSICT), 99 students taking up Bachelor of Science in Information Technology (BSIT), 45 students taking up Bachelor of Science in Computer Science (BSCS) and four (4) Pasarelles Numeriques (PN). The age distribution of the participants is shown in Table 1 which indicates that the majority of the participants as MOBA players belongs to the 19-22 age group. It is most probably because that majority of the university students, in general, has this mean age interval. It is almost consistent with the findings of Kokkinakis et al. (2017) who pointed out that MOBA players achieve a peak in performance in their mid-20's as a result of the integration of memory, tactics, strategy and reaction time. Thus, in this age group, players are still accumulating their expertise in MOBA games with a high amount of time spent.

The sample also shows that majority of the MOBA players were male (i.e., 234) and 44 players were female. It is consistent with the report of the Entertainment Software Association (2017) which shows that 60% of video game players are male. Table 2 shows the distribution of the average number of hours spent on each MOBA player. It shows that the majority of the sample spends 0.5 to 6.3 hours daily in playing MOBA games. It is a significant amount of time in building up expertise for these games.

Table 1. Age demographic profile of MOBA Players

Age	Number of Participants
27- 30	3
23–26	15
19–22	195
15–18	65
Total	**278**

Table 2. Average daily number of hours played

Average number of hours spent	Frequency
0.5- 6.3	244
6.4- 12.2	30
12.3 - 18.1	2
18.2 –24	2
Total	**278**

According to the survey initiated by Spark (2016), the top 10 most popular MOBA games for 2016 were Battleborn, Paragon, Supernova, League of Legend (LOL), Dota2, Gigantic, Smite, Heroes of Newerth (HON), Heroes of Storm (HOS) and Overwatch. Table 3 shows the MOBA games played by the samples of this study. As depicted in Table 3, the top three MOBA games usually played are Defend of the Ancient (Dota)2, League of Legends (LOL) and Overwatch. Ninety-one (91) players always played Dota2, 25 players that ever-played LOL and 20 players that ever-played Overwatch. There were also players that often played the Battleborn, Paragon, Supernova, Gigantic, Smite, Heroes of Newerth (HON) and Heroes of Storm (HOS). For brevity, Appendix A discusses a brief background of the top three MOBA games (i.e., LOL, Dota 2, and Overwatch) played by participants.

A questionnaire was distributed to the 278 students. It consists of 28 questions, among the two questions, are designed to help evaluate insincere responses. Appendix B shows the questionnaire, and the 26 items (without the two reverse questions). Each item is measured by 7-point Likert Scale with points of Strongly Agree (7), Agree (6), Slightly Agree (5), Neutral (4), Slightly Disagree (3), Disagree (2) and Strongly Disagree (1). It seeks to measure the respondents' characteristics regarding the level of acceptance of perceived enjoyment, perceived usefulness, perceived ease of use, flow, social interaction, and altruism, use context, attitude and behavior intention. It also attempts to identify the determinant factor that affects the user's intention and predictive value in determining the behavioral intention of playing online strategic video games. The questionnaire used in the research was adopted from Chen et al. (2017) that extended the TAM Model by adding external factors such as altruism, social interaction, use context, perceived enjoyment, flow, and attitude. MOBA consultants and players validated the created questionnaires to ensure the reliability of each question in each construct.

Table 3. MOBA games played

	Battlehorn	Paragon	Supernova	LOL	Dota 2	Gigantic	Smite	HON	HOS	Overwatch
Always	0	0	0	25	91	0	2	4	7	20
Very Often	2	2	1	16	58	1	5	7	12	11
Sometimes	16	16	16	55	64	16	27	35	30	34
Rarely	5	5	7	64	48	7	32	47	33	30
Never	260	260	259	124	24	259	217	190	202	189

Legend: LOL = League of Legends; Dota = Defense of the Ancient; HON = Heroes of Newerth; HOS = Heroes of Storm

3.2. Data Collection and Treatment Procedure

In speeding up the distribution of the questionnaire to the sample, a Google form is used to gather the necessary information. Students were asked to answer in their laboratory classes or even at home as long as they have an internet connection. No incentive of any form was provided to the students for participating in the survey. The data collected by the questionnaire was recorded in Microsoft Excel® program. To improve the quality of data being collected data filtering is applied. These include the following: (1) eliminate the responses of the respondents who have not played MOBA games, and (2) eliminate insincere responses through data filtering on the verification questions.

A total of 439 responses were collected from the online survey. Table 6 shows the final result in the data filtering process. Legris, Ingham, & Collerette (2003) claimed that the size of a dataset containing more than 200 responses could be considered a useful dataset. In this work, 278 was considered; thus, the data that were obtained are valid responses.

Table 4. Data filtering result

Item	Number
Insincere Responses	50
Not played MOBA games	102
Non-engaging responses (standard deviation is zero)	9
Effective Responses	278
Total Responses	439

After filtering data in Microsoft Excel®, the mean and standard deviation for each question was calculated, and the mean value of each construct was also determined. It also undergoes a convergent validity and internal reliability analysis using Cronbach's alpha and composite reliability analysis in establishing factors that are sufficiently distinct and uncorrelated. The results are shown in Table4.

Sampling adequacy was established before hypotheses evaluation in SEM was carried on to validate the applicability of the extended TAM. Hypotheses analysis was performed by checking fit indices required for SEM before finally determining the regression weights and p-values as the basis for the extended TAM model. Dataset was analyzed using IBM SPSS Amos 24.0.0 being assessed by Narayanan (2012) in the review of Software Packages for structural equation modeling to have excellent graphical interface and a well –organized and quickly accessible output format.

Table 5. Descriptive statistics and reliability analysis

Construct	Item	AVG	SD	Average	Cronbach's Alpha (Above .70)	Composite Reliability (Above 0.60)
Altruism (a)	*a1*	4.74	1.63	5.136	.755	0.770
	a2	5.51	1.31			
	a3	5.16	1.34			
Social Interaction (S)	*s1*	6.22	1.01	6.043	.849	0.862
	s2	6.10	1.08			
	s3	5.81	1.20			
Use context	*u1*	5.83	1.14	6.47	.889	0.888
	u2	5.80	1.18			
	u3	7.78	1.18			
Perceived Enjoyment (PE)	*pe1*	6.16	.96	5.72	.824	0.838
	pe2	5.67	1.18			
	pe3	5.33	1.37			
Perceived Usefulness (PU)	*Pu1*	5.11	1.29	4.893	.863	0.866
	pu2	4.66	1.42			
	pu3	4.91	1.39			
Perceived Ease of Use (PEU)	*peu1*	5.68	1.12	5.575	.819	0.832
	peu2	5.47	1.27			
Flow (F)	*f1*	5.24	1.42	5.22	.858	0.871
	f2	5.10	1.44			
	F3	5.33	1.34			
Attitude (A	*O1*	5.36	1.32	5.527	.907	0.907
	O2	5.50	1.20			
	O3	5.72	1.16			
Behavior Intention (B)	*b1*	5.21	1.29	5.40	.828	0.829
	b2	5.28	1.29			
	B3	5.71	1.17			

Legend: AVG =Average; SD =Standard Deviation

4. RESULTS AND DISCUSSION

In this section, the data gathered from the research participants are presented and interpreted.

Sampling Adequacy for Factor Analysis. The KMO test for sampling adequacy and Bartlette's test of sphericity are used to check the adequacy of data set for factor analysis (Williams, Onsman and Brown,2010). The factor analysis is shown in Table 6. As suggested by commonly used KMO measures, the sampling adequacy of this research is considered appropriate for principal component analysis.

Table 6. Factor analysis

KMO and Bartlett's Test		
Kaiser-Meyer-Olkin Measure of Sampling Adequacy.		.936
Bartlett's Test of Sphericity	Approx. Chi-Square	5400
	Df	325
	Sig.	<.001

Assessment of Fit Indices for Measurement Model. To establish the required Model fit for testing of the hypothesized model depicted in Equation 1, the Confirmatory Factor Analysis (CFA) was conducted to determine the correlation of the nine (9) constructs of the extended TAM. The measurement model estimates are shown in Figure 2 illustrating the path diagram of the CFA. Also, the following fit indices were computed: chi-square/df ratio (CMIN/DF), GFI, AGFI, RMSEA, NFI, CFI, RMSEA, and IFI. Table 7 shows that seven (7) of the eight (8) indices are acceptable. Thus, it can be concluded that the 9-Factor CFA Model fits the sample data well. The standardized and unstandardized estimates of the measurement model are shown in Table 8.

Moreover, each of the path estimates was significant at 1.0%, and the loadings among the measured variables and factors were all greater than 0.6. The indicators loaded considerably on their hypothesized construct showing the significant level of convergent validity. Thus, each of the items was accepted at this point, and convergent validity as proof of acceptability was delivered.

Table 7. Fit indices for the measurement model

Fit Index	Results	Recommended Criteria (Chen et al., 2017)
Chi-square/df ratio	2.473	<5.0
GFI	.837	>.85, close to 1
AGFI	.784	>.80, close to 1
NFI	.884	>.85, close to 1
CFI	.926	>.90, close to 1
RMSEA	.073	≤ .08, close to 0
IFI	.927	>.90, close to 1

Assessment of Discriminant Validity of the Measurement Model. Discriminant validity is tested using the square root of the Average Variance Extracted (AVE) (Hair 2010). Table 9 shows the square root of AVEs in the diagonal of the correlation matrix. Noticeably the inter-factor correlation coefficient between attitude (A) and behavior (B); attitude (A) and Perceived Enjoyment (PE); and Perceived Enjoyment (PE) and Behavior (B) are all greater than each square root of AVE indicating that the constructs are redundant (Hair et al., 2010). However, since these constructs are well established in the extant literature, they can remain as separate constructs in the model (Davcik, 2014).

Figure 2. Path diagram of confirmatory factor analysis for the of the extended technology acceptance model

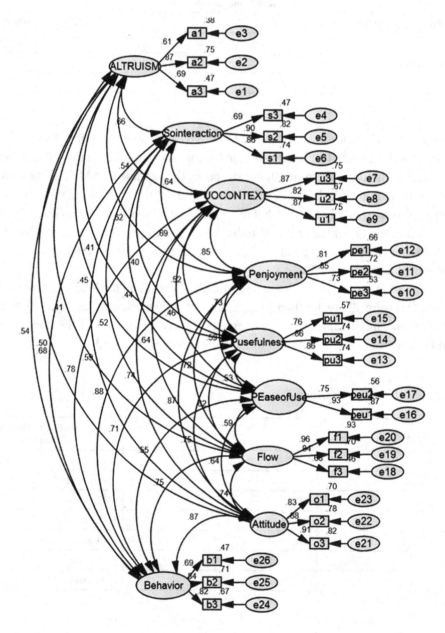

Table 8. Measurement model (CFA) estimates

Items		Factor	Standardized Estimate	Unstandardized Estimate	S.E.	C.R.	P
a3	<---	ALTRUISM	0.687	0.814	0.075	10.9	***
a2	<---	ALTRUISM	0.868	1			
a1	<---	ALTRUISM	0.612	0.879	0.09	9.744	***
s3	<---	Sointeraction	0.688	0.843	0.064	13.165	***
s2	<---	Sointeraction	0.905	1			
s1	<---	Sointeraction	0.861	0.969	0.053	18.319	***
u3	<---	UCONTEXT	0.866	1			
u2	<---	UCONTEXT	0.82	0.948	0.056	16.872	***
u1	<---	UCONTEXT	0.869	0.972	0.053	18.444	***
pe3	<---	Penjoyment	0.726	0.984	0.071	13.877	***
pe2	<---	Penjoyment	0.847	1			
pe1	<---	Penjoyment	0.81	0.78	0.048	16.328	***
pu3	<---	Pusefulness	0.858	0.976	0.058	16.894	***
pu2	<---	Pusefulness	0.859	1			
pu1	<---	Pusefulness	0.758	0.8	0.056	14.345	***
peu1	<---	PEaseofUse	0.933	1			
peu2	<---	PEaseofUse	0.748	0.901	0.078	11.539	***
f3	<---	Flow	0.678	0.672	0.049	13.761	***
f2	<---	Flow	0.839	0.891	0.045	19.998	***
f1	<---	Flow	0.962	1			
o3	<---	Attitude	0.908	0.961	0.049	19.445	***
o2	<---	Attitude	0.881	0.961	0.052	18.531	***
o1	<---	Attitude	0.834	1			
b3	<---	Behavior	0.819	1.084	0.088	12.35	***
b2	<---	Behavior	0.844	1.225	0.097	12.67	***
b1	<---	Behavior	0.689	1			

Assessing the Structural Model. The hypothesized model described graphically in Figure 1 shows the causal relationship of factors in Chen's et al. (2017) extended Technology Acceptance Model. To evaluate the hypothetical model and then determine the strength of the causal relationship, another set of model fit test was conducted. Table 10 shows the result of model fit indices for the structural model where only one (1) of the seven (7) indices is not within the acceptable range. Generally, results reveal that the model fit indices for the structural model based on the TAM were acceptable, indicating that adding several factors such as altruism, social interaction, use context, perceived enjoyment, flow, and attitude in the TAM are validated, and that post-hoc modification should not be any more conducted (Schreiber et al., 2006).

Table 9. Correlation Matrix with the square root of AVE on the diagonal

	AL	S	UC	PU	PEU	Flow	A	B	PE
AL	**0.730**								
S	0.662	**0.823**							
UC	0.540	0.638	**0.852**						
PU	0.411	0.399	0.522	**0.826**					
PEU	0.451	0.439	0.460	0.527	**0.846**				
Flow	0.413	0.524	0.641	0.619	0.589	**0.834**			
A	0.495	0.592	0.735	0.748	0.644	0.736	**0.875**		
B	0.617	0.687	0.850	0.729	0.589	0.721	0.870	**0.796**	
PE	0.541	0.683	0.776	0.708	0.546	0.748	0.867	0.879	**0.787**

Legend: AL= Altruism; S = Social Interaction; UC=Use context; PE =Perceived Enjoyment; PU = Perceived Usefulness; PEU =Perceived Ease of Use; F=Flow; A = Attitude; B = Behavior intention

Figure 7, showing accepted model based on the sample data, indicates that 81% of the variation in the behavior intention to play online video games could be estimated by using three exogenous constructs into the model such as perceived usefulness, flow, and attitude. Moreover, 84% of the attitude could be measured by perceived enjoyment and perceived ease of use. Also, 77% of the flow is solely measurable by perceived enjoyment as about 55% of perceived usefulness can be estimated by perceived enjoyment. Also, 76% of the perceived enjoyment could also be estimated by two constructs to wit, social interaction and use context while 25% of the perceived ease of use can be estimated by use context. Finally, the variation of the construct "use context" can be explained by social interaction by about 44% as social interaction construct can also be estimated by 47% percent of the variation in altruism. Thus, not only that the model is acceptable it can also be deduced that it is a good model since it captures 81%, R^2 values greater than 0.63 considered substantial (Davcik, 2014), of the variation of the endogenous construct "Behavior intention" by the inclusion of the various exogenous constructs in the model. Likewise, the results support the extended TAM as a form of replication which according to Goodboy and Kline (2017) is of the utmost importance that researchers replicate findings beyond a single study which would allow confidence in SEM analysis.

Table 12 presents an analysis of the significance of path coefficients. It can be noted that all the 12 hypotheses are supported. This result verified that behavioral intention, the tendency of a player to play more kinds of online strategic video games such as MOBA games, has been strongly influenced by attitude (H11) and moderately influenced by flow (H12) and weakly influenced by perceived usefulness (H7). The finding on the significance of attitude construct to affect behavior intention is well supported by extant literature, as validated by Greg et al., (2004), as important construct in TAM by Lopez-Bonilla and Lopez-Bonilla (2011), and as significant predictor of behavior intention by Ursavas (2011); Cheung and Vogel (2014); and Chen et al. (2017). This relationship implies that a high level of attitude in playing MOBA games substantially strengthen, direct and moderate the behavior intention of playing.

Also, the significance of flow to influence behavior intention to play MOBA is also corroborated by Shin and Kim (2008) that users' flow experience shows a much stronger impact on intention and by Hsu and Lu (2004) that flow experience is another significant predictor of intention to play online games. Csikszentmihalyi and Csikszentmihalyi (2000) have defined flow as a holistic experience when involved in specific actions. Thus, this study established that MOBA users intentional or unintentional flow feelings increase the behavior intention to use MOBA indicating that students do not feel tired of playing online strategic video games for a short period. They would not lose interest in playing the game. Moreover, they tend to ignore the time past when they started playing it. Consequently, this result indicates that the effect of flow on the behavior intention suggests that MOBA usage is a flow encounter and intrinsically fulfilling.

Moreover, the low influence of perceived usefulness to behavior intention is also upheld by Hsu and Lu (2004) as well as by Liu and Li (2011) and by Chen et al. (2017). This relationship implies that the game itself does not bring any direct benefits such as financial gains, improved welfare, among others, but the social relations brought about by the game as well as the strategy "training" they developed as the playing time may bring long-term benefits. Since the benefits are long-term, the uncertainty of these benefits is considerably high. Thus, students who are users of online strategic video games or specifically MOBA users are accepting the online game technology because it is intrinsically satisfying knowing at the same time that such are not useful in their study or has no direct impact of quality of life in general.

The findings on the positive influence of perceived enjoyment to attitude (H6) and the moderate positive relationship of perceived ease of use to attitude (H10) are well founded in the existing literature. Perceived enjoyment had a significant influence on the core constructs of the TAM including attitude (Teo and Noyes, 2011; and Hsu and Lin, 2008). Liu and Li (2011) concluded that perceived enjoyment is considered a direct predictor of attitude, but not for behavioral intention and that perceived ease of use has no significant impact on attitude. Fishbein and Ajzen(1975) have pointed out that attitude is an extension to perceived enjoyment and ease of use. For instance, if the players are enjoying while playing the game as well as able to master the rules of the game quickly, it is expected that there is a positive attitude towards playing the game. Cheung and Doug Vogel (2013) also argued that the adoption of collaborative technology is strongly influenced by peers indicating that since MOBA games are collaborative, then learning the game would be easy. Thus, the weak influence of perceived ease of use to attitude could be explained by the mean number of the age range of the research participants as the 19-22 age range has provided them a significant level of experience and to a certain extent, they are already nearing their peak of experiencing MOBA games which is at the mid-20s.

The confirmed direct positive influence of social interaction to perceived enjoyment (H2) and the direct influence of use context to perceived enjoyment (H9) are also well recognized in supporting literature. In the work of Fishbein and Ajzen (1975), they argued that behavioral intention could be predicted based on altruism, social interaction, use context, perceived usefulness, perceived enjoyment, flow, perceived ease of use and attitude towards using the game. Chen et al. (2017) also contended that offering help in the game does help much fun and social reputation among friends suggesting that social interaction plays a crucial role in increasing enjoyment. Thus, the higher the score of acceptability and interaction among players the more elevated the enjoyment in playing the MOBA games. Also, the use context construct, playing the MOBA games do not interfere with other more useful activities of the research participants, has been argued to be considered in the potential use of technology (van de Wijngaert and Bouwman, 2009). Chen et al. (2017) reasoned that "the fact that mobile social games have a low requirement on the network environment, hard devices, and storage space, it is easy for people to play anytime and anywhere." Thus, continued use due to the accessibility of the MOBA games positively influence the enjoyment of the players.

Table 10. Fit indices for the Structural Model based on the extended TAM

Fit Index	Results	Recommended Criteria (Chen et al., 2017)
Chi-square/df ratio	790.341/288 = 2.744	<5.0
GFI	.801	>.85, close to 1
AGFI	.757	>.80, close to 1
RMSEA	.079	≤ .08, close to 0
NFI	.859	>.85, close to 1
CFI	.905	>.90, close to 1
IFI	.905	>.90, close to 1

Table 11. The regression weights for the paths

Path			Regression Weights				
			Standardized Estimate	Unstandardized Estimate	Standard Error	Critical Ratio	P-value
S	<---	AL	.687	.601	.061	9.797	***
UC	<---	S	.665	.687	.064	10.777	***
PE	<---	S	.215	.218	.061	3.563	***
PEU	<---	UC	.499	.556	.065	8.506	***
PE	<---	UC	.711	.699	.069	10.166	***
A	<---	PEU	.163	.156	.042	3.719	***
F	<---	PE	.773	1.050	.075	13.942	***
A	<---	PE	.834	.906	.067	13.556	***
PU	<---	PE	.744	.930	.077	12.041	***
B	<---	A	.626	.593	.073	8.127	***
B	<---	F	.215	.163	.048	3.426	***
B	<---	PU	.147	.121	.052	2.351	.019

*** p<.001

Legend: AL= Altruism; S = Social Interaction; UC=Use context; PE =Perceived Enjoyment; PU = Perceived Usefulness; PEU =Perceived Ease of Use; F=Flow; A = Attitude; B = Behavior intention

Findings also show that the altruism influences social interaction (H1) while social interaction influences "use context" as (H3) as use context influence perceived ease of use (H8). Generally, Rachlin (2002) argued that altruism could be used to explain the people's behavior as it can be an alternative to further discuss the phenomenon of the acceptance of an information system. Ma and Chan (2014) concluded that altruism has a direct, significant, and substantial effect on online knowledge sharing behavior and since altruism refers to a condition that players help each other by giving items or gifts would result to the strength of their heroes or champions to win the game, thus affect social interaction. Likewise, social interaction influencing use context is supported by the findings of Liu and Li (2011) that being able to play a game in certain environments, such as during a commute, makes users happy, apart from the playability of the game itself. Thus, such increased social interaction would likely to encourage the use of MOBA games regardless of condition that players are situated. Therefore, it follows that use context has a weak influence to ease of use because respondents are already experienced players playing in any situation, and such play have resulted in high enjoyment.

Figure 3. Standardized Regression Weight for the extended TAM

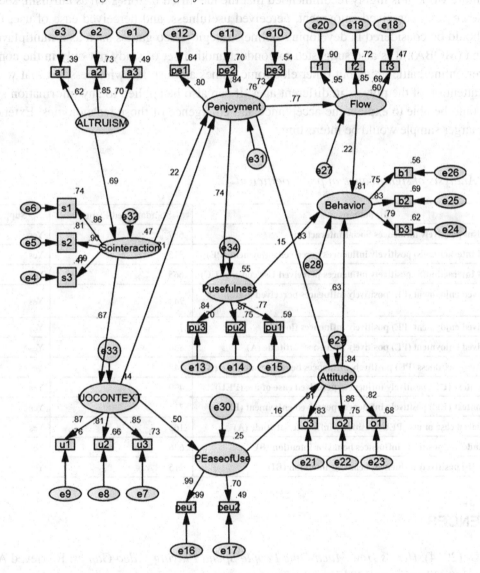

5. CONCLUSION AND FUTURE WORK

This study validated the extended Technology Acceptance Model of Chen et al. (2017) using Structural Equation Modelling involving 278 responses. The results suggest that in addition to perceived useful-ness and perceived ease of use as the original factors of Technology Acceptance Model, altruism, social interaction, use context, perceived enjoyment, flow, and attitude are significant factors that are crucial to encapsulate supplementary indicators that would help understand the design and development of online games for greater acceptance. This structural relationship supports that belief formation is still an antecedent on specific online game activity may it be for entertainment, enjoyment, and relaxation before building a positive attitude substantiated with pleasure and fun over usefulness that will consequently shape the right behavior for online game acceptance and use.

As a future work, it is highly recommended that the identified factors such as altruism, social interaction, use context, perceived enjoyment, perceived usefulness, and perceived ease of use, flow, and attitude should be considered in developing online strategic video games such as a multiplayer online battle arena (MOBA). It is also suggested to conduct another set of study not only in the context of a multiplayer online battle arena but other electronic games are also known as e-sport that was able to catch the attention of the players in different ages. It can also be applied to any information system so that we would be able to explain the acceptance and emergence of those technologies. Extending this work to a larger sample would be interesting.

Table 12. Analysis of significance of path coefficient

Hypothesis	Standardized Estimate	Supported?
(H1) Altruism positively influences Social Interaction	.687	Yes
(H2) Social Interaction(S) positively influences perceived enjoyment (PE)	.215	Yes
(H3) Social Interaction(S) positively influences perceived Use context (UC)	.665	Yes
(H4) Perceived enjoyment (PE) positively influences perceived usefulness (PU)	.744	Yes
(H5) Perceived enjoyment (PE) positively influences flow (F)	.773	Yes
(H6) Perceived enjoyment (PE) positively influences attitude (A)	.834	Yes
(H7) Perceived usefulness (PU) positively influences behavior intention (B)	.147	Yes
(H8) Use context (UC) positively influences perceived ease of use (PEU)	.499	Yes
(H9) Use context (UC) positively influences perceived enjoyment (PE)	.711	Yes
(H10) Perceived ease of use (PEU) positively influences attitude (A)	.163	Yes
(H11) Attitude (A) positively influences behavior intention (B)	.626	Yes
(H12) Flow (F) positively influences behavior intention (BI)	.215	Yes

REFERENCES

Aamoth, D. (2014). *Here's How Much Time People Spend Playing Video Games*. Retrieved August 8, 2017, from https://time.com/120476/nielsen-video-games/

Ajzen, I. (1991). The theory of planned behavior. *Organizational Behavior and Human Decision Processes*, *50*(2), 179–211. doi:10.1016/0749-5978(91)90020-T

Anderson, C. A., & Dill, K. E. (2000). Video games and aggressive thoughts, feelings, and behavior in the laboratory and in life. *Journal of Personality and Social Psychology*, *78*(4), 772–790. doi:10.1037/0022-3514.78.4.772 PMID:10794380

Anderson, C. A., Shibuya, A., Ihori, N., Swing, E. L., Bushman, B. J., Sakamoto, A., & Saleem, M. (2010). Violent video game effects on aggression, empathy, and prosocial behavior in Eastern and Western countries: A meta-analytic review. *Psychological Bulletin, 136*(2), 151–173. doi:10.1037/a0018251 PMID:20192553

Ashton, M. C., Paunonen, S. V., Helmes, E., & Jackson, D. N. (1998). Kin altruism, reciprocal altruism, and the big five personality factors. *Evolution and Human Behavior, 19*(4), 243–255. doi:10.1016/S1090-5138(98)00009-9

Bao, S., Chan, V., & Merzenich, M. (2001). Cortical remodeling induced by activity of ventral tegmental dopamine neurons. *Nature, 412*(6842), 79–83. doi:10.1038/35083586 PMID:11452310

Bean, A. M., Nielsen, R. K. L., van Rooij, A. J., & Ferguson, C. J. (2017). Video game addiction: The push to pathologize video games. *Professional Psychology, Research and Practice, 48*(5), 378–389. doi:10.1037/pro0000150

Chau, P. Y. K. (2001). Influence of computer attitude and self-efficacy on IT usage behavior. *Journal of End User Computing, 13*(1), 26–33. doi:10.4018/joeuc.2001010103

Chen, H., Rong, W., Ma, X., Qu, Y., & Xiong, Z. (2017). An extended technology acceptance model for mobile social gaming service popularity analysis. *Mobile Information Systems, 2017*, 1–12. doi:10.1155/2017/3906953

Cheung, R., & Vogel, D. (2013). Predicting user acceptance of collaborative technologies: An extension of the technology acceptance model for e-learning. *Computers & Education, 63*, 160–175. doi:10.1016/j.compedu.2012.12.003

Choi, D., & Kim, J. (2004). Why people continue to play online games: In search of critical design factors to increase customer loyalty to online contents. *Cyberpsychology & Behavior, 7*(1), 11–24. doi:10.1089/109493104322820066 PMID:15006164

Colzato, L. S., van den Wildenberg, W. P. M., Zmigrod, S., & Hommel, B. (2013). Action video gaming and cognitive control: Playing first person shooter games is associated with improvement in working memory but not action inhibition. *Psychological Research, 77*(2), 234–239. doi:10.100700426-012-0415-2 PMID:22270615

Conolly, T. M., Boyle, E. A., MacArthur, E., Hainey, T., & Boyle, J. M. (2012). A systematic literature review of empirical evidence on computer games and serious games. *Computers & Education, 59*(2), 661–686. doi:10.1016/j.compedu.2012.03.004

Creswell, J. W., & Plano Clark, V. L. (2011). *Designing and conducting mixed methods research*. Sage.

Crockett, S. A. (2012). A five-step guide to conducting SEM analysis in counseling research. *Counseling Outcome Research and Evaluation, 3*(1), 30–47. doi:10.1177/2150137811434142

Csikszentmihalyi, M., & Csikszentmihalyi, I. S. (2000). *Optimal experience: Psychological studies of flow in consciousness*. Cambridge University Press.

Curry, O., Roberts, S. G. B., & Dunbar, R. I. M. (2013). Altruism in social networks: Evidence for a 'kinship premium'. *British Journal of Psychology, 104*(2), 283–295. doi:10.1111/j.2044-8295.2012.02119.x PMID:23560672

Davis, F. D. (1989). Perceived usefulness, perceived ease of use, and user acceptance of information technology. *Management Information Systems Quarterly, 13*(3), 319–340. doi:10.2307/249008

Davis, F. D., Bagozzi, R. P., & Warshaw, P. R. (1989). User acceptance of computer technology: A comparison of two theoretical models. *Management Science, 35*(8), 982–1003. doi:10.1287/mnsc.35.8.982

Davis, F. D., Bagozzi, R. P., & Warshaw, P. R. (1992). Extrinsic and intrinsic motivation to use computers in the workplace. *Journal of Applied Social Psychology, 22*(14), 1111–1132. doi:10.1111/j.1559-1816.1992. tb00945.x

Doll, J., & Ajzen, I. (1992). Accessibility and stability of predictors in the theory of planned behavior. *Journal of Personality and Social Psychology, 63*(5), 754–765. doi:10.1037/0022-3514.63.5.754

Entertainment Software Association. (2015). *Essential facts about the computer and video game industry.* Retrieved from http://www.theesa.com/about-esa/essential-facts-computer-video-game-industry/

Ferguson, C. J. (2007). The good, the bad and the ugly: A meta-analytic review of positive and negative effects of violent video games. *The Psychiatric Quarterly, 78*(4), 309–316. doi:10.100711126-007-9056-9 PMID:17914672

Fishbein, M., & Ajzen, I. (1975). *Belief, attitude, intention and behavior: An introduction to theory and research.* Addison Wesley Publishing Company.

Frunk, J. (2013, September 2). *MOBA, DOTA, ARTS: A brief introduction to gaming's biggest, most impenetrable genre.* Retrieved May 9, 2017, Retrieved from https://www.polygon.com/2013/9/2/4672920/moba-dota-arts-a-brief-introduction-to-gamings-biggest-most

Funk, J. B. (2001). *Children and violent video games: Are there "high risk" players?* Working Paper Presented at the Playing by the Rules: The Cultural Policy Challenges of Video Games, Chicago, IL. Retrieved from https://culturalpolicy.uchicago.edu/sites/culturalpolicy.uchicago.edu/files/funk1.pdf

Gampell, A. V., Gaillard, J. C., Parsons, M., & Fisher, K. (2017). Beyond Stop Disasters 2.0: An agenda for exploring the contribution of video games to learning about disasters. *Environmental Hazards, 16*(2), 180–191. doi:10.1080/17477891.2016.1275502

Ghani, J. A. (1995). Human factors in information systems. In J.M. Carey (Eds.), Flow in Human-Computer Interactions: Test of a Model, (pp. 291–311). Norwood, NJ: Ablex Publishing Corp.

Granic, I., Lobel, A., & Engels, R. C. M. E. (2014). The benefits of playing video games. *The American Psychologist, 69*(1), 66–78. doi:10.1037/a0034857 PMID:24295515

Green, C., & Seitz, A. R. (2015). The impacts of video games on cognition (and how the government can guide the industry). *Policy Insights from the Behavioral and Brain Sciences*, *2*(1), 101–110. doi:10.1177/2372732215601121

Ha, I., Yoon, Y., & Choi, M. (2007). Determinants of adoption of mobile games under mobile broadband wireless access environment. *Information & Management*, *44*(3), 276–286. doi:10.1016/j.im.2007.01.001

Hair, J. F. Jr., Black, W.C., Babin, B.J., & Anderson, R.E. (2010). Multivariate Data Analysis (7th ed.). Pearson Education Limited.

Hong, Y., & Li, Y. (2010). The search on index system optimization of graduation design based on Cronbach's coefficient. *Proceedings of the 5th International Conference on Computer Science and Education*, 1843–1845.

Hsu, C. L., & Lin, J. C. C. (2008). Acceptance of blog usage: The roles of technology acceptance, social influence and knowledge sharing motivation. *Information & Management*, *45*(1), 65–74. doi:10.1016/j.im.2007.11.001

Hsu, C.-L., & Lu, H.-P. (2004). Why do people play on-line games? An extended TAM with social influences and flow experience. *Information & Management*, *41*(7), 853–868. doi:10.1016/j.im.2003.08.014

Johnson, J. E., Christie, J. F., & Yawkey, T. D. (1999). *Play and early childhood development* (2nd ed.). Longman.

Kilgard, M. P., & Merzenich, M. M. (1998). Cortical map reorganization enabled by nucleus basalis activity. *Science*, *279*(5357), 1714–1718. doi:10.1126cience.279.5357.1714 PMID:9497289

Kim, Y., Sohn, D., & Choi, S. M. (2011). Cultural difference in motivations for using social network sites: A comparative study of American and Korean college students. *Computers in Human Behavior*, *27*(1), 365–372. doi:10.1016/j.chb.2010.08.015

Kim, Y. J., & Park, S. B. (2006). *The Study of Online Game Acceptance Model, Modern China study*. Working paper.

King, D., Greaves, F., Exeter, C., & Darzi, A. (2013). "Gamification": Influencing health behaviours with games. *Journal of the Royal Society of Medicine*, *106*(3), 76–78. doi:10.1177/0141076813480996 PMID:23481424

Koufaris, M. (2002). Applying the technology acceptance model and flow theory to online consumer behavior. *Information Systems Research*, *13*(2), 205–223. doi:10.1287/isre.13.2.205.83

Kuss, D. J., & Griffiths, M. D. (2012). Internet gaming addiction: A systematic review of empirical research. *International Journal of Mental Health and Addiction*, *10*(2), 278–296. doi:10.100711469-011-9318-5

Kwon, O., & Wen, Y. (2010). An empirical study of the factors affecting social network service use. *Computers in Human Behavior*, *26*(2), 254–263. doi:10.1016/j.chb.2009.04.011

Lee, M., & Tsai, T. (2010). What drives people to continue to play online games? An extension of technology model and theory of planned behavior. *International Journal of Human-Computer Interaction, 26*(6), 601–620. doi:10.1080/10447311003781318

Lee, M.-C. (2009). Understanding the behavioural intention to play online games: An extension of the theory of planned behaviour. *Online Information Review, 33*(5), 849–872. doi:10.1108/14684520911001873

Legris, P., Ingham, J., & Collerette, P. (2003). Why do people use information technology? A critical review of the technology acceptance model. *Information & Management, 40*(3), 191–204. doi:10.1016/S0378-7206(01)00143-4

Lemmens, J. S., Valkenburg, P. M., & Pete, J. (2009). Development and validation of a game addiction scale for adolescents. *Media Psychology, 12*(1), 77–95. doi:10.1080/15213260802669458

Lemola, S., Brand, S., Vogler, N., Perkinson-Gloor, N., Allemand, M., & Grob, A. (2011). Habitual computer game playing at night is related to depressive symptoms. *Personality and Individual Differences, 51*(2), 117–122. doi:10.1016/j.paid.2011.03.024

Liang, T.-P., & Yeh, Y.-H. (2011). Effect of use contexts on the continuous use of mobile services: The case of mobile games. *Personal and Ubiquitous Computing, 15*(2), 187–196. doi:10.100700779-010-0300-1

Lin, J. C.-C., & Lu, H. (2000). Towards an understanding of the behavioural intention to use a web site. *International Journal of Information Management, 20*(3), 197–208. doi:10.1016/S0268-4012(00)00005-0

Lin, K.-Y., & Lu, H.-P. (2011). Why people use social networking sites: An empirical study integrating network externalities and motivation theory. *Computers in Human Behavior, 27*(3), 1152–1161. doi:10.1016/j.chb.2010.12.009

Lisi, R. D., & Wolford, J. L. (2002). Improving children mental rotation accuracy with computer game playing. *The Journal of Genetic Psychology, 163*(3), 272–282. doi:10.1080/00221320209598683 PMID:12230149

Liu, Y., & Li, H. (2011). Exploring the impact of use context on mobile hedonic services adoption: An empirical study on mobile gaming in China. *Computers in Human Behavior, 27*(2), 890–898. doi:10.1016/j.chb.2010.11.014

López-Bonilla, L. M., & López-Bonilla, J. M. (2011). The role of attitudes in the TAM: A theoretically unneccesary construct? *British Journal of Educational Technology, 42*(6), E160–E162. doi:10.1111/j.1467-8535.2011.01232.x

Ma, W. W. K., & Chan, A. (2014). Knowledge sharing and social media: Altruism, perceived online attachment motivation, and perceived online relationship commitment. *Computers in Human Behavior, 39*, 51–58. doi:10.1016/j.chb.2014.06.015

Moon, J.-W., & Kim, Y. G. (2001). Extending the TAM for a worldwide-web context. *Information & Management, 38*(4), 217–230. doi:10.1016/S0378-7206(00)00061-6

Ng, B. D., & Wiemer-Hastings, P. (2005). Addiction to the Internet and Online Gaming. *Cyberpsychology & Behavior, 8*(2), 110–113. doi:10.1089/cpb.2005.8.110 PMID:15938649

Przybylski, A., Rigby, C. S., & Ryan, R. M. (2010). A motivational model of video game engagement. *Review of General Psychology, 14*(2), 154–166. doi:10.1037/a0019440

Rachlin, H. (2002). Altruism and selfishness. *Behavioral and Brain Sciences, 25*(2), 239–250. doi:10.1017/S0140525X02000055 PMID:12744145

Rauniar, R., Rawski, G., Yang, J., & Johnson, B. (2014). Technology acceptance model (TAM) and social media usage: An empirical study on Facebook. *Journal of Enterprise Information Management, 27*(1), 6–30. doi:10.1108/JEIM-04-2012-0011

Rosen, P., & Sherman, P. (2006). Hedonic information systems: acceptance of social networking websites. *Proceedings of the 12th Americas Conference on Information Systems*, 162.

Schenk, S., Lech, R. K., & Suchan, B. (2017). Games people play: How video games improve probabilistic learning. *Behavioural Brain Research, 335*, 208–214. doi:10.1016/j.bbr.2017.08.027 PMID:28842270

Schreiber, J. B., Nora, A., Stage, F. K., Barlow, E. A., & King, J. (2006). Reporting structural equation modeling and confirmatory factor analysis results: A review. *The Journal of Educational Research, 99*(6), 323–338. doi:10.3200/JOER.99.6.323-338

Shin, D. H., & Kim, W. Y. (2008). Applying the technology acceptance model and flow theory to cyworld user behavior: Implication of the web 2.0 user acceptance. *Cyberpsychology & Behavior, 11*(3), 378–382. doi:10.1089/cpb.2007.0117 PMID:18537514

Shin, D.-H., & Shin, Y.-J. (2011). Why do people play social network games? *Computers in Human Behavior, 27*(2), 852–861. doi:10.1016/j.chb.2010.11.010

Smith, S. (2003, April 8). *Determining Sample Size: How to Ensure You Get the Correct Sample Size*. Retrieved May 8, 2017, Retrieved from https://www.qualtrics.com/experience-management/research/determine-sample-size-b/

Spark. (2015, May 5). *Top 10 MOBA Games for 2016*. Retrieved May 6, 2017, from https://www.killping.com/blog/top-10-moba-games-2015/

Teo, T., & Noyes, J. (2011). An assessment of the influence of perceived enjoyment and attitude on the intention to use technology among pre-service teachers: A structural equation modelling approach. *Computers & Education, 57*(2), 1645–1653. doi:10.1016/j.compedu.2011.03.002

Thompson, R. L., Higgins, C. A., & Howell, J. M. (1991). Personal computing: Toward a conceptual model of utilization. *Management Information Systems Quarterly, 15*(1), 125–143. doi:10.2307/249443

Trepte, S., Reinecke, L., & Juechems, K. (2012). The social side of gaming: How playing online computer games creates online and offline social support. *Computers in Human Behavior, 28*(3), 832–839. doi:10.1016/j.chb.2011.12.003

Ursavas, Ö. F. (2013). Reconsidering the role of attitude in the TAM: An answer to Teo (2009) and Nistor and Heymann (2010), and Lopez-Bonilla and Lopez- Bonilla (2011). *British Journal of Educational Technology, 44*(1), E22–E25. doi:10.1111/j.1467-8535.2012.01327.x

Van de Wijngaert, L., & Bouwman, H. (2009). Would you share? Predicting the potential use of a new technology. *Telematics and Informatics*, 26(1), 85–102. doi:10.1016/j.tele.2008.01.002

Van Der Heijden, H. (2003). Factors influencing the usage of websites: The case of a generic portal in The Netherlands. *Information & Management*, 40(6), 541–549. doi:10.1016/S0378-7206(02)00079-4

Venkatesh, V., Morris, M. G., Davis, G. B., & Davis, F. D. (2003). User acceptance of information technology: Toward a unified view. *Management Information Systems Quarterly*, 27(3), 425–478. doi:10.2307/30036540

Wang, Q., & Sun, X. (2016). Investigating gameplay intention of the elderly using an extended technology acceptance model (ETAM). *Technological Forecasting and Social Change*, 107, 59–68. doi:10.1016/j.techfore.2015.10.024

Williams, B., Onsman, A., & Brown, T. (2010). Exploratory factor analysis: A five-step guide for novices. *Australasian Journal of Paramedicine*, 8(3), 1–13. doi:10.33151/ajp.8.3.93

Wittek, C. T., Finserås, T. R., Pallesen, S., Mentzoni, R. A., Hanss, D., Griffiths, M. D., & Molde, H. (2016). Prevalence and predictors of video game addiction: A study based on a national representative sample of gamers. *International Journal of Mental Health and Addiction*, 14(5), 672–686. doi:10.100711469-015-9592-8 PMID:27688739

Yee, N. (2006). Motivations for play in online games. *Cyberpsychology & Behavior*, 9(6), 772–775. doi:10.1089/cpb.2006.9.772 PMID:17201605

Young, K. (2009). Understanding online gaming addiction and treatment issues for adolescents. *The American Journal of Family Therapy*, 37(5), 355–372. doi:10.1080/01926180902942191

This research was previously published in the International Journal of Technology and Human Interaction (IJTHI), 17(1); pages 32-58, copyright year 2021 by IGI Publishing (an imprint of IGI Global).

APPENDIX A

Background of the Top Three Moba Games

This Appendix discusses the top three games played by the research participants. These include the Defense of the Ancient (Dota) 2, League of Legends (LOL) and Overwatch. It also discusses the platform being used in playing the game.

League of Legends and Dota 2 are team-based games based on a modification for the game Warcraft 3: Reign of Chaos called Defense of the Ancients or DotA. The primary mode of Dota consists of matches played on a map where a team of five players is up against another team of five players. Overwatch features squad-based combat with two opposing teams of six players each. Players choose one of several hero characters, each with their unique abilities and role classes. The four-character roles include offense characters with high speed and attack but low defense, defense characters meant to form choke points for enemies, support characters that provide buffs and debuffs for their allies and enemies respectively (such as healing or speed alterations), and tank characters that have a significant amount of armor and hit points to withstand enemy attacks and draw fire away from teammates. Figure 2 shows the classic example of a MOBA map layout (Raizin & Sambeboat, 2013) which is divided into two parts, one side for each team.

Figure 4. A classic example of a MOBA map layout

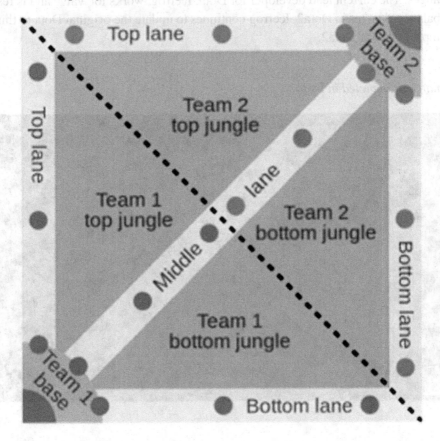

Three lanes lead out from each teams' base. The most effective strategies involve ending different characters to different lanes on the map, depending on the characters' strengths and weaknesses. Every lane has three towers. The towers serve as defense structures for each base and need to be destroyed to take down the base. Each lane periodically generates non-player characters that walk along the lane and meet with the opposing team's non-player characters. These non-player characters grant gold when killed by player characters from the opposing team, and they allow experience points to everyone close when they die. The gold can be used to buy items that make the player characters more powerful. The experience points increase the level of the player character when it reaches a set threshold. When a player character levels up the player they can choose an ability to learn or make an already known ability stronger. The skills are varied and depend on character but include effects like dealing damage to a character from the opposing team or moving a considerable distance.

Defeating a player character would reward the players with gold and experience points. The defeated player character is dead for a period and will revive in its team's base when that period is over. The goal for both sides is to destroy the opposing team's base. To make that possible a variety of strategies can be employed. Some focus one eliminating the character from the opposing team, while others apply a divide and conquer type strategy. When a group destroys the opposing base, the game ends, and they win.

Defense of the Ancient (Dota) 2

Dota2 is a game developed by Valve Corporation. It is a direct copy of the original Dota with very few gameplay changes. The current lead developer for Dota, Icefrog, works for Valve and is responsible for many of the balance changes in Dota2. Icefrog continues to update the original Dota to this day. Figure 5 shows a sample match of Dota2.

Figure 5. A match as depicted in Dota2

League of Legends

League of Legends is a game developed by Riot Games for PC. Riot Games coined the term MOBA as a genre, and the game is mostly based on the original Dota. Steve Feak was a developer on the original DotA but left development to Icefrog, the current lead developer of Dota and Dota2. Feak joined Riot Games and was part of the founding team for League of Legends which is generally considered a spiritual successor to DotA. Figure 6 shows a sample match of League of Legends.

Figure 6. A match as depicted in the League of Legends

Overwatch

Overwatch is a team-based online multiplayer first-person shooter video game developed and published by Blizzard Entertainment. Overwatch is Blizzard's fourth major franchise and came about following the 2014 cancellation of the ambitious massively multiplayer online role-playing game Titan. A portion of the Titan team came up with the concept of Overwatch, based on the success of team-based first-person shooters like Team Fortress2 and the growing popularity of multiplayer online battle arenas, creating a hero-based shooter that emphasized teamwork. Some elements of Overwatch borrow assets and concepts from the canceled Titan project. Figure 7 shows a sample match of Overwatch.

Characters in the games are known as champions or heroes in League of Legends and Dota 2 respectively. They generally have four abilities and some attributes such as health, a resource for their skills, physical defense, magical defense, movement speed, and damage. These can all be increased by buying items during a match for gold. Overwatch assigns players into two teams of six, with each player selecting one of 24 pre-defined characters, called heroes, each with unique movement, attributes, and abilities. Players on teamwork together to secure and defend control points on a map or escort a payload across the map in a limited amount of time. Players gain cosmetic rewards that do not affect gameplay, such as characters kins and victory poses, as they play the game. Characters fill different roles in the team. The positions range from fragile characters that need help from their team to stay alive in fights but deal much damage to the enemies, to the characters who remain in the midst of battle and take the loss in place of their allies. Depending on the nature, players buy different items throughout a match to reduce weaknesses of their characters and increase their strengths.

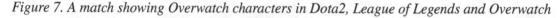

Figure 7. A match showing Overwatch characters in Dota2, League of Legends and Overwatch

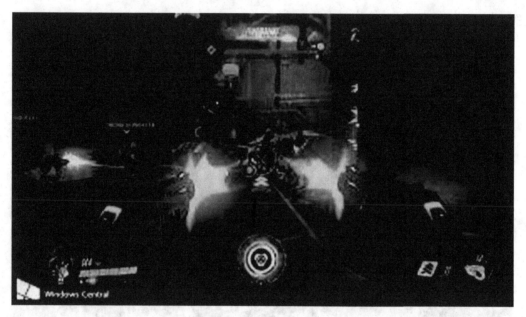

APPENDIX B

Table 13. Questionnaire

Factor	Item	Measure
Altruism (AL)	AL1	I will give my friends gifts or other in-game help.
	AL2	I often help my friends when they need help with online strategic video games.
	AL3	My friends often give me feedback when I offer to help they need for online strategic video games.
Social Interaction (SI)	SI1	I like to play online strategic video games with my friends.
	SI2	Online strategic video games provide a platform form to play games with my friends.
	SI3	I like to play online strategic video games which my friends play.
Use context (UC)	UC1	Playing online strategic video games is a way to spend free time with me.
	UC2	I will consider playing online strategic video games when I am bored.
	UC3	I will consider playing online strategic video games when I have Freetime.
Perceived Enjoyment (PE)	PE1	Playing online strategic video games is interesting.
	PE2	Playing online strategic video games brings enjoyment to my daily life.
	PE3	I always feel happy when I am playing online strategic video games.
Perceived Usefulness (PU)	PU1	Playing online strategic video games makes my life different.
	PU2	Playing online strategic video games makes my life better
	PU3	Playing online strategic video games is useful for me.
Perceived Ease of Use (PEU)	PEU1	It is easy for me to play online strategic video games.
	PEU2	It is easy for me to master the rules of online strategic video games.
Flow(F)	F1	I will not be tired of online strategic video games in a short time.
	F2	I will not lose interest in online strategic video games in a short time.
	F3	It often happened for me to ignore the time past when I play online strategic video games.
Attitude (A)	A1	It is a good idea for me to play online strategic video games during my free time.
	A2	I feel good towards online strategic video games.
	A3	I like playing online strategic video games.
Behavior Intention (BI)	BI1	I want to play more kinds of online strategic video games later.
	BI2	I will keep playing online strategic video games.
	BI3	I will play online strategic video games with my friends together.

Chapter 40
Two–Stage Non–Cooperative Game Model for Vertical Handoffs in Heterogeneous Wireless Networks

Pramod Kumar Goyal

(iD) https://orcid.org/0000-0002-8390-9273

Department of Training and Technical Education, Government of Delhi, India

Pawan Singh

Indira Gandhi National Tribal University, Amarkantak, India

ABSTRACT

In a heterogeneous wireless network (HWN) environment, performing an efficient vertical handoff requires the efficient qualitative evaluation of all stakeholders like wireless networks (WN) and mobile users (MU) and mutual selection of best WN-MU. In the literature, most of the work deals with both these requirements jointly in the techniques proposed by them for the vertical handoffs (VHO) in HWNs, leaving very little scope to manipulate the above requirements independently. This may result in inefficient vertical handoffs. Hence, this chapter proposed a generalized two-stage two players, iterative non-cooperative game model. This model presents a modular framework that separates the quantitative evaluation of WNs and MUs (at Stage 1) from the game formulation and solution (at Stage 2) for mutual selection of best WN-MU pair for VHO. The simulation results show a substantial reduction in the number of vertical handoffs with the proposed game theory-based two-stage model as compared to a single-stage non-game theory method like multiple attribute decision making.

DOI: 10.4018/978-1-6684-7589-8.ch040

1. INTRODUCTION

Heterogeneous Wireless Networks (HWN)(Pramod Goyal, Lobiyal, & Katti, 2018c) comprises of different types of Wireless Networks (WN) having a hierarchical structure. The difference in the constituent WNs are generally in terms of Network Technologies, Network Architecture & Protocols and Network Operators in the market (Trestian, Ormond, & Muntean, 2012). Fig.1 shows an HWN consisting three wireless networks; Wi-Fi, CDMA and Wi-Max overlapping each other. When a Mobile User (MU) or group of mobile users sitting in a car or a train wish to roam in an HWN environment, they may need to change the current network and connect to another network. This event is termed as Handoff. The handoff is mainly classified between two types as Horizontal Handoff (HHO) and Vertical Handoff (VHO). The HHO occurs between the same type of networks while VHO occurs between two different. In today's fast changing world, the next generation networks like 4G and 5G will all be HWNs. Even the Vehicular Ad-Hoc networks will have to be part of these networks so as to provide cloud based seamless data roaming services to the mobile users.

Like different constituent WNs in a HWN, the participating MUs may also be different. The MUs may be differentiated in terms of the service requests as real-time (e.g. voice/video call) or non- real time service (e.g. emails). Now days, the communicating devices like mobile phone or laptop are equipped with the capability to work as multi-mode or multi-home terminals. A MU with such communicating devices (Wang & Kuo, 2013) can connect with more than one different WNs at any point in time. At the same time, a WN may experience different service requests from multiple MUs. In such situations where multiple mobile nodes are competing with multiple WNs, the selection of mutually best WN – MU pair to perform the seamless and efficient Vertical Handoff (Pramod Goyal, Lobiyal, & Katti, 2017) becomes a challenging task.

Describing a WN as best in HWNs from MU's perspective depends on multiple decision factors which are termed in literature as network selection attributes or Handoff Decision Attributes (HDA) like Received signal strength (RSS), Offered Bandwidth, Delay, Jitter, Bit Error rate (BER), Velocity, Power Consumption, Distance and network usage cost etc. The HDAs may be conflicting in nature to each other like bandwidth and cost. A MU may prefer one HDA over another. Such relative preferences of users are termed in literature as User Preferences. The user preferences may be Static or Dynamic. However, the Dynamic User Preferences (Pramod Goyal, Lobiyal, & Katti, 2018b) are more useful in accommodating the changes in the values of HDAs on real time basis when a MU roam within a HWN which may result in higher user satisfaction.

Similarly, describing a MU as best from the network's perspective is depends on multiple factors like typeof service requested by the MU, requested bandwidth and expected revenue receivable from MU's etc. A WN operator generally charge different network usage cost for different type of service requests from a user. The network usage charges for voice and data services are based on per unit time (e.g. Rs / minute) and per unit data (Rs /Mb) respectively. The differential network usage cost policy force a WN to prefer one type of service request over another and prioritise the competing MU's accordingly in order to maximise its expected revenue.

The Multiple Attribute Decision Methods (MADM) (Pramod Goyal et al., 2017) based on utility theory (Zanakis, Solomon, Wishart, & Dublish, 1998) like "Simple Additive Weighting (SAW), Multiplicative Exponential Weighting (MEW), Analytical Hierarchical Process (AHP), Grey Relational Analysis (GRE) and Technique of Order Preference Similarity to Ideal Solution (TOPSIS)" are commonly used techniques to rank the available WNs. These methods can incorporate multiple & conflicting HDAs along with their

"User Preference Weights". These MADM techniques work well when a network has sufficient resources to serve one or all users at all times. However, when multiple MUs compete with multiple WNs having limited resources, the MADM techniques failed to serve efficiently. Game Theory(Pramod Goyal et al., 2018c) presents good mathematical solutions to model such multi MU – multi WN competition to find an optimum solution.

Figure 1. Heterogeneous Wireless Networks

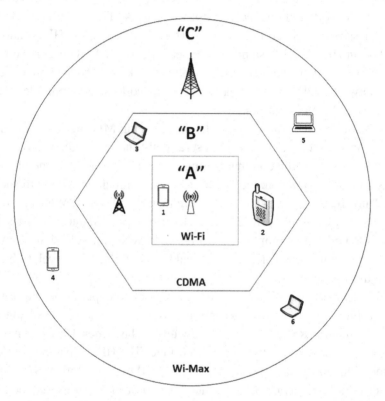

In a HWNs environment, as shown in fig.1, the selection of mutually best WN – MU pair to perform the seamless and efficient Vertical Handoff (VHO) required two important steps-

1. an efficient qualitative evaluation of different WNs & MUs, and
2. an efficient mutual selection of best WN-MU pair

in order to minimise the number of Vertical Handoffs (VHO) while maximising the profit & satisfaction of WNs & MUs respectively.

In the literature most of the work, as per my best knowledge, deals with both the above steps jointly in the techniques proposed by them for the vertical handoffs in HWNs leaving a very little scope to manipulate the above requirements independently. This may result in inefficient vertical handoffs. Therefore, in this chapter, the authors propose a generalised two stage two player non-cooperative game formulation to represent the competition among multiple MUs and multiple WNs. The network efficiency is expressed in terms of *User Payoff* receivable to a MU from a WN with all the considered handoff decision attributes. The novelty of the proposed two stage non-cooperative game model is in four ways –

1. It utilises multiple HDAs and the respective user preferences to assess the Quality of Experience (QoE) from a WN. QoE is used to assess service quality of a network from user's perspective and is a subjective measure.
2. It utilises the concept of dynamic user preferences(Pramod Goyal et al., 2018b)
3. It utilises the concept of using the WNs as game strategies for MUs and the MUs as game strategies for WNs (Pramod Goyal, Lobiyal, & Katti, 2018a) which is further explained pictorially here using a special diagram.
4. It separates the game formulation and solution (at stage 2) from qualitative evaluation of WNs and MUs (at stage 1).

The solution of the game gives a pair of WN-MU which are best for each other to perform an efficient vertical handoff. The proposed model provides a modular framework to solve the VHO decision problems using game theory. The simulations, carried out to analyse the effect of user preferences on the vertical handoffs, shows substantial reduction in number of vertical handoffs with the proposed game theory based method as compared to non-game theory methods like MADM using utility theory.

The rest of the chapter is organized as follows: Related work in section 2, Vertical Handoff overview in section 3, important concepts of Game Theory Section 4, proposed Non Cooperative Game Model for VHO in section 5, simulation and result analysis in Section 6, and section 7 states the conclusion.

2. RELATED WORK

The key challenges for an efficient network resource management in heterogeneous wireless networks are presented in (Piamrat, Ksentini, Bonnin, & Viho, 2011) along with an overview of recent solutions for vertical handoff decision making. In HWNs, The network selection is an important step for performing vertical handoff decisions which needs to consider a large number of complex and conflicting HDAs. The handoff decision factors can be static and/or dynamic (P Goyal & Saxena, 2008). The "Multi-Criteria Decision Making (MCDM)" or "Multi-Attribute Decision Making (MADM)" techniques (Obayiuwana & Falowo, 2016) are generally used to evaluate and ranked the available wireless networks for network selection in HWNs. The MADM methods are efficient and sufficient only to evaluate the various alternatives WNs for ranking by a MU while the available resources are unlimited but failed otherwise. In such situations game theory is proving an efficient tool to model and solve the VHO Decision problems in HWNs.

The SAW, MEW, TOPSIS, and GRA are prominent MADM techniques. A comparative analysis of these techniques with "SAW with Elimination Factor" method is presented in (Pramod Goyal et al., 2017). It shows that the "SAW with Elimination Factor" for the selection of best networks is more efficient among other MADM techniques as it results in less number of vertical handoffs to be occurring in a particular roaming duration of a mobile user.

A concept of Dynamic User Preferences is proposed in (Pramod Goyal et al., 2018b). The predefined "static user preferences" for the considered HDAs are moderated to accommodate the changes in current value of respective HDAs on real time basis. Such user preferences are termed as "Dynamic User Preferences". The use of Dynamic user preferences always results in less number of VHOs.

A comparative study of various types of games is presented in (Pramod Goyal et al., 2018c). There may be three types of competitions between the stakeholders of HWNs to claim the resources that is- i) competition between mobile users ii) competition between wireless networks and iii) competition between mobile users and wireless networks. It presents three non-cooperative game models to represent these three types of competitions. The researchers may use these game models as ready reference in the area of wireless networks.

A non-cooperative game between competing access network is proposed in (Antoniou & Pitsillides, 2007) to distribute a set of service requests from a set of users among a set of networks. Later a cooperative game based network selection scheme proposed in (Chang, Tsai, & Chen, 2009) to maximize number of call admissions, minimize handoff occurrence frequency, and fulfil quality of service (QoS) requirements. A user efficiency–cost ratio (PCR) based unified quantification model is proposed in (Chen, Zhou, Chai, & Tang, 2011) for evaluating the access services in HWNs. Similarly a non-cooperative game between networks to minimize energy consumption by a terminal while maintaining the desired link QoS is proposed in (Bendaoud, Abdennebi, & Didi, 2015). It considers expected QoS and expected remaining battery life time as two important handoff decision factors. A three stage non-cooperative game-theoretic framework is presented in (Dusit Niyato & Hossain, 2008) for bandwidth allocation and admission control between networks. All these papers considers only the competition between access networks to select a MU or service request and considers mostly the network aspects of the problem of network selection for vertical handoffs. A user-centric game based on user preferences for network selection (Salih, See, & Ibrahim, 2015) based on user preferences for the selection of the best heterogeneous wireless network considers only the user preferences but does not consider the network preferences for a user.

To consider the competition between users for a network, a non-cooperative game between competing users based on actual data rate of users to select the networks is presented in (Cui Yang, Xu Yubin, Xu Rongqing, & Sha Xuejun, 2011). A dynamic evolutionary game between the competing groups of users in different service areas is formulated in (D. Niyato & Hossain, 2009) to share the limited amount of bandwidth available in wireless access networks.

To consider the competition between MUs and WNs, non-cooperative games between selfishly acting users and access networks are formulated in (Cesana, Malanchini, & Capone, 2008)(Xu, Fang, & Liu, 2010)(Radhika, 2011) in order to maximize their profit while satisfying QoS for all users as well as load for networks. A matching game between users and networks (Meirong Chen, Fan Li, & Junqing Wang, 2011) consider synthetically the different requirements and targets of users and networks which guarantee the profit of both sides through obtaining stable matching. An N-person cooperative game is proposed in (Liu, Tian, Wang, & Fan, 2014) for network selection based on bankruptcy game with the combination of analytic hierarchy process (AHP). In a repeated game based scheme for vertical handoff (Fu, Li, Li, & Ji, 2014), each game is formulated as a non- cooperative strategic game between a mobile node (MU) and an access point (AP) to optimize the utility function of a network by finding a NASH equilibrium point. The payoff or utility function is defined in terms of the allocated bandwidth of a MU by an AP.

A Group Vertical Handoff decision model based on non-cooperative game is proposed in (Pramod Goyal et al., 2018a). It utilizes the concept of "Dynamic User Preferences" along with multiple handoff decision attributes. The MUs and WNs are used as game strategies against each other to reach at NASH equilibrium in order to select the best available WNs by group MUs for vertical handoffs.

All the above work, as per my best knowledge, does not separate the network evaluation with network selection and perform both the operations combined which lack the modularity in vertical handoff management. Thus this chapter proposed a novel idea of separating the analysis of worthiness of MUs & WNs from the network selection for performing the VHO. In this endeavour, the author extend the concept of dynamic user preferences and their application as game strategies developed by him earlier and published in (Pramod Goyal et al., 2018b)(Pramod Goyal et al., 2018c)(Pramod Goyal et al., 2018a).

3. VERTICAL HANDOFF

Handoff (or Handover) alludes to an occasion when a MU changes its place of connection starting with one passageway then onto the next of an equivalent or diverse wireless network. The handoffs in HWN systems can be delegated

1. Horizontal handoff (Intra-Network handoff)
2. Vertical handoff (Inter-Network handoff)
    a. Upward VHO
    b. Downward VHO

Horizontal handoff (HHO) happens when an MU moves starting with one cell then onto the next cell inside a similar wireless network. The HHOs [6] in wireless networks can be additionally delegated Intra-BSC handoff, Inter-BSC handoff and Inter-MSC handoff. The primary reasons/criteria for HHOs are: Poor Signal Quality (RSS) or Loss of Signal, Bandwidth, Traffic Load Balancing and Velocity of MU. The HHO involves three principle steps: Handoff initiation, Channel assignment, and Connection transfer / handoff execution.

Vertical handoff happens when a MU moves starting with one wireless network then onto the next various wireless network for example from Wi-Fi cell to a GSM/UMTS cell. Vertical handoffs are additionally named upward VHO and downward VHO (Pramod Goyal et al., 2017). The Upward VHO is from a lower size cell of a wireless network with higher Bandwidth to a higher size cell of various wireless network with lower data transfer capacity for example from Wi-Fi to Wi-Max. The Downward VHO is from higher size cell of a wireless network with lower transmission capacity to a lower size cell of a wireless network with higher data transfer capacity for example From Wi-Fi to Bluetooth.

The choice that for what reason to and when to perform vertical handoff in HWN is reliant on different parameters called as Handoff Decision criteria/Attributes. The handoff choice properties are principally arranged into three gatherings.

Network Related Attributes: To depict accessibility and condition of neighbouring network links for example data transfer capacity (bandwidth), coverage, use cost, delay, jitter, packet loss ratio, received signal strength (RSS), security, throughput, Signal to Noise Ratio (SNR), Carrier to Interference Ratio (CIR), Signal to Interference Ratio (SIR), Bit Error Ratio (BER) and so forth.

Terminal/User Related Attributes: To depict the cell phones/mobile device's state for example Remaining Battery Power, Speed of Mobile Terminal, and requested service type

User Preferences: To depict relative user inclinations for the different considered parameters to implement the Quality of Experience (QoE) for a mobile user. The user inclinations are expressed in terms of relative user inclination loads/weights.

The vertical Handoff Decision Process is basically comprise of three stages-

1.   Handoff data gathering,
2.   Network Selection and
3.   Handoff execution.

1.   *Handoff Data Gathering*
     This stage is otherwise called System Discovery or Network disclosure as it gathers data about the different handoff decision parameters related to user as well as networks
2.   *Network Selection*
     This stage chooses when and Where to trigger the handoff by investigating the data accumulated in before stage according to different Handoff Decision Algorithms. The Handoff Decision Algorithms for the VHO are primarily classified [7] as Received Signal Strength (RSS) Based, Bandwidth Based, Multi Attribute Decision Methods (MADM) utilizing Cost/Utility capacities, and Combination calculation dependent on Neural Network, Fuzzy Logic and Game Theory.
3.   *Handoff execution*
     This stage is the execution/implementation stage. It does the real connection transition from current wireless network to the chosen wireless network.

The network selection stage is the centre of any VHO process. The performance of every VHO Process is evaluated based on Handoff Delay, Number of Handoffs, Handoff Failure Probability, and Throughput. In light of who control the handoff decision process, the handoff control approaches are named as -

*   Network Controlled Handoff (NCHO) (In First Generation Networks)
*   Network-controlled, Mobile Assisted Handoff (MAHO) (In Second Generation & Third Generation Networks)
*   Mobile Controlled Handoff (MCHO) (In Fourth Generation/ Fifth Generation/Next Generation Networks/HWN)

4. GAME THEORY

4.1 Essential Elements of a Game

Game theory is an analytical tool to model the circumstances where explicit actions of decision makers lead to commonly clashing outcomes to one another (Charilas & Panagopoulos, 2010; Trestian et al., 2012). Such a model is called Game. The fundamental components of a game are:

Player: The individual partners who performs the strategic moves/choices. The objective of each player is to maximize his/her own payoff/profit by a choice of strategy. The players can be of two kinds Rational and Irrational. A player who consistently endeavours to augment its result is named as rational player.

Strategy: A strategy is an activity by a player which brings about a relating result to the player. The strategies can be arranged into three kinds Pure, Mixed and Dominant Strategy. The dominant strategy can be strictly dominated or weakly dominated.

Payoff: The utility that a player can get by taking certain strategy when the strategies of all the other players are fixed.

Equilibrium: An answer of the game gives the best blend of strategies of all the players which brings about the best result to every player of the game.

The games can be arranged in any of four different ways-

1. Non-Cooperative Games versus Cooperative Game
2. Static versus Dynamic Games
3. Complete Information Games versus Incomplete Information Games
4. Perfect Information Games versus Imperfect Information Games

In Non-Cooperative games, the strategies/moves/actions of players are autonomous while in Cooperative games, the technique/move of one player relies upon move of different players. In Cooperative games, the players share the data to choose their moves with the goal that all players can get best results. Here, the authors are giving the proposed model with non-cooperative game. Nonetheless, this might be stretched out to other sort of games also.

4.2 Game Representation and Important Concepts

The Non-Cooperative games (Cesana et al., 2008) are consistently of unique enthusiasm for HWNs, since the distinctive WNs constrained by various network administrators consistently attempt to augment their income without helping out some other WN, until and except if it turns out to be exceptionally important to do as such. Henceforth the authors present the idea of a game theory through non-cooperative games. The following is the proper brief portrayal of a non-cooperative game and its related significant concepts which are utilized in this paper. A Non-Cooperative Game in strategic form (or Normal Form), is a triplet-

$$G = \left(P, \left(S_i \right)_{i \in P}, \left(U_i \right)_{i \in P} \right) \tag{1}$$

Where-
  P: A finite set of rational player's i.e. $P = \{1,2,3,\ldots,n\}$
  S_i: Strategy Set for player *i*

U_i: $S \rightarrow R$, utility (Payoff) function for player *i* $\tag{2}$

$$S = S_1 \times S_2 \times \ldots \times S_i \times \ldots \times S_n \tag{3}$$

Here, S is the strategy space characterized as the Cartesian product of the individual strategy set of all the players.

Let, $S_{-i} = \{S_j\}_{j \in N, j \neq i}$ the set of "strategy sets" of all players except player *i* then $s=(s_i, s_{-i}) \in S$ will represents a *strategy profile* of player *i*. When a player $i \in P$ selects a strategy $s_i \in S_i$ in a deterministic manner i.e. with probability 1, this strategy is known as *Pure Strategy*. A strategy $s_i \in S_i$ is said to be *Dominant Strategy* for player *i* if-

$$U_i\left(s_i, s_{-i}\right) \ge U_i\left(s_i', s_{-i}\right), \quad \forall s_i' \in S_i \text{ and } \forall s_{-i} \in S_{-i} \tag{4}$$

Here, s_i' is any strategy other than s_i, belongs to strategy set S_i of player i, called as *Dominated Strategy*.

However, if

$$U_i\left(s_i, s_{-i}\right) > U_i\left(s_i', s_{-i}\right), \quad \forall s_i' \in S_i \text{ and } \forall s_{-i} \in S_{-i} \tag{5}$$

Then s_i' will be a strictly dominated strategy, otherwise a weakly dominated strategy.

4.3 Game Solutions

Nash Equilibrium(Nash, 1951) gives the best solution of a Non-Cooperative game. A pure strategy *Nash Equilibrium (NE)* of a non- cooperative game $G = \left(P, \left(S_i\right)_{i \in P}, \left(U_i\right)_{i \in P}\right)$ is a strategy profile $s^* \in S$ such that-

$$U_i\left(s_i^*, s_{-i}^*\right) \ge U_i\left(s_i, s_{-i}^*\right), \quad \forall s_i \in S_i, \forall i \in P \tag{6}$$

However, if

$$U_i\left(s_i^*, s_{-i}^*\right) > U_i\left(s_i, s_{-i}^*\right), \quad \forall s_i \in S_i \tag{7}$$

Then the NE will be strict NE.

At the end of the day, in NE, no player has a motivator to singularly go amiss to another strategy profile given that the strategy of other player's remains fixed. Two methodologies used to discover the NE in a game are – Iterative Elimination of Dominant Strategies and Best Response Function.

The *Best Response $br_i(s_{-i})$* of player *i* to the profile of strategies s_{-i} of opponents is a strategy s_i such that

$$br_i\left(s_{-i}\right) = argmax_{s_i \in S_i} U_i\left(s_i, s_{-i}\right) \tag{8}$$

There are two execution issues related with the game arrangement utilizing Nash Equilibrium-

1. Existence and Multiplicity of NE: a non-cooperative game can have zero, one or various NE
2. Efficiency: a NE isn't really the best outcome from the result point of view. Additionally if there is an occurrence of multiple NE, the selection of ideal NE is significant.

To take care of the above issues related with NE, the idea of Pareto Optimality is given. The Pareto optimality is a proportion of effectiveness to choose an ideal NE among different NE's, if exists. A strategy profile $s \in S$ is pareto-superior to another strategy profile $s' \in S$ if for every player $i \in N$ there exist $U_i\left(s_i, s_{-i}\right) \geq U_i\left(s'_i, s'_{-i}\right)$ with strict inequality for at least one player. A pareto-optimal result can't be enhanced without harming at least one player for example one can't improve the result for one player without diminishing the result for at least one other player.

5. PROPOSED TWO STAGE NON COOPERATIVE GAME MODEL FOR VERTICAL HANDOFFS

The proposed non cooperative game model for VHO is a two stage model as shown in fig.2. Stage-1 is about Handoff Information Gathering and System Evaluation. The efficiency of a WN for a MU is expressed in terms of *User Payoff* receivable from a WN. Similarly, the usefulness of a MU for a WN is expressed in terms of *Network Payoff* receivable from a MU. Stage-2 is about formulating a non-cooperative iterative game. It models the competition between multiple WNs and multiple MUs to select a mutually best WN-MU pair based on game solution using NASH Equilibrium. The *User Payoff* is calculated using Simple Additive Weighting (SAW) method in Section 3.1. Similarly, the *Network Payoff* from a MU is calculated in section 3.2. The proposed non cooperative game formulation and its solution is described in section 3.3. The proposed non cooperative game may leads to convergence only if either *MUs* or *WNs* have at least one dominant strategy. The important notations and symbols which are used in explaining the proposed game model are summarised in Table1.

The proposed algorithm comprises the following important steps-

Stage-1
    Step1: System Identification
    Step2: Handoff Information Gathering
    Step3: Payoffs Calculation
Stage-2
    Step4: Check whether (*No. of MU=0* or *No. of WN=0*)
        If yes go to step5 else go to step10
    Step5: Formulate a Non-Cooperative game between Mus and WNs (mxn)
    Step6: Find NASH equilibrium
    Step7: is NASH exist
        If yes go to step 8 else go to step 9
    Step8: Remove the optimal MU-WN pair and go to step 4
    Step9: Find the suboptimal solution and go to step4
    Step10: stop

Figure 2. Iterative Non-Cooperative Game Model for Vertical Handoffs

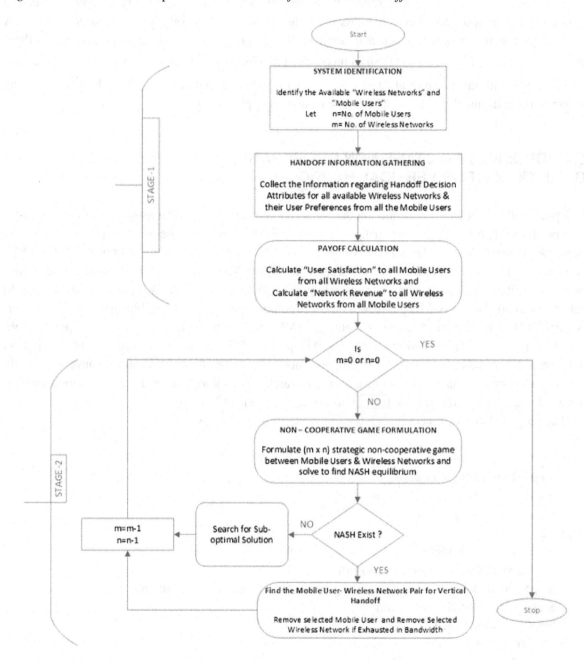

Table 1. Symbols and Notations with Description

Notations	Description
m	Number of Wireless Network (WN)
n	Number of Mobile User (MU)
p	Number of Handoff Decision Attributes
$k = \{1, 2\}$	Service Type $k=1$ Real-Time Services $k=2$ Non-Real-Time Services like email
$w_{ij,l}^{k}$	Dynamic User Preference Weight of Handoff Decision Attribute l of WN i for MU j for service type k
$u_{ij,l}^{k}$	Normalized Utility of HDA l of WN i for MU j for service type k
$A_{ij,l}^{k}$	Current value of HDA l of WN i for MU j for service type k
$A_{thij,l}^{k}$	Threshold value of a HDA l of WN i for MU j for service type k
UP_{ij}	The *User Payoff* from WN i to MU j
NP_{ij}	Network Payoff receivable by the WN i *from* MU j for service type k
C_{i}^{k}	Price of using a WN i for service type k
B_{j}^{r}	Bandwidth Requested by MU j
G	Represents a Non Cooperative Game
U	Set of MUs
N	Set of WNs
S_{U}	Set of MU's strategies
S_{N}	Set of WN's strategies
n_i	i^{th} WN
u_j	j^{th} MU
πU	Payoff MUs
πN	Payoff WNs
π	Combined Payoff matrix for both MUs and WNs

5.1 User Payoff

The efficiency of a WN is expressed in terms of *User Payoff (UP)*. We have proposed to utilize the individual utility of a handoff decision attribute rather than direct utilization of the attribute's value in order to make the User Payoff unit free inside the scope of 0 and 1. This also ensures the participation of both upward and downward handoff decision attributes on same scale. The User Payoff from WN i to the MU j is calculated as below-

$$UP_{ij} = \sum_{l=1}^{p}\left(w_{ij,l}^{k} * u_{ij,l}^{k}\right) \tag{9}$$

Where- $\sum_{l=1}^{p} w_{ij,l}^{k} = 1$

Here, the utility $u_{ij,l}^{k}$ is given as

$$u_{ij,l}^{k} = sigmf\left(x,[a,c]\right) \tag{10}$$

Where- $x = A_{ij,l}^{k}$, $c = \dfrac{A_{thij,l}^{k}}{2}$ and a is curve steepness (positive for upward and negative for downward attributes)

5.2 Network Payoff

The Network Payoff NP_{ij} is defined as the price payable by the user j to the network i for service type k, and is given as

$$NP_{ij} = C_{i}^{k} * UP_{ij} * B_{j}^{r}, \text{ i=1...m, j=1...n, k = \{1, 2\}} \tag{11}$$

Here, C_{i}^{k} is the price per unit time for voice or price per unit data for data services, receivable by i^{th} WN from j^{th} MU for service type k when the network efficiency is 100% or US_{ij} is 1.

The bandwidth requested by j^{th} MU is B_{j}^{r}. Here for the sake of simplicity, it is assumed that the MU gets the 100% of the requested bandwidth from the selected WN.

5.3 Non-Cooperative Game Formulation for VHO

It is proposed to model the competition between n MUs and m WNs as Two Player Non-Cooperative game. The Non-Cooperative game in strategic form for VHO developed in (Pramod Goyal et al., 2018c) is further expressed here pictorially using a specially designed diagram by author which is shown in Fig.3. This pictorial representation will give better understanding of the concept of using the MUs and WNs as the game strategies for the each other.

The first Player (Player 1) is the set of MUs. The second player (Player 2) is the set of available WNs. The players are assumed to be rational. Player 1 considers all available WNs as their strategy set while player 2 considers all available MUs as their strategy set for the game. A WN is represented by a set of multiple handoff attributes while A MU is represented by their respective dynamic user preferences. It is assumed that at a time one WN can select one MU only and the algorithm runs till every MU selects a suitable WN.

Figure 3. Representation of Non- Cooperative game between n Mobile Users and m Wireless Networks in strategic form

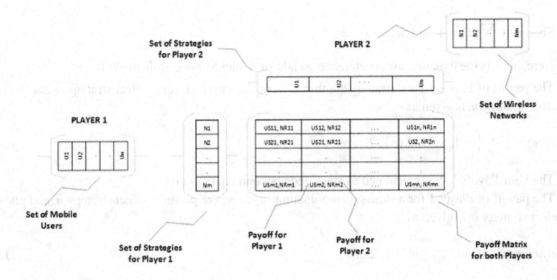

The Non-Cooperative game between mobile users and wireless networks is defined as -

$$G = (\{U,N\}, \{SU,SN\}, \{\pi_U, \pi_N\}) \tag{12}$$

Where-

$U = \{U_1, U_2, ..., U_n\}$ The Player 1
$N = \{N_1, N_2, ..., N_m\}$ The Player 2
$S_U = \{n_1, n_2, ..., n_m\}$ Strategy set for Player 1
$S_N = \{u_1, u_2, ..., u_n\}$ Strategy set for Player 2
π_U: S→R, Payoff for Player 1
π_N: S→R, Payoff for Player 2

The strategy space S of size (m x n) is defined as

$$S = S_U \times S_N \tag{13}$$

A strategy n_i for Player 1 corresponding to i^{th} *WN* is given as-

$$n_i = \{\{ ((A)_{i,l}^k, (A_{th})_{i,l}^k) \mid l=1,2,..p\}\}, i=1..m, k=\{1,2\} \tag{14}$$

Here, $(A)_{i,l}^k$ **and** $(A_{th})_{i,l}^k$ is the considered Handoff Decision Attribute and its threshold value respectively and **p** is the total number of network selection attributes.

Similarly, a strategy u_j for player 2 corresponding to j^{th} MU is given as-

$$u_j = \{\, w_{j,l}^k \mid l=1..p \,;\, k=\{1,2\}\,\},\ j=1..n \tag{15}$$

Such that $\displaystyle\sum_{l=1}^{p} w_{j,l}^k = 1$ and $w_{j,l}^k \geq 0$

Here, $w_{j,l}^k$ is the dynamic user preference weight of lth handoff decision attribute

The payoff of Player 1 for a strategy combination (n_i, u_j) where player 1 select strategy n_i and player 2 select strategy u_j is given as

$$\pi_U(n_i, u_j) = UP_{ij} \mid i=1, 2\ldots m;\ j=1, 2\ldots n \tag{16}$$

The User Payoff UP_{ij} is calculated as specified above in eq. (9) - (10)

The payoff of Player 1 for a strategy combination (n_i, u_j) where player 1 select strategy n_i and player 2 select strategy u_j is given as

$$\pi_N(n_i, u_j) = NP_{ij} \mid i=1, 2\ldots m;\ j=1, 2\ldots n \tag{17}$$

The Network Payoff NP_{ij} is calculated as specified above in eq. (11)

5.4 Game Solution

Nash Equilibrium gives an optimal solution point for any non-cooperative game where no player has a motivating force to singularly go amiss to another strategy profile given that the strategy of other player's remains fixed. The Lemke-Howson algorithm (Lemke and Howson, 1964) for discovering NE in a 2-player game is the state of art even after passing of more than 50 years. The NASH equilibrium for the proposed 2-player game is characterized as beneath

Let i and j are the index values of strategies of Player 1 (n_i) and Player 2 (u_j) respectively, and i^* *and* j^* are the index values of the strategies at the NASH equilibrium (Buttler & Akchurina, 2013). Then the pure strategy pair (n_{i*}, u_{j*}) will be in NASH equilibrium if

$$\pi_U\left(n_{i^*}, u_{j^*}\right) \geq \pi_U\left(n_{i'}, u_{j^*}\right),\ \ \forall i' \neq i^* \tag{18}$$

And

$$\pi_N\left(n_{i^*}, u_{j^*}\right) \geq \pi_N\left(n_{i^*}, u_{j'}\right),\ \ \forall j' \neq j^* \tag{19}$$

The n_{i*} and u_{j*} are the dominant strategies of player 1 and player 2 respectively which can be obtained using Best Response (BR) function also as given below-

$$\left(n_{i^*}\right) = BR_U\left(u_{j^*}\right) = argmax_{n_i}\, \pi_U\left(n_i, u_j\right),\ \ \forall i = 1\ldots m \text{ and } \forall j = 1\ldots n \tag{20}$$

And

$$\left(u_{j^*}\right) = BR_N\left(n_{i^*}\right) = argmax_{u_j}\, \pi_N\left(n_i, u_j\right), \quad \forall i = 1\ldots m \text{ and } \forall j = 1\ldots n \tag{21}$$

Here $\pi_U(n_i, u_j)$ and $\pi_N(n_i, u_j)$ are the payoff matrix for player 1 and player 2 respectively.
The payoff matrix for Player 1 for total strategy space S can be specified as-

$$\pi_U = \left(US_{ij}\right)_{mxn} = \begin{bmatrix} US_{11} & \cdots & US_{1n} \\ \vdots & \ddots & \vdots \\ US_{m1} & \cdots & US_{mn} \end{bmatrix} \tag{22}$$

And the payoff matrix for Player 2 for total strategy space S can be specified as-

$$\pi_N = \left(NR_{ij}\right)_{mxn} = \begin{bmatrix} NR_{11} & \cdots & NR_{1n} \\ \vdots & \ddots & \vdots \\ NR_{m1} & \cdots & NR_{mn} \end{bmatrix} \tag{23}$$

Then the combined payoff matrix for both the Players for total strategy space S can be given as-

$$\pi = \left(US_{ij}, NR_{ij}\right)_{mxn} = \begin{bmatrix} \left(US_{11}, NR_{11}\right) & \cdots & \left(US_{1n}, NR_{1n}\right) \\ \vdots & \ddots & \vdots \\ \left(US_{m1}, NR_{m1}\right) & \cdots & \left(US_{mn}, NR_{mn}\right) \end{bmatrix} \tag{24}$$

In case NASH equilibrium does not exist then a suboptimal solution comprising a pure strategy pair $(n_{i^\wedge}, u_{j^\wedge})$ is obtained such that

$(n_{i^\wedge}, u_{j^\wedge})$: Max $\{US_{ij}\, /\, NR_{ij}\,|\;$ i=1…m; j=1…n$\}$

Subject to: $US_{ij} > 0,\, NR_{ij} > 0$ \hfill (25)

NASH equilibrium, if exists, gives the pair of strategies (n_{i^*}, n_{j^*}) in terms of a MU and an available WN which can select each other. This MU-WN pair is expelled from further thought in next emphasis and the game is rehashed with the rest of the MU and WN till all MUs get an accessible WN. In case NASH equilibrium does not exist at all, the same set of user and networks is allowed to search for a sub optimal solution $(n_{i^\wedge}, u_{j^\wedge})$ as shown in equation (25).

6. SIMULATION AND RESULT ANALYSIS

The proposed two stage non cooperative game model for VHO is implemented in MATLAB and simulations are carried out to analyse the results. Two modules are developed to implement the Stage-1 and Stage -2 separately. The results of stage-1 are used as input to stage-2. The Stage-1 is about handoff information gathering and evaluation of MUs & WNs. The evaluation is carried out with Summative Additive Weighting (SAW). In stage-2, the Non cooperative game is formulated as two player strategic game as detailed in section 3.3 above. The game will leads to an optimal solution when at least one dominant strategy is available of either player. The simulation setup developed in (Pramod Goyal et al., 2018a) is reused here which is detailed as below.

An HWN comprising three overlapping WNs: Wi-Fi, CDMA and Wi-Max are considered for simulations as shown above in fig.1 in Section 1. The author considered the following five handoff decisions attributes –

i) Network *Bandwidth (B)*, ii) *Distance (D)* of a MU from an Access Point (AP) or Base Station Controller (BSC) of a WN, iii) Velocity (V) of Mobile Terminal, iv) *Power Consumption (P)* by a network interface, and v) Network *Usage Charges (C)*. The threshold values of the considered handoff decision attributes for all the three networks are reuse as given in *Table 2*. It is assume that all the MUs are requesting for only single service type (k=1) of voice communication.

The efficiency of the proposed game theory based method for vertical handoff is compared with non-game theory methods SAW using utility theory. Here, the authors are considering the considering the user initiated handoffs where the important consideration is always on reducing the number of handoff initiations while maximising the overall *User Payoff* as well as *Network Payoff*. The efficiency of the system is expressed in terms of total number of VHOs required to be performed by a MU for an application to be completed, since the authors are The *User Payoff* is the overall Quality of Experience (QoE) receivable from a WN by the MU while the *Network Payoff* is the total revenue receivable from a selected MU by the WN.

Table 2. Handoff Decision Attributes and their Threshold values

Network →	Wi-Fi	CDMA	Wi-Max
Network Selection Attributes ↓			
Bandwidth	54 Mbps	2Mbps	30Mbps
Velocity	1Km/Hrs	150Km/Hrs	60km/hrs
Distance	50mtr	20Km	50Km
Power Consumption	100mw	50mw	20mw
Usage Charges	10p/bps	100p/bps	50p/bps

The simulations are carried out to find the following-

1. The impact of initial connectivity of all the MUs in a particular area during the course of simulation on the system efficiency. For this, the Simulations are conducted for the following three scenarios of the MUs, when initially all the MUs are in:

    I.   region 'A' having connectivity with Net-1 (Wi-Fi) (Fig.4)
    II. region 'B' having connectivity with Net-2 (CDMA) (Fig.5)
    III. region 'C' having connectivity with Net-3 (Wi-Max) (Fig.6)

2. The impact of a particular Handoff Decision Attribute on the *"Number of VHOs"* observed by a user, in comparison to other attributes. For this, in each simulation run, there are five rounds corresponding to five handoff attributes. In each round, the authors set the user preference weight of one particular handoff decision attribute as highest and the user preference weights of other attributes equal and lower as shown in Table *3*.

Table 3. User Preference Weight Factors and Their Values

Static Weights	Round Number				
	1	2	3	4	5
W_B: For Bandwidth	**0.6**	0.1	0.1	0.1	0.1
W_V: For Velocity	0.1	**0.6**	0.1	0.1	0.1
W_D: For Distance	0.1	0.1	**0.6**	0.1	0.1
W_P: For Power	0.1	0.1	0.1	**0.6**	0.1
W_C: For Cost	0.1	0.1	0.1	0.1	**0.6**

The impact of Mobile User population in a particular duration within a considered hotspot area on the *"Number of VHOs"* to be observed by the Mobile Users.

The simulation results for finding the effect of a particular HDA on the *"Number of VHOs"* observed by a user, in comparison to other attributes are presented in fig. 7, fig.8 and fig.9. Fig.10 presents the simulation results for finding the effect of mobile user population on number of VHOs.

Fig.7, 8 & 9 consider the fixed populace of three mobile users and three wireless networks inside the HWN. The simulation results are results are exhibited regarding number of vertical handoffs resulted in one occasion of handoff initiation by all the three MUs considered for the over three situations separately. The X-Axis represents the user preference weight for a handoff decision factor which is considered as highest among others as per Table 3 in each round.

As it can be seen from Table 2 that Wi-Fi ought to be favoured network for Bandwidth and Network utilization cost, CDMA ought to be favoured network for Velocity and Wi-Max ought to be favoured network for Distance and Power Consumption as vertical handoff Decision factors. At the end of the day, if most elevated inclination is given for either data transfer capacity (bandwidth) or Network utilization cost and at first every one of the MUs are associated with Wi-Fi network, at that point they ought to be stay associated with Wi-Fi and number of vertical handoffs ought to be least in these cases. The results presented in Fig.7 prove the same more appropriately with our proposed game theoretic model in comparison to MADM based methods.

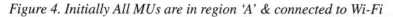

Figure 4. Initially All MUs are in region 'A' & connected to Wi-Fi

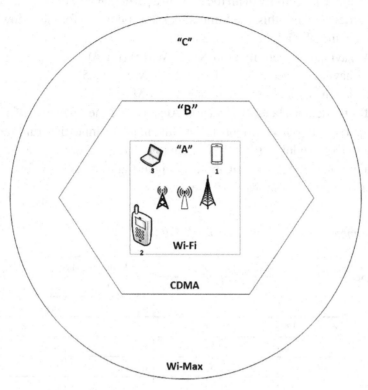

Figure 5. Initially All MUs are in region 'B' & connected to CDMA

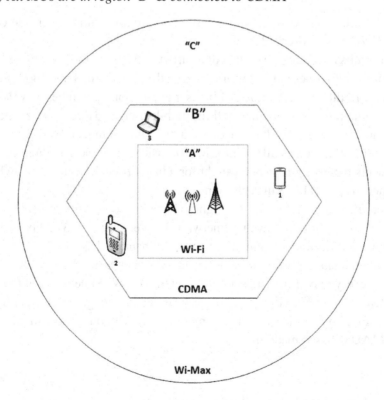

Figure 6. Initially All MUs are in region 'C' & connected to Wi-Max

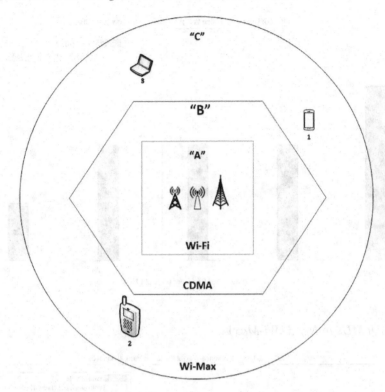

Figure 7. Initially All MUs in Net-1 (Wi-Fi)

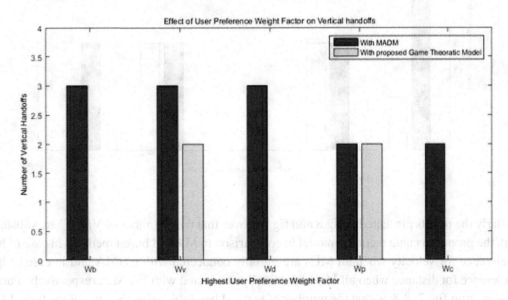

Figure 8. Initially All MUs in Net-2 (CDMA)

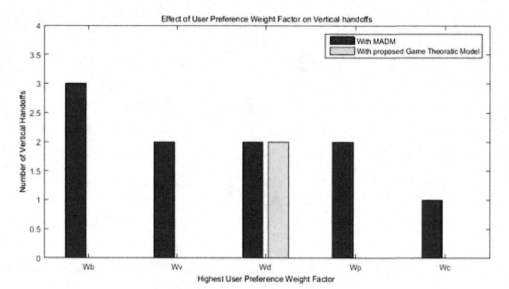

Figure 9. Initially All MUs in Net-3 (Wi-Max)

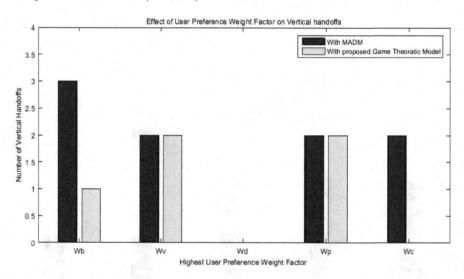

Similarly the results presented in fig.8 and fig.9 proves that the "Number of VHOs" are substantially less with the proposed game theoretic model in comparison to MADM based methods in case of highest user preference for velocity when all MUs are initially connected with CDMA and in case of highest user preference for distance when all MUs are initially connected with Wi-Max respectively. Further, it can be seen from fig. 7, 8 & 9, that the number of vertical handoffs performed by all the three MUs are always less for all the user preference weights in all situations with the proposed game theoretic model in comparison to MADM based utility methods like SAW.

Fig.10 presents the number of VHOs observed by all the MUs in a group of 3, 6, 9, 12 and 15 in one instance of handoff initiation for the three scenarios considered in fig.4-6. The user preferences of MUs for WNs are considered as predefined and fixed. The results shows that even in the situation when the competing MUs are more than the available WNs, the number of VHOs is substantially less with the proposed game theoretic model in comparison to MADM based methods.

The results presented in fig.7 to fig.10 above clearly proves that the proposed two stage non cooperative game based method does not allows all the user initiated vertical handoffs in order to maximise the User Payoff and Network Payoff. Hence the proposed game theoretic model performs better, by reducing the "Number of VHOs", during handoff decision process in Heterogeneous Wireless Networks.

Figure 10. Effect of Mobile User Population on Vertical Handoffs

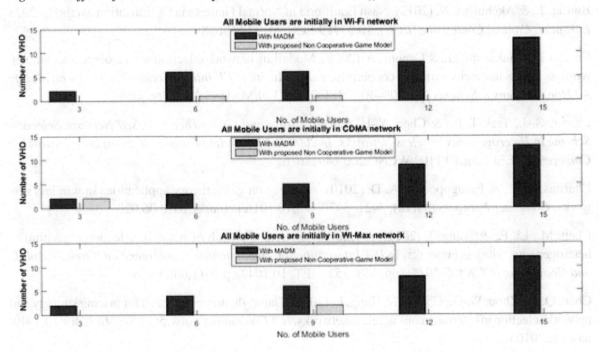

7. CONCLUSION

This chapter proposes a two stage Non-Cooperative Game model for Vertical Handoffs. This is a 2-stage modular framework. Stage-1 is used to evaluate the "Mobile Users" and "Wireless Networks". Stage-2 is used to model the competition between multiple MUs and multiple WNs using a Non Cooperative Game to select the mutually best MU-WN pair for performing VHO. The results shows that the network selection using the proposed approach in non-cooperative game model substantially reduces the "Number of vertical handoffs" in comparison to the network selection based on classical MADM based methods like SAW.

In order to effectively communicate the concept of proposed model, the authors have briefly introduced the concept of Vertical handoff and Game theory also in this chapter. This model separates the quantitative evaluation of Mobile Users and Wireless Networks from the optimal selection of the best available Wireless Networks by a Mobile User. This model can be extended successfully to apply any technique at Stage -1 while applying any other technique at Stage-2.

REFERENCES

Antoniou, J., & Pitsillides, A. (2007). *4G converged environment: Modeling network selection as a game. In 16th IST Mobile and Wireless Communications Summit.* IEEE. doi:10.1109/ISTMWC.2007.4299242

Bendaoud, F., Abdennebi, M., & Didi, F. (2015). Network selection using game theory. In *3rd International Conference on Control, Engineering & Information Technology (CEIT)* (pp. 1–6). IEEE. 10.1109/CEIT.2015.7233014

Buttler, J., & Akchurina, N. (2013). Nash Equilibria in Normal Games via Optimization Methods. *2013 European Control Conference (ECC).* 10.23919/ECC.2013.6669658

Cesana, M., Malanchini, I., & Capone, A. (2008). Modelling network selection and resource allocation in wireless access networks with non-cooperative games. In *5th IEEE International Conference on Mobile Ad Hoc and Sensor Systems* (pp. 404–409). IEEE. 10.1109/MAHSS.2008.4660055

Chang, C.-J., Tsai, T.-L., & Chen, Y.-H. (2009). *Utility and Game-Theory Based Network Selection Scheme in Heterogeneous Wireless Networks. In 2009 IEEE Wireless Communications and Networking Conference.* IEEE. doi:10.1109/WCNC.2009.4918016

Charilas, D. E., & Panagopoulos, A. D. (2010). A survey on game theory applications in wireless networks. *Computer Networks*, *54*(18), 3421–3430. doi:10.1016/j.comnet.2010.06.020

Chen, M., Li, F., & Wang, J. (2011). A game theoretical approach of network selection algorithm in heterogeneous wireless networks. In *IET International Communication Conference on Wireless Mobile and Computing (CCWMC 2011)* (pp. 148–153). IET. 10.1049/cp.2011.0865

Chen, Q.-B., Zhou, W.-G., Chai, R., & Tang, L. (2011). Game-theoretic approach for pricing strategy and network selection in heterogeneous wireless networks. *IET Communications*, *5*(5), 676–682. doi:10.1049/iet-com.2010.0249

Fu, S., Li, J., Li, R., & Ji, Y. (2014). A Game Theory Based Vertical Handoff Scheme for Wireless Heterogeneous Networks. In *10th International Conference on Mobile Ad-hoc and Sensor Networks* (pp. 220–227). 10.1109/MSN.2014.37

Goyal, P., Lobiyal, D. K., & Katti, C. P. (2017). Vertical handoff in heterogeneous wireless networks: A tutorial. In *2017 International Conference on Computing, Communication and Automation (ICCCA)* (pp. 551–566). IEEE. 10.1109/CCAA.2017.8229862

Goyal, P., Lobiyal, D. K., & Katti, C. P. (2018c). Game Theory for Vertical Handoff Decisions in Heterogeneous Wireless Networks: A Tutorial. In S. Bhattacharyya, T. Gandhi, K. Sharma, & P. Dutta (Eds.), Advanced Computational and Communication Paradigms (1st ed., Vol. 475). Singapore: Springer Singapore. doi:10.1007/978-981-10-8240-5

Goyal, P., Lobiyal, D. K., & Katti, C. P. (2018a). Dynamic user preference based group vertical handoffs in heterogeneous wireless networks: A non-cooperative game approach. *Wireless Networks*. Advance online publication. doi:10.100711276-018-1826-9

Goyal, P., Lobiyal, D. K., & Katti, C. P. (2018b). Dynamic User Preference Based Network Selection for Vertical Handoff in Heterogeneous Wireless Networks. *Wireless Personal Communications*, *98*(1), 725–742. doi:10.100711277-017-4892-x

Goyal, P., & Saxena, S. (2008). A dynamic decision model for vertical handoffs across heterogeneous wireless networks. In *World academy of science, engineering and Technology* (Vol. 31, pp. 677–682). Retrieved from http://citeseerx.ist.psu.edu/viewdoc/download?doi=10.1.1.306.7734&rep=rep1&type=pdf

Lemke, C. E., & Howson, J. T. Jr. (1964). Equilibrium Points of Bimatrix Games. *Journal of the Society for Industrial and Applied Mathematics*, *12*(2), 413–423. doi:10.1137/0112033

Liu, B., Tian, H., Wang, B., & Fan, B. (2014). AHP and Game Theory based Approach for Network Selection in Heterogeneous Wireless Networks. *Consumer Communications and Networking Conf. (CCNC)*, 973–978. 10.1109/CCNC.2014.6866617

Nash, J. (1951). Non-Cooperative Games. *Annals of Mathematics*, *54*(2), 286. Advance online publication. doi:10.2307/1969529

Niyato, D., & Hossain, E. (2008). A Noncooperative Game-Theoretic Framework for Radio Resource Management in 4G Heterogeneous Wireless Access Networks. *IEEE Transactions on Mobile Computing*, *7*(3), 332–345. doi:10.1109/TMC.2007.70727

Niyato, D., & Hossain, E. (2009). Dynamics of Network Selection in Heterogeneous Wireless Networks: An Evolutionary Game Approach. *IEEE Transactions on Vehicular Technology*, *58*(4), 2008–2017. doi:10.1109/TVT.2008.2004588

Obayiuwana, E., & Falowo, O. E. (2016). Network selection in heterogeneous wireless networks using multi-criteria decision-making algorithms: A review. *Wireless Networks*, 1–33. doi:10.100711276-016-1301-4

Piamrat, K., Ksentini, A., Bonnin, J.-M., & Viho, C. (2011). Radio resource management in emerging heterogeneous wireless networks. *Computer Communications*, *34*(9), 1066–1076. doi:10.1016/j.comcom.2010.02.015

Radhika, K. (2011). Vertical Handoff Decision using Game Theory Approach for Multi-mode Mobile Terminals in Next Generation Wireless Networks. *International Journal of Computers and Applications*, *36*(11), 31–37. doi:10.5120/4535-6451

Salih, Y. K., See, O. H., Ibrahim, R. W., Yussof, S., & Iqbal, A. (2015). A user-centric game selection model based on user preferences for the selection of the best heterogeneous wireless network. *Annales des Télécommunications*, *70*(5-6), 239–248. doi:10.100712243-014-0443-6

Trestian, R., Ormond, O., & Muntean, G. M. (2012). Game theory-based network selection: Solutions and challenges. *IEEE Communications Surveys and Tutorials*, *14*(4), 1212–1231. doi:10.1109/SURV.2012.010912.00081

Wang, L., & Kuo, G.-S. G. S. (2013). Mathematical Modeling for Network Selection in Heterogeneous Wireless Networks— A Tutorial. *IEEE Communications Surveys and Tutorials*, *15*(1), 271–292. doi:10.1109/SURV.2012.010912.00044

Xu, P., Fang, X., & Liu, X. (2010). A Non-cooperative Pairwise Matrices Game Model for Heterogeneous Network Selection. In *International Conference on Communications and Mobile Computing* (Vol. 3, pp. 387–391). IEEE. 10.1109/CMC.2010.29

Yang, C., Xu, Y., Xu, R., & Sha, X. (2011). A heterogeneous wireless network selection algorithm based on non-cooperative game theory. In *6th International ICST Conference on Communications and Networking in China (CHINACOM)* (pp. 720–724). IEEE. 10.1109/ChinaCom.2011.6158248

Zanakis, S. H., Solomon, A., Wishart, N., & Dublish, S. (1998). Multi-attribute decision making: A simulation comparison of select methods. *European Journal of Operational Research*, *107*(3), 507–529. doi:10.1016/S0377-2217(97)00147-1

This research was previously published in Cloud-Based Big Data Analytics in Vehicular Ad-Hoc Networks; pages 90-114, copyright year 2021 by Engineering Science Reference (an imprint of IGI Global).

Chapter 41
Flip–Game Engineering and Technology Methodology

Milagros Huerta Gómez de Merodio
University of Cadiz, Spain

Juan Manuel Dodero
 https://orcid.org/0000-0002-4105-5679
Escuela Superior de Ingeniería, University of Cadiz, Spain

Nestor Mora Núñez
University of Cadiz, Spain

José Mª Portela Núñez
University of Cadiz, Spain

ABSTRACT

Flip-GET has been developed with the objective of optimizing engineering practicals. The innovative element of this methodology is the use of serious games, as a complement to the flipped classroom method, in the teaching-learning process of engineering studies. This methodology uses serious games to take advantage of the capacity of motivation that video games have for the current generation of students, who have been involved with digital content, software, and electronic devices. This methodology has been evaluated using the method of case studies and by an experimental evaluation carried out in different stages, each of which has been developed during an academic course. In the experimental evaluation of the methodology, the control group carried out the practicals dividing the students into subgroups, without using the Flip-GET methodology, while the experimental group performed them with the methodology.

INTRODUCTION

Today's students are no longer the people our educational system was designed to teach. This generation of students has grown up in a digital environment, surrounded by devices such as computers, digital tablets, smartphones, etc., (Fonseca, Conde, & García-Peñalvo, 2018).

DOI: 10.4018/978-1-6684-7589-8.ch041

Most STEM students (Science, Technology, Engineering and Mathematics) are attracted by everything related to new technologies, including disabled people (Molina-Carmona, Satorre-Cuerda, Villagrá-Arnedo, & Compañ-Rosique, 2017). Especially those in which they, the students, are active participants (Freeman et al., 2014). In addition, the STEM teaching–learning process has evolved rapidly in recent times. According to Felder & Silverman (1988), the learning profiles of several engineering students are incompatible with the teaching styles of most teachers, leading to low student performance, faculty frustration and a loss to society of potentially excellent engineers.

For all these reasons, it is considered necessary to implement attractive learning environments and methodologies in the classroom.

In this chapter, the authors describe a methodology developed to solve a problem that is occurring in the practicals of engineering studies: the large increase in student numbers that is occurring in these studies leads to the ratio of students per job being higher than is desirable for carrying out practicals in an adequate way.

An analysis has been made of the different existing virtual experiences that can be implemented in the classroom. The use that teachers are making of these experiences has also been analysed. Among the virtual experiences, the most common are: alternate reality games, virtual simulation, serious games and virtual worlds. It has been proven that the use of serious games is increasing in the field of engineering education (Minovic, García-Peñalvo, & Kearney, 2016).

Ulicsak (2010) reports that the Serious Game (SG) is a successful tool for engineering students because, in addition to entertaining, it is useful to acquire skills and knowledge, as long as they are carried out properly. Therefore, this research has focused on engineering learning based on SG. In addition, analysing the teaching methodologies used currently, Flipped Classroom (FC) is a methodology that is increasingly used in the field of engineering (Toto & Nguyen, 2009, Sein-Echaluce, Fidalgo-Blanco, & García-Peñalvo, 2017). The following objectives have been established in order to improve the achievement of engineering practicals:

1. **Analyse the sustainability and effectiveness of the practicals that are currently being imparted in selected engineering studies.** With this analysis, it is possible to identify learning problems in the practical sessions, and thus to be able to find a solution to be developed by the teachers that is effective for students.
2. **Develop and implement a methodology to improve the effectiveness of face-to-face practicals.** The aim is to virtualize some practicals in order to improve their effectiveness and also to improve students' motivation. These virtualized practicals will be part of the methodology developed.
3. **Final evaluation to determine if the methodology helps students and/or teachers to improve the realization of on-site practicals.** In order to achieve this objective, an analysis will be carried out on whether the implementation of the developed methodology improves the motivation for the realization of the practicals, and if it helps the development of the competences in the subject.

In order to achieve the first objective, the current situation of engineering studies practicals has been studied and analysed for its sustainability and effectiveness. To this end, the first step was a systematic analysis of the literature on virtual educational experiences within engineering. From this analysis, the authors have concluded that the use of serious games (see KEY TERMS AND DEFINITIONS) is a promising solution for the virtualization of practicals.

For the second objective, the different methodologies that could be used to implement SG in practicals have been analysed. The selected methodology is FC. Next, a detailed study of what has been researched in the engineering studies on SG and FC has been made. There are some papers about how it is possible to combine both methodologies, but this has not been done in engineering studies. For this reason, the idea of developing a methodology for these practicals emerged, combining the use of SG in the FC.

To meet the third and final objective, the authors have proceeded to its study, implementation and evaluation throughout three academic years. Previously, the applicability of the methodology in engineering practicals has been analysed by the teachers as well as by the students.

BACKGROUND

This research is focused engineering studies practicals through serious games as virtual educational experiences. In order to achieve the aforementioned objectives, the first step has been to examine what has already been researched on the application of ICT in university education in general, and then focus on research on engineering studies.

Specifically, it focuses on practicals that use machines and/or tools, where it is desirable to be able to determine the number of students per group in the practicals depending on the space available in a job, the number of jobs and the complexity of the practical. However, this is not usually possible for organizational reasons. Generally, the number of students is the same in all practicals. There is no distinction either of the subject that is being taught, or of the difference between practicals.

Practical sessions are overcrowded, especially in the first courses. This organizational situation has the result that the student/work position ratio is not adapted to the needs of each practical. Thus, it is necessary to look for a solution that reduces the large number of students per group of practicals. It is difficult to keep all students close to the workplace to perform the practicals successfully. The solution adopted was to divide them into subgroups and divide the practicals into several phases: explanation of the practical, data collection at the workplace, report preparation and data analysis. Thus, these subgroups performed a rotational task schedule according to the phase of the practical in which they were. The main objective was that everyone had access to workplaces to perform the practical; in addition, this would serve to try to make students feel the main protagonists (while they are performing the practicals). This experience was, in part, positive, because the students did not remain as mere spectators, although they were still many students per workplace. It was also possible to involve more students, although it was not very sustainable for the teacher, because they had to repeat the explanation of the practical as many times as subgroups had been established.

The experience of reducing the number of students per workplace was positive, but not very sustainable for the teacher. It was suggested that the way of teaching this type of practical should be changed, mainly in those subjects that had the same problem. A possible solution would be to develop a methodology to help improve its performance, including the idea of combining FC with SG so that the student, through the game, learned to perform the practical before attending the classroom. It was at this moment that the Flip-Game Engineering & Technology (Flip-GET) methodology emerged.

In order to achieve the work objectives, it is necessary to start examining what has already been researched on university virtualization in general, and then to focus the research on engineering teaching.

Silvio (1998) affirms that virtualization only makes sense if it helps improve the quality of teaching by enhancing the improvement of the quality of life in general. In addition, Silvio continues to affirm that new universities and non-university higher education organizations, due to the lack of tradition and routines, would have more facility to adapt to virtualization, but have the disadvantage of a lack of accumulated excellence. Almost two decades have passed and, although the traditional universities have been "virtualized", teaching is still primarily face-to-face. He explains that it does not make sense to virtualize education if it is not going to contribute to improving it and, furthermore, he affirms that it would be more difficult for traditional universities to change their routine. It must be kept in mind that, in recent years, technology has evolved at such a rapid pace that it is the teachers who must change their habits (Prensky, 2006), since today's university students were born in the digital age (Prensky, 2012).

The experiment by Toto & Nguyen (2009) on the impact of educational practicals and the concept of active learning in engineering education must be taken into account. They state that the teaching styles of engineering professors are in conflict with the learning styles of most of their students. They decided to apply a flipped classroom-type approach to improve the teaching in engineering practicals and make better use of class time.

Cabero et al. (2010) affirm that students feel satisfied with the use of b-Learning. Their main conclusion is that it is necessary to improve teacher training in new technologies. According to López-Pérez et al. (2011), the application of b-Learning has a positive effect on the reduction of dropout rates and on the increase of pass rates. In addition, they affirm that the joint effect of the b-Learning learning activities positively influences the final grades of the students, concluding that e-Learning activities complement, instead of replacing, the traditional forms of learning. Apart from that, Adam et al. (2013) analyse the latest contributions on e-Learning application models. They also describe the advantages and disadvantages of the traditional class with regard to e-Learning, which can be used both for fully virtual teaching and for mixed teaching. It is possible to obtain more advantages by combining the advantages of each of the modalities.

Mikropoulos & Natsis (2011) carry out a review of Virtual Learning Environments (VLE), from 1999 to 2009, concluding that there is a need to investigate further the capabilities of VLEs, because there is little information on results in terms of the attitudes of users and the results of learning. Rennie & Morrison (2013) carry out a detailed study of each of the e-Learning tools, so that the reader can select the one that best suits their needs. Among the different learning tools, they analyse games and simulations. When discussing these tools, they say that a good simulation game can be a good example for learning, allowing students to manipulate and evaluate, instead of reproducing concepts. In addition, the game should be more than an exercise for the students; it should allow them to share a common experience and use that as a basis to discuss what they have learned.

On computer games and serious games (especially with respect to learning, improving training and commitment), Connolly et al. (2012) review 129 articles, concluding that to promote the use of games in learning, beyond simulations and puzzles, it is essential to develop a better understanding of the tasks, activities, skills and operations that different types of games can offer and examine how this matches the desired learning outcomes.

On the scope of this research, it should be noted that Kamp (2014), in a study on teaching in engineering, concludes that in the last two decades, while the world around us has changed at a dizzying rate, the world of education in engineering remains extremely conservative. He affirms that an engineering graduate should have a positive attitude towards lifelong learning. According to Kamp, the world has entered an era in which education in engineering will have to make fundamental changes, to take the benefits of pedagogical training and technological innovations, and prepare graduates better for the growing and different demands of the new working world. It is better to anticipate these changes and make decisions about how to adapt education than to wait for time to pass and then try to respond.

In the National Center for Education Statistics Department (NCES) of the United States, those interested in increasing the number of graduates preparing subjects related to science, technology, engineering and mathematics (STEM) performed a study (Chen, 2013), in which they analysed dropout rates. They identified the characteristics of students who leave the STEM fields and compared them with those who do not quit. In this paper, they demonstrated that the dropout rate among STEM students was higher than that of non-STEM students. Freeman et al. (2014) were concerned about the high dropout rate and/or failure of STEM students. They carried out a study in which they compared the performance of students in these subjects using traditional methodologies and active methodologies. They concluded that active methodologies not only improved the performance of the students, but also decreased the dropout rate.

Apart from that, Godfrey et al. (2013) performed an analysis on students who finished their engineering studies. They showed that the percentage of students who manage to graduate is approximately 54% of the total of students who begin these studies. Meanwhile, Rajalingam (2011) proposes patterns in Problem Based Learning (PBL) to improve the performance of engineering students. He stated that one of the reasons for the failure of these students is the misconception they have of engineering. He ends by proposing that other means be used in engineering education.

Recently, Hsu & Lin (2016) compared the use of videos with SG, as a tool for the FC. The aim was to increase the interest and motivation of students to learn computer programming and achieve higher levels of performance. Thirouard, Pidol, & Duret (2017) used Virtual Reality (VR) with FC in some lessons of their engineering classes, to take advantage of the time in the classroom. They concluded that the use of new technologies is very efficient to prepare engineering students.

In general, the application of this methodology was well received by the students, although they confirmed that they preferred to listen to the teacher "face to face" rather than watching videos outside the classroom.

Finally, Ye, Hsiao, & Sun (2018) have analysed the use of SG together with FC. In their study, they analysed whether the use of commercial video games in a flipped classroom improves student outcomes. They concluded that digital games had a positive effect on the learning outcomes of students who used the Flipped Game Based Learning (FGBL) strategy, achieving better learning results, in general, than a conference-based approach.

For the aforementioned reasons, the main hypothesis is that it can be a good choice to use Serious Games as a tool for the Flipped Classroom (Sánchez I Peris, 2015).

FLIP-GET METHODOLOGY DESCRIPTION

At this point, the process that has been followed for the creation of the Flip-GET methodology will be described. It is important not to forget the aims and contour conditions to solve the problem described above. Although this methodology has been designed with engineering studies in mind, it can be applied in other disciplines that have similar conditions and practical characteristics.

For this purpose, Instructional Design (ID) has been used, which allows the definition of a deliberate Learning Experience. ID expresses how to achieve learning objectives (Merrill, 1990).

To develop this methodology, the guidelines and specifications of the IMS Global Learning Consortium have been followed. The key task of the working group that has elaborated this specification is "to develop a framework that supports pedagogical diversity and innovation, as well as to promote the interchange and interoperability of e-learning/b-learning materials" (Koper, Olivier, & Anderson, 2003).

Of the possible specification models, the authors have selected a conceptual model. Within this model, there are different levels of aggregation, with learning design as the main level. Learning design is divided into three sub-levels: components; learning objectives and prerequisites; and method. The resources consist of the sum of components, learning objectives and requirements.

A detailed description of each of the Flip-GET components can be found in the following sections. Apart from that, the learning objectives and prerequisites will be established from the didactic method used.

Flip-GET Components

The main components of learning design are: working activities, which indicate the tasks that students and/or teachers must perform; evaluation activities, which indicate the different procedures, instruments, criteria and roles that will be used for the evaluation; the roles of the different partners of learning design; and the learning environment. The environment is where the learning will take place, connecting the activities with the necessary resources to be able to carry out the teaching–learning process.

Practical Objectives

The teacher must establish the specific objectives he seeks in the practicals before developing the necessary activities to implement this methodology. These objectives will depend on the specific competences that the professor has established for each one of them.

Since this work is focused on engineering studies, it will focus on the competences of higher engineering studies. However, the method could be applied to other STEM studies, modifying the skills required for these studies.

Activities

The different activities that make up this methodology are:

1. **Prepare GUIDE.** Elaborate a guide with the following contents.
   a. Develop a dialogue with the necessary theory for the correct understanding of what is going to be done in the practical and the necessary steps to carry it out correctly. A schematic manual on these contents can also be prepared, allowing it to be made available to the user throughout the video game.
   b. Description of the different activities necessary for the correct performance of the practical, detailing them as fully as possible and indicating possible errors when performing them.
   c. Make a flowchart of the activities described above.
   d. Prepare a question bank, as well as the possible answers, indicating at the time of the practical when the user should introduce them.
2. **Develop VIDEO GAME.** Development of the video game, taking into account, whenever possible, the following characteristics.

    a.   It is advisable to prepare the video game with variable/randomly input data. Variable data helps each student to perform new calculations every time he plays. The number of different input data should be based on the game complexity, as well as the number of students who must do it. Each one has to make their own calculations and avoid learning solutions by heart.

    b.   If the video game developing platform allows it, multimedia of the material to be used in practical must be provided. Multimedia resources allow the materials involved to be identified properly.

    c.   The video game must consist of two parts:

        i.   During the first part of the video game, a character must be introduced who will act as the "virtual teacher". The virtual teacher will explain, to students, the working sequence that must be followed to perform the practical properly. In this explanation, in addition to the necessary concepts, the student must understand what he is going to realize. It is necessary to take into account these fundamental concepts for a correct realization of the practical. All relevant concepts must be supplied, even if they are not necessarily included within the subject on which the practical is being carried out. This is essential since the student may not have acquired these concepts or may have forgotten them. All relevant concepts must be provided, in some way, within the video game. In this way, the student verifies the existing relationship between the different subjects and acquires the first basic competence. The aim of using serious games is to keep the student active. In this first part, the student is required to interact, answering questions or performing diverse actions. For example, he should choose a specific tool among others, press a specific button on a machine, etc. In order to get a high attention level from the student, the questions (and possible answers) must be clear and descriptive. The student must read different options before answering after a pause for reflection, not as a trial and error game. In the case of non-descriptive answers or performing an action (such as pressing a button), it is desirable to request an explanation of the reason for selecting an answer.

        ii.   The second part of the video game must request the student to perform a practical without any guidance whenever possible. In this part, although the student has to do the practical alone, he can get help from the "virtual teacher" if he does not answer correctly or does not know how to continue. The help will be provided with feedback, which may be: for the student to understand the reason for his error, in which case, the "virtual teacher" must re-explain the concepts where the student needs to understand the reason for the error; to indicate what the student should do when he/she does not know how to continue; or to reinforce the correct answers of the student, with some explanation that may encourage him to continue with the practical. It is very important to keep in mind that students may not have acquired certain skills they need for the correct performance of the exercise, so, the feedback, in addition to explaining the concept, should indicate in which context it should have been acquired.

3.   **Run video game OUT of the classroom.** The teacher must give access to the video game, defining how many times the student can perform the practical: one or several times, depending on its purpose.

4.   **Prepare TOOLS in the CLASSROOM**. Prepare the practicals classroom by establishing the jobs with machines and/or tools for the activity to be performed. Another additional workplace should be established. In this additional workplace, once students have collected the data from the practical,

they can perform the necessary calculations to prepare their final report. In this way the practicals workplace can be used by another student group. Although it is not desirable, if the classroom does not have an additional workplace, students can be instructed to perform the calculations and final report in another area. They may leave the additional area at any time to ask for the teacher's help.

5. **Divide into GROUPS**. Divide the students into work subgroups, within the groups already established for the practical. For this, the following will be taken into account: the number of students eligible for the completion of each practical; the number of jobs and/or tools that are available for its realization; the estimated time required for the use of each machine and/or tool.

Evaluation Activities

Each practical may have a different evaluation system, depending on its objectives. Next, the different evaluation activities proposed in this methodology are described:

- **The interaction of the student with the video game.** The teacher chooses if he wants to elaborate it such that wrong actions have a penalty in relation to the final evaluation. An example of an incorrect action can be when the student chooses a tool that is not appropriate for that stage of the practical, or if he/she responds badly to any of the questions that the virtual teacher asks during the game. The teacher, when designing the game, must define whether or not to penalize errors, as well as the number of times the student can use the video game. It may be desirable to do the practical several times, especially if the first-time performance was not adequate. If the teacher decides the game should be played just once to determine this part of the score practical, later he can provide another link to the game, which is not evaluable. In this way, the student has the possibility of practising more if he deems it necessary.
- **The attitude of the student during face-to-face practicals**. This attitude can be evaluated both by observation and by questions, with an evaluation rubric previously prepared for it.
- **When the student adopts the role of tutor**. Students can perform peer evaluation, evaluating each other using an evaluation rubric prepared by the teacher.
- **Final report.** The student must write a final document with conclusions justified from the experiments performed.
- **Final test**. This test will be designed from the contents of the practical already done in person. This test can be online, as long as the teacher can guarantee that it is the student who does it alone, without copying from other classmates.

The final mark for the practical will depend on the different evaluation activities that the teacher has prepared for each practical, weighing each of them according to its importance.

Roles

- **Role of the video game developer**. Depending on the platform that is used to create the game, this role can be played by:
  - The teacher.
  - A student who is capable of developing a video game, following the teacher's guidance.
  - An external developer.

- **Role of the student.** The student is the one who must perform the practical, both virtually through the video game and in person in the classroom.
- **Role of the tutor.** This role can be played by:
  - The teacher.
  - The student: a variant can be established in which students, once they have done the practical, can act as practicals tutors for other students. This variant can be used in the following circumstances:
    - When there are more groups than desired and a single teacher cannot attend to all the groups properly.
    - When it is necessary to evaluate a student who is acting as a practicals tutor, to observe, from another point of view, whether the student has acquired the skills that the practical required. The student can only play the role of tutor if he has done the practical correctly and the teacher has observed that he has understood correctly what was required. In addition, the student should not be left alone and should always be observed and/or advised by the teacher.

Resources

- **Video games elaborated with the contents of the practical.** These should be a virtual guide on how the practical should be carried out, explaining all the elements that are part of it, the moment at which they should be used, and the objective to be achieved.
- **A forum** or other means of online communication.
- **An electronic device** (computer, tablet, mobile phone), so that the student can execute the video game.
- **Practicals classrooms,** with space for students to perform calculations and/or reports. If the centre does not have this space, it should plan another place where this work can be done, for instance, a nearby classroom or a space reserved by the centre for group work or the library.
- **Material of the practical,** to be done in person in the classroom. The material and/or equipment that must be in the classroom.

Environment

- **Outside the classroom:** the student must have access to the video game and have a computer (or any other device from which the game can be played) to perform the practical virtually, either at home or in a public place, such as the library of the university.
- **In the classroom:** there must be all the necessary equipment to perform the practical so that the student can correctly identify all the tools that have to be used in the game.

In addition, it is desirable for the classroom to have a space where the workplaces are (with the necessary elements for carrying out the practical) and another so that the students can perform the necessary calculations, as well as writing the report on the practical, such as is shown in Figure 1.

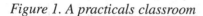

Figure 1. A practicals classroom

Learning Objectives and Flip-GET's Previous Requisites

This section details the learning objectives that are intended to be achieved with this methodology, based on the competencies and/or skills that the student must acquire after completing the practical, as well as the necessary prerequisites to be able to implement it.

Learning Objectives

Considering the general competences that university students must achieve, the following objectives are established for the student:

- The student must possess and understand previous knowledge necessary for the area of study in question. For the example in question, it could be "know how to calculate the area of the section of a spring".
- The student must know how to apply his knowledge to his work professionally. Once the virtual practical is done before attending the classroom, the student should feel more confident of putting it into practice without fear of being wrong and without requiring too much help from the teacher. It is expected that, when the student attends the practical class, he will be able to put into practice what he has learned, being able to carry out his work correctly and efficiently.
- The student must be able to understand the data and draw his own conclusions. This competence can be achieved with the preparation of the final report on the practical, when comparing and analysing the results obtained during the course of the practical.

For the transversal competences for the engineering student, the following objectives are established:

- The student must be able to solve the problems and subsequently be able to apply the knowledge to the practical.
- The student must be able to transmit what has been learned to people who are not expert in the matter. This objective will be for students who take the role of tutor, when explaining the practical to their classmates.
- The student must be able to learn independently. When doing a practical with their own hands, the student must make their own decisions at each step that must be followed to solve the practical, in order that they will remember it better.
- The student must learn to interpret technical documentation. In most engineering practicals, standardized tables (codes, geometric properties, material properties, etc.) must be used in order to perform the calculations that each practical requires. Students must be able to use these tables on their own.

For specific competences for each of the practicals, the teacher must establish his/her own objectives, taking as reference the following:

- The ability to solve both mathematical and physical problems that may arise in each of the practicals.
- Understanding and mastery of the basic concepts about the general principles of the practical and their application for the resolution of engineering problems.

Flip-GET's Previous Requisites

The necessary requirements to implement this methodology are the following:

- Teachers should not be reluctant to use new technologies.
- The practicals in which it is wanted to implement this methodology must be programmable through a video game.
- Students must have access to the video game before attending face-to-face practicals. According to the characteristics of each practical, the teacher will establish the margin of time before the students get the video game and can practise before going to the classroom, as well as the number of attempts that the student can make to practise.

Method for Flip-GET

To implement Flip-GET technology, the teacher must develop the contents that he wants the student to learn to perform a specific type of practical, through developing a video game. Subsequently, he must give access to the video game for the student to practise. Finally, the student must attend the classroom to do the practical in person and prepare a report and/or take a test about the practical. With this methodology it is intended that students acquire the necessary knowledge to solve the practical, through the video game, individually and on their own, and thus feel in charge of their own learning.

The following is a description of the steps that must be followed to implement this methodology properly, indicating who should carry out each of the activities, in what environment they should be carried out, and with what resources they should do them.

1. **Select the practical/s to implement the methodology**. First of all, the teacher must select the practical/s with which the methodology is to be implemented.
2. **Describe the content of the practical and establish the objectives**. Once the practical (s) has been selected, it will begin with one of them, describing its content and establishing the concrete goal/s that the students are intended to realize. If more practicals are selected, return to this point for each of them.
3. **Prepare the practical guide**. Based on these objectives, the teacher must prepare a guide on the practical that is descriptive enough to develop the game. Preparation of the practical guide, with its corresponding flow chart, should be done by the teacher.
4. **Development of the video game**. Then, the video game is developed. This can be the task of the teacher or an external agent to help him to elaborate it, always with his supervision. Figure 2 shows a schematic flow chart of how the video game can be structured.

Figure 2. Generic flow chart of the video game

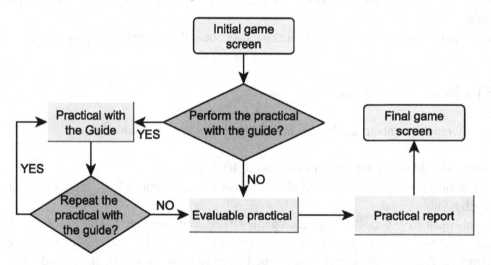

5. **Try the video game**. Once the game has been developed, it must be tested to ensure that it has no programming errors (bugs) and/or concept mistakes. This test can be done by the tutor, although other teachers and/or outstanding students can be asked to perform these tests. When the developer of the video game is the teacher himself, it is convenient to have the collaboration of other teachers, because they can detect things that the teacher (in the role of developer) may have overlooked, as shown in Figure 3.

Figure 3. Flow chart – Try the video game

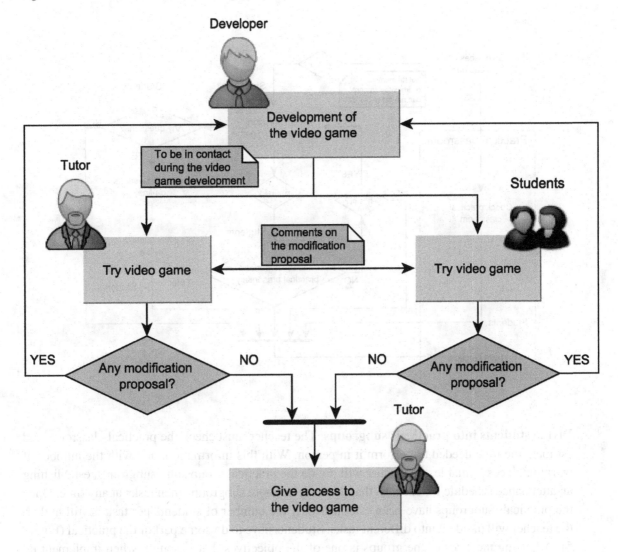

6. **Give access to the video game**. Next, the teacher must give students access to the video game. If possible, the video game must be accessible in the habitual LMS/Learning platform. If this is not possible, the teacher must provide a link to the video game for students to download and run from the device supported by the game. In addition, the teacher will enable a communication tool (for example, a forum). In the forum space, students can share questions raised during realization of the activity and resolve them. The teacher must establish time limits within which to perform the practical virtually, before attending the classroom in person.

7. **Run the video game**. Next, the student must execute the video game as many times as needed and/or the teacher has configured. Each student can share with other colleagues, and/or with the teacher, everything that is relevant to them, such as doubts raised during the realization of the virtual practical. Doubts that cannot be resolved by this medium will be clarified by the teacher in the classroom during the practical performance. The flow chart of this phase is shown in Figure 4.

Figure 4. Flow chart – Run the video game

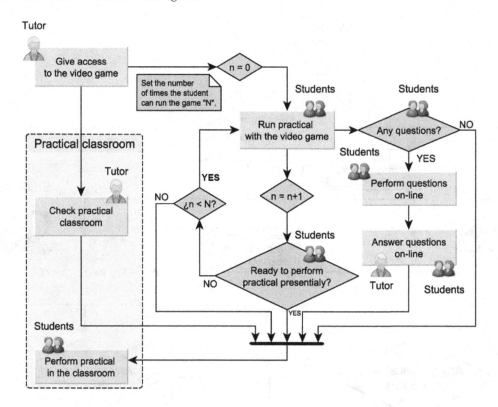

8. **Divide students into practicals subgroups**. The teacher must check the practical classroom and estimate the time needed to perform it in person. With this information, and with the number of working places available, the teacher will divide the practical groups into subgroups, establishing an attendance schedule for each, so that there are no more subgroups than tasks at any time. Once the practicals subgroups have been established, if the number of students per task is still higher, the teacher will divide it into different tasks. Students have to do some part of the practical (Figure 5). Adjusting the sizes of the groups is one of the objectives that is sought when implementing this methodology, depending on the task and the complexity of the practical. The subgroups of students must be defined to enable students to do personal work and to receive better attention from the teacher. If the teacher does not need to explain the practical repeatedly then he/she has more time to answer specific questions from the students, because they are attending the practical having already prepared the lesson.

9. **Attend practicals in person**. The student must attend, personally, the practicals in the schedule established by the teacher. All the necessary equipment must be in the classroom to carry out the practical. The student can correctly identify all the tools he has used in the video game. Ideally, the video game will have been made with real photos of the material, so that the student can correctly identify all the necessary elements to carry out the practical in an orderly manner and with knowledge of what he is doing at all times. The tutor must support the class, both to resolve any doubts that may arise when performing the practical with the video game, and to recall those steps that the student does not remember in order to continue the practical. This tutor role can be per-

formed by the same teacher or by a student selected by the teacher, according to the characteristics established in the role.

10. **Prepare the practical report**. Once the face-to-face practical has taken place in the workplace, the student will have to carry out the necessary calculations and/or the report on the practical, in the place that the teacher has provided for this activity. Each student and/or work subgroup must submit a report and/or test to the teacher, as established for evaluation.

11. **Evaluation of the practical**. The teacher will compile the different activities carried out by the students, using the evaluation activities proposed, as deemed appropriate. Finally, he will indicate the final mark obtained as a result of the realization of each of the activities evaluated in the practical, as well as if any of them needs to be repeated.

Figure 5. Flow chart – Check the classroom

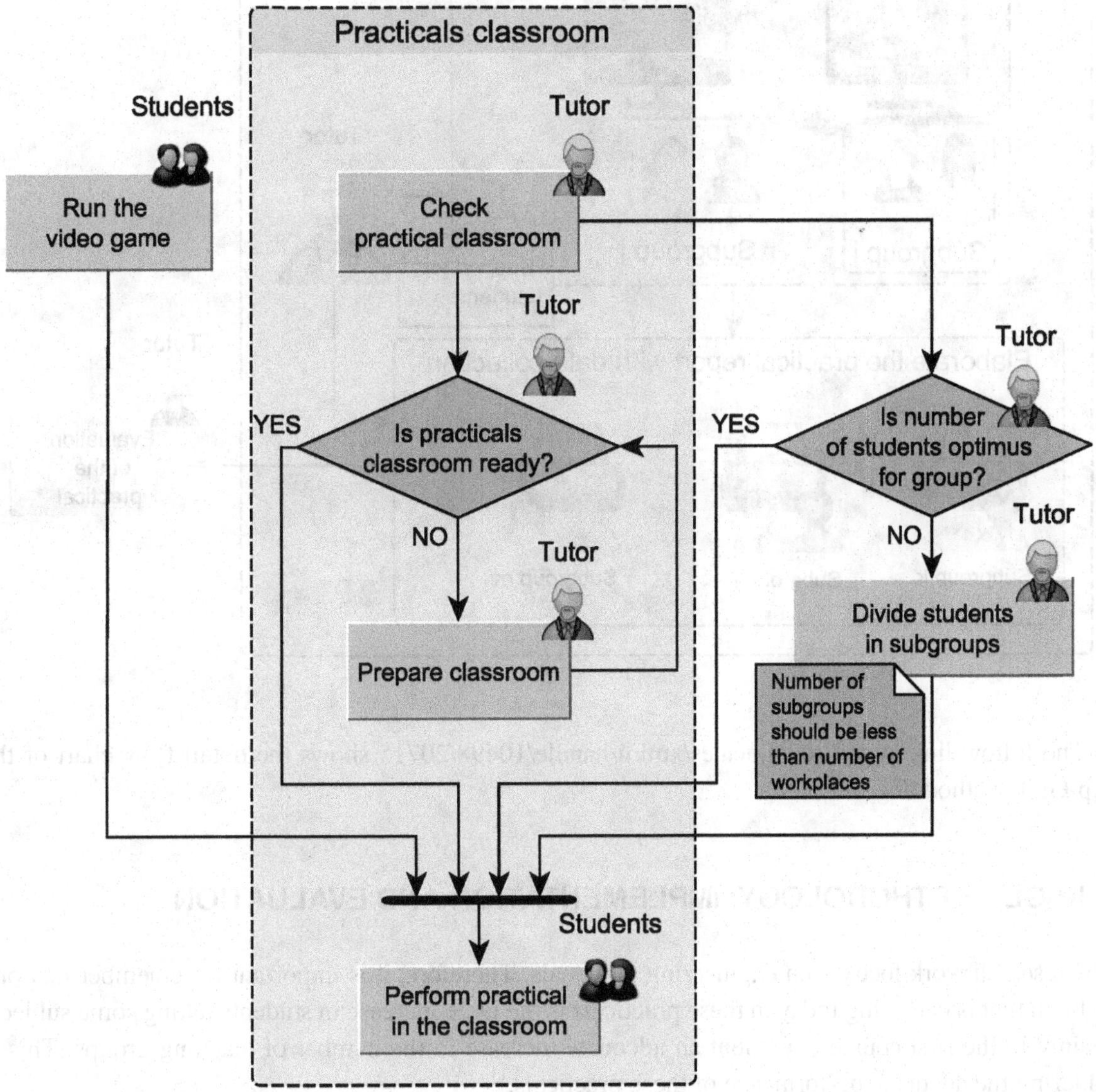

These last steps (9, 10 and 11) are shown in Figure 6.

Figure 7 shows the schematic flow chart of the Flip-GET methodology.

Figure 6. Flow chart – Practical in the classroom

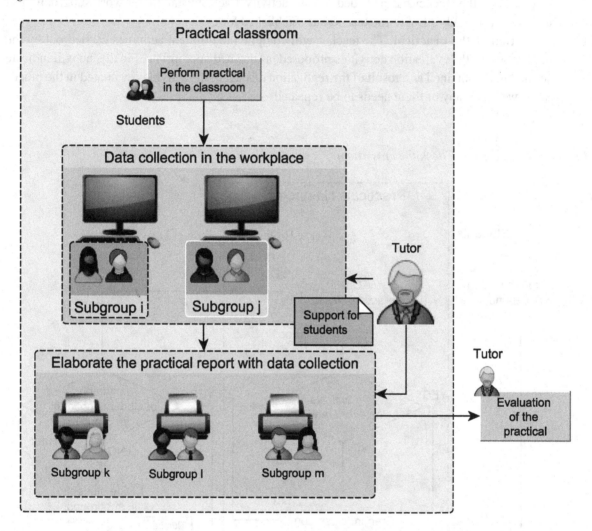

The follow link https://rodin.uca.es/xmlui/handle/10498/20715 shows the detail flow chart of the Flip-GET methodology.

FLIP-GET METHODOLOGY: IMPLEMENTATION AND EVALUATION

This research work focuses on engineering practicals. Therefore, it is important to remember that one problem that is occurring today in these practicals is the large increase in students taking some subjects (mainly in the first courses), without an adequate increase in the number of teaching groups. This is hindering the adequate performance of these practicals.

Figure 7. Schematic flow chart – Flip-GET methodology

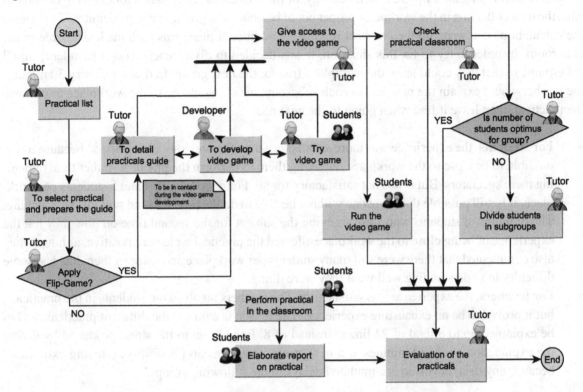

The organization of this type of practical was established in 90-minute sessions and was divided into three parts. In the first part, the teacher explains how the practical should be carried out, indicating the elements necessary to carry it out and, in some cases, explaining new concepts that are needed to be able to understand what is being done. In the second part, the students perform the practical and obtain the resulting data. In the third part, the students must produce a report on the data obtained and indicate what they have learned from the practical.

Background

The methodology used by teachers, before this research, was the following: after explaining the concepts necessary for the realization of the practical to all students, the teacher chose a student to perform the practical while others were only able to observe and perform the data collection from a distance (if they were placed near the workplace, only those in the front row would see well). Although the practical could be performed correctly, just one student performed the practical and the rest observed. Subsequently, they wrote a final report in a group, so that the individual degree of skill acquisition could not be assessed.

When the ratio per workplace is not very high, it is possible to do practicals in this way, but the problem arises when the ratio of students per workplace is very large and, consequently, students cannot do it. For this reason, as the ratio of students has increased, it has become necessary to change the way of doing practicals. Next, the steps that followed are indicated.

Before developing the Flip-GET methodology, of the 90 minutes established for carrying out practicals, the data collection in the workplace proper could be done in approximately 30 minutes. To perform the calculations and write up the practical reports, an additional place was then made available in the classroom. In order to try to fix this situation, it was decided to divide each group of students into 3 subgroups, so that they could leave the workplace free for the next group. In this way, every 30 minutes the teacher would explain the practical to each subgroup, which would go to the workplace to perform the practical, then leave it free when going to the next phase.

- **For students**, the experience was more satisfactory than the previous arrangement, because it was possible to be close to the workplace, allowing them to perform the practical, rather than remaining mere spectators. But it was not satisfactory for all. For a group with 4 and 5 students per workplace, it is still possible that someone will not be able to do the practical and will just be watching. The opinions of students who were studying the subject for the second time on how they felt the experience of being close to the workplace affected the practical were very positive, although they also commented that there were still many students per workplace and some of them had had some difficulty in understanding well what they were doing.
- **For teachers**, the experience was satisfactory. The teachers involved the students in the practicals, but it proved to be an exhausting experience. The reason is evident; the different practicals had to be explained up to a total of 24 times, instead of 8. In addition to the stress produced by giving the explanation every 30 minutes to a new group, there was no possibility of taking extra time, because any delay involved accumulated delays in the following groups.

For this reason, the teachers thought that it was necessary to redesign the way of imparting this type of practical, especially in those subjects that had the same problem. To avoid the teacher repeating the same explanation of the practical, the Flip-GET method would be used in such a way the student attended the classroom with previous training. An explanation would be given through the design of a video game, to motivate the student to pay attention. The student would have to do the practicals virtually before attending the classroom, thus being an active part of their own learning. That is when the methodology known as Flip-GET emerged.

Implementation

The subject Material Resistance was chosen for several reasons: the ratio of students/workplaces is higher than is desirable for correct performance of the practicals; in all the subjects related to this subject the same practicals are carried out; and it is taught in most engineering degrees.

Table 1 shows a summary of the data used in the different case studies, in order to give a general overview. The data collected in this table are: the objective to be achieved, if the Flip-GET methodology has been used, the number of students who did the practical, the number of subgroups into which the students were divided, and the ratio (number of students per workplace).

From here, the steps in the Flip-GET methodology described in the previous section are as follows.

1. **Choose the practical in order to implement the methodology**. In the selected subject, the practicals established are the following:

Table 1. Summary data on studies cases

Methodology		Objectives	Flip-GET	Students	Nº subgroups	Ratio
Studies cases	Case 1[1]	1	NO	202	48	4-5
	Case 2[2]	2	YES	66	18	3-4
Experimental evaluation	Control group	3	NO	33	6	5-6
	Experimental group	3	YES	26	13	2

    a.   Internal stresses in bars (3 practicals): these sessions consist of obtaining the value of the internal stresses of the bars from the deformations produced by different loads, measured with strain gauges:
        i.   Bending
        ii.   Tension
        iii.   Torsion
    b.   Buckling in bars (2 practicals):
        i.   Buckling load
        ii.   Influence of the length

From the above practicals, the first three have been selected due to their similarity in execution, and because they can be performed in the same workplace (Figure 8) and there are two units available. Once the first of the video games has been developed, the other two will be very similar.

Figure 8. Equipment FL 100 strain gauges educational system

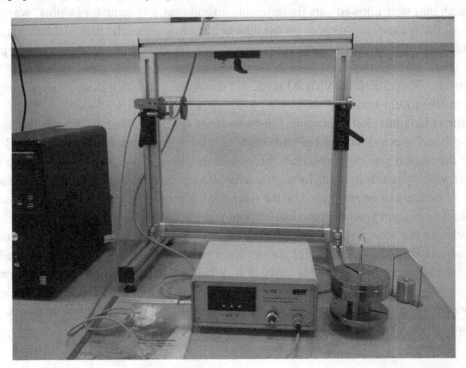

2. **Describe the content of the practical and establish the objectives**. The bending test practical consists of loading a bar with different loads, which cause internal bending stresses in the bar. In the measurement phase, there are strain gauges attached, to measure the deformations that the bar undergoes at that point, according to the different loads. After finishing the practical, the student can verify that the experimental internal stresses, which can be calculated with the data obtained by the measuring amplifier during the practical and the formulas provided in the guide, are similar to the theoretical internal stresses explained in class. Besides, they will understand better the behaviour of the elements loaded with different loads.

3. **Prepare the practical guide**. When equipment for the practicals is acquired, the selling company provides a detailed guide on its use. However, a summary for the students was elaborated.

4. **Development of the video game**. Before beginning to develop it, a flow chart of the practical was elaborated, as shown in Figure 9. The next step was to compile the necessary digital resources to include in the video game. One of them was a practical manual, summarizing the formulas that the student will need to be able to do the calculations and the final report. The student can consult this manual at any time. Finally, the evaluation was created, selecting the actions to be evaluated. Thus, once the student finishes the part of the "evaluable" video game, a final report appears, indicating whether he has performed each evaluable action correctly or has made an error.

5. **Try the video game**. The Flip-GET method proposes that the video game should be tried and tested by the developer, as well as by other people. They can detect errors and/or improvements that the developer has overlooked. In this case, the teacher had the collaboration of students who had done the practicals in person during the previous course, to give their opinion and suggestions for improvement. The development of the video games for the bending test and for the tensile test was completed.

6. **Give students access to the video game**. The final versions of the video games were uploaded to the Virtual Classroom. In order for the students to learn how to do the practical and attend the class prepared, they were allowed only five attempts. In addition, a "Forum for Doubts" was enabled. In this way, the students could check on the doubts that arose about the practical before going to the classroom. Finally, an on-line satisfaction survey was developed on the experience of performing the practical through the video game before attending the practicals classroom, and a "Forum for Comments - Suggestions for Virtual Practicals" was activated, with the aim of improving the video game in subsequent versions.

7. **Run the video game**. Before starting, the students can see the number of attempts they are allowed, the number of attempts they have already made, and the grade obtained in each attempt. In the video game, the student can see the real laboratory and should follow the conversation with the virtual teacher, who will guide him step by step on what he must do to carry out the practical properly. The guided practical can be performed by the teacher or, if the students have already played the game before, they can carry out the practical without a guide. In this case, in the first place the student must choose the necessary elements to perform the virtual practical and then the virtual teacher will indicate the data with which the student must perform it: the distance at which the hook must be located to place the load and the value of it. When the student finishes the virtual practical, he must perform the necessary calculations and produce the final report. Finally, the student can see his evaluation, which indicates the steps he has been able to perform correctly or not, as well as the time he has taken to complete the practical.

Figure 9. Flow chart – Bending test

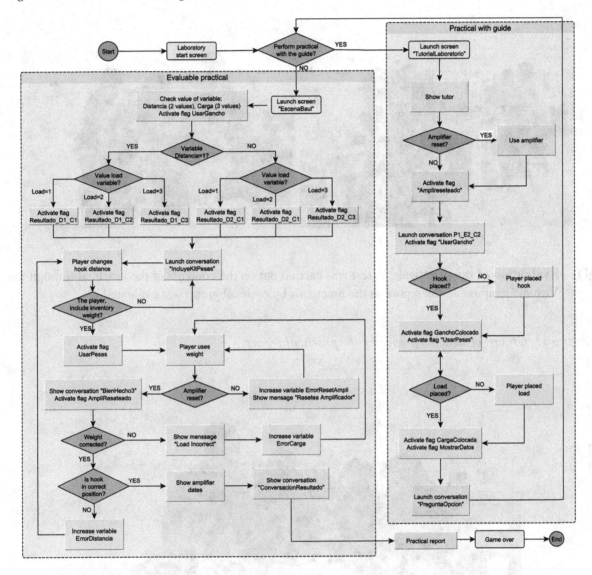

8. **Divide students into practicals subgroups**. For the practicals in question, two workplaces were available. The optimal number is 2 or 3 students per group. Due to the number of students enrolled, the students had to be divided into groups of 3/4, with a difference of 30 minutes from one to the other. Figure 10 shows the difference between 2 and 4 students per practical.

9. **Attend practicals in person**. Each practicals subgroup had a specific time. The teacher was in the classroom observing with minimal intervention. The students arrived at the classroom knowing how to perform the two practicals and they completed the data collection in 30 minutes, in comparison to the previous course where it took the same time for a single practical.

10. **Prepare the practicals report**. The students went to another part of the practicals classroom, leaving the workplace free for other classmates. Figure 11 shows a group of students writing the practical report at the tables prepared for this activity.

Figure 10. a) Groups of 2 students performing the practical b) Group of 4 students performing the practical

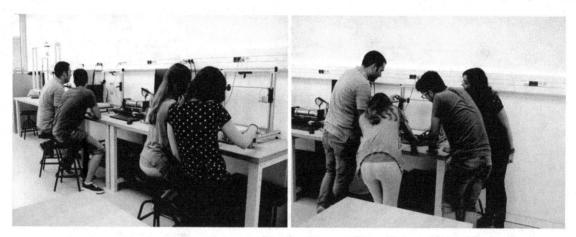

11. **Evaluation of the practicals**. A test was carried out on the contents of the practical through the Virtual Campus and the report on the practicals by each subgroup was evaluated.

Figure 11. Groups of students preparing the practical report

Evaluation

For the evaluation, two case studies have been carried out. In each case, the results obtained are shown and analysed. In order to check that the sample of selected individuals does not present a bias, two known variables have been used: the students were differentiated by gender, and the students who were performing the practicals for the first time were differentiated from the rest.

It is important to take into account, in the case studies described below, that the methodology was new for the students.

1. **Case 1. Without Flip-GET**. In each group of practicals, the students were divided into 3 subgroups, with the main objective that all students could perform the practical. In this academic course they had to take an individual test on the concepts used in the contents of the practicals, obtaining an average score of 6.8 out of 10. No difference can be seen by either gender or repeaters (Figure 12). If a hypothesis test is made, assuming that the average score of the repeating students must be higher than that of the students who are doing the practical for the first time, with a confidence level of 95%, it gives a p-value = 0.5693, in a confidence interval (-Inf, + 0.5068836). There is no evidence that the average grade of the students who had completed the practicals the previous year was higher than that of the new students. After this analysis, there is evidence that dividing students into small groups makes the practicals more effective.

2. **Case 2. With Flip-GET**. In this case, the Flip-GET methodology was applied. The result of the performance of the practicals through the video game, called Virtual Practical 1 (PV_1) and Virtual Practical 2 (PV_2), is shown in Table 2. It is observed that there is no significant difference between the types of students, or if the students are differentiated by gender. However, it is observed that the average grade for PV_2 is higher than for PV_1. This may be due to the fact that the students have already become familiar with the methodology, executing the video game with greater security and paying more attention to what is explained in it. In order to verify that the improvement in the students' mark in the second practical was statistically significant, a t-test was performed for paired samples, establishing a confidence level of 95% ($\alpha = 0.05$), where the p-value = 0.006127 <<< 0.05, so the null hypothesis of equality of the average of PV_1 and PV_2 is rejected. It can be said that there is evidence that playing the video game helped the students to do the second practical.

3. **Experimental evaluation**: For the third course, the teacher chose to combine the experience of the previous two courses. In order to compare the results, one group is for control, and the other one is experimental. The students were randomly divided into two groups, so that the control group performed the practical in the classroom, without using the Flip-GET methodology. Then, the video game was published in the Virtual Classroom, so that the students of the experimental group could play the video game before attending the classroom. Of the 40 students that remained after the filter done according to the previous criteria, 20 belonged to the control group and the other 20 to the experimental group. On this occasion, students in both the control group and the experimental group carried out the test on the subject individually, to guarantee that each student carried out his own test. Table 3 shows the average grade and the dispersion obtained by the students, differentiating it by the two groups. In this table it can be observed that the average score of the students in the control group was lower than that of the experimental group, while the dispersion was higher. To check if the improvement in the students' score in the experimental group was statistically significant, a t-test was performed for paired samples, establishing a confidence level of 95% (α

= 0.05), where the p-value = 0.1745, for a confidence interval (-Inf, + 0.360272). Because the score of the experimental group is within the range, the null hypothesis of equality of the mean of the two groups cannot be rejected. Figure 13 shows the box-plot diagram of the obtained score, differentiating it by group, in which the existence of atypical data is appreciated. Eliminating the atypical data that appear in the box-plot diagram and doing the t test again, establishing the same confidence level, 95% (α = 0.05), the p-value = 0.05638 and the confidence interval is (-Inf, + 0.024876). Now the null hypothesis can be rejected, since the p-value is outside the confidence interval, and considering that the average score of the experimental group is higher than the mean score of the control group.

Figure 12. Percentage of students who pass/fail the test

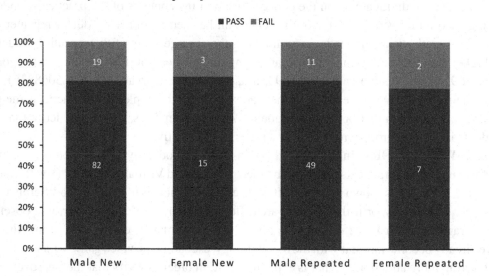

Finally, to check whether the higher average score in the test of the experimental group is obtained because it is made up of those who have obtained the best mark in the subject, the results of the test on the practical have been compared with the marks of the students in the subject. Table 4 shows these data and they are represented in Figure 14. It is observed that the number of students passing the subject is concentrated in the control group; in turn, in the experimental group, it is observed that almost all the students have passed the test, without having passed the subject.

Table 2. Average score/standard deviation of PV_1 and 2

Types of students	Average score							
Gender	Novel		Repeater		TOTAL		Standard deviation	
	PV_1	PV_2	PV_1	PV_2	PV_1	PV_2	PV_1	PV_2
Male	7.2	8.7	7.9	7.9	7.4	8.5	2.5299	1.4852
Female	7.4	8.3	6.0	8.8	7.0	8.3	2.1032	1.4428
TOTAL	7.3	8.5	7.1	8.3	7.2	8.4	2.3270	1.4450

Table 3. *Average score of the test*

Group	Average score	Standard deviation
Control	6.63	1.5937
Experimental	7.09	1.4925
TOTAL General	6.86	1.5419

Table 4. *Number of students who pass/fail the test - pass/fail the subject*

Test Subject	Control		Experimental		TOTAL
	Pass	**Fail**	**Pass**	**Fail**	
Pass subject exam	6	2	1	1	**10**
Fail subject exam	10	1	12	-	**23**
Subject exam not taken	1	-	5	1	**7**
TOTAL General	17	3	18	2	**40**

Figure 13. *Box-plot diagram – Score of practical per group*

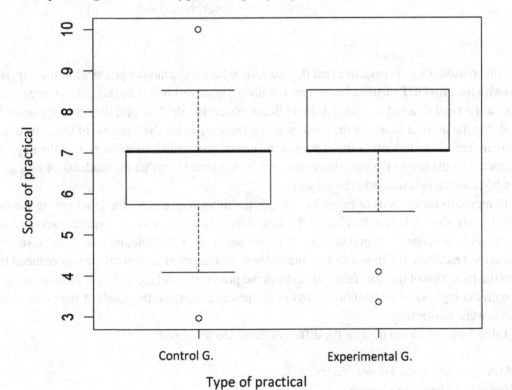

Figure 14. Number of students who pass/fail the test - pass/fail the subject

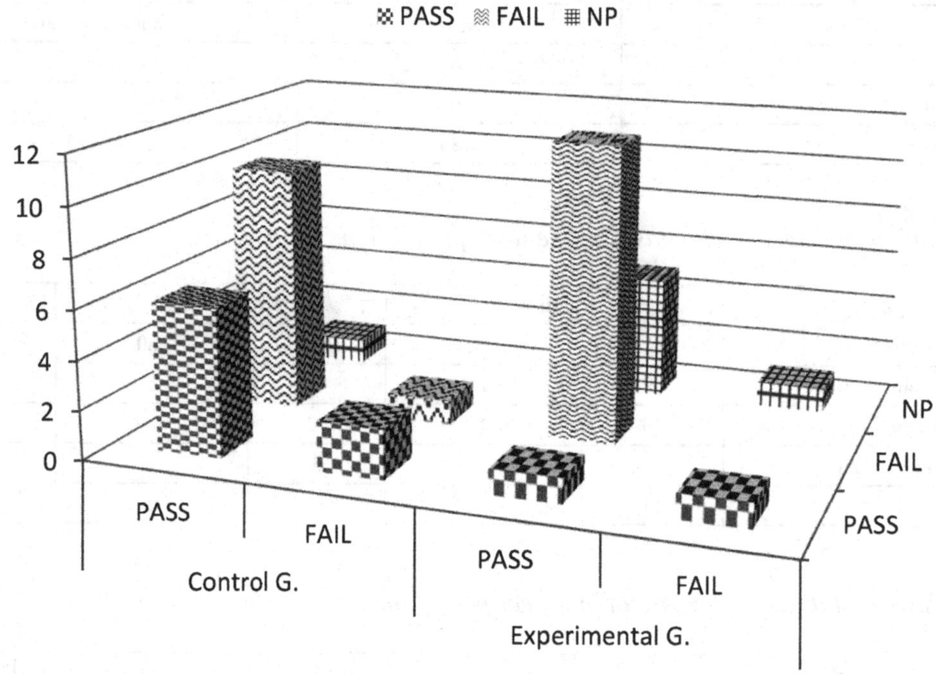

For this reason, there is evidence that the students who have done the practical in the experimental group (with the Flip-GET methodology) have obtained a good result in the practical test, even those who did not sit the final exam of the subject. In addition, observing the box-plot diagram of Figure 15, it is verified that the average score for the final exam on the subject for the students of the control group is higher than that of the students of the experimental group, so it cannot be deduced that the improvement in the marks for the test of the experimental group is due to the fact that the students of said group are those who have the best marks in the subject.

With regard to the analysis of times, in Table 5, the times required for the practicals in the different case studies are shown. When the Flip-GET methodology is introduced, the practical sessions reduced from 6 hours (4 sessions of 90 minutes) to 4 hours (2 sessions of 120 minutes). In other words, to carry out the same practicals, the time spent by the students in the practical classroom was reduced by 33%. Despite the reduction of the time taken to perform the practicals, and the different evaluations that were made with the methodology, both the results of the practical test and the result of the evaluation of the practicals were satisfactory.

In Table 5 the following data on the different cases are presented:

- Average score in the knowledge test.
- Ratio of students per workplace.
- Time spent in the classroom for one of the practicals. It must be remembered that of the 4 practicals that are currently part of the subject, this experiment was done with only 2.
- Number of times that the teacher had to repeat the explanation of the practical to the different subgroups, for a group officially established by the institution.

Figure 15. Box-plot diagram - Score groups/subjects

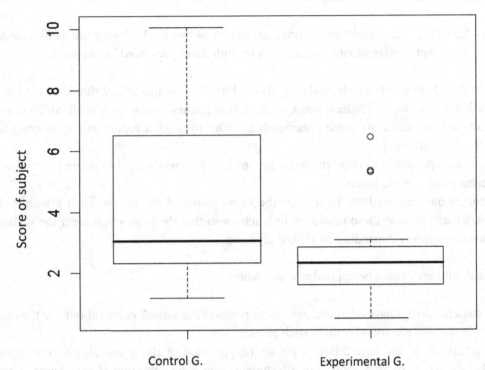

Table 5. Collection of time data in the different cases

Group Methodology	Case 1				Case 2				Experimental Evaluation			
	Score	Ratio	Time (min.)	N° (Rep)	Score	Ratio	Time (min.)	N° (Rep)	Score	Ratio	Time (min.)	N° (Rep)
Without Flip-GET	6.8	4-5	90	3	-	-	-	-	6.6	5-6	60	2
With Flip-GET	-	-	-	-	8.4	3-4	60	-	7.1	2	60	-

For the case in which the Flip-GET methodology was not implemented, Case 1, it is observed that the average score is similar. This cannot be compared with the average grade of Case 2, with the Flip-GET methodology, where the students had done the practical with the same methodology in the Experimental Evaluation, because in Case 2 very few students took the test. The sample could not be considered representative, although the score is quite good. However, if we compare the score between the students in the Experimental Evaluation, there is an improvement in the score. Therefore, it seems that the Flip-GET methodology can help improve efficiency, because they can be developed in less time with better results for the students.

SOLUTIONS AND RECOMMENDATIONS

In order to determine if the results of the implementation of this methodology are as expected, it must be borne in mind that similar situations must concur with those presented in this work:

- The practicals in which it is desired to apply the Flip-GET methodology should be similar to those described in this work. Students must work with machines and/or tools with which they have to collect data and calculate some parameters in order to make a report and/or an analysis of the results of the practical.
- It should be possible to divide the work groups into subgroups, and to rotate the students in the different phases of the practical.
- Resources must be available to develop the video games of the practicals. If possible, the institution should provide these resources to teachers so that they can implement the methodology, without completely depending on their daily work.

This methodology cannot be applied in cases where:

- The students do not have adequate devices to perform the virtual practical outside the classroom, or the institution cannot offer them such resources.
- The practicals do not have different phases (explanation of the practical, data collection in the workplace, etc.), so that subgroups of students can rotate through these phases during their realization.

The main threat to the validity is that there is not a representative sample of university teachers: all the professors who attended a seminar in which the methodology was explained to them were actively interested in introducing the new methodologies in the classroom. It is currently unknown if another teacher profile would be interested in the implementation of this methodology in their practicals, where the involvement of the teacher in implementing the methodology is essential.

As a threat to internal validity, it is important to have in mind that the development of the video game must be well designed and appropriate for the practicals. First, a specific technology has been used to create video games prepared for conversational adventures, but there are other technologies, in 3D, for instance, Augmented Reality (AR) [3], which is expected to find great acceptance by students. In addition, when implementing the Flip-GET methodology, several changes have been introduced in the way of carrying out the practicals. These changes should be implemented, one by one, to see the influence of each of them and to verify the benefit that every change provides.

In relation to the threats to external validity, the methodology has been implemented in a specific degree course. For this reason, this methodology should be implemented in other degree courses, with other types of students in the classrooms, and even in other studies in the field of STEM. In addition, in this case, the methodology has been implemented in a subject that is taught in almost all engineering studies. Another threat is that the amortization (depreciation) will not be the same for subjects that are not so widespread in engineering studies. To mitigate this threat, collaboration could be sought with other institutions that teach this subject and are interested in implementing the Flip-GET methodology.

FUTURE RESEARCH DIRECTIONS

During the realization of the present work some challenges have been tackled and successfully overcome. However, with each of these challenges new ones have been emerging: some of them could lead to interesting future works and others could complement different aspects of this work.

The most important could be handled in the short term, as discussed below.

- Implement the Flip-GET methodology in other subjects related to this subject, in order to have a more representative sample of results. Furthermore, with a larger and more diverse sample, the motivation of the students could be measured.
- Apply the Flip-GET methodology to secondary studies, in the STEM disciplines, to increase the external validity of the results with other groups, in another context and/or with other subjects.
- Develop the video games in other languages, with the objective that the students acquire transversal linguistic competence as well as being able to increase the external validity by implementing it in foreign universities.
- Develop another methodology, similar to Flip-GET, to apply to the classes of problems of engineering studies, with the aim that students can acquire skills related to the PBL.

CONCLUSION

In the previous sections the starting points of this work have been presented: the use of SG and FC applied to engineering studies. From there, the Flip-GET methodology has been developed, and it has been implemented in different case studies and has been evaluated.

Hypotheses were raised on aspects such as: if the practicals are sustainable for the teachers who teach them; if they are effective for the students; if a new methodology would improve the effectiveness of the practicals; if implementing this new methodology improves the motivation of students and teachers; and if the methodology helps the development of the competences of the subject.

From the results of the evaluation carried out, the Flip-GET methodology seems to be an effective proposal to complement traditional teaching processes, since it provides several advantages related to the development of activities and improves the acquisition of skills by students.

In particular, the following conclusions can be highlighted:

- After considering the results, it is not possible to conclude that the practicals (without the methodology) are sustainable for the teachers who teach them. It has been verified that the implementation of the methodology improves the effectiveness of the teacher, who does not have to explain the practicals continuously, in addition to which the practicals are carried out in less time. This time could be used to perform more practicals or reduce the total time required for the practicals and could be used for the acquisition of other skills. Apart from that, the Flip-GET methodology has been implemented without significantly increasing the effort on the part of the institution or the teacher.
- The authors cannot conclude that the practicals (before the methodology) were effective for the students. Nevertheless, after its implementation, the methodology improved the effectiveness for

the students: it was possible to reduce the number of students per work group and they performed them in the classroom using less time.

- Because the Flip-GET methodology involves teachers heavily, the methodology has been presented through a seminar to other university teachers, attended by teachers of STEM studies and language studies. To conclude, there is evidence that implementing this methodology motivates teachers, since 80% of the teachers who attended the seminar responded that they would be willing to implement the methodology in their classes and 20% would do so with some variations to adapt it to the subject that they teach.

- Finally, the results reveal a positive trend from the educational point of view. The students who used the Flip-GET methodology obtained better results than those who acquired the same competences through the traditional procedure. So it can be concluded that implementing this methodology helps to improve the development of the competences of the subject.

In view of these results, there is evidence that the Flip-GET methodology can solve some of the problems detected in engineering practical classes, so it is expected that its application in other subjects with similar practicals to those shown in this work can become a reality.

REFERENCES

Adam, M., Vallés, R., & Rodríguez, G. (2013). E-learning: Características y evaluación. *Ensayos de Economía*, *43*, 143–159.

Cabero, A., Llorente, C., & Puentes, Á. (2010). La satisfacción de los estudiantes en red en la formación semipresencial. *Comunicar*, *18*(35), 149–157.

Chen, X., & Soldner, M. (2013). *STEM Attrition: College students' path into and out of STEM fields*. National Center for Education Statistics 2014–001. Retrieved from http://necs.ed.gov

Connolly, T., Boyle, E., MacArthur, E., Hainey, T., & Boyle, J. M. (2012). A systematic literature review of empirical evidence on computer games and serious games. *Computers & Education*, *59*(2), 661–686. doi:10.1016/j.compedu.2012.03.004

Felder, R., & Silverman, L. (1988). Learning and teaching styles in engineering education. *Engineering Education*, *78*(June), 674–681. doi:10.1109/FIE.2008.4720326

Fonseca Escudero, D., Conde-González, M. Á., & García-Peñalvo, F. J. (2018). Improving the information society skills: Is knowledge accessible for all? *Universal Access in the Information Society*, *17*(2), 229–245. doi:10.100710209-017-0548-6

Freeman, S., Eddy, S. L., McDonough, M., Smith, M. K., Okoroafor, N., Jordt, H., & Wenderoth, M. P. (2014). Active learning increases student performance in science, engineering, and mathematics. *Proceedings of the National Academy of Sciences of the USA*, *111*, 8410–8415. 10.1073/pnas.1319030111

Godfrey, E., Aubrey, T., & King, R. (2013). Who leaves and who stays? Retention and attrition in engineering education. *Engineering Education*, *5*(2), 26–40. doi:10.11120/ened.2010.05020026

Hsu, W.-C., & Lin, H.-C. K. (2016). Impact of Applying WebGL Technology to Develop a Web Digital Game-Based Learning System for Computer Programming Course in Flipped Classroom. In *2016 International Conference on Educational Innovation through Technology* (pp. 64–69). IEEE. 10.1109/EITT.2016.20

Kamp, A. (2014). *Engineering Education in the Rapidly Changing World: Rethinking the Mission and Vision on Engineering Education at TU Delft*. TU Delft, Faculty of Aerospace Engineering. Retrieved from http://repository.tudelft.nl/assets/uuid:522e149d-3fe8-4a0e-8199-eab76297478c/310918.pdf

Koper, R., Olivier, B., & Anderson, T. (2003). *IMS Learning Design Information Model*. Retrieved from http://www.imsglobal.org/learningdesign/ldv1p0/imsld_infov1p0.htm

López-Pérez, M. V., Pérez-López, M. C., & Rodríguez-Ariza, L. (2011). Blended learning in higher education: Students' perceptions and their relation to outcomes. *Computers & Education, 56*(3), 818–826. doi:10.1016/j.compedu.2010.10.023

Merrill, M. D. (1990). Constructivism and Instructional Design. *Educational Technology, 31*(5), 45–53.

Mikropoulos, T. A., & Natsis, A. (2011). Educational virtual environments: A ten-year review of empirical research (1999–2009). *Computers & Education, 56*(3), 769–780. doi:10.1016/j.compedu.2010.10.020

Minovic, M., García-Peñalvo, F. J., & Kearney, N. A. (2016). Gamification in engineering education. *International Journal of Engineering Education, 32*(1B), 308–309.

Molina-Carmona, R., Satorre-Cuerda, R., Villagrá-Arnedo, C., & Compañ-Rosique, P. (2017). Training Socially Responsible Engineers by Developing Accessible Video Games. In *International Conference on Learning and Collaboration Technologies*. (pp. 182-201). Springer. 10.1007/978-3-319-58515-4_15

Prensky, M. (2006). *Don't Bother Me Mom: I'm learning*. M. P. House.

Prensky, M. (2012). *From digital natives to digital wisdom: Hopeful essays for 21st century learning* CRC Press. doi:10.4135/9781483387765

Rajalingam, P. (2011). *Patterns within problem-based learning: how a prior mathematics failure affects engineering diploma students* (Doctoral dissertation). Monash University.

Rennie, F., & Morrison, T. (2013). *E-learning and social networking handbook: Resources for higher education*. Routledge. doi:10.4324/9780203120279

Sánchez i Peris, F. J. (2015). Gamificación. *Education in the Knowledge Society, 16*(2), 13–15. doi:10.14201/eks20151621315

Sein-Echaluce, M. L., Fidalgo-Blanco, Á., & García-Peñalvo, F. J. (2017). Trabajo en equipo y Flip Teaching para mejorar el aprendizaje activo del alumnado. In *IV Congreso Internacional sobre Aprendizaje, Innovación y Competitividad* (pp. 610-615). Academic Press. 10.26754/CINAIC.2017.000001_129

Silvio, J. (2010). La virtualización de la educación superior: Alcances, posibilidades y limitaciones. *Educación Superior y Sociedad, 9*(1), 27–50.

Thirouard, M., Pidol, L., & Duret, P. (2017). The Use of Flipped Classroom and Gamification in Applied Powertrain Related Programs. In *International Conference New Perspectives in Science Education* (pp. 243–248). Academic Press.

Toto, R., & Nguyen, H. N. H. (2009). Flipping the Work Design in an industrial engineering course. In *39th IEEE Frontiers in Education Conference* (pp. 1–4). IEEE. 10.1109/FIE.2009.5350529

Ulicsak, M. (2010). Games in Education: Serious Games. *A FutureLab Literature Review*, *139*. Retrieved from http://www.futurelab.org.uk/projects/games-in-education

Ye, S.-H., Hsiao, T.-Y., & Sun, C.-T. (2018). Using commercial video games in flipped classrooms to support physical concept construction. *Journal of Computer Assisted Learning*, *34*(5), 602–614. doi:10.1111/jcal.12267

ADDITIONAL READING

Ertmer, P. A., Quinn, J. A., & Glazewski, K. D. (2017). *The ID casebook: Case studies in instructional design*. Routledge. doi:10.4324/9780203701041

Fidalgo-Blanco, Á., Martinez-Nuñez, M., Borrás-Gene, O., & Sánchez-Medina, J. J. (2017). Micro flip teaching - An innovative model to promote the active involvement of students. *Computers in Human Behavior*, *72*, 713–723. doi:10.1016/j.chb.2016.07.060

Fidalgo-Blanco, Á., Sein-Echaluce, M. L., & García-Peñalvo, F. J. (2017). APFT: Active Peer-Based Flip Teaching. In *Fifth International Conference on Technological Ecosystems for Enhancing Multiculturality* (TEEM'17) (Cádiz, Spain, October 18-20, 2017) (pp. Article 83). ACM.

Fishman, B., Dede, C., & Means, B. (2016). Teaching and technology: New tools for new times. In D. H. Gitomer & C. A. Bell (Eds.), *Handbook of Research on Teaching*. American Educational Research Association. doi:10.3102/978-0-935302-48-6_21

García-Peñalvo, F. J., Fidalgo-Blanco, Á., Sein-Echaluce Lacleta, M., & Conde-González, M. Á. (2016). Cooperative Micro Flip Teaching. In *P. Zaphiris & I. Ioannou (Eds.), Learning and Collaboration Technologies. Third International Conference, LCT 2016*, Held as Part of HCI International 2016, Toronto, ON, Canada, July 17-22, 2016, Proceedings (pp. 14-24).

Ibáñez, M. B., & Delgado-Kloos, C. (2018). Augmented reality for STEM learning: A systematic review. *Computers & Education*, *123*, 109–123. doi:10.1016/j.compedu.2018.05.002

Murphy, M., Redding, S., & Twyman, J. (Eds.). (2014). *The Handbook on Innovations in Learning*. IAP.

Oshima, J., Oshima, R., & Matsuzawa, Y. (2012). Knowledge Building Discourse Explorer: A social network analysis application for knowledge building discourse. *Educational Technology Research and Development*, *60*(5), 903–921. doi:10.100711423-012-9265-2

Van den Akker, J. (1999). Principles and methods of development research. In *Design approaches and tools in education and training* (pp. 1–14). Springer Netherlands. doi:10.1007/978-94-011-4255-7_1

Vlachopoulos, D., & Makri, A. (2017). The effect of games and simulations on higher education: A systematic literature review. *International Journal of Educational Technology in Higher Education*, *14*(1), 22. doi:10.118641239-017-0062-1

KEY TERMS AND DEFINITIONS

Augmented Reality: The integration of digital information with the user's environment in real time. Unlike virtual reality, which creates a totally artificial environment, augmented reality uses the existing environment and overlays new information on top of it.

B-Learning: Also known as blended learning or mixed learning, consists of combining virtual and face-to-face teaching.

Flipped Classroom: A methodology that consists of having the students start the learning work outside the classroom, so that class time is used to facilitate and enhance other processes of knowledge acquisition and practical in the classroom.

Instructional Design: The process by which learning products and experiences are designed, developed, and delivered, as well as the necessary materials, with the objective of helping the student to develop the necessary capacity to achieve certain tasks.

Learning Experience: Refers to any interaction, course, program, or other experience in which learning takes place, whether it occurs in traditional academic settings or non-traditional settings, or whether it includes traditional educational interactions or non-traditional interactions.

Serious Game: A game designed for a primary purpose other than pure entertainment. The *serious* adjective is generally prepended to refer to video games used by industries like education and engineering. The idea shares aspects with simulation generally, including flight simulation and medical simulation, but explicitly emphasizes the added pedagogical value of fun and competition.

Simulation: An approximate imitation of the operation of a process or system; the act of simulating requires first the development of a model. This model is a well-defined description of the simulated subject and represents its key characteristics, such as its behavior, functions and abstract or physical properties. The model represents the system itself, whereas the simulation represents its operation over time.

Virtual Learning Environments: Used for teaching e-learning, where the teacher takes over the role of counsellor and media designer, while the student becomes the protagonist of the training process.

ENDNOTES

[1]   Before developing Flip-GET.
[2]   All students using Flip-GET.
[3]   At present, the authors are beginning to prepare video games with Augmented Reality (AR). There is not yet enough data to draw conclusions.

This research was previously published in Innovative Trends in Flipped Teaching and Adaptive Learning; pages 77-109, copyright year 2019 by Information Science Reference (an imprint of IGI Global).

Chapter 42
Educational Games as Software Through the Lens of Designing Process

Mifrah Ahmad
ⓘ https://orcid.org/0000-0002-7908-6657
Deakin University, Australia

ABSTRACT

Educational games (EG) as learning software have become more dominant in the educational industry and have gained immense popularity. However, a constant battle between designing an EG that combines fun and educational content in delivering learning objective is a prominent challenge through the designing phase for various stakeholders involved, especially game designers. This chapter discusses three major contributions to game design fundamentals and principles and unpacks their concepts on designing EG. Moreover, an in-depth discussion of game design models/frameworks is understood. This analysis highlights issues and problems raised through the gaps existing between models/frameworks against them. This chapter proposes a combined prototyping process adopted from the discussion and emphasizes aspects required in documenting game design. With the process documented and aligned, game designers will be able to reflect a better understanding of a game design process in the industry.

INTRODUCTION

Over the past decade, educational games (EG) as learning software and the usage of game-based learning (GBL) has become more commonly used for educational deliverance, as opposed to pure entertainment, has gained immense popularity. With that, reports discussing both positive and negative impacts on usage of GBL in education and variety of ways in which the learning outcomes have been achieved. A constant battle between designing an EG that is a combination of fun and educational in delivering learning objective is a prominent challenge through an implementation phase for designers (Azadegan et al., 2014; Romero, 2015; Serrano-Laguna, Manero, Freire, & Fernández-Manjón, 2018). Games-based learning (GBL) is a pedagogical approach that utilizes EGs to support learning (Prensky, 2003). As explained,

DOI: 10.4018/978-1-6684-7589-8.ch042

GBL utilizes an appropriate set of game mechanics (the rules of EG), provides freedom for learners to recreate scenarios without having a fear of adverse reactions, and provides a problem-oriented learning process to allow learners achieve learning goals in the EG (Poulsen, 2011).

The guidelines for designing an educational computer program including (games) and make learning with computers exciting and motivating have proven to be captivating (Malone, 1983). Malone (1983) provides a checklist for designing enjoyable educational programs that include: (1) challenge (goal, uncertain outcome) (2)fantasy, (3) Curiosity (sensory curiosity and cognitive curiosity). Despite the consideration of multiple challenges discussed in this work, Malone (1983) does conclude that the capabilities of computers in making learning exciting and engaging, but designing those learning tools (games) is undoubtedly tricky when programming is considered. This shows one of the very first groundbreaking guidelines provided in educational games creating as a checklist and the consideration of programming, which leads to its relevance with game designers and designing EG. As Malone (1983) mentioned the importance of constructive feedback provided to the players, a later study painted a flow of transformation of the computer from a "work" tool to directly linking towards children, learning, and play (Ito, 2009). Ito (2009) described three main genres with descript towards academic achievements, software designed to support school content, allow children to be a part of the designed software, and lastly, engaged and explore the construction and instruction of the possibilities of using digital media. The third genre draws upon 'construction' where an emphasis on empowering kids in creating their artifacts through interactivity with the software and technology, but the work is limited to 5thD:' a system where children play a diverse range of educational software in an informal afterschool setting.' Noticeably, it doesn't focus on how to achieve the negotiation between designers, children, industries, media, or education; however, it is useful for current 21st-century digital media and the impact it has on children's learning.

Despite the research has managed to accomplish a large range of EGs that has delivered its function successfully, there have been many EGs that have reported to be a failure or unsuccessful. It is definite that game designers do not create replicas of the games that are well-recognized. With that, recent articles published has addressed the rising tension between stakeholders of the game designing process, i.e. game designers, teachers, developers, learners, students, players. Designers are required to enhance the educational tools by integrating game elements and core concepts to maximize the tools' effectiveness, to increase the possibilities of achieving learning outcomes, levels of engagement and motivation (Kalmpourtzis, 2018; Schell, 2008). Not only that, designing EG required multiple consideration of multiple stakeholders such as game designers, developers, educators, teachers, and software engineers.

Understanding the game design is a complex job. As defined: *"Design is a process by which a designer creates a context to be encountered by a participant, and from which meaning emerges"*(Zimmerman & Salen, 2004, p. 41). With game design (GD) defined a variety of game design elements and learning theories that establish and define an EG. Table 1 for examples of game design elements that are crucial (Shi & Shih, 2015). Similarly, GD is equipped with learning characteristic that adds the value of providing a good learning experience to learners. Some of the characteristics are learning outcomes, usability, user's experience, motivation, engagement, game design, user satisfaction, usefulness, understandability, performance, playability, pedagogical aspects, efficacy, social impact, cognitive behavior, enjoyment, acceptance and user interface (de Aguiar, Winn, Cezarotto, Battaiola, & Gomes, 2018; Lameras et al., 2017; Wouters & van Oostendorp, 2017). The innovative learning approach derived from EG possesses educational values or even different kinds of software applications that compile into knowledgeable aspects such as teaching enhancement, assessments, and evaluation of learner (Tang & Hanneghan, 2010).

Table 1. Game design elements and their definitions

Elements	Description
Game goals	Game designer provides what type of experience for players pursue game goals
Game mechanism	Refers to the methods prompting players to achieve the designer goals and enables smooth functioning of the virtual worlds
Interaction	Player operations that trigger the computer to generate related responses, including the interactions and conflicts between players and computers.
Freedom	An open game system that allows for player autonomy, including individual services such as the avatar.
Game fantasy	Refers to the environmental context that provides virtual world imagery
Narrative	Describes what occurs in the virtual worlds
Sensation	Multimedia presentation of the virtual worlds
Game value	Promotes players to increase their game motivation
Challenges	Refers to player efforts towards the game or personal goals
Sociality	The interaction between people through the game system including communication, cooperation, competition, and conflict
Mystery	Refers to providing a novel experience for players, including curiosity and exploration.

Source: (Shi & Shih, 2015)

Game-based learning (GBL) has been defined by identifying its principles and mechanisms (Perrotta, Featherstone, Aston, & Houghton, 2013). The principles target intrinsic motivation, learning through ''fun,'' authenticity (i.e., contextualized learning), self-reliance/autonomy, and experiential learning. Mechanisms include rules, clear but challenging goals, fantasy, progressive levels of difficulty, interactivity, player control, uncertainty, feedback, and a social element. This study focuses on the definition of GBL defined by Perrotta (2013) as it involves game mechanics that related to game design aspects. As mentioned by Perrotta (2013), studies on GBL usually focus on secondary school. This may be because of the fact that there is a little consensus between researchers and among teachers as to how games could be used for educational purposes. GBL is specifically designed to teach specific concepts or to strengthen competencies. There exist a broad scope of games including digital and non-digital ones (All, Castellar, & Van Looy, 2016; Connolly, Stansfield, & Hainey, 2009; Dondlinger, 2007; Selwyn, 2014). Digital games are developed for use in smartphones, computers, tablets, etc., whereas non-digital games exploring the use of resources such as boards, cards, pencils and papers (Connolly et al., 2009).

For GBL designing process to be effective and reliable, it is vital to provide emphasis on involving theoretical foundations with game rules, and fun with authentic learning for learners, thus, providing a precise base for learners to gain knowledge (Hays, 2005; Kebritchi & Hirumi, 2008; Schell, 2008). Hence, researchers propose theoretical frameworks for designing EG for insights between theoretical and designer's perspective. This can also be enhanced through understanding the software designer's perspective in software engineering through the established life-cycle method following strict instructions to ensure product satisfactorily. According to the prominent contributors (Kalmpourtzis, 2018; Schell, 2008; Zimmerman & Salen, 2004) in discussing educational games design, game designers reflect on a variety of concepts throughout their designing phase. When the game designers initiate the designing of EG, challenges occur in terms of planning from gathered requirements, verifying or prototyping, and cross-checking the initially designed requirements to ensure consistency and reliability. This is due to a mixture of pedagogical aspects, educational principles, motivational elements as well as game designer's own experience that influences the designing process. Combining the software designing procedures, along with educational game designing fundamental and the pedagogical concepts have challenges and issues due to its large interdisciplinary conflicts.

The objective of this chapter is to comprehend and compare a series of game design models/frameworks for designing EGs and reflect their practicality to game design fundamentals and principles established in prominent books by leading game designers/scholars: (1) *The art of Game design (Schell, 2008)*, (2) *Rules of Play: Game Design Fundamentals (Zimmerman & Salen, 2004)*, and (3) *Educational Game design Fundamentals* by Kalmpourtzis (2018). With that, the discussion on how software engineers focus on the design process of software and documentation requirements to track the crucial steps will also be compared in terms of educational game design. Therefore, this chapter attempts to provide a holistic idea based on how theoretical frameworks/models consume game design fundamentals established and how the collaboration between the designing process of EG and software design can provide a promising impression. Lastly, future direction and recommendations provide an understanding of the current approach in research for game designers, teachers, educators and software engineers.

BACKGROUND

This section mainly attempts to highlight the fundamentals/principles of educational game design through the lens of three established books on game design fundamentals (please note that due to page limitations, the author was unable to include more research). Then, a series of published models and frameworks (from 2015 to 2018) for designing EG are studied.

Observation by leading game designers, the essence of a "game" is a problem-solving or a puzzle-solving with which competence is developed through a trial-and-error and exploration learning practice (Koster, 2013; Schell, 2008). Players choose from the choices they experience in real-world and learn from those actions and feedback provided by the game, leading to an interactive learning experience. EG's remarkable motivational power includes challenges that thrills and excites players, teaches and master achievements, "It is the act of solving puzzles that makes games fun. In other words, with games, learning is the drug" (Koster, 2013, p. 40). A recent study where GBL approaches were used to enhance learning through a cross-disciplinary integrative approach; however, the key challenge is producing an effective educational game design which allows an equal balance between game playability and fun, along with the learning outcomes of the assessment of GBL (de Freitas, 2018). To find the balance between game playability and fun, and having a solid game design that is aligned with the learning outcomes of the assessment or course content, is also a challenge.

Educational Game Design Fundamentals

B.U.G designer Salen and Eric Zimmerman (CEO of the game-design studio gameLab) in *Rules of Play: Game Design Fundamentals (2004)*. "Meaningful Play" is the most crucial concept that combines actions (descriptive) and outcomes(evaluative) within a magic circle to add the emotional experience of playing games through a game system (Zimmerman & Salen, 2004, p. 27). The book evolves the discussion of game design through three major schemas in which the knowledge is organized and frames: **rules** (formal game design essential for logical and structures of game), **play** (experiential, social and representational that foregrounds the player's participation with the game and others), and **culture** (contextual design engaging larger contexts in which the games are designed and player). Consequently, proceeds on explaining the schemas in the form of a system where the elaboration on an organized system, human experience, and engagement within the context of the system was discussed in depth.

Games as a "system" contain elements such as objects, attributes, internal relationships and environment; that can be easily framed according to any game. The key concept of how the system is constructed and designed to create meaning that can engage players into a thrill and motivational feeling is always a challenge and goal. The concept of interactivity through the design of EG and its interrelation to concepts of design, systems and meaningful play discussed throughout the book to provide ease in understanding the complexity of the game design. The overall discussion of how game designers are interested in the concepts of meaning because they are involved in the creation of systems of interaction is discussed in depth. With respect to the establishment of the concepts, the book opens the door for probabilities that game designers may take in terms of social interaction, storytelling systems, cultural resistance and how each game design is visualized differently before beginning.

Lastly, the book openly challenges game designers to take into considerations of the vast potential of cultural and ethical values whilst discussing the "the play-centric" of games. Nevertheless, the critique of the book is intentionally condensed and no engagement with the interactive entertainment industry conversed. The book is a testimony to the variety of fields that game designing (game processing through iterative design approach) and game studies can potentially appeal from.

Game Design Process Through "Lens"

The art of game design (Schell, 2008), experienced in professor and game designing, discusses two major trajectories: the game design process and own advice through "the lens". The lens describes the concepts through which the design decisions are approached in terms of skill levels, mechanics, aesthetics, story and also the technological composition in industry. With the 100 lenses unfolding the designing process for designers, the discussion of each chapter unfolds from designer to experience through the game and the player and the effort of embedding each lens into a mind-map throughout the book has provided an in-depth understanding to basics of the designing process. For example, *Lens#32* The Meaning Choices (p.181), understanding the choices provided to the player are sufficient or making the player feel in charge? Or *Lens#47* The Balance (p.205) as a recommendation to apply with any occurring design problem, however, the decisions to fix the concepts and implement occurs only by the decision of programmers. Not only those, *Lens#89* The Team (p.380), *Lens#90* the Documentation (p.387), *Lens#91* The Playtesting (p.401) all fall under a very relevant yet thoughtful concepts of game designers working communicating and working respectfully, documenting the necessary concepts and testing the play of the game through player's perception.

This means putting game designer's thought out of the testing and covering essentials for game designers and engage the content for video games creatively through the design process. The mind-map includes thirty bubbles to represent new element emerging from each chapter and one hundred lenses provided can be very overwhelming information for the game designing team, who needs an urgent answer to the problem-solving or iterative approach. Despite the content list provided, it is noticeable to be confused with some identifications of the Lens names. To conclude, a creative involvement of game systems and the player working along to endorse the experience, whilst addressing crucial organizational perspective in relevance to software development methods such as spiral model, rapid prototyping and play-testing.

Game Design Principles and Cores

Educational Game Design fundamentals by an educator, game designer, founder, director and board member of several European design studios; presents a comprehensive how-to-guide on design and building world-class educational experiences (Kalmpourtzis, 2018). It combines the evolvement, pushing through concepts and learning throughout the process by providing the stand on for the reader "Games are principles and not rules" (p.7). Although rules are elaborated on their own entirety (pp. 169- 180). "Rules" are illustrating that games present rules in operational constitutive and implicit way, rules present goals and rules define ways of punishment and rewards. Kalmpourtzis highlights that game designers have the magical power to deal with challenging tasks during the educational game design process. Hence, referring to his magical triangle (p.54): players, game and learning aspects to structure basic elements and their relationships to create games evolves through the chapters.

The emphasis on the designer's struggle to ensure that the balance is maintained in the system between the realistic and imaginative context of design is rather fruitful. Explaining that games consisted of objects and placing the objects as elements to be implemented in the game lead to the betterment of gameplay (p.181). "Game Core" being the most interesting establishment, it discusses the concrete basis of any game design based on the axis of the magical triangle and providing three approaches to designing a game (p.119): the unbreakable core, the flexible core, and the hybrid core. In the same context, the perspective discussed that prototyping is a key element of game design and evaluating what has been completed theoretically as well as practically. Nevertheless, Kalmpourtzis highlights that interdisciplinary game design is always the most challenging aspects, i.e. engineer working with a game designer will differ in terms of the application of the methodology to be used in building the game.

Coexisting is nearly impossible in many cases yet there is always a way to try and provide a common language as a "tool". In relation to structuring and prototyping (the fastest and easiest way), there is an evaluation of games strategies discussed which were rather general and have been published in the previous article as well (Ahmad, 2018). Evaluating games using usability, playtesting and quality assurance approaches can highly coexist with software engineering approaches. Lastly, the documentation chapter (p.325) had a new and interesting projection of how game design document shape through the designing phase, despite mentioning the difficulties faced by designers in communicating their voice formally and that the structure of the document is never the same. Listing three types of documentation: the classic document (one or more documents), the wiki (online with indexed searches) and the forum (participatory process) (p.327).

To conclude the discussion of game design fundamentals, "lens" of game design and educational game design fundamentals and cores, Table 2 summarizes the key movement from 2004, 2008 and 2018. This shows how the published work from game designers and theorists in the field. One prominent movement can be seen that 2004 presents no interest in documenting the designing process, whilst 2008 reports a non-existing template for game designers to 2018 where a formal structure has been proposed by Kalmpourtzis (2018).

Educational Game Design Frameworks and Models

In order to provide specific models and frameworks reflecting on the criteria of game design, design process, evaluation techniques used during the game design. This section discusses the highly relevant work to show the movements of research from 2015 to 2018.

Table 2. Demonstrates the similarities, differences and concerns noticed in the studies

Books	Salen & Zimmerman (2004)	Jesse Schell (2008)	George Kalmpourtzis (2018)
Uniqueness	Three (3) major concepts: 1. Rule – formal, structured 2. Play – experiential, social, representational 3. Culture – contextual design to engage players. Key Concepts: 1. Engage Players – motivational, thrill, challenges & goals. 2. Interactivity – design, system, play.	Design aspects: 1. Mechanics 2. Aesthetic 3. Story 4. Technology in industry Lens # 100 – mind map for designers to unfold the design process.	Educational games design specific and design principles. Magical Triangle: 1. Players 2. Game 3. Learning Aspects Game Cores (3 of the designing process): 1. Unbreakable 2. Flexible 3. Hybrid Common language "tool" required. Evaluating games: · Usability · Playtesting · Quality assurance approaches Key Considerations of designing & evaluating process: · Prototyping Discusses Pedagogy with games through major learning theories.
Difference	Revolves around the three major concepts throughout.	Discusses: · Designer's thoughts (lens) · Essential game components · Engage player through experience	Discusses Schell's Design aspects and adds: · Pedagogy Documentation for Designing Games: Formally structured
Concerns/ absence	· Very niche industrial related discussion. · Very niche educational games discussion. · More on cultural context, play, and rules. · Discussion of Documentation of Games is not mentioned.	· The Mind map has 30 different points to understand which is confusing for designer's iterative work rules. · Lens names are partly confusing and could be organized better. · Documentation template does not exist.	Author Highlights: · Coexisting and interdisciplinary designing is nearly impossible. · Common language "tool" required.

1. A recent study implements a six-phase methodology, HEXA-GBL, for designing and evaluating GBL activities from a learner-centered perspective (Romero, 2015). The phases are: 1) game design activity, 2) learning objectives definition, 3) the learner-centered need analysis, and the definition of the game modalities, 4) mechanics and rules, 5) the play activity evaluation from the learning outcomes, assessment and feedback, and 6) learners' gaming and learning experience during the GBL activity. While overcoming the barriers of GBL costs and focusing on game mechanics, HEXA-GBL also prioritized the educators to operationalize with adapting processes.

2. Game-Based Learning Design Model (Shi & Shih, 2015) highlighted specific game genres making them difficult to use when the target game genre is different from default game genres applied in research. Consequently, presenting macro-level design concepts comprising of 11 key factors to provide a thinking process for assisting EG designers to integrate them into their game designing (game goals, fantasy, mechanism, game value, narrative, interaction, challenges, freedom, sociality, sensation, and mystery). With evaluation, the authors verified the usability of the model with the

performance of the factors and concluded that it can assist EG designers in developing motivational games (Shi & Shih, 2015).

3. Mechanics-Game Mechanics (LM-GM) model provides a graphical representation of game flow to establish relationships among components which translates pedagogical learning mechanics into game mechanics (Arnab, Lim, Carvalho, Bellotti, De Freitas, et al., 2015). Although it identifies abstract patterns and predefined elements to be replicated across EG, it does not expose the connection with the educational objectives to allow sustainable mechanics.

4. Recently, a framework is proposed for a blended learning environment to enhance learning outcomes and to provide a valuable strategy to facilitate both lecturers and students to obtain better educational knowledge (Jing, Yue, & Murugesan, 2015). Although it has proven a positive learning outcome, there is a need for more research work that can validate the learning-driven game design strategy.

5. In contrast, an Activity model takes accounts for the distinction between designer and instructor explicitly, therefore, the clarification of the role of the teacher/instructor in the game is needed. The game sequence representation follows the unified modeling language (UML) activity diagrams notation, which uses the shapes connected by arrows to represent the flow of the activities (Kühn, 2015).

6. MEEGA+ model (Petri, von Wangenheim, & Borgatto, 2016) was proposed to address the limitations of its predecessor regarding the lack of understanding of measurement instrument items and in terms of its validity and reliability. The MEEGA+ model has been systematically developed by decomposing evaluation goals into measures and defining a measurement instrument to evaluate the perceived quality of educational games in terms of player experience and perceived learning. The MEEGA+ model provides game creators, instructors and researchers with a measurement instrument in order to evaluate the quality of educational games and, thus, contribute to their improvement and effective and efficient adoption in practice. MEEGA+ evaluates the quality of learner assessment, thus, EG as a software, development or EG design was not included in this study.

7. A Hybrid theoretical framework that analyses a few existing design models, the learning theories embedded in them and the user experience component (de Aguiar et al., 2018). The hybrid framework is content specialist (puts developers and designer's perspectives), contains educational goals and technological aspects required around designing a game. Provides an iterative design process throughout the stages to ensure pre-production, production, and post-production are polished and enhanced. Not only that, the model includes a pedagogical approach and learning theories. Despite an immense study conducted, it is still a work in progress and the model needs to be verified or validated through the designer's and developers; to ensure its practicality, and also, the genre of games is serious games, hence, the confusion on understanding educational games and serious games is still ambiguous.

8. Another recently published work on proposing an architecture of serious game design and assessing the technology establishes through emphasizing the engaging and motivating needs of game design through knowledge of learning domain (Mestadi, Nafil, Touahni, & Messoussi, 2018). Along with that, pedagogy and game design components and their collaboration between domain content, pedagogical and playful experts lead the architecture to propose a taxonomy, representing a functional architecture for supporting the conceptual design of the game. With the help of the architecture designed, the paper reports that modification of decisions of the educational robot with affecting

a game, and responding to new updates to improve games or even reusability of the educational robot with the newly designed game is beneficial through the domain content where playful experts share the design requirements. A concern to be highlighted reducing and encapsulating experts intellectual may seem quite interesting but allowing domain experts to focus on their definitions and knowledge and not worrying on the playful aspects of letting game designers amend aspects without having them to acquire deep knowledge of domain content seems ambiguous and requires more testing to prove the authenticity of how a game design might be retrieved.

MAIN FOCUS OF THE CHAPTER

Issues, Controversies, Problems

The gap between game design and educational game design has become evident that to optimize the learning from serious games, pedagogical experts should be actively involved in the development process (Arnab, Lim, Carvalho, Bellotti, Freitas, et al., 2015; Tahir & Wang, 2018). A systematically reviewed article discussing how EGs are evaluated by including 112 relevant articles and evaluated their relevancy based on analysis factors, research design, evaluation models/methods, and the kind of instruments that are used in the research (Petri & von Wangenheim, 2017). This concludes that the majority of published articles are based on qualitative research methods, hence, they do not use a well-defined evaluation model or method. Furthermore, it highlighted that there is a need for more rigorous evaluations as well as methodological support in order to assist game creators and instructors to improve such games as well as to systematically support decisions on when or how to include them within instructional units.

The crucial experts involved in the designing process is highlighted many times. It is a challenge and substantial to ensure that collaboration between game-based learning experts, theoretical experts, game designers teachers, learners, developers, and non-technical domain experts to occur. Yet research still mentions the challenges of collaborating the experts with different intellects in one room (Kalmpourtzis, 2018). The sophistication of popularity and budget of creating EG by scratch demands a high level of the production process is also challenging to researchers and game developers. This gap was also recently highlighted in a comparative analysis study and reported two major issues in perspectives of designing EGs and models: lack of independent evaluation of EG and the need to focus on the practical application of the design models to be presentable in EG industry (Tahir & Wang, 2018). Due to lack of infrastructure capabilities including hardware and software requirements, theoretical aspects in terms of pedagogical and instructional aspects are also very crucial in designing and development process. The game industry needs to ensure that integrating an instructor in an EG can provide useful feedback to users at a run-time significance (Sinkewicz, 2015). This way bringing out the fundamentals and principles published in (Kalmpourtzis, 2018; Schell, 2008; Zimmerman & Salen, 2004) could enhance the game design process.

Designing an effective EG needs to have a clear understanding of what the desired learning outcomes are and to establish a transparent mapping amongst (Hainey, Connolly, Stansfield, & Boyle, 2011). To understand that, research methods and statistics are broad-ranging, complex, and interconnected with logical and scientific reasoning, understanding different representations of data, data analysis, interpretation of results and evaluation skills (Boyle et al., 2014). It is barely the case where domains such as gameplay, game environment, subject-matter, and learning theories interaction have been discussed in order to provide a holistic view of a particular game element. Mostly, the literature uses vaguely spread game elements that cover a large number of relationships and domains. Defining domains, playful experts, domain content in the interdisciplinary context still seems to be vaguely established (Mestadi et al., 2018).

The GBL and its diverse dimensions and characteristics make it difficult to evaluate and model. However, evaluation remains the only way to verify if the educational targets are being achieved and to detect any functional vulnerability inside the learning game. If the gaps between EG community and industry, and between academia and industry is bridged, the game development efforts could benefit all communities, including industry (Arnab, Lim, Carvalho, Bellotti, Freitas, et al., 2015; Azadegan et al., 2014). Although evaluation process can be costly, there should be a pre-modeling strategy, which can allow developer or designer to model out the elements and related elements, as well as domains that should be involved in EG actively. The collaboration between pedagogy, structural elements, dynamics and also theories in a game remains a tough task, although the research strives to provide theoretical models achieving as much as possible, yet testing their application and evaluating the proposed models is still under construction (All et al., 2016; de Aguiar et al., 2018).

Besides that, only two models cited Schell's work on "the art of game design", which is alarming as the work published in the books sets basics and establish definitions that can be adopted to ensure consistency and defined terms (2008). With respect to much work published, the questions remain untangled on what are the core values, core principles or the fundamentals; one must follow to obtain a satisfactory game design. The process of evaluating game design process using prototyping was highly discussed and seems to be promising; and it was confirmed by (Kalmpourtzis, 2018) that prototyping is the key element of designing an educational game. In terms of design, only a few models represent the idea of prototyping, however, the evaluation of EG discusses prototyping but this is still noticeably niche and needs a deeper understanding in terms of software engineering prototyping.

SOLUTIONS AND RECOMMENDATIONS

Below are a few suggestions that are carefully analyzed through the analysis of models and frameworks; to the issues mentioned above.

There is a need for researcher proposing theoretical models and frameworks to provide a legitimate ground of using definitions, game design fundamentals, structural elements of game design, or the principles of game design from the established books. This is due to the fact that every researcher understands and interprets the definitions from different articles that are written under different scenarios. Steps of software engineering prototyping and the steps to be undertaken for the game design process. This does not imply that their work is at fault, but the application of consistent terms used throughout the research will provide more engaging content to a larger group of experts. Else, the question then rises to why the mind-map to designing a game with 100 lenses of designer's experience (Schell, 2008), game rules and design fundamentals(Zimmerman & Salen, 2004) and Fundamentals of game design (Kalmpourtzis, 2018) are not being employed as they should. The in-depth procedures provide a concise yet detailed step in various aspects to visualize the position of not only game designers, but also developers, educators, new game designers, software testing teams, etc. Hence, providing a common ground and looking at the similarities of articles published and books provided game designing fundamental can assist a clarity towards designing models for game designing process.

Understanding the prototyping leads to the betterment of the game design process, there is a need to unpack how the procedure of prototyping in designing EG can be enhanced. The understanding of game designing prototyping steps through Kalmpourtzis' s fundamentals and the lens of Schell's design provides an understanding of the basic steps required for prototyping. The discussion provides a comparison and understands similarities of the prototyping steps undertaken for software engineering and the prototyping steps discussed for designing games. With the overview, the steps from software engineering prototyping can be used in the designing process of EG to clarify the requirements to ensure learning objectives and entertainment remains the equally present.

Figure 1. Proposing Combined Prototyping steps adopted for the game designing process
Source: (Kalmpourtzis, 2018; Schell, 2008; Zimmerman & Salen, 2004)

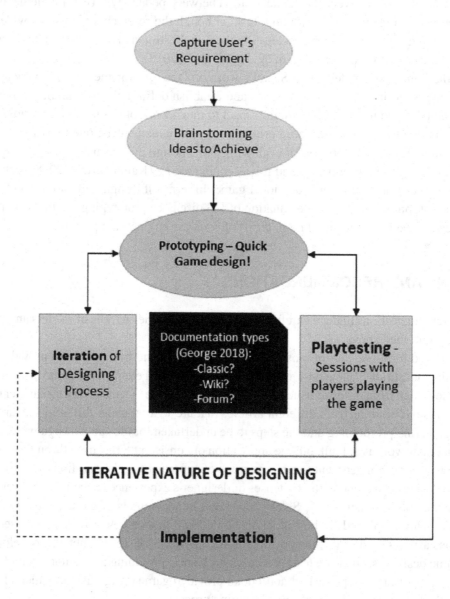

Figure 1 shows the prototyping steps discussed through the game design process in (Kalmpourtzis, 2018; Schell, 2008; Zimmerman & Salen, 2004). A commonly used and recommended (Wenzler, 2009) development method is iterative design. This is also described as a play-based design process (Zimmerman & Salen, 2004). A prototype is played, evaluated, adjusted and played again, allowing the designer or design team to base decisions on the successive iterations or versions of the game. Iterative design is a cyclic process that alternates between prototyping, play-testing, evaluation, and refinement (p. 11).

Figure 2 shows the steps undertaken in software prototyping through two different approaches: Evolutionary and Rapid throwback. Evolutionary prototyping is an incrementally refined process on the basis of customer's (players) feedback until it finally gets accepted. It saves time and effort as developing a prototype from scratch for every iteration of the process can sometimes be very frustrating for the developers. Rapid throwback is a method of exploring ideas and getting customer feedback for each prototype. A developed prototype need not necessarily be a part of the ultimately accepted prototype. Customer (players) feedback helps in preventing unnecessary design faults and hence, the final prototype developed is of better quality. These processes can be easily adopted in the game designing process as the emphasis on iterative game designing has been highly discussing in the published research. Although this requires testing on designing games, it projects a promising iterative designing approach.

Another crucial aspect to highlight is the documentation of game designing. Schell's stated that "The magic template does not exist!" (Schell, 2008, pp. 382-383). There are only two exact purposes of game documents: (1) Memory document which records decision and amendments taken place throughout the development period and, (2) Communication document, where all the stakeholders tend to communicate. Kalmpourtzis (2018) emphasized the idea of creating a document that helps individuals rather than creating problems, and stated: "game design documents are not about formalities, they are about actions!" (p. 326). Consequently, an efficient game design document contains a list of attributes: (1) never the same structure, (2) simple structure, (3) clarity of design process, and (4) Descriptive (imagery, music, videos).

Table 3 presents the most common aspects that are likely to occur in a game design document. From a software designer perspective, this can be categorized as poor management for software development, as software requirement analysis documents are required to ensure all software diagrams, content, requirements, analysis, and also the end product is quality attested (Georgiadou, 2003).

FUTURE RESEARCH DIRECTIONS

To unpack the game design process, there is a need to ensure the fundamentals, core values and the state of the art of game design is taken into consideration. This chapter attempts to comprehend the concepts, fundamentals of game design and designing process involving various experts in the field and a few recommendations to providing similarities and differences between software design and game design were discussed. Prototyping has proven to provide a good grasp on designing game and have iterative nature to test the requirements and the play of the game (Serrano-Laguna et al., 2018). Researchers have proposed prototyping tools for designing games using the iterative rapid prototyping methods (Volkovas, Fairbank, Woodward, & Lucas, 2019).

With respect to discussed literature and proposed solution, this could be further enhanced into a variety of areas in the field that could be beneficial for game designers, academicians, and researchers. The following

Figure 2. Prototyping model of software engineering combining evolutionary and throwback prototyping
Source: (Gowtham et al., 2017; Padda, Arora, Gupta, & Sharma, 2014; UsingAPA)

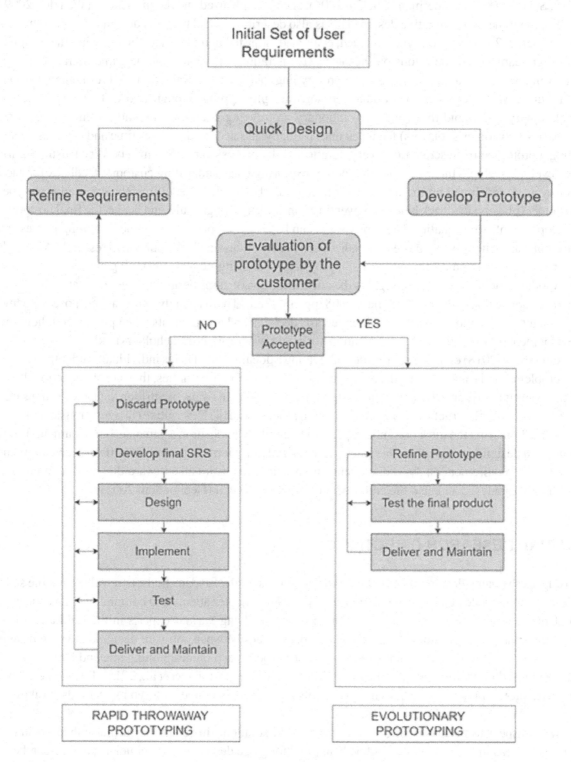

Table 3. Common aspects encountered in educational game design documents

No.	List of Aspects for an Educational Game Design Document
1.	Learning aims & Objectives
2.	Learning Methodologies
3.	Learning Theories used and their Impacts
4.	Evaluation of the Game
5.	Presentation of the game (introducing to players)
6.	Audience
7.	Audience Needs and Preferences
8.	Learning Context
9.	Game Mechanics
10.	Narrative Elements
11.	Game Characters and Abilities
12.	Connection and impact between game elements (mechanics and story of technology and mechanics)
13.	Technology Features (Related to any categories stated above)

Source: (Kalmpourtzis, 2018)

- Practicing on applying the fundamentals of game design to propose an educational game designing model EG.
- Defining terms in each model/framework proposed is a crucial necessity as there is a noticeable inconsistency.
- A template of a document is provided in Kalmpourtzis (2018, p.327) that covers common aspects every EG encounters. Perhaps, that could be easily adapted to document the design process and provides an ease of communication with other experts.
- Using the Prototyping steps clearly to achieve a more quality product.
- Testing and feedback procedures in EG could also be weighed in perspective of software engineering tools and techniques, as not all techniques could work but not all fail during application.

CONCLUSION

This chapter has discussed three prominent games designing fundamentalist alongside with various types of existing theoretical frameworks and design models which aid in designing EGs. Due to an overwhelming requirement on unpacking the complexity of the game design, this chapter discusses the models and frameworks in parallax with established fundamentals through the prominent fundamentals of game design. EG design phase also requires prototyping that has proven to be useful in iterative nature, hence, this chapter provides an overview conceptual model that game designers can adopt during the designing phase (Figure 1). The proposed conceptual model combining prototyping in game design can be similarly contrasted with software engineering prototyping (Figure 2) where throwback and evolutionary approaches can enhance the designing process of an EG. Finally, this chapter provides a further recommendation on how the software designing processes can be adopted for designing an EG and documentation of an EG thoroughly to provide a communication ground for other experts in designing process.

ACKNOWLEDGMENT

This chapter contributes part of researcher's Ph.D. study under the literature review and the researcher would like to thank Deakin University Postgraduate Research Scholarship (DUPRS) program for giving the opportunity to support and undertake the research.

REFERENCES

Ahmad, M., Rahim, L. A., Osman, K., & Arshad, N. I. (2018). Chapter: 291 Towards Modelling Effective Educational Games Using Multi-Domain Framework. In D. B. A. E. M. Khosrow-Pour (Ed.), Encyclopedia of Information Science and Technology (4th ed., pp. 3337-3347). Hershey, PA: IGI Global.

All, A., Castellar, E. P. N., & Van Looy, J. (2016). Assessing the effectiveness of digital game-based learning: Best practices. *Computers & Education*, *92-93*, 90–103. doi:10.1016/j.compedu.2015.10.007

Arnab, S., Lim, T., Carvalho, M. B., Bellotti, F., De Freitas, S., Louchart, S., Suttie, N., Berta, R., & De Gloria, A. (2015). Mapping learning and game mechanics for serious games analysis. *British Journal of Educational Technology*, *46*(2), 391–411. doi:10.1111/bjet.12113

Arnab, S., Lim, T., Carvalho, M. B., Bellotti, F., Freitas, S., Louchart, S., ... De Gloria, A. (2015). Mapping learning and game mechanics for serious games analysis. *British Journal of Educational Technology*, *46*(2), 391–411. doi:10.1111/bjet.12113

Azadegan, A., Hauge, J. B., Bellotti, F., Berta, R., Bidarra, R., Harteveld, C., & Stanescu, I. A. (2014). The move beyond edutainment: Have we learnt our lessons from entertainment games? In *Games and Learning Alliance* (pp. 77–89). Springer. doi:10.1007/978-3-319-12157-4_7

Boyle, E. A., MacArthur, E. W., Connolly, T. M., Hainey, T., Manea, M., Kärki, A., & Van Rosmalen, P. (2014). A narrative literature review of games, animations and simulations to teach research methods and statistics. *Computers & Education*, *74*, 1–14. doi:10.1016/j.compedu.2014.01.004

Connolly, T., Stansfield, M., & Hainey, T. (2009). Towards the Development of a Games-Based Learning Evaluation Framework. *Games-Based Learning Advancements for Multi-Sensory Human Computer Interfaces*, 251-273. doi:10.4018/978-1-60566-360-9.ch015

de Aguiar, M. P., Winn, B., Cezarotto, M., Battaiola, A. L., & Gomes, P. V. (2018). *Educational digital games: a theoretical framework about design models, learning theories and user experience*. Paper presented at the International Conference of Design, User Experience, and Usability. 10.1007/978-3-319-91797-9_13

de Freitas, S. (2018). Are games effective learning tools? A review of educational games. *Journal of Educational Technology & Society*, *21*(2), 74–84.

Dondlinger, M. J. (2007). Educational video game design: A review of the literature. *Journal of Applied Educational Technology, 4*(1), 21-31.

Georgiadou, E. (2003). Software process and product improvement: A historical perspective. *Cybernetics and Systems Analysis, 39*(1), 125–142. doi:10.1023/A:1023833428613

Gowtham, V., Manoj, Y., Pooventhiran, G., Praveen, A., Shivaram, R., & Kathiresan, A. (2017). Evolutionary Models in Software Engineering. *International Journal of New Technology and Research, 3*(5), 30–33.

Hainey, T., Connolly, T. M., Stansfield, M., & Boyle, E. A. (2011). Evaluation of a game to teach requirements collection and analysis in software engineering at tertiary education level. *Computers & Education, 56*(1), 21–35. doi:10.1016/j.compedu.2010.09.008

Hays, R. T. (2005). *The effectiveness of instructional games: A literature review and discussion.* Academic Press.

Ito, M. (2009). *Engineering Play: A Cultural History of Children's Software, Massachusetts.* The MIT Press.

Jing, T. W., Yue, W. S., & Murugesan, R. (2015). *Learning Outcome Enhancement via Serious Game: Implementing Game-Based Learning Framework in Blended Learning Environment.* Paper presented at the IT Convergence and Security (ICITCS), 2015 5th International Conference on. doi:10.21236/ADA441935

Kalmpourtzis, G. (2018). *Educational Game Design Fundamentals: A journey to creating intrinsically motivating learning experiences.* AK Peters/CRC Press. doi:10.1201/9781315208794

Kebritchi, M., & Hirumi, A. (2008). Examining the pedagogical foundations of modern educational computer games. *Computers & Education, 51*(4), 1729–1743. doi:10.1016/j.compedu.2008.05.004

Koster, R. (2013). *Theory of fun for game design.* O'Reilly Media, Inc.

Kühn, M. (2015). Applying Patterns when Generating Code: a Model-based Design Approach. *Proceedings of the Mulitimedia, Interaction, Design and Innnovation.* 10.1145/2814464.2814474

Lameras, P., Arnab, S., Dunwell, I., Stewart, C., Clarke, S., & Petridis, P. (2017). Essential features of serious games design in higher education: Linking learning attributes to game mechanics. *British Journal of Educational Technology, 48*(4), 972–994. doi:10.1111/bjet.12467

Malone, T. W. (1983). Guidelines for designing educational computer programs. *Childhood Education, 59*(4), 241–247.

Mestadi, W., Nafil, K., Touahni, R., & Messoussi, R. (2018). An Assessment of Serious Games Technology: Toward an Architecture for Serious Games Design. *International Journal of Computer Games Technology, 2018,* 2018. doi:10.1155/2018/9834565

Padda, E. S., Arora, E. A., Gupta, E. S., & Sharma, E. P. (2014). Review of software development methodologies used in software design. *International Journal (Toronto, Ont.), 3*(5).

Perrotta, C., Featherstone, G., Aston, H., & Houghton, E. (2013). *Game-based learning: Latest evidence and future directions*. NFER.

Petri, G., & von Wangenheim, C. G. (2017). How games for computing education are evaluated? A systematic literature review. *Computers & Education*, *107*, 68–90. doi:10.1016/j.compedu.2017.01.004

Petri, G., von Wangenheim, C. G., & Borgatto, A. F. (2016). *MEEGA+: An Evolution of a Model for the Evaluation of Educational Games*. Academic Press.

Poulsen, M. (2011). Learning by producing. In The gameit handbook (pp. 87). Academic Press.

Prensky, M. (2003). Digital game-based learning. *Computers in Entertainment*, *1*(1), 21–21. doi:10.1145/950566.950596

Romero, M. (2015). Work, Games and Lifelong Learning in the 21st Century. *Procedia: Social and Behavioral Sciences*, *174*, 115–121. doi:10.1016/j.sbspro.2015.01.634

Schell, J. (2008). *The Art of Game Design: A book of lenses*. Morgan Kaufmann Publishers. doi:10.1201/9780080919171

Serrano-Laguna, Á., Manero, B., Freire, M., & Fernández-Manjón, B. (2018). A methodology for assessing the effectiveness of serious games and for inferring player learning outcomes. *Multimedia Tools and Applications*, *77*(2), 2849–2871. doi:10.100711042-017-4467-6

Shi, Y.-R., & Shih, J.-L. (2015). Game Factors and Game-Based Learning Design Model. *International Journal of Computer Games Technology*, *2015*, 1–11. doi:10.1155/2015/549684

Sinkewicz, N. D. (2015). *A framework for designing serious games*. University of British Columbia.

Tahir, R., & Wang, A. I. (2018). Insights into Design of Educational Games: Comparative Analysis of Design Models. *Proceedings of the Future Technologies Conference*.

Tang, S., & Hanneghan, M. (2010). A Model-Driven Framework to Support Development of Serious Games for Game-based Learning. *2010 Developments in E-systems Engineering*, 95-100. doi:10.1109/DeSE.2010.23

Using A. P. A. Software Engineering | Prototyping Model. (n.d.). Retrieved from https://www.geeksforgeeks.org/software-engineering-prototyping-model/

Volkovas, R., Fairbank, M., Woodward, J., & Lucas, S. (2019). *Mek: Mechanics Prototyping Tool for 2D Tile-Based Turn-Based Deterministic Games*. arXiv preprint arXiv:1904.03540

Wenzler, I. (2009). The ten commandments for translating simulation results into real-life performance. *Simulation & Gaming*, *40*(1), 98–109. doi:10.1177/1046878107308077

Wouters, P., & van Oostendorp, H. (2017). Overview of Instructional Techniques to Facilitate Learning and Motivation of Serious Games. *Instructional Techniques to Facilitate Learning and Motivation of Serious Games*, 1-16. doi:10.1007/978-3-319-39298-1_1

Zimmerman, E., & Salen, K. (2004). *Rules of play: Game Design Fundamentals*. The MIT Press.

ADDITIONAL READING

Ahmad, M., Rahim, L. A., Osman, K., & Arshad, N. I. (2018). Chapter: 291 Towards Modelling Effective Educational Games Using Multi-Domain Framework. In D. B. A. E. M. Khosrow-Pour (Ed.), (Fourth Edition ed., pp. 3337-3347). Encyclopedia of Information Science and Technology: Hershey, PA: IGI Global.

Beatty, I. D. (2014). Gaming the system: Video games as a theoretical framework for instructional design. *arXiv preprint arXiv:1401.6716*.

de Aguiar, M. P., Winn, B., Cezarotto, M., Battaiola, A. L., & Gomes, P. V. (2018). Educational digital games: a theoretical framework about design models, learning theories and user experience. Paper presented at the International Conference of Design, User Experience, and Usability. 10.1007/978-3-319-91797-9_13

Kalmpourtzis, G. (2018). Educational Game Design Fundamentals: A journey to creating intrinsically motivating learning experiences: AK Peters/CRC Press.

Lameras, P., Arnab, S., Dunwell, I., Stewart, C., Clarke, S., & Petridis, P. (2017). Essential features of serious games design in higher education: Linking learning attributes to game mechanics. *British Journal of Educational Technology*, *48*(4), 972–994. doi:10.1111/bjet.12467

Mestadi, W., Nafil, K., Touahni, R., & Messoussi, R. (2018). An Assessment of Serious Games Technology: Toward an Architecture for Serious Games Design. *International Journal of Computer Games Technology*, *2018*, 2018. doi:10.1155/2018/9834565

Schell, J. (2008). *The Art of Game Design: A book of lenses*. Morgan Kaufmann Publishers. doi:10.1201/9780080919171

Serrano-Laguna, Á., Manero, B., Freire, M., & Fernández-Manjón, B. (2018). A methodology for assessing the effectiveness of serious games and for inferring player learning outcomes. *Multimedia Tools and Applications*, *77*(2), 2849–2871. doi:10.100711042-017-4467-6

KEY TERMS AND DEFINITIONS

Evolutionary Prototyping: Incrementally refined on the basis of customer feedback till it finally gets accepted, saves time and effort as developing a prototype from scratch for every iteration of the process can sometimes be very frustrating for the developers.

Fidelity: In the context of serious games, the concept of fidelity referees to the extent to which game emulates the real world. Mostly refers to the game environment, visual effects and response to an action from players.

Game Design Schema: A way of understanding games, a conceptual lens that can be applied to the analysis or creation of the game.

Game Environment: A dimension which collaborates game rules, objectives, subject, and theoretical aspects together as a whole to provide an interactive flow of activity.

Gameplay: This is where the rules and regulations of EG.

Model-Driven Engineering: A software development approach, focusing on the creation of models that represents the system-under-study (SUS) and subsequent generation of fully-working software artifacts from these models.

"Play-Centric Account" of Games: The formal and experiential approach to game design.

Rapid Throwaway Prototyping: A method of exploring ideas and getting customer feedback for each prototype. A developed prototype need not necessarily be a part of the ultimately accepted prototype. Customer feedback helps in preventing unnecessary design faults and hence, the final prototype developed is of a better quality

Schema: A way of framing and organizing knowledge.

This research was previously published in the Handbook of Research on Modern Educational Technologies, Applications, and Management; pages 179-197, copyright year 2021 by Information Science Reference (an imprint of IGI Global).

Chapter 43
Game Design as Literacy–First Activity:
Digital Tools With/In Literacy Instruction

Fawn Canady
Sonoma State University, USA

Ed Nagelhout
University of Nevada, Las Vegas, USA

ABSTRACT

This chapter explores pedagogical goals and classroom practices for literacy instruction with/in a digital learning environment that extends beyond the classroom. To do this, the authors developed a process for literate practices illustrated through game design. Game design is one example of a disciplinary activity that masks the complexity of writing yet provides teachers with opportunities to make visible the writing practices and genres inherent in all disciplines. Game developers are writers and game development is a 'literacy-first' activity, a process that underscores the complex and considered choices authors or designers make in specific rhetorical contexts. Pedagogical goals and classroom practices at all levels of literacy education must encourage greater collaboration, privilege informal and situated learning, and promote decision-making, student self-monitoring, and lifelong learning. The chapter concludes by describing a project framework that can be adapted at all educational levels using game design as a model.

INTRODUCTION

As our students' worlds become immersed in the digital, as our classroom practices become enacted by the digital, as our educational research spans the thresholds of the digital, and, most importantly, as learning too often becomes appended to the digital, our pedagogy must focus first and foremost on literate practices rather than digital tools. This also means that we expand the definition of literacy, which has implications for literacy pedagogies in K-12 settings and beyond.

DOI: 10.4018/978-1-6684-7589-8.ch043

This chapter explores pedagogical goals and classroom practices for literacy instruction with/in a digital learning environment that extends beyond the "classroom" to construct more transparent relationships across the range of student experiences. For us, pedagogical goals and classroom practices at all levels of education must encourage greater collaboration, privilege informal and situated learning, and promote decision-making, student self-monitoring, and lifelong learning. More importantly, these pedagogical goals and classroom practices must lead to literate practices that are personalized, rhetorical, and contextualized. To do this, we developed a process for literate practices illustrated through game design, just one example of a complex activity with the potential to make visible the writing practices and genres inherent in all disciplines.

The first section begins with the belief that literacy is not monolithic, nor is literacy simply reading or writing. Through the twin lenses of participatory cultures and multimodality, we argue that literacy is best understood in the classroom as literate practices: the results of making considered choices as part of the complex interactions among writer(s), readers, texts, and contexts (Brandt, 2011; Selber, 2004). Literacy is rhetorical. Therefore, pedagogical goals for literacy instruction must create classroom spaces and classroom activities that provide opportunities for students to make those considered choices, that allow students to interact orally, graphically, and visually in specific ways for specific purposes, and that help students develop the skills, tools, and habits of mind necessary for successful literate practices in the classroom and, more importantly, beyond the classroom.

The next section of the chapter presents literate practices as a process, one that focuses learning on development and reflection. To do this, we have created a framework that begins by rethinking game design. Game design is more than just writing code. And while writing the code for a game can certainly enhance the work of the writing classroom, the work of writers is central to game design and development. Game developers are writers, and game development is a 'literacy-first' activity, grounded in literacy research on best practices. As a process, game development underscores the complex and considered choices writers/designers make in specific rhetorical contexts through inquiry-based research, genre study, and the telling of compelling stories through multiple modes. While games inevitably invoke technology, game development draws on digital tools to support a writing process that saves the 'coding' for last: a conceptual model of literate practices augmented by, but not dependent on, technology.

The chapter concludes by describing a game development project that invites students to adapt a book for a video game. This project is appropriate for all educational levels, promotes literacy-first, and provides multimodal options. More importantly, this project serves as a conceptual framework for literacy instruction that mirrors existing literacy curricular and pedagogical objectives across contexts, allows for the use of different digital tools with/in the framework, and can be tailored for a variety of projects (e.g., digital comics, transmedia storytelling, fundraising proposal, etc.) in order to meet student-learning goals more effectively in the future.

DEFINING LITERATE PRACTICES FOR LITERACY PEDAGOGY

The "rapid digitalization of literacy" has resulted in what Mills (2010, 2016) calls the "digital turn" (p. 1). Literate practices mediated by digital media and technologies have necessitated a more expansive definition of literacy to reflect communication that is increasingly situated, contextual, and, more importantly, multimodal. Multimodality, or combining modes (e.g., aural, visual, linguistic, gestural, spatial) to make meaning, is not exclusively digital, however; the affordances of digital technology make it increasingly easier to communicate through multimodal texts (Kress, 2010). The centrality of digital multimodality is acknowledged in a recent National Council of Teachers of English (NCTE, 2016) position statement: Writing in everyday life has expanded dramatically as a result of the "important [digital] instruments of people's writing, integrated tightly, nearly seamlessly, with their composing in video, photographs, and other media" (np). Additionally, the statement underscores writing instruction that not only engages students in digital and multimodal composing, but also in "multiple, flexible models of the writing process" that include opportunities for experimentation and collaboration (NCTE, 2016). The everyday importance of multimodal digital tools should be reflected in the literacy pedagogies (LP) of school.

As entangled as our literacy practices are with digital technology, teaching is not all about the tech. If literacy is defined as "the particular ways of thinking about and doing reading and writing in cultural contexts" (Street, 2003, p. 79), then digital tools certainly affect literate practices; but technology changes rapidly, so any LP that privileges technology tools will be inherently insufficient. Rather, a literacy-first approach to teaching and learning with/in technology puts students' literate practices at the fore and encourages them to choose the best tools and modes for the purposes of their writing.

In a 'Call to Action,' NCTE (2018) recognizes that literacy encompasses digital and interdisciplinary literacies (np). By drawing on Wilhelm's (2004) learner-centered approach to reading instruction, they emphasize the following features for effective literacy pedagogy:

- Learning is social and transactional.
- Learning is an apprenticeship to a community of practice.
- Learners move on a continuum from novice to expert.
- Teachers provide assistance to the adolescent.
- Good teaching is always in the learner's zone of proximal development.
- Different students have a variety of needs, so instruction must be flexible.

While not beholden to these ideas, we acknowledge the ways they reinforce the sociocultural underpinnings of our conceptual framework for literacy instruction as a literacy-first activity and align with two theories that inspired our literacy-first practices: participatory cultures (Itō et al., 2010; Jenkins, 2009; Jenkins et al. 2016) and multimodality (Kress, 2003, 2010; Kress & van Leeuwen, 2001; Jewitt, Bezemer, & O'Halloran, 2016). Combined, we believe these twin lenses effectively conceptualize digital tools with/in literacy instruction for educators.

SOCIOCULTURAL LEARNING THEORY

In describing 'literate practices,' we refer to all of the ways that people use language and (semiotic) tools to communicate, and, for us, these communicative practices occur in the conceptual contexts of "networked publics" (e.g., Alvermann, boyd, Itō, Rheingold, etc.). While Rhizomatic Theory, which explores change, interconnectivity, and multiplicity (Deleuze & Guattari, 1987), or Actor Network Theory, which addresses technological innovation and networks of relationships (Latour, 2005), certainly offer insights for how contemporary, networked publics have shifted literate practices, we ground our approach in sociocultural theory, which is well established in educational research and more useful for our consideration of literacy-first activities, because of its emphasis on the social nature of language acquisition and the importance of considering tools and contexts in literacy learning (Vygotsky, 1978;

Wertsch, 1991). Clearly, a comprehensive review of sociocultural theory is beyond the scope of this chapter; however, features of sociocultural theory can illuminate how literacy-first digital composing projects, which can span school contexts from kindergarten to college, can be effective.

Sociocultural theory stems from Vygotsky's (1978) ideas that human consciousness is the result of a sociohistorical confluence– histories, tools, norms, languages, etc.– coproduced over time. However, sociocultural theory is not deterministic and emphasizes human agency because communication is "situated in concrete interactions that are simultaneously improvised locally and mediated by…tools and practices" (Prior, 2006, p. 55). Literacy is socially situated and dependent not only on traditional language and print-based skill sets, but in ways of doing literacy that reflect literate practices. Context, and understanding contexts for communication, is as integral to literacy learning as the cognitive (Mills, 2016; Gee, 2014; Street, 1997).

Language is learned in social contexts. Young children acquire language before coming to school, which is essentially informal learning. By the time many children arrive at school, they have acquired through exposure oral language and possibly some concepts of print, although this may be based on more formalized learning at home (see for example Heath, Gee). Vygotsky (1978) emphasizes overt instruction for more complex conventions, higher order skills such as writing or critical thinking or reading. Children require formal instruction to learn to read and write; it does not happen naturally (Gee, 2004). Similarly, assumptions that children born into a culture circumscribed by ubiquitous digital technology and media are somehow more adept with tech tools (i.e., "digital natives," Prensky, 2001) than adults of earlier generations belie the complex communication practices and media literacies necessary to fully participate in the digital contexts of society.

Despite articulated differences between acquisition and formal learning (Gee, 2004), traditional schooling does not necessarily "look" like formal learning, for the concept of "cultural processes," or things or actions important to a cultural group, can also be overt instruction through a kind of mentorship or from members in a group, what Lave and Wenger (1991) term "legitimate peripheral participation" (see also Gee, 2004). If we consider digital literacies as an important cultural process, acquisition might be as simple as swiping an iPad, moving between screens, and tapping to open apps. Children can quickly learn to work a digital device. However, like early literacy educators who show young children how books work, first with a cover, then turning pages, and, finally, recognizing that words and images convey messages, more overt instruction is necessary to help children understand the significance of digital actions (i.e., that symbols are connected to new pages, for example). More importantly, with 95% of teens reporting access to a smartphone (Anderson & Jiang, 2018), digitally mediated literate practices, or the admonition to recruit rather than ignore students' lived literacies, has added weight (New London Group, 1996).

Digitally mediated literate practices must be taught; and yet, as Mimi Itō reminds us, "much of the focus of the twentieth-century educational system is out of step with what we need today to navigate this changing ecosystem of how information, culture, and knowledge are produced and circulated" (Jenkins, Itō, & boyd, 2016, p. 97). As K-16 literacy teachers navigate various modes and resources for meaning making, they will be confronted with unique challenges that require them to "step 'out of bounds' and try new approaches in teaching learning (Jocson, 2010, p. 54). Literacy is a critical link between social and technological shifts (Rheingold, 2012, p. 54).

Participatory Culture

Fundamentally rethinking education to meet the demands of the "changing ecosystem" of a networked society underscores the importance of LPs that engage students in developing not only literacy skills, but literacy-first behaviors that are flexible and reinforce life-long learning (Jenkins, Itō, & boyd, 2016, p. 97). Participatory culture identifies the elements of informal learning that can be harnessed in more formal learning settings like schools. The definition of participatory culture can be summarized as:

A culture with relatively low barriers to artistic expression and civic engagement, strong support for creating and sharing one's creations, and some type of informal mentorship whereby what is known by the most experienced is passed along to novices. A participatory culture is also one in which members believe their contributions matter, and feel some degree of social connection with one another (at the least they care what other people think about what they have created). (Jenkins, Itō, & boyd, 2016, p. 4).

Jenkins (2016) refines this statement with "we were trying to move literacy from the capacity to produce and consume information to the capacity to participate in some larger social system" (p. 97). In other words, literacy is rhetorical and must account for the affects communication practices in context.

Participatory culture reflects sociocultural theory through the informal learning that occurs through the social engagement present in everyday literacy activities, such as social media, gaming, and digital media production (Itō et al., 2010). Informal learning offers essential 'affinity spaces' (Gee, 2003), or groups formed around mutual interests, that reflect communities of practice (Lave & Wenger, 1991) more than traditional schooling. Additionally, Itō et al. (2010) see youth participation in digitally-mediated spaces as an example of youth-centric learning that is fundamentally opposed to top-down models of schooling where the adult is the sole authority and source of knowledge and learning. However, not everyone has equal opportunities for informal learning through new media. This "participation gap" is perpetuated not only by lack of access to technology, but also the lack of opportunity to engage in informal learning through experimentation in digital spaces and similar cultural experiences (Jenkins, 2009, p. 3). Schools provide few opportunities for students to engage in meaningful ways through community-driven, informal learning in order to build essential skills and knowledge for meeting the challenges of our networked era. And we need to do better.

The literacy-first model advocated in this chapter requires not only the time to work through the iterative process, but also the student-centered inquiry and mentorship that takes place in participatory cultures. In our framework, we share Jenkin's admonition: "The more authoritative a classroom structure becomes, the less students feel that their own voice and their own choices matter, the less free they are to pursue their own passions and interests, and the less likely the curriculum is to reflect the realities of their lives beyond the classroom" (Jenkins in Jenkins, Itō, & boyd, 2016, p. 95). We anticipate that this will be met with an argument that we have heard in our own experience as teacher educators that LP must focus on discreet literacy skills before students can participate in student-centered practices. We heartily disagree. A similar paradigm shift that sees language as action, or languaging, challenges "the assumption that students first need to acquire 'competency' in language– in terms of obtaining a level of proficiency in a language or learning grammatical rules such as separating sentences with periods– as a prerequisite for engaging in literacy practices" (Beach & Beauchemin, 2019, p. 7). Instead, languaging builds relationships and bolsters the role of community in reinforcing and supporting language development. Literacy-first activity should be primary in projects that ask students to compose multimodal texts.

It is important to consider, as Alvermann (2002) has noted, "the degree to which teacher-centered instruction is superior (or inferior) to more student-centered instruction" (p. 201). Valid concerns about participatory approaches, such as those raised by Moje et al. (2000), suggest we justify how literacy instruction fits in the context of student-centered multimodal projects. Again, as Alvermann (2002) has noted, "In part, the answer to that question rests on how much one believes that meaningful content learning displaces literacy teaching. It would be false to claim that there are no tradeoffs" (p. 201).

With this in mind, we have constructed a game development framework that provides opportunities where literacy skills can be taught, as well as practiced. Specifically, the variety of texts students can create in order to develop a game creates discrete moments where overt literacy instruction can support students without detracting from the collaborative and iterative process of student inquiry, thereby making visible the ways literacy informs different aspects of everyday multimodal practices.

Informal learning, such as that which takes place in communities of practice, is based in "shared interest" in certain outcomes and a way of doing things that is dynamic and responsive to the expertise of members of the group (Lave & Wenger, 1991). The fluid mentorship and youth-centric values in participatory cultures can help teachers reframe learning experiences in literacy to engage students in the relevant application of skills and knowledge related to affinities. As we discuss in the following section on multimodality, student interests can be leveraged for more relevant and communal literacy learning.

Multimodality

Multimodality is evident at the earliest stages of literacy learning. For example, infants attend to spatial and gestural cues, as well as complex social signals, in oral language learning (Liszkowski, 2014). For children, a critical point in literacy development is realizing that marks convey meaning. Any marks. So while children see their drawing as meaning making (Narey, 2017; Albers & Sanders, 2010), formal schooling tends to distinguish it as "art" rather than a complex form of multimodal meaning-making, which means, as Narey (2017) argues, that educators still don't know "how we support their [students'] development across textual forms in our twenty-first century" (p. 2). Therefore, in keeping with other scholars who have underscored the artificial distinction between art, language, and multimodality (Albers & Sanders, 2010; Richards, 2017), we believe that multimodal composing is a rhetorical activity in which students of all ages must make considered choices to communicate for specific purposes. In other words, the aims of LP across English language arts contexts, from kindergarten to college, should be developing competency and fluency in multiple modes of communication, encouraging an awareness of a range of genres, conventions, technologies, and rhetorical contexts (Shipka, 2016), and thereby supporting students in developing "their own writing techniques fully" (Bowen & Whithaus, 2013, p. 7). This "compositional fluency" (Shipka, 2016, p. 255) enlists the experiences of learners in developing enduring literacy skills *and* dispositions.

Though there is still a gap in the multimodal composing processes of adolescents, literacy pedagogies for middle and secondary students are evident in multimodal research, principally around teachers providing scaffolding and overt instruction to support multimodal composing (Smith, 2014), and the ways multimodal composing reinforces collaborative meaning making, such as storytelling (Jocius, 2016). The nonlinear process of composing becomes more visible in multimodalities, creating spaces where different levels of expertise and knowledge in multiple modes and digital tools can come into play, encouraging a participatory approach. Other studies demonstrate how multimodal composing enhances learning through iteration by layering modes to produce a desired affect (Hull & Nelson, 2005) and/

or layering social, cultural, and linguistic identities (Domingo, 2011). While multimodality theory and research provides teachers with instructional insight and ideas, a literacy-first framework combines all of these concepts to enhance student-centered, participatory processes in the classroom that first and foremost place the onus of learning on the students and the facilitation to the teacher.

As we will describe in our game development project, multimodal, literacy-first activities are best understood as part of an iterative process that involves students in developing expectations, an approach that more closely mirrors multimodal composing practices by professionals in the 'real world' (Rowsell, 2013). And because the emphasis is on the process, assessment of some thing at the end of a series of learning experiences is instead formative, occurring throughout the project as checkpoints. A variety of assessment tools can inform this process and facilitate thinking around the important features of different genres, but, for us, Troy Hicks' (2009) MMAPS model most effectively invites students to consider the Mode, Media, Audience, Purpose and Situation in designing– and assessing– successful multimodal compositions. Additionally, students are encouraged to contribute to developing assessment tools, which can be done in connection with multimodal genre studies (Canady et al., 2018). Finally, numerous case studies of professionals working with multimodality, ranging from comic artists to filmmakers, show the prevalence of literacy-first activities where the process is multimodal, interdisciplinary and collaborative (Rowsell, 2013), which makes a case for the value of assessment that approximates the real aims of multimodal compositions in everyday experience.

Rationale for Games

Video games, besides the benefit of a genre recognizable and of high interest among students at any age, also reflect the intersection of literacy skills in the "real world." In other words, writing and visual planning is extensive before, during, and after video game design: "Most paper-based game designers follow an iterative design process, but most digital game designers do not. Typically, a commercial computer game is copiously designed in advance, with extensive storyboards and design documents often hundreds of pages long, completed before any actual game production begins" (Salen, Tekinbas, & Zimmerman, 2004, p. 12). The lead up to the prototype of a commercial game becomes more technical once players are introduced to the game: "These documents invariably become obsolete as soon as production development starts. Why? Because the play of a game will always surprise its creators, particularly if the game design is unusual or experimental" (Salen, Tekinbas, & Zimmerman, 2004, p. 12). In Nagelhout's class, the planning does not directly translate into hundreds of pages of planning; however, the expansion of an idea or concept still reflects a literacy-first approach. Our framework also aligns with Rowsell's (2013) findings about literacy as integral to multimodal professionals' work. Asking students to conduct genre studies in video games, as well as create deliverables to "sell" a game foregrounds an explicit process of literate engagement that includes multimodality. Reading and writing are essential, but we must also engage students in multimodal writing that is closer to how 'writing' is experienced in our contemporary lives.

CONTEXT FOR THE PROJECT

The game development framework began as a project in Nagelhout's electronic documents and publications course. In our many discussions about multimodal composing in the context of writing and literate practices, we conceived of an idea that could engage college students as well as early elementary children in game development as a model for digitally- and socially-mediated literacy practices. Our project description highlights literacy practices as a process, one that focuses learning on development and reflection. Our discussion is informed by the long history of process and post-process research in writing studies, rhetoric and composition studies, and literacy studies. This long history, in all of its iterations and nuances, describes at its core writing as a complex language production task requiring the integration of multiple processes, strategies, and skills (Cormier, Bulut, McGrew, & Frison, 2016). In this way, we argue that literate practices extend beyond simple reading and writing to encompass the complex interactions among writer(s), readers, texts, and contexts (Brandt, 2011; Selber, 2004). And since these practices are both cognitive and social (Cushman, Kintgen, Kroll, & Rose, 2001), our project description will encourage more collaborative activities, privilege informal and situated learning, and promote decision-making, student self-monitoring, and lifelong learning in all K-16 classrooms.

Our goal is to highlight an important trend that shows literate development, like language development, is ever in flux and recursive. From this perspective, we argue that literacy-first projects and activities must incorporate writing tasks that foreground an explicit process that student writers can examine and reflect upon as they manage their projects. But, at the same time, we must always keep in mind that students rarely progress linearly one step at a time to some sort of completion (nor should we expect them to); instead, students might take two steps forward and one step back, or progress quickly in one aspect of their writing production (planning or drafting) while progressing much more slowly in another aspect (revising or editing), or progress in one aspect (drafting) while continuously going back and forth between other aspects (re-planning or re-revising). Complex language production and literacy practices are rarely linear, and rarely a simple step-by-step process. And the evaluation of complex language production cannot be limited to a single product (Bransford, et al., 2000; Marzano, Pickering, & Pollock, 2001; Hattie, 2008).

To meet these complex language production goals, we describe a game development project that can be adapted at all educational levels, that promotes literacy-first, and that provides multimodal options. More importantly, our project serves as a conceptual framework for literacy instruction that mirrors existing literacy curricular and pedagogical objectives across contexts, allows for the use of different digital tools with/in the framework, and can be tailored for a variety of projects (e.g., digital comics, transmedia storytelling, fundraising proposal, etc.) in order to meet student-learning goals more effectively in the future.

As background for our 'literacy-first' project, we must first describe the complex nature of game development and the literate activities that encompass a set of larger processes underscoring the complex and considered choices authors/designers make in these specific rhetorical contexts. In other words, we must first acknowledge game developers as writers, and that the work of writers is central to game development. A project centered in game development engages students in literate practices that range from inquiry to research to genre study and develops important competencies for telling compelling stories through multiple modes.

For us, game development offers a certain measure of depth for all grade levels and provides the kinds of literacy activities that students can build on and carry with them into the future. First and foremost, among these are the ways that a game development project can help students understand the rhetorical choices that every writer makes in any rhetorical situation (see Figure 1).

Figure 1. The rhetorical triangle and the game design rhetorical situation

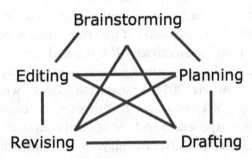

To enhance rhetorical thinking in the compositional process, we map game design features on the rhetorical triangle to provide an over-arching context and set of touchstones for student understanding.

As we describe in the next section, students, like all writers, must determine the purpose for each document they create, rather than simply responding to a teacher prompt. This student control should be a priority for all teachers of writing from kindergarten to Higher Education. For example, students should be able to distinguish the differences between the purpose for a "pitch" to investors and an advertisement targeting potential players and adjust their documents as they see fit. Since various documents may have different purposes and audiences, an ability for students to determine the purpose of a document, especially as it relates to the needs and expectations of the audience, remains one of the most important skills that a student will develop.

Student control makes them the agents of their stories, and teachers must acknowledge students as "experts" of their projects. As we describe later, agency can emerge (or be suppressed) in a number of different ways, most notably at the beginning (or brainstorming/planning) of a project and at the end (or the evaluation) of a project. Affording students the agency, the control, over their own work allows them to better understand the larger, and too often theoretical, components of any literacy project. Considerations of modes for presentation of ideas, stages of design, or the actual game depend on the knowledge, expertise and experience of the designer(s)– or interest or willingness to learn a new tool or platform. For students, an opportunity to practice a skill or engage in creative work also stimulates their interest, curiosity, and perseverance (Csikszentmihalyi, 2013, p. 327). In determining their own purpose for a project, they can make better, more informed development choices because they understand the larger context of the project, who will be engaging with the project, and why. Finally, and most importantly, giving students agency allows teacher interactions with students to be prompts and probing questions, rather than dicta and forced adherence.

Figure 2. The game design process mirrors the rhetorical writing process

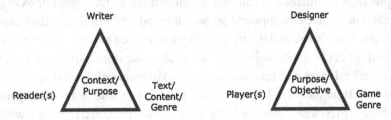

The work of game designers is the work of writers. In a literacy-first framework, the emphasis shifts from the final product to the rigor of the process (Shipka, 2009) in the classroom (see Figure 2). Considering how the process informs "core elements" of a learning environment also contributes to greater student engagement and supports intrinsic motivation (Larsen & Majgaard, 2016). The distinct difference in examining the process of game development as a literacy-first activity is to go beyond the benefits of gamification (De Schutter & Abeele, 2014) to make the work of writing visible. For example, in Fullerton's (2008) *Game Design Workshop,* game designers spend a considerable amount of time with invention, considering their own experiences with games and considering how conventions of different game genres influence play. Additionally, this "playcentric" approach is essentially the aspect of a design process in which the player or audience, in rhetorical terms, is part of the iterative process. Like writing, the process is not linear; yet, game development makes this more visible in that the audience and purpose figure prominently throughout. Game genre study is essential during invention and planning, where the boundaries of the game are considered, as well as the rules, resources, conflicts, and outcomes. Revising occurs not only in drafting stages, but also in phases where feedback loops with test players encourage designers to revisit the boundaries (Salen, Tekinbas, & Zimmerman, 2004), or at the threshold of play that mirror the rules of storytelling (e.g., suspension of disbelief) to more fully develop plot or character. Likewise, 'editing' can occur throughout the process, with each iteration, from copy editing to code testing.

A second set of literacy skills that game development offers is storytelling. Students at all grade levels need to understand that we tell all kinds of stories every day, and every project, in effect, is telling a story for a particular reason to a particular set of listeners. In a game development project, students will discover measures of depth and nuance as they are telling the story of the project, the story for the project, the story in the project, and the story from the project. As we describe in the next section, students will learn the skills to tell these different stories as they construct the different genres. They will see the different expectations more clearly when asked to create a concept statement, or analyze a game genre, or outline a storyline, or develop action flowcharts, character development, or an elevator pitch. All of these potential project elements can introduce students to different texts and different formats that all require different rhetorical choices. In other words, introducing students to these different (and actual) genres associated with game development will help them understand more concretely why we tell a story, when we tell a story, and how we tell a story.

Finally, a game development project allows students to expand their multimodal literacy skills, which grow as students determine the best means for delivering a message on screen, on paper, as a video, or as oral presentation. And while games inevitably invoke technology, and that 'coding' is often given primacy in game design, in truth, as we will show, game development actually draws on a variety of digital tools (including 'coding') that support the writing and the writing processes necessary for successful game development. Game development, we would argue, can serve effectively as a conceptual model of literate practices augmented by, but not dependent on, technology. For example, visual acuity stands front and center in a game development project, for students will see, as they explore the different genres, that the images they choose and the images they present tell a story as effectively as the words on a page. An important aspect of multimodality is that each mode does a different kind of work and that each mode will have affordances and limitations. Again, students will have to make choices.

Technology tends to steal the show because of the time, effort, and technical expertise necessary for many digital projects. Furthermore, literacy educators across K-16 contexts struggle with assessing digital or multimodal products (Hicks, 2015; Neal, 2011; Shipka, 2009, 2016). Avoiding digital technology as the focus will improve when we avoid learning activities as products. The goal is to evaluate growth and development, rather than some *thing* at the end of an arbitrarily designated time frame. Developing "compositional fluency" (Shipka 2016, p. 252) in our students should never be seen as complete when a digital tool is used or a final product is completed, but rather as an ongoing process of experimentation, iteration, reflection, and– above all– practice within different rhetorical situations. And lots of it. The thing at the end of a learning activity should be reflective of a series of developmental activities. The most significant aspect of a final product is the level of expertise evident at that particular stage of development, not the tools that went into crafting it. Again, digital technology are the tools of literacy. Not the other way around.

PROJECT FRAMEWORK

A literacy-first framework is one that identifies the ways in which literacy skills, including but not limited to writing, reading, and speaking, are central to work of multimodal composing. Our model project invites students to propose the adaptation of a favorite book for a video game. Game development is just one of many models that make visible a literacy-first framework. This project should be understood in its complexity, and should not be a one-off project, or a single-focus project; instead, this kind of project should be developed over, at the very least, an entire semester because students should be expected to develop a range of different multimodal texts in a variety of complementary genres as part of a fully articulated research and writing process. In this way, our project framework expands the common understanding of game development beyond simply writing code. As we illustrate, the complexity of writing the code for a game cannot occur without meeting all of the other expectations for comprehensive and effective game development; in other words, the work of writers should be understood as central to game development.

Game developers are writers.

Game development has been described as requiring "a playful approach but a systematic solution" (Fullerton, 2008, p. xix), which could just as easily describe a literacy-first framework that seeks to integrate digital technology into literacy instruction in a way that is student-centered and focused on developing literate practices with multimodal texts rather than simply developing skills appended to specific digital tools.

For this project, game development might include an array of genres specific to game design. A multimodal list that teachers might draw from in creating an assignment might include the following genres:

- Critical Game Reviews
- Game Genre Review
- Concept Statement
- Game Synopsis or Summary
- Adaptation Summary
- Design Plan
- Storyline
- Character Development
- Game Flowchart
- Narrative Treatment
- Game Mechanics and Rulebook

- Game Development Storyboards
- Concept Art
- Audience Analysis
- Elevator Pitch
- Ignite Presentation
- Teaser Trailer
- Game Proposal
- Production Schedule
- Market Analysis
- Marketing Campaign
- Web Site Landing Page
- Transmedia Storyboards

All of these different potential "genres," and their associated rhetorical conventions, are inherent in game design and development. And each offers specific insights into the game development process that can be learned by students. For the teacher, each of the genres can be used in different combinations for creating a variety of projects that help students of all ages build a whole range of important literacy and multimodal skills. More importantly, as we will describe shortly, each of the genres can be broken down into different deliverables in order to serve as process checkpoints. Seen in this way, these process checkpoints allow greater flexibility for fluid mentorship between students. A focus on process, as well as a focus on student interactions and collaboration through writing, relieves pressure on the teacher to make technology the sole focus of instruction. Finally, and most importantly, our game development framework can be adapted for a variety of projects (e.g., digital comics, transmedia storytelling, fund-raising proposal, etc.), which assists teachers in mirroring literacy curricular objectives across contexts by highlighting the work of writers and writing in different contexts and across disciplines.

Game Development Project Framework

This is a multimodal writing project framework that develops through an understanding of the ways that various genres support game design and development, with all aspects of the framework adaptable to a teacher's particular literacy goals for their students. As such, an important consideration for this project as a conceptual framework for literacy instruction is that student work should go through multiple drafts, with multiple forms of feedback embedded at various stages of the project. This feedback should be both higher-order and lower-order: in writing, the difference between revisions and line edits; in reading, the difference between understanding a concept and understanding a word in a particular context. More importantly, this feedback could (should) come from multiple sources: small groups of peers, small groups with the teacher, large groups with the teacher, or one-on-one with the teacher. Feedback embedded at various stages of the project process forces teachers to provide the time necessary for individual students to make connections to the work, to engage with the work, and to feel a sense of accomplishment in doing the work.

As we will show, our game development framework aligns with curricular expectations of K-12 settings, as well as the curricular objectives of the post-secondary writing course. In short, at the very least, students can be expected to

- Engage in personal reflection about experiences with, in this case, games and video games
- Participate in a peer-driven genre study to identify conventions of video games
- Consider rhetorical aspects of their writing, such as audience and purpose
- Examine similarities and differences between a book and a video game genre (using textual evidence to support those choices)
- Create a storyline for their game, such as players, objectives, procedures, rules, resources, conflict, boundaries, and outcomes (Fullerton, 2008)
- Iterate by working through a workshop process or by creating betas and "playtesting"
- Develop graphic organizers, such as a flowchart or a production schedule
- Sell an idea by creating a web landing page, an elevator pitch, an Ignite presentation, a trailer video, etc.

Likewise, these curricular objectives can also align with a set of primary pedagogical goals that model the recursivity of learning, encourage trust in multiple perspectives, and allow for the time necessary to develop quality thought. Above all, a literacy-first framework is essentially a (re)frame of mind. Starting with the kinds of work writers do in "real world" contexts that include technology, images, multiple media and modes rather than standards or discreet skills helps us change the way we *do* literacy pedagogy in the classroom. Literacy-first is a shift in thinking about the work of readers and writers.

Describing the Game Development Project Framework

In describing our framework, and the options that teachers need to consider in constructing the project, we assume the project will include a full writing process for each deliverable (brainstorming, planning, drafting, revising, editing, submission), with multiple opportunities for feedback and revision, as well as opportunities for students to help define the criteria used to evaluate the work. We also assume the project will include multiple deliverables so that students can practice working on multiple documents at different stages of the process at the same time. This allows them to understand the ways that different documents can both influence and depend on other documents, the ways that research can build over time based on the goals of a particular document, the ways that rhetorical choices change throughout the process, and the ways that different deadlines shape and prioritize their production.

While we enhance our description of the game development project framework using the specific examples outlined in Table 1, we organize the overall discussion around five primary project elements:

- Timeframe
- Project Description
- Literacy Goals
- Deliverables
- Evaluation Criteria

The first project element of our framework requires teachers to determine a timeframe for the project by defining the number of weeks that students spend on the project, along with the time students spend on each stage of the writing process. Patience is so very important in learning to write, so teachers must provide students with the time necessary for the recursivity of learning: to explore, to experiment, to give/get feedback, and to start over if necessary. An appropriate amount of time will allow for different types of composing, as Smith, Wilhelm, and Fredricksen (2013) outline: "composing to practice, composing to plan, first-draft composing, final-draft composing, and composing to transfer" (p. 47). More importantly, this contextualized process approach should further account for multimodal composing, especially, and allow student writers to move back and forth among different types of composing in different modes as they work toward publication.

Table 1. Game Development Project Framework Examples and Options

Game Development Project Framework Examples and Options		
Project Element	**Elementary** **3ʳᵈ Grade Example**	**Secondary** **9ᵗʰ Grade Example**	**Post-Secondary** **400-Level Example**
Determine Timeframe	**3-4 Week Project*** • 1 week brainstorming and planning • 1 week drafting • 1 week revising • 1 week editing & final preparations for submission	**9ᵗʰ grade 9-Week Project*** • 1-2 weeks brainstorming and planning • 4 weeks drafting • 3 weeks revising • 2 weeks editing, reflection, and final preparations for submission	**12-Week Project*** • 3 weeks brainstorming and planning • 4 weeks drafting • 3 weeks revising • 2 weeks editing, reflection, and final preparations for submission
NOTE: The timeframe may vary for each deliverable based on literacy goals		
Draft Project Description	What if you could create a video game for your favorite character or book? What would you do?	This project asks students to create a plan and proposal for adapting a specific book (or series) as a video game	This project asks students to construct initial documents for adapting a specific book (or series) as a video game
Articulate Literacy Goals	• Build on knowledge of narrative structures (e.g., setting, characterization, plot) to create a new storyline • Use the writing process to refine ideas	• Understand rhetorical context to produce effective information • Use technical and abstract content-area language appropriately • Offer organized, cohesive, and coherent expression of ideas	• Make nuanced choices based on sophisticated rhetorical awareness • Use technical language to create an effective argument • Organize and align multiple texts to achieve a single purpose
Select Deliverables	1. Story analysis (e.g., plot, setting, conflicts, etc. based on narrative arc of selected text) 2. Character/avatar chart 3. Character/avatar backstory 4. Storyboard 5. Presentation	1. Concept statement or idea proposal 2. Critical review 3. Character/avatar backstory and gameplay story options (Fullerton, 2008) 4. Game flowchart 5. Elevator pitch	1. Concept Statement 2. Critical Review I 3. Critical Review II 4. Game Flowchart 5. Five-Minute Elevator Pitch
Define Initial Evaluation Criteria	• Identifies the key features of the narrative arc of story • Articulates character in context of gameplay using evidence from text • Presents information clearly and effectively • Revised and edited	• Presents content effectively based on the specific platform • Shows clear understanding of topic • Articulates clear understanding of video game genres • Presents information clearly and effectively • Meets needs of the audience • Revised and Edited	• Presents content effectively based on the specific platform • Shows rhetorical sophistication • Articulates critical understanding of adaptation and video game genres • Presents information clearly and effectively • Meets needs of multiple audiences • Revised and Edited
NOTE: Specific criteria should be developed collaboratively with students for each deliverable		

A sample timeframe for a 12-Week Project at the post-secondary level might look like this:

- 3 weeks brainstorming and planning
- 4 weeks drafting
- 3 weeks revising
- 2 weeks editing, reflection, and final preparations for submission

It is important to point out that a timeframe should be fluid, not rigid, allowing students to develop their writing in personalized ways. Furthermore, timeframe flexibility should also pertain to the different deliverables, as some will require more time at different stages of the writing process. The goal, of course, is to allow the project to develop organically so that students can understand the time necessary to craft a successful piece of writing. For example, a third-grade teacher might want to build in time for developing independent reading skills related to standards for reading literature, as well as support for research and writing skills. This might be 2-3 weeks for reading and 6 weeks for game development. A high school teacher might consider time for literature circles to encourage peer-supported reading and choice in addition to time for developing research, writing, and revising with technology within the game development process. The teacher might determine that the standards or curriculum pacing guide for the second semester can be met in the game development framework and designate 16 weeks for the project including reading.

Second, teachers need to draft an initial project description that sets the primary goal(s) of the project without being wordy or prescriptive. In other words, teachers should avoid too much definition that will restrict students taking ownership of the project. Ideally, the teacher will offer students just enough information to get started effectively without constraining the creative outlets and research pathways.

For example, a project definition may be as simple as a single statement:

- This project asks students to construct initial documents for adapting a specific book (or series) as a video game.

Or a single guiding question:

- What if you could create a video game for your favorite character or book? What would you do?

A simple project definition allows students to ask questions, come up with their own information, design multiple research pathways, and articulate their own success as writers in this rhetorical context.

The third element of our project framework asks teachers to articulate the literacy goals for the project that are both curricular and pedagogical. For us, literacy goals are those curricular skills and strategies that students learn about, develop, practice, and possibly master as part of the project, while pedagogical goals should be student- or classroom-specific. In other words, within the grade-level curriculum, teachers must understand the needs of their students and their classroom environment in order to use the project to build in appropriate supports or target skills through deliverables. Ideally, curricular and pedagogical goals should be both abstract and (grade-level) difficult so that students can work to achieve them in the time allotted and through the concrete activities outlined in the project. More importantly, articulating literacy goals creates transparency and provides teachers with insights for selecting deliverables that will help students meet their writing goals more effectively.

For example, an initial set of secondary level literacy goals might include:

- Understand rhetorical context to produce effective information
- Use technical and abstract content-area language appropriately
- Offer organized, cohesive, and coherent expression of ideas

A set of goals like this make transparent the sophistication of the writing task for students and provides them with an opportunity for making connections between the concrete work that they are doing on the project and the abstract expectations described by state standards or common core. More importantly, goals like these allow teachers to avoid the "testing trap" described by Hillocks (2002) while helping students develop the tools and strategies necessary for successful writing.

Teachers who are concerned about meeting the standards might choose a standard and then focus on the "big idea." For example, the Common Core Standard W.9 requires students to "Draw evidence from literary or informational texts to support analysis, reflection, and research" (NGAC, 2010). A literacy goal connected to this standard for game development with literary characters might read: Use details from a literary text to develop characters, or avatars, and create familiar storylines for game play. In a third-grade classroom, Standard W.3.4 for production and distribution of writing states that with guidance and support, students "produce writing in which the development and organization are appropriate to task and purpose" (NGAC, 2010). The goal associated with meeting these standards would be more generous in order to give students some room to operate, and the assessment (discussed later) is where more specific expectations can be negotiated with students depending on the genres selected for deliverables.

Fourth, teachers need to select from the list of genres the deliverables for students to submit as part of the project. Each deliverable should be tied intimately to the literacy goals, and, in order to effectively learn about, develop, and practice before final submission, students should understand the deliverables in terms of the writing process. Obviously, the goal here is to offer students multiple opportunities to write in ways that are both interesting and relevant to them, while, at the same time, providing an introduction to new and more sophisticated kinds of writing.

For example, a secondary level project might include the following genres:

1. Concept statement or idea proposal
2. Critical review
3. Character/avatar backstory and gameplay story options (Fullerton, 2008)
4. Game flowchart
5. Elevator pitch

Each of these genres can be compressed or expanded for the level of the student and/or to help teachers meet specific literacy goals. In other words, with a little creative thinking, each of these genres can be implemented at any grade level: as text only, as visuals only, or, ideally, as a combination of both. There really are no restrictions for how teachers (or students) might define these genres and there are no restrictions for how these genres might be used in combination and/or developmentally. For example, a Game Flowchart would build on the pedagogical goal of reading literature in elementary by supporting students in demonstrating understanding of text or conveying key details through recounting the story (RL.3.1 and RL.3.2) but specific to the purpose of game play. Similarly, high school students might explore tensions and conflicts that are essential to the dramatic arc of stories *and* game design (Fullerton, 2008). And at the post-secondary level, students can offer a rhetorically sophisticated and cohesive presentation of multiple texts to achieve a single purpose.

The final element of our project framework asks teachers to create an initial set of criteria (or a rubric) for evaluating student submissions. Evaluation criteria are the measurements that students should learn about, develop, and use as a part of text development, tied intimately to the literacy goals and understood in terms of the writing process. But, as Panadero and Jonsson (2013) explain, criteria should not be seen solely as evaluative (or summative); instead, criteria should provide transparent tools for both assessing student work in-process and after submission. More importantly, criteria should also provide students with the means for owning the documents, as a tool that can negotiated and revised.

For example, general (and initial) criteria for a post-secondary project might include

- Presents content effectively based on the specific platform
- Shows rhetorical sophistication
- Articulates critical understanding of adaptation and video game genres
- Presents information clearly and effectively
- Meets needs of multiple audiences
- Revised and edited

Criteria can, and should, be an important feature for learning by students and teachers at the project level, course level, and program level (see Earl, 2003). For example, students can use criteria at the planning stage for interrogating the purpose and audience of a document more deeply and in more sophisticated ways. At the drafting stage, criteria can help students collaborate effectively on a particular document, as well as for offering feedback on drafts during peer review. Discussing whether a Game Flowchart articulates a critical understanding of plot in adapting a novel to a video game during peer review will reinforce understanding of purpose and audience. Or, at the elementary level, criteria might focus on establishing a narrator and organizing game sequences that unfold naturally (W.3.3., NGAC, 2010). Other features specific to game development such as "playtesting," or iterating with an audience, emphasize the process and can inform a refining of criteria. As students' understanding increases, they can revise the criteria specific to their genre and rhetorical purposes, thereby allowing teachers to provide consistent feedback at all stages of the writing process, as well as make adjustments in their expectations throughout the project. Hence the importance of tying deliverables to literacy goals.

CONCLUSION

For decades, literacy scholarship has considered the profound changes resulting from increased cultural, linguistic, and technological diversity (NLG, 1996). However, literacy education– and education in general– continues to reflect twentieth century models (Jenkins, Itō, & boyd, 2016). To reimagine literacy practices that make space for overt instruction, or literacy pedagogies, alongside participatory practices that privilege student-centered learning and inquiry, we created this project as a literacy-first framework. Initially implemented in the college setting, it was immediately evident that game development made visible the work of writers. With the writing process more visible, yet accessible, in game development, literacy instruction can engage all learners at all grade levels in implementing, practicing, and learning new digital and multimodal literacies.

REFERENCES

Albers, P., & Sanders, J. (Eds.). (2010). *Literacies, the arts, and multimodality*. Urbana, IL: National Council of Teachers of English.

Alvermann, D. E. (2002). Effective literacy instruction for adolescents. *Journal of Literacy Research, 34*(2), 189–208. doi:10.120715548430jlr3402_4

Anderson, M., & Jiang, J. (2018). Teens, social media, & technology 2018. Retrieved from https://www.pewinternet.org/2018/05/31/teens-social-media-technology-2018/

Beach, R., & Beauchemin, F. (2019). *Teaching language as action in the ELA classroom*. New York, NY: Routledge. doi:10.4324/9780429398537

Bowen, T., & Whithaus, C. (Eds.). (2013). *Multimodal literacies and emerging genres*. Pittsburgh, PA: University of Pittsburgh Press. doi:10.2307/j.ctt6wrbkn

Brandt, D. (2011). *Literacy as involvement: The acts of writers, readers, and texts*. Carbondale, IL: Southern Illinois University Press.

Bransford, J. D., Brown, A. L., & Cocking, R. R. (2000). *How people learn: Brain, mind experience and school*. Washington, DC: National Academy Press.

Canady, F., Martin, K., & Scott, C. E. (2018). "Song of Myself": A digital unit of study remixed. In J. S. Dail, S. Witte, & S. Bickmore (Eds.), *Toward a more visual literacy: Shifting the paradigm with digital tools and young adult literature* (pp. 101–124). Lanham, MD: Rowman & Littlefield.

Cormier, D. C., Bulut, O., McGrew, K. S., & Frison, J. (2016). The role of Cattel-Horn-Carroll (CHC) cognitive abilities in predicting writing achievement during the school-age years. *Psychology in the Schools, 53*(8), 787–803. doi:10.1002/pits.21945

Csikszentmihalyi, M. (2013). *Creativity: the psychology of discovery and invention*. New York, NY: HarperCollins. (Original work published 1996)

Cushman, E., Kintgen, E., Kroll, B., & Rose, M. (2001). Literacy: A critical sourcebook. Boston, MA: Bedford.

De Schutter, B., & Abeele, V. V. (2014, April). Gradequest–Evaluating the impact of using game design techniques in an undergraduate course. In Foundations of Digital Games. Academic Press.

Deleuze, G., & Guattari, F. (1987). *A thousand plateaus: Capitalism and schizophrenia*. London: Bloomsbury Publishing.

Domingo, M. (2011). Analyzing layering in textual design: A multimodal approach for examining cultural, linguistic, and social migrations in digital video. *International Journal of Social Research Methodology, 14*(3), 219–230. doi:10.1080/13645579.2011.563619

Earl, L. M. (2003). *Assessment as learning*. Thousand Oaks, CA: Corwin.

Fullerton, T. (2008). *Game design workshop: A playcentric approach to creating innovative games* (2nd ed.). Burlington, MA: Morgan Kaufmann Publishers. doi:10.1201/b13172

Gee, J. P. (1999/2014). *Introduction to discourse analysis*. New York, NY: Routledge.

Gee, J. P. (2003). *What video games have to teach us about learning and literacy*. New York, NY: Palgrave Macmillan. doi:10.1145/950566.950595

Gee, J. P. (2004). *Situated language and learning: A critique of traditional schooling*. New York, NY: Routledge.

Hattie, J. (2008). *Visible learning: A synthesis of over 800 meta-analyses relating to achievement*. London: Routledge. doi:10.4324/9780203887332

Hicks, T. (2009). *The digital writing workshop*. Portsmouth, NH: Heinemann.

Hicks, T. (2015). *Assessing student's digital writing: Protocols for looking closely*. New York, NY: Teachers College Press.

Hillocks, G. Jr. (2002). *The testing trap: How state writing assessments control learning*. New York, NY: Teachers College Press.

Hull, G. A., & Nelson, M. E. (2005). Locating the semiotic power of multimodality. *Written Communication, 22*(2), 224–261. doi:10.1177/0741088304274170

Itō, M., Baumer, S., Bittanti, M., Boyd, D., Cody, R., Herr-Stephenson, B., & Pascoe, C. J. (2010). *Hanging out, messing around, and geeking out*. Cambridge, MA: MIT Press.

Jenkins, H. (2009). *Confronting the challenges of participatory culture: Media education for the 21st century*. Cambridge, MA: MIT Press. doi:10.7551/mitpress/8435.001.0001

Jenkins, H., Itō, M., & Boyd, D. (2016). *Participatory culture in a networked era*. Cambridge, UK: Polity Press.

Jewitt, C., Bezemer, J., & O'Halloran, K. (2016). *Introducing multimodality*. New York, NY: Routledge.

Jocius, R. (2016). Telling Unexpected Stories: Students as Multimodal Artists. *English Journal, 105*(5), 16–22.

Jocson, K. (2010). Unpacking symbolic creativities: Writing in school and across contexts. *Review of Education, Pedagogy & Cultural Studies, 32*(2), 206–236. doi:10.1080/10714411003799108

Kress, G. (2003). *Literacy in the New Media Age*. Abingdon, OX: Routledge.

Kress, G. (2010). *Multimodality: A Social-Semiotic Approach to Contemporary Communication*. New York, NY: Routledge.

Kress, G., & Van Leeuwen, T. (2001). *Multimodal Discourse: The modes and media of contemporary communication*. New York, NY: Oxford University Press.

Larsen, L. J., & Majgaard, G. (2016). Expanding the game design space–teaching computer game design in higher education. *Designs for Learning, 8*(1), 13–22. doi:10.16993/dfl.68

Latour, B. (2005). *Reassembling the social: An introduction to Actor-Network-Theory*. Oxford, UK: Oxford University Press.

Lave, J., & Wenger, E. (1991). *Situated learning: Legitimate Peripheral Participation*. Cambridge, UK: Cambridge University Press. doi:10.1017/CBO9780511815355

Liszkowski, U. (2014). Two sources of meaning in infant communication: Preceding action contexts and act-accompanying characteristics. *Philosophical Transactions of the Royal Society of London. Series B, Biological Sciences*, *369*(1651), 1–9. doi:10.1098/rstb.2013.0294 PMID:25092662

Marzano, R. J., Pickering, D., & Pollock, J. E. (2001). *Classroom instruction that works: Research-based strategies for increasing student achievement*. Alexandria, VA: ACSD.

Mills, K. A. (2010). A review of the "Digital Turn" in the New Literacy Studies. *Review of Educational Research*, *80*(2), 246–271. doi:10.3102/0034654310364401

Mills, K. A. (2016). Possible Effects of Internet Use on Cognitive Development in Adolescence. *Media and Communication*, *4*(3), 4–12. doi:10.17645/mac.v4i3.516

Moje, E. B., Young, J. P., Readence, J. E., & Moore, D. W. (2000). Reinventing adolescent literacy for new times: Perennial and millennial issues. *Journal of Adolescent & Adult Literacy*, *43*(5), 400–411.

Narey, M. J. (2017). The Creative "Art" of Making Meaning. In M. J. Narey (Ed.), *Multimodal perspectives of language, literacy, and learning in early childhood. Educating the Young Child (Advances in Theory and Research, Implications for Practice)* (Vol. 12). Cham, Switzerland: Springer International Publishing AG.

National Council of Teachers of English (NCTE). (2016). *Professional knowledge for the teaching of writing* [Position statement]. Retrieved from http://www2.ncte.org/statement/teaching-writing/

National Council of Teachers of English (NCTE). (2018). *A Call to Action: What we know about adolescent literacy instruction* [Position statement]. Retrieved from http://www2.ncte.org/statement/adolescentliteracy/ on April 12, 2019.

National Governors Association Center (NGAC) for Best Practices, Council of Chief State School Officers. (2010). *Common Core State Standards (English Language Arts)*. Washington, D.C.: National Governors Association Center for Best Practices, Council of Chief State School Officers.

Neal, M. R. (2011). *Writing assessment and the revolution in digital texts and technologies*. Columbia, NY: Teachers College Press.

New London Group (NLG). (1996). A pedagogy of multiliteracies: Designing social futures. *Harvard Educational Review*, *66*(1), 60–92. doi:10.17763/haer.66.1.17370n67v22j160u

Panadero, E., & Jonsson, A. (2013). The use of scoring rubrics for formative assessment purposes revisited: A review. *Educational Research Review*, *9*, 129–144. doi:10.1016/j.edurev.2013.01.002

Prensky, M. (2001). Digital natives, digital immigrants part 1. *On the Horizon*, *9*(5), 1–6. doi:10.1108/10748120110424816

Prior, P. (2006). A sociocultural theory of writing. In C. A. MacArthur, S. Graham, & J. Fitzgerald (Eds.), *Handbook of Writing Research* (pp. 54–66). New York, NY: The Guilford Press.

Rheingold, H. (2012). Stewards of digital literacies. *Knowledge Quest, 41*(1), 52–55.

Richards, R. D. (2017). Young children's drawings and storytelling: Multimodal transformations that help to mediate complex sociocultural worlds. In M. J. Narey (Ed.), *Multimodal perspectives of language, literacy, and learning in early childhood: The creative and critical "art" of meaning making* (pp. 127–148). Pittsburgh, PA: Springer. doi:10.1007/978-3-319-44297-6_7

Rowsell, J. (2013). *Working with multimodality: Rethinking literacy in the digital age*. London, UK: Routledge.

Salen, K., Tekinbaş, K. S., & Zimmerman, E. (2004). *Rules of play: Game design fundamentals*. MIT press.

Selber, S. A. (2004). *Multiliteracies for a digital age*. Carbondale, IL: Southern Illinois University Press.

Shipka, J. (2009). Negotiating rhetorical, material, methodological, and technological difference: Evaluating multimodal designs. *College Composition and Communication, 61*(1), 343–366.

Shipka, J. (2016). Transmodality in/and processes of making: Changing dispositions and practice. *College English, 78*(3), 250–257.

Smith, B. E. (2014). Beyond words: A review of research on adolescents and multimodal composition. In R. E. Ferdig & K. E. Pytash (Eds.), *Exploring multimodal composition and digital writing* (pp. 1–19). Hershey, PA: IGI Global. doi:10.4018/978-1-4666-4345-1.ch001

Smith, M. W., Wilhelm, J. D., & Fredricksen, J. (2013). The Common Core: New standards, new teaching. *Kappan Magazine, 94*(8), 45–48.

Street, B. (1997). The implications of the 'New Literacy Studies' for literacy education. *English in Education, 31*(3), 45–59. doi:10.1111/j.1754-8845.1997.tb00133.x

Street, B. (2003). What's "new" in New Literacy Studies? Critical approaches to literacy in theory and practice. *Current Issues in Comparative Education, 5*(2), 77–91.

Vygotsky, L. (1978). *Mind in society: The development of higher psychological processes*. Cambridge, MA: Harvard University Press.

Wertsch, J. V. (1991). *Voices of the mind: A sociocultural approach to mediated action*. Cambridge, MA: Harvard University Press.

Wilhelm, J. D. (2004). *Reading is seeing: Learning to visualize scenes, characters, ideas, and text worlds to improve comprehension and reflective reading*. New York, NY: Scholastic.

ADDITIONAL READING

Arola, K. L., Sheppard, J., & Ball, C. E. (2014). *Writer/Designer: A guide to making multimodal projects.* *Boston, MA*. Bedford: St. Martin's.

Ball, C. E. (2006). Designerly≠ readerly: Re-assessing multimodal and new media rubrics for use in writing studies. *Convergence, 12*(4), 393–412. doi:10.1177/1354856506068366

Bazalgette, C., & Buckingham, D. (2013). Literacy, media and multimodality: A critical response. *Literacy, 47*(2), 95–102. doi:10.1111/j.1741-4369.2012.00666.x

Boyd, D. (2014). *It's complicated: The social lives of networked teens.* Yale University Press.

Cope, B., & Kalantzis, M. (2000). *Multiliteracies: Literacy learning and the design of social futures.* New York, NY: Routledge.

Garcia, A., Cantrill, C., Filipiak, D., Hunt, B., Lee, C., Mirra, N., & Peppler, K. (2014). *Teaching in the connected learning classroom.* Irvine, CA: Digital Media and Learning Research Hub.

International Literacy Association. (2019). *Digital resources in early childhood literacy development* [Position statement and research brief]. Newark, DE: Author.

Miller, S. M., & McVee, M. B. (Eds.). (2013). *Multimodal composing in classrooms: Learning and teaching for the digital world.* New York, NY: Routledge. doi:10.4324/9780203804032

Mills, K. A. (2011). 'I'm Making it Different to the Book': Transmediation in Young Children's Multimodal and Digital Texts. *Australasian Journal of Early Childhood, 36*(3), 56–65. doi:10.1177/183693911103600308

Palmeri, J. (2012). *Remixing composition: A history of multimodal writing pedagogy.* Carbondale, IL: SIU Press.

Shipka, J. (2011). *Toward a Composition Made Whole. Pittsburgh.* Pittsburgh, PA: University of Pittsburgh Press. doi:10.2307/j.ctt5hjqkk

Steinkuehler, C. (2010). Video games and digital literacies. *Journal of Adolescent & Adult Literacy, 54*(1), 61–63. doi:10.1598/JAAL.54.1.7

Vasudevan, L., Schultz, K., & Bateman, J. (2010). Rethinking composing in a digital age: Authoring literate identities through multimodal storytelling. *Written Communication, 27*(4), 442–468. doi:10.1177/0741088310378217

KEY TERMS AND DEFINITIONS

Affinity/Affinity Spaces: Interests or spaces organized around interests of the members.

Literacy-first Activity: Grounded in sociocultural theory, activities that enlist skills, knowledge, and creation around communication. It is a process that underscores the complex and considered choices authors or designers make in specific rhetorical contexts.

Multimodality: Modes (e.g., aural, spatial, gestural, visual, or linguistic) combined in a variety of ways to make meaning. Emphasis is on the unique affordances of each mode as they contribute to the meaning as a whole.

Networked Publics: New and digital media networks have become the public spaces for communication, civic participation, and commerce. Information and new knowledge creation are easily disseminated.

Participatory Culture: Cultures or affinity spaces characterized by informal learning structures such as low barriers to participation, fluid mentorship, and experimentation.

Sociocultural Theory: Language and literacy theory in which social and cultural contexts are integral to language development (including semiotics), as opposed to theories that see language(s) as rule-based and highly structured.

Chapter 44
Sustain City:
Effective Serious Game Design in Promoting Science and Engineering Education

Ying Tang
Rowan University, USA

Kauser Jahan
Rowan University, USA

Christopher Franzwa
Rowan University, USA

Marzieh S. Saeedi-Hosseiny
Rowan University, USA

Talbot Bielefeldt
Independent Researcher, USA

Nathan Lamb
Rowan University, USA

Shengtao Sun
Rowan University, USA

ABSTRACT

Recent years have witnessed a growing interest in interactive narrative-based serious games for education and training. A key challenge posed by educational serious games is the balance of fun and learning, so that players are motivated enough to unfold the narrative stories on their own pace while getting sufficient learning materials across. In this chapter, various design strategies that aim to tackle this challenge are presented through the development of Sustain City, an educational serious game system that engages students, particularly prospective and beginning science and engineering students, in a series of engineering design. Besides narrative-learning synthesis, supplementing the player's actions with feedback, and the development of a sufficient guidance system, the chapter also discusses the integration of rigorous assessment and personalized scaffolding. The evaluation of Sustain City deployment confirms the values of the serious games in promoting students' interests and learning in science, technology, engineering, and mathematics (STEM) fields.

DOI: 10.4018/978-1-6684-7589-8.ch044

INTRODUCTION

Play and technology have been combined in various interesting ways to synthesize elements of environment and story with simulations in providing real-time visualized responses (Entertainment Software Association, 2013); and to embody real world situations in which players explore, learn and solve problems (Barab, Gresalfi, & Arici, 2009). The consideration of games in education is made evident by recent and growing development in "serious games," defined by design that takes into account "(i) serious aspects that determine the pedagogical objectives such as the transmission and/or acquisition of knowledge, know-how, or information; (ii) and fun aspects which focus on the motivation and the management of end users' frustration." (Cheng, Chen, Chu, & Chen, 2015; Hocine & Gouaich, 2011). Serious games offer several strong learning-enhancement capabilities, allowing for the realization of virtual worlds that can assist students in ways that the typical classroom environment cannot (Torrente, Blanco, Moreno-Ger, & Fernandez-Manjon, 2012). In standard textbook-driven lecturing and study, visual or hands-on learners are left to find their own ways of perceiving the ever more complex concepts as they wade through a course. Currently, even hands-on approaches to learning, such as lab experiments, are limited by budgetary and safety constraints. Serious games, on the other hand, make difficult abstract concepts and large data sets accessible in ways that are more visual, interactive, and concrete, providing an opportunity to gain the attention of students who are not otherwise engaged with the content (Bosch, 2016; Callaghan, Savin-Baden, McShane, & Eguíluz, 2015; Di Mascio & Daiton, 2017; Franzwa, Tang, & Johnson, 2013; Rhodes et al., 2017). The game format provides students with a learning structure and an incentive to develop their skills at their own pace in a non-judgmental but competitive and often fun environment (Habgood & Ainsworth, 2011; Terzidou, Tsiatsos, Miliou, & Sourvinou, 2016). Vivid examples can be found in many domains, such as science and engineering discovery (Barab et al., 2009; Ma, Oikonomou, & Jain, 2011; Mavromihales & Holmes, 2016; Mott & Lester, 2006), military training (Smith, 2009; Zielke et al., 2009) and healthcare training (Menzies, 2017; Tong, Chignell, Tierney, & Lee, 2016; Wattanasoontorn, Hernandez, & Sbert, 2012).

Echoing general concerns with the current state of the US school systems, many educational groups have begun advocating curricular changes for Science, Technology, Engineering, and Mathematics (STEM) subjects. In a report of the President's Council of Advisors on Science and Technology (PCAST, 2012), higher performing students cite "uninspiring" introductory courses as a factor in choosing different majors while lower performing students struggle with mathematics due to insufficient assistance. Issues such as student interests and instructional feedback should be considered when developing any STEM serious game. While the educational value of games has long been recognized, there is significant resistance to their adoption in formal education. One problem is the amount of instructional time that must be devoted to training and practice to allow games to have a significant effect on student learning. There is a tendency for serious games to develop an all-inclusive learning system that largely leaves the instructors without the flexibility needed to create their own curriculum. Arnab et al. (2012) and Wilson (2009) argued that considerable benefit would be gained from aligning games with standards and curricula. An effective serious game relies on an instructor for focus and guidance (Egenfeldt-Nielsen, 2010). Best practices for using games in the classroom promote a strong interconnection between instructors and software, where instructors remain the driving force behind education (Wilson, 2009). A set of serious-game-based educational experiments carried out in three European countries support those research propositions (Earp, Ott, Popescu, Romero, & Usart, 2014). In particular, the study revealed the importance of tutor in guiding the learning experience although the game was tailored for self-regulated learning; the importance of carefully planned activity sequences with respect to chosen tools; and the needs for prior definition of the role and tasks of teachers.

While serious games have significant potential as instructional tools, their learning effectiveness is still understudied, mainly due to the complexity involved in assessing tangible and intangible measures in games. Such assessment is important for gaining insights into what happens when the player's capacity to make decisions in games is compromised or sabotaged, on which the most appropriate scaffolding can be provided to improve student learning. Furthermore, performance assessment enables adaptability and personalization in various aspects, such as definition, presentation, and scheduling of game contents to players (Bellotti, Kapralos, Lee, Moreno-Ger, & Berta, 2013). Chanel, Rebetez, Bétrancourt, & Pun (2011) proposed to maintain players' engagement by adapting game difficulty according to players' emotion assessed from physiological signals. Lester et al. (2013) reported a similar study where an automated analysis of fine-grained facial movement was conducted during computer-mediated tutoring. Derbali and Frasson (2010) examined players' electrophysiological responses such as galvanic skin response and electroencephalography (EEG) activity. They discovered that EEG wave patterns were strongly correlated with the increase of motivation during different parts of serious game play, while the correlation between players' motivation and their heart rate responses was insignificant. Similar study was conducted by Kramer (2007), where he found that skin conductance was positively correlated with players' performance. Besides game difficulty levels, adaptation can be seen in terms of players' guidance in game. Myneni, Narayanan, Rebello, Rouinfar and Pumtambekar (2013) developed a learning environment to help students master physics concepts in the context pulleys, where student interactions and various measures of student performance were evaluated, based on which dynamic feedback and tutoring were offered for student's misconceptions. Similar work in different learning domains were reported (Johnson, Tang, & Franzwa, 2014; Limongelli, Sciarrone, Temperini, & Vaste, 2009; McLaren, DeLeeuw, & Mayer, 2011); while a detailed design issues of such adaptive training systems were also discussed (Raybourn, 2006; Thomas & Young, 2010; Westra, Dignum, & Dignum, 2011). Apparently, the future direction of intelligent serious games calls for rigorous assessment and personalized scaffolding that allow learning to reach students at different levels.

Motivated by these remarks, this chapter presents a serious game design approach that addresses students' needs of in-game references and help, without compromising the role of the instructor in directing exploration. Four serious games were produced under the umbrella theme of "*Sustain City*" (Tang, Shetty, Jahan, Henry, & Hargrove, 2012). Each game focuses on particular fundamental science and engineering concepts and serves as a replacement for a traditional laboratory activity. In particular, *Solaris One* aims to enhance understanding of basic thermodynamic laws intuitively and mathematically. *Gridlock* offers an in-depth exploration of logic-circuit design, providing students with a realistic application of logic systems and the tools to construct and analyze the systems. *Powerville* explores the root meaning behind *Sustain City*, providing exploration of alternative energies and their impacts on a modern city. *Algae Grows Future* consists of several mini-games to connect students with the prospect of this microbe, playing a role that affects the future of the city, whether as a photosynthetic organism or fuel alternative.

Textbooks always provide example-based questions, but students can be lost in wording. This chapter presents what those textbooks intend, but in a more visual and interactive way. Although the common assumption is that today's students are well integrated with electronics and games, knowledge of common software cannot form the basis of assumption, thus the design also emphasizes scalable difficulty and usability.

OVERVIEW OF SUSTAIN CITY

In *Sustain City*, a game experiment in a course builds upon concepts gained through game experiments performed in parallel or previous courses. Students are in a better position to see the interconnection of their curricular courses and appreciate the integrated content value (Figure 1). With the context of a sustainable city, four games that focus on particular fundamental science and engineering concepts were deployed to replace traditional laboratory settings at different levels of standard curriculum and the *Project Lead the Way* curriculum. Eventually, students integrate all game modules in their senior capstone project, resulting in a fully-functional eco-city. A sustainable city is a city designed to grow and evolve in all aspects of human life without compromising the well-being of future generations. In action, *Sustain City* is an answer to the issues of curricular integration. It is not only a platform that offers expandable, modular game design, but also a motivational learning environment that emphasizes contextualized learning. Students play new roles and explore what and how their knowledge and skills combine to engineer a future ecologically healthy city. Using environmental sustainability as an authentic and engaging context for teaching core subjects promotes the 21st century skills (Church & Skelton, 2010).

Figure 1. Curricular integration and alignment

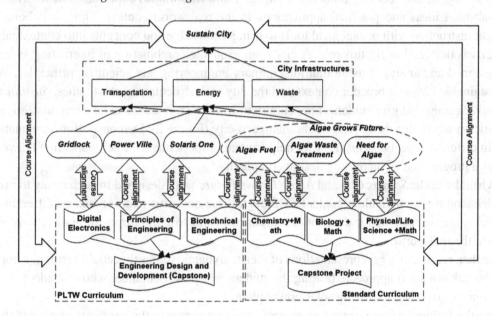

INTEGRATION OF GAME MECHANICS WITH LEARNING

The biggest challenge of serious game development is the integration of learning content with core game mechanics. Overemphasis on learning tends to "suck the fun out" of games; too much focus on playing "sucks out the learning" (Thomas & Young, 2010).

Serious games hope to leverage the interactive, entertaining medium of video games to educate students; while entertainment games start focusing on player guidance to ensure a game can teach any user how to play, regardless of skillset. In this regard, entertainment games exhibit basic educational concepts that can be emphasized in serious game design. Additionally, entire overarching gameplay concepts can be borrowed and integrated with educational content, taking advantage of the research work done in the entertainment industry. Three strategies were deployed in *Sustain City*, specifically the infusion of narrative into educational material, rewarding mechanism, and scaffolding for game navigation.

Narrative-Learning Synthesis

Students are struggling with conceptual transformation in STEM (Chen, 2007). They develop beliefs about the physical world from personal experiences or from previous schooling, in which an oversimplified definition or approach might have been taken. When encountering new knowledge in STEM, they try to fit it into their existing schema of understanding. Students often develop misconceptions when a concept does not fit logically to their schema. Hence they need transformative learning – the expansion of consciousness through contextual understanding, critical reflection on assumptions, and validated meaning by assessing reasons.

When instructors try to balance presentation of challenging concepts, facts, and learning strategies, students always feel that there are too many detailed, progressively complex theories with few "real" examples to relate. It is a constant challenge for instructors to keep students of different backgrounds, academic strengths, and learning tendencies engaged in a meaningful exploration of the relationship between abstract ideas and practical applications in the real-world context. Thus, it is beneficial to supplement instruction with pedagogical tools to bring knowledge and concepts into contextual reality. *Sustain City* is designed to fill this role. A city is an exquisite combination of interacting systems that can be designed and analyzed using multidisciplinary engineering and scientific principles. With the future sustainable city as a broader context and the city infrastructures as the themes, *Sustain City* offers narrative games that give students opportunity to learn what it means to be a scientist, engineer, or mathematician who helps design and maintain an eco-city (Figure 2). Demonstration, explanation, and practice in different aspects of *Sustain City* help students experience the interconnection between their courses as a progression of increasing design complexity.

Two virtual worlds, *Solaris One* and *Algae Grows Future* were designed in such a way to promote a deep understanding of curriculum content. Although these narrative games focus on different science and engineering concepts, their instructional goals are the same to demonstrate the applications of STEM concepts in the real world.

Rather than relying on dry representations of thermodynamic topics that could result in a boring lab, *Solaris One* takes a sci-fi approach, tasking the student as a power engineer who embarks a dangerous expedition into space to fix a failing solar power plant.

In a similar fashion, *Algae Grows Future* opens with an appeal to the emotions of players through a prologue cutscene. While the city grows from a bright and cleaning looking to overpopulated, the pollution swarming the city starts to threaten livelihoods - a little child coughs due to the smog in the city and fish struggle in the pond due to the excessive water pollution. The Mayor then calls for help "What can save us from this plague that has infected our city?" These appeals give the players an interesting motive and drive to complete the game.

Repetition, as one of the most basic key learning techniques, can be very powerful but tends to result in disinterest from students who either grasp a subject immediately or get bored of the same concept presented in the same format over and over again. Careful game design ensures that repetition is hidden behind variation such as a changing setting/environment or tweaks to the gameplay structure (Coyne,

2003). In *Solaris One* and *Algae Grows Future*, repetition is manifested as a constant demand for players to understand the same concepts in solving problems; while variation is introduced through degrees of difficulty and increasing levels of challenge.

Figure 2. Screenshots from sustain city: (a) Overview of sustain city; (b) power ville; (c) gridlock; (d) Solaris One; (e) algae grows future

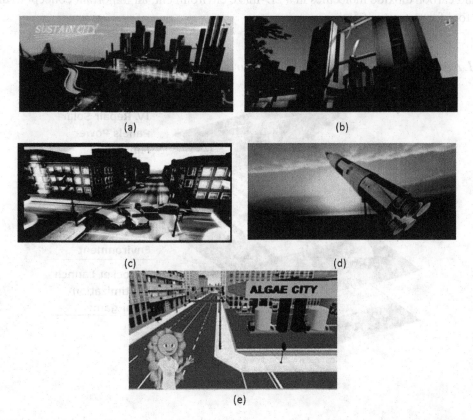

(a)

(b)

(c)

(d)

(e)

Solaris One consists of three stages (Figure 3). The first stage finds the player aboard an old Saturn V rocket that has been retrofitted with a new engine system. To successfully launch the rocket and exit the earth, players must correctly route the control system's energy into five different nodes. The nodes represent one of the two engines mounted on the rocket. The second stage starts when the rocket lands at the space station. To patch the power system, players must manufacture fuses that require metal ore mined from the asteroid. To obtain the ore, they must first fix the mining drill's cooling system pipes. Finally, they have to place fuses made out of different materials into fuse slots that will both endure the heat created by the standard wattage and correctly break with overcurrent.

The idea of repetitions is resembled in *Water Purification* module of *Algae Grows Future* with a tutorial and three traditional levels of pipe games with increasing difficulty (Figure 4). The tutorial teaches players how to play the pipe game, which is to choose the right pipe structures that connect the water input and output with maximum numbers of algae scrubs to achieve optimal purification results. Variations appear in the next three game levels in terms of pipe structure complex, the number and types of algae scrubs. These levels expand educational content to prevent cognitive overload for players. Additionally, players receive more time exposure to the material in order to maximize the content learned. Increasing complexity through the additional components and aspects added in each subsequent level of the module prevents the player's ennui. To prevent boredom, a mini-game was scheduled between the first and second levels of the pipe module, where players are led to inside the pipe, observing what is happening to purify water. This mini-game, a reminiscent of Pacman, challenges players to chase nitrogen and carbon dioxide molecules in a 2D-maze environment, an important concept to understand algae as a tool for water purification.

Figure 3. Layers of sophisticated gameplay in Solaris One

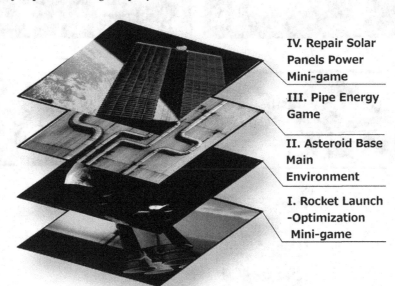

IV. Repair Solar Panels Power Mini-game

III. Pipe Energy Game

II. Asteroid Base Main Environment

I. Rocket Launch -Optimization Mini-game

The narrative design of a game can be an incentive to drive a player forward. *Solaris One* relies substantially on the idea of layers/levels for high fidelity. First, the game and mini-games are presented in a story, which is integrated into the game world environment logically. Second, all mini-games in *Solaris One* share an overarching goal of restoring power to the space station. Completing a mini-game not only provides the access to the next level of challenge, but also adds to the final goal: enabling the eco-city to receive power from the solar power plant. When players go through layers of challenge, they have to transcend levels of knowledge to achieve higher understanding, they are then getting closer to the truth, an understanding of the way things really are.

The narrative of *Algae Grows Future* serves as a vehicle to drive student learning. All modules in *Algae Grows Future* are designed logically to hold players' interest (Figure 5). The first module, *Water Purification*, comes naturally to the game when players encounter a polluted pond. After understanding how useful algae is, players start to think how to grow algae more in *Need for Algae* module to help the city in different venues. While excess algae is in production, more fun gameplay takes place where algae becomes solutions to a multitude of problems. Players power the public transportation system using an algae-ethanol fuel and make practical products out of algae like pharmaceutical gel, cosmetics, and surfboards.

Figure 4. Layers of sophisticated gameplay in Solaris One

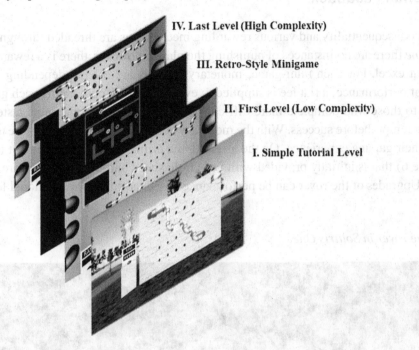

Figure 5. Logic of sophisticated gameplay in Solaris One

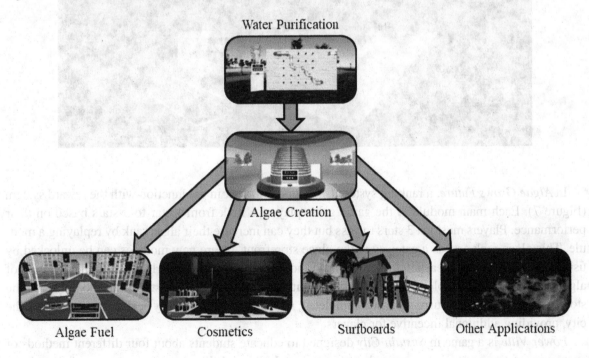

Supplemental Feedback

Experiential consequentiality and various rewarding mechanisms are threaded throughout *Sustain City*. In *Solaris One* there are no instances of punishing the player; however, there is a reward system in place for those that excel. For each mini-game, monetary rewards are offered depending on performance. Regardless of performance, a flat fee is supplied to every player for completing each game. Bonus cash is rewarded to those who complete more difficult problems, complete problems faster, or have lower numbers of attempts before success. With the monetary bonuses, players can purchase upgrades or perks to improve their gaming experience. On the asteroid, the primary form of movement for the player is a rover (Figure 6) that is initially provided with very little speed and no special features beyond surface movement. Upgrades of the rover can be performance based, aesthetic, or additional features.

Figure 6. The rover in Solaris One

In *Algae Grows Future*, a ranking system is designed to work in conjunction with the reward system (Figure 7). Each main module in the game gives players a rank from 1 star to 5 stars based on their performance. Players must get 3 stars to pass but they can increase their algae rank by replaying a module. This algae rank acts as a gateway to the algae storefront, where new modules can be unlocked by using the rank. As stated earlier, these storefront modules focus on real-world and commercial uses of algae. Students who complete any main module with five stars can access storefront modules. All the storefront modules yield currency when completed, which can be used to buy aesthetic upgrades for the city, providing additional incentive for players.

Power Ville is a game in *Sustain City* designed to educate students about four different methods of energy generation and their impact on the environment. In *Power Ville*, players take a consulting engineer role to investigate what form of electricity generation the city should pursue within the constraints of the city budget and power requirements. They talk to different experts to learns the pros and cons of each on available form of energy. With all the information collected, players use a simulator to determine the environmental impact of each form of energy and its feasibility as a power source (Figure 8). After the simulation, players can use a design tool to create a hybrid energy system solution that provides sufficient enough power for the city within the given budget (Figure 9). The tool scopes the city into different areas that can be powered by different sources of players' choice. When players make a decision, the information is dynamically updated with the amount of power that can be generated versus the demand and the amount of budget required versus available. The updates show how the decision helps or hinders the optimization goal. The ability to use a portion of each type of power generation instead of a single type for the final solution has many benefits. First, there is less likelihood of a student guessing a correct answer to a problem with more options. Further, choosing partial power production is a more realistic situation as many cities buy power from neighboring areas as an alternative or supplement to building their own power supply.

Players' final decision—the selection solution and the results of other in-game activities—is reported to the mayor. The quality of solutions is evaluated by a pre-programmed scoring method. Figure 10 presents two possible outcomes. When a player ranks coal as the power source with the least environmental impact, his or her preliminary understanding was criticized as a one-star decision. On the other hand, the correct understanding of the environmental impact of the four power sources was rated as a four-star decision.

Figure 7. The ranking system in Algae Grows Future

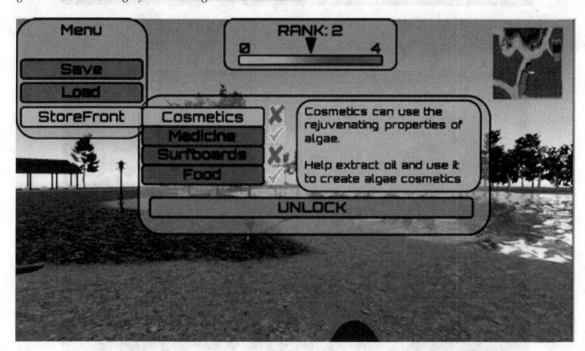

Figure 8. The simulation tool in Power Ville

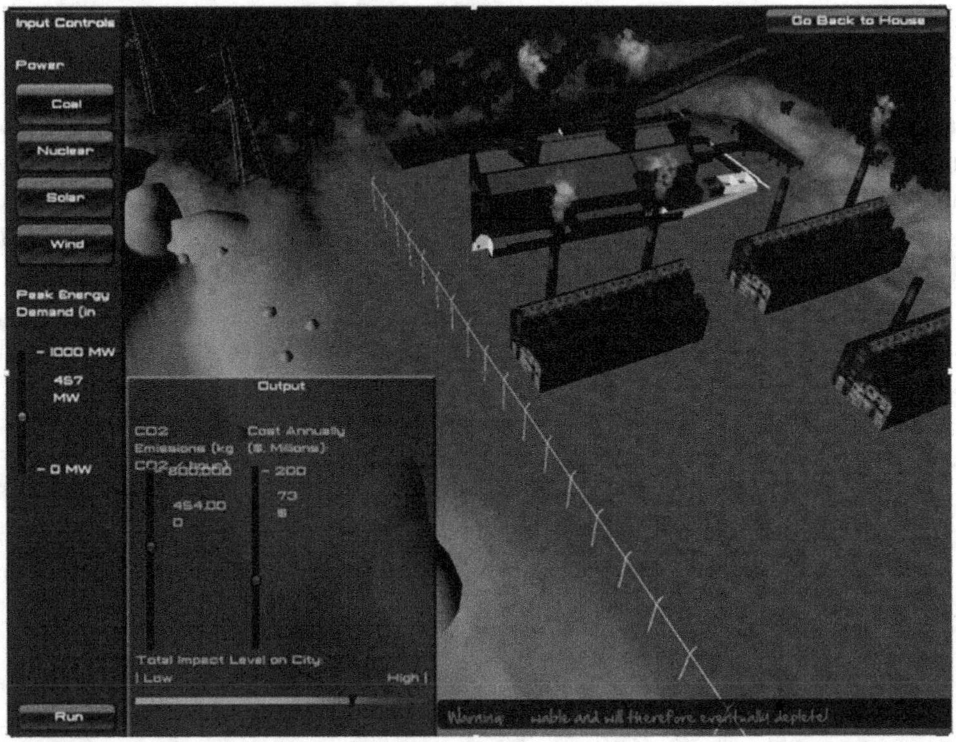

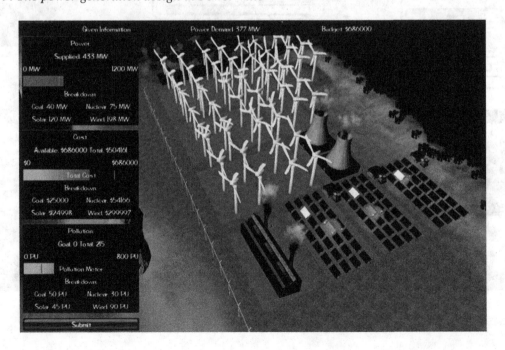

Figure 9. The power generation design in Power Ville

Figure 10. Examples of players' solutions in Power Ville

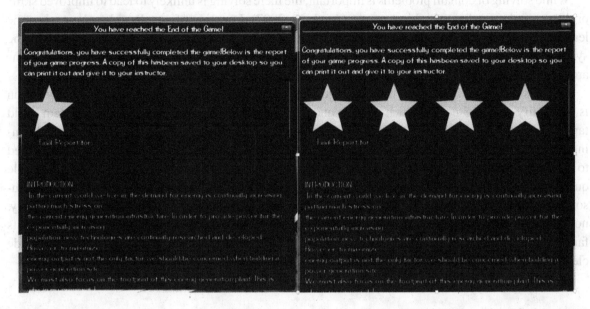

Player Guidance

When dealing with an education-based game, the challenge to teach players how to play and guide them through the game world becomes greater. It must guide students with various backgrounds throughout the game without direct instructor interference. For example, highly self-motivated students often take full advantage of opportunities presented in games to discover knowledge on their own. For students who lack of motivation and prior knowledge, more structured approach might be needed in games to offer them necessary incentive and instructional support. *Sustain City* takes the approach of incremental learning where learning concepts are built slowly over layers of game play such that students can ease into all aspects of a topic, avoiding frustrations that might dissuade them from learning.

Although *Solaris One* can be viewed as a layered learning experience, it is better to look at one of the mini-games to better explain the concept. The pipe-game within *Solaris One* is one of two main events on the asteroid portion of the game. The pipe game asks the student to construct pipe structures that obey given sets of rules such as length or heat transfer rates. Each chamber is unique and creates situations such as an extreme cold chamber where the player must move the liquid in the pipe with the lowest heat loss possible, or an extremely hot one where players wish to guard the liquid from the temperature and aim for maximum insulation. To introduce the interface and concepts, there are a series of challenges that increase in difficulty, never introducing more than one new unique game mechanic at a time. At its simplest, the game merely asks the player to play around with the interface, watching the result. Regardless of player actions, the next level will progress when they choose to move on. Next, the game simply asks the player to complete a pipe path, ignoring any parameters for heat loss or pipe material. The levels continue in this way until equations are introduced into the player's choices. By this stage, the natural progression of the levels should allow players to solve the problem on their own.

While solving of domain problems is important, the mere solving is unlikely to lead to improved skills or deeper understanding of subject matter (Anohina, 2007). Learning often takes place best when the learner is actively involved in the cognitive processes of problem solving and receives feedback from the system on how to be more metacognitively adept. In *Sustain City*, a series of metacognitive interventions are integrated with the experiential games to offer rigorous assessment and personalized scaffolding.

Not all students are alike. The first step in guiding a player through any difficulty in game navigation is to identify students' needs, which is when and what problem the player has. If a game system could tap into how individuals learn differently and equip them with learner-specific tactics, student's learning outcome will be optimized. In *Sustain City*, a series of progressive question prompts are designed to pinpoint where breakdowns occur in the context of in-game problem-solving. Figure 11 is a sample question prompt in *Gridlock*. Those questions are tied to the goal, knowledge and facts of problem-solving stages and administered within the game context. If students answer those questions correctly, no references are forced onto them while there are still options for help should they choose. If students fail, additional resources, such as tutorials and live videos of experts solving similar problems, are made clear to them and students may go through the resources to progress to the next level.

Figure 11. Sample question prompt in Gridlock

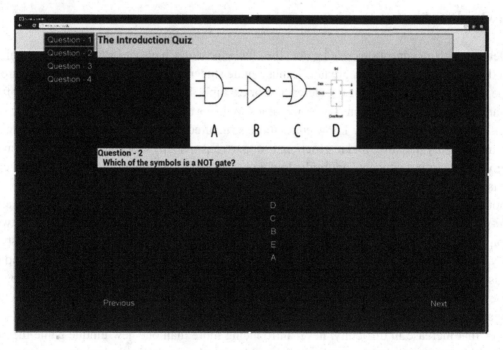

The question prompts also provide players instant information about their current knowledge of the problem, their weakness in understanding or where they should seek improvement. Such feedback is automatically updated whenever players submit answers to question prompts. The KWS method (What I **K**now-What I **W**ant to Know- What I have **S**olved) is a structured metacognitive tool in the games to help students to be aware of their own learning process. The more they know themselves, the more they can control goals, dispositions, and attention, and the better they become successful learners. In the initial design, KWS was a three-column chart structure (Figure 12) to activate students' prior knowledge by recalling what students know about a problem (K), to motivate students to read/think by asking what they want to know (W), and finally to review which part of the problem has and has not been solved (S). This intervention is usually implemented in classroom environment with instructors' facilitation. In a virtual environment, students are often left alone with to explore and figure out problems themselves. The lack of guidance makes the implementation of such intervention difficult because not all students are motivated to use it without facilitation.

Figure 12. Original KWS structure in Sustain City

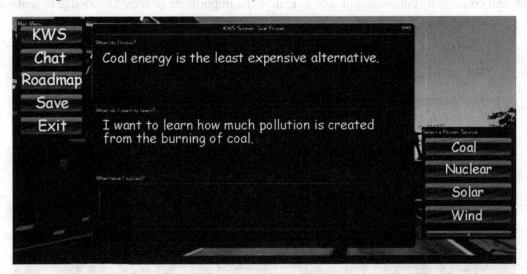

The second implementation of KWS affords the game system to take the facilitator role. Instead of asking students to write down what they know and do not know, and what they have solved, the game connects KWS with the question prompts. When players fail, the system immediately informs them what went wrong (Figure 13). Based on players' answers and other information gathered from their gameplay, the system selects guidance tailored to their specific needs (Figure 14).

Another useful metacognitive tool is learning roadmap. It provides study guides for students to find relevant information and to capture key concepts in study materials (Tang et al., 2011). Depending on game content, a road map in *Sustain City* might be a task list. In *Power Ville,* the task list guides students to navigate through game assignments and retrieve important information (Figure 15). The road map might also be a set of suggestions designed to lead students through a problem-solving process by directing attention to key ideas and suggesting the application of proper skills, such as the one in *Gridlock* (Figure 14).

One vivid example of the seamless integration of intelligent metacognitive tutoring with a narrative-based game can be seen in *Gridlock*, a content-specific game in digital electronics that invites students to investigate solutions to automatic traffic light control for a 4-way intersection. An automatic traffic light is a typical engineering invention that made the lives of common people safer and more convenient. For the development of the future eco-city, its design inevitably appears in the agenda of the city master plan and becomes an essential task of this game module. For students to design a full-functioning traffic light control, they should realize from the design specification that it is a typical sequential circuit, from which they have to apply their knowledge of finite state machine to complete the design. Thus, the game is partitioned into three problem-solving steps: problem statement comprehension, state machine design, and state table design. At each milestone, players are prompted with a series of questions that are tied to the goal, knowledge and facts of the specific problem-solving stage. Based on players' responses, the game system immediately prompts players either to move on with the design or to use the roadmap for additional helps. At the end, players' solution is validated where they are able to visualize the consequences of their design. A good traffic light design would follow correct sequence and specific timing, otherwise accidents reoccur due to the bad logic design. In this sense, students are engaged with societal and community concerns and able to realize the importance of their knowledge to make a difference in people's life.

Figure 13. KWS in Gridlock

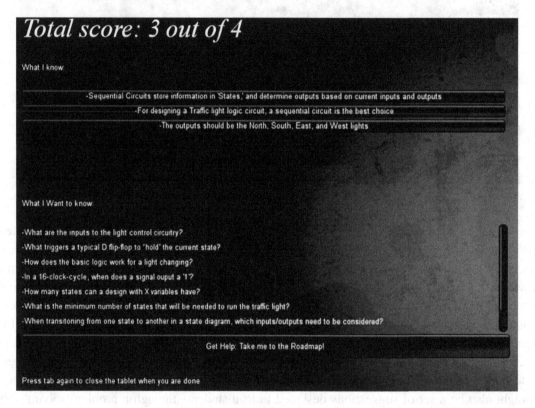

Identifying what happens when a player's capacity is sabotaged in problem-solving and providing tailored help to individual player's are two challenging tasks in the game design. The data needed to understand the student's knowledge level can only be acquired through observation of the learning process. Therefore, any attempt to developing an accurate guidance solution needs an algorithm to allow the decision-making process to accumulate past experience to a pertinently defined set of data structures, and at the same time, exploit the "knowledge" captured in the data set towards improving the overall system performance. The idea was implemented in *Gridlock* using a k-nearest neighbor (*k*NN)-based close-loop control (Figure 16). Each player is thoroughly evaluated at individual game stages on their understanding of the material. The results of the evaluation and other factors that represent players' behavior and understanding are classified to determine if a player masters the required material before proceeding to the next section of the game. Such classification is cascaded from one game stage to another, reinforcing the system understanding of student domain knowledge. If a student is found lacking in some area of the information, immediate feedback and detailed help are provided to the student to acquire the knowledge.

Figure 14. The roadmap in Gridlock

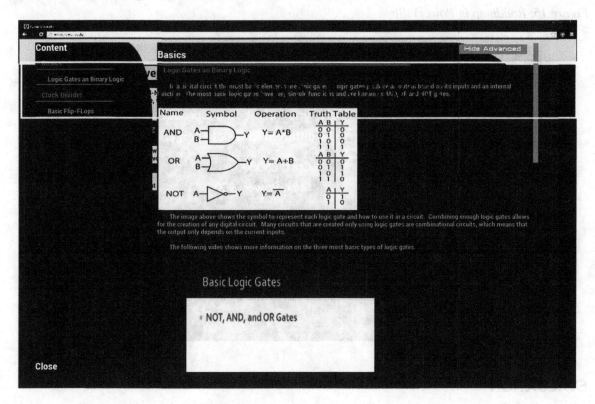

The kNN-based game system consists of three interactive modules: Student Module, Expert Module, and Pedagogy Module (Figure 17). The Student Module is responsible for the timeliness of system knowledge of the student reflected in the student model. The game system provides different measures to capture student real-time actions. Besides tracking student answers to prompted questions and student online communications, an additional measure is added to gather information, such as the time spent on individual tasks, student frustration on task, and the frequency of reviewing a specific portion of the help documentation. Students' responses to those assessment queries then serve as observed evidence that is kept in the student model and will be accumulated as the prior knowledge for future decision making. The Expert Module functions as a black box. With the inputs of student actions in the game, it classifies how well the student knows the material for the assignment. Such classification is subsequently adjusted every time new observed evidence on student actions is obtained from the game system, which helps to bring the maintained value estimates closer to the ones corresponding to the observed student behavior.

Meanwhile, the classification is fed into the pedagogy module where a mapping algorithm determines which sequence of prompts and cues in *Instruction Database* is proper to the knowledge level of the student. To work nicely with the partitioned game, the entire *Expert Module* consists of *r* instances, each of which has two components, *Knowledge Database* and *Expert Model*, built specifically for its corresponding problem section. Eventually, all *Expert Module* instances are cascaded to offer reinforced classification where the outcome from one section is not only used to guide the instructional helps that are tailored to individual student knowledge level, but also provided as an input feature to the next section

Figure 15. Roadmap in PowerVille

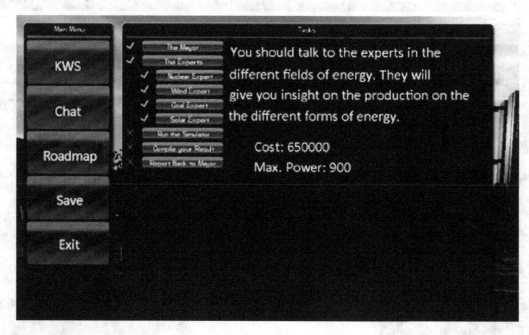

EVALUATION

To date, *PowerVille, Gridlock,* and *Solaris One* were piloted in both pre-engineering and engineering classrooms. A mixed methodology was utilized for evaluation and assessment that triangulated understanding for how the serious game system with metacognitive interventions impacted student interests and learning. Three research questions as presented in Table 1 guided the project assessment. Methods included surveys and focus group interviews.

As shown in Table 2, the instrument used for evaluation sought to determine student attitude towards the game scenario and problem-solving, and the utility and usefulness of the various metacognitive tools built into the games. In particular, students were surveyed about how helpful the tools were and how often they used them during the games. Two open-ended questions were also designed in the survey to have students select the most/least useful tools and provide their justification. Note that there are differences in requirements of the games, so not all survey items were presented to all players. Compared to *PowerVille, Gridlock* and *Solaris One* are more content-specific and require players to have basic mathematics and certain knowledge (e.g., circuit design in *Gridlock* and thermodynamics in *Solaris One*). In addition, the games also increase in visual sophistication and narrative complexity from *PowerVille* to *Solaris One*. As stated earlier, *PowerVille* is focused on a single decision, a recommendation for choosing a power source for a city. *Gridlock* requires programming of digital circuits to regulate traffic flow through an intersection, including representing the solution in circuit-diagram software. *Solaris One* requires overcoming a series of problems to repair a failing power station in space, all of which depend on understanding fundamental thermodynamics equations.

At total of 254 students completed the surveys (152 *PowerVille*, 71 *Gridlock*, and 31 *Solaris*). Levels of experience with video gaming were higher for *PowerVille* (64% gaming at least weekly) and Gridlock (72%). Fifty-two percent of Solaris players reported gaming at least weekly. Students generally felt themselves to be aware of the content, although as noted later in this section, players generally increased scores on content assessments after playing the games.

Figure 16. The system architecture of the kNN-based game system in Gridlock

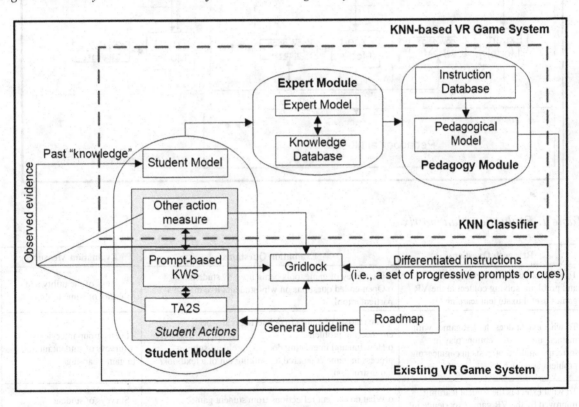

Utility and Usability of Metacognitive Interventions

As shown in Figure 18 and Figure 19, students had few problems figuring out how to use the tools, but of the three core supports, Road Map was the most popular, since that tool, in students' words, *"kept reminding me what I did and what I have to get accomplished,"* and *"hints necessary concepts"*. When KWS was used alone as a three-column chart in *Power Ville*, there was not a direct purpose that required responses to the intervention; thus students were not focused on deeply the learning modeled in such support. Once question prompts were connected with KWS to facilitate student reflection, more students started to appreciate their value. "The question prompts let me know that I was on the right track and gave me confidence in what I was doing," students wrote, "they reiterate the concepts from the lectures needed to beat the game." Although students perceived chatting as an important tool, it was not used frequently. In students' own comments, "it serves no purpose since we were in the same room" and "lab partners are in the room while [game] lab is in progress".

Figure 17. The cascading kNN system model

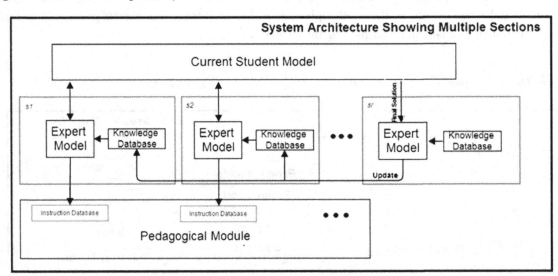

Table 1. Evaluation plan matrix

Research Questions	Evaluation Questions	Evaluation Measures
To what extent is the metacognitive and problem- solving content in the VR games useful to student learning?	o Frequency of game tools being used by students o Open-ended questions on why students like/dislike a particular tool	- Surveys of the utility and usability of game tools
To what extent does the VR games with metacognitive interventions play in fostering student interests in engineering problem-solving?	o The realism of games in delivering real-world engineering problems o How fun and interesting does the problem-solving process in game compared to working out of a textbook/ lab instruction	- Focus group interviews - Surveys of student interests in game learning
To what extent is the student learning improved by the VR game experience in general?	o What do student reflections from student game experience reveal about their learning	- Surveys of student conceptual learning

Table 2. Comparison of modal survey responses across games

	Attribute	Power Ville N=152	Gridlock N=71	Solaris N=31
Experience	Video game experience (Rarely/ <Weekly/ ≥Weekly)	≥Weekly: 64%	≥Weekly: 72%	≥Weekly: 52%
		Rarely: 22%	< Weekly: 18%	Rarely: 26%
	Content Experience (None/Some/Very)	Somewhat: 55%	Very: 54%	Very: 65%
		Very: 36%	Somewhat: 41%	Somewhat: 29%
Interest (Not/ Somewhat/ Very)	Interest in scenario	Somewhat: 66%	Somewhat: 54%	Somewhat 65%
		Not very: 22%	Not very: 24%	Not very: 23%
	Interest in problem	NA	Somewhat: 54%	Somewhat 61%
			Very: 31%	Not very: 23%
Relative effectiveness	Text comparison (Inferior/ Similar/ Superior)	Similar: 45%	Similar: 48%	Similar: 44%
		Superior 37%	Superior: 39%	Sup/Inferior: 28% (tie)
Perceived results	Increased skills	NA	NA	Agree: 65%
				Disagree: 17%
Utility of Game Tools (Not/ Somewhat/ Very)	Informational videos	Very: 50%	NA	NA
		Somewhat 40%		
	Simulator	Very: 43%	NA	NA
		Somewhat: 39%		
	Power Optimizer	Somewhat: 44%	NA	NA
		Very: 34%		
	Road map	Very: 43%	Somewhat: 41%	NA
		Somewhat: 41%	Not very: 37%	
	Online chat	Not very: 50%	Not very: 67%	NA
		Somewhat: 34%	Somewhat: 26%	
	Know/Want to know/Solved (KWS)	Not very: 57%	Not very: 48%	NA
		Somewhat: 30%	Somewhat:39%	
	Question Prompts	NA	Somewhat: 56% Very: 24%	Somewhat 40% Very/Not very: 30% (tie)
	Manual	NA	NA	Very 43%
				Not very: 30%

Interests and Motivation

Students were asked to compare the game experience to covering the same material in a textbook. The survey had six dimensions, showing the percentages of respondents at each level of Less Than/Same As/ More Than a textbook (Figure 20). The question about realism of the engineering task was not asked of the 152 *PowerVille* players; all other questions were presented to all 254 students in the sample.

- How much did the problem seem like a realistic engineering task?
- How interesting was the problem?

Figure 18. Percentages of students selecting resources to keep or retain

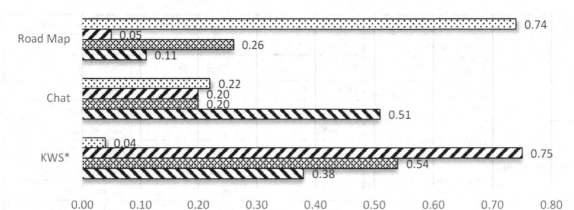

Powerville Keep (N=127) Powerville Omit (N=123) Gridlock Keep (N=70) Gridlock Omit (N=69)

Figure 19. Students' use of and attitude toward metacognitive tools, median values

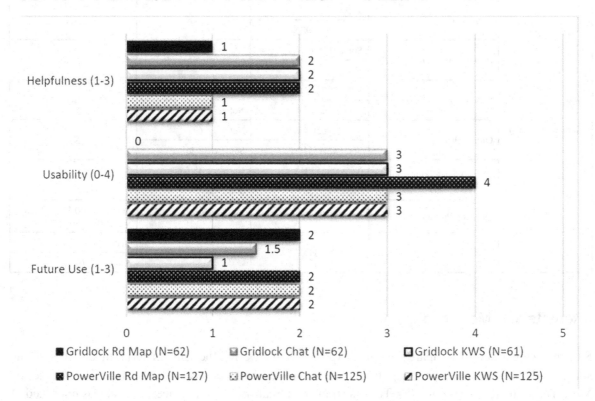

■ Gridlock Rd Map (N=62) ▨ Gridlock Chat (N=62) ☐ Gridlock KWS (N=61)
▧ PowerVille Rd Map (N=127) ▨ PowerVille Chat (N=125) ▨ PowerVille KWS (N=125)

- How much fun was the process?
- To what extent did you have the resources to solve the problem?
- How much did you learn?

- To what extend did you increase you understanding of the content?
- To what extent did you increase your interest in this type of engineering?

Interest in the game scenario was consistently moderate. Given that students reported themselves to be frequent video game players, it is likely that these simulations were being compared to commercial products with sophisticated narrative and production values. Most students found the simulations to be comparable or better than similar content presented in a textbook. The particular advantages of the games are that they were rated more fun and interesting. Students commented " *The more realistic the scenario, the better. I enjoy working on real-world problems because I feel it better prepares me than simply designing a circuit that performs some random function*", and "*I thought the movement in the game encouraged me a little more to make it work*".

Figure 20. User comparison of games to textbooks

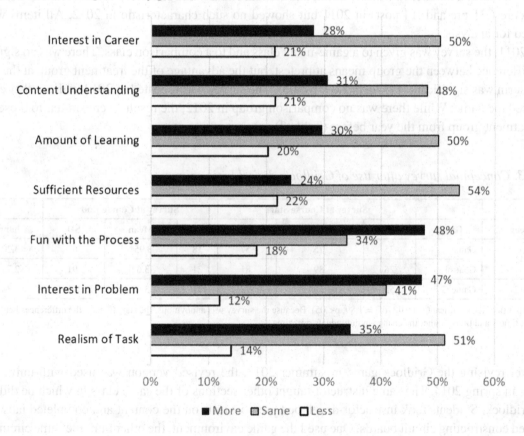

Results of textbook comparisons were similar for *PowerVille* and *Gridlock*. *Solaris One* players had similar responses to the interest and fun questions, but were less likely to say the game exceeded textbooks in terms of resources, learning, understanding of the specific content, and interest in thermodynamics, probably due to the relative experience of the *Solaris One* players. Sixty-five percent said they had extensive experience with thermodynamics equations before playing the game, as opposed to 42% of

Gridlock players with experience in sequential circuit design, and 36% of *PowerVille* players with prior knowledge of energy efficiencies. The *Solaris One* effect on content knowledge was positive; however, the more experienced thermodynamics students may have felt they had less to learn.

Conceptual Understanding

The efficacy test of *Gridlock* was conducted in a lower-division college level digital logic course at Rowan University. Surveys measuring student understanding of core concepts were given to game-using and control sections to rate students' proficiency on core concepts. Response options on each item ranged from zero to five (unfamiliar to proficient).

The 19-item Digital Logic survey used for this assessment had high internal consistency (α=.92 pre and .86 post in fall 2011, α=.93 pre and .94 post in fall 2012). Principal Component Factor analysis showed a single factor explaining 80% of variance. No other factor had an eigenvalue greater than 1. Item 5 ("Present a number in Binary, Octal, and Hexadecimal") had relatively low correlation with the total score (.31 pre and .14 post) in 2011 but showed no such characteristic in 2012. All items were retained for analysis.

In 2011, the survey was given to a game-using class and to a comparison class. There was no significant difference between the group means at pretest, but the advantage of the treatment group at the end of the term was significant (t [37df]=1.89, p<.05). The survey was repeated in 2012 with another class that used the game. While there was no comparison group in 2012, the results were similar to those for the treatment group from the year before (Table 3).

Table 3. Conceptual survey after use of Gridlock, digital logic course

Year	Group	Survey at Course Start			Survey at Course End			
		N	Mean	SD	N	Mean	SD	Change
Fall 2011	Game	35	.75	.57	18	3.95*	.67	3.20
	Control	26	.89	.81	21	3.62	.91	2.73
Fall 2012	Game	55	.59	.72	51	3.95	.71	3.36

*Group difference significant (t-test[37df] = 1.89, p<.05). Because the survey was anonymous, the statistic tests the differences between groups at time 1 and time 2 rather the change in individuals over time.

After revising the Gridlock game in summer 2013, the revised version was used with university classes in spring 2014. The same instructor taught other sections of the same class in which he did not use Gridlock. Students took instructor-developed pre/post tests on the content and completed labs that required constructing circuit boards. One used the game environment, the other built the same circuit on a development board. Table 4 summarizes the lab grade and test results for the two conditions. Scores are reported as percentages of the total possible. The data are paired and balanced; students who did not take both pre and post tests were deleted. The Gridlock group had an obvious advantage in terms of lab performance - more than a standard deviation. The advantage for Gridlock on test score gain was also positive, but only about .10 of a standard deviation, and not statistically significant. The gain for the Gridlock students may have been constrained by a ceiling effect: the group had higher mean scores to begin with, and thus had less room for improvement.

Table 4. Gridlock course test and lab results, computer architecture course

Group	Test Pre %	Test Post %	Lab %
Control N=13	48.81	62.54	70.08
SD	35.20	34.38	12.02
Gridlock N=19	76.29	93.11	83.84
SD	29.66	6.33	10.14
Total N=32	65.13	80.69	78.25
SD	34.33	26.71	12.76

Fourteen students who piloted *Solaris One* in spring 2015 also took an instructor-developed content assessment on thermodynamics. This class did not have a control group. The gain for the pilot group was close to half a standard deviation (Table 5), but was not significant because of the small sample size (t[13df]=1.93, p=.076). As with some of the other pre/post comparisons, the effect size may also be constrained by a ceiling effect. Sixty-five percent of the *Solaris One* students considered themselves to be very familiar with the game content, and both the pre and post distributions are negatively skewed (a high proportion of high scores). Nevertheless, 60% of the students agreed that the game enhanced their design and problem-solving skills, and 70% agreed that the game enhanced their theoretical and analytical skills.

Table 5. Solaris pre-post content assessment

N=14	Pre	Post	Total
Mean	7.39	8.86	8.13
SD	3.08	2.88	3.02

OVERALL FINDINGS

The evaluation above indicates that the interactive games of the *Sustain City* series were perceived by users to be as useful as traditional texts, and more fun and interesting. When compared to traditional units on the same topics, *Gridlock* produced greater learning gains. A pre/post pilot without control using the thermodynamics game (*Solaris One*) produced comparable effect sizes in its small sample. Measurable effects may depend on prior knowledge and experience of users. Two challenges were encountered in the development of *Sustain City*: identifying the appropriate level of preparation for each game content and addressing an increasingly sophisticated student user accustomed to commercial games.

Careful consideration should be taken in integrating any technique meant to boost fun in a serious game. If the fun is prioritized too greatly, a player could become either distracted or halt progress completely in pursuit of a reward. Based on general play-testing and student feedback, five concrete concepts are recommended around which to design a game that promotes fun and minimizes frustration while maintaining a balance between fun and learning.

- The educational content should be woven into a narrative that exists outside of norms, including unusual settings and story.
- Player guidance is most effectively implemented by slowly stacking core concepts rather than providing all instruction at once.
- Supplemental feedback can be realized by rewarding the player with some kind of spendable virtual currency or "points."
- More attention shall be paid to the implementation format of the metcognitive strategies in games to achieve the best student learning outcome.
- Machine learning and sensor informatics can be integrated with serious games to allow adaptation and personalization that overcome the shortcomings of a "one-size-fits-all" learning model.

As many serious games are at least in some degree simulation, it is far too common that the context is a predictable setting such as a hospital room for medical education or a laboratory for science. In focus testing, this study found that students responded far more enthusiastically to the sci-fi setting of *Solaris One* than to the straight-forward city structure of *Sustain City* despite the considerably more challenging content. Unless the environment is an essential component to the educational topic, this strategy can be implemented without taking away from the core content. Thus, there is no negative impact on the learning component. The only barrier in a practical sense is that skilled artists are required to construct such an environment and story, potentially raising the cost of development.

Player guidance is usually implemented through text based instruction, or some kind of bulleted guide. Guidance can refer to navigating a game's environment and story, and teaching core educational content. Although it may be enticing to provide large guides that offer the student with all information necessary, such guides were largely ignored. In fact, even if smaller snippets were provided, the student would skip quickly through them to arrive at the gameplay. It is more beneficial and enjoyable to the student when games slowly introduce concepts through example and player experience, providing guides as a backup. Doing so forces the player to tackle smaller tasks that naturally stack to accomplish larger ones.

Players react very strongly to forms of reward that exist within a virtual world. The mobile and casual gaming market relies on players' desire to accumulate virtual currency, often in exchange for real world currency. Providing players the ability to accumulate virtual cash is a better alternative to a letter grade or a percentage. The key design decisions weigh on the methodology for spending the currency. It was effective to rely on purchasable upgrades that affect gameplay, such as enhancing the performance of a rover. Although it can provide a huge boost to the fun content of a serious game, the addition of a reward system also runs the biggest risk of distracting the player. In this study, it is still possible for a student to remain inside the "fun" section of the game without ever proceeding, however the environment and story proved compelling enough that this was never the experience.

Awareness and monitoring of one's learning processes with a repertoire of strategies that the learner can apply as required by different circumstances are increasingly recognized as critical for success. The pilot of *Sustain City* confirms that such metacognitive awareness on the part of students can be improved through systematic and direct instructions on strategic thinking in games. However, the seamless integration of metacognitive interventions with game mechanics presents an implementation challenge quite different from that in a traditional classroom. Any serious game development shall consider the strategy to motivate and track student use of metacognitive interventions to maximize their impact. In a virtual game, players are often left alone to explore and figure out problems themselves. This self-paced learning structure actually makes it difficult for metacognitive interventions such as KWS. The original KWS in a three-column chart structure was not much appreciated due to the lack of facilitation. Once question prompts were connected with KWS, student reflection was guided, allowing players to acknowledge its value.

More and more students are unable to achieve learning successfully in a "one-size-fits-all" teaching model that offers only minimal, identical instructions to every student in a class. The marriage of sensor informatics, statistical inference, and serious games opens an opportunity to alter the situation and to assist instructors in offering "just-in-time" instructional support tailored to individual needs. In particular, rigorous assessment and characterization of players' activities has to be in place first, where user profiling, task characterization and their relations are modeled (Bellotti et al., 2013). Such assessment includes in-game measures that is integrated with game logic without interfacing with game playing experience, and external measures using various neurophysiological sensors. The assessment offers insights into the most appropriate scaffolding to improve student learning when the learners' capacity to make decisions is compromised; and how to provide feedback without distracting players from the immersive experience.

CONCLUSION

This chapter presents an approach to serious games design that attempts to balance fun and education that are so often considered separately. The successful response to the many design challenges is made evident through four game examples, *Powerville, Gridlock, Solaris One,* and *Algae Grows Future*, where each subsequent game evolves to meet student feedback and experience. An evaluation of the three games, *PowerVille, Gridlock* and *Solaris One* was conducted in several pre-engineering and engineering classrooms, where over 200 students worked with the games as the replacement of traditional laboratory activities. Results from student surveys and focus group interviews showed that the games were perceived as effective in promoting student learning. It was easy and useful to work with the game system, and more beneficial than working with the same problem solving in paper and pencil. The integration of game mechanics with rigorous assessment opens a new opportunity to offer students personalized learning experiences (Johnson et al., 2014; Tang & Shetty, 2011).

ACKNOWLEDGMENT

This work is supported in part by the National Science Foundation grant #OCI-1041306, #EEC-0935089, and #IUSE 1610164.

REFERENCES

Anohina, A. (2007). Advances in intelligent tutoring systems: Problem-solving modes and model of hints. *International Journal of Computers, Communications & Control, 2*(1), 48–55. doi:10.15837/ijccc.2007.1.2336

Arnab, S., Berta, R., Earp, J., de Freitas, S., Popesci, M., Romero, M., … Usart, M. (2012). Framing the adoption of serious games in formal education. *Electronic Journal of e-Learning, 10*(2), 159-171.

Barab, S. A., Gresalfi, M., & Arici, A. (2009). Why educators should care about games. *Teaching for the 21st Century, 67*(1), 76-80.

Bellotti, F., Kapralos, B., Lee, K., Moreno-Ger, P., & Berta, R. (2013). Assessment in and of serious games: An overview. *Advances in Human-Computer Interaction, 2013*, 1–11. doi:10.1155/2013/136864

Bosch, N. (2016). Detecting student engagement: human versus machine. In *Proceedings of the 2016 Conference on User Modeling Adaptation and Personalization* (pp. 317-320). ACM.

Callaghan, M., Savin-Baden, M., McShane, N., & Eguíluz, A. G. (2015). Mapping learning and game mechanics for serious games analysis in engineering education. *IEEE Transactions on Emerging Topics in Computing, 5*(1), 77–83. doi:10.1109/TETC.2015.2504241

Chanel, G., Rebetez, C., Bétrancourt, M., & Pun, T. (2011). Emotion assessment from physiological signals for adaptation of game difficulty. *IEEE Transactions on Systems, Man, and Cybernetics. Part A, Systems and Humans, 41*(6), 1052–1063. doi:10.1109/TSMCA.2011.2116000

Chen, J. C. (2007). Application of transformative learning theory in engineering education. *Proceedings of the 1st International Conference on Research in Engineering Education*, 1-6.

Cheng, M. T., Chen, J. H., Chu, S. J., & Chen, S. Y. (2015). The use of serious games in science education: A review of selected empirical research from 2002 to 2013. *Journal of Computers in Education, 2*(3), 353–375. doi:10.100740692-015-0039-9

Church, W. & Skelton, L. (2010). Sustainability education in K-12 classroom. *Journal of Sustainability Education*.

Coyne, R. (2003). Mindless repetition: Learning from computer games. *Design Studies, 24*(3), 199–212. doi:10.1016/S0142-694X(02)00052-2

Derbali, L., & Frasson, C. (2010). Players' motivation and EEG waves patterns in a serious game environment. In *Proceedings of the International Conference on Intelligent Tutoring Systems* (pp. 297-299). Heidelberg, Germany: Springer. 10.1007/978-3-642-13437-1_50

Di Mascio, D., & Dalton, R. (2017). Using serious games to establish a dialogue between designers and citizens in participatory design. In M. Ma & A. Oikonomou (Eds.), *Serious Games and Edutainment Applications* (pp. 433–454). Cham: Springer. doi:10.1007/978-3-319-51645-5_20

Earp, J., Ott, M., Popescu, M., Romero, M., & Usart, M. (2014). Supporting human capital development with serious games: An analysis of three experiences. *Computers in Human Behavior, 30*, 715–720. doi:10.1016/j.chb.2013.09.004

Egenfeldt-Nielsen, S. (2010). *Experiential eLearning: an ID model for serious game*. Retrieved from http://www.egenfeldt.eu/papers/overview_serious_games.pdf

Entertainment Software Association. (2013). *Essential facts about the computer and video game industry*. Retrieved from http://www.theesa.com/facts/pdfs/esa_ef_2013.pdf

Franzwa, C., Tang, Y., & Johnson, A. (2013). Serious game design: Motivating students through a balance of fun and learning. In *Proceedings of the 5th International Conference on Games and Virtual Worlds for Serious Applications* (pp. 1-7). IEEE. 10.1109/VS-GAMES.2013.6624239

Habgood, M. J., & Ainsworth, S. E. (2011). Motivating children to learn effectively: Exploring the value of intrinsic integration in educational games. *Journal of the Learning Sciences, 20*(2), 169–206. doi:10.1080/10508406.2010.508029

He, X., Wang, Y., & Cao, Y. (2012). Researching on AI path-finding algorithm in the game development. *Proceedings of the International Symposium on Instrumentation & Measurement, Sensor Network and Automation, 2*, 484-486 10.1109/MSNA.2012.6324627

Hocine, N., & Gouaich, A. (2011). A survey of agent programming and adaptive serious games. In P. Yolum, K. Tumer, P. Stone, & L. Sonenberg (Eds.) *Proceedings of the 10th International Conference on Autonomous Agents and Multiagent Systems*. Taipei: Academic Press.

Johnson, A., Tang, Y., & Franzwa, C. (2014). kNN-based adaptive virtual reality game system. *Proceedings of the 11th IEEE International Conference on Networking, Sensing, and Control*.

Kramer, D. (2007). Predictions of performance by EEG and skin conductance. *Indiana Undergraduate Journal of Cognitive Science, 2*, 3–13.

Lester, J. C., Ha, E. Y., Lee, S. Y., Mott, B. W., Rowe, J. P., & Sabourin, J. L. (2013). Serious games get smart: Intelligent game-based learning environments. *AI Magazine, 34*(4), 31–45. doi:10.1609/aimag.v34i4.2488

Lim, C. W., & Jung, H. W. (2013). A study on the military serious game. *Advanced Science Technology Letters, 39*, 73–77.

Limongelli, C., Sciarrone, F., Temperini, M., & Vaste, G. (2009). Adaptive learning with the LS-plan system: A field evaluation. *IEEE Transactions on Learning Technologies, 2*(3), 203–215. doi:10.1109/TLT.2009.25

Ma, M., Oikonomou, A., & Jain, L. C. (2011). *Serious games and edutainment applications*. London: Springer. doi:10.1007/978-1-4471-2161-9

Mavromihales, M., & Holmes, V. (2016). Review of research in games-based approaches with examples in engineering education. *CARN International Conference*. Retrieved from http://eprints.hud.ac.uk/id/eprint/30187/

McLaren, B. M., DeLeeuw, K. E., & Mayer, R. E. (2011). A politeness effect in learning with web-based intelligent tutors. *International Journal of Human-Computer Studies, 69*(1), 70–79. doi:10.1016/j.ijhcs.2010.09.001

Menzies, T. A. (2017). *Surgical skill and video games: a meta-analytic review* (Unpublished undergraduate thesis). Concordia University.

Mott, S. L., & Lester, J. (2006). Probabilistic goal recognition in interactive narrative environments. *Proceedings of the 21st National Conference on Artificial Intelligence*.

Mourning, R., & Tang, Y. (2016). Virtual Reality Social Training for Adolescents with High-Functioning Autism. *Proceedings of IEEE International Conference on Systems, Man & Cybernetics*, 9-12. 10.1109/SMC.2016.7844996

Myneni, L. S., Narayanan, N. H., Rebello, S., Rouinfar, A., & Pumtambekar, S. (2013). An Interactive and Intelligent Learning System for Physics Education. *IEEE Transactions on Learning Technologies*, 6(3), 228–239. doi:10.1109/TLT.2013.26

President's Council of Advisors on Science and Technology. (2012). *Report to the President: engage to excel: producing one million additional college graduates with degrees in science, technology, engineering, and mathematics*. Retrieved from http://www.whitehouse.gov/sites/default/files/microsites/ost p/pcast-executive-report-final_2-13-12.pdf

Raybourn, E. M. (2006). Applying simulation experience design methods to creating serious game-based adaptive training systems. *Interacting with Computers*, 19(2), 206–214. doi:10.1016/j.intcom.2006.08.001

Rhodes, R. E., Kopecky, J., Bos, N., McKneely, J., Gertner, A., Zaromb, F., ... Spitaletta, J. (2017). Teaching decision making with serious games. *Games and Culture*, 12(3), 233–251. doi:10.1177/1555412016686642

Smith, R. (2009). The long history of gaming in military training. *Simulation & Gaming*, 41(1), 898–920.

Tang, Y., & Shetty, S. (2011). Adaptive virtual reality game system for personalized problem-based learning. *Proceedings of the 8th IEEE International Conference on Networking, Sensing and Control*, 1-6. 10.1109/ICNSC.2011.5874957

Tang, Y., Shetty, S., Jahan, K., Henry, J., & Hargrove, S. K. (2012). Sustain City – a cyberinfrastructure-enabled game system for science and engineering design. *Journal of Computational Science Education*, 3(1), 57–65. doi:10.22369/issn.2153-4136/3/1/7

Terzidou, T., Tsiatsos, T., Miliou, C., & Sourvinou, A. (2016). Agent Supported Serious Game Environment. *IEEE Transactions on Learning Technologies*, 9(3), 217–230. doi:10.1109/TLT.2016.2521649

Thomas, J. M., & Young, R. M. (2010). Annie: Automated generation of adaptive learner guidance for fun serious games. *IEEE Transactions on Learning Technologies*, 4(3), 329–343. doi:10.1109/TLT.2010.32

Tong, T., Chignell, M., Tierney, M. C., & Lee, J. (2016). A serious game for clinical assessment of cognitive status: Validation study. *JMIR Serious Games*, 4(1), e7. doi:10.2196/games.5006 PMID:27234145

Torrente, J., Blanco, A., Moreno-Ger, P., & Fernandez-Manjon, B. (2012). Designing serious games for adult students with cognitive disabilities. In *Proceedings of the International Conference on Neural Information Processing* (pp. 603-610). Heidelberg, Germany: Springer. 10.1007/978-3-642-34478-7_73

Wattanasoontorn, V., Hernandez, R. J. G., & Sbert, M. (2012). Serious games for e-health care. In Y. Cai & S. Goei (Eds.), *Simulations, Serious Games and Their Application. Gaming Media and Social Effects* (pp. 127–146). Singapore: Springer.

Westra, J., Dignum, F., & Dignum, V. (2011). Guiding user adaptation in serious games. In F. Dignum (Ed.), Lecture Notes in Computer Science: *Agents for games and simulations II* (pp. 117–131). Heidelberg, Germany: Springer. doi:10.1007/978-3-642-18181-8_9

Wilson, L. (2009). *Best practices for using games and simulations in the classroom: Guidelines for K-12 educators*. Washington, DC: Software & Information Industry Association.

Zielke, M. A., Evans, M. J., Dufour, F., Christopher, T. V., Donahue, J. K., Johnson, P., ... Flores, R. (2009). Serious games for immersive cultural training: Creating a living world. *IEEE Computer Graphics and Applications*, 29(2), 49–60. doi:10.1109/MCG.2009.30 PMID:19462634

ADDITIONAL READING

Project Lead The Way (PLTW). (2018). *Our K-12 pathways: cohesive, hands-on learning experiences*. Retrieved from https://www.pltw.org/

Tang, Y., Shetty, S., Henry, J., Jahan, K., & Hargrove, S. (2011). Interactive and collaborative games promoting metacognition for science and engineering design. In M. Zhou & H. Tan (Eds.), *Advances in Computer Science and Education Application. Communications in Computer and Information Science* (pp. 405–412). Heidelberg: Springer. doi:10.1007/978-3-642-22456-0_58

KEY TERMS AND DEFINITIONS

KWS Method: A structured metacognitive tool in serious games that can help students to be aware of their own learning process.

Sustainable City: A city designed to grow and evolve in all aspects of human life without compromising the wellbeing of future generations.

Transformative Learning: Expansion of consciousness through contextual understanding, critical reflection on assumptions, and validated meaning by assessing reasons.

Chapter 45
Towards a Role–Playing Game Procedural Dungeon Generation Strategy to Help Developing Working Skills

Esteban A. Durán-Yañez
Tecnológico Nacional de México IT Aguascalientes, Mexico

Mario A. Rodríguez-Díaz
Tecnológico Nacional de México IT Aguascalientes, Mexico

César A. López-Luévano
Universidad Politécnica de Aguascalientes, Mexico

ABSTRACT

This chapter describes the insights towards a proposal to integrate a procedural content generation strategy in a computer role-playing usable and accessible learning video game for gaining replayability to encourage engagement and motivation in learners. In order to explain the contextual issues of the topic, the chapter includes a discussion on how computer role-playing video games impact the skills considered crucial for the work in the future—abstraction, system thinking, experimentation, and collaboration—emphasizing the importance of usability and accessibility to ensure effectiveness of the proposal. A first approach of a computer role-playing video game is presented to provide an illustrative example. The prototype will serve for future evaluations with people for usability and accessibility.

INTRODUCTION

Role-playing is an activity that has been present in the development of the human being since the beginning of civilization, and nowadays takes several forms, including video games, that has become the biggest entertainment industry and has proved to be an important tool for education.

DOI: 10.4018/978-1-6684-7589-8.ch045

Video games for learning represents a power alternative to develop useful skills and competencies in students (Barr, 2018). Engagement becomes video games an effective learning tool which may be potentiated by blending it with face-to-face approaches, it seems that said strategy do enhance student motivation and can be associated with behavioural change (De Freitas, 2018). In this context, a "*critical component of an engaging game is delivering content to player with incrementally increasing the challenge*" (cited by Adellin, Khuan, & Gertrude, 2019, p. 1); this concept is strongly related to the concept replayability or reply value, which broadly speaking consist in provide gamers the possibility of continue playing a game after its first completion (Adellin, Khuan, & Gertrude, 2019). One important tool to give video games replayability is the use of procedural content generation (PPG), which is currently popular in industry since is suitable to generate several elements of video games with high cost-benefit value, these elements include the construction of levels for platform games, and dungeons (Volkmar, Mählmann, & Malaka, 2019).

Replayability could enhance the experience of players in role-playing video games for education but it is very important to reinforce said strategy with usability and accessibility aspects (Darin, Andrade, & Sánchez, 2018). In this scenario, traditional usability aspects (Nielsen, 1995) should be complemented by including important aspects in such as mobility, multiplayer interactions, enjoyability, fun, satisfaction, storyline, customization, social connectivity, multimodal interaction, among others (Yanez-Gomez, et al., 2019). The goal of usability in this context is to provide user-friendly environments that foster learning in a more attractive, intense, and challenging way to help students in learning a variety of complex skills and abilities (Slootmaker, et al., 2018). Additionally, role-playing videogames should consider the configuration and functionality of the interface within the same game, and control over scenarios (dungeons) and main and secondary characters (Lee & Song, 2019).

Accessibility lies in the same level of importance; in fact, a product cannot be called usable without consider accessibility basics in its design process. As explained in (Bierre et al. 2005) "*While specific needs vary from person to person, the common issue is the same. The need to address accessibility in gaming is real. The number of people interested in gaming transcends age, gender, income, and disability. The disabled are often misunderstood and underestimated in terms of potential and participation*". Accessibility directly affects players experience and, therefore, to the effectiveness of the video game's purpose. Designing accessible video games include devices for control and interactions with user interface (Compañ-Rosique, et al., 2019). Related to said requirements (Tyagi, Choudhary, & Majumdar, 2019) found three families of accessibility issues that players currently face: (1) Don't receive feedbacks; (2) No identification of in game responses; (3) No way to provide the input from the various input devices used. In this way it is necessary to have strategies, approaches, and/or tools that result in video games that can be enjoyed and played by people independently of their skills to operate or perceive things in order to them feel included (Cairns, et al., 2019). (Smith, & Abrams, 2019) particularly explained said general context of video games accessibility from the vantage point of educational perspective, emphasizing that the gamification of learning procedures should foster equity and access to instructional materials for all the students including those with auditory, cognitive, neurological, physical, speech, or visual disabilities.

Literature that integrate the whole context is limited and it has not been found researches that explain in detail the procedural dungeon generation that takes into consideration usability and accessibility aspects during settings of said scenarios. In order to contribute to filling this gap here is proposed first approach for a procedure that provide more control for players allowing the selection of the role that the player must take when using certain character class in a role-playing game having high replayability by adapting its game environment or dungeons considering the character classes. Additionally, multimodal interactions will be offered to users for comfortable control and configurations including narrative and affordances relating specific learning activities and character roles abilities. By doing this, the player could get a better experience intended for the character class chosen encouraging engagement.

BACKGROUND

Role-playing

Role-playing can be seen in several activities of human behavior, like childhood playing, arts, rituals and storytelling. People have always lived limited by constraints imposed by the time they live in, its geographical location, cultural, economic and political situation, so they often use fantasy for healthy development. As people are younger, they dream about their future, like kids wanting to be a superhero, a cowboy, a famous singer, etc. But as we grow, we often do not follow the path we fantasize about as children, adapting ourselves to the constraints imposed by adulthood reality.

Several artistic and cultural expressions offer a relaxation from the expectations imposed by the society, those expressions include theatre, movies, music and video games. Some cultural critics manifest that art offers a healthy liberation to the mind, while others consider that excessive indulgence in fantasy makes people forget about real-life problems. Regardless of opinion about fantasy and art, it is a strong element in culture, worthy of study and important for understanding how people develop its minds (Bowman, 2007, 2010).

Tabletop Role-Playing Games

Traditional tabletop role-playing games has its origins in Dungeons & Dragons, a tabletop game like others but radically different, it is a role-playing game, it is a game where its participants control fantastic characters in a world that exists only in the imagination of the players (Ewalt, 2013). Of course, there are several others tabletop role-playing games such as Shadowrun and The Dark Eye.

Dungeons & Dragons was created by Gary Gygax and Dave Arneson in 1974 (Gygax & Arneson, 1974) and gets its inspiration from several narratives and literary work sources, being the stories of J.R.R. Tolkien, like Lord of the Rings (Tolkien, 1954), its mayor influences, it is based mainly on stories of brave knights and wise and elder mages fighting against evil forces (Ewalt, 2013). A typical gaming session in a role-playing game, the players find themselves immersed in huge caves where they look for treasures and have to fight with terrible monsters, in this kind of game there is a very important figure known as the Dungeon Master, who is the person in charge to guide the players through their adventure.

A fundamental characteristic in role-playing games is that each player takes a special role from a character belonging to a certain class. A character class refers to the profession or the kind of adventurer, this determines not only the character role, but the possibilities that it has in the game. This can be defined as a subset of characteristics and abilities owned that differentiates it from the other characters (Pantaleev, 2012).

In Dungeons & Dragons there exist three main character classes: fighters, magic-users and clerics (Gygax & Arneson, 1974). The fighters character class defines brute force and high constitution, can use armors and has a lot of health points (Voorhees, 2009), the mages character class, on the other hand, needs intelligence, wisdom and dexterity, can not use armors and have few health points, the clerics character class is capable to use magic that restores its health and to give protection, they can use armors.

Video Games

Video games have their origins since the first days of modern electronic computers, being Alan Turing the first person to write a computer Chess Program in 1947. Through the industry of video games as we know nowadays has its roots in the 70s, with important pioneering engineers like Ralph Baer, Steve Russell and Nolan Bushnell (Kent, 2001).

Nowadays many consider the video games industry a young one, and that is truly being in its sixth decade, but are an economic sector encompassing dozens of job disciplines and employing thousands of people worldwide. As an industry it has grown from being a niche sector to the mainstream market, being the most profitable entertainment industry.

Modern devices for playing computer games owe many of its advances by the necessity for faster and better hardware, like sound cards, graphic cards and processors to play video games. Similarly, in the software part, the video games industry has motivated many innovations in the fields of graphics algorithms and artificial intelligence techniques.

There exists a lot of debate whether video games, as a whole medium, can be considered a form of art or not, though there is no doubt that video games include many forms of artistic expression: sculpture, painting, music, acting and literature. The hardware that runs video games is just a vehicle for the creativity and vision of creators (video games developers) where unlike other media, the consumer (player) is an active participant, rather than a passive observer (Donovan, 2010).

Nowadays exists several video games genres and subgenres, being the following the wider and most recognized:

1. **Action:** Games that emphasize hand-eye coordination and motor skills.
2. **Simulation:** Refer to those games that are designed to model natural or manmade systems or phenomena.
3. **Strategy:** The main objective is to think skillfully and make planification.
4. **Adventure:** The mechanics of adventure games are mainly to solve puzzles by interacting with the game world or characters.
5. **Sports:** Designed to model real-life or fictional sports, with competitivity in mind.
6. **Role-playing:** Role-playing video games are based on tabletop games.

Role-Playing Video Games

Computer role-playing video games are a very special video game genre that holds the traditional role-playing experience but presenting it by means of a computer screen instead with a bunch of miniature figures and a map as traditional games (Barton, 2007, 2019). With the combination of role-playing elements with video games, the pioneering designers of computer role-playing and their players realized that role-playing video games were more than the sum of their parts, those games were a lot more than role-playing games computerized equivalents.

Akalabeth: World of Doom is considered one of the earliest computer role-playing video game, it was released in 1979, this video game was designed by Richard Garriot, who was an experienced Dungeons &

Dragons Dungeon Master and member of the Society of Creative Anachronisms and Renaissance Fairs. The video game industry has changed a lot since Garriot released Akalabeth, but the same foundations still remains leveling up characters, acquiring the best armors and weapons and fighting against ever more powerful enemies.

There is important to make a distinction between computer role-playing video games and Japanese role-playing video games, both genres share some characteristics, but there exist some key differences, being storytelling the principal: in computer role-playing video games, often the players control a single customizable avatar that along the way develops its abilities and end up meeting other characters that join their crew and form bonds with them, eventually progressing as a team through the main story, emphasis is often placed on choice, giving the player the opportunity to turn its actions towards evil or good, meanwhile in Japanese role-playing video games, rather than an avatar, the player is given a predefined main character or a group of main characters and the story is a quest from an ultimate evil, giving the player some choices to determine parts of the game, but it is usually a much more clear ending with a focus on a cinematic experience. So the main difference between those genres is the capacity to decide the type of character to play with and its development, as well as the capacity to decide what to do on the story, having a lot more freedom in computer role-playing video games.

MAIN FOCUS OF THE CHAPTER

Issues, Controversies, Problems

Education and Video Games

Video games is not an industry extent of controversy, through its history there have been blames for increasing aggressivity in users (Anderson, 2004; Anderson & Bushman, 2001), or being addicting (Toker & Baturay, 2016), causing in users difficulty in regulating the amount of time spending on playing (Ogletree & Drake, 2007) or even provoking different health issues like motion sickness and postural problems (Chang, Pan, Tseng, & Stoffregen, 2012; Merhi, Faugloire, Flanagan, & Stoffregen, 2007; Stoffregen, Faugloire, Yoshida, Flanagan, & Merhi, 2008).

On the other hand, a lot of research has been made to study the effect of videogames in education, showing that the support of education in video games helps students to learn better (McDaniel & Telep, 2009; Sevilla, Santini, Haya, Rodriguez, & Sacha, 2012; Vlachopoulos & Makri, 2017; Zheng & Gardner, 2017), considering the study of particular topics like English (Yang, Chen, & Chang Jeng, 2010; Yen, 2011), mathematics (Chiu & Hsieh, 2017), geology (Chen, Yeh, & Chang, 2016), even for human skills (Chiang, Lin, Cheng, & Liu, 2011; Daniau, 2016; Jang & Ryu, 2011; Su, Chiang, James Lee, & Chang, 2016).

When learning is active, experiential, situated, problem-based and provides immediate feedback it is most effective, according to modern theories of education (Boyle, Connolly, & Hainey, 2011). And video games appeared to offer those features. Education integrates new technologies to support its processes, nowadays technological applications, video games and simulations are widely used by formal education institutions (Vlachopoulos & Makri, 2017).

According to (Reich, 1991) on his book The Work of Nations, there are four basic skills that are critical for the workplace in the future:

1. **Abstraction:** Is the capacity for the human mind to put order in the chaotic, highly entropy, the world we live in, by the recognition of patterns and meanings and the classification of the information we receive by our senses, so it can be manipulated in new ways. Abstraction is the very essence of symbolic analysis.
2. **System Thinking:** This refers to the capacity to identify causes and consequences, to be able to see in the world the different systems interacting forming the reality, but also, being able to see the relationships between different systems identified by abstraction, seeing the world as a whole allows for new discover opportunities.
3. **Experimentation**: The capacity to test different options to note causes and effects in a systematic and orderly fashion allows to a better understanding of the world. In order to learn higher forms of abstraction and system thinking, the experimentation is imperative.
4. **Collaboration**: Being able to collaborate, communicate abstract concepts effectively, and achieve consensus is a skill very important for symbolic analyst, who seem to work in an unrelated way, but they must communicate their findings and ideas among the team.

Role-playing games generally are composed of rulebooks and bestiaries and are played by using miniature figures in maps previously defined where the players are situated, discover treasures, challenges and advance through a story (Gygax & Arneson, 1974). It those rulebooks are included data tables with ability points for each character class, this has allowed that the players experiment with those points and learn to play with each one of the character classes. This learning process is an empirical one, while it is true that the players know which character class is the most appropriate to perform (and they know how to do it), there is not documentation that cites each case or that facilitates the identification of the conditions where each character class is better than the others.

Most activities are better learned by doing, rather than just by studying. In computer role-paying video games normally the designers give few advices to players and encourage them to experiment with controls and commands, making this a process of discovery. The gamer that begins to play a new computer role-playing video game normally acts as a scientist, devising theories based on observations and then making experimentations, to understands how this virtual world works (Barton, 2019), this shows us two of Reich's skills: system thinking and experimentation (Reich, 1991). According to (Gee, 2003): "Video games situate meaning in a multimodal space through embodied experiences to solve problems and reflect on the intricacies of the design of imagined worlds and the design of both real and imagined social relationships and identities in the modern world."

Gaming experiences allow for better learning of game mechanics than reading the video game manual, by observing the effects of different parameters in the video game, the gamer can learn about its meaning in a better way than by reading its description in manual or tutorial. This works in the same way in much of a formal educational system: we may read an memorize facts, but outside of context or real experience they do not mean anything, and we do not get real understanding of underlying mechanics this way. This argument do not says that the videogames necessarily teach us how important concepts works, those concepts maybe do not have importance in the real world as they could be lore specific for the video game or something not very useful outside of the game world, the important thing is the teaching of mental habits that those games demand and reward that end being more important than much of the disembodied learning we get in formal learning systems. By instead of memorizing definitions of a textbook, the gamer thoroughly internalizes this critical thinking, getting better knowledge than a boring science class (Barton, 2019). The ability to abstract knowledge from a realm and apply it to another is a skill undervalued in formal education systems, and is another of the skills described in (Reich, 1991).

According to (Moses, 1986), statistics are a body of methods for learning from experience, this also applies to computer role-playing video games, that as been said before, are complicated statistical models that model the game mechanics, systems and simulations, using mathematical formulas with different parameters for computing probabilities. And allow the player to learn about how those mechanics work by playing the video game, the gamer normally is unable to know the exact formulas but get an idea of how they work by their experiences at playing. What happens at schools is the opposite, the students learn the formulas, but will hardly know what they model if they are not applied in a context.

The other skill described by (Reich, 1991) is collaboration. Countless education experts stress the importance of collaborative learning; students learn more by discussing topics among them, ratter than just listening a teacher. Players must frequently work together to learn to play a Massive Multiplayer Online Role Playing Game, a subgenre of computer role-playing video game, that one of their principal mechanics is the collaboration online of lots of gamers around the world, and differently to tabletop role-playing games, the online element facilitates the reunion of groups of players. One inconvenient, though, is that the online experience allows for anonymous usage, with the possibility to leading to problems of toxic communities (Paul, 2018). On the other hand, single player computer role-playing video games can also teach effective collaboration, in some occasions better than massive multiplayer online role playing games, as they allow the player to control more than a single character, in a crew of adventurers with complementing abilities, allowing for a tactical thought by using the different perks, making the successful party of adventurers the one that successfully leverage strengths and weakness of their members.

One problem with computer video games is that the experience they offer eventually can become boring or finally it ends, offering no more surprises to the player.

SOLUTIONS AND RECOMMENDATIONS

Computer role-playing video games are descendants form the tabletop role-playing games and are based on them, having inherited many of their characteristics, but as we commented before, there are fundamental differences. The tabletop role-playing games benefit enormously form the players and the Dungeon Master ability to improvise story and add surprising elements at any moment, this characteristic is limited for computer role-playing video games. On the other hand, computer role-playing video games can perform millions of complicated operations per second on its relying hardware, allowing the use of complicated systems of rules impractical for tabletop role-playing games. This allows for more complex game play (Pantaleev, 2013), allowing for several stats that the characters can have.

In role-playing tabletop games, the dungeons are designed by hand by the dungeon master. In Dungeons & Dragons, in the tome The Underworld & Wilderness Adventures it is shown how to create a dungeon with interconnected level segments (Appelcline, 2013).

Procedural Content Generation

The main idea behind procedural content generation is that an asset is not generated manually by human designers, but by computers executing a well defined procedure (X. Short & Adams, 2017). To avoid losing control over the design process, it is desirable that humans can still influence the final product by adjusting the parameters of the procedure (Hendrikx, Meijer, Van Der Velden, & Iosup, 2013). By content we can refer to several elements in a video game: levels, maps, game rules, textures, stories, items, quest, music, weapons, vehicles, characters, etc (Shaker, Togelius, & Nelson, 2016).

Vander Der Linden, Et. Al, (Van Der Linden, Lopes, & Bidarra, 2014) identifies five reasons to use procedural content generation in video games:

1. Agile content generation of content correctly structured (A. M. Smith & Mateas, 2011).
2. Replayability, with a big diversity of results (Hastings, Guha, & Stanley, 2009; G. Smith, Gan, Othenin-Girard, & Whitehead, 2011). Another reason to use procedural content generation is to increase the replayability, by allowing to generate new content in real time, if this new content has enough variety this can allow the creation of endless games (Togelius, Yannakakis, Stanley, & Browne, 2011).
3. Save time and money in videogames creation (Tutenel, Bidarra, Smelik, & Kraker, 2009). One of the main reasons to use procedural content generation in video games is to reduce production costs, nowadays video games industry has grown to the point that production is a bottleneck in both game budgets and product time to market (Iosup, 2009; Kelly & McCabe, 2007; Lefebvre & Neyret, 2003; Smelik, Kraker, Groenewegen, Tutenel, & Bidarra, 2009).
4. Generate the basis for the adaptability of video games to the players (Lopes & Bidarra, 2011; Yannakakis & Togelius, 2011).
5. The creation of designs that helps creativity (Shaker et al., 2016).

An important aspect to consider about procedural content generation is to perceive this as the solution to problems of content generation. This problem is defined as the necessity of being able to generate content under certain rules or through the fulfillment of definite properties. The following is a list of common properties that it is desirable to take into account in the procedural content generation (Shaker et al., 2016):

1. **Speed:** Speed requirement, when it is desirable that certain result is achieved in a specific time lapse.
2. **Reliability:** Is the capacity to be able to satisfy a given quality criteria.
3. **Controllability:** The generation of the content needs to be controllable in some sense, so there can be specified some aspects of the content to be generated.
4. **Expressivity and Diversity:** Being able to offer results that are enough different among themselves.
5. **Creativity and Credibility:** It is a good thing that the result not look like it has been designed by a procedural content generator.

Procedural Generation of Dungeons

Inspired by maps (dungeons) in tabletop role-playing games, the computer role-playing video game Rogue is created in 1980, developed by Michael Toy and Glenn Wichman; this video game is one of the first to employ procedural content generation of dungeons in real time (Hendrikx et al., 2013), from the release of this title on forward there have been a derivation for other video games that generate dungeons procedurally, creating a new genre of video games known as "Rogue-like" (M. R. Johnson, 2017). One of the most outstanding aspects of this genre of video games known as roguelikes is the creation of dungeons in an automatized way, without a doubt, this genre marked a milestone in procedural content in video games (Garda, 2013).

A dungeon can be defined as a labyrinthic environment, consisting mostly of interrelated challenges, rewards, and puzzles, tightly placed in time and space to offer highly structured gameplay progressions, this close control over gameplay pacing is an aspect which sets dungeons apart from other types of levels. In this sense, a dungeon is not only the physical structure of the gameplay space, but also the set of challenges and rewards that shape it. A kind of content generated procedurally that results very interesting is precisely the generation of levels for dungeons, this because to the peculiar relationship between Rhythm, Playability and Space. (Adams, 2002). As has been seen before, there exists diverse computer video games that use procedural content generation, and even there exists al whole genre of those (roguelikes). In all those cases the procedural generation comes from a set of parameters that try to control the result.

A well designed dungeon is the one that offer a good game play experience and has the next elements: interesting level architecture, adequate rhythm, realism, intelligent foes, advance previews, non linearity, takes care on the inclusion of new elements, balancing resources, adequate difficulty (Lopes & Bidarra, 2011).

There are used several techniques to generate dungeons procedurally, some of them are the following:

1. **Agent Based Dungeon Growing:** Usually, a single agent dig tunnels and create rooms in a sequence (Shaker et al., 2016).
2. **Space Partitioning Approach:** There is made a subdivision of the game play space into disjoint subsets so that any point in the space lies in exactly one of these subsets (Shaker et al., 2016).
3. **Cellular Automata:** Cellular automata are widely studied in computer science and other sciences as models of computation, growth, development, physical phenomena, etc. though somewhat simple to understands its basic concepts (L. Johnson, Yannakakis, & Togelius, 2010).
4. **Grammar Based Dungeon Generation:** Developed to formally describe structures in natural language are modeled by a finite set of recursive rules that describe linguistic structures in a way that also describes how to generate them (Adams, 2002; Dormans, 2010).
5. **Genetic Algorithms:** Search-based evolutionary algorithms that try to find an optimal solution to an optimization problem, a genetic representation and a fitness function are required (Ashlock, Lee, & Mcguinness, n.d.; Hartsook, Zook, Das, & Riedl, 2011; Valtchanov & Brown, 2012).
6. **Constraint Based Method:** Generation is based on a constraint solving approach where constraints are expressed as rules with parameters that place nodes in relation to fixed terminal nodes (Roden & Parberry, 2004).
7. **Machine Learning:** A relatively new paradigm to generate dungeons procedurally, it consists on machine learning models trained on existing content (Summerville et al., 2018).

For the development of the procedural dungeon generator, it is considered to use an artificial neural network because one of the key elements is the ability to learn. A neural network is not just a complex system, but a complex adaptive system, meaning it can change its internal structure based on the information flowing through it, typically it is achieved through the adjusting of weights. There is considered to use a reinforcement learning approach.

There has not been found evidence that procedural dungeon generated computer role-playing video games generate the dungeons considering the role or character class. There has only been found in some sources (Adams, 2002; Forsyth, 2016; Hendrikx et al., 2013) that the only considerations for dungeon generation are the same aspects: size, complexity, difficulty, realism, topology, etc.

Development of Procedural Dungeon Generator for Computer Role-Playing Video Games

Currently, a computer role-playing video games is in development by the indie games studio Ogre Pixel, the development team consist of nine specialists that include game designers, programmers, visual artists and artificial intelligence scientists. The project is called Swipy Fantasy. It is expected that the Swipy Fantasy video game to be released in the first quarter of 2021.

The video game Swipy Fantasy is a casual roguelike adventure game where the player fights nasty creatures by drawing swipes to perform attacks, the game perspective is a 2D top down view, its game mode is a single player adventure with a team or party of adventurers controlled by computer but with the direction of the player, the player can configure the kind of behavior it desires for its party members. The target audience is for people of approximately between the ages from 10 to 35 years old who are fans of fantasy casual mobile games and also for fans of classic roguelikes and computer role-playing video games like Rogue or Tibia.

In Swipy Fantasy video game there are several stats that will define the combat and mechanics results, being the following the most important:

- **Maximum Health Points:** Capacity to live for the character.
- **Maximum Magic Points:** Capacity to use magic movements by the character.
- **Regeneration of health:** How quickly the character recovers health points.
- **Regeneration of Magic:** How quickly the character recovers magic points.
- **Damage:** The basic damage the character can inflict when it attacks.
- **Armor:** The capacity to absorb damage when the character is attacked.
- **Evasion Rating:** The capacity to dodge attacks, making the enemies attack ineffective.
- **Dexterity:** How fast can the character attack.
- **Speed:** Movement speed in the game world.
- **Range:** How far the character can inflict damage.

The values of all those stats depends mainly of the character class, but also can be raised when the character gets experience and raises its level. Besides the stats can be modified positively or negatively by the equipment the character uses, for example, a heavy armor rises the player armor but reduces its speed and dexterity.

The character classes available are based in the classic Dungeons & Dragons classes. Their attributes are modeled by different value combinations of the stats previously described. The character classes can be also controlled by the computer, and are the following:

- **Knight:** The Knight, represented in Figure 1, is a strong melee attacking hero, with short range, has a high resistance to damage but is somewhat slow on its movement. Its artificial intelligence behavior consist on staying quiet and close range attack enemies one by one.

Figure 1. Knight, conceptual art.　　　　　*Figure 2. Archer, conceptual art.*

- **Archer:** The Archer, represented in Figure 2, is a hero that has medium attacking power with a very long range attack, have medium resistance to damage and is fast moving. Its artificial intelligence behavior consist on keeping distance form its closest enemies, its shooting long range attack simulates arrows.
- **Wizard:** The Wizard, represented in Figure 3, has a very powerful attack and also a long range of attack, but it is ratter weak to damage and slow on its movement. So its artificial intelligence behavior is to keep the distance from enemies and use its powerful long range attacks.
- **Healer:** The Healer, represented in Figure 4, is mainly a support unit for its partners, it has a weak attack with short range, medium resistance to damage and medium speed of movement, though it has the capacity to improve his stats and from its party members, also can heal both partners and himself. The artificial intelligence tries to keep distance from enemies and concentrates on raising its partners abilities, also helps its partners with low health.

Figure 3. Wizard, conceptual art.　　　　　*Figure 4. Healer, conceptual art.*

Swipy Fantasy video game will feature autonomous moving and behavior agents that will offer the player challenges in accordance with the game play style of the character class chosen. The foes will adapt their behavior depending on the class the character uses, trying to offer the player the best experience intended for the player character class. For this, there is in development a proprietary physics and artificial intelligence engine that models effectively the movement steering behavior for actions to seek, flee, arrive, pursuit, evade, wander, obstacle avoidance, wall avoidance, interpose, hide, path following and offset pursuit.

For the Swipy Fantasy video game there will be included both antagonist characters (enemies, bosses and non player characters), as well as good or neutral characters (shopkeepers, and other party members). The main gameplay revolves mainly in character interaction, either combat or otherwise, and each of these elements can be complex. The types of characters to be present and their artificial intelligence are the following:

- **Enemies:** The common enemies that are present in large quantities in the video game, they are the main source of experience for the character, have a statistical behavior that depends on their basic stats. There exists a vast variety of them. Can use complex behavior patterns, including running away, healing themselves, fighting in groups, surround the player, use complementary attach methods and so forth.

- **Bosses:** Larger, more complex game characters, either humanoid or creature, found at the end of sections or levels after defeating a horde of lesser enemies. Are very specific, usually unique characters that can break previous rules. That is why are heavily scripted with special attacks and behaviors that only they can perform.

- **Non Playable Characters:** Can be defined as anybody in the game that is not a human player. Usually refers to characters in the game that the player can interact with in ways other than combat. Non playable characters are generally not very intelligent; they usually do not have to be. Anything they add beyond information or story advancement is just flavor for the game. So their intelligence limits to path following and grammar systems.

- **Shopkeepers:** Special non player characters that do business with the player: buying and selling gear, teaching the player new skills, and so on. Shopkeepers usually are not much smarter than regular non player characters, but what differentiates from them is that they require special interfaces and additional programming, so they seem intelligent when doing transactions, they take in account for their prices if they like or dislike the player.

- **Party Members:** Members of a player´s adventuring party are also special non player characters, except that they travel with the player, and are either completely controlled by the player or have artificial intelligence code associated with them.

FUTURE RESEARCH DIRECTIONS

As future research directions, it is considered to:

1. Identify characteristics and game play ways for the different character classes of computer role-playing video games.

2. Identify key design elements for dungeons that can improve the game experience for each of the character classes in computer role-playing video games.

3. Identify a mechanic to measure the Flow (Borderie & Michinov, 2016; Cowley, Charles, Black, & Hickey, 2008; Csikszentmihalyi, 1991; Velikovsky, 2014) and the game experience through the data recompilation from the player.

4. Define an algorithm for the procedural dungeon generation with an approach to key design elements that can improve the game experience for each character classes of computer role-playing video games.

5. Examine the Flow and the game experience in a prototype where it is generated dungeons procedurally applying key design elements that can improve the game experience for each character classes of computer role-playing video games.

CONCLUSION

Role-playing is an activity performed historically by humans, since ancient times in the form of childhood playing, arts, rituals, storytelling, etc. It is considered that role-playing is an important activity for healthy brain development. In modern times there exists a subculture around role-playing that is expressed in performances, tabletop games and more recently in videogames.

Being, nowadays, video games the biggest entertainment industry in the world, it has a huge impact on culture and economics. Besides the doubtless importance on the economic aspect, video games also represent an important repository of creativity and a medium of artistic expression. Because of those both reasons, a lot of research has been made on the negative and the positive impacts of playing digital games. In the educational field, there exists a lot of research about the video games capacity to help students acquire values, skills and knowledge, that have demonstrated its utility on the field.

Computer role-playing video games help to the development of a set of skills considered as critical for the workplace in the future: abstraction, system thinking, experimentation and collaboration. In this case engagement is a feature to exploit from role-playing video games.

A constraint in video games is that eventually the game play becomes repetitive or it ends, an option to mitigate this is by using procedural content generation, that consist in creating new content by algorithmic means, this increases the replay value of the video games.

This in-progress computer role-playing video game will aimed to help developing learning skills previously mentioned. This video games will consider the use of procedural dungeon generation using artificial neural networks with a reinforced learning approach. This algorithm will take the character class chosen by the player to give it the best experience. Besides, the game in development will use a proprietary artificial intelligence engine that will enhance the player experience considering the chosen character class. The proposal will be oriented to integrate both traditional and video games usability aspects, together with accessibility elements addressed to encompass all disabilities including auditory, cognitive, neurological, physical, speech, and visual by considering multimodal interfaces, narrative, and affordances.

REFERENCES

Adams, D. (2002). *Automatic Generation of Dungeons for Computer Games.* University of Sheffield. Retrieved from https://pdfs.semanticscholar.org/2502/0f8d955aee07b7dd49a3ec 23b1f2a8cf1d06.pdf

Adellin, R., Khuan, C. T., & Gertrude, L. D. (2019, May). Conceptual Framework Puzzle Game with High Replayability. *Journal of Physics: Conference Series, 1228*(1), 012070. doi:10.1088/1742-6596/1228/1/012070

Anderson, C. A. (2004). An update on the effects of playing violent video games. *Journal of Adolescence, 27*(1), 113–122. doi:10.1016/j.adolescence.2003.10.009 PMID:15013264

Anderson, C. A., & Bushman, B. J. (2001). Effects of violent video games on aggressive behavior, aggressive cognition, aggressive affect, physiological arousal, and prosocial behavior: A Meta-Analytic Review of the Scientific Literature. *Psychological Science, 12*(5), 353–359. doi:10.1111/1467-9280.00366 PMID:11554666

Appelcline, S. (2013). *The (Not-So) Secret Origin of D&D.* Retrieved from http://dnd.wizards.com/articles/features/not-so-secret-origi n-dd

Ashlock, D., Lee, C., & Mcguinness, C. (n.d.). *Search-Based Procedural Generation of Maze-Like Levels. Academic Press.*

Barr, M. (2018). Student attitudes to games-based skills development: Learning from video games in higher education. *Computers in Human Behavior, 80*, 283–294. doi:10.1016/j.chb.2017.11.030

Barton, M. (2007). *The History of Computer Role-Playing Games Part 1: The Early Years (1980-1983).* Retrieved from Gamasutra website: http://www.gamasutra.com/view/feature/132024/the_history_of_ computer_.php

Barton, M. (2019). *Dungeons and Desktops Dungeons and Desktops The History of Computer Role-Playing Games (2nd ed.).* Taylor & Francis. doi:10.1201/9781351273404

Bierre, K., Chetwynd, J., Ellis, B., Hinn, D. M., Ludi, S., & Westin, T. (2005, July). Game not over: Accessibility issues in video games. In *Proc. of the 3rd International Conference on Universal Access in Human-Computer Interaction* (pp. 22-27). Academic Press.

Borderie, J., & Michinov, N. (2016). Identifying Flow in Video Games. *International Journal of Gaming and Computer-Mediated Simulations, 8*(3), 19–38. doi:10.4018/IJGCMS.2016070102

Bowman, S. L. (2007). The Psychological Power of the Roleplaying Experience. *Journal of Interactive Drama.*

Bowman, S. L. (2010). *The Functions of Role-Playing Games: How Participants Create Community, Solve Problems and Explore Identity.* Jefferson, NC: McFarland & Company, Inc., Publishers.

Boyle, E., Connolly, T. M., & Hainey, T. (2011). The role of psychology in understanding the impact of computer games. *Entertainment Computing, 2*(2), 69–74. doi:10.1016/j.entcom.2010.12.002

Cairns, P., Power, C., Barlet, M., & Haynes, G. (2019). Future Design of Accessibility in Games: A Design Vocabulary. *International Journal of Human-Computer Studies*, *131*, 64–71. doi:10.1016/j. ijhcs.2019.06.010

Chang, C. H., Pan, W. W., Tseng, L. Y., & Stoffregen, T. A. (2012). Postural activity and motion sickness during video game play in children and adults. *Experimental Brain Research*, *217*(2), 299–309. doi:10.100700221-011-2993-4 PMID:22210118

Chen, C. L. D., Yeh, T. K., & Chang, C. Y. (2016). *The effects of game-based learning and anticipation of a test on the learning outcomes of 10 th grade geology students. Eurasia Journal of Mathematics, Science and Technology Education.* doi:10.12973/eurasia.2016.1519a

Chiang, Y. T., Lin, S. S. J., Cheng, C. Y., & Liu, E. Z. F. (2011). *Exploring online game players' flow experiences and positive affect. Turkish Online Journal of Educational Technology.*

Chiu, F. Y., & Hsieh, M. L. (2017). *Role-playing game based assessment to fractional concept in second grade mathematics. Eurasia Journal of Mathematics, Science and Technology Education.* doi:10.12973/ eurasia.2017.00659a

Compañ-Rosique, P., Molina-Carmona, R., Gallego-Durán, F., Satorre-Cuerda, R., Villagrá-Arnedo, C., & Llorens-Largo, F. (2019). A guide for making video games accessible to users with cerebral palsy. *Universal Access in the Information Society*, *18*(3), 565–581. doi:10.100710209-019-00679-6

Cowley, B., Charles, D., Black, M., & Hickey, R. (2008). Toward an understanding of flow in video games. *Computers in Entertainment*, *6*(2), 1. doi:10.1145/1371216.1371223

Csikszentmihalyi, M. (1991). Flow: The psychology of optimal experience: Steps toward enhancing the quality of life. *Design Issues*, *8*(1), 80. doi:10.2307/1511458

Daniau, S. (2016). The Transformative Potential of Role-Playing Games—: From Play Skills to Human Skills. *Simulation & Gaming*, *47*(4), 423–444. doi:10.1177/1046878116650765

Darin, T., Andrade, R., & Sánchez, J. (2018, January). CLUE: A Usability Evaluation Checklist for Multimodal Video Game Field Studies with Children Who Are Blind. *Proceedings of the 51st Hawaii International Conference on System Sciences.* 10.24251/HICSS.2018.034

De Freitas, S. (2018). Are games effective learning tools? A review of educational games. *Journal of Educational Technology & Society*, *21*(2), 74–84.

Donovan, T. (2010). *Replay: The History of Video Games.* Yellow Ant Media Ltd.

Dormans, J. (2010). Adventures in level design: Generating missions and spaces for action adventure games. *Workshop on Procedural Content Generation in Games, PC Games 2010, Co-Located with the 5th International Conference on the Foundations of Digital Games.* 10.1145/1814256.1814257

Ewalt, D. M. (2013). Of Dice and Men: The Story of Dungeons and Dragons and the People Who Play It. In *American Journal of Play.* Scribner Book Company.

Forsyth, W. (2016). Globalized Random Procedural Content for Dungeon Generation. *Journal of Computing Sciences in Colleges.*

Garda, M. B. (2013). Neo-rogue and the essence of roguelikeness. *Homo Ludens, 1*(5), 59–72.

Gee, J. P. (2003). *What video games have to teach us about learning and literacy*. New York: Palgrave Macmillan.

Gygax, B. G., & Arneson, D. (1974). *Dungeons & Dragons*. Academic Press.

Hartsook, K., Zook, A., Das, S., & Riedl, M. O. (2011). Toward supporting stories with procedurally generated game worlds. *2011 IEEE Conference on Computational Intelligence and Games, CIG 2011*, 297–304. 10.1109/CIG.2011.6032020

Hastings, E. J., Guha, R. K., & Stanley, K. O. (2009). Automatic content generation in the galactic arms race video game. *IEEE Transactions on Computational Intelligence and AI in Games, 1*(4), 245–263. doi:10.1109/TCIAIG.2009.2038365

Hendrikx, M., Meijer, S., Van Der Velden, J., & Iosup, A. (2013). Procedural content generation for Games: A Survey. *ACM Transactions on Multimedia Computing Communications and Applications, 9*(1), 1–22. doi:10.1145/2422956.2422957

Iosup, A. (2009). *POGGI: Puzzle-based online games on grid infrastructures*. Lecture Notes in Computer Science. doi:10.1007/978-3-642-03869-3_39

Jang, Y., & Ryu, S. (2011). Exploring game experiences and game leadership in massively multiplayer online role-playing games. *British Journal of Educational Technology, 42*(4), 616–623. doi:10.1111/j.1467-8535.2010.01064.x

Johnson, L., Yannakakis, G. N., & Togelius, J. (2010). Cellular automata for real-time generation of infinite cave levels. *Workshop on Procedural Content Generation in Games, PC Games 2010, Co-Located with the 5th International Conference on the Foundations of Digital Games*. 10.1145/1814256.1814266

Johnson, M. R. (2017). The Use of ASCII Graphics in Roguelikes: Aesthetic Nostalgia and Semiotic Difference. *Games and Culture, 12*(2), 115–135. doi:10.1177/1555412015585884

Kelly, G., & McCabe, H. (2007). Citygen: An interactive system for procedural city generation. *Fifth International Conference on Game Design and Technology*.

Kent, S. L. (2001). *The Ultimate History of Video Games: From Pong to Pokémon and Beyond - The Story Behind the Craze that Touched our Lives and Changed the World*. New York: Three Rivers Press.

Lee, S. H., & Song, D. H. (2019). Functional usability analysis of top Korean mobile role playing games based on user interface design. *Indones. J. Electr. Eng. Comput. Sci, 13*(1), 123. doi:10.11591/ijeecs.v13.i1.pp123-128

Lefebvre, S., & Neyret, F. (2003). Pattern based procedural textures. *Proceedings of the Symposium on Interactive 3D Graphics*. 10.1145/641514.641518

Lopes, R., & Bidarra, R. (2011). Adaptivity challenges in games and simulations: A survey. *IEEE Transactions on Computational Intelligence and AI in Games, 3*(2), 85–99. doi:10.1109/TCIAIG.2011.2152841

McDaniel, R., & Telep, P. (2009). Best Practices for Integrating Game-Based Learning into Online Teaching. *Journal of Online Learning and Teaching / MERLOT*.

Merhi, O., Faugloire, E., Flanagan, M., & Stoffregen, T. A. (2007). Motion sickness, console video games, and head-mounted displays. *Human Factors*, *49*(5), 920–934. doi:10.1518/001872007X230262 PMID:17915607

Moses, L. E. (1986). *Think and Explain with Statistics*. Penguin Books Australia.

Nielsen, J. (1995). *10 usability heuristics for user interface design*. Nielsen Norman Group.

Ogletree, S. M., & Drake, R. (2007). College students' video game participation and perceptions: Gender differences and implications. *Sex Roles*, *56*(7-8), 537–542. doi:10.100711199-007-9193-5

Pantaleev, A. (2012). In Search of Patterns: Disrupting RPG Classes Through Procedural Content Generation. Proceedings of the The Third Workshop on Procedural Content Generation in Games, 4:1-4:5. 10.1145/2538528.2538532

Pantaleev, A. (2013). *In Search of Patterns: Disrupting RPG Classes through Procedural Content Generation*. doi:10.1145/2538528.2538532

Paul, C. A. (2018). *The Toxic Meritocray of Video Games, Why Gaming Culture is the Worst*. Minneapolis, MN: University of Minnesota Press. doi:10.5749/j.ctt2204rbz

Reich, R. (1991). The Work of Nations: preparing ourselves for 21st century capitalism. In *The Work of Nations*. New York: Vintage Books.

Roden, T., & Parberry, I. (2004). From artistry to automation: A structured methodology for procedural content creation. *Lecture Notes in Computer Science*, *3166*, 151–156. doi:10.1007/978-3-540-28643-1_19

Sevilla, C., Santini, S., Haya, P. A., Rodriguez, P., & Sacha, G. M. (2012). Interdisciplinary design of videogames: A highly motivating method of learning. *2012 International Symposium on Computers in Education, SIIE 2012*.

Shaker, N., Togelius, J., & Nelson, M. J. (2016). Procedural Content Generation in Games. In Retrogame Archeology. doi:10.1007/978-3-319-42716-4

Short, X. T., & Adams, T. (2017). Procedural Content Generation in Game Design. Taylor & Francis.

Slootmaker, A., Nadolski, R., Kurvers, H. J., Hummel, H. G. K., & Koper, E. J. R. (2018). Usability of the EMERGO player environment for scenario-based serious games. *Human-Computer Interaction*.

Smelik, R. M., De Kraker, K. J., Groenewegen, S. A., Tutenel, T., & Bidarra, R. (2009). A survey of procedural methods for terrain modelling. *Proceedings of the CASA Workshop on 3D Advanced Media in Gaming and Simulation (3AMIGAS)*.

Smith, A. M., & Mateas, M. (2011). Answer set programming for procedural content generation: A design space approach. *IEEE Transactions on Computational Intelligence and AI in Games*, *3*(3), 187–200. doi:10.1109/TCIAIG.2011.2158545

Smith, G., Gan, E., Othenin-Girard, A., & Whitehead, J. (2011). PCG-Based Game Design: Enabling New Play Experiences through Procedural Content Generation. *Proceedings of the 2nd International Workshop on Procedural Content Generation in Games Article No. 7*. 10.1145/2000919.2000926

Smith, K., & Abrams, S. S. (2019). Gamification and accessibility. *The International Journal of Information and Learning Technology, 36*(2), 104–123. doi:10.1108/IJILT-06-2018-0061

Stoffregen, T. A., Faugloire, E., Yoshida, K., Flanagan, M. B., & Merhi, O. (2008). Motion sickness and postural sway in console video games. *Human Factors, 50*(2), 322–331. doi:10.1518/001872008X250755 PMID:18516842

Su, Y. S., Chiang, W. L., James Lee, C. T., & Chang, H. C. (2016). The effect of flow experience on player loyalty in mobile game application. *Computers in Human Behavior, 63*, 240–248. doi:10.1016/j.chb.2016.05.049

Summerville, A., Snodgrass, S., Guzdial, M., Holmgard, C., Hoover, A. K., Isaksen, A., ... Togelius, J. (2018). Procedural Content Generation via Machine Learning (PCGML). *IEEE Transactions on Games, 10*(3), 257–270. doi:10.1109/TG.2018.2846639

Togelius, J., Yannakakis, G. N., Stanley, K. O., & Browne, C. (2011). Search-based procedural content generation: A taxonomy and survey. *IEEE Transactions on Computational Intelligence and AI in Games, 3*(3), 172–186. doi:10.1109/TCIAIG.2011.2148116

Toker, S., & Baturay, M. H. (2016). Antecedents and consequences of game addiction. *Computers in Human Behavior, 55*, 668–679. doi:10.1016/j.chb.2015.10.002

Tolkien, J. R. R. (1954). *The Lord of the Rings*. George Allen & Unwin.

Tutenel, T., Bidarra, R., Smelik, R. M., & De Kraker, K. J. (2009). *The role of semantics in games and simulations*. Computers in Entertainment. doi:10.1145/1461999.1462009

Tyagi, M., Choudhary, C., & Majumdar, R. (2019). A Study on Gaming Engines Accessibility. In *Advances in Interdisciplinary Engineering* (pp. 33–41). Singapore: Springer. doi:10.1007/978-981-13-6577-5_4

Valtchanov, V., & Brown, J. A. (2012). Evolving dungeon crawler levels with relative placement. doi:10.1145/2347583.2347587

Van Der Linden, R., Lopes, R., & Bidarra, R. (2014). Procedural generation of dungeons. *IEEE Transactions on Computational Intelligence and AI in Games, 6*(1), 78–89. doi:10.1109/TCIAIG.2013.2290371

Velikovsky, J. (2014). *Flow Theory, Evolution & Creativity*. doi:10.1145/2677758.2677770

Vieira, E. A. O., Da Silveira, A. C., & Martins, R. X. (2019). Heuristic Evaluation on Usability of Educational Games: A Systematic Review. *Informatics in Education, 18*(2), 427–442. doi:10.15388/infedu.2019.20

Vlachopoulos, D., & Makri, A. (2017). The effect of games and simulations on higher education: a systematic literature review. International Journal of Educational Technology in Higher Education, 14. doi:10.118641239-017-0062-1

Volkmar, G., Mählmann, N., & Malaka, R. (2019, November). Procedural Content Generation in Competitive Multiplayer Platform Games. In *Joint International Conference on Entertainment Computing and Serious Games* (pp. 228-234). Springer. 10.1007/978-3-030-34644-7_18

Voorhees, G. (2009). The character of difference: Procedurality, rhetoric, and roleplaying games. *Game Studies*. Retrieved from http://gamestudies.org/0902/articles/voorhees

Yanez-Gomez, R., Font, J. L., Cascado-Caballero, D., & Sevillano, J. L. (2019). Heuristic usability evaluation on games: A modular approach. *Multimedia Tools and Applications, 78*(4), 4937–4964. doi:10.100711042-018-6593-1

Yang, J. C., Chen, C. H., & Chang Jeng, M. (2010). Integrating video-capture virtual reality technology into a physically interactive learning environment for English learning. *Computers & Education, 55*(3), 1346–1356. doi:10.1016/j.compedu.2010.06.005

Yannakakis, G. N., & Togelius, J. (2011). *Experience-driven procedural content generation*. IEEE Transactions on Affective Computing. doi:10.1109/T-AFFC.2011.6

Yen, L. (2011). *Promotion of Student Problem-Solving Skills, Motivation, Knowledge Acquisition and English Proficiency level Using an Interactive Computer Game*. ED-MEDIA.

Zheng, R., & Gardner, M. K. (2017). *Handbook of Research on Serious Games for Educational Applications*. IGI Global. doi:10.4018/978-1-5225-0513-6

ADDITIONAL READING

Barton, M. (2019). *Dungeons and Desktops Dungeons and Desktops The History of Computer Role-Playing Games (Second edi)*. Taylor & Francis. doi:10.1201/9781351273404

Bowman, S. L. (2010). *The Functions of Role-Playing Games: How Participants Create Community, Solve Problems and Explore Identity*. Jefferson, North Carolina: McFarland & Company, Inc., Publishers.

Cowley, B., Charles, D., Black, M., & Hickey, R. (2008). Toward an understanding of flow in video games. *Computers in Entertainment, 6*(2), 1. doi:10.1145/1371216.1371223

Donovan, T. (2010). *Replay: The History of Video Games*. Yellow Ant Media Ltd.

Ewalt, D. M. (2013). *Of Dice and Men: The Story of Dungeons and Dragons and the People Who Play It. American Journal of Play*. Scribner Book Company.

Gee, J. P. (2003). *What video games have to teach us about learning and literacy*. New York: palgrave macmillan.

Kent, S. L. (2001). *The Ultimate History of Video Games: From Pong to Pokémon and Beyond - The Story Behind the Craze that Touched our Lives and Changed the World*. New York, USA: Three Rivers Press.

Paul, C. A. (2018). *The Toxic Meritocray of Video Games, Why Gaming Culture is the Worst*. Minneapolis: University of Minnesota Press. doi:10.5749/j.ctt2204rbz

Reich, R. (1991). *The Work of Nations: preparing ourselves for 21st century capitalism. The Work of Nations*. New York: Vintage Books.

Shaker, N., Togelius, J., & Nelson, M. J. (2016). *Procedural Content Generation in Games*. Retrogame Archeology; doi:10.1007/978-3-319-42716-4

Short, X. T., & Adams, T. (2017). Procedural Content Generation in Game Design. Taylor & Francis.

KEY TERMS AND DEFINITIONS

Artificial Intelligence: According to many authors, artificial intelligence can be hard to be described, but we can reduce it to two actions: (1) a set of technics and methods used to allow any device to perceive its environment and make decisions that maximize its chance of successfully achieving its goals, mimicking a living being brain. (2) Capability of a machine to learn and perform narrow, repetitive and/or delicate tasks, for example an IA focused in predict words according to the context of the writer and previous sentences will not be able to predict the amount of money a person will spent next year.

Character: Is the complete simulation of a being (a person, an animal, an imaginary creature, etc) inside a computer game, this may include the ethnicity, height and weight, gender, psychological, cultural and regional properties, skills and abilities, dressing styles among other features. The equivalent in the real world would be an actor inside a theater play. Some characters are playable, and others have the purpose of give information, be the enemy or simply allow the player a better immersive experience of a simulation.

Education: Process which aim is to achieve the learning of a student, this can be measured as skills, values or knowledge that will help the student take the best possible decision in similar tasks reviewed in the educational system.

Flow: In terms of gaming, flow is a state of fulfillment where the player feels the game is in optimal conditions for his own level of experience, not too difficult nor too easy, increasing the loyalty and sense of personal achievement. There is an entire theory constructed around explaining this concept, it is not only limited to the field of games, any human activity can be described in terms of passion and boringness, concepts that are the pillars of this construct.

Game: Is the proposal of a fictional scenery that includes the goal(s), a set of rules and the structure of the development and the quantity of players per game (single person or by teams). A game can be played for fun or with educational purposes due the real-life simulation inside it. It can also represent unreal situations.

Indie Game Studio: It is an abbreviation of "independent game studio". This is a company that typically have fewer economic resources than a well know brand. However, many times an indie development disrupts the common constraints imposed by the market and the players achieve better experiences due the development of new technologies or styles.

Procedural Content Generation: A set of tools and methods that helps game developers the creation of sceneries algorithmically instead of manually. For example, if you have a set of three types of traps (mood, ice or fire) and you choose to put random traps in a narrow space like an aisle the software must be capable of adapt the space and the trap type and react according to the character approaching it.

Replayability: When a player has achieved all the goals of a game, if the game offers alternate endings, secret missions, additional characters, increasing scores and rewards or any other mechanism that keeps the interest of continue playing the game is called replayability.

Role Playing: Is the action of taking a certain job or activity inside a group of beings (teacher, student, janitor, policeman, etc.). Talking about games, it means specifically becoming a character inside a simulation. In computer science role playing will be selecting a certain type of warrior, agent, scientist, driver, or any other job description the game needs. The main purpose of taking a role in a game is develop the skills the character have, and make easier the task needed to achieve the games goal.

Video Game: In computer science, a game is a software that typically include graphical, sound, text and other multimedia combination aiming to simulate a real or unreal world situations to entertain the players in a single or collective way.

This research was previously published in UXD and UCD Approaches for Accessible Education; pages 274-296, copyright year 2020 by Information Science Reference (an imprint of IGI Global).

APPENDIX

Yuji Nakamura via bloomberg.com in his article "Peak Video Game? Top Analyst Sees Industry Slumping in 2019" has a deep analysis about the annual revenue of the videogame industry from 1971 to 2018, and if we compare this data with Pamela McClintock's article "Global Box Office Revenue Hits Record $41B in 2018" via the Hollywoodreporter.com about the film industry in the past 5 years we can clearly see that videogames surpass films by far, in fact, we can highlight that in 2014 Game industry revenue was 2.5 times the Films revenue globally speaking and by 2018 it has become 3.36 times, also we can see the film industry has reached a top and has flattened its incomes.

If we make a similar comparison with the music industry and using the data collected from IFPI (International Federation of the Phonographic Industry) Global Music Report 2019 // State of the Industry, we can clearly see that the differences are even more drastic going from 6.33 times in 2014 to 7.25 times in 2018 as can be seen in Table 1.

Table 1. Video games vs films and music revenues expressed in billions of US dollars.

Year	Video Games	Films	Music
2014	91.2	36.4	14.3
2015	97.1	38.4	14.8
2016	107.7	38.8	16.2
2017	122	40.5	17.4
2018	138.5	41.1	19.1

And if we express this data as a graphic, Figure 5, for visual comparison purposes we can point the fact how films are not growing at the same rate as videogames or music, even if music is the lower of the three of them it has a constant increase.

Figure 5. Video games vs. films and music revenues expressed in billions of US dollars.

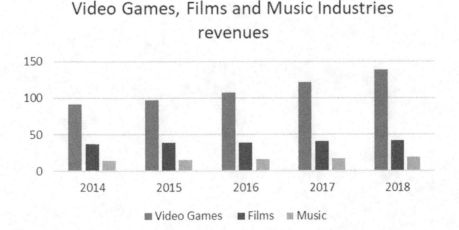

Section 4
Utilization and Applications

Chapter 46
Probability and Game

Alessio Drivet
Geogebra Institute of Turin, Italy

ABSTRACT

Probability is generally concerned with dealing with problems of a random or uncertain nature. The fact that it arises and develops from the analysis of gambling is something that cannot be overlooked. From the point of view of teaching, in addition to historical aspects, it is important to point out the importance of putting students in front of situations that, if not known, can lead to incorrect behavior and pathological attitudes. For this reason, the authors tried to emphasize not only the theoretical aspects, but above all the certainty that you always play "against the dealer" with an expected loss assessable for the various games.

INTRODUCTION

The probable is what usually happens. ~ Aristotle

Probability has historically been created precisely to study the game and in particular gambling, in general to deal with problems of a random or uncertain nature, the so-called aleatory problems. It is not surprising that the etymology of the word gambling and the word aleatory are similar: both derive from the word dice (*az-zahr* in Arabic and *alea* in Latin). Dice and betting were also well known in ancient Greece. An example is provided by mythology: playing dice, the gods divide the universe: Zeus gets the sky, Poseidon gets the sea, Hades loses and finds himself in the underworld.

Even the Romans can be regarded as remarkable gamblers. It is known that they bet almost everything, from gladiator fights to chariot races, from the launch of astragals to lottery tablets during the holidays dedicated to the god Saturn.

One of the most famous treatises on the game dates back to 1283. Alfonso X (2007), King of Castilla and Leon (Spain) wrote the *Libro de los Juegos*. In the text it is said that an Indian king had proposed to three wise men to reflect on what is worth more between luck and intelligence. One wise man takes the side of intelligence, another of luck, and the third argues the importance of both. The king asks to

DOI: 10.4018/978-1-6684-7589-8.ch046

demonstrate these positions concretely, and the three wise men take chess, dice and the last one games based on a board (such as backgammon) as proof.

In the Middle Ages, gambling became compulsive in Europe. The chronicles of the time speak of numerous edicts aimed at limiting the game, which, in places as bad as taverns, but also special gambling dens had taken on an incredible dimension. The Italian term *baratteria* (barratry) indicated precisely who kept a gambling dealer; the term was born in the 13th-14th century and the chronicles tell us that many municipalities taxed the game. *Barattiere* was also the one who, having a public role, was bribed for money. The accusation of barratry could be profoundly serious and also used to strike political enemies. At the State Archives of Florence is preserved the book where all the court sentences issued in that period were recorded. On March 10, 1302 it reads: "Alighieri Dante is condemned for barratry, fraud, falsehood, malice, unfair extortion practices, illicit proceeds, pederasty, and is sentenced to 5000 florins of fine, perpetual disqualification from public office, perpetual exile, and if you take him, at the stake, so that he dies. In the fourteenth century, with the introduction of modern cards, an adaptation of the previous ones coming from the East, new forms of game appear.

As time goes by, the games find an accommodation in small pavilions, called *casine*, a term that then evolves into "casino". The first real modern casino was built in 1861 in the Principality of Monaco and only in 1931 did the state of Nevada legalize gambling, making Las Vegas the gaming city par excellence. Other states followed suit and today gambling is widespread almost everywhere.

These few considerations would be enough to highlight how rich the history of gaming is and the space that would deserve analysis in the school environment. As Siew Pei Hwa (2018) says: "Play-way method involves act of seeing, hearing, saying and doing, which makes it easier to remember". Some difficulties, however, arise because many teachers do not have a clear picture of the spread of the phenomenon while students are frequently the protagonists, especially since the possibilities of online gaming became more popular. The study of gambling must consider both mathematical and psychological aspects. The study of gambling must consider both mathematical and psychological aspects. It is now well established among scholars that the accuracy of probability judgments is poor, as is familiarity with numbers. Some scholars such as Cosmides & Tooby came to explain the fact in evolutionary terms: according to them evolution has not consolidated *ad hoc* processing tools. Another interesting aspect is that, according to Drazen Prelec (1988), the human mind tends to overestimate small probabilities and underestimate high ones, which determines that the point of coincidence between probability and its estimate is for a value that is not, as one might suppose, 0.5 but coincides with a mathematically more interesting value: $p = 1/e$. The author has constructed a non-linear transformation of probabilities into "decision weights" $w(p)$. If we try to represent this characteristic we get the following graph (Figure 1):

This mechanism makes the individual think he can win with greater probability than the real one, plus the *sunk cost bias* that consists of continuing in the game because you have already invested a lot of money, energy, time.

An interesting field of research concerns a behavior that involves our cognitive system. Let's just think about the difference in attitude between finding a four-leaf clover in the meadow (unlikely event) and finding a poppy (much more likely event). In the first case the event, linked to luck, creates a short circuit between improbability and mental representation of desirability, probable events are instead easily structured in terms of rationality. A similar mechanism occurs in the game, if one wins, he thinks he is "lucky" and therefore can continue to play without taking into account that the probability of continuing to win may be extremely low. It is this behavior that contributes to what has been called *gambler's ruin*, widely described in literature. To give an idea we use a simple example.

Figure 1. Prelec diagram

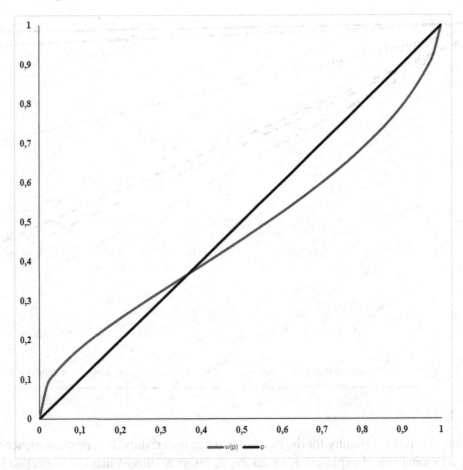

Two players compete for heads and tails, if heads *A* wins $1, if tails *B* wins $1, the game ends when one of them has exhausted his capital. Apparently it is a fair game. But let's suppose that the available capital is not the same: *A* has $10 and *B* $50.

We can represent it all as the random journey of a placeholder on a flat route with at the extremities two bars, the first place 10 steps to the left of the initial position and the second to the right 50 steps from the initial position. What is the probability that the placeholder will fall into one of the two bars, i.e. that one of the two players will run out of capital?

When the game develops a hypothetical gain and loss line oscillates around the zero-gain line (being the game fair) but the oscillations can be more or less wide: if the line exceeds a player's availability, he has lost everything. Those who have less money available are more likely to lose first. In general, the probability of winning depends on the ratio between the initial capital of each player and the sum of the two players' capital. So the probability of winning for *A* is given by $p_a = 10/60$ and for *B* by $p_b = 50/60$.

The problem becomes even more dramatic if you participate in a game where the dealer has a better chance of winning. In this case it is interesting to compare the "loss coefficients" of some extremely popular games according to Canova and Rizzuto (2016) (Figure 2):

Figure 2. How much you can lose in various games

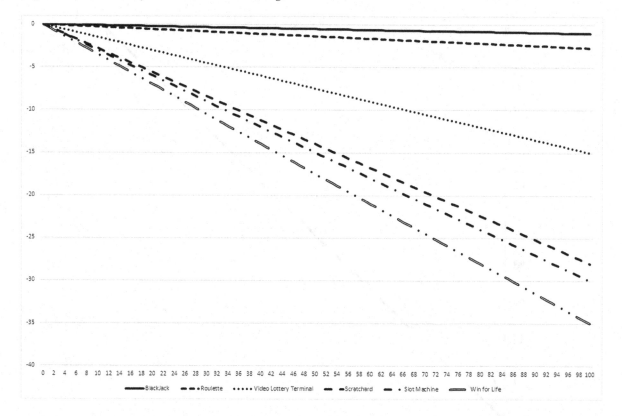

Underlying this is the difficulty for the mind to manage uncertainty. It is no coincidence that many, not finding a rational causal explanation for an event, resort to almost magical concepts. Everything could be enclosed in a question: can superstition influence events?

The term superstition refers to practices that are intended to reject supposed negative influences. Many actions are avoided by players: never knock before rolling the dice, never cross your fingers, never touch the cards before they are all served at the table, etc..

These brief considerations are just the tip of the iceberg of an issue that affects the daily life of the population, not just the players. For this reason it would be essential to provide all the tools for under-standing random phenomena, starting from school.

Returning to didactics, according to Siller & Maaß (2012), teach probability through gambling: "is a very authentic one, so that the students can discuss a real-life problem which could be found in their near environment".

All educational experiences in this sense have shown that betting is an emotionally charged activity, involving the individual as a whole. Leveraging this can stimulate the student to reflect on these issues, also exploiting the mechanism of playful adhesion.

In the chapter will be presented, mixed, both board games and some particularly significant games of chance.

ORCHARD

The first game presented is certainly the simplest, but not trivial in terms of probabilistic reasoning.

It is a cooperative game aimed at pre-schoolers. The board has four trees loaded with fruit that must be picked by the players: apples, pears, cherries and plums. A raven wants to take advantage of the opportunity to seize the fruits. The game is regulated by throwing a dice that shows the colour of the fruits on four sides, on the fifth side a basket (if it comes out you can pick two fruits of your choice) and on the sixth side the image of the raven. Depending on the result of the throw the children collect one or two fruits, but if the raven comes out one of the nine pieces of the puzzle representing the animal is placed on the board to compose the drawing of the raven (Figure 3).

Figure 3. Orchard

The game ends when the players have collected all the fruits or the puzzle is completed.

The game is simple, but it is less simple to answer the question: what is the probability that the children are winners?

The modeling of the game itself is not difficult and a tree graph can help us, each launch corresponds to 6 different outcomes, but after n throws the possible results are 6n. Even eliminating the basket so as not to complicate the analysis too much (if its symbol comes out, the die is thrown again and therefore it is as if we had a five-sided die), there are too many cases. Let's try a simplified version of the game (Bibbona et al,2014) tree with two fruits and a puzzle consisting of three tiles and using a coin; if heads come out the children collect the fruit, if tails come out they put a crow tile on the board..

Now we can build a simplified tree diagram (Figure 4).

Figure 4. Simplified Orchard Graph

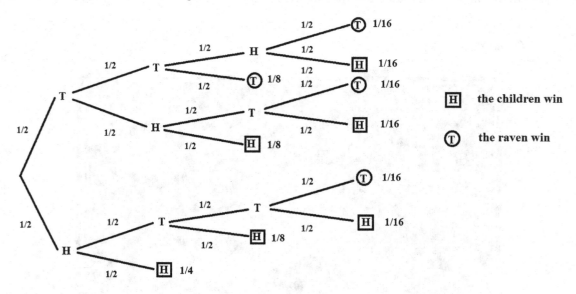

The maximum number of rolls is 4, i.e. $n_{fruits} + n_{raven} -1$. As you can see the probability of the children winning is 11/16 while the crow is left with a more miserable 5/16.

Even using an old programming language such as BASIC you can achieve the theoretically expected result. Here is a possible program:

```
FRUITS = 2
RAVEN = 0
RANDOMIZE
INPUT "# GAMES    ", n
FOR I = 1 TO n
    DO
        COIN = FIX(RND * 2) + 1
        IF COIN = 1 AND FRUITS > 0 THEN FRUITS = FRUITS - 1 ELSE FRUITS = 2
        IF COIN = 2 AND RAVEN < 3 THEN RAVEN = RAVEN + 1 ELSE RAVEN = 0
    LOOP UNTIL FRUITS = 0 OR RAVEN = 3
        IF FRUITS = 0 THEN win = win + 1
        IF RAVEN = 3 THEN lose = lose + 1
```

```
NEXT I
PRINT "% WIN", win / n * 100, "% LOSE", lose / n * 100
The VBA version for Excel does not differ much:
Sub OrchardGame()
fruits = 2
raven = 0
n = InputBox("# games")
For i = 1 To n
    Do
        dado = Int(Rnd * 2) + 1
        If (fruits > 0 And dado = 1) Then fruits = fruits - 1 Else fruits =
2
        If (raven < 3 And dado = 2) Then raven = raven + 1 Else raven = 0
    Loop Until fruits = 0 Or raven = 3
        If fruits = 0 Then win = win + 1
        If raven = 3 Then lose = lose + 1
Next i
Range("A2") = "% win"
Range("A3") = "% lose"
Range("B2") = win / n * 100
Range("B3") = lose / n * 100
End Sub
```

Generalizing, an interesting case assuming an unbalanced coin where the probability of heads is p and the probability of tails $q = 1 - p$, you will have $P(T) = p^2 + 2 p^2 q + 3 p^2 q^2$.

The problem becomes more complicated when you switch to regular play. In this case the number of trees becomes 4 with 40 fruits, the pieces of the puzzle rise to 9 and in addition there is the variant of the basket. For the analysis of this type of problem with multiple objectives, see an article by Paul J. Campbell (2007). A simplified version that is easier to program could include the elimination of the basket and the presence of a single tree with 40 fruits.

RISK

It is a board strategy game, published in 1957 under the title *La conquête du monde* and later in the United States under the name *Risk*. In Italy it was published in the variant called *RisiKo!* (Figure 5).

The goal of the game is to achieve a predefined but secret and different goal for each player. It may consist in the conquest of a number of states, the conquest of two or more continents, the entire planisphere or the annihilation of an opponent. The scoreboard on which a game develops represents the world divided into 42 territories grouped in 6 continents. At each moment of the game each territory is occupied by one player's armies. Each participant commands a group of armies, identified by the color of the tanks, with which they occupy their board territories, attack the territories occupied by the other players and defend themselves against attacks. When a goal is achieved the game ends and the player

Figure 5. Italian variant of Risk

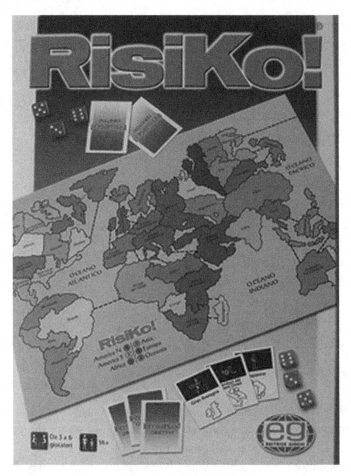

who has achieved it has won. The rule foresees that the attacker (A) and the defender (D) roll from 1 to 3 dice, to be compared in pairs in order of value, in case of equal dice, the defender wins.

The simplest situation is when *A* and *D* compete with one die each: *D* wins if the number obtained by throwing his die is greater than or equal to that of *A*.

Built the Table 1 of the 36 possibilities, which represents the *sample space*, you can see that *A* wins with probability $15/36 = 5/12 = 41.7\%$ while the chances are obviously greater for the defender.

Let's suppose instead that *A* attacks with two dice, while *D* defends with 1 dice: in this case *A* wins if at least one of his results is greater than D's. The calculation of A's probability of winning is now a bit more complicated as the possible cases are already $6^3 = 216$. What happens can be displayed with a graph in which the attacker collides head-to-head with the defender and, in case of defeat, uses the second die.

It should be noted that if *A* loses the first fight (with probability 21/36), this affects what happens afterwards; in other words, the events are not independent: it is therefore necessary to use conditional probability: that is, we must calculate p(A wins the second shot | A loses the first shot). Once the calculations have been made, we can see that the probability that *A* wins the second fight is only 10/36. At this point, the tree (Figure 6) becomes:

Table 1. Results in the toss of a dice

		Striker					
		1	2	3	4	5	6
Defender	1	D	A	A	A	A	A
	2	D	D	A	A	A	A
	3	D	D	D	A	A	A
	4	D	D	D	D	A	A
	5	D	D	D	D	D	A
	6	D	D	D	D	D	D

Figure 6. Risk Graph 2 vs 1

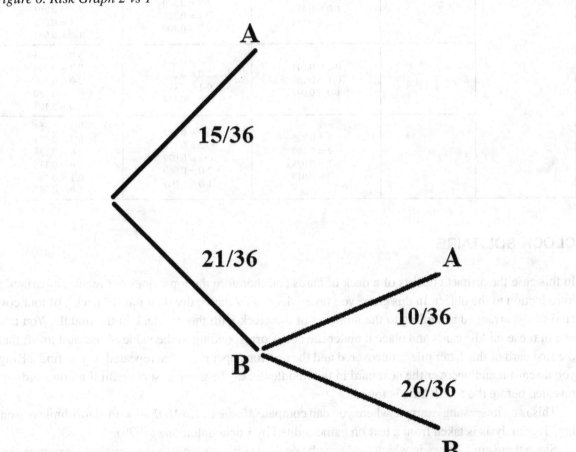

What happens in general if *A* and *D* play with a different number of dice or are repeated attacks to be considered?

From a strategic point of view it is always advantageous for *A* to roll the maximum number of dice. So when the attacker rolls three dice against two, three against one or two against one, he has a slight advantage, otherwise the advantage is all of the defender. The analysis is not trivial, it is a typical case where it is convenient to use a program to simulate a large number of lots and empirically verify the probability. The method (already seen) used to draw estimates through simulations is called *Monte Carlo Method*; it is used to find solutions to mathematical problems that are difficult to deal with. To give an idea of the odds involved, the results of 20000 virtual fights can be examined (Table 2).

Table 2. Summary table of simulations

		Striker		
		1	2	3
Defender	1	1-0 = 0.417 0-1 = 0.583	2-0 = 0.579 0-1 = 0.221 1-0 = 0.200	3-0 = 0.658 2-0 = 0.203 0-1 = 0.072 1-0 = 0.067
	2	0-2 = 0.741 0-1 = 0.162 1-0 = 0.097	0-2 = 0.444 2-0 = 0.225 0-1 = 0.177 1-0 = 0.154	3-0 = 0.375 0-2 = 0.208 2-0 = 0.180 0-1 = 0.130 1-0 = 0.107
	3	0-3 = 0.825 0-2 = 0.130 0-1 = 0.028 1-0 = 0.017	0-3 = 0.615 0-2 = 0.176 0-1 = 0.079 2-0 = 0.069 1-0 = 0.061	0-3 = 0.384 0-2 = 0.173 3-0 = 0.138 2-0 = 0.115 0-1 = 0.108 1-0 = 0.082

CLOCK SOLITAIRE

In this case the artifact consists of a deck of cards and therefore the topic does not require a particular introduction to the object. In this game you take a deck of 52 cards, divide it into 13 decks, of four covered cards, arranged according to the numbers of the clock with the last deck in the middle. You take one of these middle cards and place it under the deck corresponding to the value of the card itself; then the first card of this latter pile is uncovered and the previous operations are repeated. If you find a King, you discard it and uncover the next card in the middle deck. The game is successful if all the cards are revealed before the fourth king is found.

This is an interesting example where you can compare *Monte Carlo Method* with algorithmic reasoning. The analysis is taken from a text on games edited by Lucia Salomone (1979).

Since there are 52 ways in which cards can be dealt, it is not possible to systematically examine possible distributions. Then you can play a certain number of games on the computer, assuming the fraction of successful solitaires in the sample as an estimate of the probability. The order of the cards is due to chance and is influenced only by the initial distribution. The probability of winning, on average, is 1 in 13. If you do not have a computer to check the result, you can use a different solution based on reasoning. To predict from the beginning if the game will succeed, simply know the value of the last card of each bundle! Figure 7 shows a possible configuration.

Figure 7. Final configuration of the solitaire

Each position of the clock is matched to a corresponding value of the cards, so one coincides with the Ace, two with 2, ..., eleven with Jack, twelve with Queen.

Then you draw a line from each of the 12 card values to the card that occupies the corresponding place, for example: the card that is placed on the one is a Queen and therefore must be connected with Q. The card placed on the two is a nine and then connects with 9, the card placed on the three is a four and then the connection must be made with the next card, which is a four, and so on. In practice, for each card, the connections are indicated as shown in Figure 8.

The representation of the connections is then transformed into a graph (Figure 9).

The game is won if and only if the graph of the connections between the last cards is a tree that includes all thirteen decks.

For example in this case the solitaire will succeed because the graph is connected.

Figure 8. Solitaire connections

SLOT MACHINE

A slot machine is a gambling machine, now widespread not only in casinos but also in many Internet sites. Even a slot/money box (Figure 10) can serve to introduce different concepts.

The aim of the game is to achieve a winning combination of the figures that appear on the reels. To play the game you have to insert a coin and then pull the lever that operates the rollers, wait for the rollers to stop and check if the combination is winning or not. The odds of winning vary depending on the type of slot. Taking a cue from the slot machine in the figure we can see that there are three wheels and five symbols: BAR, cherry, apple, 7, \$. Lowering the arm the three wheels slide independently to form an arrangement between the $5 \cdot 5 \cdot 5 = 5^3$ possible. Suppose you win if you get a triple BAR or a triple 7 or two BAR and a 7 or two 7 and a BAR. In total you have eight winning combinations because the triple 7 and the triple BAR have only one occurrence while the other two can each be presented in three different ways. For example: 7 7 BAR, 7 BAR 7, BAR 7 7.

The probability of winning is therefore $8/125 = 0.064$. How much should you get from a bet if the game was fair, i.e. both the player and the machine operator did not have an advantage?

Figure 9. Solitaire graph

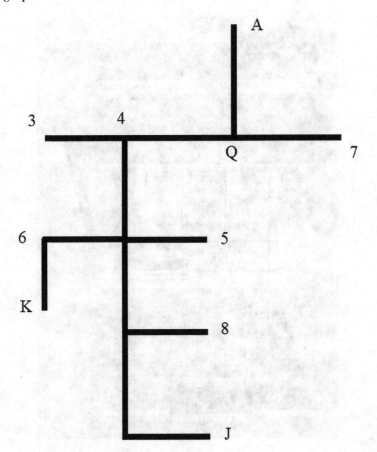

From this consideration we can take a fundamental concept, that of *Mathematical Expectation* or, more simply, *Expectation*.

The Expected value is the product between the sum S to be won and the probability p to win:

Expectation = S • p

Returning to the case of the slot machine, if the bet is \$1, the $S • 0.064 = 1$ should apply in case of victory.

Obtaining S, we have:

$$S = \frac{1}{0.064} \approx 15.6$$

In reality the slot manager does not give this amount to the player but retains part of it as remuneration, so the game is unfair.

Figure 10. Slot machine – money box

Following an example set by Jean-Louis Boursin (1986), we now shift our interest to a situation where there are two slot machines. Let's first take as a reference the previously calculated probability of winning (0.0064). Next to it (without our knowledge) there is a slot machine which, due to a malfunction, sees this probability increased by a factor of ten (0.064). What is the probability that, choosing at random one of the two, the win (V) or the loss ($\overline{V}$) depends on the use of the faulty one (F) or the not faulty one ($\overline{F}$)? The answer depends on the type of question being asked, for example we can ask ourselves what the probability is:

1. If I play a game and I win it;
2. If I play a game and lose it;
3. If I play two games and win them both;
4. If I play two games and lose both;
5. If I play two games and lose one, I win the other.

The answers can be found using a tree graph (Figure 11):

The solution is to be found by applying Bayes' Theorem. If I play a game and I win, the probability that this victory is due to the use of the broken machine is remarkably high:

$$P(V|F) = \frac{P(\bar{F} \cap V)}{P(\bar{F} \cap V) + P(F \cap V)} = \frac{0.0032}{0.0032 + 0.032} = 0.909$$

If I play a game and lose it, then I get:

$$P(\bar{V}|F) = \frac{P(\bar{F} \cap \bar{V})}{P(\bar{F} \cap \bar{V}) + P(F \cap \bar{V})} = \frac{0.4968}{0.4968 + 0.468} = 0.485$$

If I play two games it is necessary to continue the calculations by going further through the branches but the reasoning does not change. Summarizing the results you will have (Table 3):

Figure 11. Tree of the two slot machines

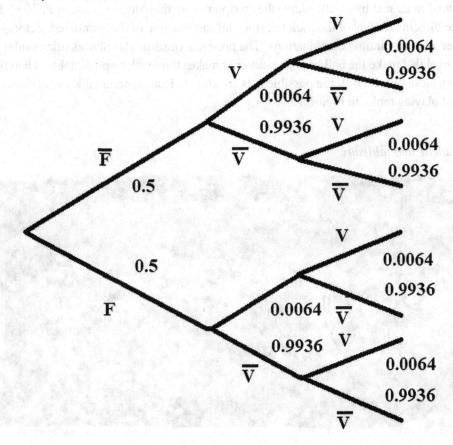

Table 3. Probability of the two slot machines

Question	Probability
1. If I play a game and I win it;	0.909
2. If I play a game and lose it;	0.485
3. If I play two games and win them both;	0.990
4. If I play two games and lose both;	0.470
5. If I play two games and lose one, I win the other.	0.904

ROULETTE

Roulette is a gambling game of Italian or, according to other sources, French origin. It consists of a disc, divided into 37 sectors (38, in American roulette with 00) numbered from 0 to 36 and colored alternately in red and black, while the zero (0), like the double zero (00) when present, is normally colored green; the disc is rotated in its seat by an attendant (the croupier) who then throws a ball at it. The ball, rotated in the opposite direction to that of the roulette, stops falling into one of the numbered sectors, determining the number and the winning combinations. The presence of some rhombuses (diamonds) placed on the roulette wheel that make the ball bounce randomly makes the result unpredictable. Then there is the tableau, a green cloth on which all the possible bets are shown. Roulette and tableau are shown together, as in the actual playing table, in Figure 12.

Figure 12. Roulette and tableaux

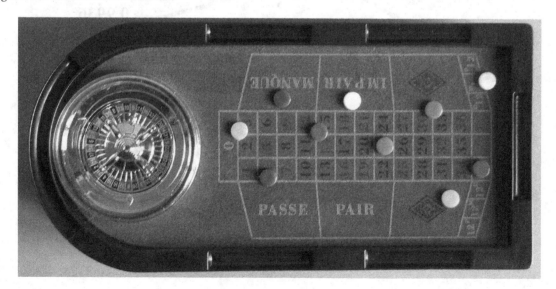

While the slot machine, seen above, is an object known to most students, typical casino games do not often have the same notoriety and therefore it would be useful to show how they work. There are excellent virtual reproductions of the roulette game on the net. The problem is that, almost always, online simulations offer, in addition to the possibility of playing for free, also that of playing for real money with the risk of sponsoring certain sites, albeit in good faith. To avoid this, it is preferable to turn to the few versions not explicitly linked to betting sites or, better, to use the equipment readily available in any toy store in the classroom.

The combinations and payments per unit of bet are those in Table 4:

Table 4. Table of bets

Name	Payments
Straight/Single (single number)	35
Split (contiguous pair)	17
Street (transverse)	11
Corner/Square (four contiguous numbers)	8
Six Line/Double Street (two contiguous transversal)	5
Dozen bet (first, second or third)	2
Column bet (first, second or third)	2
Even or Odd	1
Low or High (1-18 or 19-36)	1
Red or Black	1

Roulette, like all games of chance, guarantees the dealer a mathematical percentage of advantage over the player, which in the case of French roulette is about 2.70%. If you bet on a number the probability of winning is 1/37 and that of losing 36/37, betting a \$ the expected "gain" is $35 \cdot 1/37 - 1 \cdot 36/37 = -0.027$. If roulette is American the losses double because the numbers are 38.

Repeating the calculation for the other combinations can verify that the result does not change. For example, if you bet on red or black, the relationship $1 \cdot 18/37 - 1 \cdot 19/37 = -0.027$ applies. As a result, there are no systems or techniques that guarantee a secure win.

Many players thought they could beat roulette: the best-known method is doubling the bet (martingale). The system is, at least in appearance, simple. Suppose we use the minimum bet, which we suppose is \$10, on the red. If it comes out red I win \$20 and then I have a balance of +\$10. If it comes out black or the zero that is green (it's worse for roulette with double zero) I bet red again, doubling the bet to \$20, so I bet \$30. If it comes out red I win double, i.e. \$40, and then my balance is positive again. If unfortunately this color doesn't come out I keep betting on red, doubling the bet again, and so on, until finally it comes out red and I end up with a balance of +\$10. So I can think that, sooner or later, I will be able to gain from this strategy and in any case not to be at a loss. Too bad the method only works if I have unlimited money available. In fact at some point I may not have enough money to make continuous doubles. Also, casinos impose a cap on bets (suppose it is \$2000). After seven bets I have to bet \$1280 and if I don't win I've lost \$2550 but I can't keep playing doubles. The probability of such a threatening event is not as low as you might think:

$$P = \left(\frac{19}{37}\right)^8 = 0.0048$$

So the question arises: am I willing to risk losing \$ 2,550, about once every 200, to earn \$ 80, if it comes out red at most eight times?

Despite the broad and motivated mathematical justifications that advise against believing in the possibility of beating the dealer in the long run, there is still a proliferation of sites on the Internet where they sell out amazing strategies to win. Many players have tried to perfect a game system thinking they are skilled enough to beat the wheel. In this regard I would like to recall an anecdote that happened years ago in a casino, I observed a player who did not place bets but noted the results in a booklet building a fairly complicated scheme. After a certain time a smile appeared on his face, he put all his chips on the green table and relaxed in his chair. Needless to say, he lost everything and, more than disconsolate, he was stunned by the failure.

A more scientific approach is based on an analysis that takes into account some fundamental parameters such as knowledge of the initial position, speed and acceleration of the ball (Small & Tse), the problem lies both in the definition of the initial position (as we will see in chapter dedicated to Chaos) and the need to mount a digital camera above the wheel, a procedure obviously prohibited by casinos.

An interesting study on the link between skill and chance is due to Dreef et al (20010. According to the authors the outcome of any game depends on learning and chance. The ability to improve, with learning, one's performance allows an expert to increase the winnings compared to a beginner.

The random aspect affects the increase in winnings of a player who not only knows the rules of the game, but also knows what may depend on the case. Synthetically: the skill (S) can then be expressed as the ratio between learning (L) and the sum of learning and randomness (R):

$$S = \frac{L}{L+R}$$

Poker is a typical example: any player who only knows the rules of the game but has no knowledge of the odds, will not improve his winnings by playing. So learning is unlikely to significantly increase your winnings; poker is a game that mixes skill and chance. If we then consider the game of roulette then the skill, defined as above, gives us as result 0, i.e. the game of roulette is a game of pure chance.

Speaking more generally of the *gambler's ruin* we must mention Abraham de Moivre (1667- 1754) who managed to solve this classic problem by demonstrating that in a fair game the chances of ruin are inversely proportional to the capital available to play. Even in a fair game against a dealer with unlimited monetary availability, ruin is certain; this is even more true in a game like roulette, which is clearly not fair.

For a lot of players, this is a discouraging news (though hardly accepted). All gambling games involve a loss that represents the dealer's remuneration. So there's no chance? Two losing games, according to the physicist Juan Parrondo, can be set so that when played one after the other, they become winners. This is a surprising result in game theory called Parrondo's paradox, named after its discoverer. For the explanation we follow (with some modifications) the indications contained in an article by Harmer and Abbott (1999). Game *A* consists of flipping a coin that has a chance of winning a little less than half, let's say with a small bias like 0.005; the probability of winning (p = 0.4995) is such that it is a long losing game. The *B* game consists of playing with two particular dice. The rule is that, if our capital is a multiple of a whole number (Harmer and Abbott (1999) use n =3), we play with an octahedron and we win if face 1 comes out so with low probability of victory (p = 1/8); we play with a tetrahedron and we lose if face 1 comes out so with favorable probability of victory (p = 3/4). It should be easy to convince yourself that the combination of these two strategies leads overall to a loss, the advantage of playing with the tetrahedron does not compensate the losses of when I use the octahedron. Here the paradox comes into play: both games are losers, but if we alternate them, for example playing AABB, this periodic change leads to a rapid increase in capital. Starting with a certain capital, after a large number of games we see a positive *Average final capital*.

Presented as a game the paradox may seem a futile exercise, in fact it is widely used in game theory, engineering, the study of population dynamics, the diversification of financial risk, etc..

BLACKJACK

Although there is no total agreement, many scholars in the history of blackjack believe that this game dates back to Vingt Et Un ("21" in French) played in 17th century casinos in France. The only The only certain thing is that there is official news of Blackjack in 1623, in a local press there is an article dedicated to gambling that mentions it.

Players are dealt cards whose value is equal to the number that appears on the card except for figures that are worth 10. The Ace is the only card that can have two values: it can be worth 11 or 1, in this case it is said that the hand is soft. The goal is to get a score as close to 21 as possible. This value must not be exceeded, because in that case the player, or the dealer, "bust". Often it is thought that the goal of the game is to get as close as possible to 21, without exceeding this number, actually the goal of Blackjack is first of all to beat the dealer without exceeding 21. This aspect affects the game strategy.

To play you must place the bet in the appropriate box. After the players have made their bets, the dealer distributes two cards to all those sitting at the table and also gives two cards to himself (Figure 13). One of the dealer's cards is always uncovered. The other card, covered, is called the "hole card". Most casinos around the world prefer an "uncovered game" where the cards are placed face up next to the bet, there are other casinos that prefer the "covered game" where the cards are placed face down and the player has the right to look at them.

Once the distribution has taken place, players can exercise different options. If with the first two cards you do not have a "Blackjack" (21) in your hand you can:

1. Stay: you reject other cards and keep your score;
2. Ask for card: you can ask for "card" as many times as you want;
3. Split: if the first two cards are of the same value, you can split them, to play two separate hands, automatically betting the same amount;
4. Doubling: you can double the bet but in this case the dealer only needs one card.

At this point the dealer must pull paper with a score less than or equal to 16 and stay with 17 or more. The possibilities for the dealer are closely tied to its first card value, as shown in Table 5:

Figure 13. Blackjack table

Table 5. Advantages and disadvantages based on the dealer's first card

Dealer Show Card	% Of Dealer Bust	Player Advantage %
2	35.30	9.8
3	37.56	13.4
4	40.28	18.0
5	42.89	23.2
6	42.28	23.9
7	25.99	14.3
8	23.86	5.4

Some statistical calculations have made it possible to elaborate a "basic strategy" of play which, considering the uncovered card of the dealer and the two initial cards of the player, suggests what is more convenient to do. A different technique is based on counting cards that have already been issued. When the deck is "full" of aces and cards with a ten value, the player places high stakes. When the deck has more low-value cards such as two to six, it is advisable to make small bets or leave the table.

To understand how this strategy works, we can see a film, 21: based on the story of a group of MIT students who, between 1980 and 1990, bankrupted numerous casinos by counting cards.

REVOLVER

A game not to be experienced as potentially lethal, but very well known, is called Russian roulette. The rules are simple: a six-shot revolver has only one bullet in the drum, in turn the participants aim the weapon at their temple and pull the trigger risking, of course, to die. A famous Russian roulette scene is present in the film *The Deer Hunter* with Robert De Niro. The film features three American soldiers captured during the Vietnam War and forced to play this type of roulette. The game goes on until all but one of the competitors are killed.

In our case the object/stimulus (Figure 14) is represented by a card of the game known in Italy as the *Merchant at the fair* which is played with two decks of special cards with typical figures.

Figure 14. Paper with a revolver depicted

36 – IL REVOLVER

Leaving aside the bloody and senseless aspect of the game, you can formulate some questions whose answers depend on the conditions in which the game takes place.

Assuming there are six players taking turns at shooting each time the drum:

1. What are the chances of dying on the first try?
2. Is it better to try your luck first, second... or last?

The answers are a typical example of the application of conditional probabilities.

By indicating with $P(E_i)$ the probability of the first player to die at gunshot i, you obviously have $P(E_1) = 1/6$. Furthermore $P(E_2|\bar{E}_1) = 1/5$; $P(E_3|\bar{E}_1\bar{E}_2) = 1/4$; ...; $P(E_6|\bar{E}_1 ... \bar{E}_5) = 1$. Note that $E_2 = \bar{E}_1E_2$, $E_3 = \bar{E}_1\bar{E}_2E_3$; ...; $E_6 = \bar{E}_1 ... \bar{E}_5E_6$. Applying the composite probability theorem you have $P(E_1) = 1/6$, $P(E_2)$

$= P(\bar{E}_1)P(E_2|\bar{E}_1) = 5/6 \cdot 1/5 = 1/6$; $P(E_3) = P(\bar{E}_1) \cdot P(\bar{E}_2|\bar{E}_1) \cdot P(E_3|\bar{E}_1\bar{E}_2) = 5/6 \cdot 4/5 \cdot 1/4 = 1/6$; $P(E_6) = P(\bar{E}_1) \cdot P(\bar{E}_2|\bar{E}_1) \cdot P(\bar{E}_3|\bar{E}_1\bar{E}_2) \cdot \dots \cdot P(\bar{E}_5|\bar{E}_1 \dots \bar{E}_4) \bar{E}_4 P(E_6|\bar{E}_1 \dots \bar{E}_5) = 5/6 \cdot 4/5 \cdot 3/4 \cdot 2/3 \cdot 1/2 \cdot 1 = 1/6$.

As you can see, it is indifferent to try your luck in any position.

If you consider only two players the problem changes. By indicating with P(A) the probability that *A* dies, and with P(B) the probability that *B* dies occurs:

1. 1st round P(A) = 1/6 = 0.17 (ends the game); P(B) = 5/6 • 1/6 = 0.14; probability that nobody dies 5/6 • 5/6 = 0.69
2. 2nd round P(A) = 5/6 • 5/6 • 1/6 = 0.11; P(B) = $(5/6)^3$ • 1/6 = 0.09
3. 3rd round P(A) = $(5/6)^4$ • 1/6 = 0.08; P(B) = $(5/6)^5$ • 1/6 = 0.06.

At this point we can generalize the reasoning; we can say that P(B) = 5/6 • P(B). This happens at every turn, because, to win, *A* must pass his turn, whose probability is 5/6. If no one dies, the conditions return identical to the starting situation: it is as if he hadn't played. Moreover, since one of the two must die P(A) + P(B) = 1.

Solving the simple system in the two equations:

$$\begin{cases} P(B) = 5/6 \cdot P(A) \\ P(A) + P(B) = 1 \end{cases}$$

you get

P(a) = 6/11 and P(b) = 5/11.

An additional question could be the following: if there are two bullets is it better to shoot straight away or make a spin?

The problem of Russian roulette does not end with the consideration that it is a crazy game, in fact mathematicians and psychologists have tried to deepen the subject in terms of *Expected utility*. The Expected utility theory is based on the hypothesis that, under conditions of uncertainty, the utility can be calculated as a weighted average of utilities in every possible state, using as weights the estimated probabilities of the occurrence of possible events. We follow the reasoning of Kahneman & Tversky (1979): "Suppose you are compelled to play Russian roulette, but are given the opportunity to purchase the removal of one bullet from the loaded gun. Would you pay as much to reduce the number of bullets from four to three as you would to reduce the number of bullets from one to zero? Most people feel that they would be willing to pay much more for a reduction of the probability of death from 1/6 to zero than for a reduction from 4/6 to 3/6. Economic considerations would lead one to pay more in the latter case, where the value of money is presumably reduced by the considerable probability that one will not live to enjoy it". Experimental research (Wu & Gonzale, 1996.) based on risky decision-making processes shows that people systematically violate the principle of expected utility.

Remaining always in the field of firearms one can remember what is considered the paradox of the three gunslingers.

Three gunfighters *A*, *B*, *C* challenge each other to a duel by placing themselves at the vertexes of an equilateral triangle. They will shoot one at a time until there is only one survivor; each can choose who to shoot. What is interesting, from a probabilistic point of view, is that the skills of the three gunfighters are not the same: *A* when he shoots hits 100% of the time, *B* 80% of the time and *C* only 50% of the time.

To help the weakest are supposed to shoot first C and then B to shoot. What does *C* have to do to have the best chance of winning? Paradoxically, he has to shoot high!

It's not good for him to shoot the strongest of the gunfighters because, assuming he can eliminate him, he only has a 20% chance of surviving when it's B's turn. In the second phase *B* won't shoot him, he'll shoot *A*. There are two cases: if he hits him it will be *C* who will then shoot B with a 50% chance of hitting him; if he doesn't hit *A* he will obviously shoot B and kill him with certainty. At this point the turn is up to *C* who can hope to hit *A*.

Summing up, you can see that *C*, firing in the air the first time, has a higher probability of survival.

BACKGAMMON

One of the oldest games is Backgammon, whose origin dates back more than 5000 years. A similar game was also present among the Greeks. The current rules, dating back to 1931, can be traced back to the president of the Racquet and Tennis Clubs of New York. The players have 15 checkers that move (one clockwise and the other counterclockwise), based on the throw of two dice, along 24 arrows (Figure 15). Players must, if possible, move the checkers according to the number indicated on each dice, the same checker can be moved twice, if the throw generates a double result the player must play each dice twice. The game's aim is to be the first to move all their checkers off the board. If you play a money stake, there is also a doubling dice that allows you to win (or lose) a double amount every time a player uses it.

This is a probabilistic optimization game that requires careful evaluation of positions and is influenced by the possibility of doubling the stakes before each shot. Also in this game enters the concept of Mathematical Expectation.

This can be clarified with an example, suppose that the final position, where the move touches the grey, is the one shown in Figure 16. The grey has two checkers on arrows 2 and 3 while the white has two checkers on points 23 and 24, remember that the white checkers move clockwise and the grey ones counterclockwise.

Let's consider what the probability is for grey to let his checkers out with a throw. He will win unless one of the dice comes up with face 1. Since the possible results in the throw of two dice are 36 and 25 are the combinations that do not present the one, the probability of victory is 25/36 = 0.694. Now, before launching, he can choose to double or double the $ 1 stake. If he doesn't double, although the odds are almost 70%, his expected earnings per game is 25/36 • 1 - 11/36 • 1 = 24/36 = $ 0.39. If it doubles, two things can happen: white gives up and grey's equity becomes $ 1, given that it wins; if white accepts the doubling, the hope of grey doubles becoming 0.39 • 2 = 0.78 $. This is certainly not a good situation for the white that must decide how to minimize losses; especially assuming multiple games, it is not convenient for him to be renouncing.

Figure 15. Backgammon

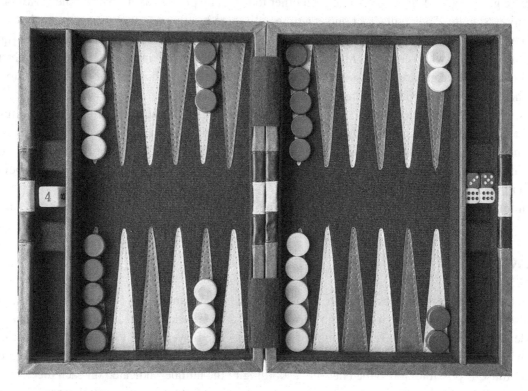

Figure 16. Final position of a Backgammon game

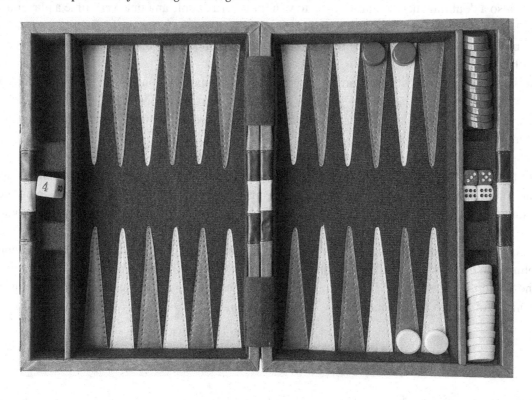

CONCLUSION

As we have already had occasion to clarify, we must distinguish between games and gambling. In the first case we can talk about situations in which a real (or at least realistic) situation is simulated and therefore can play an important role both for training and learning. War-gaming, business gaming, backgammon, etc. are effective tools for teaching. Already in the 1970s, Jerome Bruner (1965) highlighted the usefulness of simulation in the school field.

Gambling requires a different kind of consideration. This is because there are important behavioral aspects. A 2018 research carried out in Italy by the ISS (Higher Institute of Health) showed that 18 million adult Italians have gambled (out of a total population of 60 million): of these, more than 13 million play in a 'social' way, 2 million have a low-risk profile, 1400000 have a moderate risk, 1500000 are problem gamblers. Leaving aside the pathological game which represents a real disease, one is struck by people's total ignorance of the main probabilistic rudiments.

FUTURE RESEARCH DIRECTIONS

Games can play an important role in learning probability as students can test themselves by concretely discovering numerous concepts. Immersed in an engaging role (the kids want to win) you can measure an incomparably higher involvement than that obtainable in a normal lesson. "There are some studies revealing that game-based learning enriches the learning environment, improves the students 'performance, increases the students' motivation, provides the opportunity to work with the group and provides a fun learning environment". (Koparan, 2019).

In this sense, a fruitful research path could guide us towards the operational verification of the introduction of these supports in teaching or, at least, in the proposition of elements capable of arousing greater awareness of the implications of this issue.

Seeing this approach simply in a playful way is wrong, just think of the tumultuous development, in the field of artificial intelligence, of genetic algorithms (stochastic optimization techniques based on evolution). Well, all the texts that describe applications in industry, medicine, genetics, etc. cite the Roulette-wheel selection as a randomized generative basis.

REFERENCES

Alfonso X (King of Castile and Leon), & Calderón, R. O. (2007). *Libro de los juegos: acedrex, dados e tablas; Ordenamiento de las tafurerías*. Fundación José Antonio de Castro.

Bibbona, E., Boggiatto, P., Carypis, E., De Simone, M., & Panero, M. (2014). *Gare e giochi Matematici: Studenti all'opera*. Ledizioni.

Boursin, J. L. (1986). *Les structures du hasard: les probabilités et leurs usages*. Le Seuil.

Bruner, J. S. (1965). *Man: A course of study*. Educational Services, Incorporated.

Campbell, P. J. (2007). Games of chance with multiple objectives. *Metrika, 66*(3), 305–313. doi:10.100700184-006-0112-5

Canova, P., & Rizzuto, D. (2016). *Fate il nostro gioco*. Add Editore.

Cosmides, L., & Tooby, J. (1996). Are humans good intuitive statisticians after all? Rethinking some conclusions from the literature on judgment under uncertainty. *Cognition, 58*(1), 1-73.

Dreef, M., Borm, P., & van der Genugten, B. B. (2001). *A New Relative Skill Measure for Games with Chance Elements*. Tilburg University.

Eastaway, R. (2008). *How Many Socks Make a Pair?* Surprisingly Interesting Everyday Maths. JR Books Ltd.

Harmer, G. P., & Abbott, D. (1999). Losing strategies can win by Parrondo's paradox. *Nature, 402*(6764), 864–864. doi:10.1038/47220

Hwa, S. (2018). Pedagogical Change in Mathematics Learning: Harnessing the Power of Digital Game-Based Learning. *Journal of Educational Technology & Society, 21*(4), 259–276.

Koparan, T. (2019). Teaching Game and Simulation Based Probability. *International Journal of Assessment Tools in Education, 6*(2), 235–258. doi:10.21449/ijate.566563

Li, L. B., He, S. H., Li, S., Xu, J. H., & Rao, L. L. (2009). A closer look at the Russian roulette problem: A re-examination of the nonlinearity of the prospect theory's decision weight π. *International Journal of Approximate Reasoning, 50*(3), 515–520. doi:10.1016/j.ijar.2008.10.004

Prelec, D. (1998). The probability weighting function. *Econometrica, 66*(3), 497–527. doi:10.2307/2998573

Roberts, F., & Tesman, B. (2009). *Applied combinatorics*. CRC Press. doi:10.1201/b12335

Salomone, L. (1979). *Raccolta di giochi a due*. A.P.E. Mursia.

Siller, H. S., & Maaß, J. (2012). Learning mathematics or losing money - betting as a topic for mathematics education. *Teaching Mathematics Applications, 31*(2), 65–83. doi:10.1093/teamat/hrs005

Small, M., & Tse, C. K. (2012). Predicting the outcome of roulette. *Chaos (Woodbury, N.Y.), 22*(3), 033150. doi:10.1063/1.4753920

Tversky, A., & Kahneman, D. (1979). Prospect theory: An analysis of decision under risk. *Econometrica, 47*(2), 263–291. doi:10.2307/1914185

Wu, G., & Gonzalez, R. (1996). Curvature of the probability weighting function. *Management Science, 42*(12), 1676–1690. doi:10.1287/mnsc.42.12.1676

ADDITIONAL READING

Hays, R. T. (2005). *The effectiveness of instructional games: A literature review and discussion (No. NAWCTSD-TR-2005-004)*. Naval Air Warfare Center Training Systems Div Orlando Fl. doi:10.21236/ADA441935

Kordaki, M., & Gousiou, A. (2016). Computer Card Games in Computer Science Education: A 10-Year Review. *Journal of Educational Technology & Society*, *19*(4), 11–21.

Lipowski, A., & Lipowska, D. (2012). Roulette-wheel selection via stochastic acceptance. *Physica A*, *391*(6), 2193–2196. doi:10.1016/j.physa.2011.12.004

Monaghan, J. (2016). Games: Artefacts in gameplay. In *Tools and Mathematics* (pp. 417–431). Springer. doi:10.1007/978-3-319-02396-0_18

KEY TERMS AND DEFINITIONS

Expectation: The arithmetic mean of a large number of independent realizations.

Expected Utility: The attractiveness of an economic opportunity.

Gambler's Ruin: A gambler with finite wealth, playing a fair game will eventually and inevitably go broke against an opponent with infinite wealth.

Monte Carlo Method: Algorithm that rely on repeated random sampling to obtain numerical results.

Sunk Cost Bias: Expenses paid for previously that are not affected by current or future decisions.

This research was previously published in Examining an Operational Approach to Teaching Probability; pages 163-193, copyright year 2021 by Information Science Reference (an imprint of IGI Global).

Index

N

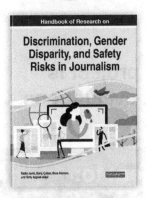
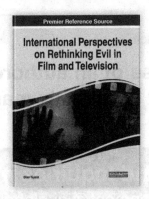

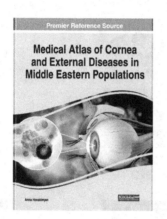

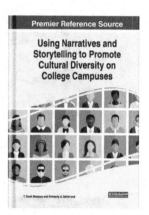

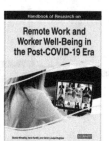

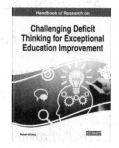

Printed in the United States
by Baker & Taylor Publisher Services